United Nations University Series on Regionalism

Volume 34

This book series offers a platform for innovative work on (supra-national) regionalism from a global and inter-disciplinary perspective. It started with the World Reports on Regional Integration, published in collaboration with other UN agencies, and now publishes theoretical, methodological and empirical contributions related to various themes on interregionalism from academics and policy-makers worldwide. All book proposals are reviewed by an International Editorial Board and final approval on manuscripts also comes from the board.

The series editors are particularly interested in book proposals dealing with:

- comparative regionalism;
- comparative work on regional organizations;
- interregionalism
- the role of regions in a multi-level governance context;
- the interactions between the UN and the regions;
- the regional dimensions of the reform processes of multilateral institutions;
- the dynamics of cross-border micro-regions and their interactions with supra-national regions;
- methodological issues in regionalism studies.

Accepted book proposals can receive editorial support from UNU-CRIS for the preparation of manuscripts.

Please send book proposals to: pdelombaerde@cris.unu.edu and lvanlangenhove@cris.unu.edu

Christian Ghymers

Independence, Federalism and Regionalism in Latin America: An Analytical Anthology of Francisco de Miranda's Writings (1790-1811)

Springer

Christian Ghymers
IRELAC and RTI/UCLouvain
Bruxelles, Belgium

ISSN 2214-9848 ISSN 2214-9856 (electronic)
United Nations University Series on Regionalism
ISBN 978-3-031-96937-9 ISBN 978-3-031-96938-6 (eBook)
https://doi.org/10.1007/978-3-031-96938-6

This Springer imprint is published by the registered company Springer Nature Switzerland AG
The registered company address is: Gewerbestrasse 11, 6330 Cham, Switzerland

Source: Painting, oil on canvas, by Georges Rouget, François Miranda, General of the Army of the North in 1792, Palace of Versailles collection, room 1792

"Citizen, to rest or to be free, one must choose!"

Pericles
Cited by Thucydides
(end of IVth century B. C.)
History of the Peloponnesian War,
(Translated from J. de Romilly)
Robert Laffont, 1990

In homage to the emblematic precursor of Latin American democratic integration and to all the citizens of this region, victims of their populist caudillos

Foreword

The person of Francisco de Miranda and his project of emancipation of Hispanic America have appeared, until recently, as distant and distorted as a consequence of pseudoscientific historiography aimed at exalting the role of Simón Bolívar and highlighting as original to him the conception of a political union among the Hispanic American countries after independence. This historiography, too, with a few exceptions, such as those of Caracciolo Parra, A. Polanco Alcántara, and José Luis Salcedo-Bastardo, has insisted on attributing to Miranda a role that he did not have at all in the fall of the First Republic of Venezuela.

The work of Professor Christian Ghymers rescues, with the presentation of the numerous key texts written by Miranda, the contribution of political philosophy and constitutional thought as a Precursor of a pragmatic democracy adapted to Latin America. The project of the emancipation of Hispanic America and its conception as both external and internal decolonization through the integration of countries, based on a pragmatic vision of the difficult and complex problem of governance of the extensive, plurinational, and pluricultural state that was to emerge from a colonial regime, are presented with crystal clarity by the author, which already makes the reading of this work great interest. But no less merit, and which makes this reading more meaningful and attractive, is the analysis, together with the presentation of the respective texts, of the concept of governance developed by Miranda. This is important not only because it was a pioneering concept ahead of its time, but perhaps mainly because it contributes to the study and examination of current governance problems, both in Latin America and the rest of the world.

Thus, Professor Ghymers' book is indispensable reading and study for anyone interested in the complex geopolitical conditions that prevail in the world today.

Santiago, February 2025

Professor with tenure, University of Chile, Miguel Castillo Didier
Director of the Center for Byzantine
and Neohellenic Studies
Santiago, Chile

Bibliographical Sources and Conventions

The bibliographical references in the original text have been revised, extended, translated, and updated to allow a more fluid reading. To facilitate the reading, and due to the character of this book as an anthology, we opted for three different kinds of presentation of the bibliographical sources:

1) For the respective reproduced texts, after each document, the multiple sources used for copying or translating the original texts are mentioned under the sub-title "Sources".
2) The bibliographical references on which the comments to the documents are based are placed at the end of each chapter and Annex.
3) The details of these references (volumes, pages) are placed in the footnotes.

In addition, the three most important sources used in this work are referred to in a shorter format in the footnotes as follows:

- *Archivo* [1929–1950] refers to the first edition of Miranda's Archive, edited by volume in Caracas and La Habana.
- *Columbeía* [1978–now] refers to the second edition in Spanish of this Archive, edited by the Presidency of the Republic in Caracas.
- *América Espera* [1982] refers to the first anthology of Miranda's writings, edited by Salcedo-Bastardo for the Ayacucho publishing house in Caracas.

Competing Interests The author has no competing interests to declare that are relevant to the content of this manuscript.

Contents

About the Author

Christian Ghymers is Vice-Chairman of the Robert Triffin International (RTI-University of Louvain-la-Neuve) and President of the Interdisciplinary Institute for Relations between the EU and Latin America and the Caribbean (IRELAC). He is a Belgian economist university-graduated from Liège (1969) and Louvain (1971), "*Agrégé de l'enseignement supérieur* [equivalent to PhD, 1980]. As an academic, he was Professor of International Economics with tenure at ICHEC—Brussels Management School (1977–2013) and taught also in France (IESEG at Lille, CEFI at Aix-Marseille II, University of Chile, IMF Institute in Vienna-JVI, and ENA Strasbourg). He was a researcher at IRES/UCLouvain on business cycle analysis and forecasting (1970–1972, 1975–1978) and in CERNEA/Paris Nanterre (1983–1986). He specialized in international economics, crisis management, regional integration, governance issues, and Latin American and African policy.

As a civil servant, he was successively an economist and an adviser at the National Bank of Belgium (1978–1986) in charge of competitiveness, exchange rates, and external adjustment, Visiting Fellow at the New York Fed and the Brookings Institution on monetary policy (1984), adviser at the DG ECFIN of the European Commission (1986–2008) on policy coordination issues, at the UN ECLAC-CEPAL (2000–2004) on crisis management and regional coordination, and at the IMF Institute-Joint Vienna Institute (2009–2011) on international monetary issues, Euro crisis, and EU policies.

He has mainly published on policy coordination and international monetary issues, as well as on Latin American economic issues and history.

He was awarded the O'Higgins Order (Chile) and the Miranda Order (Venezuela).

List of Contributors (Annexes)

Professor John Dunn, Emeritus Professor, Cambridge University.
Professor Miguel Castillo Didier, University of Chile, Director of the Center for Byzantine and Neohellenic Studies, Santiago.

Chapter 1
Origins and Purpose of This Book

This analytical anthology of Francisco de Miranda's political thought fills a void. Until now, there was only one excellent compilation of texts, edited by Salcedo Bastardo in 1982 for the Ayacucho collection. However, it included broader themes and presented the texts chronologically without providing contextual explanations or thematic analysis of their contents. The idea of organising the texts with analytical comments arose from the joint efforts of the author with the faithful and essential support of David Chacón—the contemporary historian who best knows the pro-emancipation hero—to look to rescue the contribution of the political and constitutional philosophy of the "most universal of Latin Americans".

What is the purpose of this book? Miranda's case raises fascinating questions, not only for bringing a new light on the process of Latin American independence but also on the geopolitical context and the European involvements in which Miranda formed his singular project of emancipation through the creation of a universal republic and had to evolve, as well as on this crucial period of revolutions and wars that shaped our Western world. Furthermore, such a journey in the company of Miranda's political thought raises an epistemological question: considered to be a "precursor" in political ideas (as we sustain in this book), Miranda constitutes an emblematic case of a universal problem that faces historians: *how to make history without rebuilding the past under the influence of our present values* and ideologies? This is the critical debate that the "*Cambridge New School of History of Political Thought*" (or in short "Cambridge School") opened half a century ago and deserves careful attention. Miranda's political thinking presents a textbook case for raising what seems emblematic of the objectivity problem in history. Indeed, by definition, naming Miranda as the "Precursor" automatically implies a judgment. This assessment also involves examining the degree of pertinence of a precursor's proposals for future situations or today's world, mainly since Miranda was primarily focused on issues of governance and regional and socio-ethnic

C. Ghymers, *Independence, Federalism and Regionalism in Latin America: An Analytical Anthology of Francisco de Miranda's Writings (1790-1811)*, United Nations University Series on Regionalism 34,
https://doi.org/10.1007/978-3-031-96938-6_1

integration. Consciously or not, this means to evaluate his thoughts that were formulated more than two centuries ago, with some present values and considerations. In addition to questioning the historian's objectivity, the case of Miranda's thought also raises the more systemic issue of the precise scope of the Cambridge conception of the history of political thought. Therefore, it was necessary to dedicate a specific section of this chapter to trying to clarify our position in such a complex epistemological debate.

Furthermore, I soon realised through my research that analysing Miranda's actions and thoughts could contribute to addressing deep-seated governance issues, not only in Latin America and its stagnation in regional integration, but also in the current globalised world and the socio-political challenges of our multicultural societies. It might be constructive for opposing the new emerging political philosophy launched by the "Dark Enlightenment thinking",[1] [Nick Land 2012] or the Neo-Reactionarism [Peter Thiel 1995, 2009] against Enlightenment values, observed in the United States. This new movement—radically contrary to Miranda's political views—has been prepared and developed in the last 20 years [Curtis Yarvin alias Mencius Moldburg 2007, 2008], focusing on the axiomatic belief in the incompatibility of freedom with democracy. Consequently, this thought takes the debate back more than two centuries to the time of Miranda's arguments, thus showing its degree of topicality. Neo-reactionarism, assessed by many political scientists as a updated version of fascism, favours authoritarian forms of government, wanting to instate a techno-feudalism, i.e. a capitalist corporate power as the organising force in society and the privatisation of government. This movement opposes the empiricist views and claims an antidemocratic return to traditional forms of society decided by a few CEO pretending to own a single truth, denying the separation of powers, like in fascist and Nazi regimes. Miranda's precursory views of democracy and the threat of totalitarism were already warning and fighting against the centralisation of powers, with still valid arguments today.

An essential aspect of this book, by trying to assess the degree of precocity of Miranda's ideas, is the confrontation with the delicate methodological question of knowing to which degree this exercise would correspond to a mere evaluation of the past with the concepts and conceptions of today, as the Cambridge School has been

[1] The **Dark Enlightenment** or Neo-Reactionarism (NRx) is a new ideology developed in the 2000s in the US. Coined by philosopher Nick Land [2012] and based on Thiel and Sacks [1995] and Thiel [2009], a billionaire, tech-investor, on Curtis Yarvin, alias Mencius Moldbug [2007, 2008], and Marc Andreessen [2011], also a techno-investor. This radical far-right ideology provides a philosophical basis for being back to anti-democratic order, assessing through a lens of Darwinism that the Enlightenment was an error because humanism, democracy, and quest for equality are responsible for the decay of Western civilisation, proposing a revolution to strengthen a capitalist corporate power opposed to democracy and civil rights for efficiency reasons, based upon techno-control through Artificial Intelligence and pseudo-scientific racism. It recently invaded part of the Silicon Valley's elites and some Republican political actors like Steve Bannon, Donald Trump, Michael Anton and Senator James D. Vance. This emerging philosophy is a return to a kind of absolutism and a domination of the executive power over the other two branches, in total opposition to the constitutional regime Miranda fought for.

objecting it since several decades. In fact, behind this key question lies the risky issue of assessing the relevance of how the Cambridge method is applied and of some of its extensions. From the start, we announce the options for our work. Although adhering to the fundamental concern of Cambridge, we cannot extend it to the extreme of denying specific individuals the ability to promote in advance what society ultimately decides. History—always written or dominated by the victors—has yet to do justice to the genuine precursor of the emancipation of Latin America and the Caribbean. Based on my personal experience as an economist closely involved in policy-making and governance issues, I became aware of the relevance of some of Miranda's contributions to governance for my own work, both within the European Union institutions and during my technical advisory missions to various governments, especially in Latin America, Africa and Central and Eastern Europa. Therefore, I decided to systematically search the writings and their context of this denied hero, especially rescuing all texts (or fragments) that could have a constitutional or political relevance, primarily in matters of regional and social integration.[2]

In this way, *the first idea* of the present book was born: to rescue what could be viewed as advanced and valuable thoughts regarding governance that had been hidden or discarded by the interests of local or doctrinal oligarchies or not adequately assessed by official historians. In my analytical journey in the study of Latin American revolutions, I realised that knowing Miranda's activities better would benefit historians' tasks and citizens' understanding of their past and its manipulation. My conviction was reinforced when I had the opportunity to be confronted with the abusive instrumentation of Bolivar in Venezuela by the late Hugo Chavez, with whom I had personal discussions (and clear divergences) on Miranda's role and thinking, and especially on the historical revisionism undertaken by the "*Chavist socialism of the XXI century*". Consequently, this project became a personal crusade for restoring Miranda's figure, which had practically disappeared or distorted by the so-called "Latin American experts" influenced by hegemonic ideological currents of the twentieth century, both in Latin America and Europe. In particular, I was convinced that Miranda's key messages would have been beneficial for preventing the fatal consequences of Chavism for Venezuelan people and Latin America.

The *second idea*—based on our conviction that singular persons and events weigh heavily on other determinants of history—is that the saddest betrayal organised by a small part of "patriots" against Miranda in 1812 allowed for Bolivar (one of the main conspirators against his chief) to usurping his leadership throwing Miranda's constitutional emancipation into collective oblivion. The resulting

[2] The crucial advancement and pragmatism of Miranda's integrative ideas drew especially my attention for being helpful to my own work at the service of the European Commission at the end of the 1980s and during the '90 s when I was involved in the discussions on subsidiarity in the preparation and implementation of the Maastricht Treaty, the single currency implementation, and my following work on policy coordination in the EU. They were also inspiring in parallel with several of my modest technical contributions to regional integration in Africa, Latin America, and Central and Eastern Europe.

abortion of the internal part of Miranda's decolonisation vision and the triumph of Bolivar's "caudillism" could explain the lack of socio-economic development of the whole region. This thesis, of course, necessitates deep debates.

The *third most recent idea* is the future debate, which should appear with the present emergence of a return to antidemocratic forms of government, which are in clear opposition to Enlightenment values and Miranda's ideas of separation of powers.

The difficulties surrounding the publication of this book, which can also be viewed in part as an analogy revealing some current features of Latin American obstacles to socio-economic development, contributed to its delayed release. I embarked on this exciting adventure within Latin American societies and their historians, both Latin American and European, in the 1990s and early 2000s.

This adventure provided me with a unique opportunity to immerse myself in the intimacy of Latin American cultures. I discovered essential aspects of the use—and abuse—of history for political and social purposes in this region, as is the case elsewhere. Simultaneously, this fantastic journey challenged the dominant academic criticisms of the "teleological" aspect of my purpose: the issue of subjectivism in the history of political thought has to be dealt with, all the more about a precursor hero whom, by definition, the political proposals were innovating concerning his historical context and constraints. Our interpretations could easily be considered teleological explanations that reconstruct the past from the prevailing ideas and values of a later time. Indeed—by definition—assessing a Precursor's ideas implies inevitably an explicit degree of judgement based upon subjective present conceptions, exposing the whole work to the criticism of the *Cambridge New School of History*. Although my training in history (as well as my discipline in economics) makes me consider being a fair adherent to this school, when trying to apply it to Miranda, I realised that his case provides an exciting opportunity to question some radical interpretations of the Cambridge method. Miranda's thinking and actions are emblematic of dealing with a past innovator while trying not to be biased by posterior evolution. This epistemological aspect is present in my own research and was explicitly debated at several international conferences where I had the opportunity to present my views. Chapter 3 focuses on this methodological issue.

After having undertaken the organisation of three successive high-level international seminars[3] (Brussels in 2001 in the Egmont Palace under the auspices of the Belgian Presidency of the EU, Santiago of Chile in 2002 under the patronage of the University of Chile, and Santiago again in 2003 in a symposium selected by the 51st

[3] The proceedings of these three seminars were all published:

Ghymers, C. & Grisanti, L.X. [2001], *Francisco de Miranda, l'Europe et l'intégration latino-américaine*;

Ghymers, C., [2002], "Influencia del Maestro sobre el Discípulo: el papel de Miranda y O'Higgins en la singularidad del caso chileno y de su gobernabilidad";

Bohórquez C & Ghymers, C., (eds), [2006], *El papel de Miranda y de su generación en la emancipación latinoamericana: identidad, integración regional y gobernabilidad,*

International Congress of Americanists, and several conferences in Europe[4] and Latin America,[5] dedicated to Miranda and the history of emancipation, I was invited, in 2005, on the initiative of the Director of the Bolivar Hall of London, Gloria Carnevali, and HE Alfredo Toro Hardy, the Ambassador of the Bolivarian Republic of Venezuela, to deliver a speech at two conferences, one in London and the other in the University of Cambridge, about my interpretation of Miranda and his constitutionalist views. From these lectures, some academic interests emerged to re-read Miranda's contribution. With the support of HE the Ambassador of Venezuela, Alfredo Toro Hardy and Gloria Carnevali, a specific "Panel on Miranda" was organised at the University of London the following year, in May 2006, by Professor James Dunkerley at the Institute for the Study of the Americas. This event coincided with President Chávez's visit to London, during which he expressed his support for the event. The ambitious purpose of Venezuelan authorities was to utilize my own insights into Miranda's thinking to draw European academic attention to the intellectual values and advances the Venezuelan precursor had achieved in comparison with Europe and the US. This academic panel brought together the three main research centres on Latin America of the United Kingdom. It was composed by renowned historians: James Dunkerley and John Lynch from the University of London; Malcolm Deas from St. Antony's College, Oxford; Geoffrey Hawthorn and John Dunn, both from the University of Cambridge. The latter, dedicated to the history of political thought, is considered one of the founders and pillars of the Cambridge School of History of Political Ideas. These eminent British academics were very interested in listening to and criticising an alternative view about this precursor, which presents some peculiarities not so widely known. Furthermore, as explained below in the Methodological Chap. 3, the debate led directly to an epistemological confrontation with John Dunn and his vision as a founding father of the Cambridge School.

This second event was again co-organized and co-financed by the Bolivar Hall of the Bolivarian Republic of the Venezuelan Embassy, whose director also took charge of translating into English a part of the political texts of Miranda with Professor Dunkerley from the University of London, which had previously required from me to select these texts as a preparation of the panel colloquium. The panellists received these translated texts in advance.[6] I take this opportunity to express my deepest gratitude to Gloria Carnevali for her initiative and duty devotion. This initiative, promoted by President Chávez himself for the prestige of Venezuela, from the very place where Miranda conceived and organised the revolutions in Latin America, had also programmed—under request from Venezuelan authorities—that these

---

[4] In Brussels, London, Cambridge, Louvain-la-Neuve, Paris, Vienna, Budapest, Szeged, Waterloo (Belgium).

[5] Santiago de Chile, Coro & Caracas (Venezuela).

[6] This anthology includes more documents than those presented in the London seminar. I thank Professor Donkerley and Gloria Carnevali for their English translations for the London event; however, I revised these and translated numerous additional translations. I support the full responsibility for these translations.

political texts of Miranda and the minutes of the London panel would be published by the University of London, with the financing of Venezuelan Presidency. Unfortunately, for reasons that were never formally explained, the Venezuelan public funds, especially earmarked (and carefully transferred each budgetary year from 2006 to 2009) by HE Ambassador Toro Hardy and Director Gloria Carnevali for this publication, were not used for their legitimate purpose once a new Ambassador arrived in London. At this moment in 2009, Gloria Carnevali was also removed from her position as the head of the Bolivar Hall. Therefore, the announced publications (in Spanish and English versions) never materialised. Later, I had other publishing possibilities in Vienna. Still, the global economic crisis of 2008–09, followed by the euro-area crisis, impacted my priorities and professional commitments as a European Commission macroeconomist, preventing me from completing the editing work on this publication.

This edition attempts to overcome these flaws and obstacles, albeit with a 20-year delay. Therefore, the objective is to announce, in the most didactic manner, the importance and relevance of the message of the Venezuelan, known as the Precursor or "Protolíder" of Latin-American Independence. We attempt to reconstruct the evolution of the political thought of one of the most remarkable figures in Latin American history, who paved the way towards a pragmatic view of democratic governance and socio-ethnic integration. Unfortunately, Miranda's ideas were never implemented and fell into the garbage of history, or at best, they were qualified as a utopia. This book diverges from studies that focus on the most anecdotal aspects of his life, which tend to overshadow his genuine value. All translations from Spanish and French into English are my responsibility.

The texts selected in this book, which were classified in great themes and arranged chronologically, present what we value as a fabulous multi-racial and multi-cultural project that would have been the largest Republic of its time, endowed with the most modern democratic governance to date, and which could have represented the best hope for improving governance, human rights, regional integration and socio-economic development. We aim to highlight the extraordinary path of this humanist-Creole within the context of Enlightenment ideas, specifically in a particular geopolitical context, and the way he conceived and shaped a new multicultural synthesis that would have led to a new political system of democratic governance, logically more adapted to foster inclusive development in Latin America. This revolutionary vision pretended to be able to make up for the inheritance from the colonial and racial oppression of the Inquisition and the economic under-development imposed by commercial protectionism and the social divisions of the absolutist colonial order.

To better understand the purpose of this research, the original documents' internal layout is preserved, respecting their overall structure. Miranda's explanatory body and notes are also preserved, except for the original language. When necessary, the documents were translated into English from Spanish or French, or in some cases, from translations already available in other works.

According to our contextual method, discussed later in Chap. 3, which interprets historical facts within their original context, each document is preceded by a systematic explanation of its historical context, serving as a general introduction, along with a brief synthesis of its content and specific bibliographical sources.

Most of the valuable documentation presented here has been revised and updated by David Chacón, based on the editions of Miranda's Archive, published under the title "Archivo del General Miranda" (Archive of General Miranda) [1929–1950] as well as in the Spanish version under the title "Colombeía" [1978 - unfinished] . Likewise, we revised the translation of José María Antepara's work [1810][7] called *La Emancipación de la América del Sur: ... (The Emancipation of South America ...*

In the same way, this work publishes the context of the documents from which the extracts have been taken so that we can see it as a whole.

In the case of the insufficiently known "Letter of Viscardo", its importance both for Miranda's thought and for the emergence of Latin American identity recommends attaching it extensively in the additional appendix, translating it into English, and modernising its spelling and punctuation. However, to avoid modifying Antepara's criterion, the paragraphs are in square brackets, indicating the observations in footnotes. As it contains multiple referential information, it is enriched with a set of explanatory notes to make the erudition presented by the author more comprehensible. It was also compared with the original prints in French, which are housed in the National Library of Paris (PC 70), and Spanish, deposited in the "Archivo General de Indias" in Seville (State Section, file 70).

The book is supplemented with extensive and brief biographical information about the individuals or notable events mentioned in the documents, as well as contextual sections.

Although conceived and written under my own responsibility, it is worth mentioning the high-value work undertaken by the Caracas historian, Dr. David Chacón, who guided me throughout my research and generously shared all the necessary information about Miranda that he had collected during a research tour spanning more than 30 years. The rigour of the sources' analyses, the bibliography, and David Chacón's analysis contributed significantly to this publication. I am also especially grateful to Professor Miguel Castillo Didier from the University of Chile for his constant support and his permanent availability to share his analysis on Miranda. I would like to thank both of them warmly, although I take full responsibility for the ideas, interpretations, and writing in this book.

August 2024, Christian Ghymers,
Priory St Christol, Provence, France

[7] This 1810 publication, signed by Antepara, a friend of Miranda, was written with Miranda under his direct control at a time when the British government, for trying to keep good relations with Spain, prohibited him from publicly interfering from London into Spanish colonies. See Chap. 8, document 8.1.

References

Andreessen, M., [2011], "Why Software is Eating the World". Life & Culture. *The Wall Street Journal.*

Antepara, J. M., /Miranda, [1810], *La Emancipación de la América del Sur: ... (The Emancipation of South America: historical and explanatory documents that show the plans that have been in progress, and the attainments made by General Miranda-, For the achievement of such objectives during the last twenty-five year,* printed by R. Juigné, No 17, Margaret-Street, cavendish-Square, 1810, re-edition by David R. Chacón Rodríguez, [2005] Fundación Hermano Nectario María, Caracas 2005. Serie: (Francisco de Miranda; t. 2).

Bohórquez C & Ghymers, C., (ed.), [2006], El papel de Miranda y de su generación en la emancipación latinoamericana: identidad, integración regional y gobernabilidad, Memoria del del Simpsio Historia, 51Congreso Internacional de Americanistas, Santiago de Chile, Association Internationale Andrés Bello, Caracas.

Ghymers, C. & Grisanti, L.X. [2001], *Francisco de Miranda, l'Europe et l'intégration latino-américaine*, ed. Versant Sud, Louvain-la-Neuve.

Ghymers, C., [2002], "Influencia del Maestro sobre el Discípulo: el papel de Miranda y **O'Higgins** en la singularidad del caso chileno y de su gobernabilidad", *Revista del Instituto O'Higgiano de Chile*, n° 19, Santiago.

Land, N., [2012], The Dark Enlightenment, https://keithanyan.github.io/TheDarkEnlightenment.epub/TheDarkEnlightenment.pdf.

Miranda, F. de, [1929–1950], *Archivo del General Miranda*, ed. Vicente Dávila/Rubén González, Caracas/La Habana.

Miranda, F. de, [1978-en curso], *Colombeía*, edición de la Presidencia de la República, Caracas.

Moldburg, M. [2007], A Formalist Manifesto, https://www.unqualified-reservations.org/pdfs/formalist_manifesto.pdf.

Moldburg, M., [2008], Patchwork: A Political System for the 21st Century, https://www.unqualified-reservations.org/pdfs/patchwork.pdf.

Thiel, P. and Sacks, D., [1995], The Diversity Myth: Multiculturalism and the Politics of Intolerance at Stanford, Independent Institute, Michigan University.

Thiel, P., [2009], The Education of a Libertarian, CATO Institute, https://www.cato-unbound.org/2009/04/13/peter-thiel/education-libertarian/.

Yarvin, C., [2007, 2008], see Moldbug, M.

Chapter 2
Overview of Miranda's Political Thought

2.1 Introduction: What Is a Precursor?

Two centuries after the independence events of a region whose emancipation is still unfinished, it is advisable to re-examine and rescue the political and constitutional contributions—unjustly discarded, forgotten, or undervalued—of one of the most lucid and universal of Latin Americans. The priority of his commitments to the Latin American cause and his personal choices as a man of action made Miranda a reasonably pragmatic man, apparently not attached to theoretical considerations but always guided by a set of profound philosophical inquiries and guiding ideas. He left no academic treatise or a large volume of political writings. He did not even pretend to invent a new political principle. Nevertheless, his remarkable value lies in the way he combined the best ideas of the Enlightenment to propose a rational, workable governance that would lead to development and social inclusion. His entire journey implicitly referred to a balanced philosophy—the result of his vast personal experiences throughout the US, Europe, Russia, and Turkey—setting structured theoretical principles that deserve as much attention as the best treaties of political science for their operational value-added. In particular, it should be emphasised that his emancipatory plan corresponds to what is called today the creation of a universal republic: no discrimination, representative democracy characterised by strict separation of powers warranting free debates. His emancipating project was built on two steps: first, to achieve complete external (political) independence, allowing for the implementation of an internal (ethnic-social) decolonisation in a second step. This broader view makes Miranda not only an anti-colonialist and anti-imperialist precursor but also—what was never highlighted—an anti-racist precursor, contrary to the thinking of his time and especially of Bolivar and other liberators,

C. Ghymers, *Independence, Federalism and Regionalism in Latin America: An Analytical Anthology of Francisco de Miranda's Writings (1790-1811)*, United Nations University Series on Regionalism 34,
https://doi.org/10.1007/978-3-031-96938-6_2

except his Chilean disciple Bernardo O'higgins[1] [Ghymers, 2002] and his Haitian ally [Dalencour, 1955], Alexandre Pétion.[2]

Miranda is often considered the Precursor of the independence of Latin America. However, the concept itself raises the question of defining a precursor and then determining the criteria to use under this definition. In Latin America, especially in Venezuela and Colombia, the nickname "Precursor" has a condescending tone, referring to the initiator of a mission that only the single Liberator Bolivar could carry out. This image of Miranda as the loser, implicit but strong in Venezuela,[3] further glorifies Bolivar. The point of view adopted in this work is distinct and differs from having initiated a factual process that was later implemented by others. For us, the concept encompasses the overall characteristic of seeing beyond his historical context—and well beyond the other Libertadores—and showing a clear advance in his political thinking with respect to his historical context, announcing what would later be considered a modern democracy. We are conscious that such a claim is blatantly contrary to the basic principle of the *New Cambridge School of History,* which is to prevent judgements of the past with posterior ideas. It is, however, the major characteristic and component of our thesis.

This is why it is necessary to open the broader methodological question of objectivity in history and to use Miranda's case as a concrete test for questioning the accuracy of some interpretations of the Cambridge School of History. Chapter 3 deals with this methodological aspect. The basis of our position is that observing *the natural selection that emerges in the historical facts two centuries after Miranda's time should allow us to provide an objective criterion for measuring the degree of forwardness of his political thinking* with respect to his time while limiting the risk of rebuilding history with our present conceptions. Nevertheless, our "objective"

[1] **Bernardo O'Higgins Riquelme** (1778–1842), influenced by Miranda with whom he conspired from London, became the "Libertador" for Chile, the founder of the Chilean democratic Republic. In particular, he was favourable to the native Mapuches (Indians) proposing an agrarian reform for them. However, his successors never implemented it. Only recently some limited attributions of grounds were effective. We consider that he gave an initial orientation favouring the rule of law in Chile. See our article [Ghymers, 2002];

[2] **Alexandre Pétion** (1770–1818), Franco-Haitian mestizo who fought as a French soldier in 1791 in the Haitian revolution against slavery, he participated with France in the expulsion of the British and Spanish troops from Haiti in 1798, he was opposed to the racist anti-white policy of the slave leader Jean Jacques Dessalines, and had to go into exile in France; he returned to Haiti with the French troops in 1802, but changed his camp when Napoleon betrayed the general Toussaint Louverture, the head of the black Haitian people who was made prisoner by Napoleon's order. Pétion contributed then to the independence of Haiti (proclaimed in 1804 by Dessalines) but, in favour of a liberal republic, he opposed Dessalines 'absolutism (who had proclaimed himself emperor), and, after several internal struggles, a senate elected him, president of the republic in 1807 until he died in 1818. In 1806, he provided crucial logistical help to Miranda's expedition to disembark in Coro. He will do the same with Bolivar in 1816.

[3] This image was even made explicit through Michelena's romantic painting, depicting Miranda imprisoned in his Spanish cell in La Carraca (near Cadix). This became the most popular image that associates him with a resounding failure, antinomic and instrumental to the triumph of the single deified Liberator Bolívar.

criterion relies on a "subjective" postulate that the so-called natural selection between political ideas and regimes over time would offer the possibility of assessing some progress in governance. This hypothesis effectively constitutes an evaluative judgement as to whether our present political regimes would be ethically better than those of the old regime, later totalitarianism, or contemporary illiberal autocracies. Recognising that this is a subjective option, Cambridge's possible criticism highlights its limits by leading to indeterminacy: denying that our Western democracies constitute progress in governance compared to the past would also lack an objective basis. Although this might be true, it illustrates the very fact that it is impossible in history not to refer implicitly at one moment to some "values". Despite the inherent indeterminacy of politics, our proposed criterion offers the advantage of being observable and verifiable in the facts, regardless of the historian's political preferences or the assessment of which regime is considered "better" than others. The Precursor's accuracy is objectively measurable anyway through the degree of forecast of observable posterior regimes, whether they were "good or bad", democratically chosen or not. On this factual basis, we consider that the degree of forwardness of political ideas on democratic governance can be reasonably assessed by comparison with both the dominant ideas of that time and those of later political thinkers, including contemporary ones.

At the same time, it is possible to evaluate objectively to what degree an intellectual position is "revolutionary". We use the simple qualification of *revolutionary* for any actor who wants and proposes operationally to change one system for what he pretends to be a better one for the purposes and objectifiable results of governance, acknowledging that, nonetheless, the «objectifiable» results are always assessed with respect to ethical criteria. So, we coin a definition of a "political *Precursor*" as *a revolutionary innovator who can identify in advance what democratic governance would be able to provide to ensure a higher degree of individual rights and political participation, with expectations of better welfare for its citizens.*

Some Cambridge school representatives opposed my thesis in the 2006 academic panel organised by the University of London on Miranda's political ideas. John Dunn, in a radical position, challenged my view of Miranda as a revolutionary as well as a precursor of modern democracy, sustaining—as one of the founders of the *Cambridge School*—that for reaching my conclusions, it was inevitable to commit the methodological sin to use present values for assessing the past. Although acknowledging the importance and legitimacy of such questioning, we precisely sustain that Miranda's example could also provide a test case to question the genuine degree of objectivity when applying this Cambridge criterion, at least for some excessive extrapolations, like Dunn's positions presented in the 2006 London Panel and reproduced in Annex 2 (see Chap. 3, Sect. 3.3 and Annex 2).

This questioning can be presented in the following (caricatural) binary way: Which interpretation would be the most subjective?

- To consider that some dissident thoughts (manifested in the past against the dominant thinking), which announce a development observed later, could not be

precursory (Dunn's Cambridge interpretation of Miranda[4]) because these past ideas should be seen either as an abusive retro-projection of our current values or alternatively as a pure coincidence
- Or to recognise that precursor ideas issued in an adverse context would be advanced proposals of what future values would actually be implemented in our societies; such a conclusion resulting from an objective observation of thinking evolution up to now (*our interpretation*).

We think that both versions participate in a certain degree of subjectivity. The second interpretation—which is ours—does not necessarily imply having a teleological vision based on an abuse of references to our current conceptions, given that it involves *comparing historical facts with present facts* in an analysis of the contexts (respecting the method of Cambridge). On the contrary, the first interpretation—which is not necessarily that of the entire Cambridge school—appears more arbitrary because decreeing that it would be fortuitous or subjective for a hero of the past to issue political formulas that were applied later seems to be more dogmatic than describing them as precursors. Denying the historical fact of the existence of thinkers or actors ahead of their time and context, solely on the argument that the future offers some similarities with their ideas, cannot be more objective than observing the historical similarities in the complex process of value creation and evolution.

This corresponds to an explicit dogmatic bias, which exposes the risk of excluding, in principle, an innovator with respect to the dominant conceptions of an era. This logic leads to the limit of rejecting the meaning of the concept of "precursor"—at the cost of losing a part of the historical context—under the non-objective argument of limiting the facts to the dominant paradigms of the past due to the elimination of those whose only fault would be to get too much closer to later values. Furthermore, we claim that analysing the astonishing insight of a political thought ahead of its time is a legitimate and essential part of history because the evolution of thought is objectively observable and not necessarily subjective, even if, by definition, we inevitably observe the past through influences—conscious or not—of the present values and principles.

Behind our argument lies the even more profound question of whether it would be possible to reach a genuine contextual analysis, as made by Cambridge, without any implicit reference to the present. At the limit, there is the paradox of committing the same error that the Cambridge school denounces: using today's ideas to deny any advance to Miranda instead of using them to perceive his lucid advance in his time. What would be the most severe error?

Our position highlights the value of comparative analysis of contemporary views in enhancing our understanding of the past, a perspective we consider fully compatible with Cambridge's views. Thanks to Cambridge's questioning, "emphasising the subjective character" of our analysis opens a broader debate that extends to the

[4]Dunn's extreme position [2006] does not necessarily reflect those of his school. See Dunn's text of his intervention in the London panel of May 2006 in Annex 2.

social function of history. This is why this book requires dedicating some development to epistemological aspects after the following synthesis of our thesis.

2.2 Synthesis of Our Interpretation of Miranda's Political Thinking

The objective of our research is to contribute to restoring the universal value—the character of the "intellectual heritage of humanity"—of Miranda's contribution, updating the words proclaimed in 1794 by the French writer and politician Antoine Quatremère de Quincy [1794][5] in defence of this exceptional hero of freedom, already unjustly imprisoned by order of the coup plotter Robespierre for expressing moderate opinions and for that being condemned as necessarily politically guilty[6]: "*Miranda no longer belongs to any country, it is a kind of common property, inviolable*".[7]

The central axis of this work is to argue that Miranda developed a revolutionary project of governance adapted to Latin America, whose underlying political thought has not yet been sufficiently analysed. Our interpretation suggests that his political project presents a precursory conception of the fundamental principles that have been progressively imposed on contemporary Western democracies.

We sustain that Miranda's political attempt, despite not having been implemented,[8] constitutes an incontestable historical fact of significant interest, both for having failed and for his forward vision. The analysis of his ideas helps better understand both the development difficulties and the defects of the Latin American republics that emerged from the colonial empire, thus contributing to the identification of the challenges of democratic governance. The reasons for Miranda's failed emancipation plan and the determinants of the apparent initial success of his opponents carry important messages for today's world, in addition to shedding new light on

[5]**Quatremère de Quincy** (1755–1849) was a French architect, archaeologist, philosopher, art critic and politician. In charge of the creation of the Pantheon of Paris (1791–93), he was imprisoned during the Terror and denounced with Miranda in his famous "Letters to Miranda", the looting of works of art by Napoleon's armies in the occupied countries. He defended the imprisoned Miranda in a pamphlet, "*Précis sur Miranda*", [1794], published in Paris by Barrois l'aîné and reprinted in 1989.

[6]Robespierre [Miranda, *Archivo*, 1929] pressured the Court president, who had proof of Miranda's innocence, to convict him: "Miranda should not be judged with evidence but politically" advice from Robespierre to Montané, president of the Revolutionary court [*Archivo*, Vol. XII p. XXXVI of the Introduction]. Later, Robespierre had this fair, professional judge arrested and cynically sent to share Miranda's prison.

[7]Quatremère de Quincy, [1794, 1989], *Archivo* ... op. cit. Vol. XII, p. 434; translated from French], also reprinted in French [1989] *Lettres à Miranda*, and also translated in Spanish [1998] *Cartas a Miranda sobre el desplazamiento de los monumentos de Arte de Italia.*

[8]Is a fact that Miranda's constitutional project could not be implemented. However, this historical fact cannot simply be considered a failure of his ideas, but rather a personal failure that remains to be analysed and explained.

significant past events and their interpretations by historians and political scientists. In particular, Miranda's complex relationships with British and French leaders prompt us to reexamine the Franco-British wars during this period of significant transformation. Chap. 11 is specifically dedicated to a detailed analysis of the vicissitudes of the ambiguous British attitude towards Miranda's proposals, showing, among other conclusions, that this cynical selfish ambiguity turned mainly against the own interests of the "*perfide Albion*".

History has demonstrated a long series of monstrous errors in governance, and this "groping process" has had direct consequences, from which we opt for the hypothesis of a historical process of action-reaction, which could appear to be the emergence of a natural selection of political ideas. Therefore, this hypothesis leads us to explicitly apply an empirical, although controversial, method to Miranda's ideas, comparing them with what has been progressively tested and selected by our societies during the two subsequent centuries. Drawing lessons from the past, these ideas are widely accepted today by consensus or a clear majority of citizens. The result shows that Miranda's vision was a precursor in the sense that his ideas of governance ultimately prevailed, at least in the Western world, until 2024. We are aware that our point of view is subjective, but common sense suggests that objective reality indicates Western societies have progressively adopted these principles to achieve what is considered better governance today compared to the past. Even if a popular majority opted for another system of governance tomorrow, the current democracy would have been historically announced by Miranda, in *tempore non suspecto*. To deny this view would mean to think that our current democratic regimes were not chosen but emerged by chance, without any objective reason to be considered "better" than past absolutism or totalitarism. Demonstrating the opposite requires identifying the "actors of change" and the origin of their ideas.

Therefore, it is not useless to recognise Miranda's exceptional ability to imagine better than others what would be most appropriate for what is seen today and in recent decades as political progress in comparison with Miranda's time—and especially in contrast to what the "successful" Liberators did—as well as in comparison with the repetition of the "Jacobin system" under subsequent totalitarian regimes that he tirelessly denounced as a major danger for democracy, and which is becoming topical again with the present drift towards illiberal regimes. Undoubtedly, this perspective necessarily draws on contemporary values and ideas to interpret the past. Of course, our method is subject to valid criticism. It must remain open to discussion, as it opposes different schools of thought, particularly the Marxist ideologies of the "sense of history" and certain principles of the "new school of thought" of Cambridge historians.

Applying our method of comparing Miranda's proposals with current consensual principles leads us to highlight the extraordinary ability to combine the new fundamental principles of the Enlightenment and adapt them in an innovative way to solve the aporia, or systemic contradiction, between individual freedom and the interests of all citizens, by applying very empirical principles: allow, institutionalise, guarantee pluralistic debates, and accept majority choices.

Behind what seems an obvious or common-sense recipe today, Miranda's fundamental democratic principle rests on a pragmatic anthropology that allows him to reduce it to a minimum of ideological postulates. Contrary to dominant thoughts from Plato to Rousseau and his followers, he did not rely on absolute rights. Miranda, just like his friend Alexander Hamilton,[9] does not believe in the concept of "political virtue" of the human being, but in his rational capacity to conceive and build an institutional system through written constitutions able to limit the political power through mechanisms of separation of powers and counterweights that allow these separate powers to control each other. To this end, the three constitutional powers must be on the same footing and have the means and incentives to remain autonomous. This supposes four postulates or conditions to function:

- First, *popular sovereignty* was claimed by the Enlightenment, with the people's government serving as the source of authority to establish the legitimacy of institutions and their three branches of power.
- Second, this power of the people cannot be confused with "popular power," meaning that political control by the people must be exercised through a representative system based on regular elections; the people cannot govern directly. The so-called "popular power" implies that the legislative branch would inevitably impose its power over the other two, as historical experience demonstrates without any exception, always leading to totalitarian tyranny.
- Third, the representative system must be based on credibility and trust, so that the people have confidence in the institutions and their ability to monitor the different powers professionally in the general interest. That implies an active role in public opinion, the consent of which allows political authority
- Fourth, the *axiom of the pre-eminence of fundamental human rights* over any other ideological principle: «A *free government views all men equally ... a homicide is always a homicide, whatever its origin. When you confuse your oppressors, do not imitate their tyranny ...*[10]" «*no man will be above [*the laws*] or will be*

[9] **Alexander Hamilton** (1757–1804), one of the founding fathers of the United States, one of the authors of the United States Constitution, and principal author of the "Federalist Papers" published under the pseudonym Publius from 1787 to 1788 in the New York press, to expose the federative doctrine that allowed the approval of the US Constitution. He played a fundamental role in the economic and financial policy of the United States that allowed the success of this federal republic. He is the founder of the Federalist Party, Jefferson's political adversary. He died in a duel provoked by Aaron Burr, Jefferson's vice-president, for his criticism of Burr's ethical conduct during the electoral campaign of 1804. Hamilton had close ties of friendship with Miranda, and Miranda's constitutional ideas were inspired by the discussions that were held. Miranda's constitutional ideas were inspired by the discussions that both had during Miranda's stay in the United States in 1784. They remained in epistolary contact. In 1798, both expressed great distrust towards Jacobin France for the same reasons. Although the "Federalist Papers" did not appear in the lists of Miranda's books established for sale in 1828 and 1833, it seems clear to us from the similitudes between their key principles that Miranda was aware of or at least discussed the fundamental issues with Hamilton. Most likely, Miranda took this fundamental book to Venezuela when he left London in 1810, explaining its absence in his house in London. Xavier Reyes Matheus [2010] details the same conviction of Hamilton's influence on Miranda in his work, while Daniel Betti [2008] underlines the similitude in both revolutionary thinkers in his paper; see also Sect. 4.6 in this book.

[10] Chapter 9, document 9.2, translated from Spanish, [*Archivo* ... op. cit Vol. XVI, p. 119].

able to transgress them with impunity; The poorest in the State will be under their protection as much as the richest.[11]

The similarity between Miranda and Hamilton on these basic philosophical postulates draws attention. The reasons are their common sources from Hume, Locke, and Montesquieu, together with the crucial exchanges the two revolutionaries had in New York in 1784 and after these first exchanges. Their shared view was that they believed human behaviors could be channeled by institutions capable of motivating common interests across social groups, provided that they impeded the domination of legislative power over the executive and the judiciary. Both were opposed to slavery and racial discrimination and advocated for social and ethnic integration. They also warned the US government about the growing risk that France might attempt to seize the Spanish colonies, thereby posing a threat to US democracy.

The combination of the above principles aims to make a strict separation of powers feasible through a representative legislative power, which thus acts as a filter. Miranda reinforces this through restrictive electoral criteria, known as a "censitarian" vote, and an appointed senate. Having suffered personally from the unbalanced power of the popular deliberative assemblies during the French Revolution,[12] Miranda proposes a "*mixed democracy*" that simultaneously prevents popular power from imposing itself on the executive and the judiciary, while also providing the means to exercise popular sovereignty through regular elections. The purpose was to mitigate the abuses and tyranny resulting from the centralisation of powers. He wants [Antepara/Miranda, 1810] a «*government for the people, controlled by people, but not directly governed by the people*[13]». A direct democracy based on popular power would prevent an effective separation of powers, subjecting the government and judges to popular emotions and violence, thereby eradicating pluralism and freedom. This explains why he opposed the principle of excessive control over the executive, as the French Revolution had abused this principle by multiplying "deliberative" bodies. He wanted a proper balance of powers on an equal footing to achieve an executive with adequate power of action but controlled to prevent anarchy or tyranny; what was clearly missing from all the governments of the Revolution, from the Girondins and the Jacobins to Napoleon (see Chap. 6, document 6.3, in Context). His diagnose of the French Revolution illustrates particularly his clear-sightedness when comparing his analysis with the multitude of historians' views up to now. It is only with Timothy Tackett's work [2015] that a similar explanation of the Terror was implictly generated by the Revolution without adequate constitutional conception.

---

[11] Chap. 9, document 9.5 Proclamation to be issued upon landing in Brazil, 1806, translated from Spanish [*América Espera*, op. cit. Document 132, p. 351–353].

[12] Miranda, as we will explain, was significantly influenced by his experiences during the French Revolution, by the imbalance caused by the excess of power of the deliberative assemblies over the executive (Girondin regime during the Convention 1792–1793) as well as the opposite excess when the legislative ruled during the tyranny of the Jacobins (Robespierre 1793–1794), and also when by reaction the power shifted radically to the executive (Thermidor, Directory, and the dictatorship of Napoleon in the Consulate and Empire).

[13] Antepara, J. M., [1810], *South American Emancipation* … op. cit., section 14, "Adequate political dissertation to be followed for South America".

Miranda's "mixed democracy" is based on the permanent interaction of checks and balances between independent powers that exert pluralistic or critical pressures, allowing, through free and open debates, for better information and education of voters, who then decide with sovereignty the type of society that suits them. They, in short, can judge and sanction the government through regular elections, although they do not directly govern. Considering Miranda as a mere liberal defender of the social order is an error based upon an explicit ideological bias that corresponds to pretending to own an "absolute truth" for the sake of human progress. On the contrary, Miranda's democracy is not ideological but merely empirical, based on the observed principle that all power leads to abuse; therefore, the only solution is that the different branches of power limit each other's room for manoeuvre. Such mutual control works only when the three powers are separate and independent. For this reason, he proposes *limiting popular power to its function of periodic control* through regular elections, not so much for ideological reasons, but rather out of pragmatism, observing that when popular power dominates, it leads to tyranny and the denial of human rights.

It is interesting to note the similarity between his philosophy of governance progress and the modern scientific method: scientific progress results not from ideologies but from open debates about the facts of experimentation and its possible errors or deficiencies. Accepting this in politics constitutes fundamental human progress by relativising the role of political ideologies, whose role must be limited to a value judgment, i.e., an explicit political choice that citizens must validate through open debates. This means recognising that "truth" does not exist in politics, but only in free societies' choices. This constitutes a total *revolutionary break*, not only in comparison with the old regime, but above all, with other revolutionaries and even the current political movements, including the emerging anti-democratic movement in the United States coined "Dark Enlightenment" (see Chap. 1) or Neo-Reactionarism (NRx), which relies entirely on ideological axioms.

Is limiting access to voting and opting for representative parliamentary formulas a loss of democracy? Ideologically, this is clearly the case. However, in the historical context of Spanish America, Miranda's political choice is overall a measure to protect a nascent democracy from what he saw as the greatest threat to democracy, as he had experienced personally with the Jacobin drift of the Terror, which perverted the French Revolution. For him, as for Hamilton in the US, a sustainable democracy cannot let the people govern directly. The «popular power» in polarised societies with unequal education does lead necessarily to an antidemocratic regime, as the radical left (from the Jacobins to Venezuelan "Chavism[14]") demonstrates by

[14] **Chavism** is a radical left-wing populist political ideology based on the ideas of **Hugo Chavez** (1954–2013), who promoted a socialist revolution in the early 1980s, which he called the Bolivarian Revolution. However, based on a personal interpretation of Bolivar's ideas, mixed with some of Rousseau and Marx's principles as well as with some personal elements imported from Christianity, which he synthesised later in the "*Socialism for the twentieth century*", a radical left ideology against neo-liberal and market economies, this very populist program became dominant in political life in Venezuela, leading to the democratic election of Hugo Chavez as President of Venezuela, and his successive legal four re-elections until his death, despite a clear tendency to a weakening of democracy with a growing autoritarism. The movement has continued under his neo-marxist

confusing "democracy" with direct "popular power" applied through dominant people's assemblies. History shows, at least until today, that popular power, when it dominates the executive and the judiciary, transforms any well-intentioned political regime into totalitarian power.

Miranda's democratic governance thus becomes an evolutionary and open process, subject to the scrutiny of public opinion through counter-powers, such as the press and independent bodies established in his constitutional projects. Miranda necessarily belongs to the category of revolutionaries/decolonisers since his only objective was to change the political regime in two linked sequences: first, complete independence from the Metropolis (*external decolonisation*), and thanks to it, to acquire the possibility to organise a representative system of filtered democratic sovereignty able to guarantee pluralism (*internal decolonisation*), which, in turn, requires to set consensus on institutions able to channel popular emotions and their violent potential. In this way, he was a moderate revolutionary who prioritised achieving a complete but progressive decolonisation through a smooth transition, without violence, thanks to establishing a new constitutional order. This rule of law should allow for a gradual social change with cohesion if cooperation between classes and ethnicities is organised explicitly. The process of social change that Miranda hopes for cannot be imposed by ideology, but rather by the democratic exercise of seeking consensus, aided by the power of education.

Thus, we believe Miranda was genuinely revolutionary in precisely trying to counteract radical and ideological revolutionaries, which constitutes an interesting paradox that political scientists or philosophers have not often emphasised. Therefore, Miranda designed a visionary formula of governance able to decolonise both externally (independence) and internally (emancipation) by integrating, developing socio-economically, and educating the whole citizenship—Indians included—to citizen freedom for meeting the challenge of making sustainable a great federation of heterogeneous peoples that the colonial regime had segmented into castes and ethnicities to keep them subdued.

Miranda's democracy is conceived as an evolutionary process of permanent search for open debates capable of evaluating governability, controlling the executive, and redeeming its errors because there is no single political truth with a single direction of History. However, he believes in human progress and a possible path to emancipation only if a wise, integrative, and educative institutional framework can channel social movements and particular interests to ensure what he calls "rational

disciple, the interim President Maduro, who was elected as President with 50,6%. He amplified the systemic weakening of democracy with centralisation of powers and anti-economic policies, strengthening the discretionary power of his party and the Army. The catastrophic economic results, joined with the recurrent violations of Human rights and the rule of law, combined with systemic electoral frauds, the corruption and the untransparent, autocratic governance, have led the country to unprecedented disaster with about eight million emigrants (a quarter of its population). According to our estimation, the GDP per capita fell from 11.000 US$ in 2011 to around 2.000 US$ in 2021, an unprecedented historical record of economic contraction in world history.

freedom.[15]" This concept corresponds to an institutional order that simultaneously protects individual freedom and society's common interests by guaranteeing permanent pluralistic debates, thus ensuring a "trial-and-error" process capable of self-correcting errors necessary for progress in socio-economic and human development. The word "rational" implies that individual freedom is justified if it does not compromise society's goals. This is a pragmatic response addressing the fundamental human aporia between the individual and society. Miranda's formula attempts to channel the centrifugal forces resulting from the inevitable acephaly, which he expected to follow the rupture with the absolutist Spanish monarchy in the problematic context of dual and multicultural societies.

The governance regime that Miranda conceived constitutes a novel synthesis—the first—between the utilitarianism of J. Bentham (that is, the individualistic liberal thought that led to modern neo-liberalism), the community natural law of J. J. Rousseau (that is, the social thought which led to socialism and Marxism). The Miranda's proposal was a pragmatic attempt to reconcile "freedom" and "equality" (or "fraternity") by setting the innovative idea concerning liberalism that individual freedom requires a collective dimension, not merely for protecting individual rights but also limiting them for protecting common goods and goals. Furthermore, Miranda added the precursory idea of incorporating some indigenous components of American culture to this innovation in his synthesis. This cultural initiative was not taken seriously and was even perceived by many historians as mere exotic folklore. It was not understood that he adopted an effective cultural relativism, a considerable advance over the dominant, fanatical Euro-centric world of his time, which has persisted until very recently or even prevailed in many cases. Today, with the benefit of two centuries of experience with the abuse of the superiority complex of the old continent and the excesses of radicalisation of its two ideological poles (liberalism versus socialism), Miranda's humanist path continues to chart a timely path for our democratic and multicultural societies to face the challenges of globalisation. Even further, behind Miranda, one can perceive a questioning of our own Western way of thinking in a binary manner,[16] but that is another intellectual debate outside the scope of this book.

Although he imported several concepts from the Anglo-Saxon political regimes (the United Kingdom, the United States, especially A. Hamilton), the 'Republic of Miranda' copies neither the American formula nor the French one but proposes a new type of governance that, although Miranda failed to implement it in Latin America effectively, announces and advances what the European Union has, with difficulty, discovered much later: the use of a common ethos capable of making compatible and of taking advantage of different national identities. His proposal relies on a specific sense of democracy in which the popular power is channelled through a double representative and geographical dimension. This two-tier system is essential to ensure the effective division of powers (see later) together with the

[15] Specific concept of Miranda, see Sects. 4.1 and 4.2 in this book.

[16] On this epistemological dimension, see Ghymers, C. & Gonzalez, C. [2016].

purpose of integrating both regional and socio-ethnic heterogeneous peoples. This principle was later dubbed "subsidiarity[17]" and is constitutionally anchored in the Treaty of the European Union [2010]. It allows both to base a legitimate central power that would make it possible to build a new identity progressively while ensuring the necessary local autonomies and the protection of their citizens from the State, political oligarchies and the central power.

2.3 Is Miranda a Political Philosopher?

Let's be clear from the beginning. Miranda does not belong to the same category as the most significant political thinkers of his time, such as the authors of the "Federalist Papers" Hamilton and Madison, or others like Jefferson, Bentham, Paine, Montesquieu, Rousseau and Condorcet. Miranda cannot either be considered a «philosophical precursor» since he did not invent (and never intended to) the basic principles—such as written constitutions, representative democracy, separation of powers, tolerance and human rights, republicanism, subsidiarity, etc.) on which his precursory contribution in governance and decolonisation is built. Most authors do not consider him a political philosopher. Nevertheless, he left key ideas and essential documents. Still, most importantly, he had concrete life and action options on the field, manifesting a long-range project with an indisputable scope of political philosophy well before his time, making him a «precursor statesman».

Two reasons tend to reinforce and mutually explain why Miranda is, however, not considered an influential political thinker. First, the advanced character of his ideas and behaviours left him unfairly undervalued by his contemporaries and History. By definition, a "precursor" means, in other words, "it is his fault to be right before the others", making him necessarily objected to or rejected by his contemporaries. «*After all, you don't get the moniker 'The Precursor' through timely triumph but early failure*» [Betti, 2008]. Second, the short and eclectic character of his political texts, whose purpose was to provide operational responses to specific events and operational needs in a given and dated geopolitical historical context, could explain why historians have not paid sufficient attention to his thoughts. These two combined factors force the historian or political analyst to undertake a challenging exercise of interpretation of contingent facts and extrapolation of contextual positions, which must be assessed in reference to options and principles deduced from Miranda's actions and according to the values he defended throughout his life. Thus, historians are led into the realm of pure philosophical and political inquiry, where objectivity does not exist by definition. This also highlights the limitations of the method employed in this work, acknowledging beforehand the inevitable degree of subjectivity that affects this work due to the inherent nature of the chosen theme.

[17] **Subsidiarity**: the political principle of governance incorporated in the Treaty of the EU [2010, Art. 5 § 3] that states that decisions should be made at the most appropriate level for reaching their objective, see Sect. 4.4 in this book.

Nevertheless, which other method would seem able to draw exciting debates and lessons for understanding the historical orientations adopted by the caudillos who prevailed over Miranda and, consequently, drove the whole region in the opposite direction?

References

Antepara, J. M., [1810], *South American Emancipation*, ed. by R. Juigné, 17 Margaret Street, London, Re-edited by Chacon, D. [2005] and also by Editorial Ayacucho [2009].

Betti, D. [2008] «*American Revolutionaries: Alexander Hamilton & Francisco de Miranda*», 2008. Available at SSRN: https://ssrn.com/abstract=4410146 or https://doi.org/10.2139/ssrn.4410146

Dalencour, F., 1955], *Francisco de Miranda et Alexandre Pétion : l'expédition de Miranda*, Librairie Bernard Levrault et Dalencour, Paris & Port-au-Prince.

Dunn, J., [2025], Annex 2 of this book, "Miranda as Prematurely Professional Revolutionary", unpublished draft presented in 2006 Conference in London.

European Union, [2010], Version consolidée du Traité sur l'Union Européenne, Office des Publications de l'UE, Luxembourg.

Ghymers, C., [2002], "Influencia del Maestro sobre el Discípulo: el papel de Miranda y O'Higgins en la singularidad del caso chileno y de su gobernabilidad", *Revista del Instituto O'Higgiano de Chile*, n° 19, Santiago.

Ghymers, C & González. [2016] "Intercultural Management: Bridging the Cultural Divide – CELAC – Europa", in *Management interculturel et affinités électives, Europe - Amérique latine et Caraïbe, pour contribuer à un développement durable* , by CERALE- Centre d'Etudes et de Recherches Amérique Latine - Europe, and ESCP Europe Business School, Paris.

Miranda, F. de [1929–1950], *Archivo del General Miranda*, ed. Vicente Dávila/ Rubén González, Caracas/La Habana.

Quatremère de Quincy, [1794, 1989], Précis sur Miranda, ed. Barrois l'aîné, Paris, re-published as *Lettres à Miranda*, ed. and also translated in Spanish [1998] *Cartas a Miranda sobre el desplazamiento de los monumentos de Arte de Italia,* ed.

Reyes Matheus, X. [2010], "*Mas Liberal que Libertador: Francisco de Miranda y el Birth of Modern Democra cy in Europe and America*", FAES Foundación editorial, Madrid.

Tackett, T., [2015], *The Coming of Terror in the French Revolution*, Harvard University Press.

Chapter 3
Methodological Aspects: Resolving the Conflict Between Objectivity and Assessing Precursory Ideas

3.1 The New Cambridge School of Political Thought

From a methodological point of view, Miranda offers an exciting test case for an essential methodological debate between historians, particularly with the "Cambridge School[1]" [Pocock, 1962; Skinner, 1969; Dunn, 1968]. This school aims correctly to recover the original meaning of the ideas issued by their authors according to their environment and historical context without interference with posterior thinking. It is characterised by *analysing the socio-economic and ideological context* in which a particular way of thinking was developed and expressed in written form or discourse. Even though we consider ourselves as belonging to this school of thought,[2] Miranda's case offers us an exciting opportunity to test the limitations—or even some contradictions—in the extended interpretation that a few authors of this

[1] John Pocock, Quentin Skinner, and John Dunn are the most known representatives, forming the "Triumvirate this **Historian school to intellectual history and political thought** shaped in Cambridge at the end of the sixties and characterised by a deep analysis of the original historical context of political texts and ideas. Although these three authors are considered the fathers of this New School, they could be "*understood as a long consequence of Seeley's determination at the foundation of the Historical Tripos in the 1870s to relate history and politics to each other*" [Alexander, 2016].

[2] As already shown clearly by the structure of this book, I adhere without any reserve to the general principle that any political text and corresponding idea must be analysed in their specific milieu, not only the historical surrounding context of the time but also of their author, trying to recover the precise questions to which the political or philosophical texts were designed to answer at a specific moment. This principle is broader and older than the "*New Cambridge School*" and simply sets that political thought should be studied historically—that is, explicitly, not in contemporary terms. From this obvious principle emerges the more complex issue of subjectivism, which has no clear-cut or "binary" solution in the sense that not only objectivity does not exist as such, but also subjectivism is not necessarily the opposite of objectivity according to how the analyst explains how he works.

C. Ghymers, *Independence, Federalism and Regionalism in Latin America: An Analytical Anthology of Francisco de Miranda's Writings (1790-1811)*,
United Nations University Series on Regionalism 34,
https://doi.org/10.1007/978-3-031-96938-6_3

school apply for pretending to abstract from the posterior relevance that past ideas could have today for us [Skinner, 1969].

Although this Cambridge school recovers various positions and nuances, a common principle is that the "objectivity" of a historian implies that their research on past thoughts cannot be influenced by the subsequent relevance these ideas may have today. This looks great and is very useful for self-analysing objectivity and denouncing many abuses.[3] Still, it might also lead to contradictions as history cannot be limited to describing past events, especially regarding the history of political ideas. History has a social and cultural function for understanding the past, inevitably for its implications for the present and future, making it impossible for historians of political thought not to draw conclusions that bear on present-day debates. Consciously or not, this opens the question of possible interferences of political options in the interpretation of facts. More than a problem of objectivity, this question raises another key issue: the relationship between political thought and history, which has been a main characteristic of Cambridge's historical teaching and research since the 1870s. As explained by James Alexander [2016],

> for a century, almost all the major figures in Cambridge agreed that history and politics should be related but disagreed about how to do it. The writings of Seeley, Sidgwick, Acton, Maitland, Figgis, Barker, Oakeshott, Cowling, Laslett, Runciman, Dunn, Skinner and others attempted to relate history and politics.

Political science emerged in this context of the development of the history of political thought, which suffered from a fundamental ambivalence about its relevance to actual politics. Cambridge historians "*sometimes claimed that if the history of political thought were good history, then it would eschew any simple attempt to relate past theories to the present, but at other times they claimed that good history could enable us to restore the relation between past and present theories*". This contradiction has not been solved.

As Michael Oakeshott[4] and many others have argued, politics does not occur independently of specific human beings in specific historical eras; therefore, political theories must be analysed "historically." However, the results are not merely of historical significance, but also hold significance for contemporary political theory and its challenges. This means that the objectivity versus subjectivism qualification has no "scientific solution". The Cambridge School warns rightly against the "teleological" temptation of reading the past in function of the present. Still, it exposes a contradiction, as history is often seen as a means to an end, which is the understanding of our societies, not only past societies, and even this past tends implicitly to be viewed through the lens of some present influences. Even when contextualising the

[3]The recent case of the unbolting of statues of characters linked to or considered colonialists or slaveholders illustrates the need for rigorous analysis and deeper public debates to prevent populist simplifications.

[4]**M. Oakeshott** (1901–1990), English conservative philosopher and historian, trained in Cambridge before WWII, later became a Professor of Political Science at the London School of Economics (LSE). He does not belong to the "New Cambridge School" but to the previous Cambridge School. See Oakeshott [2006], *Lectures in the History of Political Thought*.

writings and an author, it is impossible to do so entirely independently of current views.[5] Pretending the contrary, although looking "objective", means to deny the function of history, which would become useless by studying "the past for its own sake"! Aware of this "antiquarianism", the triumvirate formed by Skinner with John Dunn and John Pocock has adapted its views later (and each of them in different ways), considering that history and philosophy had to be fused at a higher level where they would, in effect, become the same thing. This evolution, joined to many criticisms, has settled in a more moderate form of contextualism [Charette & Skjönsberg, 2020; Alexander, 2016] even among the Cambridge school, and a more pragmatic consensus seems to appear around the mutual dependency that political theory needs the history of political thought and vice versa. Even Skinner [2008] said in an interview

> To write history is not in the least to stop doing philosophy; rather, it is a way of doing philosophy, of raising questions that either have or ought to have relevance for us here and now. That this is so important to me, for I think that historians ought to be willing to explain why the study of the past matters, and I don't feel that they ask that question often enough.

We share Alexander's diagnostic [2016] that "*... the concomitant exclusion of political science, political philosophy and political theology has, if anything, left the Cambridge school with what I would argue is a highly eroded capacity to say anything about politics at all*".

3.2 Our Conception of Objectivity in History

According to our views, three different considerations should be combined to ensure an analysis which tries to be as objective as might be possible in history:

- First, as the New Cambridge School rightly argues, the contextual determinants, especially the cultural society's dominant ideas and philosophical views, being considered at a specific time, must be the reference basis, including the global aspects.
- Second, precisely in parallel as a necessary complement, the other views or intellectual dissident movements must be assessed compared to the existing mainstream with their contextual basis and attempt to identify their origins or determinants and their possible posterior impacts.
- Third, and this is the core issue, to try to explain the results of the conflicts and to issue an interpretation of the consequent events or their chronological development, distinguishing between endogenous, exogenous, and stochastic factors.

---

[5] Scientific works in Quantum Physics, psychology, and neurology tend to demonstrate that "the point of view could create the phenomenon." Although not necessarily relevant to other disciplines, it is inspiring to know that Quantum Physics sets that any observation is affected by the observer: everyone sees a different truth because, in a way, everyone is creating what they see.

The first two components could and should be objectively executed. Still, the third one requires an analysis of the determinants that implies—consciously or not—an inevitable assessment when making the necessary comparative analysis. Who could pretend this crucial step is feasible without interfering with present ideas and values? Such an assessment, even based upon scientific explanation (or econometric models), needs a "system of reference", i.e. is necessarily relative to a posterior time and to present values because referring only to dominant ideas of the past does not bring any value added to the historical analysis for understanding changes, but remains limited to a mere description of historical facts without any possibility to make sense through a comparative analysis. This comparative analysis between mainstream and *minority ideas gains all its meaning only in relation to posterior (or present) values*. Therefore, such a reference to our present ideas is not only inevitable but also necessary for understanding and assessing the emergence of "new ideas" in their context and the resulting social evolution that sustains innovation as well as the resistance to changes or regressions. Social events are based on forces in conflict; the results of these struggles compose history, but other factors also act, and the factual outcomes must be interpreted. This assessment requires comparing them with potential alternative results. This comparison is inevitably "subjective," but it cannot be rejected as "subjectivity" as far as it remains a part of a genuine historical analysis, remaining fully aware of its "relativity" and degree of explicit subjectivism. Therefore, we even maintain that a dose of conscious subjectivism is necessary for generating helpful debates and making it possible to issue explanatory hypotheses, giving a social role to history and making sense of the historian's work in contributing to the debates that shape a democratic society.

We firmly believe that any comparative analysis makes it inescapable—consciously or implicitly—to be influenced by present ideas and values. Pretending to be radically isolated from today's views might only be feasible at the expense of part of the content of the analysis. It could lead to a worse bias than explicitly accepting some interferences with our own reference system. Indeed, radical objectivity, in fact, tends to reduce the scope of the analysis, with the danger of seeing any change as due to stochastic or exogenous determinants, as was demonstrated by John Dunn's interventions in the panel on Miranda in 2006 in London.[6] Such a radical method means limiting or even impeding the analysis and understanding of the dynamics of innovation and social movements. We firmly believe that the degree of adequacy or divergence of ideas presented in a specific historical context compared to subsequent conceptions provides essential information. This information must be analysed explicitly and carefully in reference to these posterior or contemporaneous conceptions, with the aim of identifying relative positions, drawing upon the results of the perceived evolution to look for a possible "historical path" and its hypothetical determinants. It is illusory to pretend to be able to analyse a context without assessing dissidents and minority views existing in the same context, something that—of course—is never and cannot be purely objective. Under the condition of

[6] See following sections and Annex 2.

being explicitly acknowledged, such an imperfect objectivity seems analytically superior to the search for absolute objectivity, which would result in being sterile, impeding a valuable assessment for society and the future. Wouldn't history be considered a social science? We pretend that this assessment step is inherent to the nature of History, which is dynamic and is, therefore, condemned to be rewritten and re-assessed at each period. Permanent rewriting of history is necessary to prove the inescapable reference to the present. It is a process of criticism for studying the emergence of new ideas, the degree of innovation or the qualification of "novelty" itself, and so the evolution of ideas, beliefs, and societies. Therefore, it is essential to consider that other evolutions would have been possible even if they failed. Potential alternatives always exist and must be assessed in their own context to understand the existing forces at stake. Denying this step transforms the real world into unanalysed and sterile chaos, i.e., renouncing an understanding of human reality and cultural dynamism, rendering history a useless art, and even exposing it to the dangerous virus of an "apolitical" illusion.

Let's be concrete about Miranda's case. We consider it worthwhile to examine the relevance of his positions for our time, in order to make a more acute and pertinent analysis of Miranda's concepts and actions, making this relevance an operational criterion in our own method. On the contrary, applying strictly the "Cambridge" principle of objectivity to Miranda's or other precursors' thinking might expose succumbing to a hidden type of subjectivism that would remove—and even impede—the interest in analysing Miranda's revolutionary thinking. The risk of this bias could create a dangerous illusion.

3.3 A Concrete Case: The 2006 Debate with John Dunn's Views on Miranda as a Precursor

The most explicit demonstration of the loss of historical content and sense to which leads a radical application of the Cambridge obsession for objectivity in history is given by the pejorative reduction of Miranda's thinking by John Dunn—one of the most famous pillars of the Cambridge school—when he participated as discussant in the London panel on Miranda's political thinking in 2006 (Annex 2, the paper he sent me after the event[7]). Therefore, this methodological section must seize Dunn's presentation to illustrate the above arguments.

[7] See Annex 2, Dunn, John, "*Miranda as Prematurely Professional Revolutionary*", unpublished paper presented in answer to the conference given by C. Ghymers in the "Panel on Miranda" organised by Professor James Dunkerley, in the "Institute for the Study of the Americas" of the University of London in May 2006 with the participation of the Professors Malcolm Deas, St. Antony's College, Oxford, John Dunn, University of Cambridge, Christian Ghymers, Brussels Management School, Geoffrey Hawthorn, University of Cambridge, John Lynch, Emeritus Professor of Latin American History in the University of London.

Dunn considers Miranda an "*incoherent thinker*" who proposed "*a nebula of government forms*" without evaluating the risks implied by his governance proposals. This extreme interpretation through the Cambridge method leads him to put into question Miranda's historical status: "*the indeterminacy of Miranda's historical status—Precursor clairvoyant or largely inadvertent, and precursor to just what?*[8]" denying him even a role as a genuine "*revolutionary*" for considering it as "*self-attributed*" and assessing that his role could be merely due to "*external circumstances*" and not to his political ideas or own analysis. Even the concept and status of Precursor and revolutionary are downgraded by the qualification of a "*premature professional revolutionary*" given to Miranda, as well as considering—wrongly—that "*there are no surviving traces of any commitment to mixed government*" and, as regards the Jacobin defect and the Thermidorian[9] abuses, Dunn sees—also wrongly -"*no rejection* [by Miranda] *of its structure of authority, or of the arbitrary relation between that authority and the society*" because he thinks that Miranda adopted the "*flagrantly unjust principle of action with a French provenance which, far from being a Jacobin innovation went back at least as far as Cardinal Richelieu*".

For those knowing Miranda's factual path, texts and constant strategy, it is straightforward to demonstrate that Dunn's interpretation is not only wrong but in contradiction with the Cambridge principle of broad contextualisation: Miranda's primary purpose (and well in advance compared to most of other Latin American patriots) was always to change the governance in Hispanic America radically, not for taking-over the Metropolis privileges, what most of the other patriotic rebels wanted, but for emancipating through good governance, what sets the basis of a genuine de-colonialization of the whole societies. Wouldn't that be the standard definition of a revolutionary? Wasn't he seen—in this past context—as the major threat to the established colonial and social regime, not only by the Spanish (and even Portuguese) authorities but also by the British ones, the Catholic Church, the ruling social class, and the white creoles? The incumbent powers precisely perceived his constitutional proposals in his time and context as an especially coherent attack "against their interests". Such a perception dates back to his time and does not reflect any interference with current values. The writings and acts of Miranda (which are historical facts) demonstrate precisely the contrary to what Dunn said, pretending erroneously that Miranda did not evaluate the consequences of his propositions. On the contrary, he was permanently worried about the risks that any revolution or regime could pose [Miranda 1929, quoting his letter dated 1798], and

[8] Dunn, J., ibid.

[9] The **Thermidorians**, named according to the month of Thermidor (July 1794), during which a coup against Robespierre overthrew him as a result of a conspiracy to arrest, convict and kill him through a coalition of Jacobins and other deputies of the Convention, who felt threatened by his arbitrary regime of "Terror" but who, above all, wanted to take advantage of the tyrant's powers for their own benefit. Miranda opposed them since they did not change these arbitrary powers that betrayed the revolution. Their regime led to the Directory regime endowed with a new constitution establishing an undemocratic republic managed by the same bourgeois up to Napoleon's coup in 1799.

much more than his successful rivals: "*I fear equally and maybe even more, anarchy and the revolutionary system!* [10]". Therefore, his priority and his actions [Antepara, 1810] in opposition to his contemporaneous revolutionary actors, were to assure, through written constitutions and the rule of law, an evolving and coherent governance framework in order to:

> To save the country from the danger of all the unjust and illegal acts that would result from an interval in which it was without government, and from all the evils of a momentary anarchy, so difficult to avoid when passing from one government to another.[11]

His formula was very pragmatic: first, to ensure a democratic transition through elected Municipal Councils; second, to establish the security of people and property, which constitutes, for him, the critical criterion of the success or failure of a revolution:

> "Nothing is more important in the cause of liberty that [this] security" and "if when a people rise to destroy all that is opposed to good government, they form a firm resolution to respect persons and property, it may be predicted that if they maintain this security, will lead your society to success.[12]"

In the most explicit terms, Miranda warned about the risks of any change in political regime:

> ... you must fear staining it [independence] with irregular procedures. Detesting crimes of all kinds, carefully avoid the movements of anarchy. Remember that revenge for crimes belongs only to the courts of justice; that a homicide is always a homicide, whatever its origin. When you confuse your oppressors, do not imitate their tyranny. It is not your idea to replace an irregular government with another similar one, to replace an oppressive regime with another oppressive regime; to destroy an old tyranny with a new tyranny; in a word, to establish upon the ruin of a foreign despotism, the reign of another despotism no less cruel, that of license and anarchy?[13]

Reducing the risks of instability and abuse of power inherent to social changes was a constant guideline of his emancipation plan, and he even gave the operational details in his book written with Antepara in 1810 in London: "*Let us now see how these General principles apply to the notable and specific case before us ....*[14]". The comparison between the observed results of the independence wars and the expected results of Miranda's emancipation project should be part of any historical analysis exercise, obliging us to explicitly identify the forces in conflict and the supposed explanatory factors.

Miranda had identified carefully and well in advance the risks of social and racial violence that would emerge with the acephaly implied by a revolution. To channel these risks, he consistently advocated in favour of adopting a careful preventive

---

[10] See Chap. 10, document 10.3.1. Letter to John Turnbull, January 12, 1798.

[11] See Chap. 8, document 8.2., document 6.2. "*El Colombiano*", extracts from n° V, 15 May 1810.

[12] Ibid.

[13] Chapter 9, document 9.2. Proclamation "*A los pueblos del Continente Colombiano alias Hispano-América*», London 1801.

[14] Chapter 8, document 8.1. § 14.

strategy structured through a new legal order cleverly articulated and based upon a democratic movement at the most basic level, the municipal councils, but coordinated with a systemic division of powers and a delegation to a strong central executive, something that for not having been implemented in the first Republic of Venezuela in 1811, and à fortiori by his successors after his capture by the Spanish army in 1812, demonstrated that he was right as shown by the bloody and definitive damages provoked by the rejection of Miranda's formulas.

Dunn wrongly said that the reference to a "mixed government" disappeared, that the consequences of upheaval were not adequately taken on board, and that Miranda had espoused French centralism like any Jacobin.[15] These gross mistakes manifest a lack of context analysis, directly contradicting his own method. Miranda was always radically and obsessively opposed to the Jacobins and any centralisation of the constitutional powers. Miranda's recurrent obsession has been since 1795 to find a way to impede Jacobinism from extending and polluting Latin America. There are several dozen references in his writings and remarks warning about the threat of the "*abominable French system*" and the need to "*... forming a stable government on radically opposite foundations to the French system*[16]*...*" as well as any abuse of deliberative assemblies on executive responsibility; his concept of "*mixed government*" (see Chap. 5, Sects. 5.1 and 5.2.1) is not linked to a Monarchy but to the filters for preventing abuses of popular power (senate and elective criteriums), whatever being a republic or a monarchy, even when he referred to Pitt[17] his proposal of a *hereditary Ynca*. This formula was in the direct line of Montesquieu, who considered the British regime to be republican despite being headed by a monarch. All the proofs are provided in the original texts presented in this book.

Is the concept of "Precursor" meaningless? We sustain that it makes sense only by comparing two different moments and contexts of history. This comparison enables historians and social scientists to understand, by definition, the degree of innovation in a specific context that represents a precursor's thought. Therefore, this comparison of contexts enables the measurement of the obstacles to the Precursor's ideas, his role, and his potential contribution to history. Dunn's interpretation illustrates clearly the contradictory nonsensicality of a too-radical application of the Cambridge objectivity principle. His analysis of the context tends to reproduce merely the historical fact that, contrary to Bolivar, Miranda failed. However, he doesn't provide any analysis of the reasons explaining what he names "*the Bolivar success*" or Miranda's failure. This indicates a precise absence of an objective assessment of the forces in conflict. Such a lack is the opposite of the contextual analysis Cambridge advocates for! Dunn acknowledges that he could not explain Bolivar's success, but only the political independence, finding it "*hard to go beyond the turmoil of hurt, frustration, disappointment, and confusion in which his gigantic*

[15] **Jacobin**: radical political revolutionary movement on the extreme left of the French Revolution, see Chap. 5, Context, note n°4.

[16] Chapter 10, document 10.3.9. Miranda's letter to W. Pitt, 19 March 1799.

[17] **William Pitt the Younger** (1759–1806) was prime minister of the United Kingdom from 1783 to 1801 and again from 1804 until his death.in 1806, see Chap. 5, note n°6.

struggle ended'.[18] Would it not be an à-priori Anglo-centric judgement that he would consider Latin American people unable to go beyond mere military independence as Bolivar did?

If objectivity should mean just listing past facts as the only possible evolution, what would be the meaning of the historian's search, tasks, and social role? This narrow conception rejects the consideration of subsequent events and consequences when assessing political ideas. This corresponds to a disavowal of any possibility of an effective selection process, as dictated by history, and, thus, at the limit, the denial of any positive evolution in human thinking. Such a narrow Cambridge interpretation of historical objectivity leads to neglecting the interesting Miranda's approach to seeking a coherent system of governance. Without these references to contemporary ideas, any change of regime risks appearing as a random walk, driven solely by exogenous factors or individual actions ("Cleopatra's nose"). Although individual actors are essential to contextual research, they are vulnerable to weakening analytical explanations. How do we consider alternative events to have been possible? Miranda's project represents an alternative history that could have been realised and whose explanation of his failure must be evaluated; otherwise, historians would be writing a deterministic history that accepts bloody revolutions as the only natural changes to the existing order or fortuitous evolutions.

3.4 Miranda as an Aristotelian Philosopher

In clear opposition to John Dunn's reductive interpretation, we argue that our empirical method, grounded in a different understanding of contextualism à la Cambridge, enables us to demonstrate that Miranda must be considered a genuine political philosopher. Indeed, precisely by using the historical context and dominant conceptions of his time as a reference, it is possible to emphasise the scope and coherence of his plans and actions, thereby pointing to the implementation of an emancipatory governance system that makes genuine social change possible.

Contrary to Dunn's position, we sustain that assessing the revolutionary content of Miranda's plan does not necessarily mean an interference with present conceptions. Miranda's opposition against the dominant principles of his time is merely an objective fact. To decide that this opposition, because it is close to today's values, would be a biased view of the past, corresponds to a necessarily subjective evaluation: any dissident would become an accident! The fact that his positions and proposals were close to contemporaneous ones cannot be sufficient to judge that our views are biased by posterior ideas. On the contrary, considering that Miranda's dissident ideas would result from chance or accident, as Dunn said, is an evident lack of objectivity.

[18] Dunn [2006], Annex 2, op. cit.

As expressed by Miranda [1805], he dedicated his entire life "*to studying the wise principles that lead humanity to happiness in order to implement them for the benefit of his homeland*[19]", that is, the search for an ideal governance system. Nonetheless, his search is singular because of the way he wanted to implement his reforms, which was "à-la-Aristoteles", i.e., inductively. He was not seeking to implement the "ideal society" alongside the ideological principles of an absolute revolutionary ideal "à la Plato". Miranda was a sociological analyst shaped by Greek culture but opted against Plato's political philosophy in favour of Aristotle's. As defined by Pierre Aubenque [1979], Aristotle's politics cannot be a science based on absolute principles like geometry. Still, it comes close to the art of a physician because life and human society are dominated by contingency due to indeterminacy, thus escaping absolute necessity. Therefore, facing uncertainty, it is necessary to build a political system able to respond to human aspirations for progress empirically and one step at a time (to "*open the path by walking*"); this means identifying step by step on the field and depending upon circumstance each orientation that leads the citizens to benefit and progress. In this system that does not respond to any absolute truth, debates and dialogue are the essential engines of democratic search, unlike Plato. Miranda's political philosophy is clearly framed in this relativist and pragmatic line, which bases a prudent approach to progressive construction through deliberative and adaptive processes, making room for experimentation and error correction. Such a method is similar to the technique applied in science: scientific progress does not come from ideologies but from debates among peers about the results of reproducible experiments. Therefore, the executive power had to be able to make effective decisions to engage in experiments. The essential controls by the legislative and juridical bodies need to be "ex-post" but strong. Thus, experiments chosen at one moment should not be paralysed "ex-ante". The recipe requires fine-tuning a genuine balance of powers, with no dominance of one body over the others.

Such a constant search is evident in all his political writings, and even more so in his actions and behaviour. The texts that outline his line of action have not been compiled into a single published document yet. This is the purpose of this anthology, and it consists essentially of gathering and analysing:

- the five constitutional projects for Latin America (1790, 1797, 1801, 1808, and one dateless in between),
- a synthetic account of the supposed constitutional project for Brazil in 1806 with a proclamation, both attributed to Miranda,
- a pamphlet on the crisis of the French Revolution of 1795,
- a significant part of Antepara's book of 1810 (attributed to Miranda's hand), and the review "El Colombiano" also signed by Antepara
- his main successive political "Proclamations", and
- a series of excerpts from contextual letters sent to relevant political leaders or thinkers.

[19] Chapter 10, document 10.3.22. Miranda's letter to W. Pitt, 13 June 1805, translated [*Archivo* … op. cit Vol. XVII, p. 216].

- his main interventions in the Supreme Constituent Congress of Venezuela in 1811.

This is a highly heterogeneous work, whose essential texts do not exceed approximately 100 pages. Still, the present book presents them systematically, accompanied by a contextual introduction for each document, including historical comments and detailed bibliographical information. To these documents, we added a specific analysis of his relations with the successive British governments, as his persevering strategy with London reveals the coherence and foresight of his political ideas, visible in his actions on the ground, not only in his writings. In particular, the confrontation between British strategies and Miranda's geopolitical vision—something that, by definition, does not rely on present values—allows us to confirm his pioneering nature and our method.

3.5 Is the Precursor of Latin American Independence also a Precursor in Political Thinking?

It is an undeniable fact that Miranda is the precursor of independence. But not only. He carried out this role through a constitutional project aimed at establishing complete emancipation through continental and social integration, which would implement "domestic" decolonisation. According to current historical criteria, this should qualify him as a significant precursor in the field of political philosophy. Furthermore, upon closer analysis of his political thinking, I see his precursor role in political thought as even more significant. However, these aspects remain insufficiently understood and are not widely shared among historians and political analysts.

Miranda does not seem to stand out from the average Enlightenment thinking. Early in life, he embraced the principles of Humanism, Rationalism, faith in progress through education, and the development of empirical knowledge, as well as a tolerant yet critical deism towards the clergy and the Church's abuse of power. Politically, he expresses a radical opposition to the absolutist government, to colonialism and imperialism. He proposes establishing a republican government anchored in written constitutions, capable of organising and warranting an effective separation of powers (in Montesquieu's line) through representative and federal democracy. At the same time, he also radically opposes the Jacobins and other violent revolutionaries, who seek to impose popular systems where powers are confused or centralized through popular assemblies and exposed to emotional impulses instrumentalised by a few leaders or a caudillo. However, he also opposed the excessive control of the executive by the legislative or "assemblies," which impedes effective governance by the executive, leading to anarchy or tyranny. Not sufficiently observed, Miranda adopted an early non-racist, non-Eurocentric view, contrary to most Enlightenment thinkers.

Regarding the economic regime, his closeness to Bentham and Mill's utilitarianism defines him as a classical and liberal economist who seeks to open the harbours to free trade as a means of accelerating economic, technological, and socio-cultural development, and to promote an emancipating entrepreneurial culture. Finally, yet importantly, socially, he is considered the facilitator of developing an entrepreneurial and enlightened middle class, which is called to gradually replace the traditional Creole elite. Furthermore, in his last writings in London [Miranda 1810, Grases 1966, Salcedo Bastardo 1982], he emphasises the need for social policies that facilitate cooperation between social and ethnic classes, which, in his view, is a prerequisite for ensuring good governance, a condition that is itself necessary for a successful revolution and prosperity. Although moderately, he questions explicitly the nation's traditional domination relationships by a social, political, and ethnic minority:

> The establishment of good government ... depends on mutual sacrifices for mutual happiness. A bad government is one in which one class makes many sacrifices and another very few. In this case, the rich tyrannise the poor, the poor tyrannise the rich, or people of one origin tyrannise those of another lineage.[20]

> Whenever the interests of two sets of people are combined together in one concern, if the entire management be left to one, it is evident that this managing set will draw, by degrees, all the advantages to their own side and throw all the disadvantages to the other ... so far is this inequality sure to proceed as to ruin the interest itself, and destroy all national prosperity.[21]

> Anarchy exists when the different classes of society contend for unjust privileges and are not animated by a spirit of reconciliation.[22]

In these phrases, the rejection of "internal" colonial racism (which remained very present after the Latin American independence), which he saw as contrary to nature and human development.

Because Miranda did not invent any of these values or principles, many authors do not consider him more than an emblematic case of the Enlightenment's optimistic humanism. Many recognise that he synthesises all the emerging values in his time very well. Some others believe that he was a utopian idealist, a naive dreamer whose revolutionary moderation was adapted neither to his emancipatory project nor to his region and the dominant forces of his time. They consider that he failed for these reasons. This view contrasts with those who see him as an opportunistic pragmatist or a utilitarian and materialist bourgeois. Very few capture his most advanced specificities, in particular, his vision of a society without political, racial, or social discrimination:

> Every citizen will participate in the legislature. The laws will be made by those who must obey them, and no man will be above them or will be able to transgress them with impunity; The poorest in the State will be under their protection as much as the richest.[23]

---

[20] Chapter 8, document 8.2, extracts translated from the newspaper "*El Colombiano*", [*América Espera*, document 161 p. 432].

[21] Chapter 8, document 8.1. Antepara [1810] ... op. cit. §14.

[22] Chapter 8, document 8.2, translated from *El Colombiano*, n° IV, May 1810, [*América Espera*, op. cit document 161, p. 433].

[23] Chapter 9, document 9.5 "*Proclamation to be issued upon landing in Brazil, 1806*", translated [*América Espera*, op. cit. p. 351–353].

That means a higher degree of prescient character in relation to the modern world than most thinkers of the Enlightenment. That means recognising a specific precursor character of the contemporary world, given that today's world was built on these premises. Nevertheless, most conventional interpretations reduce his own singular richness of thought and his actual political contribution to the bare minimum. The fact that Miranda did not develop his arguments explicitly or elaborate theoretical principles, but instead gave priority to action by identifying direct, workable solutions, tends to hide the more profound, implicit principles and the originality of his own contribution, enshrined in his constitutional formulas of governance. Many historians have viewed him merely as an importation of ideas from others, without appreciating the truly novel character of his constitution and the creative way he operationalizes these ideas, drawing upon empirical experiences. His main original ambition, insufficiently noted, was to articulate two pillars of a democratic process:

1. to start a non-violent process of significant social changes by anchoring it in the rule of law through a written constitution relying on elected "cabildos" (municipal councils), the basis of the social and political structure in the colonies.
2. and betting upon the potential social cohesion provided by the historic opportunity to have the common goal of emancipation beneficial for almost all the people, as far as specific socio-economic reforms would consolidate social integration and build an American identity, not by à-priori ideologies

Would not such a "courage of moderation" be a precursory principle of our social democracies?"

He was especially aware of the fragmented interests produced by an intentional system of castes, exposed to the danger of bloody socio-ethnic eruptions in case the process of change would not be legitimately anchored since the beginning, and legally well-structured for eradicating unfair privileges. However, he firmly believed that, under the condition of acting carefully in time, a legal order based on elected municipal councils (Cabildos), which in turn send representatives to a federal level, could replace the colonial order and guide the process of change by channeling conflicts into pluralistic debates. In this way, he thought it was possible to organise economic development in a backward and caste-segmented society, thanks to a more just legality that allowed class cooperation and the effective decolonisation of India.

In addition, the permanent pragmatism of his political thought tends to be undervalued by the inevitable dogmatic interpretations—whether they are implicit or not—that any analysis of political thought implies. For example, Miranda's cautious moderation in areas of social change, property rights and popular democracy is even considered by some on the left side as an opportunistic weakness or as a too-cautious bourgeois biased by an anti-revolutionary alienation,[24] that is to say, to classify him as a less "advanced" thinker, not so much as a genuine precursor.

[24] A typical case is the Venezuelan historian Carmen Bohórquez [1998], whose ideological option outweighs her admiration for her hero Miranda, (see her nevertheless excellent book *Francisco de Miranda, Précurseur des indépendances de l'Amérique latine*, L'Harmatan, Paris, 1998, p. 285).

Contrary to this à-priori view, our own contextualisation allows us to sustain the opposite interpretation; in other words, his political moderation and his respect for human rights despite the dominant values of his time, constitute the proof of a precursory insight of the risks that were threatening democracy in a society of castes, affected by centuries of colonial oppression, which accumulated social resentment and ethnic tensions. Since these divergences in interpretation stem from evaluative analyses of the kind of society in which historians or analysts want to live, evaluating the precursory character of Miranda's political thinking becomes, by definition, a political problem without a truly objective solution. Anyway, the absence of explicit references to present judgements could not warrant a better, more objective analysis; faced with the risk of implicit references, it seems safer to make them explicit, as this book chose.

3.6 Our Criterion for assessing the "Precocity Degree" of Miranda's Political Thoughts

Given the inability to neutrally treat a historical actor's political thinking and behaviour, we suggest clarifying this debate through a certain degree of empirical positivism. For us, the criterion for determining the forwardness character is merely the ability to glimpse into the future at the time of its formulation. Our method relies upon a probabilistic hypothesis about the historical selection of ideas and governance systems. That means to *define as objectively "precursory" any political idea that announces what later becomes an acknowledged reality, whose general application and durability can be objectively observed, whatever the historian's positions in favour or contra would be*. It is not about judging the situation of the past with today's ideas, but about observing and measuring the objective capacity to forecast the future or the ability to warn or favour changes that become a later reality in a given moment in history, independent of our value judgements.

Applying this criterion allows one to establish the degree of extension and "earliness" character of Miranda's political thinking. This allows one to evaluate in which measure this historical actor achieved more than others in glimpsing fundamental issues, not only of his time but also for today's world, regarding governance in several regions. We merely apply this empirical method to Miranda's ideas, comparing them with what has been progressively tested and selected by our societies during the two subsequent centuries. Drawing lessons from the past, these ideas are widely accepted today by consensus or a clear majority of citizens. The result shows us that Miranda's vision was a "precursor" in the sense that his ideas of governance finally mainly prevailed in the Western world, at least until 2024, when populist pressures and post-truth illiberal regimes seem to repeat the 1930s drifts. Although it is clear that Miranda—from today's perspective—is not an inventor as far as the essential political principles are concerned (republicanism, representative democracy, separation of powers, tolerance and human rights, federalism with subsidiarity, gender equality, social cohesion etc.) on which his political proposals are based—the operational combination of these principles that characterises his governance methods, is genuinely a precursory recipe compared with his contemporaries, for his creative realism and his appropriate dynamic balance. Even in our times, Miranda's way of governance remains pertinent, not only for improving our governance realities, but also for facing the emerging debates which oppose democracy and authoritarian ideas, like the Neo-Reactionarism[25] against Enlightenment values, observed in the United States. This recent movement brings back the governance issue from more than two centuries ago, giving more value to Miranda's arguments for democracy.

Thanks to his eagerness for pragmatic solutions, Miranda undertakes an incomparable and frenetic search (considering that it was the constant and obsessive work of a lonely person) for a political system capable of overcoming colonialism by proposing to integrate a dual and multi-ethnic society while respecting both individual freedom and the sense of the American community. For that reason, he perceives better, and before the thinkers of his time, the fundamental contradictions inherent to the societies of his time and the potential threats they pose to the future of democracy. The evolution of his constitutional positions demonstrates that he perceived the essentials of the challenges that future democratic governance implies. Therefore, we sustain the thesis that Miranda distinguishes himself from other thinkers of his time for being able to analyse, in an original way and with exceptional lucidity, the components of a sustainable democratic regime in multi-ethnic societies. His character as a genuine precursor of modern governance results more from his realism than his idealism, contrary to what many authors think, especially British historians and Marxist thinkers.

Independent of the respective ideological positions that determine the classification (and evaluation) of Miranda's ideas, his case provides important lessons to historians and social scientists when debating the advanced character of his expositions, which has yet to be done correctly until now.

References

Alexander, J. [2016] "The Cambridge School, c. 1875 to 1975", *History of Political Thought* 37, p. 360-86. http://www.ingentaconnect.com/contentone/imp/hpt/2016/00000037/00000002/art00007

Antepara, J. M./ Miranda, F. de, [1810], The Emancipation of South America, printed by R. Juigné, No 17, Margaret-Street, Cavendish-Square, 1810, re-edition by David R. Chacón Rodríguez, [2005] Fundación Hermano Nectario María, Caracas 2005. Serie: (Francisco de Miranda; t. 2).

Aubenque, P., *Histoire de la philosophie* — contribution pour le commentaire d'Aristote, Paris, Vrin, 1979

Bohórquez, C. [1998], *Francisco de Miranda, Précurseur des indépendances de l'Amérique latine*, L'Harmatan, Paris.

[25]Thiel [1995, 2009], Moldbug [2007, 2008], Land [2012]. See references in Chap. 1.

Charette, D. and Skjönsberg, M. [2020] "State of the Field: The History of Political Thought", History published by The Historical Association and John Wiley & Son Ltd.

Dunn, J., [1968], "The Identity of the History of Ideas", *Philosophy* 43.

Dunn, J., [2025] Annex 2 of this book, "Miranda as Prematurely Professional Revolutionary", drafted in 2006.

Grases, P., [1966], ed. *El Colombiano de Francisco de Miranda y dos documentos Americanistas*, Instituto Nacional de Hipódromo, Caracas.

Miranda, F. de, [1805], Miranda's letter to W. Pitt, 13 June 1805, translated [Archivo … op. cit Vol. XVII, p. 216].

Miranda, F. de [1810], El Colombiano, N° V, May, re-printed in Salcedo Bastardo [1982] *America Espera*, Biblioteca Ayacucho, N° 100, Caracas

Oakeshott, M., [2006], Lectures in the History of Political Thought. Thorverton: Imprint Academic.

Pocock, J. [1962], "The History of Political Thought; A Methodological Enquiry", in Laslett, P. & Runciman, W. eds., *Politics, Philosophy and Society*, Basil Blackwell.

Salcedo Bastardo, J. L., [1982], *América espera / Francisco de Miranda*; Biblioteca Ayacucho, n°100, Caracas.

Skinner, Q. [1969], "Meaning and Understanding in the History of Ideas", *History and Theory*, Vol. 8, No. 1 (1969), pp. 3-53, Wesleyan University, Middletown, USA

Skinner, Q. [2008] School of Advanced Study, Making History, University of London, 2008, https://archives.history.ac.uk/makinghistory/resources/interviews/Skinner_Quentin.html

Chapter 4
Miranda as a Precursor of Current Democratic Governance

4.1 The Concept of "Rational Freedom[1]" as the Basis of Miranda's Political Views

Miranda's leading innovations in the political field are concentrated in his constitutional governance formulas, which operate an original synthesis of the best ideas of the Enlightenment for operationally combining the fundamental principle of individual freedom with the community's interests. This combination is intended to solve the universal "Gordian knot" faced by any political regime with pragmatism: How can we operationally make compatible and balanced both an efficient political power and the respect for individual freedom? How do we balance collective and personal rights simultaneously?

His answer is based on a structured concept of freedom as a process rooted in institutions and education: "*freedom is nothing other than justice wisely administered*"[2] and "*no people without philosophy and great instruction can preserve their freedom*".[3] This process is the key to progress, which does not happen spontaneously; it must be built by institutions and a government of laws[4] [Miranda, 1929].

Miranda does not pretend to seek a political truth in the sense of an absolute value that would resolve the rivalry between human values and the conflicts of ideas between cultures and periods. He believes in the universal value of pluralism as a means of opening the path towards improved governance. As the definition of freedom is a self-responsibility process, always in a state of construction and exposed to

[1] Chapter 10, document 10.4.5 and 10.4.10, translated [A*merica Espera*...op.cit. p 370 & 382].

[2] *Archivo* ... op. cit. Vol. XXIII p. 524–525.

[3] *Archivo* ... op. cit. Vol. IV, p. 11.

[4] *Archivo* ... op.cit. Vol. XV p. 233.

C. Ghymers, *Independence, Federalism and Regionalism in Latin America: An Analytical Anthology of Francisco de Miranda's Writings (1790-1811)*,
United Nations University Series on Regionalism 34,
https://doi.org/10.1007/978-3-031-96938-6_4

risks and permanent questioning, Miranda does not believe in absolute or sacred dogmatic principles that would always dictate the actions of men in history. He does not think that changing the social structures or the political regime would be sufficient to return to or generate Rousseau's "good man". However, his thinking rests on some elementary and pragmatic principles everyone can observe: good governance—which requires tolerance and cooperation across classes and ethnicities[5]—leads to socio-economic development. Good governance [Bastardo 1982, quoting Miranda, 1801] relies also on the principle that "*a free government views all men equally*[6]", while "*anarchy exists when the different classes of society contend for unjust privileges*"[7] [Bastardo 1982, quoting Miranda, 1810]. The method builds on a "trial and error approach" (groping), exposed to the permanent criticism of a free and pluralist debate, which constitutes the only practicable recipe for anti-abuse power. He is convinced that the colonial system must disappear as the first necessary condition (absolute independence). Still, it is not sufficient to ensure the "emancipation of the peoples": he believes it essential and possible to create a robust institutional formula to set the rules of a pluralistic game that will allow for channelling peacefully the conflicts of values in collective decisions in a way that always respect people while managing to value common interests and taking care of the long-run interests. This dynamic and open process allows for minimising of the risks that the political power always represents for personal freedom without removing the possibility of the action of this power when it comes to improving the individual's final freedom, which is the only final community's purpose and what the chosen political system is supposed to warrant. However, this requires a strong constitution that restricts the community's influence on the individual in essential values such as tolerance to protect individual freedom (which, later, I. Berlin [2002], in line with some anti-Enlightenment authors, defines in 1958 as "*negative freedom*"[8]). However, he went further by attempting to give meaning to this freedom, in line with the rationalism of the Enlightenment (what Berlin defines as the opposite of his "*positive freedom*").

This attempt to combine negative and positive freedom—to unite the two antagonistic poles of the Enlightenment—is audacious because it addresses the fundamental aporia of human society: how to reconcile freedom with social life? His attempt is genuinely innovative and remains valid today. The implicit philosophy of this attempt is to correct the individualist bias of Anglo-Saxon utilitarianism by supplementing it with the introduction of a teleological dimension but trying to avoid both the political dogmatism of the "law of nature" ("yus naturalism[9]") of the Enlightenment and the dogmatic view opposed to the Enlightenment (such as E. Burke, Herder, de Maistre and others).

[5] Chapter 8, document 8.2., *El Colombiano*, extracts translated [*America Espera*...op.cit.]

[6] Chapter 9, document 9.1, "Proclamation to the people of the compatriots from London", May 1801, translated [*América Espera*. [1982]..op.cit. p. 263–270].

[7] Chapter 8, document 8.2 ibid.

[8] Berlin, I., [1958/1969], reprinted in 2002.

[9] Ius natural or natural law, system of deductive laws based on intrinsic values of human nature that should be superior to positive laws.

How? Merely by letting people seek the purposes of their society that bring together a majority of citizens, without imposing à-priori any ideology other than tolerance and free debates, acknowledging that no one and no ideology has a monopoly on the truth. Furthermore, subjective values evolve in each society; organising the free search for this teleological dimension through pluralist debates and "checks-and-balances" would be sufficient. This corresponds to a "*trial-and-error*" process capable of self-correction, betting on the capacity for rationality when freedom is protected through human rights. Miranda names this pragmatic process "*rational freedom*[10]". It is an essential contribution to political thought, as it allows for a fair balance between individual freedom and the shifting value judgements expressed by parliamentary majorities. This new interpretation of freedom is the key to our reading of the Precursor's pragmatic contribution to philosophy and political thought. Although all of Miranda's analysts agree that Miranda is a hero and an apostle of freedom (he calls his "favourite deity"), the content of the values he defended and promoted has not been adequately analysed. In addition, the lack of detailed philosophical texts and the pragmatic nature of his concept necessitate seeking explanatory complements in his actions and contexts, resulting in a lack of proper analysis and numerous divergences in interpretation.

Although Miranda was strongly influenced by Bentham's utilitarianism[11] and the economic liberalism of the classic British economists, we do not share the reduction of his philosophy with these liberal schools. Nor can it be assimilated to a disciple of Rousseau—the opposite current—even though he is inspired by many of the same roots for introducing a teleological aspect in his definition of freedom, relying on the rule of law. He also selectively used some of his ideas, notably when defending himself against the Jacobins, to argue in the same field using their own source.

Miranda would be the first to propose an operational synthesis between Anglo-Saxon utilitarianism ("à la Bentham") and the communitarianism of Latin cultures ("à la Rousseau"), whose extreme pole is Jacobinism ("à la Robespierre") and later what is called communism or Marxism-Leninism. Furthermore, and noteworthy precursory, he completes this original synthesis of Western cultures with some elements of the American natives' cultures, such as the sense of community and nature. The function of this synthesis is to provide a concrete answer to the background problem of rational governance in multicultural societies emerging from colonial absolutism: how to reconcile individual freedom with the "common good" or how to achieve social inclusion and personal ownership among the newly emancipated citizens in a new political community. In other words, the issue to be addressed was managing a new republic comprising heterogeneous ethnic and cultural groups with their own identities and autonomous powers, without compromising human rights, personal freedom, and local idiosyncrasies. For him, emancipation requires

[10] Chapter 10, document 10.4.4 translated [*América Espera* [1982] op. cit. Document 142, p. 370].

[11] **The utilitarian doctrine** created at the end of the eighteenth century by **Jeremy Bentham** (1748–1832) is an ethical philosophy that establishes that an action or policy must aim to generate the maximum well-being for the maximum number. It is the basis on which neo-classical political economy and economic liberalism (Stuart Mill) were built.

individual freedom oriented by common goals and a shared American identity, but respecting local idiosyncrasies, something that has to be defined constitutionally (subsidiarity, fixing the geographic competence according to the efficiency of the policies, see section 4.4 below).

The operational recipe for this delicate balance has been present since his French experiences. It is specified in most of his writings, but especially in his latest texts published in London, where he explains that it consists of the combination of five priority principles[12]:

1. to avoid a power vacuum by temporarily depositing it in the Councils of each district, whose members must be elected by the neighbourhood
2. to firmly ensure the safety of all people and property
3. to prevent "*the sacred intervention of religion*" through a separation of Church and State
4. to ensure equality among all citizens (to eradicate the "internal colonialism" that independence would not necessarily change)
5. to centralise at the federal level only the very few policies dedicated to the common interests (defence and diplomacy, customs and money, justice and human rights)

At the historical moment in which Miranda conceives and formulates his constitutional proposals, two opposite political interpretations of freedom and happiness are developed from utilitarianism on the one hand and from the "Natural Law" ("*yus naturalism*") on the other. These two interpretations, from which Miranda imports some elements, will lead to the division of political philosophy over the two following centuries. This philosophical conflict has been transformed into a genuine political schism since the end of the eighteenth century. On the one hand, representative liberal democracy has led to an ideological radicalisation towards individualist liberalism. On the other hand, a popular democracy has led to the opposite radicalisation expressed in "popular power", contrary to freedom, ultimately driving toward totalitarianism. The first trend—the liberal one—is dominated by a concept of "*negative freedom*" (absence of restrictions on the individual's self-determination), which will lead to the excesses of materialistic liberalism, which is quite visible nowadays. In the second, a teleological concept of "*positive freedom*" predominates (individual autonomy only finds its meaning when prioritising the accomplishment of the human essence along a collective purpose to which the individuals must be submitted). This second trend is a biased extension of the Christian and Thomistic conception of individual freedom, which must respect the community's interests and goals. However, in the eighteenth century, the atheist reaction readjusts the finalities of social life in a very materialist sense without reference to either God or Christian values or personal self-arbitrage. As a result, the finalities were turned aside towards a hypostasis of community that would lay the basis for communist

[12] Chapter 8, document 8.2., *El Colombiano*, n° V, May 1810, translated [*America Espera* [1982], op. cit.].

abuses against individual freedom and Human rights. Very clearly, Miranda, drawing lessons upon his personal persecutions under the French Revolution, perceives this dangerous deviation of democracy towards a "*popular power*" that he describes rightly as "*bloody freedom*[13]".

This fundamental schism regarding the meaning of "freedom" and "democracy" will decisively influence the world over the next two centuries. Miranda perceives it with extraordinary lucidity when warning repeatedly and explicitly against the threats that weigh on the future of democracy and freedom, in case they do not firmly assure a balance between freedom and power. Operationally, this requires the protection of people and property. By the way, Miranda was not the only, nor the first, opponent of the Jacobin tyranny; however, he was a singular opponent, being one of the very few who did not belong to the conservative movement or the anti-Enlightenment and anti-rationalist movement. Therefore, he was a paradox because he was a moderate revolutionary with pragmatic and disinterested priorities who believed in the feasibility of managing a regime change without violence by warranting democratic pluralism and ensuring human rights by law.

History teaches us that Miranda was right[14] when seeking an in-between path; therefore, he fulfils our criterion of "advancement" among his contemporaries (and many others nowadays). This led him to take a clear position in defence of individual freedom, not as an opponent of the revolution but, on the contrary, for ensuring the triumph of genuine emancipation, i.e., in coherence with the enlightened ideology and the goal of providing greater popular happiness through more rational governance.

Miranda always considered that putting individual freedom under community power was a fatal error ("*the key principle execrable from the Couthon and Robespierre that the individual interest must be sacrificed on behalf of the public interest is the basis on which their tyranny was founded*[15]"). In France, he saw the birth and development of a bloody revolutionary political regime built on an abusive concept of freedom ("*...fatal consequences of the French republican system that Montesquieu calls the extreme freedom*[16]"). His fears of expanding such a French system explain why Miranda would later assume a defensive position, which is translated into an evolution of his constitutional thought towards a greater reluctance against universal voting rights. For tactical prudence, he wanted to limit popular power. The clearest example is the evolution of the proposed electoral system in his successive constitutions, which has become increasingly restrictive over time. Starting with the 1790 version of ample universal suffrage ("*all the citizens of the*

[13] According to the Memories of Dukess of Abrantés, cited in *America Espera*, [1982], op. cit. document 62, p. 186.

[14] As explained in Chap. 3, this affirmation manifests our explicit disagreement with some radical interpretations of the New Cambridge School's method.

[15] Chapter 6, document 6.3. This shows clearly his opposition to Rousseau's meaning of freedom.

[16] Chapter 10, document 10.16. Miranda's letter to John Adams, President of the United States, 24 March 1798.

Empire will choose the House of Commons[17]"), Miranda—who, in 1784, criticised the system of the United States, whose right to vote was based on an economic criterion—changed, when adopting in his 1801 project suffrage reserved to the citizens who had, in the provisional government of this transitory phase, an annual income of 36 pesos (more or less US $ 36 of this period[18]) at the minimum, or who were owners, in the formula of a definitive federal government, of a minimum of 10 "arpens" of land (between 1.3 and 3.4 ha according to the chosen definition of the voluntary unclear size of an "arpent"). However, Indians had been turned into voters automatically through an agrarian reform that granted, by constitutional law, the required quota to most of them.[19] In the 1808 version, preoccupied with the risk of a power vacuum in the period between the fall of the colonial regime and the organisation of a new regime, these criteria to satisfy for being an active citizen became more restrictive with the view to give higher guarantees to the powerful Creoles (without whom the revolution could not be peacefully undertaken). The purpose was to show that the risk of social violence and popular power would be under control. However, his clear choice in favour of freedom and his defensive evolution over time in the face of the increasing risks of tyranny (or totalitarianism, using contemporary language) does not mean that he was merely an individualist liberal, but that he better perceived the danger of incoherence in the thinkers of his time.[20]

Indeed, the other thinkers of the end of the eighteenth century stumble the fundamental contradiction between their conceptions of freedom and the moral prescriptions considered necessary to be able to live in society, becoming, on one side, too individualistic when rejecting the concept of "natural laws" (like Bentham) to the detriment of the general interest and social cohesion, and on the other, too "collectivist" at the detriment of the individual and justice when deifying the natural laws (Rousseau and his Jacobin followers) with a dogmatic view of individual freedom necessarily submitted to the community.

Although Miranda certainly shows an apparent asymmetry when denouncing solely the risk of hypostasis of the community and not the risk of social injustice resulting from the excess of liberal individualism, his thought demonstrates his

[17] Chapter 5, document 5.2.1. Constitution proposal of 1790.

[18] This could be estimated to correspond to the purchasing power in 2021 of 800 $ per year; see explanations in Chap. 5, document 5.2.2. in Context.

[19] Chapter 5, document 5.1.3. Constitution proposal of 1801.

[20] In fact, history also shows us that most of the intellectual support given to the Marxist movements in Western Europe during the twentieth century was also based upon this logical contradiction, denounced by the Oxford philosopher, Isaiah Berlin [2003], who accused them of being the "betrayers of freedom". After the fall of the Berlin Wall, many testimonials acknowledged the late awareness that their emotional idealism impeded them from seeing the contradiction between their libertarianism, which led them to react against the defects of Western democracies, following their unjustified bias towards Marxist ideologies and the "popular democracies". This bias reflects the excessive binarism inherent in Western thought. The flaws of Western democracies do not mean that Marxism alone could solve the lack of democracy and the social problems. History shows that Marxist regimes have failed in both democratic and social terms. Is this not a precursory proof that Miranda did not wait so many years to realise the danger of radical ideologies to democracy?

awareness that the integration and social cohesion process cannot result from "laissez-faire". The State must organise it within a legal framework that allows for both freedom and good governance, making general education a collective good open to all inhabitants, while eradicating unjust privileges. His definition of good governance[21] makes it explicit that it is not about liberalism but about organised cooperation between social classes, which implies:

> "... sacrifices that [social and ethnic classes] make mutually in favour of mutual happiness" in opposition to a situation in which "one class makes many sacrifices and another very few, and in this case, the rich tyrannises the poor, or the poor tyrannises the rich; or else people of one origin tyrannise those of another lineage[22]..."
>
> Anarchy exists when the different classes of society contend for unjust privileges and are not animated by a spirit of reconciliation.[23]

Therefore, Miranda combines the liberal individualism of utilitarianism with the communitarian elements of his ardent humanist conviction, which contains an implicit teleology. Individual freedom needs to be channelled through a rational collective order that makes "*the situation of private citizen not only pleasant and eligible but a good example ... in being submissive to the laws of their country and a useful member of the society to which they belong*". On the one hand, his pragmatic, utilitarian option places him clearly in the field of the defence of "*personal freedom, the basis of all civil happiness*[24]" against the Jacobins and "*their so-called French Freedom ... where atrocious crimes are committed without punishment, true freedom cannot take place*[25]". On the other hand, his humanist side prevents him from becoming just a mere liberal because he seeks to build a social inclusion of different ethnic groups in the same citizenship through a proactive legal order. That is what he synthetically means by his "*rational freedom*" concept. Although he did not explain it explicitly, his ethical positions and actions concerning freedom during his whole life offer an already sustainable basis to affirm that he does not correspond neither to "negative" freedom from Bentham's English liberals nor to its opposite "positive" freedom of Rousseau's French movement that tries to impose a dogmatic natural order. For Miranda, convinced of the capacity of society to build transparent institutions, "*freedom is anything but wisely administered justice*[26]", which means legal procedures that allow for public interventions under the control of pluralist debates. This rationalist perspective tries to balance dogmatic elements (value judgements) and the capacity to search for progress that arises from the self-interest of the individuals. It contains more Aristotelian and Thomistic echoes than utilitarian ones, as they do not stem from a "laissez-faire" concept or an absolute

---

[21] Chapter 8, document 8.2, *El Colombiano*, N°IV, May 1810, translated from *América Espera*, [1982], op. cit. document 161, p. 432.

[22] Ibid.

[23] Ibid, p. 433.

[24] Chapter 10, document 10.17. Miranda's instructions to Caro, 6 April 1798.

[25] *Archivo*... Vol. XXIII, p. 324.

[26] *Archivo*... Vol. XXIII p. 524–525.

truth. His concept of freedom operationally rests on the combination of representative democracy that filters popular power but launches a dynamic pressure and control of the political pluralism and the individual "free will" that permits "opening a path by walking".

4.2 Political Pluralism as the Corollary of Rational Freedom

Miranda thus conceives a constitutional project aimed at ensuring social and economic progress. The primary tool for achieving this goal was a suitable allocation of powers to transform conflicts and counteract centrifugal forces into an integrating cooperative process. Such cooperative dynamic balance can only give results if individual utilitarianism is compensated by a "teleological" dimension granted by the feeling of belonging to the community, that is to say, social values and collective goods that will allow for the creation of a sufficient degree of social cohesion without threatening the effective practice of tolerance in front of divergent voices.

At first glance, this idea of opting for an intermediate option seems simplistic, common-sense or utopian pretension. However, it is remarkably modern once one realises that the starting point is the rejection of any "dogma" or imposition of any "truth" other than to allow for an organised tolerance in public debates that address question to accountable policy-makers. This means that the search for the ideal mix between individualism and the common good is à-priori undetermined but under permanent scrutiny. Such relativism constitutes a genuine socio-political innovation in his context, which makes all the difference between Miranda's definition of democracy and the Jacobin or its opposite, utilitarian schools.

Indeed, adopting an absolute purpose, as in the Jacobin order, the ideal city of Plato, or the Marxist project, makes tolerance perceived as an obstacle or a threat to the common good. Therefore, to determine what this "common good" is or what composes these collective purposes, Miranda moves away, stepping ahead, from most of the philosophers, not only from the eighteenth century but also the later currents, when trying not to fall into dogmatism. This new position fosters political pluralism as a method of dynamic governance, based on the absence of a single political "truth," thereby preserving a free collective search for consensus. Was it a banality in Miranda's time? What are similar projects in his time or even currently underway? Let's remark the interesting exception of neo-Marxist Antonio Gramsci [1929–1935, posthumously published in 1947], who views the role of civil society as the realm of debates and consent, allowing the state to govern as long as it can build an active consensus among citizens. Such a position, expressed almost one century after Miranda, shows that this method escapes from the traditional left-right opposition. Gramsci rejects the Marxist state worship that results from equating political society with civil society, as was done by the Jacobins and fascists. He believes the proletariat's historical task is to create a society in which civil society prevails over political society.

This constitutes the most advanced and essential aspect of his precursory singularity, allowing him to maintain a delicate balance between individualism and communitarianism, while simultaneously safeguarding individual freedom and collective projects. Miranda rejects the "messianic natural order" of his century (yus naturalism), which is an ideological pressure towards a new form of absolutism prevalent in his time, such as the "natural laws à la Rousseau", already announcing the "sense of history à la Marx". These ideologies pretend to determine the general interest deductively and, from it, impose a new moral value in politics. Miranda, like Gramsci later, escapes this ideological trap by merely *replacing subjective doctrines with the undetermined but more objective empiricism of political debates*. His innovative solution is also the simplest, as it only requires a basic framework of human rights that must prevent any abuse of power, from the popular assembly and executive power, against the people, since they are the ultimate goal and not the means. This simple and pragmatic way of being less dogmatic—that is to say, pluralist—in politics is atypical, not only for his time but also because it announces the most advanced way of relativistic thinking of the thinkers of our contemporary time. Therefore, by applying our precocity criterion again, we consider Miranda's pluralism a brilliant advance compared to the neglect of most historians and the radical leftists (self-proclaimed as "progressists") who view him as a late, conservative bourgeois.

The essence of Miranda's implicit argument can thus be reconstructed:

- from the fact that there is no universal truth in politics but pure judgements of values, there is necessarily a plurality of possible paths, and nobody has the right to impose "his single solution";
- on the contrary, the competition of ideas must be promoted through open political debate, which should allow for making errors but correcting them through building a new majority;
- but this "trial-and-error" process opens up a high risk of conflicts between irreconcilable positions concerning social purposes; therefore, the essential function of the political system is its capacity to process these divergences in a civilised way and to take advantage of the dynamic of innovations created by the open debates;
- this is why the constitutional system must consecrate the tolerance principle for protecting the individual (negative freedom), the only possibility for promoting efforts to search for solutions to dogmatic conflicts and to fight the ignorance that restrains progress and peaceful dialogues;
- at the same time, the constitution must organise and protect the right of the people to choose the values (positive freedom) that bring together a majority of representatives to appoint a government according to a process of recurring elections;
- however, this legislative power cannot degenerate into a popular power dominating the current management of the two other powers (separation of powers) directly.

In Miranda's rational democratic philosophy, the collective purposes cannot be determined beforehand by any standard, historical or religious order. Still, they can only be chosen by self-determination through a sovereign and pluralist political debate. Therefore, Miranda is concerned about how to ensure the organisation of this debate, which cannot be developed spontaneously and could only result from an institutional framework established through constitutional mechanisms that guarantee a balance between powers and social groups regarding minorities. This balance is intrinsically a component of democratic work, but it is necessarily evolutionary and relative, without the preexistence of any single formula.

Thus, Miranda could also be seen as the true Precursor of a dynamic conception of the democratic political system: democracy cannot be a stable order but a dynamic one exposed to risks. There isn't a definitive formula; democracy is a continuous building process, employing a "trial-and-error" method within an evolutionary social system. Miranda announces, therefore, the present relativism and political pluralism in opposition to the implicit totalitarianism of a "natural order" or a deterministic historical, philosophical, or theocratic order that excludes, by definition, the very concept of political opposition and tolerance. It is not by coincidence that all the political regimes that abide by a dogmatic order (or religious, or in a historical sense) end the freedom of the press and opinion because these regimes try to introduce a perfect standard order legitimised (or not) by people, to criticise them can only be a result of ignorance, madness, or corruption, as declared by Rousseau and his totalitarian followers. Miranda was one of the few who understood that Robespierre, as a revolutionary once in power, would inaugurate the idea of ending this freedom of the press and the opinion that he had previously claimed for conquering power. This universal attitude of the revolutionaries does not stem so much from the perversion of power itself, but rather from the implacable logical coherence of the type of naturalistic philosophy based on a perfect order that the "incorruptible" precursor of totalitarianism sought to impose. By the definition of the ideal natural order that these governments pretend to be the only ones capable of implementing, combined with the supposed infallibility of the decisions of popular assemblies (again, as set by Rousseau), there is no room left for any opposition. In these revolutionary regimes, Rousseau's logic means an implicit but inescapable totalitarianism: personal freedom and free will make sense only by submitting themselves to the "law of nature" or the sovereignty of the popular power. Under such hypotheses, for example, asking for a free press when a revolution prevails necessarily becomes something useless or anti-revolutionary, and the opponents could only be seen as antisocial, alienated or corrupted by foreign interests.[27]

[27] Unfortunately, there are a lot of examples in the history of totalitarian regimes, but even in the present time and in Latin-American governments, which still pretend to be democratic. Some of the leftist political parties in Europe consider these governments positively as "progressist", as was the case with Cuba, Venezuela under the Chavez/Maduro regime and Nicaragua. This ideological option means to believe in a sense of history that implies that an abuse of human rights is judged differently when committed by an auto-proclaimed "progressive" regime. At the same time, it is condemned when committed by a liberal or right-wing regime.

In philosophical terms, according to several twentieth-century authors and our own analysis, this implacable totalitarian logic was directly derived from Rousseau's thought. Despite being considered, especially in France, as a "freedom lover", his teleological conception of liberty implies an excessive submission of any individual to the community, given the reference to a naturalistic dogma imposed on the whole society as essential to the human being. Rousseau tried to solve the contradiction between two natural principles—individual freedom and the community's authority—by claiming that they are the two sides of the same coin, but subordinating unfairly the first one to the second one in a disguised way by using the following argument: both principles being natural laws, since nature cannot have made them opposed to each other. Therefore, Rousseau adopts an arbitrary definition of freedom that subjects persons arbitrarily to the social group. The individual can only be truly free if he accepts that he can choose only what corresponds to his authentic social nature as decided by the popular assembly. This philosophy is a deviated extension of the ontological Christian Thomism. Still, he evacuates God for re-emplacing it by the "great benevolent legislator", the single owner of legitimate sovereignty, which is the sovereign people once it gathers in popular assemblies. This kind of assembly, also by the "Law of Nature", cannot be wrong. According to Rousseau [cited by Touchard, 2005]

> "the individuals must hand over their interests to the community because, like that, they obey themselves and therefore do not lose freedom at all[28]". "Society has the right to force men to be free ... since when they lose their political and economic freedom, they become free in a superior, deeper, more rational, more natural way than only the dictator ... or the assembly knows [cited by Berlin, 2002][29]". "If the individual wants the chains because this choice is an expression of their nature ... a man chained by himself is not imprisoned ... since control by itself means freedom [Berlin, 2003][30]".

Miranda's conceptions of freedom and pluralism are radically opposed to those of Rousseau. Miranda [1801][31] categorically opposed this type of revolution, proclaiming:

> ... a homicide is always a homicide, whatever its origin. When you defeat your oppressors, do not imitate their tyranny. It is not your idea to replace an irregular government with another similar one, to replace an oppressive regime with another oppressive regime, to destroy an old tyranny with a new tyranny; in a word, to establish upon the ruin of a foreign despotism, the reign of another despotism no less cruel, that of license and anarchy?

Nevertheless, Miranda even used some of Rousseau's sentences in his tactical interest to defend himself better when he was unfairly imprisoned in France by the

[28] Rousseau J.J. cited by Touchard, J., [2005], in *Histoire des idées politiques*, Vol II PUF, Paris, p. 424, translated from French.

[29] Rousseau J.J., cited by Berlin, I., [2003], *Freedom and its Betrayal*, ed. Henry Hardy, Pilmico, London, p. 47, 49.

[30] Rousseau J.J ibid., p. 43, 44, 49.

[31] Miranda, F. de [1801], Chap. 9, document 9.2, "*To the people of the Columbian continent (Alias Hispanic America)*", translated from Spanish [*Archivo*... Vol. XVI, p. 108–120].

Jacobins' disciples of Rousseau. Still, he did that by selecting only Rousseau's texts that were in favour of personal freedom.

4.3 Miranda's Concept of Democracy

Sometimes, Miranda's caution regarding violent revolutions and personal freedom makes historians consider Miranda a "conservative revolutionary" with a less "democratic" orientation than others. It is true that, in the philosophy of the eighteenth century and etymologically, democracy means "government by the people themselves". This understanding would tend to limit the concept to direct democracy, as seen in popular assemblies, or the predominance of legislative power over other forms of governance. Even the election principle was once considered by some authors to be "an aristocratic" principle, that is, the power given to the best ones, rather than a purely democratic way of governance by the people. For Miranda, the only stable democracy that respects both personal freedom and happiness is not only a representative democracy (as opposed to a direct democracy) but also an effective separation of powers that impedes any one power from dominating the others. Within this framework, a dynamic of pluralist debates enables the reduction of the risks associated with populism and the emotional violence inherent in popular power.

Furthermore, Miranda [1810][32] poses the question of the size of the representative formula: "*The most important question which occurs here is, whether the national representatives shall be elected by the members of the Cabildos, or by the electors of these members*." His answer consists of finding an optimum between two opposite risks:

> … we shall state the grand principle which ought to guide in the deliberations of this kind. There is one danger in rendering the basis of a representation too wide. There is another danger in rendering it too narrow. In rendering it too wide, you incur the inconveniences of the ignorant and precipitate passions of the vulgar. In rendering it too narrow, you incur what is still worse, the mischief of bribery and corruption. If the Cabildos' electors formed a too-wide basis, there is reason to dread that the Cabildos themselves would form one too narrow. The difficulty, however, might probably be overcome by establishing provincial assemblies for the members of which almost all the inhabitants might have a vote, while the great national legislature was elected by the members of the Cabildos alone.[33]

His conception of democracy radically opposes the dominant ideas during the French Revolution. Both Girondins and Jacobins opposed the separation of powers, submitting the executive to the legislative power organised in a regime of assemblies.[34] Following the fall of Robespierre, a conservative reaction led to a

[32] Antepara/Miranda, [1810], op. cit. Chap. 8, document 8.1. §14.

[33] Ibid.

[34] See Chap. 5, document 5.2.2. in Context.

counter-trend, characterized by a gradual increase in executive dominance in the subsequent regimes (Directory, Consulate, Empire).

For example, although assimilated to the Girondins' party during the French Revolution, Miranda was already opposed to the Girondins' constitutional project of 1792/93 (Convention's Constitution Committee chaired by Condorcet [1793][35]). His criticisms were that the Girondins had excessively locked in executive power through a too numerous and short-term permanence of collegial government (eight members under a rotating presidency for only two weeks) under permanent control of deliberative bodies, which were given to the legislative bodies (elected each year), thereby concentrating all power. The following project [June 1793], named "Constitution of Year I" or Jacobins' Constitution directly written by Saint-Just[36] [1908] and Robespierre, was even more unbalanced, claiming a generalisation of elective assemblies, impeding any effective separation of power but reaching a total concentration of authority in the hands of the Convention (legislative power) while the executive was decentralised and powerless in front of the popular deliberative assemblies. Contrary to what most analysts concluded, the Jacobins' constitution did not permit centralisation of government or administration: it aimed for the executive to be divided, submitting it to the "sovereignty of the people," which warrants the unity of the state. This focus on "unity" for the sake of the Revolution was the argument for controlling the process through the concentration of power, achieved by a manipulable legislative dominance. Therefore, the centralist character of the Jacobin regime was effective, but only at the legislative level, not at the executive level, which was decentralised and under the permanent control of elected bodies. The Jacobin centralisation worked by channelling the legislative branch to mandate Robespierre to interpret people's natural rights without intermediaries or countervailing power. The Jacobin ideology was based on the ideological pursuit of total unity between the people, their republic, and their representatives, to the extent that no intermediary body could be tolerated between the people and the assemblies. By extension of this unrealistic principle of total unity, any opposition would be counter-revolutionary for creating division among the citizens. Therefore, the Jacobin totalitarian regime imposed a geographical centralisation (opposed to any

[35]The **Girondins' constitutional project** was elaborated by an 8-member committee under Condorcet's chairmanship and presented to the Convention in February 1793. However, it was never enacted because its prominent authors were arrested and executed by Robespierre's regime, which overtook the government in a coup on June 1, 1793. The Jacobins immediately imposed a more radical constitution, based on Rousseau's principles and the concept of direct democracy, which was enacted in June 1793 as the Constitution of Year I of the Republic.

For Condorcet's project (in French) see:

https://fr.wikisource.org/wiki/Plan_de_Constitution_pr%C3%A9sent%C3%A9_%C3%A0_la_Convention_Nationale; for the Jacobins' Constitution of Year I of June 1793 (in French), see http://www.gauchemip.org/spip.php?article1091

[36]**Louis Antoine Léon de Saint-Just** (1767–1794), known as the "Angel of Death", was a Jacobin leader during the French Revolution, a close ally to Robespierre, promoted extreme violence against any opposition to the Revolution, is considered a precursor of totalitarianism (both its fascist and communist versions). Killed by guillotine together with Robespierre (Thermidorian coup, July 1794).

federalism) and a permanent search for exclusion of all possible opponents as "bad citizens" who must be eliminated, with the paradoxical result that their republic was unable to integrate people but only to launch an exponential trend for division. Even hatred became a tool for imposing the unity of the Republic [Saint Just, quoted by Rouvillois, F., in Escande, R., 2008].[37]

Miranda's views were built on the opposite method and ideology: his method was the search for inclusion and the control of conflicts by channelling them by the rule of law and institutional federalism; his ideology was dominated by realism and practical solutions, with no abstract idealism of unity or people but workable decentralisation and cooperation among citizens preventing violence and popular emotions.

The key to warranting Miranda's separation of powers was an adequate constitutional balance of powers able to filter popular emotions or violence and impede populist manipulation. Such a balance results from promoting the dynamics of pluralist debates, which is only warranted in the absence of legislative power domination, except through the ex-post, recurrent electoral sanction. The philosophical principle of "sovereignty of the people" is impractical for current affairs and should be restricted to the main political orientations to ensure efficient governance by giving the executive the mandate to undertake practical actions.

For Robespierre and Saint-Just, who closely followed Rousseau, democracy should be the opposite: only direct democracy, through popular assemblies, allows for generating freedom and people's happiness. Relying upon the belief in natural order, Rousseau and Robespierre consider that happiness comes from virtue, which consists of respecting the purely natural state, which spontaneously would grant personal freedom. For Miranda, virtue is rather concrete and consists of respecting human rights and the laws settled by the community in a constitutional framework, which are always temporary and imperfect solutions to the permanent tension between individual freedom and social authority. Miranda denies the belief that natural laws or absolute values would exist that could determine the boundaries between individual rights and the common interest. Only an imperfect and human process of groping ("trial-and-error process") through pluralist exchanges can establish this ever-changing and approximate, yet always rectifiable, boundary without violating human rights.

Miranda's [1929] essential democratic criterion on governance is when the Republican system gets to "*provide powerful means of action to ensure individuals well-being while being countered if it damages these same individuals*[38]", given that

---

[37] Saint-Just exposed the need to educate the people to hate as a means to awaken the citizens and inspire them to love the fatherland, as seen in Saint-Just, Oeuvres Complètes, edited by Charles Vellay, Charpentier et Fasquelle, [1908], Vol. II, p. 361, quoted by Rouvillois, F., [2008], "Saint-Just Fasciste?" in *Le Livre Noir de la Révolution Française*. This was not only a philosophical debate, as evidenced by the numerous crimes against humanity. For example, the Vendean genocide, the thousands of executions, and the punishment of the city of Lyon, ordered by Robespierre to be entirely eradicated for being considered too moderate (the execution of this decision started and affected many persons, but was finally not achieved).

[38] Testimony of L.A. Champagneux included in *Archivo*...op. cit. Vol. XIV. p. 367, translated from French.

the political system and its executive branch, which is the State, must have no other purpose than this. For Miranda, however, the fulfilment of this ideal is constantly threatened by the inevitable trend of political power to abuse, regardless of the Government's formula. Therefore, the political system cannot rely on a dogma—whatever it is—but only under the permanent control of a collective, open, and revisable research process, which requires setting the rules of the game: guarantee mechanisms and countervailing powers or "check-and-balances" so that the purpose of the political regime (people's freedom) could effectively be warranted. These rules and guarantees render it unrealistic and dangerous to let the people govern directly, given the irrational and emotional nature of crowds or popular assemblies, which are generally susceptible to manipulation by an elite or a caudillo. However, people remain the basis of sovereignty, which does not mean that it must exercise it at all levels or permanently, but that it must participate through the delegation in favour of competent representatives and their periodic revocation—but not at each moment—through periodic, regular elections. To this end, Miranda [1810] states that:

> political science tricks itself ... by confusing the design of a Constitution with its management ... its design should only apply the principle 'everything for the people, but without the people' ... . because it is not always possible to control popular violence ... On the contrary, if there is one thing (in a democracy) that the people must do, it is to conduct the national business according to the rules of the constitution to manage the Constitution and control its application ... in this use of power, it is necessary to entrust to people, and that is purely salutary[39].

Furthermore, when the people are compounded by different ethnic groups, as in the case of Latin America, he warns against any discrimination:

> Whenever the interests of two sets of people are combined together in one concern if the entire management be left to one, it is obvious that this managing set will draw, by degrees, all the advantages to their own side, and throw all the disadvantages to the other; ... so far is this inequality sure to proceed up to destroy all national prosperity; witness Sicily, Poland, and all other countries where a feudal aristocracy has swallowed up the power of the people .... So far, therefore, it is from being true that in carrying on the business of a constitution you can do no good ... without the influence of the people ... after it is introduced, abundant checks against any irregular impulse of the people[40];

It is now clear that Miranda's conception of democracy and governance is particularly antagonistic to Rousseau's, upon which the Jacobin and its Marxist totalitarian deviation were built:

- for Rousseau, by postulate, the only democratic assembly is the popular one; people cannot delegate to elected representatives (only if there are permanently revocable mandates) nor create intermediate bodies that would fall under "vested interests" game, while, for Miranda, only the representation of people by election

[39] Chapter 8, document 8.1, Antepara, [1810], *The Emancipation of South America*, London.

[40] Ibid.

allows to warrant a democratic control in the big countries or to avoid falling into tyrannical centralism;

- for Rousseau, powers should not be separated or controlled by "checks-and-balances" for not weakening popular legitimacy, while, for Miranda, only the separation of powers based on a dynamic of permanent mutual vigilance and pluralist search, reinforced by autonomous bodies and institutions, could warrant the democratic character and avoid the risk of "elective despotism" in case to get the same majority controlling all of the three powers;
- for Rousseau, the people gathered in assembly is always right since, by postulate, the assembly issues the popular will, which, by definition, always respects the public interest when it has the power, while for Miranda, who, by personal experience, does not believe in the invisible hand of the common sense of people or of any government, any power tends to be abusive by its own nature and there is no reason why people should not be oppressive; on the contrary, people are often irrational, subjected to "irregular impulses" and "violent passions" that destroy both justice and democracy as demonstrated by the excess of the French revolution;
- for Rousseau [quoted by Touchard, 2005], "*the social pact gives the political body the absolute power over its members*", and "*society has the right to force men to be free*[41]", while Miranda [1798] is opposed to any absolutism that coerces the individual, but he wants to "*introduce freedom by soft means and wisely*[42]";
- for Rousseau, the people are absolutely sovereign by natural law. In contrast, for Miranda, the people's sovereignty is relative. It needs to be acquired through the results of the interplay of three branches emanating from the people, providing the information that enables it to change and sanction governments periodically as a result of elections, and acknowledging that errors can occur but can be self-corrected;
- for Rousseau and his disciples, the sovereignty of the people and the power of the state are the same; therefore, for them, federalism leads to division not only in the state but also in the people and the republic, being so against the sovereignty of the people. In contrast, for Miranda, only federalism allows for a workable democracy with realistic cooperation between different local identities, which leads to effective sovereignty.

Miranda thus announces modern and pluralist democracies by rejecting Rousseau's direct democracy and his "popular power." He proposes a monitoring power exercised by several intermediate bodies, combined with a popular power limited to exercising a periodic veto through the option of revoking only periodically the representatives and choosing others or confirming them for a limited legislative period.

[41] Rousseau J.J., cited by Touchard J. [2005], op. cit. p. 425–426.

[42] Chapter 10, document 10.3.2., Miranda's report on his arrival in London … 16 January 1798.

4.4 Subsidiarity[43] as the Necessary Geographical Dimension of Democratic Governance

An essential and original component of Miranda's formula to balance the three power branches is the geographical dimension he gave to the distribution of their competence fields. Miranda combines the two principles of modern governance, which are also the key to successful regional integration:

1. the separation of powers for ensuring their mutual monitoring and
2. Geographic subsidiarity ensures a protective decentralisation of local authorities and individual people in exchange for the centralisation of very few geographical matters for which the common interest could be better served.

The added value of this combination lies in activating the balancing forces of mutual surveillance and competition between branches and geographical levels of power, thereby ensuring the operational effectiveness of an effective separation of the three powers.

This "geographical dimension of democracy" is Miranda's response to Montesquieu's objection [1748] against the "*Republican system that is only long-lasting in small territories*[44]" and to Rousseau's pessimism, who considered that "*more than human abilities were needed to govern large nations*[45]". In Miranda's time, a republic was considered an archaic system that could only survive in small territories, such as trading cities. It was believed that the more extensive both territory and population, the more centralisation of power was necessary to prevent anarchy, and it was even more challenging to ensure democratic power, so it increased the chances of tyranny in big countries or empires.

To deal with this risk, the Republican Miranda conceived a constitutional dynamic solution based on a geographical combination of the principle of separation of powers by organising a successive delegation of power in a federal pyramid: each lower level choosing its representative members, which in turn select their representatives for choosing the successive ones for the next upper level up to the head of the Federal Republic. This mechanism offers several essential and unique elements that contribute to the originality of the proposed governance formula.

The first characteristic is the geographic dimension of "subsidiarity," i.e., the distribution of powers between successive, concentric geographical entities. This is one of Miranda's original and essential contributions to his conception of a federal

[43] Miranda never used the word «subsidiarity» but based entirely his Federalist views on its meaning. The Treaty of European Union [2010] includes this principle in its Titre 1, Article 5, §3 "*The Union shall act only if and in so far as the objectives of the proposed action cannot be sufficiently achieved by the Member States, either at central level or at regional and local level, but can rather, by reason of the scale or effects of the proposed action, be better achieved at Union level*".

[44] Montesquieu, *l'Esprit des lois*, VIII, 16.

[45] Chapter 6, document 6.3, *Miranda's Political Pamphlet* … op. cit. Translated from French.

government for Hispanic Latin America and also, according to some Portuguese documents,[46] for Brazil.

This contribution must be viewed in the context of strong opposition in France to any form of federalism. For example, Saint-Just [quoted by Rouvillois, 2008] declares federalism intrinsically immoral since it undermines popular sovereignty: "*Unity is not limited to the government but to all interests and relations between citizens*",[47] assimilating "*any immorality to a federalism in civil rights*".[48] Miranda's constitutional ideas were shaped between 1790 and 1801, when France was under the influence of centralist ideas and Jacobin power, not only under Robespierre's regime but also under Napoleon's deviation towards a Jacobin caudillismo.

Furthermore, Miranda's new formula not only announces but also goes beyond what the European Union enacted in the Maastricht Treaty (1992) with the so-called "principle of subsidiarity". This principle that Miranda did not name as such is bi-dimensional: it allows for both substantiating a strong specific central power in very few areas, necessary for developing a new identity and acting efficiently, but also for decentralising all the other powers to warrant the required local autonomies, to protect the citizens from the State, from the political oligarchies, and also to lean on the primary and genuinely American institution of the town councils ("Cabildos"[49]), provided that they would be handed to popular control by democratic elections which include the native Indians.

The subsidiarity that Miranda proposes is more comprehensive than the initial interpretations of liberal Anglo-Saxon or Dutch Protestants who promoted it. Still, both were single-dimensional: they aimed only to protect the individual from the State. While it is true that Miranda's subsidiarity reinforces the protection of individual persons through the explicit use of the geographical dimension, it is a dynamic, bi-dimensional approach that also points to strengthening the federal central power, albeit in minimal policy areas. This limitation ensures a permanent dialogue between the two levels of governance (local and federal) and escapes Montesquieu's objection against the republican system at that time. Paradoxically, his choice of centralising some critical decisions at the federal level responded to the concern of ensuring the autonomy of the other levels of government for all remaining policies, thereby warranting better respect for individual rights and democratic control. The individual welfare should be improved as a result of some centralised powers.

---

[46] Chapter 5, documents 5.3.

[47] Saint-Just, [2008], *Œuvres Complètes*, op. cit Vol. II p. 373.

[48] Ibid, Vol. II p. 271.

[49] The "**Cabildo**" was the first Spanish colonial institution established by the Conquistadors to govern a territory from its municipality in a decentralised and collegial manner. It granted the cities various levels of self-rule and unique sets of laws decided by representatives of all the property-owning adult males of the city and its dependent territories. The distance and difficulty of communication with the Metropole gave this municipal council a key role in managing the territories of the Colony, despite the Spanish absolutist regime. These cabildos played a central role in Miranda's plans and constitutions as well as in the effective historical process of independence.

This is the second important aspect of subsidiarity. Miranda especially feared the risk of excessive centralisation of the Jacobins, given that efficiency requires the strength of the Executive Branch to be proportionate to the number of citizens. Miranda [1795] thought that:

> a democratic form of government … [is not possible by centralisation] … in such a big a country … [such as France where] … the Caesars, the Alexanders, and their fellows would become dangerous citizens.[50]

In addition, this risk was significantly more pronounced in a republic at the mercy of "elective despotism," driven by "the popular irrationality and the violence of passions" that could be triggered in popular assemblies and lead to tyranny due to the confusion of powers. Indeed, in Miranda's republic [1795], the people must be the basis of the sovereignty of the three branches of power. Therefore, as already seen by Madison and Jefferson in 1787–88 and confirmed in the "Reign of Terror" of Robespierre's Republic (1793–94), the separation of powers cannot be guaranteed if popular power directly controls the three branches. However, as a passionate Republican, Miranda refuses the mixed monarchical solution of the British, which involves handing over powers to three social classes with opposing interests and requiring mutual surveillance to ensure the game of autonomous "checks and balances" is fulfilled. He also rejects Jefferson's solution of a weak Republican federal power and bicameral deliberation (Senate and House of Representatives).

> All politicians agree that the more populated the nation, the stronger the executive power must be. However, they have not perceived the need for this power to be stronger in proportion to the degree of freedom citizens enjoy[51].

Miranda's formula manages to reduce the two major risks for democracy, which are anarchy (excessive freedom) and tyranny (which crushes freedom in the name of national cohesion), through a double movement: an increase in the guaranteed freedom at local and personal level (autonomies of the Town Councils and Provinces) and an increase of the federal executive power, but only in the three essential fields required for managing efficiently the common destiny:

- legal framework and human rights,
- defence and external relations,
- custom union and monetary union.

Everything else should be handled and decided upon at the decentralised level, where both efficiency and legitimacy are higher. Furthermore, flexible mechanisms for constitutional changes through qualified majorities are organised from the centre, i.e. a majority at the Federal Congress or from a majority of local parliaments (States). Moreover, additional guarantees against the confusion of powers arise from the representative principle, which operates as a filter against the radicalism of popular assemblies when preventing people from governing directly. According to

[50] Chapter 6, document 6.3, *Miranda's Political Pamphlet …*, July 1795 op. cit.

[51] Ibid.

Montesquieu, the election of representatives allows for the selection of the most skilled and wise rulers. Miranda prefers this elective filter to the birth privileges one. In his successive versions of the electoral vote, he strengthened the natural tendency of the election system that leads people to delegate to the most qualified individuals, which became more restrictive after his experience in France, where the fear of the Jacobins, supported by popular power, was evident (see Sect. 4.3).

We must consider that Miranda's formula [1795] promotes political debate, not only between elected representatives and the other two powers, but also in the dynamic exchanges between different geographic levels within the three constitutional powers, aiming to defend or define their respective specific competencies. It promotes a dynamic pursuit and control (checks & balances) that assures an effective separation of powers. In addition, this formula also provides accountability mechanisms to which presidents, ministers, and other senior public officials are subject.

> Thus, the government would be given stability only through a wise division of powers. All the established authorities come to watch over mutually because all of them are interested in the continuation of the constitutions from which they come, and this is why they are all united against whoever tries to attack one of them … Since tyranny is only due to the fatal confusion of powers. … it is necessary for freedom to divide them scrupulously and make impossible this monstrous confusion[52] ….

4.5 Miranda and the Spanish Colonial Regime

Miranda [1805] presented his legal arguments in terms of international law and from political, moral, and economic perspectives in several texts. His most explicit text is "*The Succinct Relationship of the Current State of the Spanish Colonies in South America, 1805.*[53]", which is too long to be reproduced in this book. This is a geopolitical and strategic vision that highlights England's interests in joining the emancipation of Spanish America, given that the Spanish colonies serve not only as a financial source for the French Jacobin for their goal of destroying the British Empire but also because Britain could benefit from «*the immense resources which those countries offer and which will make her the most powerful nation on Earth*[54]». He then argues in very modern terms against colonialism and racism that impeded the development of Spanish America. He shows an evident empathy for the Indians and mestizos, whom he considers to be the Americans. He precisely describes the mechanisms of the inhumane regime of the colonies, with the exploitation of the Indians that led to depopulation and the trafficking of enslaved Black people and racism, with a hierarchy of castes that served to divide and thus maintain Spanish domination. It explains in detail the policy of domination, which involves the

[52] Chapter 6, document 6.3 *Miranda's Political Pamphlet* …. op. cit.

[53] *Archivo* … op. cit. Vol. XXI, p. 199–281.

[54] Ibid. Vol. XXI, p. 200.

destruction of American manufacturing by a colonial monopoly that increases costs and prohibits industrial activities, as well as agricultural and mining development. This results in the absence of collective goods, such as education, health, and public works, leaving the people in misery. Spain *"shut out every kind of rational information in America ... they avail themselves the double engine of religion and arbitrary power*[55]*»*. as well as the persecution of educated Creoles and the prohibition of contacts with the outside, the promotion of superstition and the fear of hell, the obligation of annual confession, the segregation imposed by whites, the unfairness of the administration of justice, all pointing to domination by the Metropolis.

> No part of the conduct of Spain appears to be directed to the country's welfare, but on the contrary seems calculated to render it as miserable as possible[56]». Miranda sheds light on "how deeply Spain has studied the way of separating the interests of all the classes that make up the society of America ... and consequently ... how difficult ... it is to form a plan of independence...[57].

After analysing the dispositions of the populations to rise against Spain, he presents a detailed study with numerical data on the military and strategic state. He emphasises the advantages that England could get by leading an emancipation movement. He concludes that it would be significant economic progress for the entire world and to achieve lasting peace.

4.6 Miranda and Political Economy

Miranda is an economist in the broadest sense of the political philosophy of the Enlightenment: without having written much about the economy, nor even having developed an accurate written economic policy, as a man of action, he had a very precise reference scheme in which economic preoccupations were essential for his project. In perfect coherence with his political thought, the economy is an integral and even crucial part of Miranda's emancipation and integration (socio-ethnic-geographical) projects defined above, in a conception very close to Hamilton's. Miranda also seeks to find the "best of the republics" to warrant the highest degree of people's happiness, which he considers as passing through a socio-economic development that determines political evolution and vice versa. To Miranda, this development process depends on the institutional factors defined in the most modern and contemporary concepts. In this sense, Miranda—who witnessed during his extended stay in London the start of the Industrial Revolution, being able to compare England with the other countries of his time—has a perception equivalent to say (in today's language) that economic growth factors are internal to the socio-economic system or that sustainable growth is essentially endogenous for being

[55] Ibid. p. 210.

[56] Ibid. p. 218.

[57] Ibid p. 256.

linked to the quality of governance and national institutions. Thus, Miranda appears to be also a precursor of contemporary economic theory, rather than a mere classical economist of his time, such as Ricardo, Mill, or Malthus.

In fact, with Miranda, one cannot notice any perception of diminishing returns threatening the prosperity of the world or America, contrary to David Ricardo's theory. On the contrary, he proclaims total confidence in progress driven by society's internal factors, when institutions provide credibility in stability, security, and financial parameters. These factors result from national governance and make investment in knowledge feasible and its translation into productive activities, generating positive effects on social and fiscal conditions. This rests on the modern concept of increasing returns generated by knowledge, although he does not explicitly mention this concept.

Although Miranda did not elaborate on his model of growth or its exact mechanisms and components, all the key factors of the so-called "endogenous growth theory" are highlighted in his preoccupations: human capital, technology, innovation, dissemination of knowledge, trade liberalisation, and the import of "know-how". These economic growth determinants depend on the institutional context that ensures political and social order, the rule of law above arbitrary interests, the credibility of financial and fiscal conditions, the fight against harmful monopolies, etc. Through these factors, we can perceive an implicit vision of economic growth as a self-sustaining process, provided that the constitutional and institutional basis allows for promoting this process. In this sense, Miranda already perceived the basis of the contemporary theory of development and endogenous growth, with ideas such as the importance of combining individual incentives with public goods that markets cannot provide spontaneously, like education, as well as the stability of institutions and the rule of law.

What are the inspiration sources of such an advanced and lucid perception of the causes of prosperity? We know that Miranda did not write any explicit economic theory. However, his writings (or those signed by others under his direct instructions, such as James Mill and Antepara) contain many direct references to economic principles. Furthermore, explicit references or indices exist relative to specific sources of inspiration that could be detected from his personal contacts, travels, and ground experiences.

The first clue of a significant source is his study journey in the emerging United States of America in 1783–1784 and, more precisely, his exchanges of views with Alexander Hamilton in 1784. There are at least two concrete proofs of Hamilton's significant impact on Miranda: the first is what his friend Quatremère de Quincy wrote about how Miranda benefited from his contacts with the revolutionaries from the United States independence. The second is the explicit reference to Hamilton that Miranda [1795] wrote in his pamphlet on the French Revolution.

In addition, facts show that Miranda enlisted Hamilton [1787] in his endeavour to extend the American Revolution to the South, with the same conception of changing the world by «*establishing good government from reflection and choice*[58]» to create a process of prosperity that would become the motor of political unity. Both revolutionaries shared the same views on needing a federal constitution warranting the separation of powers by ensuring that they could watch permanently over each other. Their shared view was based on centring the governance issue on the credibility of government and institutions in shaping public opinion and facilitating free debates, with the working of checks and balances, rather than on «popular power», which they saw as an ideological concept and a threat to prosperity and democracy. In 1798, they agreed on the priority of acting preventively to impede France from taking over the Spanish colonies, considering that this would be a dangerous threat to America. Hamilton supported Miranda's plan for an alliance between the US and Britain to free Spanish America.[59] They even agreed to declare war on France.[60] For both, anarchy and the open contempt for law were their true arch-nemesis. Both sought to unite separate colonies into one political union, with the express purpose of establishing a large open market. As analysed by Daniel Betti [2008]:

> They espoused and worked toward creating political and economic systems of greater cooperation, integration, and openness. They intended these larger political systems to foster prosperity among all classes and provide the opportunity for new skills and trades to flourish. This kind of thought is distinctly cosmopolitan, especially compared to the narrow agrarianism prevalent among Jeffersonians.

Another significant indication of the impact of Miranda's journey in the United States, particularly under Hamilton's influence, is the evolution of Miranda's ideas. When Miranda arrived, he held a classical opposition between trade/wealth and democracy/virtue, a concept from Plato and developed in Europe (Rousseau). In contrast, Hamilton advocated that trade and manufacturing were the motor of prosperity, which would anchor democracy and shared identity, leading to a federal union. Miranda's ideas underwent a radical transformation under Hamilton's influence. He understood that prosperity, democracy, and federalism were closely interdependent. Like Hamilton, he recognised that farming, manufacturing, and trading were closely linked in a reinforcing cycle of growth and innovation, provided the state played an active role in creating the necessary infrastructure, education and stability in monetary, financial, and fiscal domains.

Later, Miranda worked closely with the economist James Mill [1808, 1809] in London to publish an essential article in the influential Edinburgh Review.[61] This

[58] Hamilton, A., [1787], *The Federalist Papers*, N°1, Introduction.

[59] The conflict provided the opportunity—named the «**quasi-war**»—that France created by seizing the US ships as a retaliation for the US's non-payment of a loan made by the old French regime. Hamilton was in charge of preparing an army for this purpose, named second in military command to George Washington.

[60] This plan failed because President Adams, who was very hostile to Hamilton and Miranda's ideas, opposed it.

[61] «*The Emancipation of Spanish America*», which Miranda did not sign since the British government prohibited Miranda from creating problems for the Spanish regime in the hope of preventing

article demonstrates the mutual benefits that Britain and Spanish America would gain from the emancipation of Spanish America. Their demonstration was directly based on the economic *law of comparative advantage*[62] and developed very advanced geopolitical ideas on the possibility of escaping from Napoleon's aggressive continental trade blocks by creating an alternative trade route with the Americas. This demonstration was not only of strategic interest for both Britain and Spanish America but also had a tactical aspect for Miranda, who based his plan on attracting British economic interests to justify their support for the emancipation of Spanish colonies as a way to resist Napoleon's aggression.

Furthermore—and even more singularly—Miranda and Mill [1809] launched the visionary idea of «globalisation through trade», allowing Japan and China to «*soon receive important changes in ideas, arts, manners and institutions*» by «*obtaining direct access to them [regions of Asia] across the Pacific Ocean ... immense would be the traffic which would immediately begin to cover that ocean ... all the riches of India and China would move towards America. All the riches from America would move towards Asia*» Miranda confirmed his ability to formulate a global vision of the external impact his plan could provoke by increasing the world's prosperity when, with the academic authority of Mill, he raised the question that the emancipation of Spanish America could, very probably, attract China and Japan in the same kind of openness for triggering their economic development.

The fact that Miranda does not elaborate further on his conceptions of this process of endogenous growth could indicate that he was informed of ideas that he probably found evident in his contemporary readings. In addition to Hamilton and his reading of Adam Smith, James Mill, and Adam Smith's contemporary James Steuart, the most likely candidate would be Emmanuel Kant [1795], who is not known as an economist but published important ideas in 1784, which likely influenced Miranda's concept of political economy. In particular, Kant—another great precursor in various domains—brilliantly announced what is now the current theory of endogenous growth by complementing the concept of the 'invisible hand' with the same idea applied to the search for and creation of knowledge, which, for him, is the real cause of development: rivalry (competition) between individuals pushes them to make efforts to accumulate knowledge and to progress individually,

Spain from joining France against Britain. This article in the Edinburgh Review of January 1809 (N° 26, Art. 2) was attributed to the economist James Mill (Miranda's friend). Later, an extended version with the same title was published as a book in 1810 under the name of another Miranda's friend, José Maria Antepara (see Chap. 8, document 8.3). Miranda also wrote an article for the Edinburgh Review, but signed by Smith [1809] on the Jesuit Molina's book describing Chile.

62 The law of comparative advantage is the basic principle of economics that explains the rationality of specialization in production. Applied to international trade, this model shows the principle that even when a country's firms, factories, and workers are less efficient than others in producing all goods, it is beneficial to open trade with those others to benefit from the productivity increase generated by the specialisation where its disadvantages are the lowest for benefitting also from the foreigners' higher productivity through international exchanges. Attributed to David Ricardo in his 1817 publication, this principle was already used by James Mill and Miranda. Mill [1808] had dedicated another book to the subject in his "*Commerce Defended*".

resulting in mutual external effects of general progress of culture (i.e. an accumulation of ideas available to everybody, these crucial "non-rival goods" that produce positive external effects on productivity i.e. increasing returns) that is the origin of economic progress. Kant [1795, 2006][63] explicitly detected the mechanism that rests on the non-declining returns resulting from the accumulation of ideas through the external effects of individual accumulation, which turns it social, similar to Smith's "invisible hand".

> ... in such a precinct as the civil union is, these inclinations have after-ward their best effects; just like trees in a forest, precisely because each of them seeks to take the air and the sun from the other, are constrained to look for them above themselves, and thereby achieve a beautiful straight growth; whereas those in freedom and separated from one another, that put out their branches as they like, grow stunted, crooked and awry. All culture and art that adorn humanity, and the most beautiful social order are the fruits of unsociability, through which it is necessitated by itself to discipline itself, and so by an art extorted from it, to develop completely the germs of nature.

Further research on Kant's possible influence on Miranda should be necessary. In the catalogues published by Sotheby in 1828 and 1833 [Uslar Pietri, 1979] for the auction of Miranda's library, only 3200 books (approximately half the total) were listed. Kant's works do not appear on this list. However, either important books were likely dispersed between 1810 and 1828/1833, or Miranda brought with him some essential books.

The entire concept of Miranda's Latin America's emancipation rests on the idea that the Iberian colonial regimes and their institutions were the key obstacles to the region's social, intellectual and economic development. Political independence was a prerequisite for implementing a type of government that would allow for the institution-building process (in the current Anglo-Saxon sense, see Douglass North [1990][64]), ultimately leading to the eradication of poverty through economic and social progress. Miranda thinks (too) optimistically that Colombia's underdevelopment compared to England and the United States would only be a governance problem that could be solved quickly once the emancipation process achieves the implementation of institutions that foster good governance. However, for geopolitical reasons, he added a supplementary condition to establish a tripolar international cooperation among the democracies of Europe (the United Kingdom), North America and South America.

The importance attached to international cooperation among democracies was already highlighted in his early texts, where he presented his geopolitical strategy in 1790[65] to the government of William Pitt and again in the Paris Act of 1797.[66] In these documents, he explained the need for a geopolitical, strategic alliance among

---

[63] Kant, I., [1795] "Idea for a Universal History from a Cosmopolitan Perspective" in Toward Perpetual Peace and other writings on Politics, Peace and History. Reedited in 2006.

[64] We can see it more in-depth in the definition given by Douglass North [1990], Nobel Prize in Economics 1993,

[65] Chapter 5, document 5.2.1. 1790.

[66] Chapter 7, Paris Act, 1797.

the three democratic poles of the world in order to resist the totalitarian and mercantilist threats of absolutism (in 1790) and Napoleonic Jacobinism (in 1797). His geopolitical plan was to promote an open world, not only commercially (trade and tariff agreement) but also to production factors and undertaking (capital, men and ideas), but in a regulated world, both to ensure peace through international rules and also to ensure the public good of macro-stability through monetary cooperation.

What is the content of Miranda's development policy? As a reader of Adam Smith's "Wealth of Nations" from its right publication—and, just like other liberal thinkers of his time, Miranda considers freedom of trade and settlement without any monopoly as a necessary condition for the development of nations. However, he does not believe trade and economic liberalism are sufficient conditions. First, because the individual freedom that he defends together with the utilitarians (Bentham) and others as Kant only works if there is a stable legal and social framework able to supply the essential collective goods for economic development: a non-arbitrary government, the popular education, the security of people, of the goods and the respect for contracts, the credibility of policies—features that did not exist in Hispano-America—but which he considers necessary [Miranda 1795]. His recipe was to build emancipation on political independence, plus a written constitution that could channel the revolution legally and impede its natural tendency to fall into either anarchy or tyranny through an adequate institutional order prepared in advance, thereby promoting social inclusion. That means a solid but limited State, systematic popular education, respect for intellectual property and the creation and maintenance of the productive infrastructure.

> … the national paper [currency] would not have its value if we did not give enough solidity to the government … [and] if we do not prove that with the ability to satisfy our creditors, we have still the firm desire to fulfil our commitments punctually. Bad faith harms more than insolvency because a poor state can become solvent. Still, it is not ordinary for an unjust government to respect its promises. As long as government arbitrariness diminishes, the confidence of those who contract with it increases because they know its power to break its commitments disappears. The roots of credit are, therefore, solvency and good faith. But neither one nor the other can be insured as long as the State has not taken a strong and invariable base[67]…

In Miranda's thinking, we can perceive an economic doctrine far from liberalism and based on a proactive development policy, i.e., a deliberate policy to create the necessary legal and institutional framework. For Miranda and his concept of 'rational freedom', this means that the framework should allow not only respect for individual freedom and protection from arbitrary Government, but also be conceived to orient individual incentives, as given by the markets, towards social integration and the common good. A concrete example of this concern is his measures for combating fertile lands that are left uncultivated, forcing landowners to work on them and produce, under the threat of losing their right to vote or their eligibility for certain positions if this requirement is not met.

[67] Chapter 6, document 6.3. Translated from French, *Political Pamphlet*, op.cit.

In agreement with his most advanced contemporaries—the classic economists—Miranda [1805, 1929] points to socio-economic development not only for his Colombia but for the whole world in a pioneering vision of "globalisation" that he presents as a large and clearly anti-mercantilist "win-win game" for humankind.

> Let us now for a moment contemplate the Spanish colonies in a state of liberty and having the free use of all the benefits which nature has so amply bestowed upon them, the Isthmus of Panama and other points opened by canals serving as communications between Asia and Europa. America forming of its treasures a Bank for the payment of the industry of every nation on earth. What activity, what animation will be spread all over the world through such an event. .... Finally, in whatever manner we contemplate the independence of Spanish America, we must admit that it would be a general advantage to the human race and particularly to England[68]....

4.7 The Political Opposition Between Miranda and Bolivar

The relationship between the two independentists and, above all, the elimination of Miranda by Bolívar constitute, according to our reading of history, a key element of the destiny of Latin America, significantly since the cult organised in favour of Bolívar and the consequent manipulation of history, prevented a genuine evaluation of his policy by historians. History, being written by the winner and his followers, has not yet been able to take into account the consequences of the undemocratic political regime established by the Liberator, who consecrated himself as the only Liberator and encouraged the spread of caudillismo. Subsequent oligarchs exploited his quasi-deification to maintain power without socio-economic change. They were even protected by laws[69] that prohibit damaging the image of the Liberator, applicable to both Venezuelans and foreigners, which perpetuates the manipulation of culture by successive governments. Such worship of Bolívar means that no other hero could legally surpass him as the only one capable of achieving independence successfully. This very technique was recovered, even by the only leader—Hugo Chávez—who sincerely tried to achieve true emancipation, that is, the "second" independence, but which Bolívar did not even want to undertake.

This Chavista technique for manipulating opinion through the "bronze memory"—which excludes any historical debate on the political content of this "second"

[68] *Archivo*...op.cit. Vol. XXI, p. 232 and 237.

[69] In addition to Art. 1 of the Bolivarian Constitution of Venezuela [1999], which bases the republic on the doctrine of the Liberator, the law of 10/28/2022 imposes the obligation to respect and train on the doctrine of the Liberator, in addition to regulating the use of the name, titles, signature and effigy of the liberator; repealed the previous law of 06/20/1968. It should be noted that the 1968 law prohibited using the Liberator's name in political propaganda or activity, while the new law in force repealed this prohibition. Thus, the direct politicisation of the country's history and the political manipulation of the Liberator is officially recognised and sanctioned by law. The Chavist regime stands out in the legal order by imposing a precise political doctrine on all citizens and resident foreigners by law. It even intends to preserve the doctrine of the Liberator also at the international level.

revolution—also recuperates Miranda, reducing him to the misleading role of "precursor of the Liberator". However, in doing so, Chavism fell into its own trap by believing that the effective method of the "first" independence would necessarily be also effective in the "second", a flawed assumption as demonstrated by the facts. Furthermore, Chávez focused essentially on anti-imperialism and anti-market, trusting dogmatically that the "popular power" would amplify democracy, another wrong assumption. The method was incorrect. In this way, Chávez perpetuated Bolivar's betrayal of Miranda. That is, he betrayed effective democracy. Given that Bolívar applied policies radically contrary to the democracy proposed by Miranda, it was not coherent to attempt true emancipation with the measures and techniques of a leader-dictator. The only thing that could result was a repetition of the Liberator's failure as a democrat. So it was with the gradual fall of the Bolivarian Republic of Venezuela into dictatorship.

It is historically accurate that Bolívar militarily achieved the political ("external") independence of several Latin American countries, while Miranda could not make it, since he was impeded by Bolívar's betrayal in 1812. However, Bolívar limited himself, like almost all[70] the leaders of the other independent republics, to what is now called the "first" side of independence without achieving the "second" side, i.e., the "internal" decolonisation or democratic emancipation, which was Miranda's true objective in his emancipatory crusade. The facts, not the speeches, demonstrate that Bolívar implemented the opposite: a dictatorship that preserved the oligarchs for two centuries.

This difference between Miranda's plan and Bolívar's genuine attitude contradicts the official interpretation of a Miranda precursor of Bolívar, reducing it to almost nothing. It is worth remembering a few painful historical facts:

- First, from a military point of view, the fall of the first republic was not due to Miranda—who did not suffer any military defeat in Venezuela (see Annex 3 by M. Castillo)—but mainly due to a personal failure of Bolívar, who, through his fault,[71] was responsible for the fall of the fortress of Puerto Cabello, the critical point of the defence of the republic, which Miranda had entrusted to him as such.
- Second, Bolívar's consequent betrayal that handed Miranda over to the royalist enemies made Bolívar the leading cause of the elimination of Miranda's plan. Bolívar's subsequent attitude of opposition to his master tends to confirm his guilt, both psychologically and in the justifications he gave a posteriori. In par-

[70] The exception was Bernardo O'Higgins, Miranda's closest disciple.

[71] The topic is, of course, highly controversial (see Sect. 4.8). Still, it is enough here to remember Bolívar's written confessions (in his messages to Miranda) that proved his direct responsibility and fault, as well as the subsequent silence that he always imposed on the subject, leaving the single affirmation that he only acted by patriotism for killing the betrayer responsible of the defeat. Another psychological indication was at the end of his life, the strange textual repetition of Miranda's exclamation when Bolivar arrested him, "*Bochinche, bochinche (useless noises), these people can only make stupid noises*". This might be interpreted as acknowledging that Miranda was right.

ticular, in the *Cartagena Manifesto* issued by Bolivar [1812], in which he blames, without naming him, Miranda for the failure of independence:

> … certain good visionaries who, imagining aerial republics, have sought to achieve political perfection, presupposing the perfectibility of the human lineage. So we had philosophers for leaders, philanthropy for legislation, dialectic for tactics, and sophists for soldiers.

From the betrayal of his mentor to the enemy in exchange for personal safe conduct, Bolívar not only adopted an orientation radically opposed to the paths towards a democracy opened by Miranda but also made the "first" independence the gravedigger of the "second": Bolívar extended the military dictatorship used during the war for the first independence to his attempt for a second independence. No democracy or internal decolonisation prospered, and slavery and exploitation of the Indians were reestablished.

It is disconcerting to observe the radical manipulation of the Liberator's legacy by Hugo Chávez to portray him as the precursor of his Bolivarian revolution and twenty-first-century socialism. The worst thing is not so much the historical fraud of investing Bolívar with socialist ideas but, above all, the paradox of thus recognising that the Liberator was not able to achieve the "second" independence that Commander Chávez intended to accomplish two centuries later with the same Bolivarian ideology and with the same caudillo methods. Furthermore, and even more severely, by making it appear that Bolívar was the precursor of his "twenty-first-century socialism," Chávez thus explicitly recognises his desire to implement a Jacobin regime opposed to genuine democracy and human rights, despite the historical failures of similar attempts everywhere. Tragically, the same flawed method yielded the same unsatisfactory results. Chávez and Bolívar were fervent disciples of Rousseau and "popular power," just like the revolutionaries in history and the sad list of many dictators. Despite the obvious facts that both the Liberator and Commander Chávez failed to achieve the necessary "second" independence, debates among historians—amazingly—do not yet focus on the failures of the Jacobin thought of the Liberator and Commander Chávez. On the contrary, the official version attributes these failures to exogenous forces, such as imperialism, complicit local oligarchs, and international markets.

The fact that the same arguments are still used today in Caracas as the basis of the regime, two centuries later, to blame the external and internal enemies of the people for the repeated failure of Bolivarian-Chavism is an indication of the disaster that the manipulation of history through the cult of Bolivar has caused. To this day, it seems impossible to get away from the Bolivarian myth so profoundly rooted in Latin American culture that it has fostered anti-democratic caudillismo.

4.8 Miranda's Eviction by Bolívar in 1812

Bolívar handed Miranda over to the enemies of the Republic on July 31, 1812.

This is a historical fact that no one contradicts. It reveals a tragic and emblematic story in which Venezuelan citizens achieved what the Spanish enemies had unsuccessfully tried to do for more than three decades: stifle the democratic threat embodied by Miranda, with significant impacts on the political future of Latin America.

The controversy lies in interpreting the Master's betrayal by his disciple, a narrative that lacks objective evidence but is rich in clues and contradictory versions. This adds a layer of interesting intrigue and subjective interpretation to the historical analysis.

According to Bolívar's version—which became the single official one—the capture of Miranda was highly patriotic. The young pro-independence officer, in an emotional reaction of patriotism, wanted to punish his military chief and Head of State, Miranda, for his supposed "betrayals", by having him shot for treason, given that he had negotiated a truce with the enemy after accusing him to be guilty of the military disaster through his incompetence. Furthermore, the rumour was that he was escaping with the monetary reserves of the republic. This version is completed by the story of this young romantic patriot being impeded from achieving his punishing plan because the Spanish troops arrived by surprise and seized the prisoner he wanted to kill. If his attitude was driven by patriotic passion, why wouldn't he have shot him when he organised the capture several hours before? Furthermore, the young patriot later pretended to demonstrate his heroism by daring to reject the passport offered by the Spanish chief as a reward for the capture of Miranda, which the Spanish attributed to Bolivar. However, this version has no other witness than a friend from the Spanish side. Undeniably, the facts are that he accepted the only passport offered to his "patriot" group and used it to escape from the Spanish troops with Miranda's boat.

Despite the lack of formal evidence, we are inclined to believe the alternative version by deduction, which suggests a conspiracy in which Bolívar participated voluntarily and with premeditation. This inclination remains a hypothesis based on psychological factors, which, when emphasised, can help convince and persuade of the validity of this interpretation. The arguments are:

1. Bolívar could not accept Miranda's sanction against him after having failed in the mission entrusted to him by Miranda to defend the most crucial position in Puerto Cabello, giving access to Caracas; Miranda excluded him from the Army, as required by Bolivar himself according to his written confession demanding such a sanction (sent in a letter to Miranda on July 12, 1812). He recognised his military fault and responsibility for the disaster in this letter. For the son of the most powerful family in Venezuela, it was unacceptable to be sanctioned by the son of a Canarian citizen, socially considered to be only a second-class citizen. This frustration heightened his awareness of the political differences between him and his master.
2. Bolívar's elimination of Miranda may have been a strategic move to escape his fate, "killing three birds in a single shot": to restore his rank, save his reputation by appearing more patriotic than his boss, and potentially pave the way for him to take over Miranda's role [Picon-Salas, 1946], similar to the concept of the

"death of the father." This strategic aspect of Bolívar's actions may help us understand the calculating nature of his decisions, which characterise him in his past and future actions.

3. The official explanation of an emotional excess of patriotism is not credible. It makes no sense that five days after the conclusion of the armistice at the port of La Guairá, eighteen days after learning that the government had unanimously decided to ask for that truce and confessing his personal responsibility for the defeat that forced Miranda to negotiate that armistice, the young man would have been still in such emotional disarray. Furthermore, the cease-fire was not Miranda's decision, but the government's, which approved it as the only remaining option. All the wealthy families considered it the least damaging option because it was not surrendering to the enemy, but, thanks to Miranda's negotiation, the only alternatives were either to escape and continue the fight from outside or to accept Spanish restoration. Bolívar, excluded from the army, went to the port to try to benefit from the clauses of that pact, seeking to escape and avoid continuing to fight there. Miranda had ordered not to authorise any navigation before his arrival. As instructed, he arrived at the port, the last, and immediately embarked on his ship to sail before the Spanish troops came to the haven. Bolívar coldly lured him into a trap, convincing him to postpone his departure and disembark to wait on land, telling him the lie that he had negotiated a better armistice thanks to his family contacts who were about to arrive at the port; he only arrested Miranda several hours later, when he was sleeping, in the middle of the night, when the Spanish army was close to entering the haven. A sudden emotional reaction of ardent patriotism could not easily account for this entire chronological sequence. Instead, this looks very much like a coldly prepared betrayal, betting on Miranda's sense of duty that made him delay his departure for the benefit of his country. Furthermore, it is also unbelievable to pretend that, at this moment, Bolívar would have wanted to continue fighting when a beneficial ceasefire agreement had been sealed, the oligarchy did not want to fight, and troops and arms were missing. Our analysis suggests that his behaviour demonstrates an attempt to use Miranda's escape clause to usurp his master's role and resources, thereby continuing the combat from outside under his leadership, as a means to recuperate his honour.
4. In the conspiracy in which Bolívar participated, a rumour was launched that Miranda was betrayed for money, being bought by the Marqués and Monteverde. This rumour provides an easy excuse for capturing Miranda and avoiding the appearance of being anti-patriotic, especially since Miranda had sent the rest of the public treasury on the ship waiting for him. This rumour, totally contrary to Miranda's behaviour and values, was demonstrated to be absurd by most witnesses and explained by the interests of two other betrayers, Miguel Peña and Manuel Maria de las Casas [Henríquez, 2001; Parra-Pérez, 1943]. Later, in the archives of the Republic as well as in the British Archives, documents proved that these monetary resources were allocated to buy arms and munitions to continue the patriotic fight from Cartagena. Seizing Miranda could also mean

seizing these resources. This plan failed since Miranda's boat managed to sail when the British Captain realised Miranda was betrayed.

5. In his subsequent written explanations in November and December 1812, Bolívar changed his version of the causes of the loss of the Republic. He gave contradictory explanations for the military disaster. In November, he blamed Miranda for the defeat, contradicting his July letters to Miranda, in which he acknowledged that he was personally responsible. In December, he listed many causes in his Cartagena Manifesto, again without mentioning his responsibility for the loss of Puerto Cabello. Nine of the ten causes listed are not Miranda's responsibility at all. On the contrary, he took up Miranda's arguments, which he shared utterly. However, he added a tenth element (that we had already mentioned above in Sect. 4.7.) [Bolívar 1812], which deserves attention and is repeated here because this criticism reveals his political ambition, demonstrates his profound opposition to Miranda's views and announces the authoritarianism of the future Libertador:

> … certain good visionaries who, imagining aerial republics, have sought to achieve political perfection, presupposing the perfectibility of the human lineage. So we had philosophers for leaders, philanthropy for legislation, dialectic for tactics, and sophists for soldiers.

4.9 Conclusion

This book does not disguise the author's personal admiration for the universal citizen of Caracas, who has the capacity to anticipate the future. Methodological arguments are presented to explain the criteria that justify it. Independently, it also pretends to be a sincere tribute to the native of Caracas who dedicated his entire life to a cosmopolitan ideal of freedom, non-discrimination, and peace, founded on the necessary alliance of Europe and the Americas, as well as the respect for the indigenous population. We see him as a genuine «universal republican», the most advanced of all liberators, an authentic anti-racist and anti-colonial humanist. The pragmatic formula of democratic governance proposed by Miranda was a genuine innovation, not a copy of the American or French constitutions. It was an original mix of colonial Habsburg, Roman, Anglo-Saxon and indigenous institutions.

In this work, we interpret and measure in detail the scope of the political thought of the Precursor of the independence of the Latin American republics. Such a purpose necessarily raises profound epistemological questions, as the case of this hero transforms into a test case about objectivity in history: is it possible to analyse the political thought of a historical figure without being influenced by our present values? This kind of search for objectivity is not only unrealistic but would also prevent any interpretation, as perfect objectivity—as a limit—would reduce history to a useless, sterile list of stochastic events. On the contrary, this book attempts, through systematic contextual analysis, to identify innovative ideas and proposals formulated by Miranda in opposition to his context and to compare them with what was later considered the standard of democratic governance. The Precursor's accuracy is objectively measurable by referencing factual elements through the degree of forecast of observable posterior regimes, whether they were "good or bad", democratically chosen or not.

Miranda's most unique and advanced ideas were, first of all, distancing himself from any ideology except the basic principles of peaceful life in a society that rests on cooperation by protecting the equality and freedom of each person through the separation of powers. The Constitution's task is to defend these fundamental principles, while dogmatic options must be expressed legitimately through legislative initiatives, subject to public debate and autonomous counterpowers. Secondly, in the application of Human Rights, the purpose of achieving complete emancipation of the colonies is understood as external decolonisation (independence as a means), allowing an internal one, that is, socio-ethnic inclusion (as the goal).

His conception of democracy was less ideological than any other in the past, except for the fundamental option for a representative system based on a strict separation of powers according to the following complementary principles:

- The essential thing about democracy is to ensure an effective separation of powers. Therefore, democracy cannot be compatible with an executive directly controlled by the legislature or under a popular power subject to the emotional overflow of masses or violence.
- The people cannot govern directly, contrary to the classic definition of "*government of the people for the people*", but must be "*a government only for the people but not by the people*"; periodic elections of representatives warrant the indirect sovereign control of the people.
- These elections are guided by a permanent public debate that must be open and with an effective guarantee for free opinion and popular education. This allows any ideological option to be democratically formed by a majority due to these debates, with respect for human rights and other autonomous powers and counter-powers.
- A democratic regional integration requires strict subsidiarity with limited but strong federal power in very few policies, for which the lower geographical political level cannot manage better. The interpretation of this geographical subsidiarity is an evolving process that stimulates the separation of powers.

This system deserves to be studied more deeply than it has been the case. We even think that it should be spread because it has managed "to pass the test of History", that is to say, to resist the Darwinian selection of political regimes and philosophical ideas, fulfilling our empirical criterion for being considered authentically of precursory character. The "advance" of Miranda has much more value in its realism than those of other precursors of systems that later failed to reach what they announced and provoked a terrific infringement of human rights. In particular, and in clear opposition to an aspect of the contextual School of the new history of Cambridge, the best way to evaluate ex-post the intrinsic value of his political contributions of Miranda is by checking his visionary capacity to warn against the risks of tyranny that he perceived in the "popular power" and direct democracy, which Rousseau advocated for, and which was applied frantically by Robespierre as well as most other dictators up to now.

Additionally, although slightly more implicit in the proposed system, his conception of economic development as a self-sustaining process that depends essentially on institutional conditions guaranteeing good governance marks a considerable advance that aligns with the most advanced economic theories currently prevailing.

Our central thesis is that Miranda glimpsed "in tempore non suspecto" the fundamental dilemma of democratic governance and perceived the necessity to try a synthesis of the two primary positions that divided the European thinkers of his time: on the one hand, the Anglo-Saxon utilitarians and the economic liberals, and on the other hand, Rousseau's communitarianism and its derivative towards the Jacobin centralisation of powers. History showed that these two schools of thought became the two sides of an antagonistic geopolitical world, whose excesses of liberalism and centralism have caused—and continue to do—endless victims and costly policies.

Miranda's intermediate governance solutions continue to provide realistic insights not only to Latin America but also to contemporary debates when addressing the challenges of today's globalised world, particularly in the operational definitions of freedom, democracy, regional integration, and development, as well as in explaining the fundamental mechanisms of endogenous economic growth. His argumentation could even be opportune in the recent debate, which emerged in the United States with the so-called "Dark Enlightenment"[72] (see Chap. 1) about the compatibility between democracy and freedom.

That leads us to a double enigma that deserves more attention if we want to better understand the structural weaknesses of Latin America and the Caribbean:

Why wasn't Miranda successful in his time?

Why do his proposals still need to be analysed after having been neglected or insufficiently assessed by historians?

References

Antepara, J. M./de Miranda, F., [1810], *The Emancipation of South America*, printed by R. Juigné, No 17, Margaret-Street, Cavendish-Square, 1810, re-edition by David R. Chacón Rodríguez, [2005] Fundación Hermano Nectario María, Caracas 2005. Serie: (Francisco de Miranda; t. 2).

Berlin, I., [2002, 1958], "Two Concepts of Liberty" in Berlin, I. *Four Essays on Liberty*, London: Oxford University Press. New ed.

Berlin, I., [2003], *Freedom and its Betrayal: Six Enemies of Human Liberty*, ed. Henry Hardy, Pimlico, London

Betti, D. [2008] *American Revolutionaries: Alexander Hamilton & Francisco de Miranda*. Available at SSRN: https://ssrn.com/abstract=4410146 or http://dx.doi.org/10.2139/ssrn.4410146

[72] Land, N. [2012], Yarving, C./Moldbug, M. [2007, 2008], Thiel, P., [2009]; see references in Chap. 1.

Bolívar, S., [1812], Cartagena Manifesto, available in Spanish on http://www.analitica.com/bitblioteca/bolivar/cartagena.asp

Condorcet's constitution project (in French), (1793), https://fr.wikisource.org/wiki/Plan_de_Constitution_pr%C3%A9sent%C3%A9_%C3%A0_la_Convention_Nationale

Constitution of the Bolivarian Republic of Venezuela, [1999], https://venezuela.justia.com/federales/constitucion-de-la-republica-bolivariana-de-venezuela/

Gramsci, A., [1929, 1947], Notas sobre Maquiavelo, Prison Notebooks [Quaderni del Carcere] (translated eds. by Joseph Anthony Buttigieg II; 1947–2019). (3 volumes). Columbia University Press.

Hamilton, A., Madison, J., Jay, J. [1787, 1982], *The Federalist Papers*, reedition by Wills, G., Bantam Books, New York.

Henríquez, G., [2001], *Historia de un Archivo: Francisco de Miranda*, Reconstitución de la memoria, Fundación por la Cultura Urbana, Caracas.

Jacobins' Constitution of Year I of June 1793 (in French), http://www.gauchemip.org/spip.php?article1091

Kant, I., [1795, 2006] "Idea for a Universal History from a Cosmopolitan Perspective" in *Toward Perpetual Peace and other writings on Politics, Peace and History*. Reedited by Pauline Kleingeld, Yale University Press.

Miranda, F. de [1929–1950], *Archivo del General Miranda*, ed. Vicente Dávila/ Rubén González, Caracas/La Habana. Miranda, F. de, "Proclamation to the people of the Colombian continent", May 1801, translated from Salcedo Bastardo, *América Espera* [1982]. op.cit. p. 263–270].

Montesquieu, C. L., [1748], *De l'esprit des lois*, Barrillot & Fils, Genève. https://classiques.uqam.ca/classiques/montesquieu/de_esprit_des_lois/de_esprit_des_lois_tdm.html

North, D., [1990], *Institutions, Institutional Change and Economic Performan*ce, Cambridge University Press.

Parra-Pérez, C. [1943], *Páginas de Historia y de Polémica*, Litografía del Comercio, Caracas.

Picón-Salas, M., [1946], *Miranda*, Editorial Losada, Buenos Aires.

Rouvillois, F., [2008] « Saint Just fasciste ? » in Escande, R. *Le Livre Noir de la Révolution Française*, Les Editions du Cerf, Paris.

Saint Just/ Charles Vellay & others eds. [1908] *Oeuvres complètes*, Paris.

Salcedo-Bastardo, J. L., [1982], *América espera / Francisco de Miranda*; Biblioteca Ayacucho, n°100, Caracas.

Smith, J., [1808] *Commerce Defended. An Answer to the Arguments by which Mr. Spence, Mr. Cobbett, and Others, have attempted to Prove that Commerce is not a source of National Wealth*, C. and R. Baldwin, London. https://oll.libertyfund.org/pages/james-mill-commerce-defended-1808

Smith, J./Antepara/Miranda, [1809], *The Emancipation of South America,* Vol. XIII, N° 25, January, Art. 2, p. 227; https://hetwebsite.net/het/schools/edreview.htm

Smith, J./Miranda, [1809], "Molina's Account of Chili", Vol. XIV, N° 28, July, Art. IV, p. 333, *The Edinburgh Review* https://hetwebsite.net/het/schools/edreview.htm

Touchard, J., [2005] *Histoire des idées politiques*, 2 vol. PUF, Paris.

Uslar Pietri, A., [1966], Los Libros de Miranda, Ediciones del cuatricentenario de Caracas.

Chapter 5
The Constitutional Projects for Hispanic America and Brazil

5.1 Overview of the Five Projects for Spanish America and One for Brazil

Miranda's successive constitutional projects are the most significant part of his political texts. They synthesise the dream of integrative governance, which the precursor had encouraged throughout his life. His primary purpose was to establish the most appropriate way of governing Spanish America, aiming to catch up with the Anglo-Saxon democracies through an original synthesis between these Anglo-Saxon cultures and the French one, while respecting local and indigenous idiosyncrasies. This new governance formula also pointed to making possible a strategic geopolitical alliance of democracies against autocratic or absolutist regimes. Although well-known by historians who specialise in this subject, these texts have yet to be genuinely analysed, resulting in a sub-evaluation of their innovation and neglect of their revolutionary potential.

With exceptional sobriety for this kind of text, these projects synthesise the essentials of the federal model of governance that Miranda proposed for Hispanic America. This was an outstanding project regarding its integration and inter-cultural ambition, its constitutional innovations in governance and the extent of its geographical coverage. It would have formed the larger Democratic Republic of the time, and its purpose was to launch the most advanced social, ethnic, and geographical process of integration and decolonisation.

These constitutional projects were written between 1790 and 1808, and they were contemporary with the first written constitutions in Europe, but were earlier and more modern than the European liberal constitutionalism of the nineteenth century, which arose in Cadiz (Spain) as a symbol of the theoretical and practical fight against the old regime. The constitutional movement of Cadiz (1810–1812) that served as an

C. Ghymers, *Independence, Federalism and Regionalism in Latin America: An Analytical Anthology of Francisco de Miranda's Writings (1790-1811)*,
United Nations University Series on Regionalism 34,
https://doi.org/10.1007/978-3-031-96938-6_5

inspiration for Constitutional Texts in other countries is significantly less advanced than Miranda's projects, despite Cadiz's text being conceived more than one decade later (or even two decades compared to the 1790 text) than those of the Precursor. This demonstrates the advancement and great political maturity of the humanist general, who formulated a pragmatic version of a more modern Democracy that would have prevented the ideological manipulation of popular power that he had observed during the French Revolution. In this way, Miranda was a visionary for conceiving a pragmatic formula for a more modern Democracy. His main objective was to provide the necessary institutional structure for channelling the independence aspiration towards a complete but progressive emancipation process through the rule of law and popular education. Proposing electoral filters to prevent populism, his fundamental idea was to warrant a profound, peaceful change when the colonial structure was on the verge of collapse. This change aimed to replace the colonial order with an autonomous democratic system capable of facilitating a progressive process of socio-ethnic inclusion. The purpose was to eradicate ethnic, social, and religious discrimination in order to promote production and trade, thereby fostering economic development.

This process of conquering citizen freedom and development was based on an original conception of a pragmatic and less ideological democracy. The five successive constitutional projects he delivered for Spanish America and the project for the Brazilian federation (this one is attributed to him) show that more than a fighter for Latin American independence, Miranda was the central axis of the conception and organisation of a long-term revolutionary strategy and a visionary promotion of modern democratic governance warning against the ideological manipulation of popular power he had observed in France. But being the loser of this democratic struggle, most historians have mainly perceived his role as a precursor of independence to the detriment of his ability to formulate an operational synthesis of the most advanced ideas of governance of his time and, above all, to protect Latin America from Jacobinism by adapting in a pragmatic way democracy to Latin American realities. Our interpretation is that, being defeated by the "caudillismo", the independence process remained biased and unable to achieve genuine emancipation, which was Miranda's purpose for independence.

Miranda was looking for concrete formulas capable of channelling the conflicts and the social forces that would inevitably be released by the collapse of the absolutist Empire through institutions that would monitor each other to ensure an effective separation of powers following Montesquieu. To translate it into an operational, institutional architecture, he was inspired, in addition to his deep knowledge of the Greek and Latin world, by three experiences: positively by the British pragmatic equilibrium reached with its parliamentary regime, as well as his journey in the emerging republic of the United States and overall by the federalist ideas of Alexander Hamilton [1787, 1982], but also negatively by the French disequilibrium resulting from the missing autonomy of constitutional powers due to the dogmatic principle of popular power. He concludes that a genuine separation of powers is the only effective way to guarantee rights and freedoms to citizens against the inherent tendency of all political power to abuse. Moreover, he was indisputably the first to base political independence on a specific American identity, endowed with a constitutional framework that integrated all its components, whether social, ethnic, or regional. Likewise, its projects for a federal constitution are based on the principle of geographical subsidiarity, which is radically opposed to the French Jacobin rule of "one-size-fits-all." His constitutions announced what the European Union was trying to achieve two centuries later: strong federal powers but strictly limited only to three areas: external defence/diplomacy, economic and monetary union, and human rights (gender, justice, free opinions and elections), while all the other policies remaining decentralised for the realism of efficiency and for protecting the different local identities.

For him, regional, social, and racial integration was necessary for transforming political independence into a process of lasting emancipation and sustainable socio-economic development. Written constitutions could only ensure this process by setting a new legal and institutional framework rooted in local and indigenous institutions and cultures.

These innovative aspects of his constitution proposals rely on the combination of the following principles:

1. Democracy comes from popular power, but this power has to be limited to regular elections, which sanction the executive but do not interfere with its current management: "*all from the people and for the people but nothing by the people*."
2. The solution is a "*mixed government*[1]", taken by Miranda from Aristotle, Polibius (with the Roman Republic experiences), Hobbes, Locke, Vico, Kant, Hamilton and Madison, to balance the powers to prevent anarchy or tyranny for maintaining stability thanks to a mixture of the different forms of government (aristocracy, democracy and tyranny) and the development of autonomous «checks & balances». Miranda's constant preoccupation was to prevent the excess of popular power through a representative system that limited legislative power via electoral (adjustable) filters and a combination of elected representatives with designated senators appointed by the Head of the executive, based on objective merit but subject to the permanent action of autonomous "checks-and-balances" mechanisms.
3. The separation between the three branches of power (legislative, executive, judicial) for preventing any disequilibrium through each watching the others in a permanent dialogue and with a partial participation of the Head of the executive (Monarch or elected President) to each of them. The constant concern is a limitation of popular power to avoid an "elective tyranny" if the three powers were controlled by popular assemblies subject to the masses' emotions.
4. The federal nature of the proposed regime distributes the powers and policy responsibilities geographically according to their respective efficiency in an adjustable way: in contrast to current views (and especially the French ones) presenting federalism as opposite to democracy, his federal option points to develop a progressive integrative dynamism (totally absent in French thinking preoccupied to impose a radical single "truth" in a "one-size-for-all" philosophy),

[1] For theoretical analysis, see Morrow, J. [1998].

which respect local identities while contributing to building awareness of common interests; Miranda's federal formula announces what will be named later the principle of "*subsidiarity*" and will be re-discovered two centuries later; it combines strong powers entrusted to the federal level only when they are more efficient and more beneficial for all the regions, with the decentralisation principle for all other areas for preserving local autonomies and dynamism. The frontier between the federal and regional powers is adaptable according to precise processes of qualified majorities, either initiated by the popular base or the top level, but always ratified by three-quarters of the legislative.

5. The representative system is structured in a geographical pyramid based on direct voting at the basis of the level of the "cabildos" (the traditional municipal institution), followed by pyramidal successive delegation by voting to designate their representatives at the subsequent national and federal levels. His texts focused on protecting Americans from the risks of the tyranny-anarchy cycle (which he had experimented with in France) and the risk of geographic fragmentation.

The first version of Miranda's constitution was written in 1790 and was one of the very first proposals of European constitutional texts. After the first modern constitution was conceived in the US (signed in 1787 and ratified in 1789[2]), Poland was the European precursor to adopting written constitutionalism[3] in 1791. The first Polish constitution, also known as the "Government Law," was a set of fundamental laws enacted by the Assembly, commonly referred to as the "Dieta" or Polish parliament, and later became known as the Constitution of 3 May 1791. In this document was introduced the principle of the division of power into three independent branches: Legislative Body (Bicameral system), Executive Power (the King, as head of government, was who presided over the Council of Ministers called "Guardia de Leyes"), and Judiciary (Independent Court), which abolished the election of kings by introducing a hereditary monarchy. It was the second fundamental law written worldwide and the first in Europe since the time of the Greco-Roman era.

The National Constituent Assembly of France, at the beginning of the French Revolution, promulgated its first Constitution in 1791, accepted and signed by Louis XVI on September 3 of the same year. It was the first written constitution to establish a constitutional monarchy. Miranda witnessed the failure of this formula and the popular violent insurrection of the commune of Paris organised by the Jacobins[4]

[2] The US Constitution was signed in the Philadelphia Convention by each of the representatives of the Confederate States of America and subsequently ratified by a short majority of three votes by the people in conventions through representatives, becoming a Federation (although the US Constitution was never voted on by universal suffrage).

[3] Before the US and Polish Constitutions, the Republic of San Marino enacted a written text in 1600. The Corsican Republic claimed independence from the Genoa Republic in 1755 with a constitutional text (written by Pauli, who later came into contact with Miranda), and Armenia too in 1773, but failed to establish a republic.

[4] **Jacobin**: Radical republican movement—comparable to the contemporaneous extreme left—inspired mainly by Robespierre and Saint-Just. They claim that people's sovereignty must imply a

in August 1792, followed by elections in September 1792, which proclaimed the First Republic and established the Girondins' government.[5]

The original text of the ***second Miranda's constitutional Project*** disappeared. Only a few comments on its content are available in Miranda's diary. It was written in Paris at the end of 1797 before seeking refuge in London. The police persecuted him due to his strong opposition to the Directory and to the emerging Napoleon Bonaparte, whom Miranda perceived as an ambitious potential César who would threaten world peace.[6] Miranda had only one original exemplar of his second version

---

centralised single power, rejecting, therefore, Montesquieu's separation of the three powers and imposing direct popular democracy, drawing upon an interpretation of Rousseau's ideology, leading to an effective centralisation of powers in the hands of the legislative body by dividing and submitting the executive one. The name "Jacobin" originates from the location in Paris where an association of political supporters of the Revolution convened. Initially, it encompassed almost all revolutionaries, but it was radicalised to regroup a minority, yet very influential, fringe, first designated as the "Montagnards" (for occupying the upper part of the assembly), later referred to as the "Jacobins". They wanted to remove the King and impose a popular republic. They indeed imposed increased ideological totalitarianism justified by the dogmatic belief of single popular sovereignty, which excludes any pluralism or opponents; this led inevitably to violence, first with the popular insurrection of August 10, 1792, and from then to an escalation towards the dictatorship of "Terror" imposed by Robespierre with his 'coup d'état' on the May 31/June 01, 1793, until its fall in the end of July 1794 under an opposite coup led by the members of his own party who felt in danger to be eliminated themselves by the Robespierre's exclusion principle that claimed the unity of popular sovereignty and so a single central legislative authority.

[5] **Girondin**: the moderate left-wing political movement, supporting the revolution and controlling the majority in the French Parliament from 1791 to 1793. Its name comes from the fact that the deputies from the Bordeaux region (La Gironde) were dominant in the moderate group, which was formed when supporters of the revolution were divided between moderates and extremists (Jacobins) in the wake of the King's attempt to escape from France. However, this moderate group of «bourgeois» encompassed a wide range of heterogeneous ideological currents, lacking any cohesion beyond counteracting the Jacobins' rise and opposing the conservatives. However, they failed to stabilise France because of a lack of adequate power in the hands of the executive. Indeed, the constitutional order at that time was based on many deliberative assemblies, with liberal democratic representation but an insufficient separation of powers. Miranda was perceived as a Girondin member, although he was critical of their positions and fully aware of the flaw in an unbalanced repartition of powers (a centralised legislative having superior power facing an excessively decentralised executive).

[6] **Napoleon**: Although very well-known, this famous military dictator and brilliant military strategist, who conquered most of Western Europe and tried to modernise and integrate the countries of Europe, but by force, knew Miranda in Paris before carrying out his "coup d'état" and becoming popular. Napoleon, arising from within the Jacobin agitators, represents the exact opposite of Miranda. He spilt blood all over Europe, contributing significantly to further nationalist reactions and subsequent bloodshed and European divisions, still tangible nowadays. He was born in Corsica on August 15, 1769. After one decade of "*military successes*", he became influent on the government (Directory). He organised two "self-coups" for maintaining in power the corrupted Jacobins in 1797 and 1799, taking power as First Consul, and the 18th of May of 1804 he proclaimed himself Emperor of the French and King of Italy under the name of Napoleón I. He was consecrated in Notre Dame in the presence of Pío VII. He was finally defeated by the Seventh European Coalition organised by England in the Battle of Waterloo (18th of June of 1815, in Belgium). A few days later, he was exiled to the British island of Santa Elena, where he died on the 5th of May 1821. The balance of his role remains controversial since he can be attributed to many millions of deaths

of the constitution when he arrived in London in January 1798. Still, the English Prime Minister, William Pitt,[7] who received him in priority, was so impatient to get it that Miranda was forced to hand over his original. Even though Miranda made Pitt commit to giving it back to him, he never recovered his single copy.

The *third version* of the constitution, from 1801, is the most complete one and includes Miranda's ideal views. We will analyse it in detail in Sect. 5.2.2.

The *fourth document, dated 1808*, is a tactical, conservative adaptation of the 1801 version in a less democratic sense. The aim was to persuade the powerful Creoles not to fear an election that would introduce independence. By restricting popular access to voting and eligibility through the imposition of patrimonial criteria, the process could be gradual, thereby preventing social turmoil. In other words, diminishing the "degree of democracy" would ensure that the Creoles would perceive the systemic change as less drastic, more manageable, and not directly opposed to their interests. Faced with the probability of the fall of the Spanish regime as a consequence of the invasion of the Iberian Peninsula by Napoleon (that Miranda [1978] had foretold 10 years before[8]), it was crucial not to frighten Creole people—whose support was essential to attract them against the Spanish authorities and to avoid a bloodbath. Therefore, Miranda intended to give the Creoles more guarantees to alleviate their fears of too-rapid social changes, which could threaten his plan and derail the peaceful transition. It is worth highlighting the insight of Miranda in foreseeing in 1808 this risk of bloody civil war and racial conflict between the white colonists and the Native Americans in case of the absence of a robust constitutional order for controlling the changes. The frightening events of Saint Domingue, first since 1791, had been impacting mentalities and were repeated in Mexico in 1810, destroying the revolution.

The fifth, not yet published, is, in fact, an intermediate draft that mixes elements from both the 1801 and 1808 projects. It is undated and titled "draft." David Chacón discovered it in the Spanish archives. This version suggests that Miranda was willing to adapt his constitutional texts pragmatically to local realities according to different contexts. This version sets much lower election criteria and import duties.

---

and victims, feeding nationalism in Europe. He also reinforced French Jacobin culture, its juridical machismo, and nationalist protectionism, while promoting social mobility and the modernisation of the French administration.

[7] **William Pitt** (1759–1806), nicknamed "the Younger" to distinguish him from his father, William Pitt (1708–1778), Count of Chatham, who was also Prime Minister of England from 1766 to 1769. His son served as Prime Minister for 24 years, from 1783 to 1801 and from 1804 to his death in 1806. He belonged to the "Tory" philosophy, favourable to landowning aristocracy and a robust monarchical power, as opposed to the "Whigs", who were more liberal and favourable to a strong Parliament.

[8] Chapter 10, documents 10.15, 10.16, and 10.17. Miranda's letters to Prime Minister Pitt, President John Adams of the United States, and James Hamilton were all written in March 1798. Hamilton fully agreed with Miranda on the threat of French Jacobinism to democracy in America, to the point that he advocated for a war against France and was responsible for preparing the US army for this option.

***For Brazil*, a constitutional plan is attributed to Miranda**, according to a series of secret diplomatic documents discovered by the historian André Fugier[9] [1930] and analysed by C. Parra-Pérez[10] [1936, 1943] in the Portuguese diplomatic archives. They are dated 1806. Nevertheless, there is no formal proof that Miranda was the direct author and organiser of a revolutionary uprising against the Portuguese colony in Brazil. However, the content reveals ideas and styles so close to Miranda's that they could be considered authentic testimony of his main constitutional ideas. There are only two possibilities:

1. The insurrectionist plan was effective, created secretly (to prevent an English reaction in defence of the Portuguese ally) by the precursor in connection with the Lusitanian liberal party, either from London or later from New York, and denounced by an English (or American) spy for money, or
2. this plan was invented by a brilliant English (or American) scammer who was very well-informed about Miranda's constitutional ideas and documents, utilising his exclusive information to gain credibility and extract money from the Portuguese government.

Whatever the reality of this plan, these diplomatic sources deliver authentic information about what was perceived as Miranda's views in 1806, like a journalistic report in real-time. Even in the case of a pure scam, the manipulator understood Miranda's constitution and project perfectly.

The first document is intended to synthesize Miranda's ideas soundly. It was written by an English trader from Liverpool who denounced Miranda's plan to benefit himself by claiming a reward from the Portuguese authorities.

The second one—introduced in Chap. 9 with the prominent others of Miranda's proclamations—is intended to be a copy rewritten by the same spy of the independence declaration project for Brazil. Miranda's supposed aim was to implement this plan after the landing of forces to defeat the Lusitanian colonial regime.

According to the spy/fraudster, the denounced military expedition to the Brazilian coasts would have taken place in link with—but just after—the success of the planned landing in Coro (Northern coast of Venezuela) against Spanish colonies. The Coro invasion was intended to remain secret and was scheduled to take effect in July or August 1806, but it ultimately failed to overthrow the Spanish authorities.

---

[9] **André Fugier** (1896–1976), French historian. See: Fugier, André.: *Napoléon et l'Espagne: 1799–1808...* -Paris: Felix Alcan, 1930 (Dijon: Darantière). 1929.2 v.; 25 cm. (Library d'Histoire Contemporaine.). Facs. intercal. Recent translation to Spanish: Fugier, André (1896–1976): *Napoleón y España, 1799–1808*/André Fugier; traducción del francés, 2008.

[10] **Carraciolo Parra-Perez** (1888–1964), Venezuelan historian and diplomat, specialist of Miranda's life and discoverer of the Archives of the Precursor in 1926 in the Cirencester castle of the family of Lord Bathurst. This Minister of War and Colonies secretly hid Miranda's archives after Bolivar arrested Miranda in 1812. When Lord Bathurst left his ministry, he took the archives to his castle in Cirencester, Gloucestershire. When the boat with Miranda's archives escaped from La Guaira and arrived in Curacao under the care of Miranda's secretary Leleux, the British Governor referred to his minister Bathurst, who asked him to send these documents to Downing Street.

Although these two documents are genuine original letters sent to the Portuguese ambassador in London—whose dates perfectly match the preparation of Miranda's secret operation in Coro—there is no sufficient proof that Miranda was the direct author of an actual conspiracy against the Portuguese colonial empire, or just a scam using his ideas to threat Portuguese government for selling them as genuine strategic information. Nevertheless, valid sources indicate authentic and rigorous information about the constitutional ideas ascribed to Miranda in 1806. Therefore, these constitutional texts can be considered as worthy historical documents.

It seems perfectly coherent that Miranda could have conceived this parallel plan for Brazil, as he had always envisioned a continental and federative approach to decolonization, leading to genuine emancipation. Additionally, it was perfectly logical that this plan against Portugal's colonies had to be kept even more secret than Miranda's project to land in Spanish colonies, given that Portugal and Britain were strategic partners. He could not risk provoking an adverse reaction from his British ally. Nevertheless, there is no formal proof of his direct implication in Brazil. It remains unclear whether Miranda would have effectively dealt with emancipating Brazil.

We carefully verified the authenticity of the letters between the Portuguese ambassador in London and his government in the official Portuguese diplomatic archives.[11]

5.2 The Five Projects for Hispanic America

5.2.1 First Constitutional Project for Spanish America, 1790

Context:

This synthetic document was written to be handed to William Pitt. The idea was to obtain the support of the British government. In 1784, after failing to get Washington's direct military involvement in his emancipation plan, Miranda was convinced that international assistance was indispensable for the diplomatic and military success of a liberal revolution in Latin America. In June 1789, after a 4-year trip studying European political regimes and seeking future geopolitical alliances, Miranda finally decided to settle in London. The reason was that he thought that England was the only European country whose socio-political structures were open and reliable, so they could provide him with a sufficient guarantee of freedom of expression and the possibility of active networking, two conditions for being operational for conceiving, managing, and carrying on his democratic/subversive plan of colonial emancipation.

[11] Archivos Torre de Tombo, Lisboa. The author thanks the Director of the Archives for her pleasant cooperation in 2006.

On the 14th of February 1790, Thomas Pownall[12] suggested that Miranda visit William Pitt for the first time (he had seen him before at an official dinner in 1789) in his country house in Hollwood, Kent. The interview took place in the context of the new conflict between England and Spain, which was disputing the ownership of the northwestern coast of the Pacific. In Noodtka Sound (now Canada, Pacific coast), the Spanish navy seized British ships and blocked their commerce. In 1790, news arrived in London, provoking intense public reactions against Spain. This fact opened an excellent opportunity for Miranda's plan to justify a British military expedition to South America. On the other hand, England was divided over the issues of the French Revolution and Republicanism at that moment. Miranda and Thomas Paine[13] participated in these debates, defending the revolution against the conservative Edmund Burke,[14] with the idea of convincing the English government of the advantages for the United Kingdom in fighting against the Spanish colonial regime. In his diary, he notes that he gave Pitt an action plan to implement once England had declared war on Spain. On March 5, Miranda sent Pitt his first proposal regarding the wishes of Spanish America. These comprise a compendium of circumstances which justified English intervention. It also explains the Spanish policy of excluding Creoles from public functions and the censorship of the Inquisition, which prohibited reading helpful or instructive books, thereby preventing the colonies from assuming their own government. In addition, he provides a list of the American Jesuits expelled by the Spanish regime and assigned to residence, mainly in Italy. This intellectual elite could have been very useful in supporting the Spanish-American liberation and in assuming control of the public administration of the newly independent territories, serving as replacements for the Spanish colonial administrators. On the 13th and the 27th of March, he sends Pitt some new works. In May, he met in secret with Pitt and Lord Grenville.[15] On August 3, 1790, Miranda

[12] **Thomas Pownall** (1722–1805), a member of the British Parliament, former governor of Massachusetts and of other American states, a friend of Miranda, British activist of the cause of the American independence of the North but also of Latin America, supported Miranda in London from its first steps, providing him financial resources and his connections with the government and his advanced ideas. He was especially active in his efforts in 1800 and 1801 with the British government to secure the necessary diplomatic and military support to execute Miranda's plan, which would have made it possible to mitigate the risks of anarchy or tyranny in Spanish America while supporting the United Kingdom's strategy. He finally did not make it.

[13] **Thomas Payne** (1737–1809) was an English-born American Founding Father, philosopher and political activist promoting actively in the American and the French revolutions; condemned as seditious in the United Kingdom, he fled to France, where he was involved in the Revolution and also arrested as Miranda by Robespierre in 1793, but remained Jacobin.

[14] **Edmund Burke** (1729–1797) was an Anglo-Irish statesman, economist, philosopher, member of the British Parliament, and a leading figure of conservatism opposed to the French Revolution. Not to be confused with William Burke, who published a pamphlet promoting British support for emancipating South America (see Chap. 10, document 10.4.5., note & document 10.4.14., note), nor with the British spy James Florence Burke (see note 36 in Chap. 11).

[15] **William Wyndham Grenville** (1759–1834), cousin and Interior Minister of William Pitt in 1790, before becoming Pitt's Foreign Affairs Minister from 1791 to 1801 and returning as Prime Minister after Pitt died in 1806. Grenville was very influential in Parliament, pro-aristocratic and

gave him his government project for the Spanish Indies after carefully analysing Pitt's sensibilities. This text complemented Miranda's plan that involved England in a political-military operation in South America to implement a modern democracy and a free-trade system. Nevertheless, on October 28, 1790, Pitt achieved on his side a diplomatic agreement with Spain ("Nootka Sound Agreement"), avoiding an expensive war impeding Miranda's plan's realisation. Following this change in strategy, Miranda and Pitt fought (*"I've been sold for a trade treaty,"* Miranda says). Miranda demanded the restitution of his documents, something that Pitt did very reluctantly, taking until March 1792 to return only a part of the documentation provided by Miranda.

Content:

This first proposal incorporates British aspects for strategic reasons, being monarchic but with specific original characteristics. The text contains only ten articles[16] on establishing a "mixed" government system. According to Miranda's terminology, this means organising the cooperation of the three autonomous powers to sanction the laws and mutually control each other through a combination of popular power with moderating mechanisms for balancing respective powers. The strict separation of powers ensures a limitation of popular power to prevent an "elective tyranny" from emerging by dominating the other two powers.

- The Parliament is elected by universal popular suffrage without economic restrictive criteria
- The Senate members ("*Caciques*") are not elected but designated by the Inca (Head of State) among high-level categories of civil servants or military, i.e. among a kind of aristocracy by merits, not by birth origin; they named the Ministers ("*Ediles*") with the agreement of the Head of State ("*Inca*")
- Ministers ("*Ediles*") account for public expenditure management before the parliament for public buildings and before the senate for other expenses.
- The separation of powers is combined with a hereditary monarchy (the *Inca*), whose prerogatives are limited by the legislative chambers,
- But the Inca participates in the decisions of the three branches as a channel of dialogue across powers and to moderate the conflicts
- Two autonomous entities act as countervailing powers: the censors and the auditors («Quaestors»), whose members are selected by elections. The censors ensure a kind of "democratic accountability" over the designated senators, and the auditors control all financial accounts and uses of public money by the ministers and the Inca.

suspicious of Miranda, who was Republican and had fought alongside Washington in the US against the UK. Contrary to Miranda, Grenville was in favour of military intervention in Europe and opponent to Henry Dundas (Minister of the Interior from 1791 to 1794, Minister of War from 1794 to 1801, and of Admiralty from 1804 to 1805), who was always a supporter of Miranda's plan of a maritime war in America in order to get a lever upon France and to establish English supremacy at lower cost.

[16] For comparison purposes, the US Constitution of 1789 had only 7 articles, and the French one from 1791 had 210 articles.

- The Inca appoints the judges from a list presented by the autonomous judicial power
- The revision of the constitution depends upon a qualified majority of two-thirds at initiative either of both chambers or by the judges with the Inca, but in both cases, the ratification requires a qualified majority of three-fourths of the Chambers or the judges, respectively.

Miranda's constitution, inspired by Montesquieu and British history, starts with the territorial formation and the analysis of the mixed government system, which is a consequence of the three branches of power that sanction and control the laws. Each branch controls the others to prevent tyranny and centralization of power.

On the list of documents remitted to William Pitt on the negotiations carried out by Miranda [1790, 1929][17] in London from 1790 to 1792, document number 7 was the Plan for the Formation, Organization, and *Establishment of a Free and Independent Government in South America.*

Sources:

Original text written in French. Found in *Public Record Office*. William Pitt, first Earl of Chatham Mss: Papers 30/8/345–1. ***Papers relating to South America***. There is a copy of the original one in the Archivo de la Academia Nacional de la Historia. Caracas. **Colección Caracciolo Parra-Perez**: Papeles relativos a Miranda y a la independencia de Venezuela. Chatham Mss. 345.

Published in:

Gil Fortoul, José: **Obras completas**/Historia Constitucional de Venezuela/ -Caracas: Ministerio de Educación. Dirección de Cultura y Bellas Artes. Comisión Editora de las Obras Completas de José Gil Fortoul, 1953., mapas pleg.; 1954. Vol. 1 p. 173–174. Summary.

Archivo del General Miranda. Negociaciones. 1777–1810.—Caracas: Tipografía Americana. Vol XV. p. 110, appears only the title in French of this draft constitution in the list of the documents handed over to W. Pitt: «*Plan pour la forme, organisation, et établissement d'un gouvernement-libre, et indépendant dans l'Amérique méridionale*», but the text is missing in the Archivo as well as in Colombeia.

Warning: many historians make confusion between the successive projects, presenting the 1790 version as the given project to William Pitt in January of 1798, among which we can mention:

José Luis Salcedo Bastardo en su obra: **América espera**/Francisco de Miranda; – Caracas: Ayacucho library n°100, 1982, p. 208–210. This text is incorrectly presented as the 1797 version handed over to W. Pitt in January 1798, which he never returned to Miranda (as indicated in his Archivo, Vol. XV, p. 205, «Esquisse de Constitution 6.6»).

[17] *Plan pour la forme, organisation, et établissement d'un gouvernement-libre, et indépendants, dans l'Amérique Méridionale.* In: *Archivo* Vol. XV & in *Colombeia.* Vol. IX.

Batllori, Miguel, S.J.: **Del descubrimiento a la Independencia: estudios sobre Iberoamérica y Filipinas**/prólogo de Pedro Grases.- Caracas: Universidad Católica Andrés Bello, 1979. XIII, (Colección Manoa; 20).

Zeuske, Michael.: **Francisco de Miranda y la modernidad en América = Francisco de Miranda e a modernidade na América**/estudio de Michael Zeuske; [translation to Portugues, Miguel Freitas da Costa].- Madrid: Fundación Mapfre Tavera; Aranjuez: Doce Calles, [2004]. (Prisma histórico; 2). Texts in Spanish, French and Portuguese.

Text:

Project for establishing a Free and Independent Government in South America, 1790.

ON THE TERRITORY

The State integrated by the Latin-American colonies will have the following borders: in the north, the line that passes along the Mississippi River, from its mouth to its source, from there, following the same straight line west along 45° of northern latitude until it reaches the Pacific Ocean. To the west, the Pacific Ocean, from the point mentioned above to Cape Horn, includes the islands at a 10-degree distance from the coast. To the east, the Atlantic Ocean goes from Cape Horn to the Gulf of Mexico and from there to the mouth of the Mississippi River. Brazil and Guyana are not included in these demarcations. The islands along the coast will not be part of this state, as it is a continent large enough for land-based and agricultural power. Nonetheless, and as an exception, the Island of Cuba will be preserved because the harbour of Havana is the key to the Gulf of Mexico.

ON THE FORM OF GOVERNMENT

This must be mixed, like that of Great Britain. It will consist of a hereditary executive power, represented by an Inca named Emperor.

UPPER CHAMBER (SENATE)

The Senators or "Caciques" designated by the Inca will make up the High Chamber. The appointment will be for life but will not be hereditary. Only the Censors will have the authority to ban Senators from the chamber. Simple disqualification will entail exclusion. Selection will be from the class of citizens who have already served honourably in the first offices of the Empire, fulfilling functions such as General, Admiral, Judge of the Supreme Court, Censor, Town Councillor or Controller (Quaestor). The number of senators will be fixed. This number must always be complete.

LOWER CHAMBER (HOUSE OF COMMONS)

The citizens of the Empire will elect it. Its numbers are fixed. The members receive no salary, but they are eligible for re-election. While in office, their persona will be inviolable, except in cases involving capital crimes. Each legislature (parliament) will last 5 years.

ON JUDICIAL POWER.

The Inca will elect its members from a list of the most distinguished citizens of the Judicial Body. Their office will last for life, and they can only be removed from it under charges of and subsequently for corruption trials. The judges' salaries will be substantial, so a comfortable livelihood protects them from prevarication. In this respect, the English High Courts are a model to follow.

THE CENSORS

These will be two in number. They will be elected by the people and ratified by the Inca. Their term of office will last 5 years. They can be re-elected. Their primary function is to oversee the good conduct of the Senators, whom they can exclude from the Senate by mere dismissal, by inscribing their names on slates. They will also oversee the morals of the young, especially in schools and among Teachers.

THE EDILES (Ministers)

To be elected by the Senate for 5 years and confirmed by the Inca. They will be responsible for the great thoroughfares of the Empire, the harbours, the canals, the public monuments, the national festivities, etc. At the end of every 5 years, they will present their accounts before the House of Commons on the funds allocated to public buildings and before the Senate on all matters concerning buildings, monuments, and projects undertaken and completed.

THE QUAESTORS (Auditors)

The House of Commons will appoint them for a term of 5 years, and the Inca will confirm them. They will be re-eligible. Their primary function is to watch over the code of conduct of those in charge of the Treasury, national forest keepers, and customs officers ... In other words, to protect the public interest in all financial matters

ON LAW-MAKING

Following the English model, the three powers must sanction the passing of the laws. The laws can only be statutory, emanating from the Constitution itself. If they happen to contradict the state's constitutional laws, the courts will consider them null and void.

STEPS TO RECTIFY A CONSTITUTIONAL LAW

If two-thirds of both Houses consider it convenient to modify a constitutional law, it would be the Inca's duty to refer it to the judges of the High Court of Justice and put the proposal to them, which must then be sanctioned by two-thirds of both houses. If three-quarters of all the judges, including the Inca, who will have the right to vote, approve the law, this comes into being and the Constitution is modified. If, conversely, two-thirds of the judges and the Inca present a proposal, and three-quarters of both houses sanction this, then the law is enacted, and the Constitution is modified accordingly. The reform occurs without convulsions and blood-curdling fights in the political body.[18]

[18] Miranda defines the territory of the new state as extending from the middle line of the Mississippi River in the North, up to the Cap Horn in the South. Similar ideas are also expressed in paragraph 9 of the Act of Paris, signed on December 22, 1797 (see Chap. 7).

5.2.2 Second Constitutional Project for Hispanic American Colonies, 1797/98

Context:

After 18 months in French prisons waiting in the "corridor of death", Miranda was condemned to the guillotine by Robespierre's regime[19] of Terror and shared the situation of the victims of political persecution; he was finally released in January 1795, 6 months after Robespierre's fall. He was one of the first victims of the Jacobins,[20] personally persecuted by Robespierre *"for being politically wrong"* despite being a fair defender of the Revolution and one of its highest-ranking military officials, but as a moderate "Girondin". He also became the last political prisoner of Robespierre to be released after the fall of the Jacobins' regime. The main reason was that the Thermidorians,[21] who eliminated Robespierre, also opposed Miranda's democratic views. Despite his negative experiences with the French revolutionaries, he decided to stay in Paris because he hoped France would return to the ideology of freedom of the initial French Revolution. His interest was not only to contribute to the triumph of his conception of the revolution ("mixed democracy") but also to benefit from the French doctrine and export his revolution by getting the French military and diplomatic support for his anti-colonial political project in America. These two reasons were inseparable because military support would make sense only if the Revolution ensured the emancipation of other countries, not in the case of their submission to another form of centralised power under the Jacobins. Therefore, the Precursor believed that his political mission to Hispanic America would make sense only after contributing to rebalancing the French Revolution by preventing the drift toward Jacobin tyranny.

---

[19] **Maximilien de Robespierre** (1758–1794), a lawyer and politician of the French Revolution, was the head of the Jacobin movement that radicalised the Revolution, utilising Rousseau's principles of direct democracy to impose a totalitarian interpretation of the people's interests. He instigated successive popular insurrections that led to the «coup d'état» imposing the regime of Terror (1793–1794), with the centralisation of powers under his authority. He was overthrown and guillotined in July 1794 by a coalition of Jacobins and deputies from the centre and right wings, all united by the fear of Robespierre's dogmatic zeal, which threatened the interests of most intellectuals and politicians.

[20] See footnote 3 of this Chap. 5. The **Jacobins** were radically opposed to the **Girondins**, who also supported the Revolution but in a moderate and less dogmatic orientation. Miranda was assimilated into the Girondins, who were fiercely persecuted by Robespierre, who had most of them executed by guillotine, including the Girondist elected deputies. Miranda was imprisoned and sentenced to the guillotine with them. Still, his connections succeeded in postponing his execution, and Robespierre was overthrown just before the final deadline fixed by Robespierre himself in July 1794 (see Chap. 6, note n°111).

[21] The "**Thermidorians**" were the members of the French Convention who overthrew Robespierre with a coup on the ninth of the month of Thermidor (24 July 1794) and who organised a conservative republican regime after the «Terror». This "Thermidorian coup" was a broad reaction to eliminating Robespierre and his tyrannical regime of "Terror". However, this reaction was used to maintain a corrupted new oligarchy in power.

When Miranda offered his military services to the French Army on 22 August 1792 in defence of the Revolution and of the French territory invaded by the Austro-Prussian coalition,[22] the French authorities committed to rewarding him with military support to his South American plan once the invaders had been repelled. At the end of 1792, he was indeed offered the opportunity to lead a military expedition in Santo Domingo, but to restore French colonial authority on this island, which was in rebellion against France, something he considered incompatible with the democratic emancipation plan he had conceived for Spanish America. Therefore, he refused this unfair proposal, hoping for better offers later when France stabilised. Unfortunately, the situation deteriorated sharply with the Jacobins' coup in 1793 and the consecutive arrest of Miranda. He was jailed from July 1793 until January 1795. Condemned to the guillotine without any judgment, his execution was cancelled with the fall of Robespierre 2 days before the scheduled date. Nevertheless, the new regime (Thermidorian Convention), which purported to end the tyranny of popular power, tended to be controlled by a new emerging class that was preoccupied solely with its own power and interests. They maintained the centralisation of power but opted for a reversed imbalance with a strong executive branch dominating the legislative branch. Thus, this regime, the Directory, fell into the opposite disequilibrium but arrived at the same abuse by centralising powers in the hands of a few ex-Jacobins, who became very unpopular. The result was another form of tyranny, one that allowed the Directory to remain in power,[23] against which the anti-Jacobin Miranda protested, accusing the Directory Regime (1795–97)[24] of violating

[22] **First European coalition** (1792–97) against the French Revolution formed by Austria and Prussia (and extended later to England and Spain) as a reply to the French government's declaration of war against Austria in April 1792. This decision was made by the Girondin government, which sought to export the revolution as a means to unite the nation against an external enemy, with the King's agreement for other, undisclosed reasons. In July, the invasion of France began, accompanied by a threat against the French people if they did not restore the French King to his full power. In reaction, the crowd stormed the Royal Palace and overthrew the King in August 1792. On 22 August, the Minister of War asked Miranda to join the French Army, which was in need of professional high-ranking officers due to political emigration, as the Royal Army was predominantly commanded by aristocrats.

[23] Most citizens opposed the corrupt persons in place, but not so much against the Constitution of 1795. Faced with this "moral insurrection" in 1797, the minority in power used all means, including recalling some Jacobins, to maintain their advantages and looked to the Army, where Bonaparte appeared as the right Jacobin to end the risk of a democratic demand.

[24] **The Directory** (1795–1799) refers to the regime established by the Thermidorians and is the name given to the final four years of the French Revolution, succeeding the Convention (1792–1795). The power was in the hands of five Directors, who governed France from 1795 when it replaced the Committee of Public Safety. On 9 November 1799, it was overthrown by Napoleon Bonaparte in the Coup of 18 Brumaire and replaced by the French Consulate. Initially, the new governance method purported to prevent the Jacobin concentration of power and enacted the new constitution of Year III (1795), which opposed the Jacobin constitution of Year I (1793). The dominance of the popular assemblies, which had led to a concentration of power in the legislative branch, was reversed: a dominance of the executive emerged, also leading to the concentration of power. The result was another instability, marked by coup attempts, election manipulations, and shifting alliances between the royalists and the Jacobins, all aimed at maintaining power in the

its own constitution of 1795. He was again persecuted and arrested, unfairly accused several times under false denunciation—either by the left (Jacobin) or by the right (Royalist) for being a foreigner and perceived as a potential alternative leader.

In the face of these growing difficulties, and due to a confluence of various factors (see further details in Chaps. 6 and 7, context), Miranda realised that his dream of France being the ideal partner for his project was dead. Indeed, the successive regimes failed to set up a democratic government. Miranda, who promoted pacific arguments, opposed all consecutive governments for their lack of separation of powers and ambition of territorial conquests. He owns the record of political persecutions: the democratic Girondins (1792–93), the "popular power" abused by the Jacobins' tyranny (1793–94), the abusive executive power of the "republic without democracy" of the Thermidorian (1794–95), transformed into the conservative Directory (1795–97) and the neo-Jacobin one (1797–99) leading to the Napoleon dictatorship, all launched successive political persecutions against him at variable degrees, from death (guillotine) to accusations, arrests or expulsions ("dry guillotine"). All the more, he was worried about what he perceived long before others as the inevitable rise to power of a "*Cesar or an Alexander*" («caudillos»). He personally knew Napoleon, who was looking for power and popularity with his victories in Italy and Austria and who organised the Jacobin coup of 1797. Finally, according to his explanations, "*the monstrous alliance between the French Republic and Spanish monarchy*" directed against England convinced[25] him that his emancipation project could not thrive *in* Paris. Despite the removal of Robespierre and the disputed role of the Jacobins, Miranda changed his mind. He viewed Paris as dominated by a dangerous centralist culture, unable to ensure "habeas corpus" and human rights, making democracy a scam. He understood that the Tyranny relied upon a more deeply rooted feature, unable to implement an effective separation of powers, and not only the fact of a small, deviating group with left-leaning ideology.

As soon as the beginning of 1797, Miranda considered the alternative to return to London. He sent Pedro José Caro,[26] his agent, to London with a detailed memorandum [1797][27] addressed to the British cabinet, thanks to the intermediary of John

---

hands of the Directory. This situation paved the way for two successive "self-coups" in 1797 and 1799, not for ideological reasons but merely to maintain a few corrupted ex-Jacobins in power, restoring the Jacobin method. Miranda was declared "persona non grata" in France, and newspapers were censored, leading to Napoleon's dictatorship.

[25] From ratifying the agreement between France and Spain, Miranda understood that France would not be the expected ally. Miranda referred to the Second Treaty of San Ildefonso of August 18, 1796, which established a defensive and offensive alliance between France and Spain against England. Miranda wrote to Turnbull in January 1797 to see a possible contact with Pitt.

[26] **Pedro José Caro** (?-1803), Cuban, arrived in London in 1796 seeking help from England to make New Granada independent (Venezuela, Colombia, Panama, Trinidad and Guyana); without result, he settled in Paris, where he met Nariño and later Miranda, He became his agent from 1797 to 1799 when he betrayed Miranda.

[27] *Archivo*...Vol. XV, p. 180–184.

Turnbull,[28] Miranda's faithful English friend. This letter argued the need and possibility of a change of regime in Latin America to ensure independence from any other nation, which would benefit England, provided it received its help. Caro waited without results from March to June, and then he returned to Paris. As a consequence of the self-coup of 18 Fructidor 1797[29] (September 4, 1797) in Paris, organised by Napoleon from Italy, Miranda was banned by the Directory and persecuted by the political police under the Jacobins (and Joseph Fouché, his love rival and Napoleon's agent).

Several factors obliged Miranda to opt for London and restart his cooperation with Pitt, despite their sharp dispute in 1792 and his reputation as a republican for having defended revolutionary France in the war against England since 1793.

- First, he was banned from France;
- second, London seemed again to him the most adequate regime and place for the development of his plans;
- third, England had entered into war against Spain,[30] which was an essential condition for Pitt's government to support him (precisely what was not the case in 1790 as a result of the diplomatic agreement reached by Pitt and Grenville to avoid a distant conflict).
- Fourth, Napoleon's expansionism had directly threatened England, and Miranda's opposition to Napoleon could help restore his credibility.

Accordingly, at the end of September 1797, he sent Caro back to London to inform explicitly the British government,[31] via Turnbull and Joseph Smith (Pitt's secretary), that he was willing to return to London and resume his cooperation with Pitt. This cooperation appeared to be highly likely to be favourable to both sides. However,

[28] **John Turnbull** (1750–1816), a banker and English businessman, very influential in the British government, was the financier of Miranda's plans and his lifelong friend. He met Miranda in Gibraltar in 1775 or 1777 when he was an officer of the King of Spain, and they became close friends from that point on; Miranda even proclaimed him as executor of his testament and tutor to his children when he left London to prepare for his expedition to Coro. More details in footnotes.

[29] **The "18 fructidor"** coup (4 September 1797) against the Royalists and the moderate deputies was executed by General Augereau (who was sent to Paris by Bonaparte). This coup tried to restore a neo-Jacobin (left) power by eliminating the centre-right opposition. From July 1797, Bonaparte used the Army as a threat against the legislative power, which was dominated by a centre-right majority, with even a monarchical conspiracy uncovered, and this served as an opportunity to reject the last election results won by the right wing. Inspired by the three neo-Jacobin members of the Directoire, the purpose of the coup was to maintain power despite losing the legislative elections and to consolidate control over all powers. They expelled 198 centre-right deputies from the chambers and condemned 53 of them to the "dry guillotine" (deportation to Guyana), as well as the two conservative Directors and Pichegru, the President of the Chamber, but also Miranda, who tried to oppose this coup, he considered as equivalent to Robespierre's method.

[30] The Anglo-Spanish War resulted from the **Second Treaty of San Ildefonso** (August 1796), which established a Franco-Spanish alliance and common war against Great Britain. In February 1797, the British Navy won the battle of Cape St Vicente (Portugal coast) and, in the Caribbean, took the Island of Trinidad (in front of Venezuela)

[31] *Archivo*...Vol. XV, p. 185.

Miranda's strategy was necessary to prevent any ideological ambiguity that could have led him to be associated with the Republicans and the Jacobins. The French Republican regime was regarded in England as a significant calamity shortly after the attempt to land French troops in Ireland in 1796[32] with the aim of installing the Republicans into power, while France was planning another landing under Napoleon's command[33] to end the British monarchy and its representative regime.

Despite the political context in England, which did not expose the regime to any real republican risk of revolution, the events of 1792 in France were skilfully used by the government of Pitt to suppress radical groups and to impose British conservatism. Nonetheless, the repressive measures taken in 1794 (suspension of "Habeas Corpus") and in 1795 (Anti-subversive laws of the "Two Acts") had provoked a reaction, fueling radicalism towards a clandestine republicanism that even might support a French invasion. In this highly sensitive context, Miranda had to provide explicit assurance of his political credibility and reliability vis-à-vis the British government, particularly after his role as the top general of a republican army, which London perceived as an enemy of the British Crown and its democratic mixed system.[34]

[32] **Theobald Wolfe Tone** (1763–1798) was the head of the Irish Republican rebellion. He sought and secured the support of France, which set up an expedition of 45 ships with 14,000 soldiers headed by General Hoche. Due to unforeseen hostile weather conditions, the French landing attempt failed in December 1796. Hoche undertook a new attempt, which was aborted too. In 1798, an Irish rebellion was defeated in June, and in September, a new French expedition failed, to which Wolfe participated under French uniform. Arrested and condemned to death, he committed suicide in jail.

[33] Being back from glorious victories and looting in Italy, Napoleon was officially charged in October 1797 by the Directory to organise the previous project from 1793–94 to invade England, which had been abandoned for economic reasons. Napoleon worked intensively on this project from Dunkerque in 1798 but ultimately postponed it, preferring the more manageable and less risky Egyptian campaign to enhance his own prestige. He never abandoned his dream to impose his law and to submit to the British Empire. He resumed his plan in 1801, when Britain was isolated following the Peace of Lunéville, which ended the war with Austria. The fear of Napoleon's plan contributed to pushing Britain to sign the Peace of Amiens (1802). Still, Napoleon pursued his ambition to invade England, deciding to organise an unprecedented inter-armies invasion in November 1802 (well before the end of the Peace of Amiens, which was concluded with England until May 1803. In two years, 1294 small boats, 359 cannonballs, 456 cannon boats, and 540 transporters were built. Nevertheless, the French Navy, united with the Spanish and Dutch allies, remained inferior to the British Navy. This is why Napoleon planned to disperse the enemy by sailing the vessels and frigates towards America to lure the British, before secretly returning to protect the operation in the Channel. This plan failed and led to the Trafalgar defeat, comforting Napoleon's idea that to dominate England, it was first necessary to conquer Europe. In 1810, he again considered another invasion plan.

[34] "**Mixed Democracy**" refers to a system where the different powers and groups of society (monarchy, aristocracy, and the people) are associated to balance each other. More precisely, for Miranda, this system implies overall to moderate the power of the people (the legislative power) through a representative system that cannot dominate the other powers, in order to preserve the strict separation of powers, and which can control but not interfere in daily government or justice. Miranda believed that the executive power had to be strong in current management, but strictly democratically controlled through recurrent popular elections that choose the main options. The

In December 1797, Miranda carefully prepared his return, given his appointment with Pitt. To strengthen his bargaining power, he wrote two complementary documents, especially designed to convince the British government about his plan:

1. The "*Paris Act*" (see Chap. 7) that explains his pro-British geopolitical Project. This Project aims to give him a more official character (or legitimacy), thereby lending credibility to his cooperative intention with Pitt. He conceives and produces "official" documents, creating an itinerant coordinating college (baptised the "Board of Deputies") that gave him a formal mandate on behalf of the patriots. Whatever the actual representativeness, this document is a synthesis of his critical geopolitical thoughts (American identity and unity, necessity of an international alliance with British and US democracies)
2. A second draft of a federal constitution whose purpose was, among other things, to give Pitt assurance of his anti-Jacobin options (which anyway were sincere and constant) so that Hispanic America would not fall into what Pitt called "*calamities of the abominable system of the French*".

   The mixed character of his governmental proposal was the key, where the "democratic" power of the legislative assembly was moderated in the English line by an aristocratic senate and a hereditary Monarch, the opposite of the Jacobins and the Bonapartists. The Republican Miranda accepted, for a tactical reason—according to our analysis—a constitutional monarchy as a means to mark his choice against the dangerous and deceptive direct democracy à la Rousseau of the Jacobins, thereby counterbalancing his republican reputation. In fact, the difference between a "mixed" democratic republic and a constitutional monarchy was not so significant for Miranda: Montesquieu himself considered that the English monarchy had a republican character in the essential sense of limiting the powers of the executive. Besides, the ideological difference between Miranda and the French Jacobins was not tactical but fundamental and constant in his philosophical and constitutional thinking: Miranda already opposed the first monarchical constitution of France in 1791 and the three following republican attempts: the 1792/93 Girondins' draft, the 1793 Jacobins of Year I and the 1795 Thermidorian reaction of Year III. The Girondins' governance in 1792/93 was excessively deliberative, paralysing the executive. This imbalance provoked the Jacobins' reaction towards further centralisation of all powers, disguised behind a manipulated supremacy of legislative assemblies (popular power), through a concentration of power in the hands of the Convention, combined with a decentralised executive branch at the levels of Municipalities and revolutionary local committees. In turn, this radical ideology and its manipulation of "democracy" provoked a conservative reaction. This led to a non-democratic republic due to a reversed imbalance with a too-centralised executive facing a frail legis-

definition of Miranda, although republican, converges with the English one towards a representative system that filters the popular power and feeds public debates through checks-and-balances bodies so that no power can dominate the others, each one watching the actions of the others.

lative branch, favouring the consolidation of a corrupted new class of enriched oligarchs.

Miranda cleverly identified the roots of French instability in the imbalanced relations between the branches, leading either to anarchy or tyranny. Therefore, he unambiguously opposed both the failed "popular democracy" of the two first republican constitutions and the conservative one (Thermidorian constitution of Year III), which betrayed the revolution. His deep conviction was the necessity of a "*mixed government*" inspired by the pragmatic British system for warranting the separation of powers through autonomous «checks & balances» for moderating the direct popular power, but also for making possible, when necessary for governing, a robust executive power but always controlled ex-post by the legislative power.

The report Miranda [1929] wrote about his interview with Pitt explicitly confirms the importance of the mixed monarchic character of his project to satisfy Pitt's desire. This report also confirms that Miranda's strategy was effective, as he successfully addressed two key questions that Pitt posed to him upon his arrival in London: on whose behalf is he negotiating? And what form of government does he propose?

At that moment, William Pitt was interested in listening to Miranda again because he had written to him in letters stating that he no longer wanted to cooperate with France to help England, which was threatened by the French despotic bias. Indeed, Pitt was very afraid of a conjunction of worrying events against the interests of the United Kingdom:

- the defection from Prussia and Spain (Basle Treaty, July 22, 1795) in the first coalition against France,
- the offensive Alliance concluded between France and Spain against England (San Ildefonso Treaty, July 22, 1795),
- the active cooperation of the French, Spanish and Dutch when the British naval officers led to a severe mutiny,
- and above all, the actual plan of French landing in England that Napoleon was preparing under instruction from the Directory when he came back victorious from the Italian campaign (in October 1797),
- in the context of the systematic support of the French to the Irish,[35] Scottish[36] and English[37] Republicans.

[35] After the failed attempt of General Hoche to land in Ireland in 1796, other plans of invasion were prepared. In August 1798, another attempt led by General Humbert managed to disembark but was then crushed to the ground, and a third attempt occurred in October 1798, which took place in Donegal Bay; this one also failed, while Napoleon was officially in charge of forming the "Army of England" to invade the island and to end the British democratic monarchy.

[36] In January 1797, British police discovered the Scottish plan for a revolution to proclaim a republic with a well-organized movement called "United Scotsmen". It was banned in July 1797. In January 1798, some details of the organisation and the conspiracy were discovered, which seriously alarmed Pitt.

[37] Since the American Revolution, an internal intellectual debate in Britain has pitted the Monarchist and republican camps against each other. Prominent figures of the republican camp were Mary Wollstonecraft, William Godwin and Thomas Paine, one of the activists of the US Revolution and

Pitt aimed to resist and debilitate France in order to prevent the expansion of French republicanism in his country and America. Besides, Henry Dundas,[38] close to Pitt and favourable to Miranda's plans, had been Minister of War since 1794, and he was opposed to the Foreign Secretary (Lord Grenville) 's positions. Grenville wanted to fight France on the continent and not overseas. Furthermore, he thought that Miranda was a dangerous Republican activist.

In this period before the formation of the second anti-French coalition (that Pitt achieved only in September 1798), Miranda represented an attractive strategic option, which explained that Prime Minister Pitt was immediately available to the South American activist and waited for him on Downing Street on the 15th of January 1798 all day long (but Miranda's trip was delayed on the road to London). The next day, Pitt welcomed him into his home in Hollwood. This unusual eagerness explains that Miranda, contrary to his habits, did not have time to take a copy of the original manuscript text of the second draft of the constitution. When Pitt saw it, he got very insistent on keeping it; Miranda, although reluctant due to the precedent in 1790–92, did not want to risk losing his lever upon the powerful British chief and accepted, setting explicit conditions to recover this document (reminding himself the previous difficulties he went through to make Pitt give him back the documents related to his first constitution project). Despite the precautions, it is known that Pitt never fulfilled his commitment, and he never returned the document to Miranda. This is the reason why the document disappeared.

In parallel with the negotiations with Pitt, Miranda also made contacts with the US Ambassador to London, Rufus King,[39] to whom he also provided information on

Constitution. With the French Revolution, the debate worried the government, especially with Thomas Paine's personal involvement in Paris, who was promoting the French invasion to end the Monarchy in the United Kingdom. The fear of a revolution in England began early in 1792, with the rapid development of political clubs creating pressure on Parliament to reform the electoral system. Although not revolutionary, but reformist, these societies, such as the London Corresponding Society, were wrongly suspected to be linked to the French Jacobins with the French events of August 1792, triggering a collective fear in the British elites, developing an anti-Jacobin phobia, convinced that a domestic conspiracy was in preparation inside the Kingdom. The mutinies in the Royal Navy in 1797, followed by the arrest of the United Englishmen in February 1798, increased this paranoid worry, which was an exaggeration [Dziembowski, E., 2023]. However, other documents, such as the Castlereagh correspondence, attest to the constant concerns about French republican interference in Britain [Vane, C., 1848].

[38] **Henry Dundas** (1742–1811) Scottish jurist and politician, close to Miranda, Home Secretary from 1791 to 1794, in charge of the Ministry of the Indies from 1793 to 1801, Minister of War from 1794 to 1801 and First Lord of Admiralty from 1804 to 1805. Elevated to the title of Viscount of Melville in 1802. His policy was to develop the "*Blue Water*" strategy, i.e. betting first on the global sea control and not so much on the European continent (see Chap. 11).

[39] **Rufus King** (1755–1827), considered one of the "founding fathers" of the U.S.A. and their constitution, Hamilton's close friend and political militant in the Federalist ranks, was designated Ambassador in London by G. Washington, where he brilliantly performed from 1796 to 1803. He adopted advantageous positions for Latin American emancipation; he received the documents of Peruvian Father Viscardo and entrusted them to Miranda (to see Annex 1: Letter to the American Spaniards). He actively supported Miranda's views, in contrast to the administration of the U.S.A., which never wanted to help Miranda.

his political plans, and from which he received the famous "*Letter to the American Spaniards*" written by the Peruvian Jesuit in exile, Father Viscardo (see Annex 1). As explained below (see the Paris Act of 1797, Chap. 7), Miranda sought to garner support for his plan for a future Spanish-American federation's geopolitical alliance with the two Anglo-Saxon democracies, aiming to counter France's totalitarian ambitions. Alexander Hamilton [1961] fully shared his views on the need for a coalition between Britain and the US to free the Spanish colonies and counteract the perils of French imperialism in the Americas [Betti, 2008].[40] As tensions rose between the US and France in 1798 with the so-called «quasi-war», Hamilton returned to the Army in July 1798 as a major general and served as the Army's inspector general and second in command to Washington for organising the army in the prospect of a war against France. Despite the positive reports written by Rufus King[41] and the active support of his friend Alexander Hamilton [Syrett, 1974], who proposed a military defensive intervention in South America,[42] the president of the United States, John Adams,[43] categorically refused to help Miranda and to endorse Hamilton's plan for pre-emptive action against France and Spain. Adams viewed Hamilton as a dangerous competitor and Miranda as a utopian, because he believed that Latin American people would be able to establish democracy. Adams [1856][44] viewed his Southern neighbours as inferior beings, unable to govern themselves.

Content:

The little we know about its content comes from Miranda's diary, copied below. Clearly, the context of the time described above explains that this project was tactical, intended primarily to seduce Pitt and to clean Miranda of any Jacobin Republican characteristics. Although Miranda was already a convinced republican, his moderate ideology brought him closer to the concept of "British mixed democracy," that is, a system with filters and autonomous "checks and balances" able to channel or moderate popular power. For him, accepting a monarchical system was not a genuine philosophical change but an alternative method entirely consistent with his constitutional ideas. Nevertheless, Miranda was upset because he could not retrieve his manuscript from the British politician's hands, with whom he had no sufficient trust regarding the future of his emancipating project.

---

[40] Chapter 10, document 10.3.6, Miranda's letter to Hamilton, April 1798; Miranda's letter to Hamilton, October 1798 in *America Espera*, document 81 p. 233–234; See, especially Hamilton, A., [Syrett, H.], "The Stand IV." *The Papers of Alexander Hamilton* (PAH), vol. 21, 412–418. and "Hamilton to Miranda," 8/22/1798, PAH vol. 22, 155–156.

[41] In particular, see the letters from Rufus King to President Adams as well as letters between Hamilton and King.

[42] In April 1798, Hamilton published a series of anonymous polemics entitled "The Stand," in which he argued against French imperialism, which was preparing to take over Spain and its American empire.

[43] **John Adams** (1735–1826), second president of the United States (1797 to 1801), after serving as vice-president under Washington's presidency; before that, he was a diplomat and one of the United States' founding fathers. He was hostile to Hamilton and Miranda.

[44] Adams, J., [1856], *The Works of John Adams, by his grandson Charles Francus Adams*, Boston, Little, Brown and Company, (10 vol). 1856.

Sources:

Drafted in French, a report from Miranda's diary about the content of this second project of the constitution:

In: Colombeia. Vol XVIII. Document 3969. *Esquisse de Constitution* 6.6. N° 10 Correspondent au N° 46 of the classification (Draft of Constitution). p. 86.

In the **original Archive**. Vol. 1, fol. 150 of negotiations appears with number LXVI, corresponding to n° 10 de 1797 in the file with an empty page. There is an error in the original one. It corresponds to n° 46.

In **the Archive of General Miranda**. -Caracas: Typography Americana. Vol XV. Negotiations. 1777–1810. p. 205 and p. 264–269;

Colombeia. Vol XVIII. Document 3968. Miranda's arrival in London and interview with Pitt. p. 79–85. In the original Archive. Vol. 1. Negotiations. fol. 151–154.

In: **América Espera**, Salcedo Bastardo, op.cit. p. 205–207.

Text:

(from Miranda's diary January 1798)

Outline of a Constitution

This paper was initially delivered to Mr Pitt at our Conference on my arrival here (January 1798) at Hollwood. "It seemed so good to him that he begged me to leave him, believing this would alleviate all difficulties. In fact, on the contrary, I did not receive any further answers on the matter, nor could I retrieve this interesting paper.

It is a monarchist Project with an aristocratic chamber.

As it is seen, Miranda himself confirms that this version got lost. Salcedo Bastardo, as well as many others, confuses this text with the 1790 version.

In the narration of the interview of the 16 of January of 1798 with Pitt, Miranda exposes:

Mr Pitt, who came to me without delay … reminding me that 8 years ago … we had met for the first time … that now the circumstances were very different … because England was in open war with Spain … [but] in the name of whom or by whom [I was negotiating] and if I could get an official document giving me (if possible) a mandate….

> And coming now to another point, he added (although England does not intend to mix for any reason in the government of my future country), what is the form or system of government designed to be established in this Country? I replied that it was very similar to Great Britain; it must be made up of a House of Commons, another of nobles, and a Ynca, or hereditary sovereign! Very well, he told me. Well, suppose a system by way of France would be introduced into the country. In that case, I assure you (he replied vividly) that we would instead prefer Spanish Americans to continue for a century as obedient subjects under the oppressive government of the King of Spain than to see them immersed in the calamities of the abominable French system! … Very well, I said, and it is precisely to avoid such contagion, and to guard against the Gallic influence in time, that we have thought of emancipating ourselves immediately; and form an alliance with the United States of America and England in order to unanimously combat (if necessary) the monstrous and abominable principles of the alleged French Liberty! … And so that you see that these are the same opinions, that my compatriots profess, here I have the draft of the Constitution project that is believed to be more suited to the spirit and views of our Americans; and that the commissioners of that country have sanctioned. He read everything carefully and, arriving at the article of the hereditary Ynca, he gave a big assent, lowering his head—and at the end, he said, because all this is very well, and I do not perceive any difficulty in the whole,

but as it is such a serious matter, at the moment, I can't tell you more for now. You will have a more formal and decisive answer very soon! I made clear that the frankness and simplicity with which I had proceeded allowed me to wait as soon as possible for a follow-up to the matter and that I expect to get the same treatment... Very indeed, he replied, and this is always the best way to end matters promptly and with mutual satisfaction. He still asked me when I had arrived in London. I replied that it had not been until yesterday after five. This question, it seemed to me, could perhaps be aimed at knowing if I had not been able to form here, after my arrival, the Draft Constitution, etc.... but my prompt reply apparently satisfied him, and I repeated that he should not misplace the draft of the projected Constitution since I had no copyleft. I only left it to him because of the urgency that he manifested to me ... which he acknowledged!

5.2.3 *The Third Constitutional Project for Hispanic America, 1801*

Context:

At the beginning of 1800, Miranda believed he had finally convinced the British authorities to give him the necessary military support. Nevertheless, for diplomatic reasons, the English government changed its strategy again and denied this cooperation. In March 1800, Miranda was so disappointed that he gave up. He did not want to continue trying to convince the ambiguous government of Pitt, so he asked him for a passport to leave the country and return to his country or the United States. However, the government denied him the document several times. Finally, Pitt let him go, and in September, he got the official agreement to leave the UK. The only (and long-lasting) reason Pitt denied Miranda the passport was to use him in his European policy by showing Spain that England had control over Miranda, impeding him from acting outside of London. Pitt's strategy was to try to weaken the alliance between Spain and France against England, demonstrating that he still had the power to either let or impede Miranda from triggering his revolutionary actions against the Spanish Empire. Miranda became an involuntary instrument in British European diplomacy for years. Miranda was aware of Pitt's blackmail, but in a way, he had been so sure that the French threat to British democracy and industrial interests would eventually compel Pitt to include his own emancipation plan for the sake of the British Empire and industry.

To break up this blockade, Miranda played the risky game of responding to Pitt with his own blackmail by showing the British government that he could also offer his services to France, the enemy, by moving again to the French side in exchange for military support. He sent another disciple, Pedro Fermín de Vargas,[45] to Paris to

[45] **Pedro Fermín de Vargas** (1762–1813?), a Colombian citizen, was considered the first economist in New Granada of his time. A fellow student and friend of Antonio Nariño, he went to London in 1799 to join Miranda and support his strategy for 4 years before separating due to differences over military strategy. Antonio Nariño (1765–1823) Colombian patriot, first president of the revolutionary state of Cundimarca (Santa Fé de Bogota, capital of the Viceroyalty of New

bargain with Napoleon for a visa for Miranda. Miranda feels so cornered and disappointed by London's diplomatic myopia that he prefers to use the slight chance of being able to channel Napoleon's lust for power as blackmail over Pitt: whether he could carry out his plans with the French dictator or whether the fear of such a prospect would force Pitt to break out of his procrastination and opt for the lower risk that his plan represents. Miranda remains convinced (just like Hamilton in the US) that Napoleon will not be able to resist taking over the Iberian colonies, which is necessary to finance his fight against the British empire. Therefore, he wants to counter the risks of Jacobin governance on the ground. By offering to serve Napoleon, Miranda did not alter his doctrine regarding colonialist Jacobinism and dictatorship. Still, he believed he could fight it more effectively from within, gaining speed on the ground and reducing the threat posed by the "French system" so far away from Paris. In other words, he wanted to demonstrate to Pitt and his conservative ministers his determination to even opt for an alternative that would create worse effects for London. He hoped to prove that his initial plan was the most attractive to the British and thus reestablish his worth. The British government was indeed taking a risk by not effectively supporting his Spanish-American emancipation formula. Miranda could never understand the Pitt government's lack of geopolitical vision, which was counterproductive in that it comforted the British mortal enemy in the event of a Napoleonic initiative in South America. Moreover, coordination between France and the United States could have been carried out to the detriment of an excluded England. Miranda knew that Napoleon had that addiction to risk that Pitt so lacked. He thought that Napoleon, whom he had met personally in Paris, could have bet on him and, therefore, in the worst-case scenario (if Pitt had not reacted), would give him the possibility of influencing the course of events from within to limit the damage that the Jacobin virus could have on his constitutional revolution.

Therefore, Miranda played a card towards Napoleon, expecting to get the means of action either by setting a deal with the emerging dictator or making the prudent Pitt change his mind when realising that abandoning Miranda's plan would be riskier for the UK than helping him. Indeed, not cooperating with Miranda would expose the UK to having to confront Napoleon later in a much stronger position and to lose the geopolitical and commercial advantages resulting from opting for Miranda's dream of a democratic alliance between Britain, the USA and Colombia[46] (as formulated in 1797 with the "Paris Act"). He also knew that Pitt's cabinet was divided between H. Dundas, Ministry of War, the main partisan of the strategy to use the control of the sea, convinced by Miranda's geopolitical views, and Grenville, Minister of Foreign Affairs, opposed to Miranda and convinced that Napoleon had

Granada) from 1811 to 1813, anti-federalist, he divided the independence movement, he lost the battle of Pasto in 1814 and was jailed in Spain until 1820. Bolivar named him Vice-President of Colombia for a while, but he resigned in July 1821, and ran as a candidate for the Presidency in August 1821, facing Bolivar, he lost.

[46] Colombia was the name Miranda launched to designate the great federation, grouping the four Spanish viceroyalties into a single entity from the Mississippi to Tierra del Fuego.

to be defeated on the continent and not oversea.[47] Miranda never could understand this weakness of Pitt's government, which implied strengthening the "French enemy to death," a move that might even provoke a division between Britain and the US in case of a French alliance with the US to take over South America and exclude England.

For all these reasons, thanks to a visa from Napoleon, Miranda managed to return to France 3 years after escaping the French police. He settled in Paris from October 1800 until March 1801. He again contacted his lover, the pretty and heroic Delphine de Custine,[48] when Fouché[49] (his rival in love to conquer Delphine) arrested him for being anti-Jacobin and accused him of being an English spy. Thanks to his political contacts, he managed to be free, but probably[50] mainly because of Delphine's influence upon Fouché—Miranda was expelled from France once again.

---

[47] For a detailed analysis of the relations of the British cabinet with Miranda, see Chap. 11.

[48] **Louise Eleonore Melanie Sabran, Marquise of Custine**, was born in Paris on March 18, 1770, and died on July 13, 1826, in Bex, Switzerland. Nicknamed "the Queen of Roses", she was described as the nicest woman in Paris. She belonged to one of the oldest aristocratic families related to the kings of France. She met Miranda in prison during "The Reign of Terror", when he was imprisoned alongside her father-in-law, General de Custine, who was guillotined in August 1793, and her husband, the Marquis de Custine, who was guillotined in January 1794. Delphine remained in close contact with Miranda but was also imprisoned with Joséphine de Beauharnais (who later became Napoleon's wife). Through her contacts outside, it seems that the three managed to postpone their execution to the guillotine. Delphine and Miranda fell in love in these tragic circumstances. The final date imposed personally by Robespierre to kill Miranda was scheduled for the end of July 1794; however, the coup against Robespierre occurred three days prior. Delphine was liberated by chance in September 1794 and contributed to the liberation of Miranda, the last political prisoner to be released, in 1795. Delphine shared Miranda's democratic ideology in addition to acting as an emancipated woman. She engaged in a strange parallel love affair with the powerful Fouche, a Jacobin spy and later the Directory's chief of police, which could have probably allowed Miranda to escape the political police from 1795 to 1797 and again under Napoleon in 1801. After Miranda's leave for London, Delphine found consolation in the arms of the diplomat and writer René de Chateaubriand, with whom she was mistress for 20 years. Their remains are buried near Fervaques (Calvados). See: Parra-Pérez, C., [1927, 1950]; also Maugras, G. & Croze-Lemercier [1912].

[49] **Joseph Fouché** (1759–1820) was a notorious Jacobin known for his extreme cruelty in repressing the Revolution's opponents. He accused people without evidence and executed them without fair trials to please Robespierre. As a corrupt and opportunistic individual, he played a role in overthrowing Robespierre and established dubious contacts with France's enemies. After serving as a denouncer in hidden missions at the behest of the Jacobin political police, he was appointed Minister of Police by the Directory in 1797. There, he prepared Bonaparte's coup d'état of 1799, which led to his appointment as police minister.

[50] We have no precise document to confirm it. Due to the sensitivity of the situation, it is evident that there are reasons why such interventions do not appear in Delphine's letters, and there is no proof but deductions: Delphine is linked to Fouché and a close friend of Josephine, the wife of the First Consul. Given that Delphine is known to have acted on behalf of various people and friends of Miranda, it would be hard to imagine that she would not act on behalf of the person who was her lover and to whom she swore "eternal friendship." The fact that Delphine used to have Miranda and Fouché as lovers simultaneously could support this deduction. Miranda was very discreet about his relationship with Delphine for several reasons. According to Parra Pérez, Miranda's macho culture led him to break up with Delphine due to jealousy. We believe that the Miranda-Delphine relation-

During this period, in February and March 1801, the cabinet of William Pitt had to resign due to Pitt's failure with his plan for the political emancipation of Irish Catholics. Besides, the new government, formed by Pitt's opponent, Addington,[51] favoured establishing peace with France. Miranda arrived in London on April 26 under a false name, worried about the position this new government could take regarding him and due to French intentions in Latin America. Thanks to his friends Turnbull and Ponwall, he immediately entered into direct contact with the new Minister, Nicholas Vansittart,[52] and he managed to convince him of his interest in his plans for England. He hoped that this new government would be less procrastinating than Pitt. However, at this moment, Miranda was once again conscious of the growing risk that a possible peace treaty between England and Spain would undermine his plan. Therefore, he is once again pushy to get a decision of British military-political support. On May 2, 1801, Miranda presented himself before the new government to express his views, having prepared two proclamations, a military regulation, and a new draft of the constitution, which he submitted to the government of Addington.

The internal English political context had changed: the excesses of the French Revolution and its expansionist tendencies had reinforced the citizens' support for British conservatism, ultimately ending the radical republican movement. Supported by a large majority, the government no longer feared the banned popular social movements. On his side, Miranda felt that he was better known in London as an anti-Jacobin and pro-British figure, and he trusted that he could openly argue for a republic, albeit one very different from the French experience, by transposing a *mixed regime* into a federal republic for Spanish America. His government's formula is called mixed because it strongly opposes the Jacobin kind of Republicanism, which is based solely on manipulated popular power. It also differs from the Directory reaction, which is characterised by a too-centralist executive in front of a too-weak legislative power. The Republic of Miranda relies on British-inspired guarantees to foster a representative system with filtered access to voting and eligibility based on restrictive criteria, such as owning a minimum amount of land or

ship was more substantial, being instead an alliance from the death corridor to fight for the same ideal of progress and democracy, utilising their complementary talents, each with their comparative advantage. Miranda's letters to Delphine disappeared, and only some of Delphine's letters to Miranda were discovered by Parra-Perez [1927, 1950].

[51] **Henry Addington** (1757–1844), William Pitt's friend and member of the British parliament from 1784, was proclaimed Prime minister in March 1801 to replace William Pitt, negotiated The Peace of Amiens with Napoleon, ending the second coalition against Napoleon, but leading it to another war against France in 1803, which will be fatal to him and will contribute to the return of Pitt to the power in 1804. He was proclaimed Viscount of Sydmouth in 1805 and worked in British politics, serving as Pitt's minister in 1806 and other cabinets. In 1812, he became the Interior Minister until 1822, opposing the recognition of the Latin American republics and the emancipation of Catholics.

[52] **Nicholas Vansittart (1776–1851)** was Pitt's political ally and quickly attached to Miranda's plans, Deputy Minister of Finance (1801–04) in Addington's Government, who succeeded Pitt in 1801, and future Finance Minister. He was Miranda's friend.

having a minimum income. His purpose is to channel the risks of emotional overflows from a popular power that doctrinaires could manipulate, as he had observed closely in the French case.

Regarding the issue of the advancement of his thought, one might think that reducing access to voting with economic criteria manifests a lack of "advancement", but it would precisely be judging the past with current values. Our analysis involves situating it correctly in its context, which precisely justifies defending democracy by avoiding a universal vote in an unprepared society. Who would be the most pioneering? He who proposes a universal vote leading to dictatorship and eventually the disappearance of the vote, as history demonstrates, or he who reduces access to voting to guarantee the separation of powers and respect for human rights with a change without violence, but who was impeded from implementing it?

Content:

The third constitution project is clearly "mixed" in the British sense, as it limits popular power by strictly protecting the separation of powers. However, it is explicitly republican. It reflects the more elaborated formula of Miranda's political ideals and integration strategy for ensuring a sustainable emancipation process. Miranda's regional integration concept encompasses the social, ethnic, and economic perspectives between Latin American cultures. This constitution project marks a rupture with the dominant ideas, both in terms of being a republic and a federal one. The French ideology held that a republic could not be federal and remain democratic, as the people's sovereignty could not be divided. In London, to be a Republican in 1801 was not self-evident; the idea of a republic was being discredited everywhere by French excesses, but Miranda sought to solve difficulties by drawing lessons from these failures. He conceived an original federal combination of three geographical levels of governance (what would be named later subsidiarity), with a strict separation of powers, but giving strong power to the current management of the central executive in only very few federal fields, under the control of counter powers (*checks and balances*) and submitted to people recurrent votes on fundamental orientations. The representative democratic character was established through pyramidal electoral filters to create a representative system and prevent the diversion of popular power. While it is essential for Miranda that the people have an influential voice through periodic democratic control of elections, popular assemblies can never interfere with the government's daily management, as this would prevent popular passions and social violence. Still, the control of the executive's conduct according to the rules of the constitution must be exercised by the people.

It is structured in two parts, thus demonstrating the pragmatism of its author. The first part, characterised as a provisional government, of immediate application as a substitute for the Metropolis authority to avoid falling into an acephalous power during the transitional revolutionary period and ensuring a 'change without convulsions', an essential feature of Miranda's plan, obliging him to restrict the right to vote according to an economic criteria. The second part is the definitive formula, qualified as a federal government once the new institutions are democratically legitimated and adequately implemented. This federal governance scheme organises governments in each vice-royalty, without prejudice to a common legal framework, to ensure the necessary integration for lasting emancipation. This purpose was a fundamental principle in Miranda's thinking: emancipation was achieved through regional integration, ensuring both the formation of an identity with geopolitical weight and the economic sustainability of independence.

Regarding these principles, one can also ask who is the precursor compared to those who proposed separate republics or Napoleonian dictatorial centralism.

The Miranda Archive contains additional comments by the author related to exchanges on specific points, which are reproduced after the constitutional text.

Many authors (see sources) have confused this "progressist" version with the following (1808), which was a more conservative one, adopted for tactical reasons due to the context.

Sources:

Original text written in French.

Archivo del General Miranda. Negotiations. 1800-1804. La Habana: Editorial Lex. Vol. XVI. p. 151-159.

Colombeia. Vol. XIX, p. 627–640, version translated to Spanish. In the **Archivo Original del General Miranda**. Vol. III. Negotiations, pages 88–107, comprise several rough drafts of sketches of the provisional and federal governments, which, when collated, present some variants. A Spanish version is also in "*Archivo General de Indias*" in Seville.

Warning: It has been copied with errors by different historians, presenting the 1801 version while using the 1808 version (a more conservative adaptation for tactical reasons). That is the case of:

Ruíz Chataing, David., Mondolfi, Edgardo.: **Miranda, la aventura de la libertad. Antología,** Caracas: Monte Ávila Editores, 1991, 2 vols. (Biblioteca del Pensamiento Venezolano José Antonio Páez; núm. 3). Vol. 1 p. 241–247.

América espera/Francisco de Miranda; Caracas: Biblioteca Ayacucho n°100: p. 285–292.

Academía Nacional de la Historia, [1961], **El pensamiento Constitucional Hispanoamericano hasta 1830**, Vol. V, Venezuela, Sesquicentenario de la Independencia, Caracas.

Mariñas Otero, Luis, Comp.: **Las Constituciones de Venezuela**/Madrid: Cultura Hispánica, 1965. (Las Constituciones Hispanoamericanas; 17).

Villarroel, Miguel A.: **Miranda primer legislador de América.** Caracas: Imprenta Nacional. OCI. Ediciones del Instituto de Estudios Históricos Mirandinos. 1970. Includes index.

Zeuske, Michael.: **Francisco de Miranda y la modernidad en América = Francisco de Miranda e a modernidade na América**/estudio de Michael Zeuske; [traducción portugués, Miguel Freitas da Costa].—Madrid: Fundación Mapfre Tavera; Aranjuez: Doce Calles, [2004]. (Prisma histórico; 2). Spanish and English texts, Spanish and Portuguese studies. See: p. 176–186.

Text:

1801: "Outline for a Provisional Government" and "Outline for a Federal Government".

1. OUTLINE FOR A PROVISIONAL GOVERNMENT

London, 2nd May 1801

All authority that emanates from the Spanish Government is ipso facto abolished. All laws not included in this project will remain unchanged.

(a) **ELECTORATE**

The Electorate consists of the inhabitants born or established in the country, whatever their caste, as long as they are 21 years of age, have sworn allegiance to the new form of government and American independence, have an annual income of 36 piastres[53] [NA: 800 dollars de 2021] are children of a free father and mother, do not work as paid servants and have not suffered criminal penalties.

(b) **MUNICIPAL COUNCIL ("Cabildos »)**

The Spanish authorities will be replaced by the "Cabildos" and Councils of the different cities, which will comprise one-third of the chosen representatives from the Indians and people of colour in the Province; the Municipal elections must confirm these designations. No member of those Cabildos or Councils can be less than 25 years old or have property smaller than ten arpents of cultivated land [NA: 1.3 or 3.4 ha].[54]

[53] **Piastre** was a name for the **Spanish peso** or Spanish dollar, used in the Americas. It was equivalent to the currency the United States introduced in 1792 at par with it (at 371.25 grains = 0.7735 troy ounces = 24.0566 g.) as defined by Alexander Hamilton, who arrived at these numbers based on a treasury assay of the average fine silver content of a selection of worn Spanish dollars. The peso was widely used as the first international currency, used in Europe, the Americas, and the Far East. It was also used in French as the word for the United States dollar (for example, in the French text of the Louisiana Purchase). The value of a Spanish peso or piastre was equivalent to one dollar or a peso (24 g of silver at 0.89) or a Haitian gourde. Translated into purchasing power in 2021, this annual income of 36 piastres (36 dollars in 1800) would correspond to about US$ 800 per year, less than the average income at that time. We estimate that the GDP per capita was around US $ 1.400 measured in purchasing power of the dollar in 2021 by adjusting Angus Maddison's results [1995] of US 700 in purchasing power of 1990 (we multiplied it by 2 for inflation between 1990 and 2021). This indicates that the Miranda criteria were moderately restrictive, allowing for significant vote participation that was not limited to wealthy citizens, excluding only non-integrated individuals. Indeed, the rich category represented a relatively small share of the population; thus, the impact of income inequality, although high, had a limited effect on the average income. However, Miranda did not seem willing to provide a too definitive benchmark for this, maintaining an interpretation room for manoeuvre according to the audience he wanted to convince.

[54] **Arpent**: the measure of this criterion for acceding to vote and to be a candidate to election also remains vague because it allows for fixing the degree of filtration of the "popular power" of the system. Miranda left it probably ambiguous in order to preserve a significant margin of manoeuvre (a factor of 2.49): the Arpent would be equal to 1.3 or 3. 4 ha (or 3.24 and 8.46 acres) depending on whether the French or Spanish definition is applied. It is not clear in the original French text: Miranda writes "Arpens", but the old French and American territorial measures were the "arpent"—which is equivalent to 0.846 acres or 0.34 ha —while the old Spanish agrarian measure was written "Arpendes" which was much smaller being equivalent to 0.32 acre or 0.13 ha. According to David Chácon, the Spanish measure is smaller since it corresponds to the Roman measure "Square Act", which had a length of 36 m, equivalent to only 0.13 ha. In this interpretation, the condition to access the quality of voters was to own only 1.3 ha. Due to Miranda's penchant for importing Roman concepts, Chácon's interpretation may be proper. The correct translation is Arpendes (from the Latin Arapennis). The ancient Spaniards used this surface measurement, which, according to

The Indians and coloured people will be spared the fulfilment of this last condition in a single instance.

The Cabildos will select two members and all the district's citizens to be designated as mayors, who, as was done in the past, will oversee the administration of justice and the police during this time of war. These nominations should fall on citizens of proven honesty, no younger than 30, and with an annual income of at least 300 piastres [NA: or Spanish peso, i.e., purchasing power of 6.667 dollars of 2021].

ASSEMBLIES

The Cabildos will choose one or several representatives (proportional to the town's size) from its members and among all the district's citizens to form a Provincial Assembly. This assembly will be in charge of the general government of the whole Province until a Federal Government is established.

The Assembly members shall be over 30 and have an annual income of at least 500 piastres [NA: i.e. equivalent to US $11.111 in 2021]. The Assembly will select two citizens, known as "Cuaracas," from its members or from the citizens of the Province to be in charge of activating and executing provincial laws during the war. They will be at least 30 years of age and have an income of 500 piastres.

The existing laws will remain in effect until they are replaced. The following will be *ipso facto* abolished:

1. Every tax or personal burden for the Indians or any other citizen;
2. All duties on imports and exports to and from the country. Only a tax of 5% on imports and 2.2% on exports will be maintained; there will be no restrictions on the kinds of manufactures and goods that can be imported into or exported from the country.

All laws related to the hateful Inquisition Tribunal will be allowed. Religious tolerance is a principle of natural right, and the Colombian people always recognise the Catholic, Apostolic, and Roman religions as their national religion.

MILITIA

The militia, along with the armed forces, will be under the command of one citizen nominated by the Assembly and confirmed by the Electorates (*Comicios*) of the Province: he will hold the title of *Hatunapa* [General] of the Colombian armies and his authority will last if the war or until a Federal Government is formed. His principal duty will be to organise the army and defend the country, and to this effect, he will have all his officials sanctioned by the Assembly. The Assembly will nominate

San Isidoro de Sevilla, was a Roman linear measurement equivalent to 120 feet, approximately 36 m long. Ten arpendes correspond to an area of 1.3 ha in our time, which was little for the Americans; that is, it was enough to give the vote to the stable, popular layers and exclude only the adventurers. Through this filter, Miranda wanted to avoid a Jacobin scenario of popular power. However, his "censitarian" criteria were significantly less than what was required in most of the US at this time (for example, Jefferson in Virginia set 25 acres, or 10.1 ha, as the minimum voting quota). The "censitarian" vote (or the selective vote based on economic criteria) became more prevalent than ever after the disastrous French example of universal suffrage during the "Terror" period, as seen in the constitution of 1793. In the second sense, "Arpent" would be the measurement used by the French for an area of 3.4 ha.

three people to form a secret consultative body to advise the *Hatunapa* on all matters concerning his office.

The funds necessary to maintain, move, or garrison the army will be obtained by requisition of the Commanding General until the Assembly can make a final arrangement on this issue. The Hatunapa is responsible for the administration of all these interests and for the use he may make of his powers. The Government will have the right to request an account at the end of his term of office.

CLERGY

During the war, the clergy will be under the command of a General and Apostolic Vicar named by the Assembly. The priests from all the provinces will also be nominated or at least confirmed by their parishioners.

REGULATIONS

Foreign citizens who did not settle or marry in the country before our Declaration of Independence will not enjoy the rights of American citizens unless they can claim 6 years of continuous residence or have participated in two campaigns of the American armies. The legislature will, nonetheless, be able to grant those rights in exceptional cases or when it considers it convenient.

Those inhabitants of any category who refuse to take the oath of fidelity will be confined inland, in particular locations determined by the Government for the duration of the war. Permission to leave the country will be granted immediately to those who request it. The real estate or property of any kind that they leave behind will be faithfully administered in their absence once administration costs and general taxes have been deducted. When peace is re-established, they will be free to return to the country as foreigners, and their property will be restored to them. But those who have voluntarily served in the armies against their Fatherland will be expelled for life.

Every citizen who breaks the oath of fidelity to the country will be persecuted by the magistrates and severely punished according to the laws of the State.

(In the Original Archive, in the margin of this document, we can find the following comments made to Miranda by someone he consulted about the topic).

ELECTORATE:

Never use Roman or European names already used, but only American names, if they already exist; if not, they can be created, except the words Cabildos and Municipalities; why wouldn't they use the words Congress, Assembly, etc.?

TRADE "*Ne quid nimis*, never have too much trade and flee from that English obsession".

Colombian: "If the name of *Colombia* is adopted to designate the new Republic, its inhabitants should be called *Colombians*; this name is much more resonant and majestic than *Colombinos*.[55]".

2. PROJECT FOR A FEDERAL GOVERNMENT

AMERICAN CITIZENS ARE:

[55] *Archivo* ... Vol. XVI. 1938. p. 154–159. Translated from French.

Colombeia. Vol. XIX. 2006. Document 4570. Project for a Federal Government. 628–632. In the original one Vol. III. fol. 88–96 vto.

1°- All who were born in the country of a free father and a free mother;

All foreigners who are established and married in the country take the oath of fidelity to the new Government or, if single, participate in three campaigns for American independence. Otherwise, they will keep their foreign status. Nonetheless, the legislature will be able to confer those rights in exceptional cases when it considers it convenient.

AMERICAN ELECTIONS

These assemblies will consist of all American citizens who comply with the qualifications required by the Constitution, have landed property of at least ten arpens[56] of cultivated land, and are at least 21 years old. The Government will ensure that those Indians who do not have sufficient property receive ten arpens if they are married and five if they are single.

Citizens who do not comply with these requirements will not be able to vote in the Elections, but they will not lose the other rights they are entitled to as peaceful citizens.

MUNICIPAL COUNCILS (CABILDOS)

These bodies consist of a certain number of citizens from the district, appointed by active citizens. They will form a body of electors (with a vote) to represent the provinces.

Their principal duties are to police and run the internal administration of the townships, as well as to designate the people who will be part of the Provincial Assemblies.

Members of the Municipal bodies will be over 25 years old and have an annual income of at least 500 piastres [NA: US $2689 in 2021].

PROVINCIAL ASSEMBLIES

These Assemblies will consist of several people chosen among the active citizens of the American Empire. They will be responsible for health matters and the provincial administration. To this end, they can enact administrative laws applicable only within their Province and that do not conflict with the general rules. They will, therefore, submit them to the Legislative Body, which will sanction them for their application or give the reasons for their refusal without delay in the same year.

The members of the Provincial Assemblies will elect among American citizens the people who will constitute the Legislative Body and have the right to present petitions before it. They must be at least 30 years old and own a minimum of 30 acres of real estate.

The term of office of these authorities will be 5 years; they will likewise elect two American citizens to hold the post of Executive Power in the Province for 5 years. The latter will hold the title of Curacas; they must be at least 40 years old and own at least 150 arpents (approximately 195 ha) of cultivated land.

LEGISLATIVE BODY

[56] Equivalent to 1.3 or 3.4 ha or 3.24 to 8.46 acres (see above note n° 55).

The Legislative Body will consist of representatives named by the different Provincial Assemblies (*Amautas*[57]) in proportion to the number of inhabitants of each Province who are citizens of the Province from which they come. They will own 150 arpens [NA: 195 ha] of cultivated land and be at least 35 years old. This Assembly will be called *the "Dieta Imperial" and will be the sole authority to dictate laws to the entire* American Federation.

A simple majority of votes will pass these laws. However, they will be submitted to the sanction of the Executive Power, which has the right to reject the proposed law if it explains its reservations in doing so. If Dieta votes the same law by two-thirds after this, the Executive Power will accept the new decision and implement it immediately as a law of the Empire.

If the Dieta, by a majority of two-thirds, finds that a constitutional law needs reform or change, the Executive Power will submit it to the different Provincial Assemblies for their approval; if three-fourths of the Assemblies accept it, then it will be passed and made effective. Conversely, the Assemblies can take the initiative, and if three-fourths of the Dieta approve the law, it will become a constitutional law and take effect.

Their positions will be for a maximum of 5 years. Their members cannot be re-elected.

EXECUTIVE POWER

The Executive Power, named by the Dieta Imperial, consists of two citizens chosen from those of the whole Empire; they should be 40 years of age, own property of 200 arpens [NA: 26 or 68 ha], and should have exercised at least one of the great offices of the Empire. An interval of 5 years must be adhered to for the re-election of one or both.

The members of the Executive Power would have the title of *Incas*, a venerable name in the country.

One Incas will remain in the federal city, near the Legislative Body, and the other will tour the Provinces of the Empire.

The Incas will name two citizens to exercise the office of *Quaestors* or administrators of the Public Treasury; two for the post of *Ediles* who will build and repair the roads of the Empire; and two citizens under the title of *Censors* will draw up the census of the Empire, supervise public education and look after the preservation of proper behaviour. The *Censors*' age will be at least 45, while that of the Quaestors' and Councillors' will be 40. Their office has a term of only 5 years, and new appointments will be made immediately.

Several Quaestors will be present in the Provinces and Armies, with the sole responsibility for receiving public income, paying the armed forces, and other related tasks, all in conformity with the laws and rulings of the Empire.

In all Provinces, there will also be Ediles, who, as they do in the Capital, will look after the welfare of the cities, public buildings, churches, aqueducts, sewage,

---

[57] **Amautas**, Quechua word meaning a wise and experienced person who, in the Indian communities, has moral authority and a specific executive power.

public markets, weights and measures, etc. They will censor theatre productions and oversee all matters concerning public games, festivities, and other events.

The *Censors* will also have delegates in the Provinces, with the instruction to establish the census in the manner adopted in the Capital. The census will be passed punctually to the Government every 5 years to determine with exactitude the condition of the population throughout the Empire. They will also examine whether citizens are working their land correctly, whether they have been unmarried for a long time, and whether they have behaved bravely during the war, among other factors.

The Incas will be responsible for administering the nation. Despite their immunity during office, their public functions can be terminated, and they can be accused and judged before the Supreme National Court.

The Executive Power's primary duty is to oversee the security of the Empire; it can, accordingly, wage a defensive war in the event of foreign aggression; however, it cannot prolong it without the consent of the Colombian Council. Under no circumstances can it declare war without the permission of the Council, and this Body's authorisation will be required to carry it beyond the limits of the Empire.

JUDICIAL POWER

This power is vested in the judges who preside over the various courts in the Provinces. In agreement with the provincial assemblies, the Executive Power will single them out in provincial elections, as many as it considers necessary.

The Inca will confirm or reject the election of the judges as determined by the polls. If he denies the election, he will warn the Dieta, which will call for new elections if it ratifies the denial. If the Inca confirms the election, the judge will be legitimised, and he will take office.

The judges will be active citizens no younger than 40 years of age. They are not removable, and the appointment is for life, except in case of malfeasance. If such were the case, they would be accused before the Dieta, which will examine the charges. If it does not find them sufficient, it will reject the accusation; if it accepts them, this will be passed on to the Supreme National Court (the only court qualified to judge the Incas).

The constitution of law courts and the trial by jury will conform precisely to those in England and the United States of America. Initially, a special jury will be named until the mass of citizens acquires the habits of freedom. The jury will only hear cases involving civilians and crimes.

The executive power will name the Supreme National Court (High Court), which will consist of a president and two judges, elected among the other national judges. This Court will know of matters related to the Rights of People ("*Derecho de Gentes*"), to treaties with foreign powers, and will judge the magistrates and all those other citizens accused of malfeasance or other crimes against the State.

RELIGION

The Catholic, Apostolic and Roman Religion will be the national religion, and the Provincial Council, summoned for this purpose, will determine the hierarchy of the American clergy. Since the Constitution admits absolute religious tolerance, no citizen will be harassed for religious beliefs. The ministers of the Gospel will not be hindered in any of their functions, and to this effect, they will be excluded from all civil or military action.

Likewise, this rule will be applied to the agents of the Judicial Power, who are no less necessary than helpful in exercising their functions. Therefore, every *public notary or lawyer* will be excluded from military service and civil functions.

Every person who sells their property loses the precious right of citizenship and can only recover it when they have acquired the necessary amount.

Magistrates will punish those who neglect the cultivation of their land for 2 consecutive years, as per the law.

The *Federal City*, to be established at the most central point, possibly the Panama isthmus, will bear the august name of Columbus. This name, a tribute to the explorer who discovered this beautiful part of the Earth, carries the weight of history and the promise of a new beginning.[58]

Comments were made to Miranda by someone to whom he consulted regarding their opinion.

(In the Original Archive, they are noted on the margin of the third project).

Incas—the introduction of this Inca Word is accurate and may have a significant impact. Still, we must also introduce the *Zipa term*, which refers to the title held by the sovereigns of the vast country known today as the *New Kingdom* before the conquest. It should be pointed out, and this is important, that these two sovereigns were effective. The first court was held in Bogotá, a significant city at the time, which is now a small town near Santa Fe. He was above the second one, who lived in Tunja. All these details, and many others, must be present in the various descriptions published in the Spanish language about the new Kingdom; they must be verified.

Quaestors and Councillors—Neither *Quaestors* nor *Councillors*. The Indians of paganism (as Spanish people say), whose government was not as despicable as it is thought, had officers who fulfilled these functions. If other names should be set, I would prefer *Treasurers* or *Argenteros*, although it is a form of barbarism, and Guards or Curators, which is currently another form of barbarism.

Censors.—Here, you have Magistracy par excellence, and I think it cannot be practised well before being 40 years old. More than two would be needed. That of the Romans was not exercised, but in Rome, yours will take place in all parts of a large empire. The word Censor does not have a complete meaning; It is mainly related to the census of citizens. The Censors must be the guardians of *morality* and *customs*, which are too despised in our wise Europe. Sound practices are almost always the safeguard of habits; their perpetual change can be attributed to most of the absurdities that afflict, debase and will soon lead to the destruction of our civilised nations. *More*…Romans said this expression makes a lot of sense. Alas, the legislator who forgets about it!

Religion.—We must necessarily speak of the Pope, the head of this Church.

[58] *Archivo*….op.cit., Negotiations. Vol. III. f. 93. From page 94 to page 107, this document is repeated as a draft.

5.2.4 *The Fourth Constitutional Project for Latin America, 1808*

Context:

Blocked in England by the persistent British reluctance to support his emancipation plan for Spanish America, Miranda was finally authorised to leave London in August 1805 to organise a military landing in Venezuela alone. This autonomous expedition would not get British support, but he expected to arm it from New York in July/August 1806. Finally, his landing did take place in Coro, Venezuela, but it was a big failure. He was betrayed after Pitt's death (January 1806) by his British successors and by H. Popham,[59] a high-ranking Navy officer and former collaborator of Miranda, who had secretly and in parallel organised his own plan to first seize Montevideo and Buenos-Aires in a piracy operation in April 1806 for his profit. He hoped his expedition would be legitimised as a colonial extension of the British Empire that would be profitable for British industry. Indeed, despite being carried out without either the Navy or government authorisation, the pirate expedition was quickly backed by the Grenville cabinet and amplified with the illusion of becoming a populist colonial conquest of the entire Southern Cone of America. However, both imperialist operations ended in a very humiliating military disaster, with Argentinian patriots capturing the British troops.

After his own failed expedition, Miranda stayed until 1807 in Trinidad, a British island strategically located off the coast of Venezuela, with some hopes that new events would provide him again an opportunity. It was the case as the situation in London evolved slowly in favour of his thesis due to the geopolitical situation that turned contrary for England and made Miranda's warnings very tangible. British authorities realised:

- the need to draw lessons from the disaster in Buenos Aires that—according to Miranda—was inevitable. He had announced the impossibility of a British operation being successful without prior coordination with the Creole independence movements
- the deterioration of England's industrial prospects in Europe as a result of the Berlin decree (December 1806) imposing the continental blockade,

[59] **Sir Home Riggs Popham** (1762–1820) was a Royal Navy commander who fought against the French during the Revolutionary and Napoleonic Wars. He created a signal code for boats adopted by the Royal Navy in 1803, contributing to the Trafalgar victory in 1805. He was a Member of Parliament from 1804 to 1812. Between 1787 and 1793, he participated in commercial ventures on the Eastern Sea, including contraband trade. From 1794, he was active in the war against France in Flanders, Denmark, and the Red Sea. In 1804, Pitt commissioned him to work on Miranda's plan to contribute to the emancipation of Spanish colonies. In January 1806, he recaptured the Cape of Good Hope from the Dutch, where he conceived his pirate expedition to La Plata, betraying Miranda (see Chap. 11) and attempting a colonial conquest, which ultimately ended in total disaster. The Navy dismissed him for sending him to the Spanish war against Napoleon, where he won various battles, and he was promoted to Rear Admiral in 1814.

- Napoleon's successive military victories against Austria (Austerlitz, December 1805), Prussia (October 1806), Russia (June 1807)
- the secret information relating to the treaty concluded between Napoleon and Alexander first, Tsar of Russia, in Tilsit (July 1807), which anticipated a maritime attack of England by France with the Danish and Portuguese fleets,
- Napoleon's invasion of Portugal and Spain (October–November 1807).
- The negative impact on England's image of the preventive attack decided by Minister Canning[60] in Copenhagen (August–September 1807) to seize the Danish fleet.

In this context, Miranda received the support of several influential people, from the King's sons to General Arthur Wellesley[61] (future Duke of Wellington), who had the mission to overthrow Napoleon and prevent his influence in America. General Wellesley requested Miranda's return to London to act as his adviser to organise the fight against Napoleon's expansionism and prepare a specific military operation in Latin America based upon naval supremacy, returning so to the traditional strategy of the "Blue Water" policy[62] that Miranda had been pushing since 1790 (see Chap. 11). It was the moment Miranda wrote his fourth version of Colombia's federative constitution.

As announced and feared by Miranda since Napoleon's return from the Italian campaign a decade ago, the Emperor invaded the Iberian Peninsula at the end of 1807 to overthrow the two absolutist thrones. Napoleon's purpose was to complete his commercial blockade against Britain and seize the financial resources from the two colonial empires in order to stifle the power of the emerging English industrial revolution and its parliamentary democracy. This Bonapartist expansion strategy provoked a reaction (both in England and Creole America), providing the expected

[60] **George Canning** (1770–1827), Tory politician, British Minister of Foreign Affairs from 1807 to 1809 in the Portland cabinet; he was already vice-minister of Foreign Affairs in the Pitt government from 1795 to 1799 (then he also knew Miranda) and acted as "anti-Jacobin" by editing a weekly magazine of the same name in 1797 to 1799. As Minister of Foreign Affairs, he was very opposed to his colleague Castlereagh, War and Colonies Minister, who provoked him and wounded him in a duel in 1809, removing him from power until 1816 when he returned as Minister of India (Board of Control) until 1821, becoming Minister of Foreign Affairs again until 1827 when succeeded the Prime Minister from April to August 1827 before he died. He sought to prevent South America from entering the French sphere of influence. In this, he was successful and helped guarantee the independence of Brazil and the Spanish colonies, thereby supporting the Monroe Doctrine and aiding British merchants to open new markets across South and Central America.

[61] **Arthur Wellesley** (1769–1852), **Duke of Wellington**, general in chief, victorious against Napoleon in Portugal (1809), Spain (1812–13), France (1814) and finally in Belgium with Waterloo (1815). He was also a British politician; Miranda was his adviser until 1808 to help him defeat Napoleon.

[62] The **"Blue Water" policy** (1689–1815) refers to the priority of developing a military navy that allowed British supremacy. It results from the British insular character combined with the widespread distrust towards a land army, which was always seen as a possible instrument of monarchical despotism. However, this priority had weakened by the Miranda period, and Pitt's government was divided between pro and con maritime operations. See Chap. 11 and Baugh, D., [1988]; also, Brewer, J., [1994].

political opportunities for organising a revolutionary change in America. However, based on his French revolutionary experience, Miranda feared a violent and bloody revolution, which would have unleashed popular ethnic passions accumulated over three centuries of colonial abuses. The weight of the past exposed Latin America to high risks of civil wars with subsequent political fragmentation that would have been fatal to Miranda's democratic project of economic development and the operational sustainability of emancipation through peaceful continental integration.

Therefore, he attempts to implement his strategic plan quickly, which relies on the mobilisation of the popular base through the Municipal Councils ("Cabildos"), encouraging them to form advanced representative revolutionary boards («Juntas»). These elected representatives would have implemented a single federative constitution at the same time as an anchor for political change through a democratic legitimacy (election) and also to serve as an integrating pillar between each vice-royalty renamed "Provinces". However, Miranda's revolutionary plan, implemented through the "Cabildos" (Municipal Councils), required the support of the Creoles—and especially that of their oligarchs—to avoid a civil war. Therefore, he had to adapt his constitutional text to one that was acceptable to the local oligarchy.

Miranda arrived home in London on January 1, 1808, and immediately resumed negotiations with the new British cabinet, led by the Duke of Portland[63] through the ministers Castlereagh[64] and Canning. The purpose was again to obtain British military support to prevent South America from falling into Napoleon's hands.

However, once more, the British support for Miranda was cancelled in June. This time, it resulted from the general uprising of the Spanish people against the French (unleashed on May 2, 1808). The British government sought to capitalise on this guerrilla. On July 12, 1808, it ordered that Wellesley's expedition, mounted with Miranda and about to sail towards South America, was diverted to the Iberian Peninsula to fight against Napoleon on the Continent directly. Although Wellesley invited Miranda to remain in charge of this radically different mission, he protested

[63] **William Henry Cavendish, Duke of Portland** (1738–1809). Whig politician and leader who became Tory at the end, Prime Minister in 1783, later Home Secretary in Pitt's government from 1794, remaining Minister in all cabinets and succeeded to Grenville as Prime Minister in 1807 up to resigning in 1809 for health reasons but being dominated by the disputes between his two main Ministers Canning and Castlereagh.

[64] **Robert Steward, Viscount of Castlereagh** (Dublin, 1769–1822), Irish Tory, was a Minister for Ireland (1798–1801) in Pitt's government. He fought for the emancipation of the Catholic Irish, suppressing the Irish Rebellion of 1798, and was instrumental in securing the passage of the Irish Act of Union of 1800. He joined the Addington office (who succeeded Pitt) as India's Minister (Board of Control) and was appointed War and Colonies Minister in the last year (1805) of Pitt's second government (1804–1806), who also appointed him as his Deputy Prime Minister; he quitted when Grenville took over in 1806, and he came back to War and Colonies Minister together with Portland in 1807 until 1809 (he had to leave due to his dispute with his colleague Canning which led to a shocking duel wounding Canning) and he came back later to the same Minister post from 1812 to 1822, carrying out a key role in the fight against Napoleon, in the Congress of Vienna and the suppression of slave trade. Later, as a supporter of firmness during the economic crisis that shook Great Britain, he advocated in 1817 the suspension of the Habeas corpus and repressive measures. He became very unpopular and also paranoid. He committed suicide in 1822.

vehemently and decided to act on his own again, modifying his approach. His new strategy involves two complementary pillars: the network of disciples and agents that he had progressively built in his numerous contacts from London and that he expanded to the main cities of the four vice-royalties, and an actual propaganda campaign organised with several articles published under nicknames [Smith 1809, Antepara 1809, 1810], in British newspapers (The Political Herald, the Morning Chronicle, the Edinburgh Review,) and with his book (Antepara [1810][65] and his magazine "El Colombiano [1810][66]"). Faced with the resilience of the colonial regime, drawing lessons from his failures, Miranda considered it necessary to utilize the existing social structure and bet on the local oligarchies, who could potentially benefit from independence. Therefore, he adapts his political discourse to avoid alarming the influential Creoles. It is a step back to be able to start a dynamic of changes without violence. To this end, he changes his constitutional project in a very conservative sense to win the support of the powerful social class.

In July 1808, he attempted to implement his new strategy to promote an endogenous revolution from within the local administrations. Miranda disseminated his new constitutional project in the following months and sent letters to the principal Municipal councils (Caracas, Buenos Aires, Lima, Santiago, Quito, Mexico, Santa Fé de Bogotá, and Havana). He tried to activate his political network (prepared in advance in London from his home with Bernardo O'Higgins[67] in 1798), insisting on the need to start by forming "a representative municipal body" (elected) with which each vice-royalty would be able to proclaim legitimately both its independence and its federative union with the other Cabildos. Miranda [1808] especially warns that the purpose of this municipal movement ("Juntas") is not at all similar to what is appearing in Spain with the municipal "juntas" that are being created "*in Oviedo, Seville, Madrid, etc.* [Against the invasion of France and] *which have minimal compatibility with the interests and authorities of our provinces in America*[68]". These "juntas" were indeed created to defend the Spanish King and the integrity of the Empire. At the same time, Miranda planned to organise radical independence from the Metropolis to eradicate the absolutist monarchy and implement a new democratic order.

Content:

His fourth draft of the federal constitution is almost identical to the third one, which means that it is a federal republic with subsidiarity in both directions, that is,

---

[65] Chapter 8, document 8.1.

[66] Chapter 8, document 8.2.

[67] **Bernardo O'Higgins Riquelme** (1778–1842)," Libertador" of Chile, the illegitimate son of the Viceroy of Peru, His father sent him secretly to London as a student, where he was trained by Miranda for preparing Chilean independence (1810–1817), becoming the Head of the Chilean army, he proclaimed independence and became the first "Director Supremo" and founder of the Chilean Republic (1818–1823). He played a decisive role in founding the republic on constitutional order and the rule of law more than in any other country. See Ghymers, C., [2002].

[68] Chapter 10, document 10.4.7. Miranda's letter to Marqués del Toro, Cabildo of Caracas, July 20, 1808.

central solid powers in only three federal fields (monetary & economic matters, foreign policies, justice) and all other powers and governance remaining decentralised towards their most efficient level (subsidiarity). The differences with the 1801 text are purely tactical. They explain the peculiar context of a direct attempt to convince the Creole oligarchy, which, in fact, held the effective power. Miranda realises that the independence process inevitably exposes the risks of internal fights for seizing local power, coupled with a deep socio-ethical potential conflict. He was fully aware that announcing a rapid social change in advance, although he knew the change was desirable and inevitable in the long term, would make the local oligarchy worry about their own interests. This explains the more selective filters than in the 1801 version, which introduced the right to vote (based on higher income criteria) and to be elected. However, his own philosophy makes him believe in the possibility of social progress under the condition of triggering a "trial-and-error" process. This dynamic was expected to channel the demand for changes progressively and peacefully, thanks to his constitutional balance of powers in a legitimate "mixed system" based on open debates. In his journal "El Colombiano" in London, he explained in 1810[69]: "*...the greatest current obstacle to the establishment of independence is the fear that many good men have of seeing their people and their properties compromised if the established order is changed*". Also, he explains that «*whatever form and mutation is made in government*, the "sacred principle"—which is the basic criterion of a good sustainable governance—is to warrant "*the security of all people and their properties*" [in the period] "*between the dissolution of the ancient regime and the establishment of the new regime*" (see Chap. 8, document 8.2).

Therefore, the key was to be more gradual and not appear too revolutionary in terms of socio-political and ethnic aspects. Thus, he adapted his 1801 constitution with much more restrictive eligibility requirements for voting and being elected. However, in the text for the provisional government, Indians could vote anyway but not be elected if their monetary income did not reach a critical amount. However, for the post-war federation, the agrarian reform meant that married Indians would receive only 6.5 ha, while a minimum of 65 was required for voting. In the 1801 version, married Indians would have automatically received the right to vote through the agrarian reform, which involved the restitution of arable land sufficient for them to be active citizens with voting rights. Miranda also adds the role of the *constitutional dictator* in case of emergency. He aimed to address the fear of a lack of operational executive power in the event of war. So, he introduces a specific procedure for demonstrating the ability of his democratic formula to address exceptional situations, such as war, by concentrating legally the necessary powers as far as possible but only temporarily, under democratic control according to strict procedures and without compromising fundamental citizen rights.

[69] Chapter 8, document 8.2. *El Colombiano*, n°V, 15 de Mayo 1810 [Grases 1966].

This fourth project is often presented by mistake as his 1801 project or as the only one, creating a conservative bias, anti-democratic and many interpretation errors.

Sources:

Written in Spanish.

Warning: wrongly copied by J. Gil Fortoul as the 1801 project in Gil Fortoul: **Historia Constitucional de Venezuela**. 4th Edition. Caracas, Venezuela: C.A. Tipografía Garrido. Ministerio de Educación. Dirección de Cultura y Bellas Artes. Comisión Editora de las Obras Completas de José Gil Fortoul. 1954. Vol 2°. p. 331–339. Also reproduced in Mondolfi: **Miranda La Aventura de la Libertad**. Vol. 1 p. 253–256, as well as in Salcedo Bastardo, op. cit. But *presented wrongly* as being the 1801 project.

Text:

London, 1808

1. - PROJECT FOR A PROVISIONAL GOVERNMENT

All authority that emanates from the Spanish Government is ipso facto abolished. All laws not included in this project will remain unchanged.

ELECTORATE (*COMICIOS*)

The Electorate consists of the inhabitants born or established in the country, whatever their caste, if they are 21 years of age, have sworn allegiance to the new form of government and American independence, have an annual income of 50 pesos,[70] are children of a free father and mother, do not work as paid servants and have not suffered criminal penalties

MUNICIPAL COUNCILS (*CABILDOS*)

The Spanish authorities will be replaced by the Cabildos and Councils of the different cities, with one-third of the members chosen from the Indians and people of colour in the Province; the Municipal elections must confirm these designations. No member of those Cabildos or Councils can be less than 35 years old or have property smaller than 20 "*fanegadas*"[71] of cultivated land; the Indians and coloured people will be spared the fulfilment of this last condition in a single instance.

The Cabildos shall select two from their members and all the district's citizens to be designated as mayors, and who, as was done in the past, will oversee the administration of justice and the police in this time of war. These nominations should be

[70] **Peso**: Miranda, now addressing his Spanish compatriots as a priority, expresses the values of Latin American pesos (not anymore in piastres as in the 1801 version, although the Spanish piastre was synonymous with peso or dollar). Latin America's predominant currency, the eight "reales" coins (or escudos), from which the US Dollar was created, with the same value (27gr of 0,892 silver). This means a more restrictive level of income, 50 pesos against only 36 in the 1801 version.

[71] **Fanegada**: A Castilian agricultural measure approximately equivalent to 64/100 of a hectare. The condition for being a Municipal council member was to own at least 12.8 ha (compared to only 1.3 ha in the 1801 version, using the old Castilian measures of "Arpense", see note n°43).

made to citizens of proven honesty, no younger than 35, and with an annual income of at least 300 pesos.[72]

ASSEMBLIES

The Cabildos will choose one or several representatives (in proportion to the town's size) from their members and among all the district's citizens to form a Provincial Assembly. This assembly will oversee the general government of the whole Province until a Federal Government is established.

The Assembly members shall be over 35 and have an annual income of at least 400 pesos. The Assembly will select two citizens, known as "Curacas", either from its members or from the citizens of the Province, who will oversee the activation and enforcement of provincial laws during the war. They will be at least 40 years of age and have an annual income of 500 pesos.

The existing laws will remain in effect until they are replaced. The following will be *ipso facto* abolished:

1. Every tax or personal burden for the Indians or any other citizen;
2. All duties on imports and exports to and from the country. Only a tax of 15% on imports and 20% on exports[73] will be maintained. There will be no restrictions on the kind of manufactures and goods imported into or exported from the country.
3. All laws related to the hateful Inquisition Tribunal. Religious tolerance is a principle of natural right and will be allowed in general: the Colombian people always recognise the Catholic, Apostolic, and Roman religion as their national religion.

MILITIA

The militia, along with the armed forces, will be under the command of one citizen nominated by the Assembly and confirmed by the Provincial assembly: he will hold the title of *Hatunapa* (Generalissimo) of the Colombian armies, and his authority will last as long as the war or until a Federal Government is formed. His principal duty will be to organise the army and defend the country, and to this effect, he will have all his officials sanctioned by the Assembly. The Assembly will nominate three people to form a secret consultative body to advise the Hatunapa on all matters concerning his office.

---

[72] An income level much higher than the average income impeded Indians or low-class workers from being elected. The local oligarchy perceived this concession as necessary to make independence acceptable, that is, impeding Indians or low-class workers from being elected.

[73] These criteria are much more protectionist than in the 1801 version (only 5% on imports and 2.5% on exports); this is a clear signal to the rentist class benefitting from the mercantilist policy of the Empire. This measure thus appears as a temporary gift for buying appears thus as a temporary gift for buying support from the local establishment. Miranda was a free trader, considering that protectionism was a colonial way to impede the development and emancipation of dominated territories and block the international exchange of ideas.

The funds necessary to maintain, move or garrison the army will be obtained by requisition of the Commanding General until the Assembly can make a final arrangement on this issue.

The Hatunapa is responsible for the administration of all these interests and the use he may make of his powers. The Government will have the right to request an account at the end of his term of office.

CLERGY

During the war, the clergy will be under the command of a General and Apostolic Vicar named by the Assembly. The priests from all the provinces will also be nominated or at least confirmed by their parishioners.

REGULATIONS

Foreign citizens who did not settle or marry in the country before our Declaration of Independence will not enjoy the rights of American citizens unless they can claim 6 years of continuous residence or have participated in three campaigns of the American armies. The legislature will, nonetheless, be able to grant those rights in exceptional cases or when it considers it convenient.

Those inhabitants of any category who refuse to take the oath of fidelity will be confined inland, in particular locations determined by the Government for the duration of the war. Permission to leave the country will be granted immediately to those who request it. The real estate or property of any kind that they leave behind will be faithfully administered in their absence once administration costs and general taxes have been deducted. When peace is re-established, they will be free to return to the country as foreigners, and their property will be restored to them. But those who have voluntarily served in the armies against their Fatherland will be expelled for life.

Every citizen who breaks the oath of fidelity to the country will be persecuted by the magistrates and severely punished according to the laws of the State.

2. PROJECT FOR A FEDERAL GOVERNMENT

American citizens are:

1. All those who were born in the country of a free father and a free mother;
2. All foreigners who are established and married in the country take the oath of fidelity to the new Government or, being single, participate in three campaigns for American independence. Otherwise, they will keep their foreign status. Nonetheless, the legislature will be able to confer those rights in exceptional cases when it considers it convenient.AMERICAN ELECTIONS

These assemblies will consist of all American citizens who comply with the qualifications required by the Constitution, have a landed property of at least 100 "fanegadas" of cultivated land and are at least 21 years old. The Government will ensure that those Indians[74] who do not have sufficient property will receive ten

[74] In this version, directly addressed to the Cabildos (not yet elected), that is to say, to the Creole oligarchy, Miranda increases from 1.8 to 65 ha (× by 36) the criteria to access to vote, and the land quota of his agrarian reform only increases from 1.8 to 6.5 ha (× by 3.6) making very difficult for the Indians to participate to the elections. Given that in all other versions, the purpose of Miranda

"*fanegadas*" if they are married and five if they are single. The citizens who do not comply with these requirements will not be able to vote in the Elections, but they will not lose the other rights they are entitled to as peaceful citizens.

MUNICIPAL COUNCILS (CABILDOS)

These bodies consist of a certain number of district citizens appointed by active citizens. They will form a body of electors (with a vote) to represent the provinces. Their principal duties are to police and administer the internal affairs of the townships and designate the individuals who will be part of the Provincial Assemblies. Members of the Municipal bodies will be over 35 years of age and have an annual income of at least 500 pesos.

PROVINCIAL ASSEMBLIES

These Assemblies will consist of several people chosen among the active citizens of the American Empire.

They will be responsible for health matters and provincial administration. To this end, they can enact administrative laws applicable only within their Province that do not conflict with the general rules. They will, therefore, submit them to the Legislative Body, which will sanction them for their application or give the reasons for their refusal without delay in the same year.

The members of the Provincial Assemblies will elect among American citizens the people who will constitute the Legislative Body and have the right to present petitions before it. They must be at least 30 years old and own real estate property of at least 30 fanegadas.

The term of office of these authorities will be 5 years; they will likewise elect two American citizens to exercise in the Province the post of Executive Power for 5 years; they will not be younger than 40 years of age, and they must be the owners of at least 150 *fanegadas* of cultivated land.

LEGISLATIVE BODY

The Legislative Body will consist of representatives named by the different Provincial Assemblies (Amautas) in proportion to the number of inhabitants of each Province who are citizens of the Province from which they come. They will own a minimum of 150 *fanegadas* of cultivated land and be at least 35 years old. This Assembly will be called the Colombian Council and will be the sole authority to dictate laws to the entire American Federation; a simple majority of votes will be required to pass laws. But they will be submitted to the sanction of the Executive Power, which has the right to reject the proposed law if, in doing so, it explains its reservations. If, after this, the Council votes the same law by two-thirds, the Executive Power will accept the new decision and will implement it without delay as a law of the Empire

If the Council, by a two-thirds majority, finds that a constitutional law needs reform or change, the Executive Power will submit it to the various Provincial Assemblies for their approval; if three-fourths of the Assemblies accept it, then it

---

was to give the vote to married and stable Indians, this change is interpreted as a forced concession to the oligarchy when he was asking for their support, relying on the expected democratic dynamics once the colonial regime would be eradicated.

will be passed and made effective. Conversely, the Assemblies can take the initiative, and if three-fourths of the Council approve the law, it will become a constitutional law and take effect.

EXECUTIVE POWER

The Executive Power, named by the Colombian Council, consists of two citizens chosen from those of the whole Empire; they should be 40 years of age, own property of 200 fanegadas, and should have exercised at least one of the great offices of the Empire. The two members of the Executive Power will remain in office for a term of 10 years. For the re-election of one or both of them, an interval of 10 years must be adhered to.

The members of the Executive Power would have the title of Incas, a venerable name in the country.

One Incas will remain in the federal city, near the Legislative Body, and the other will tour the Provinces of the Empire.

The Incas will name two citizens to exercise the office of "Quaestors" or administrators of the Public Treasury; two for the post of "*Ediles*" (Ministers) who will build and repair the roads of the Empire; and six citizens under the title of "Censors" will draw up the census of the Empire, supervise public education and look after the preservation of proper behaviour. The Censors' age will be 45, while that of the Quaestors' and Councillors will be 40. Their office has a term of only 5 years, and new appointments will be made immediately.

Several *Quaestors* will be present in the Provinces and Armies, with the sole responsibility for receiving public income, paying the armed forces, and other related tasks, all in conformity with the laws and rulings of the Empire.

In all Provinces, there will also be *Ediles*, who, as they do in the Capital, will look after the welfare of the cities, public buildings, churches, aqueducts, sewage, public markets, weights and measures, etc. They will censor theatre productions and oversee all matters concerning public games, festivities, and other events.

The Censors will also have delegates in the Provinces, with the instruction to establish the census in the manner adopted in the Capital. The census will be passed punctually to the Government every 5 years to determine with exactitude the condition of the population throughout the Empire. They will also examine whether the citizens are working their land correctly, if they have lived together for a long time unmarried, behaved bravely during the war, etc.

The Incas will be responsible for administering the nation. Despite their immunity during office, their public functions can be terminated, and they can be accused and judged before the Supreme National Court.

The Executive Power's primary duty is to watch over the security of the Empire. Accordingly, it can wage a defensive war in case of foreign aggression but cannot prolong it without the consent of the Colombian Council. Under no circumstances can it declare war without the permission of the Council, and this Body's authorisation will be required to carry it beyond the limits of the Empire.

In cases of extreme necessity, the Council will decree the nomination of a Dictator (with the same power that Rome gave its dictators, and the office will last only 1 year). The Incas will elect the person who will fulfil this sacred post. The

Dictator must be at least 45 years old and have already served in one of the first offices of the Empire.

JUDICIAL POWER

This power is vested in the judges who preside over the various courts in the Provinces. In agreement with the provincial assemblies, the Executive Power will select as many candidates as necessary for provincial elections.

The Inca will confirm or reject the election of the judges as determined by the polls. If he denies the election, he will warn the Council, which will call for new elections if it ratifies the denial. If the Inca confirms the election, the judge will be legitimised, and he will take office.

The judges will be active citizens no younger than 40 years of age. They are not removable, and their appointment is for life, except in case of misconduct. If such were the case, they would be accused before the Council, which would examine the charges. If it does not find them sufficient, it will reject the accusation; if it accepts them, this will be passed on to the Supreme National Court (the only court qualified to judge the Incas).

The constitution of law courts and the trial by jury will conform precisely to those in England and the United States of America. Initially, a special jury will be named until the mass of citizens acquires the habits of freedom. The jury will only hear cases involving civilians and crimes.

The Executive Power will appoint the Supreme National Court (High Court), consisting of a president and two judges, who will be elected from among the other national judges. This Court will know of matters related to the Rights of People (*Derecho de Gentes*), to treaties with foreign powers, and will judge the magistrates and all those other citizens accused of misconduct or other crimes against the State.

RELIGION

The Catholic, Apostolic, and Roman Religions will be the national religion, and the Provincial Council summoned for this purpose will determine the hierarchy of the American clergy. Since the Constitution admits absolute religious tolerance, no citizen will be harassed for religious beliefs.

The ministers of the Gospel will not be hindered in any of their functions, and to this effect, they will be excluded from all civil or military action.

Likewise, this rule will be applied to the agents of the Judicial Power, who are no less necessary than helpful in exercising their functions. Therefore, every public notary or lawyer will be excluded from military service and civil functions.

Every person who sells their property loses the precious right of citizenship and can only recover it when they have acquired the necessary amount.

Magistrates will punish those who neglect the cultivation of their land for 2 consecutive years, as per the law.

The federal city will be established at the most central point (maybe the Panama isthmus) and will bear the August name of Columbus,[75] to whom we are indebted for discovering this beautiful part of the Earth.

5.2.5 *The Fifth or Alternative Version (Draft) of the Constitutional Project for Latin America (Undated)*

Context:

Similar to the two previous projects, Miranda's primary concern was to establish a coherent institutional order that would protect Latin America from the risks of anarchy and Jacobin tyranny. This intermediate text reveals the author's hesitation in setting the point of the census filter and the degree of commercial protection. In this version, the criteria for voting and being eligible are less restrictive than in the two other versions. The import duties are also much lower.

Content:

It is an anonymous and undated document titled *Draft of Provisional Government B and Federative Government C*. It is a draft that combines elements of the 1801 and 1808 projects; the differences are minimal and relate to the criteria of votes and eligibility, likely intended for use in the event of favourable conditions for support from the Creole oligarchy. It indicates the pragmatism and preoccupation for adapting the democratic degree to the context and local acceptance.

Sources:

Written in Spanish, not yet published, discovered by David R. Chacón Rodríguez in the *Archivo General de Indias, Sevilla, Sección Estado. Legajo, 81. N°. 74.*[76]

Text:

OUTLINE FOR A PROVISIONAL GOVERNMENT B

All authority derived from the Spanish government is ipso facto abolished. However, the existing laws will remain in full force, except for those specified later.

ELECTORATES (*Comicios*)

To substitute another one, Elections or meetings of all the inhabitants of the native countries, or established in it, of whatever caste they may be, provided they have reached the age of 21 that they have sworn American independence, who have an annual income of 36 pesos (NA In the version 1808 appears 50 pesos); that they are born to a free mother and father; that they are not domestic servants, nor have they suffered defamatory punishment.

---

[75] Miranda's handwritten note: If the name of Colombia is adopted to designate the new republic, its inhabitants should be called Colombians; this name is more sonorous and majestic than "Colombinos".

[76] Collated with the one that appears in the *Archivo*. Talks. 1800–1804. Havana: Lex Editorial. Vol. XVI. p. 154–159.

MUNICIPAL COUNCILS (*Cabildos*)

These elections will elect several citizens, proportionate to the population of each district, to form the councils and town halls of the different towns and cities. These bodies will increase their membership by a third, attributed to Indian and coloured people from the district. No member shall be less than 25 years of age, nor with a property less than ten fanegadas (NA In the version 1808 appears 100 and in 1801 20) of arable land.

/fol 1v°./ The Indian and coloured people will only be exempt, for now, from this last circumstance.

The Municipal Council (Cabildos) will choose at will from among its members or from the mass of the citizens of the District two people who are called Mayors and who will be in charge (as in the past) of the distribution of justice, or from the mass of the citizens of the District, two people who are called Mayors, and who will be in charge (as in the past) of the distribution of justice, and of the district police during the war. Care will be taken to ensure that these elections select people of recognised integrity, older than 30 (NA In version 1808 appears 35) years, and whose annual income is not less than 300 pesos.

ASSEMBLIES

The Cabildos will appoint one or more members from among themselves or the other citizens of the District (according to this population) who will form a Provincial Assembly in charge of the general government of the entire Province until the Federal government is established.

The members of this Assembly are required to be no younger than 30 years [NA in the one of 1808 appears 35] and to have an annual income of at least 400 pesos (in the one from 1801, there are 500)

The Assembly will name from among its members, or from the number of citizens of the province, two persons named *Curacas*, who will be in charge of activating and enforcing the provincial laws during this time of war. These will have a minimum age of 30 [NA in 1808 appears to be 40] years and an annual income of 500 pesos.

The current laws will remain in effect until better ones are established.

/fol 2/ However, the following will be abolished.

1 any personal tax or tribute on the Indians or other citizens.
2 all duties on imports and exports of the country, which will be reduced to 5 [NA in 1808 appears 15] % on the former, and to 2 1/2 [NA in 1808 appears 20] % on the second, being free the entry of all kinds of manufactures and merchandise, and the exit of all types of productions.
3 all the laws related to the hateful tribunal of the Inquisition. Religious tolerance, being a principle of natural law, will be allowed. The Colombian People recognise the Roman Catholic Apostolic religion as the National Religion.**MILITIA**

The militia and the entire armed force will be placed under the direction of an American Citizen, appointed by the Assembly and confirmed by the provincial electorates. He will hold the title of general-in-chief ("*Hatunapa*") of the Colombian armies, and his authority will remain in effect until the end of the war or until the establishment of the federal government. His primary obligation will be the organisation of the armies and the defence of the country. To this end, he shall have the power to propose all officers to the sanction of the Assembly, which shall appoint a Commission of three Persons to whom he shall secretly communicate the military plans and operations. Etc.

The funds necessary for the subsistence, lodging, and movement of the armies will be paid by the Provinces at the General-in-chief's request until the Assembly has formed a definitive Regulation on this urgent matter, responsible for its administration as well as the use of the powers conferred on him for this purpose. The Government has the right to check his accountability when leaving his post.

CLERGY

The Clergy will remain under the Vicar General's Direction, whom the Assembly will appoint during the war. The priests of the entire province will also be named or confirmed by their respective parishioners.

REGULATIONS

All foreigners who were not established or married in the country before the declaration of our independence will not enjoy the rights of American Citizens unless they reside in the country for 6 continuous years or make 2 [In the 1808 version, it appears 3] campaigns in the American armies. The Legislature may, however, in particular cases, grant these rights to the persons it judges on purpose.

The inhabitants of all kinds who refuse to take the oath of fidelity will be obliged, during the war, to withdraw into the

/fol 3/country in the places assigned to them by the government.

Those who wish to leave it will obtain a license without delay and will be able to enter again, as foreigners, and recover possession of their property, in case they would have been left behind, which will be faithfully administered in their absence with no other deduction than that of simple administration expenses and general tax. Those who have voluntarily taken up arms against their homeland will be forever banished from it.

Every citizen who has sworn an oath of allegiance to the country has the misfortune to betray it, and it will be brought before the magistrates and punished severely by the laws.

OUTLINE FOR A FEDERATIVE GOVERNMENT

Are American Citizens: 1° all born in the country of free father and mother. 2° All foreigners who, being established and married in the country, take an oath of fidelity to the new government or who, not being married, make two campaigns for American independence; otherwise, they will remain in the alien class. The Legislature may, however, in particular cases, grant these rights to those it deems appropriate.

/fol 3v°.//**AMERICAN ELECTIONS**

These assemblies shall comprise all American citizens with the qualities the Constitution requires.

These qualities are: a territorial property of 10 "*Fanegadas*" [NA, in 1801, 10 arpents appear, that is, less land, and in 1808, 100 *Fanegas*] of arable land at least, and an age no younger than 21 years. The government will take care to distribute to each Indian citizen who does not have sufficient property 10 *Fanegadas* [NA in that of 1801 are arpents, that is, less land but enough to be able to vote] of arable land for the married, and five for the unmarried.

Citizens who lack these qualities will not have a vote in the assemblies, but this does not prevent them from enjoying other rights, such as passive Citizenship.

MUNICIPAL COUNCILS

The assembly will choose several representatives from among the district's active citizens to form the municipal bodies.

Its main functions are the politics and interim administration of cities or villages, as well as the election of members who must form the provincial Assembly. The age of these municipal representatives will be at least 25 [NA in the 1808 version appears 35] years, and they will have an income of at least 500 pesos.

PROVINCIAL ASSEMBLIES

These Assemblies will be composed of a certain number of citizens chosen by the municipal bodies from each province's general mass of active Citizens.

/fol 4/

Their obligations will be to ensure the health and administration of the province, to which effect they may make administrative laws which will not extend outside the province, nor will they impede the progress of the general rules. They shall also appoint among the American citizens of the respective provinces those who must compose the legislative body and have the right to petition this same body. Their age will not be under 30 years, and they should each have no less than 100 [NA in 1808 it appears 30] *fanegadas* of property land. The duration of these authorities will be 5 years.

They will also elect two citizens from across America to serve as executive power in the province for a term of 5 years. They will hold the title of *Curacas* and must be at least 30 years [in 1801, it appears 40] or own at least 150 Fanegadas of land.

LEGISLATIVE BODY

The legislative body will be composed of *Amantas* (sic) representatives appointed, as has been said, by the different assemblies of the provinces, in proportion to the population of each one. They must have a property of at least 150 Fanegadas of land, and the age must be at least 30 years [NA in 1801 appears 35].

This Assembly shall be known as the Colombian Council and shall alone have the power to enact general laws for the American Confederation. These laws will pass with a simple majority of votes, but they must be sanctioned by the executive power, which will have the right to return the bill with its observations to the Council. However, if, despite these observations, the Council votes for the same law by a majority of two-thirds of its members, the executive power will be compelled to comply with it by having it executed immediately.

If two-thirds of the Diet find that any constitutional law must be amended, the executive power will be obliged to pass it to the provincial assemblies to take their opinion on it, and if three-quarters of these agree with the vote of the Diet, the law will be amended. The assemblies, and vice versa, will also have the initiative in this part, and if three-quarters of the Diet agree, the result will be the same as the previous one, and the proposed law will be admitted and put into effect.

The powers of the representatives to the Diet will not last more than 5 years, but they may be re-elected for the subsequent Diet.

EXECUTIVE POWER

The Colombian Council will appoint this power. He will choose among all the citizens of the Empire two persons older than 40, who own property of 200 Fanegadas, and have exercised at least one of the significant positions of the empire. The individuals who secure this position will hold it for 5 years and cannot be recruited until after another 5 years. They will carry the title of *Yncas*, a venerable name in the country.

One of the *Yncas* will remain constantly close to the legislative body in the Federal City, while the other will visit the provinces of the empire.

The *Yncas* will appoint two Citizens for the function of *Questors* (Quaestors) or administrators of the public treasury: Two others for that of *Ediles*, mainly responsible for the preparation and repair of the great roads, and two others with the title of Censors who will make the census of the empire, will watch over public instruction, and the preservation of good customs. The requisite age for these jobs will be 32 years [NA in the 1801 version, appears not less than 45 years, nor 40 for the *Ediles* and *Questors*] and will not exceed 5 years.

Several Questors, both in the provinces and in the armies (provincial and military), will be in absolute charge of collecting public receipts, paying the troops, and other related tasks, as mandated by the laws and regulations of the empire.

In all the provinces, there will also be *Ediles* (councillors), who, like those of the Capital (urban), will be in charge of the care of the Cities, public buildings, temples, aqueducts, sewers, etc., as well as the public markets and weights and measures. They will also review the theatre performances in advance and have exclusive direction of the public games and parties alone.

There will also be Censors in the provinces taking charge of the census of all citizens, according to the form prescribed by the Capital. This Census will be sent punctually every 5 years to the government, thus providing a complete cadastre of the entire empire. The Censors will further examine whether citizens take care of their land, whether their marriages are long deferred, and whether they have shown courage in war.

All these charges will be removable at the will of the executive power. The jobs mentioned above, or any others that are of the nomination of the executive power, may not be occupied by the members of the legislative body unless an interval of 2 years elapses after they have left their legislative function.

JUDICIAL POWER

The judiciary will comprise judges presiding over the different provincial courts. They will be named by-elections in the respective provinces, and their number will be determined by the executive power, with the agreement of the Provincial Assemblies, to establish the number of courts necessary. The *Ynca* will approve or disapprove of the election results, and in the latter case, it will send its disapproval to the Diet. If fair, the assembly will hold a new election; otherwise, the judge is legitimately elected and endowed with the charge. The judges will have the qualities of active citizens and be at least 32 years of age [NA in 1808 appears 40].

These charges are not removable and lifelong, unless of prevarication; in this case, they will be brought before the National Supreme Court, which alone can pronounce her dismissal.

The court forms and the sentences by juries shall be consistent with those of England and the United States of America. Until the mass of citizens is more educated to live in freedom, a special jury will be appointed. They will absolutely judge all civil or criminal matters.

The executive branch will appoint the National Supreme Court, which will be composed of a president and two judges chosen from among the national judges. This Court shall judge all matters relating to the law of nations, to treaties with the / fol 6/foreign powers, and finally/will judge all public officials accused of prevarication or any other state crime.

RELIGION

The Roman Catholic religion will be the national religion, and the hierarchy of the American clergy will be arranged in a provincial council convened for this purpose. The Constitution will admit complete tolerance, and no citizen will ever be concerned about their religious opinions.

The clergy and ministers of the gospel shall not be disturbed in any way in exercising their functions, to which effect they shall be excluded from all Civil or military employment.

Citizens who get rid of their lands will lose the precious right of Citizens until they acquire the portion necessary to recover it. The magistrates will fine those who neglect the culture of their lands for 3 consecutive years.

The Federal Capital will be founded at the most central point (perhaps in the Panama Isthmus) and will have the august name of Colombo, to whom the world owes the discovery of this beautiful portion of the earth.

5.3 The Constitutional Plan for the Brazilian Federation Prepared for a Revolution in Brazil in Connection with the Emancipation Expedition to Coro in 1806

Context:

Between June and the beginning of October 1806, a fantastic epistolary exchange unfolded between the Portuguese ambassador in London, Domingo Antonio de Sousa Coutinho, and a Liverpool merchant, Archibald Campbell, who presented himself as a spy and whistle-blower revealed a dual emancipatory conspiracy that Miranda was preparing against the governments of Spain and Portugal. The conspiracy aimed to revolutionise Brazil with a military disembarkation, seizing the opportunity provided by another planned disembarkation in Venezuela against the Spanish Empire to make the whole of Latin America independent of its respective metropolis.

Assessment of Miranda's involvement:

The fact that the letters were written before Miranda landed in Coro at the end of July 1806 gives the case an undeniable historical value. Whether written or not by Miranda, the ideas exposed in these letters deliver an indisputable testimony of Miranda's ideology. In July 1805, Miranda referred to a plan proposed by Liverpool traders providing boats for 10.000 soldiers.[77] This might have provided an opportunity for treason. The English whistle-blower claimed money from the Portuguese government in exchange for infiltrating the conspiratorial network and providing the names of Miranda's Lusitanian accomplices, as well as the locations of conspiracy and disembarkation. The precise amount of money required was justified, alluding to the benefits he had to forgo by not continuing to be part of this conspiracy as a commercial supplier to the insurgents. The announced operation in Brazil was to be closely coordinated with the operation in Venezuela, although the former was presented as totally dependent on the previous success of the latter. The primary objective of this coordination was to bring down both colonial empires simultaneously and establish two democratic regimes based on similar political constitutions.

Unfortunately, it has not been possible to find further information on this operation until now, nor has a concrete stance been taken by the Portuguese government, except that the ambassador at the highest level considered this complaint a severe threat. He decided exceptionally to classify it as ultra-secret, to the point that he dispensed with any intermediary (even writing the letters to Lisbon himself). Therefore, he informed only the Minister and the King, without using any other channel or creating an official record. The Ambassador also decided to conduct a confidential investigation into Campbell and his colleague, Rawson. These researches confirm the actual existence of these persons but with little helpful information, except that they were not very important persons. This fact further increases the mystery of the case.

The accuser's letters stopped when the news about Miranda's unsuccessful landing in Coro came out in London. However, it cannot be deduced that this was a fraud because the operation's completion in Brazil, as clearly stated from the beginning, depended on its success in Venezuela. Miranda's plan for landing in Coro, which took place between July and August of 1806, had dates and details that match so closely with the data and content of the letters of the denouncer that Miranda's involvement acquires an undeniable presumption of credibility.

Besides, the strict parallelism with the Coro Operation means that the betrayer was closely informed of the secret operation to Coro. Would it be a simple and complete counterfeit invented in England by only extrapolating the Coro project to Brazil? This doesn't look to be the case because:

- first, Miranda had organised his landing in Venezuela from the United States and Haiti; of course, the British Ambassador in the US and the US government were informed;

[77] Chapter 10, document 10.3.23. point IV, [*Archivo*...Vol. XVII, p. 245].

- second, the time necessary for any information from the United States or the Caribbean to arrive in England prevented the details of the Coro expedition from being known in real time;
- third, the denouncers seem to be ordinary persons without adequate knowledge of constitutional issues;
- fourth, the content of the letters about the political ideas fits so perfectly with Miranda's precursory proposals that it looks impossible to be merely invented or copied by common crooks.

That suggests that even in cases of fraud, these documents should have a concrete basis, such as one of the possible abandoned initiatives by Lusitanian patriots. From their potential conspiracy, the well-informed fraudsters could have decided to use it to extract easy money from the Portuguese power.

However, even in this hypothetical fraud scenario, what can be said about Miranda and his possible involvement with Brazilian rebels? Was it also a subtle invention organised to increase fear pressures on the Portuguese regime? Or was it also based upon Miranda's actual or potential plan and contacts for a continental revolution?

Although no definitive proof has been discovered until now, several elements converge to support the possibility of a precise link between Miranda and the Brazilian patriots. The accuracy and originality of the constitutional and political contents reported by the spy, its adequacy to the Brazilian case, the operational details and the correct announcement of the Coro landing, the copy of a Proclamation of Miranda (see Chap. 9, document 9.5. below), all these elements reveal factual contributions, directly or indirectly, from Miranda himself. Anyway, these elements could not have been the product of fraudsters' creativity. A simple merchant like Campbell or Rawson could not conceive, with coherence and without exaggeration, such sophisticated ideas so in advance of the current concepts.

In particular, three precise elements are in favour of the authenticity of Miranda's direct contribution to his plan for Brazil:

1. In the text of the Proclamation of the Independence of Brazil copied by the denouncer in August or September of 1806 (Chap. 9, Proclamations of Miranda, document 9.5.), the announcement of Napoleon usurping the throne of the Braganza is mentioned. However, this event was a personal prediction of Miranda, which did *occur 16 months later*, in December 1807, as a result of a secret negotiation between Napoleon and Spain through the Treaty of Fontainebleau, signed on the 27th of October of 1807 in the French city of that same name.[78] This forecast is equivalent to a personal signature from Miranda

[78] **Treaty of Fontainebleau (1807)**, bargained and concluded on 27 October 1807 between Manuel Godoy and Álvarez de Faría, in the names of the Spanish King Carlos IV de Bourbon and Napoleon Bonaparte. It stipulated the Franco-Spanish joint military invasion of Portugal (which had joined England). France and Spain aspired to the division of Portugal into 3 strips by the Douro and Tagus rivers, the North being reserved for the queen of Etruria, the South for Godoy and the centre for future negotiations with England, including the authorisation for the French troops to cross over

because he had mentioned such a probability only in confidential diplomatic letters that the merchant Campbell could have accessed only in the case that he was part of (or very close to) an actual conspiracy with Miranda. Indeed, the Precursor in France, between 1795 and 1797, feared and opposed a French invasion of Spain and Portugal, and was the first and only person to announce this invasion. Still, he did so in a very reserved way, for example, through personal correspondence with the President of the United States in 1798.[79] This information supports the thesis that Miranda contemplated an uprising in Brazil, in the event of a probable French invasion of Portugal, according to him. In a mind like Miranda's, such a forecast would have implied being ready to support such an uprising.

2. The content of this Proclamation develops not only the visionary philosophical conceptions of Miranda but also accounts for a style typical of this humanist that seems impossible to have been invented or even imitated. On the other hand, the philosophical positions subtly balanced in the proclamation could not have been written by fraudsters, as that would imply precise knowledge and a perfect interpretation of Miranda's original ideas, which were considered very advanced for that time. Therefore, they did not fit with the culture of marginal smugglers. The additional fact that this Proclamation does not correspond to excerpts from existing texts of Miranda for Spanish America, combined with the previous observations, leads us to think that this Proclamation could only be written by Miranda himself, either well before the Coro project or even in parallel with it, in order to prepare for the possibility of an extension of the movement in case of success in Coro. Another reason in line with Miranda's continental vision was the interest in a constitutional convergence between Spanish America and Brazil, which would speed up their integration.
3. The almost-absence of reference to the case of Brazil in Miranda's Archive seems rational from the point of view of his priorities and his strategy to prevent a conflict with the British government, the support of which he depended so much. Portugal was a key ally of England, and Miranda did not want to expose himself to diplomatic complaints from Lisbon, which would have jeopardised British support for its first priority, Colombia.

However, assuming the existence of Miranda's plan for Brazil, it cannot be clarified whether the Brazilian part of the conspiracy was a reality or only an extrapolation in Miranda's mind. In this hypothetical case, Miranda would have written a new constitution for Brazil in secret, with proclamations, to be ready in the most optimistic scenario of a general extension of the political upheavals against both colonial empires. According to Miranda's geopolitical perception, it is conceivable that his

the Spanish territory, thus being the antecedent of the subsequent French invasion of the Iberian Peninsula leading to the Spanish revolution of Independence of 1808 and the beginning of the end of Napoleonic successes.

[79] See Miranda's letters to President Adams, Prime Minister Pitt, and Hamilton in Chap. 10, documents 10.3.3, 10.3.4, and 10.3.5, all in 1798.

landing in Venezuela could trigger a broader revolution, extending to Brazil, in the event of a French invasion towards Portugal and Spain. It should also be noted that Lusitanian patriots were active in London, and some were in contact with Miranda. In this possible assumption, it is presumed that the denouncer had privileged access to Miranda's ideas and operational plans, i.e. through a very close "contact" with whom Miranda was very confident. In this case, Campbell would merely be a go-between, concealing the betrayer's identity. It should also be noted that in one of the letters, the denouncer provides the exact names of two British boats involved in the conspiracy, and the Portuguese Ambassador confirmed their existence and itinerary with Lloyd's.

At this point, two sub-hypotheses remain plausible:

- Either the plan was effective, and a betrayer inside Miranda's circles directly informed the scammer.
- Or was the plan just an obsolete possibility, giving Miranda's co-operator/contact ideas to make money without betraying any reality? Even in this case (or in the case of ignoring the dates or the precise connections between Venezuela and Brazil), as soon as this betrayer/scammer learned about the Coro project, he might have imagined by his own deduction a possible link between both landing plans. A fortiori, in the case that Miranda would have abandoned (or failed to establish the necessary Brazilian contacts), a profitable opportunity would have arisen. Nevertheless, this hypothesis implies that the real brain of this scam was not a mere trader or smuggler but a very high-rank diplomat and/or an intimate "betrayer", for example, from the Pitt's close circle or the United States, informed by the preparation in New York of the Coro expedition and its failure.

Deductive hypothesis on the identity of the traitor or crook: Whatever the involvement of Miranda in the texts for a project of the Brazilian constitution, a betrayer or a crook intervened to extract money from the Portuguese authorities. Nevertheless, the way the denunciation was made, even in the hypothesis of a scam, the existence of a brilliant mind endowed with exclusive knowledge not available to many people at this time was necessary. Although there is no formal proof to designate a culprit, in terms of probabilities, it is fitting to orientate further investigation on a controversial figure in American history which concentrates several of the outstanding abilities for being the betrayer or the crook: Aaron Burr, ex-vice-President of the United States. Several elements give convergent and precise presumptions to the hypothesis that Aaron Burr had a conflict of interest with Miranda's plan for the independence of the Spanish colonies:

- Aaron Burr had many opportunities to be perfectly informed about Miranda's views: as a member of Jefferson's government, in close contact with his political rival Hamilton (who shared Miranda's ideas and supported his emancipation plan), but also for his close and ambiguous relations with the Ambassadors of England and Spain.
- Jefferson dismissed Burr in March 1805 for suspicion of conspiracy.

- Burr knew Miranda well; they had mutual animosity; they precisely met in Philadelphia in December 1805, when Miranda was travelling from New York to see Jefferson and Madison in Washington for asking military assistance before sailing to Coro.
- Burr informed the Spanish Ambassador on the Coro objective of Miranda; indeed, Spanish authorities took critical preparatory measures to repeal the invasion
- Burr established a plan of conquest of part of Mexico and even planned to provoke a secession of part of the South of the United States to «erect a great Southern Empire» under his rule [Burr, T., 1902].[80] Such a big plan was proved later, and he was arrested in 1807 for treason, but, amazingly, despite evidence about Burr's proposals to Britain and Spain to foment secession in the US, an unclear trial [Hoffer, 2008][81] failed to condemn him [Stewart, D., 2011].[82]
- It was also proved in his trial that Burr conspired with the Ambassador of England (Anthony Merry), some Mexican local authorities, and even the Ambassador of Spain (Carlos Martínez de Irujo y Tacón), from whom he received payments, the idea being that Burr pretended to dismantle the United States, objective interesting for Spain and Britain.
- Burr was also in need of money to finance his private army
- Making the denunciation from London was much safer for him than in the US.

In addition, the chronology indicates the possibility that Burr to have sent to his agents in England the instructions and contended for organising the extraction of money from the Portuguese Ambassador once Miranda's expedition to Coro had effectively sailed from New York (February 1806). At this moment, the Spanish military took measures to oppose Miranda's landing in Venezuela. Burr escaped the US territory and followed his project from England, where he arrived in 1808. He tried to get the British government's support for taking over Mexico. He was expelled from Britain in 1809, and in 1810, he offered the same project to Napoleon[83] without no further success. He amazingly entered into a close relationship with Jeremy Bentham, Miranda's friend, who nicknamed him «the Emperor of Mexico».[84]

In the Miranda Archive, however, there are two enigmatic references to Portugal or Brazil, which might open more hypotheses:

1. The first, in a 'journal note' dated July 1805, where he expresses his fear that "*Mr Pitt has been negotiating with my person... and that he has offered to Portugal the same bargaining as what he did with Spain: to maintain its neutral-*

[80] Burr Todd, C., [1902], *A General History of the Burr Family*, Knickerboker Press, New York, p. 94

[81] Hoffer, [2008], *The treason trials of Aaron Burr*, University. Press of Kansas.

[82] Stewart, D. O. [2011]. *American Emperor: Aaron Burr's Challenge to Jefferson's America*. New York: Simon & Schuster.

[83] Ibid, p. 287–289.

[84] Ibid, p. 281.

ity and independence against England assures of not disturbing its colonies…[85]". This information might confirm Miranda's concern about a possible diplomatic complaint from Portugal if he conspires with the Brazilian patriots. It could also indicate that the denunciation had come from Pitt's direct environment shortly after his death. Still, such sensitive information was limited to very few people trusted by Pitt. The fact to sell for money such information would then be due either to the mere venality of a discarded diplomat or instead to an additional British manipulation of Miranda's reputation for their geopolitical interests by making the Portuguese government more aware their regime was exposed—like Spain—to imminent external risks that would recommend a stronger alliance with the UK and its Royal Navy.

2. The second, dated January 10, 1808, is much more explicit and offers indices of the existence of a plan for Brazil since it refers to "*it cannot be feared that* [the Viceroyalty of New Granada] *interferes with the preparations that now are made in Brazil.*[86]". Miranda had returned from his failed Coro expedition a few days earlier. He could have continued to contact the Lusitanian patriots shortly before arriving in London and, obviously, by prudent reserve, kept it highly secret so that the British government would not be aware. Indeed, after the Coro expedition, Miranda resided in Trinidad for more than a year, one of the places mentioned by the spy where the conspirators were hiding arms for invading Brazil. It may be part of the arms used in Coro, given to the Brazilian rebels by Miranda.

Despite these uncertainties, whether true or not, the plan for Brazil's emancipation reveals interesting information on Miranda's thinking on constitutional and political aspects at that time. From the previous analysis, two highly probable hypotheses can be deduced:

- a genuine Miranda conspiracy for Brazil, directly or not, or
- an invention of someone who was very well informed and able to extrapolate Miranda's thinking to the case of Brazil for unclear reasons.

In both cases, and regardless of whether the letters are from a real spy or a skilled fraudster, they provide the historian with a journalistic service, demonstrating the most valuable features of Miranda's authentic constitutional ideas as they were conceived in 1806, according to our own contextualist method. It seems perfectly coherent that Miranda could have conceived this parallel plan for Brazil, given that he always had a continental vision for emancipation. Nevertheless, there is no formal proof of his direct implication in Brazil.

Content:

The revolution must be without any violence and respectful of persons and properties, but an agrarian reform will be organised, and nobody will be above the law. A federal organisation in 30 districts electing each at universal suffrage (for men),

---

[85] Chapter 10, document 10.37.3, taken from *Archivo….* Vol. XVII, p. 248.

[86] Chapter 10, document 10.4.5. Miranda's letter to the British Minister Lord Castlereagh.

10 deputies forming a Parliament named the «*Council of Brazil*» for 3 years; these 300 deputies elect 30 of its members to set a Senate, the «*Supreme Council of Brazil*», and appoint for 4 years a *Prime Minister* who has a veto on the proposed legislation but remained accountable to the legislative power.

Sources:

They were translated from Portuguese. The complete original documents (a set of 58 letters sent by the "spy"/denunciator written in English, including the reports in Portuguese from the hand of HE the Ambassador) are in the Instituto Arquivo Nacional da "*Torre do Tombo*", in Lisbon,[87] identified with the reference: *MNE CX 725.*[88] In 2006, the author checked the complete and perfect authentication of the original and the copies made by Parra-Perez in 1935. The Parra-Pérez copies are also kept in *Archivo de la Academia Nacional de la Historia* (Caracciolo Parra Pérez. Papeles de Miranda. Armario VII. Carpeta 11).

Published in Spanish under the title:

Miranda y la independencia del Brasil, in el *Boletín de la Academia Nacional de la Historia*.- Caracas. Año XIX. N° 73, enero-marzo 1936, p. 146–153. Later, Caracciolo Parra Pérez (1888–1963), reprinted on pages 135–142, in his book *Páginas de Historia y de Polémica*.- Caracas: [s.n.], 1943 (Lit. del Comercio). as well as in the book of Nucete Sardi, José Vicente (Mérida - Estado Mérida: 4-8-1897 – Caracas, Venezuela, 12-11-1972): (Comp.): *Documentos Mirandinos. Prolegómenos de la Emancipación Iberoamericana*/Caracas, Venezuela: [Edit. Ávila Gráfica]. - 1950; Instituto Panamericano de Geografía e Historia. Comisión de Historia. Comité de Orígenes de la Emancipación. Publicación N°. 9. Véase: p. 94–104.

Later published also in:

Historia de la Primera República de Venezuela/Caracciolo Parra Pérez; – Caracas: Fundación Biblioteca Ayacucho, Impresión 2011. (Colección Clásica; 183).

Some of these documents are reproduced and translated in Spanish and without critical analysis of their context and authenticity, in the book ***América espera/* Francisco de Miranda**; J.L. Salcedo Bastardo, Caracas: Biblioteca Ayacucho, 1982 n°100, doc. N° 73, p. 344–353,

It is also helpful to consult Fugier, André:

Napoléon et l'Espagne: 1799–1808... París: Félix Alcan, 1930 (Dijon: Darantière) 1929.2 v. ("Biblioteca d'Histoire Contempe."). See Vol. II. p. 63. Note 2.

Napoleón y España, 1799–1808/André Fugier; traducción del francés - Madrid: Sociedad Estatal de Conmemoraciones Culturales: Centro de Estudios Políticos y Constitucionales, 2008. See Cap. V. Talleyrand y el proyecto portugués, p. 417, 422 a 424.

Texts:

[87] Created in 1378 to archive all the documents from the Portuguese royal chancellery.

[88] Lisbon Ministry of Foreign Affairs. Legation in London. On May 8. (Reproduced in *Le Moniteur* on the 16th. Sousa Coutinho a Aráujo, April 5. Secretissimo). August 4, 1806, with a voluminous Miranda file.

5.3.1 Denunciation of Miranda's Conspiracy to Invade Brazil in a Letter to HE, the Ambassador of Portugal in London, Warning About Miranda's Conspiracy to Invade Brazil

Report to Lisbon[89]

Liverpool, 24 June 1806

Thank you very much, dear friend, for your punctual delivery of my message, which I received yesterday morning and today. As you had asked, Mr. Hobhouse was kind enough to come twice with your letter to deliver it to me in my own hands. When I said in my last communication that I expected to be reimbursed the £ 2500 that I would lose if this expedition were discovered, I assumed that His Excellency [NA: Domingos Antonio de Sousa Coutinho[90]] had the discretionary power of his Court to give me that assurance, but seeing that this is not the case and knowing the importance of the information, as well as the danger of delay in such a critical period, I will cease from my first proposition and proceed to reveal as much of this extraordinary matter as I have come to know, except certain circumstances and names that as an honourable man I am not free to reveal at this time, trusting in the high honour of His Excellency and the generosity of his Court, without seeking any other assurance on his part than his statement and ours that he will state the whole matter and do whatever he considers adequate to get my loss reimbursed. As for my acquaintance with Miranda and his behaviour in London, that would be tedious and uninteresting. Suffice it to say, and his Excellency will notice my words, that they deserve attention. Whoever supposes that Miranda has embarked on a speculative adventure, depending on the casual attendance of a few disgruntled people in America, without the endorsement or recognition of any Power, is entirely wrong. The fact is that he attempts a long and well-arranged expedition, invited by thousands of his compatriots, who are ready to help the expedition with their lives and resources, that a powerful military manoeuvre of diversion will be made in his favour and that probably from here in a few months the Spanish power in that part of the globe will have disappeared. If I had the freedom to reveal specific names and facts, you would see that his attempt would be assisted by a great and powerful Government, against which the Spanish have no means to resist, but on this subject, I have no freedom to say more; "tempus exalux rerum", will give results and will see

[89]The original letters are in English but were translated to Spanish in *America Espera*, [1982], op. cit., which we again translated back into English after having checked them in Portuguese diplomatic archives.

[90]**Domingos António de Sousa Coutinho**, first Marquis of Funchal (1762–1833), ambassador of King of Portugal in London (1803–1814). He was intensely involved in secret diplomatic negotiations at this time as Portugal openly sided with Britain and refused to join the Continental System; Sousa Coutinho was instrumental in arranging the details of the transfer of the Portuguese court to Brazil with British Foreign Secretary George Canning.

that Miranda is not a gross adventurer, but rather a bold, active and enterprising commander and, I think he has been very successful.

I cannot say precisely when the expedition to Brazil was decided. Still, I have reason to suppose that it was part of Miranda's great plan from the beginning and that a similar attempt accompanied every step taken in Spanish America to prepare the people for revolution on Portuguese territory. Among those people who were associated with the project from the beginning is a gentleman from Brazil, a man with unlimited wealth and a restless character with immense ambition; I have heard his name frequently (but since this was some time ago, I cannot remember it today; but I know that he has a son or brother also a native of Brazil, who is currently in Lisbon and is one of the conspirators). For his wealth and influence, this gentleman greatly benefited Miranda, both in England and America. He expressed an insatiable will to be an active patriot for his own country; he used all the resources that a man of his fortune and influence had to prepare the minds of the people in Brazil to break their commitment to the Portuguese Government. In this business, he was mightily assisted by some priests he had managed to convince for his own purposes. Great incentives have been offered to those who join this association. In short, everything possible to win them to this cause has been rehearsed. They have had enough ingenuity to show that France and Spain were about to unite their arms to overthrow the present Government of Portugal and seize Brazil and that the present association was not so much to separate from the Portuguese Government as to avoid falling under the rule of Spain; In short, the plan has been carefully studied by men of considerable talent and endorsed by others of great fortune and influence in the Colony; nor do I pretend to be aware of all the details, but they will be found in hand of the conspirators, as well as the names of all those interested, both in Portugal and in Brazil. The entire plan is now almost ready to be executed. In about 2 weeks, the two gentlemen in charge of the project here will leave for Lisbon, where they will meet the rest of the associates and proceed to Madeira. There, they will embark on a North American ship that will land on the island as if it were for wine; the vessel will appear as owned by a citizen of the United States on its way to the East Indies, protected by this ruse. His course will not be interrupted. The actual object of his journey will not be suspected. From Madeira, they will have to go to Santo Domingo, where they have a large stock of weapons, provisions and everything necessary for their big expedition; all the detailed explanations will be found in the abovementioned papers. My knowledge of these facts is due partly to General Miranda himself and partly to one of the gentlemen currently in London, who has urged me to join the expedition, which I have so far declined because of my business commitments. I am convinced that if I proposed to participate in the project, it would allow me to obtain any other required information. Still, for reasons of personal friendship, I will undoubtedly stipulate that the Government of Portugal protect his person and property. I will see that they do not leave England without my knowledge, and His Excellency can trust that I will give him the most timely information through you of that intention to leave. The way to take advantage of this information is to keep it reserved to the least possible because I know with certainty that the conspirators have friends in the Court of Lisbon who would find out if anything escaped.

Once those two gentlemen are traced to Lisbon, it will be easy to trace them to Madeira. They arrest all the heads of the operation with all the papers related to the plot. I have received the £ 198 compliant banknotes and will forward this in a few days to Manchester, from where I will go to Stockport, Leeds and the other manufacturing towns and then to Scotland, but if you forward your letters as last via Liverpool, they will follow me. Believe me, your very sincere friend,

Archibald Campbell

P.S. The old Winaughton died and gave as heritage to his son in Africa an amount of £ 17.000.

Liverpool 8 July 1806

I am grateful for your favour on the fifth of the current. Since my last letter to you on the 30th of the previous month, I have had several conversations with Jennings about his current expedition. From what I have been able to gather, I will endeavour to give His Excellency any information that may be useful. Still, it is necessary to note that although Jennings has told me a great deal about the general features of the plan, there is various detailed information, such as names of places and people, etc., which he has reserved because, as he says, it is not necessary to mention names; yet his servant has promised, if I pay him well, to get me whatever names I need. I must confess that I would not be entirely pleased or interested in this way of proceeding or in any other if it weren't for a matter of public concern and one in which I feel I am doing a good job. I discovered something I did not know until then: that the European part of the conspiracy is only waiting for Miranda's information. If his success meets their expectations, they will not waste time leaving for America. If he succeeds in this expedition, I think that the Portuguese Government will find it challenging to prevent a revolt in its Colonies unless it immediately takes the preventive measures that the magnitude and necessity of the matter require. When you hear Jennings's account, it can be genuinely assumed that most of the Crown officials and all the Clergy in that country are involved in the conspiracy; at least, I believe many people secretly favour the revolt, but they do not dare to acknowledge their feelings until a decisive blow is struck. As regards the natives and the inhabitants of the interior of the country, he declares that they are unanimously in favour of the conspirators and ready to join them as soon as they are given notice; he has particularly mentioned the names of Pernambuco, Porto Seguro, Rio de Janeiro, Paraiba and São Paulo as prominent in the confederation; the last place mentions it as a place of refuge for several of the leaders before the plan was partially executed. They have already sent a considerable quantity of arms and ammunition to the country's interior, primarily through Rio de Janeiro. I have also learned from him that they have a substantial park on the island of Trinidad; by the way, according to their relationship, it must be immense, and all of it is acquired by subscription among Brazilians. They have an agent in Trinidad who is currently dealing with all correspondence with Europe. At this moment, I have received his letter of the fourth, in which he says that His Excellency intended to arrange for him to go [to the port of] Deal in order to find out something about Isabela. In my opinion, it will not succeed; you can be sure that they are on notice and will only mislead you, but I will find out from Jennings' servant his true destiny, or I am very wrong: the guy appreciates me and likes money so that I have it on both sides; he indeed has the opportunity to see the papers of his master, but by what means it is not for me to find out; he tells me that Jennings expects at any moment for a Mr. Corry from New York, who has been a very active agent of the people involved in this matter; he says that the time when (J.) will leave England will be determined by the information he receives from this Mr. Corry. Jennings's servant promised to show me the letters his boss will receive from America. Therefore, something will be drawn from them; if Miranda is defeated, the plans for Brazil will end there; if he succeeds, warn the Court of Portugal. You will hear from me again very soon.

Your faithful server,
Archa. Campbell

5.3.2 Secret report from the Portuguese Ambassador in London to His Minister

Top Secret:

Finally, I am taking the resolution to send to Your Excellency, using this safe shipment, including the letters I previously announced to you.

I have been hoping for almost 2 months to achieve a result that would satisfy me and leave no doubt in the minds of H.R.M and V. Excellence. But now that I face the challenge of continuing, I am afraid to delay the news more, and I believe that it is my obligation to make Your Excellency judge its importance by yourself.

In the first days of June, I received the attached letter to p. 1, accompanied (or preceded, I do not remember well) by a note that I lost. In it, I was asked to indicate in writing a safe person to whom to trust a secret of the highest importance. I replied that you should write directly to me, and I received the letter dated June 10.

In reply, I proposed a meeting in writing to discuss a date for speaking directly with Mr. Arch. Campbell, at any place Mr. Rawson would indicate in the letter, p. 5, of June 11.

Have H.E. the patience to go through the following letters, and you will see that Mr. A. Campbell attributes to General Miranda in the first place and to his associates, the project of revolutionising Brazil; that he claims to have a party formed in that kingdom; that Mr. Jennings, whose servant he claims to have bribed, is a man who has lived in Spanish America, and Brazil, and is one of Miranda's agents, who has insured him to participate in this project; that there is an arms depot in Brazil; that the commissioners will be distributed throughout the interior after landing on the coast with the help of smugglers, as he says, (and I have evidence), by people employed in the government of various captaincies.

You will see, Your Excellency, that his first advice is to capture on the Island of Madeira or Sta. Catalina, these commissioners who are to go aboard the ship Isabelle Cap. Green—which should be now in Lisbon and will surely be smuggling off the coast of Brazil because that is the current way used by the traffickers who dispatch to the customs offices of Río de la Plata, and this is what is advertised on the Lloyd's list.

After my observation that by not knowing who the conspirators were, one could do more harm than good and that it was improper to hijack a ship without evidence, this step could involve difficulties with the United States, &&&.

After the little result obtained from reading Jennings' papers (as he says), his opinion is to infiltrate the expedition with a reliable man associated with it.

I replied that I did not know anyone to propose to him and that, in short, it was necessary first to report everything to Your Excellency.

Of all the questions I have asked him about the nature of the project, the quality and quantity of weapons, the number of people, the place of "Rendez-vous" here and in Brazil, and the names—finally—of the Brazilian leaders, it was this last point that has been the most difficult to get an answer to. Alleging my reluctance to make vague accusations that could compromise innocent people, Your Excellency will see his answer in the letter of July 19 (page 43).

So, I do not see anything sure or even probable in all this information. Still, instead of the two ships, Isabelle (Cap. Green) and Ruby (Cap. George Bunker), they have to arrive at Madeira Island and then unload contraband off the coast of Brazil. I see no other truth or probability in this expedition than contraband with these fast sailing cutters. I tried to find out, through the Police, what kind of men were both this Mr. Arch. Campbell and Mr. Rawson. From the 1st. I am waiting for information from Liverpool, and I already know that he is a merchant of the Established House. Still, of these travellers and traders who go with their own resources to Africa and America, from the second, Mr. Rawson, I made the Police members follow him. All I have discovered so far is that he is a Dutchman who lives in some sense in hiding and, indeed, is a modest person.

I must warn Your Excellency that the police magistrates, both in this city and in Liverpool, were not informed about the reason for investigating Mr. Arch. Campbell and his relationship with me; I have only asked them to tell me about these men's normal behaviour and qualifications.

No one but me has read these letters—this affair, while imperfect, remains highly secret. Please, Your Excellency, consider the matter and advise me on how I should proceed.

These men, especially Mr. Arch. Campbell, who seems to want the money he thinks he lost (1 and 2500 lbs.) as a reward, does not ask me for any money at the moment—and I hardly think they ask for even the 100 guineas from Jennings' servant.

If we are to be associated with these men, a conditional and secret promise would not be hurtful.

To completely neglect information of this kind seems to me to be dangerous. Spreading it is even more dangerous. In short, Your Excellency will think and design to order what should be done, begging for the approval of S.A.R. so that this business remains exclusively in the hands of Your Excellency, whom God will keep for many years.

(a) Mr. Domingo Antonio de Sousa Coutinho

5.3.3 Political Project for Brazil 1806 (Attributed to Miranda)

London, 4th of August 1806

One of the first steps to take in Brazil (see the proclamation) is to arrest all Government Officials, their wives, children, etc., and hold them hostage to ensure the people of the conspirators against harm or punishment. This was determined to be the most viable way to prevent the severe punishment of those involved in the rebellion, as they were convinced that if they could demonstrate to the crowd that they were not in danger of joining the flag, there would be no man who hesitated to join the conspiracy.

This deserves careful attention.

5th of September 1806

That day, Jennings showed (to Rawson) the headings of the plan for the new Government of Brazil, plus other documents related to the same topic and a large trunk full of proclamations in several languages to be distributed around that country; he also showed me the copious correspondence he has maintained with the leaders since 1797, in which many of his designs are revealed. Apparently, they intended to attempt the Independence of the Colonies before the last governor-in-chief was recalled. Still, whether the new one was aware of this, or for other reasons unknown to me, the plan was abandoned for the time being and deferred to a more favourable opportunity; on that occasion, they had decided to make that first attempt of the new plan for the Government in San Salvador and then in more distant locations (a resumé in so far as I can recall it), which would have been entertaining.

Brazil would be divided into 30 districts, and each district would be subdivided into another 10, thus creating 300 minor divisions altogether; each division would send a Member to a free, elected and representative Council named the Council of Brazil; those members would all be elected by the people of their respective district; each male individual older than 21 would be part of the representation. Each member would have to write the name of the person he thinks is most eligible as a representative and will insert it in a box placed for that purpose in a principal church; a month after the day of the elections, the box would be opened, and the person whose name appeared most frequently, would be elected. Similarly, when the Elective Free Council meets, it would select among its members 30 men well-known for their talent, integrity and experience to form what would be called the Supreme Council of Brazil; it would also appoint one of them to fulfil the function of Prime Minister or Great Elector; this office would last 4 years, but the two Councils would be elected every 3 years, thus leaving the people the freedom to choose their legislators. They would promulgate laws and civil and military regulations, establish taxes and order and control the distribution of public funds; the decision would be by majority in both assemblies; the Great Elector has the power to agree or disagree with these resolutions, although any member of the Assemblies can subject his conduct to investigation and judgement at the end of his period; in that case, a Council called the Emergency Council will have been nominated, until the circumstances allow for the application of the adopted measures.

A draft proclamation of the Brazilians copied in English at the time of the landing also probably indicates Miranda's participation:

… "We have weapons, and we are men. The Portuguese government has ceased to be legitimate in Brazil. The tyrant of France usurped that throne and intends to seize those rich and fertile provinces as part of her conquest. But will the Brazilians calmly submit their neck to the yoke of a tyrant?

May our motto be Liberty or Death.

Brazilians, we are hereditary owners of the land, and we must not allow the terror of being treated as rebels to influence our spirits for a moment … ".

The conspirators hope to be able to gather an army of 40,000 men, a necessary number in a country as extensive as Brazil.

5.3.4 Proclamation to Be Issued During the Invasion of Brazil

See in Chap. 9 Miranda's main Proclamations, document 9.5.

5.3.5 Short Comment from the Betrayer/Scammer

"There was more information, mainly regarding Miranda's supposed success in the Spanish provinces and exhorting the Brazilians to follow their example, but I did not have the opportunity to copy it."

References

Academía Nacional de la Historia, [1961], *El pensamiento Constitucional Hispanoamericano hasta 1830*, Vol. V, Venezuela, Sesquicentenario de la Independencia, Caracas.

Adams, J., [1856], *The Works of John Adams, by his grandson Charles Francus Adams*, Boston, Little, Brown and Company, (10 vol).

Baugh, D., [1988], "Great Britain's 'Blue-Water' Policy, 1689–1815," The International History Review 10:1 (February 1988): 33–58.

Betti, D. [2008] «American Revolutionaries: Alexander Hamilton & Francisco de Miranda», 2008. Available at SSRN: https://ssrn.com/abstract=4410146 or http://dx.doi.org/10.2139/ssrn.4410146

Brewer, J., [1994], *The Sinews of Power. War, Money and the English State, 1688-1783*, London, Unwin Hyman, re-edited Routledge, 1994 [1989]

Burr Todd, C., [1902], *A General History of the Burr Family*, Knickerboker Press, New York.

Dziembowski, E., [2023], *La main cachée, une autre histoire de la Révolution Française*, Perrin, Paris.

Fugier, A., [1930], *Napoléon et l'Espagne: 1799-1808*, Felix Alcan, Paris.

Ghymers, C. [2002], "Influencia del Maestro sobre el Discípulo: el papel de Miranda y O'Higgins en la singularidad del caso chileno y de su gobernabilidad", *Revista del Instituto O'Higginiano de Chile*, n° 19.

Grases, P., [1966], *El Colombiano de Francisco de Miranda y dos documentos americanistas*, Instituto Nacional de Hipódromos, colección venezolanista.

Hamilton, A., Madison, J., Jay, J. [1787, 1982], *The Federalist Papers*, reedition by Wills, G., Bantam Books, New York.

Hamilton, A. [1961], *The papers of Alexander Hamilton in 27 vols*. Eds Harold Syrett & Jacob Cooke, New York: Columbia University Press,

Hoffer, [2008], *The treason trials of Aaron Burr*, University. Press of Kansas,

Maugras, G., de Croze-Lemercier, P., [1912], Delphine de Sabran Marquise de Custine, Plon, Paris.

Maddison, A. [1995], Monitoring the World Economy 1820 – 1992, Development Center Studies, OECD, Paris.

Miranda, F. de [1929-1950], *Archivo del General Miranda*, ed. Vicente Dávila/ Rubén González, Caracas/La Habana.

Miranda, F. de [1978 – still in publication], *Colombeía*, Edición de la Presidencia de la República, Caracas.

Morrow, J, [1998], "Mixed Government, Balanced Constitutions and the Separation of Powers", in: *History of Political Thought*. Palgrave, London. https://doi.org/10.1007/978-1-349-25939-7_10

Parra-Pérez, C., [1943/1936], *Paginas de Historia y de Polémica*, Litografía del Comercio, Caracas.

Parra-Pérez, C., [1950], *Miranda et Madame de Custine,* Bernard Grasset, Paris

Salcedo-Bastardo, J. [1982], *América espera / Francisco de Miranda*, : Biblioteca Ayacucho, n°100, Caracas.

Syrett, H. ed. [1974], *The papers of Alexander Hamilton,* Columbia University Press, New York

Stewart, D. O. [2011], *American Emperor: Aaron Burr's Challenge to Jefferson's America*. Simon & Schuster, New York.

Vane, C. Marquess of Londonderry, [1848], Memoirs and Correspondence of Viscount Castlereagh, Henry Colburn, London. https://archive.org/details/memoirscorrespon001cast

Chapter 6
Miranda's Political Manifestos in Francia (1795)

6.1 General Miranda's Manifesto to the Representatives of the French People, Paris, Prison "La Force", 2 January 1795 (13 Nivôse)

Context:

After the Nootka Sound Agreement and the Escorial Treaty[1] (October 1790), signed by William Pitt with the Spanish government, temporarily sverted a costly war against England, Miranda's efforts to gain the support of London were lost. Hence, he turned towards revolutionary France, which Miranda had defended from London alongside Thomas Paine [1791, 1792][2] against the conservative criticisms of Edmund Burke [1790].[3] As a result, he had the opportunity to come into contact with the revolutionaries and developed close ties with the moderate party, known as the Girondins. Miranda arrived in Paris on March 23, 1792, when his "Girondin" political friends took charge of the government after the fall of the conservative government appointed by the King. Implementing the constitutional monarchy, approved in September 1791, was destined to end the revolution peacefully.

[1] It is also known as the **First Nootka Convention**. It was concluded between Spain and England, committing to several areas (fishing, navigation and trade) relative to the Pacific Ocean and the South Seas and referring to the colonial settlements on the Northwest coast of America. The Count of Florida Blanca and Alleyne Fitz-Herbert signed it in San Lorenzo el Real on October 28, 1790.

[2] **Thomas Paine,** see Chap. 5, document 5.2.1., note n°12 and Chap. 10, document 10.2.10. note n°38. He wrote *The Rights of Man* to answer Edmund Burke's attacks against the French Revolution.

[3] **Edmund Burke**, see Chap. 5, document 5.2.1., note n°13. He wrote *Reflections on the Revolution in France*,

C. Ghymers, *Independence, Federalism and Regionalism in Latin America: An Analytical Anthology of Francisco de Miranda's Writings (1790-1811)*,
United Nations University Series on Regionalism 34,
https://doi.org/10.1007/978-3-031-96938-6_6

However, the political situation deteriorated, marked by the typical difficulty of cooperation between the legislative and executive branches, exacerbated by the conflict between the left and the right, as well as the attitude of the European monarchies hostile toward the revolution.[4] The Girondins wanted to end this external threat, and the Minister of Foreign Affairs, Dumouriez,[5] urged the King to declare war (April 1792) on the Emperor of Austria, brother of Queen Marie-Antoinette. Miranda, who had broken with Pitt, saw in this new democratic regime— the Constitution of 1791 established a mixed government with separation of powers— that was intended to export its liberal revolution to the world, an alternative favourable to developing his emancipation plans for Latin America. However, in August 1792, France was defeated and invaded by Austria, which had allied with Prussia, marking the first coalition against revolutionary France. Miranda was requested by his Girondin friends to help defend the French Revolution with his experience as a professional military. The deal was that in exchange for this emergency help, he would later get reciprocal military support from France to liberate his homeland.

---

[4]Declaration of Pillnitz, August 1791, by the Emperor of Austria and the King of Prussia, promoted by the French aristocrats in exile, threatening the French population in case of harming the French Monarchy, an argument used by the Girondins to justify the export of the revolution to the other European dynasties. This declaration had very counterproductive effects on French opinion, making the monarchy appear linked to outside enemies.

[5]**Charles-François Dumouriez** (1739–1823), a career military officer in the King's army, joined the Revolution to support a constitutional monarchy, began his political career in the Jacobin ranks in 1790 (before extremists dominated the movements), a friend of La Fayette, Mirabeau and Danton. In 1792, he was appointed general. When the conservative cabinet fell in April 1792, the Girondins, who entered the monarchical government, appointed him Minister of Foreign Affairs; he immediately declared war on the Austrians but was dismissed in June 1792. After August 10, 1792, Danton commissioned him as general of the Northern army, replacing La Fayette, who had defected. His mission was to stop the invasion of the first coalition (Austria and Prussia). Miranda was required to reinforce him. They won together the battle of Valmy. However, Dumouriez's orders not to continue the fight to eliminate the Prussian threat looked like a tactical error or a suspect arrangement. The Prussian army withdrew outside France. There might be that Dumouriez already had in mind at that time a plan of alliance with them in case of the radicalisation of the Jacobins. Another hypothesis would be a corruption deal between Danton and the enemies. Instead of pursuing the Prussian, Dumouriez opted to invade Belgium with Miranda to expel the Austrians for extending France up to "natural borders". He left Miranda in charge of the army in Liège to return to Paris, where he undertook political manoeuvres with the Girondins against the Jacobins. At the end of January, looking for an external victory, he decided to invade the Netherlands, against Miranda's opinion. The Austrians took advantage of this dispersion to counterattack on the Eastern border of Belgium, leading to a dramatic French defeat on March 18, 1793, after which Dumouriez defected and passed to the Austrian side (see following note). He accused Miranda of being the cause of his military disaster and lived in exile. In 1800, he used to advise the British government in London against France and tried to discredit Miranda's reputation. With Napoleon's invasion of the Iberian peninsula in 1808, he worked for the Portuguese and the Spanish, inspiring the guerrillas' strategy against the French. In 1812, he advised the general Wellesley (Duke of Wellington) and his minister Castlereagh to overthrow Napoleon (a position occupied previously by Miranda in 1807–08).

The French Minister of War, J. Servan[6] and the Mayor of Paris, J. Pétion,[7] insisted in August 1792 that Miranda accept the Field Marshal (Brigadier General) rank to help stop the Prussian attack on the Ardennes. He finally accepted on August 24, but under conditions that excluded participation in the conquest of territories and avoidance of confrontation with Spain, and went directly to the North to reinforce the general-in-chief of the Republican army, Dumouriez, on September 6. Miranda achieved immediate symbolic military successes in Morthomme, Briquenay on 12/09, and he played a significant role in the more decisive victory at Valmy, on 20/09, which had a crucial psychological impact, marking the first victories for the revolutionary army.

He was promoted to Lieutenant General, and, as the government considered attacking Spain, he was proposed to lead a military expedition first against the rebellious slaves to re-establish French power over Santo Domingo before dedicating himself to removing Madrid's tutelage over Spanish America. However, Miranda considered this a "colonial" offer incompatible with his own emancipation plan, which he had exposed before to the government in Paris at the end of October. Therefore, from Liège, where he was defending the revolution, he diplomatically rejected this offer at the end of 1792.

Promoted deputy of the commander-in-chief of the Army of the North, but also in disagreement with the desire for territorial conquests in Belgium and Holland of his chief Dumouriez, Miranda noted with anguish the increasing risks of a confrontation between moderate Girondins and radical Jacobins. This internal division could oblige the Army to choose its camp, interfering dangerously with the revolution strategy. Indeed, in early 1793, Dumouriez wanted to impede the Jacobins from taking power[8] either by bringing a fast military success in Holland and Belgium that

---

[6] **Joseph Servan** (1741–1808) was a career military man. A Girondin revolutionary, he was appointed Minister of War in May 1792 in the Girondin government. He resigned in October 1792 as minister to command the Pyrenean army. Arrested by Robespierre during the Terror, he was released after the tyrant's fall and rejoined the military until his retirement in 1807.

[7] **Jérôme Pétion** (1756–1794), revolutionary lawyer and leader of the Jacobin family at the beginning of the Revolution, was elected Mayor of Paris in 1791 and progressively distanced himself from Robespierre and the Jacobins. After the September 1792 massacres, he left the Jacobins and moved to the Girondin group. He resigned as Mayor of Paris to become the first president of the new legislative assembly, named "Convention". After Robespierre's coup of May 31, 1793, he was arrested to be executed as an opponent. He managed to escape but was persecuted for a year. He committed suicide with two other Girondins so as not to be executed in June 1794.

[8] Dumouriez, uneasy about the growing power and the repeated manoeuvres towards a coup by the Jacobins (Republicans), wanted to take the lead in the conflict between moderate Girondins and extremist Jacobins, trying to break the deadlock between the King and Parliament that had paralysed the country. He planned to strengthen his power through a decisive military victory against the Austrians, which would have enabled him to prevail in Paris against the Jacobins' totalitarian plan. In the event of defeat, he would negotiate a political-military agreement with the European courts, offering peace in exchange for overthrowing his republican government and imposing as king the young Prince Egalité (Louis-Felipe de Orléans), who was a Girondin like himself and Miranda. Anyway, he planned to stabilise the new constitutional monarchy's regime and end the revolution. Miranda, despite sharing Dumouriez's fears about the Jacobin manoeuvres towards

he would attribute to the young Prince Egalité (Louis Philippe d'Orléans[9]) or, in case of defeat, by turning back his army against the republican government for re-establishing a constitutional monarchy with Orléans. With this monarchy, he expected to be able to bargain for a peaceful arrangement with the Austrians and the other European monarchies [Parra-Perez, 1925].[10] Already in conflict with the Convention, the failure of his conquest of Holland and the disaster in the East of Belgium led him to seek an immediate victory in Belgium before being sacked by the Convention. Therefore, he took excessive risks, ignoring Miranda's information and advice. Miranda suspected an unclear attitude and had already realised the anti-republican attitude of his boss, who intended to prepare a return to a monarchy. Miranda made it very explicit that he was vehemently opposed. He had also observed the growing lack of coherence in Dumouriez's military strategy, which included extending the combats too far in the North and East, sending Miranda to take over Maastricht without the necessary artillery, and reducing the rear defences on the Aachen side. The incapacity of his colleague, General Valence,[11] to defend the frontier with Prussia caused the French army to retreat, forcing Miranda to lift the siege of Maastricht and leave Liège. Dumouriez, coming back from Holland, took over the command and dismantled Miranda's sound strategy for defending Louvain and Brussels.

He then obliged Miranda – his only general with clear republican conviction - to execute an unprepared suicide attack on the most robust wing of the Austrian army

power, did not want to betray his word as a constitutional officer and made it known to Dumouriez that he would remain faithful to the government and the Convention, refusing to accept that the army would interfere in internal politics. He even warned Dumouriez that, if necessary, it would go so far as to prevent the treason of its chief, Dumouriez. As a result, Dumouriez tried to get rid of Miranda by throwing him into a trap with a fatal military order to attack the most robust part of the Austrian army in the Neerwinden battle. His plan (see note 12 below) was to eliminate Miranda, using him either to ease his own victory or, in case of defeat, to blame him for the disaster. Therefore, he accused Miranda of the loss of Belgian territories, influencing many French historians, despite the facts and sequencing of this battle

[9] **Louis-Philippe d'Orléans** (1773–1850), nicknamed "Prince Egalité", became later King of the French with the revolution of 1830 that overthrew the Bourbons. He was the son of Louis-Philippe de Orléans, the Duke of Orleans, the wealthiest man in France and a supporter of the Revolution, who voted for the death of his cousin, King Louis XVI, and who was also guillotined by Robespierre in 1793 as a result of his son's escape with Dumouriez. Louis-Philippe always respected Miranda, with whom he shared the battles of the Army of the North in 1792–93. He ordered, once King in 1830, that the name of Miranda be engraved on the Arc de Triomphe of Paris with the list of heroes of the Revolution, and also put Miranda's portrait in the "Galerie des Glaces" with the Revolution's military heroes of the Palace of Versailles.

[10] See the complete analysis and proofs in Parra-Perez, C. "Miranda et la Révolution Française", Paris, 1925.

[11] **Jean-Baptiste Cyrus de Valence** (1757–1822) was a nobleman who joined the French Royal Army, but he adhered to the French Revolution; becoming general in Dumouriez's team, he was involved in Dumouriez's failed plot against the Convention and defected in April 1793. He returned to Napoleon's empire as a General. He participated in the campaigns in Spain and Russia.

in Neerwinden[12] (between Liège and Brussels) in order to ease the success of Orléans on the right wing of the battle. According to most French versions,[13] the disaster of Miranda's cavalry would be the cause of the defeat of the republican army in Belgium. These versions proved false because Dumouriez's defeat started before Miranda's retreat. In charge of the rear guard, Miranda reached to organise an orderly withdrawal of the French troops. Still, upon arriving in France, he was accused of betrayal and complicity by Danton and Robespierre following the defection of his boss, Dumouriez, who had switched sides, escaping with the young Prince Egalité (Louis Philippe d'Orléans) on April 3, 1793. Imprisoned in April and tried in Paris, Miranda was accused of Dumouriez's faults but, in fact, for being too critical of the Jacobins. Surprisingly, he was first acquitted on May 16, to the unanimous decision of the Revolutionary Tribunal (he had proven the incoherent written orders he received from Dumouriez). Still, the inexorable logic of Jacobin extremism uses the context of external threats to eliminate any democratic political debate, organising a coup and putting in jail all the Girondin deputies as well as Miranda and other democrats. Robespierre imposed a fanatic tyranny based on a manipulated popular consensus through the activism of the ideological "*Sociétés de pensées*" [Cochin, 1921][14] controlled by the Jacobins. The Jacobin phenomenon is the ideological clubs' usurpation of the people's will.

---

[12]The **Battle of Neerwinden** [March 1793] was a military disaster for which French historians generally attributed responsibility to Miranda. A more rigorous examination quickly shows—just as Miranda did it to convince his accuser, the Jacobin Fouquier-Tinville, that he was innocent—that Dumouriez ordered him to commit a suicide attack on the left front without respecting several elementary criteria and against Miranda's information and tactical opinion. Dumouriez's idea was to kill two birds in a single shot by sacrificing Miranda and thus eliminating an honest but embarrassing witness, whose sacrifice would have forced the Austrian troops to immobilise most of the defence on this left side (the strongest because the headquarters was there with the Emperor's son), thus making easier for Dumouriez and Principe Egalité to win by collapsing the right front and outlining the left side blocked by Miranda. Dumouriez planned to ease the victory and attribute it to Orléans in order to return to Paris, where he would crown him and expel the Jacobins. The last straw is that Miranda was unduly accused of complicity with Dumouriez by the Jacobins, especially by Marat.

[13]These versions rely only upon Dumouriez's memoir, but the chronology proven by witnesses as well as by the Austrian archives demonstrates these versions to be false. They tell that Dumouriez and Orléans were obliged to fall back before knowing that Miranda was defeated, too, contrary to Dumouriez's comments pretending that he was obliged to abandon his victory because of Miranda's faults (see Parra-Perez, C., [1925] op. cit, also Miranda's Archivo, in Vol. XIV and XII, Introduction).

[14]These ideological societies were political clubs, Masonic lodges, or intellectual groups that acquired a decisive role in manipulating and usurping public opinion to radicalise the revolution, drawing upon Rousseau's concept of direct democracy. Their political pressures are responsible for the derive towards Terror by imposing an antagonism between ideology and the real world, following Augustin Cochin [1921]. This «forgotten» historian was the first to provide a deeper analysis of Jacobinism, presenting it as a usurpation of the «popular sovereignty» by small ideological groups imposing their own will above all other principles. Cochin was ignored in France for ideological reasons up to the rehabilitation by François Furet [1978] *Penser la Révolution française*.

Miranda is a lucid witness and one of the first victims of this process of ideological inquisition, which served to manipulate public opinion for taking power and imposing a radical centralisation of the legislative power facing a weak and decentralised executive, submitted to the popular power usurped by the philosophical groups, along with Rousseau's thinking. On the first of June, 1793, Robespierre seized control with a subtly prepared coup and immediately decided to imprison the Girondins, especially Miranda [1929], knowing he was innocent, but on the charge of a crime of opinion ("because *Miranda should not be judged with proofs but for being guilty politically*[15]"). The judge who had acquitted Miranda was arrested for this reason. This extremist wing of the Jacobins considers itself directly inspired by Rousseau's philosophy, claiming to possess the truth, having derived it from the sovereign people, who cannot be mistaken, and pretending, through opinion manipulation, to be the people themselves. Therefore, the revolution requires the physical elimination of all opponents, especially the Girondins, as a priority. Miranda, considered the "sword of the Gironde", thus shares for more than a year the anguish of the victims of Terror condemned to the guillotine. It is difficult to explain how a foreigner like Miranda managed to escape his execution in such a xenophobic environment of Terror. The most probable hypothesis is that he would have been saved by the manoeuvres of Delphine de Custine, who had met him when she visited her father-in-law, General de Custine, Miranda's colleague, also imprisoned on false accusation as Miranda, and executed in August 1793, and shortly after, his son, Delphine's husband, Adam de Custine, also wrongly accused and unfairly imprisoned together with Miranda. Delphine had planned her husband's escape [de Custine, 1843],[16] but he rejected her plan at the last minute. He was executed on January 4, 1974. Delphine's efforts in defence of her father-in-law and her husband drew suspicions about her, and she was arrested, too and sentenced to the guillotine. During her interrogations, she had managed to seduce and bribe one of her guards,[17] who had access to the Fouquier-Tinville's[18] office. Each day, the public prosecutor

[15] According to Robespierre's letter sent to Montané, the court President, who had declared Miranda innocent because the facts and proofs demonstrated he was innocent. See *Archivo*..., Vol XII, Introduction, p. XXXVI. Robespierre even sent this judge to jail with Miranda for pretending he was not guilty. This frightening argument by Robespierre anticipates the "Stalinist judgments" in the USSR.

[16] Astolphe de Custine was Delphine's son.

[17] According to Gaston Maugras & de Croze-Lemercier, in *Delphine de Sabran, Marquise de Custine*, Plon, Paris 1912, p. 247–249. He was a young mason named Jérôme, according to the testimony of Delphine's son, Astolphe de Custine [1843], who tells it in detail in his famous work *La Russie in 1839*. Delphine used this method so that her own execution could be postponed; however, Miranda is not mentioned. Nevertheless, since her late husband had recommended Miranda to care for her and they had become lovers, it seems logical that her system was extended to Miranda. When Robespierre fell, there remained very few prisoners to be guillotined, including Miranda and Delphine. She later helped the young Jacobin Jérôme, who was in turn under indictment by the anti-Jacobins and organised his escape to America, probably with the contacts provided by Miranda in America.

[18] **Fouquier-Tinville** (1746–1795), the fearsome Jacobin, the public prosecutor of the revolutionary court, created in March 1793 by the Convention to judge the enemies of the revolution and the

of the Revolutionary Court prepared a stack of personal files, listing the ranking of persons to be executed the following day. She asked this guard to put her husband and Miranda's files at the bottom of the stack, postponing the guillotine's daily schedule. It is also known that her friend and cell-mate, **Joséphine de Beauharnais**, acted similarly[19] thanks to the complicity of a copyist in the Office of Detainees, dependent on the Public Safety Committee, **Charles de la Bussière,**[20] who reached to make her order of execution to disappear, and who also saved Delphine [Audoubert 1988], and very probably Miranda too,[21] just as he did so for many others innocents [Lienart 1804]. However, Robespierre realised the suspicious delay in the execution of Miranda and fixed his irrevocable execution at 12 Thermidor (July 30, 1793). Two days earlier, Robespierre himself was arrested and executed on July 28 as a result of the Thermidor coup organised by members of his own party, frightened by the acceleration of his policy of suspicion and mass executions.

However, Delphine and Miranda remained imprisoned as suspects without being prosecuted by the new authorities. They were considered dangerous by both sides: the royalists were aware of their republican sympathies, while the Jacobins viewed them as opponents to their centralisation of power. Two months later, Delphine was released by pure chance, but Miranda stayed until January 1795. His political positions, favouring the separation of powers and opposing territorial conquests, continued to be poorly perceived by both the left and the right, in addition to his foreign status and contacts in London. He was the last political prisoner to be released; despite the many efforts of his Delphine, his friends, and the defence campaign in the press, he organised himself from his jail. The document sent to the Convention's representatives is one of several pamphlets he printed and distributed to achieve justice.

---

betrayers of homeland, who had acquitted Miranda in May 1793 but who soon concentrated in Robespierre's regime the functions of both arrest and investigation, accusation, trial and execution, and even decided on many executions without accusations or evidence or condemnation, even making generic accusations with executions of groups of innocent people, using cannons for speeding up the logistics of death sentences. He was the leading actor in the mass executions during the Terror and was tried in 1795 and sentenced to the guillotine.

[19] See Biography of Joséphine de Beauharnais.

[20] **Charles de la Bussière** (1768–1808) was a theatre actor and a little-known hero. Saint-Just employed him in the Committee of Public Safety as a clerk, copying the records of those convicted by the Revolutionary Tribunal. Without hesitation, he saved his unjustly imprisoned colleagues from the Théâtre Français. Then this "just" continued at a grand scale, managing to save the lives, in addition to Delphine's, of more than 2000 victims of Terror, probably a historical record. Among others, he freed the Marquise de la Villette, Madame de Buffon, Talleyrand's uncle, the anthropologist Volney, the banker Delesserre, Madame de Vassy, the writer Florian, the Vicomte de Ségur, Madame de La Fayette, and the Prince of Monaco. Even at Robespierre's death, he threw 924 files of defendants still in prison into the Seine. See Nadine Audoubert [1988] *Un bouffon sous la terreur,* and also Nicolas Lienart [1804] sur Charles Hyppolyte La Bussière.

[21] There is proof that de la Bussière's system was used for Delphine and Josephine, but Miranda's name did not appear on the known list. Nevertheless, it is a fact that Miranda's execution was strangely postponed without any other explanation.

Content:

Eloquent pamphlet arguing the incoherence of being both the first victim of the Terror and the last one to remain in prison without accusation or trial despite the end of the Terror. His arguments extend beyond his own case, seizing the opportunity to try to be helpful to France and an idealistic Republic by teaching the Convention deputies universal political philosophy. Miranda warns them eloquently on three critical defects of their regime:

- "*People must know that tyranny still exists here*" and was not only due to Robespierre but to the French governance system, which proves with his case to be unable to warrant freedom and justice
- the presence of xenophobic culture, which denies the revolutionary principles and damages the dignity of the French people.
- The abuse of philosophical principles by a small minority speaking in the name of the people[22] or the Nation for their own oligarchical interests. Very subtly, he cites the philosopher upon whom the Jacobins relied most, J.J. Rousseau,[23] using his warning against sacrificing individual rights for the sake of the group. This is precisely the contrary[24] principle that the Jacobins extract from Rousseau for strengthening the grip of a few upon the majority, for concentrating the powers, and submitting individuals to the social group.

Sources:

Written in French
Becerra. Vol. II. p. 430–437.
Colombeia. Vol XVII. Document 3631. p. 47–60.
América Espera. Document 59. p. 170–175.

Text:

2 January 1795 (13 Nivose)
To the Representatives of the French People

... qui autem non defendit, nec obsisit, si potest, \ injuriae, tam est in vitio, quam si parentes, aut amicos, aut patriam deserat. (Cic. de off. L. I, cap. VII)

[22] This is what Augustin Cochin [1921] demonstrated one century later, see *Les sociétés de pensée...*, op. cit.

[23] Robespierre, like many other revolutionary thinkers and leaders, was a strong disciple of Rousseau, using Rousseau's principle that individual rights must be submitted to the power of the people by natural law. This axiomatic affirmation allows for concentrating all the powers in deliberative assemblies, which must control the two other branches for imposing the single "truth" of popular power (see the Oxford criticisms of Rousseau, which must control the two other branches for imposing the single "truth" of popular power (see the Oxford criticisms of Rousseau, i.e. Isaiah Berlin [2003]. Miranda, who was fundamentally opposed to "popular power" as a means of governance, was using Rousseau to defend himself by employing the arguments of his enemies.

[24] Most authors wrongly consider Miranda an adept of Rousseau. This was only true when he travelled to the US at the beginning of his life, while all his ulterior principles and actions demonstrate the contrary. Those authors rely only on the many references in his writings. Examples are Antonio Egea Lopez, [1983], in *El pensamiento Filosófico y Político de Francisco de Miranda*, and John Dunn [2006], see Annex 2.

[... and whoever does not defend the oppressed, being able, is as guilty as if he abandoned his parents, his friends or his homeland].

Citizens:

Before the National Convention, I denounce a crime, the investigation and persecution of which constrain liberty.

This crime often occurs in the impunity of a great wrongdoer or the persecution of an innocent person.

There are many ways to kill liberty, but none is so deadly to the Republic as the impunity of crime or the prescription of virtue.

Society does not exist where a member of the social body can insult justice with impunity, that is, can attack that part of the body which looks after its security through the repression of the criminals.

Society does not exist where the social body allows one of its members to be oppressed, for the consequence from the part to the whole is direct and necessary.

One of these crimes against liberty exists in the illegal incarceration of my person, which I denounce before the National Convention.

Either I am guilty; in this case, a crime is committed against society by leaving me unpunished. In this case, I demand that I get a legal penalty because I prefer to die free by the enforcement of the law than to live as a slave, that is, in contempt of the law and by the will of another.

Or I am innocent, and then a crime is also being committed against society by keeping me in jail without judgment, but what am I saying? Without daring to confess the accusation, and according to the declaration of the current Junta of General Security, without there being any charges pressed against me. In this case, I demand my liberty in the interest of the social body, hurt in my person by the tyranny of which I am a victim.

I beg the Convention to decide between two such strange alternatives, the furtherance of which is a transgression against society and, for me, a torment worse than death.

In 1792, I accepted an honourable office repeatedly offered to me to defend French freedom against the League of Despots. My destiny seems to be to be a soldier in this cause always and under all circumstances.[25]

During my command, no matter what intrigues threatened to compromise the outcome of the French Revolution, indeed, no other man in France was less liable to suspicion for having taken part in those maneuvers, simply because nobody informed me more strictly about his conduct than I did myself.[26]

---

[25] Miranda's note: See statements by Thomas Paine, Stone, Barlow, T. Christie, Sabonadiére, etc., in the process of General Miranda before the Revolutionary Court. See also Miranda's *Archivo*, Vol. XII, Introduction.

[26] Miranda's Note: If there is anyone whose conduct could be subject to examination in this regard, I confess that it would be that of the Commissioners expressly sent to monitor Dumouriez's conduct in Belgium sometime before his defection and that, instead of to prevent him from doing so, they have allowed him to do everything he wanted to deliver the conquered countries as well as the armies of the Republic to the enemies of the State; and that they have arrested, without wanting to

Since my position put me under suspicion, the acting Juntas of General Defence and Vigilance asked me to submit to them all the circumstances of my behaviour. The most thorough investigation resulted in the decision to eliminate any suspicion. This report was drowned by the intrigues of Lacroix and others, who believed that their connivance with Dumouriez would come through at the Convention, and they obtained, without decorum, my transfer to the Revolutionary Tribunal.

The tribunal held nine sessions to discuss the set of accusations that had accumulated against me, including intrigue and perfidy. All of them were dispelled and disappeared before the sun of justice. I emerged from that ordeal like a man who needed no justification: I received a civil crown, to put it more strongly. No juror did not include praise in his declaration, praise I do not claim to deserve, but that at least shows the opinion about myself that the debates gave to justice. I will never forget the affection that a large multitude showed me after the sentence, taking my lawyer and me in public manifestations of joy along the streets, as only a generous people can show when innocence triumphs after long oppression.

The triumphs of good men are the defeats of the wicked. Those who viciously wished my doom fired their battery of calumnies, and from that rampart, inaccessible to innocence, they attacked me with their poisonous darts. According to them, the boxes where I kept my books were full of rifles: my travelling memoirs and correspondence with foreigners. Everything was broken into, and they only found calumny. It was deemed necessary, in the end, to find crimes to be committed by me in the future, to snatch from me the possibility of proving their spuriousness. They imagined a project for me to travel to Bordeaux. Cambon announced it to the tribune of the Convention,[27] and although there were no indications, nor could there ever have been, of that trip, Pache, under that ridiculous pretext, gave the order to apprehend me.[28] Since then, 18 months have gone by, and still, I waste away under chains. Eighteen months in which I have been dragged from prison to prison, without resources of any kind, without knowledge of what happened after my absolution, to my horses and coaches, without once receiving my salary, neither for the time I

listen to him, the only superior officer of the army who said and had written since March 21 to the constituted authorities that Dumouriez was no longer acting in good faith. However, they agreed that this officer, who had known him closely for several months, had supported the decrees of the Convention with more force than any of his colleagues and had consistently manifested the most republican spirit and the most perfect submission to the law on all occasions. (See the report signed by Lacroix, Danton, Gossuin, Merlin de Douai, Treilhard and Robert, Commissars to the Army in Belgium, printed by order of the National Convention, p. 41). The first two are the ones that motivated the order that led to my separation from the army at the time of the betrayal; the others signed it with confidence, as Lacroix and Gossuin declared in General Miranda's trial before the Revolutionary Court.

[27] *Colombeia,* Vol. XVI, doc. 3548.

[28] Miranda's note: It is very extraordinary that a member of the Committee of Public Safety came, during the session of the last 2 Brumaire, to distort this report in such a strange way that it puts my name in place of Dillon, then accused of Capetism. I don't think Delmas did it intentionally, but the error is gross and highly objectionable. (See *Le Moniteur*, 4 Brumaire and Cambon report, July 11, 1793. Old style).

served the Republic at the head of its armies or during my imprisonment; without being able to obtain the slightest support from the banks; reduced, finally, to live with the debris of a library, part of which I have had to sell to survive. In other words, I spent more than 18 months waiting for tyranny to get tired of me. But being so fully committed to the glorious task of combating tyranny, I declare that I will wear it out.

I am determined to show Europe, and also America, that in France, I have the exclusive privilege of persecution. I want to see if, after being the first victim of Robespierre's tyrannical system, I will, thanks to his disciples, also have the joy of being its last, and then will come to light, at least, how remote I was from sharing the atrocious and tyrannical opinions of those infamous enemies of liberty, and how it was out of my power to offer any resistance.

There is something glorious about being the only suspicious man in France, that is, the last barricade behind which tyranny has entrenched itself. It is curious to see how many different meanings the word "suspicious" has concerning me. Obviously, and to have an apparent pretext for persecution, I was suspected of complicity with Dumouriez. Immediately after, when it was proven that I was not his accomplice but his victim, I fell under suspicion for being a republican but not a revolutionary (this was on the 31st of May). Soon after, I fell under suspicion for federalism, and now, when that denomination can no longer be a pretext for oppression, I am suspected of Capetism.

Finally, if Robespierre and his accomplices had ruined public affairs, as almost happened, it would not have been surprising for me to be proscribed as a friend of liberty, a legitimate suspicion I would never have denied.

I acknowledge that this destiny, unexpected to me, encourages me to bear with it. And since you have the cruelty of not wishing to find me guilty, afraid maybe that I may discover guilt in others, and since I am deprived of the favour of an accusation to snatch from me the glory of defence and justification, I give in to the invisible hand of an indefinable tyranny.

But it will not be said that I will not use this to the advantage of the French Republic. People must know that tyranny still exists here since I remain in chains and without accusation, without motives and with the confession that there are no charges against me. It is necessary for the French who escaped from the 10,000 Bastilles of the decemviral tyranny to be aware that these Bastilles await them, and they are ready to open their doors to them again if only one man, arbitrarily, is still imprisoned in them. They must know that the weight of my chains hovers over them as much as over me and that the whole social body is attacked if there is an unpunished culprit or an innocent man in jail.

The execrable maxim of the Couthons and Robespierres that individual interests must be sacrificed to the public interest is the basis on which they founded their tyranny. It is the infernal axiom with which men like Tiberius and Philip II of Castile subjected and mortified many of the human species before them. I have known that certain members of the Security Junta, lacking legitimate reasons, had given such a doctrine as the cause of my detention, a doctrine they call political and supported my status as a foreigner.[29]

May I ask then by which law I am granted French citizenship when the sacred duties it embodies are weighed upon my head? When it has been acknowledged that I have fulfilled them with exactitude, and yet I must be persecuted, am I stripped of them to become a foreigner? Am I then a Frenchman only when I fulfil my duties but not when I claim my rights as such?

If it were the case that the success of public liberty depends on the deprivation of my personal liberty, the sacrifices that I have already made prove that I would be capable of further abnegation, but since simple common sense screams that that alleged reason of state is nothing but a pretext for persecution, I will refute it with the gravest and most profound authority on democracy. J.J. Rousseau says:

> You must not believe that you can hurt or cut an arm without the head feeling the pain, nor is it believable that the general spirit will allow a member of a state to harm or destroy another, no more than a man in his right mind would let his fingers pull out his eyes. Personal security is in such a way connected to public confederation that without taking into account human weakness, this convention would be dissolved if only one citizen perished in a State when he could have been saved; if only one were detained in prison and one legal case was lost to evident injustice; because once the fundamental conventions are infringed, we cannot see what rights nor what interest would keep the people in social union, unless it were restricted by the only force that produces the suspension of civil state.
>
> In fact, is it not the pledge of the nation's body to provide for the preservation of the last of its members with as much care as for all the others? And the welfare of one citizen, does it affect less the common cause than that of the whole State? Tell us that it is suitable for one citizen to perish for the rest. I shall admire this sentence on the lips of a worthy and virtuous patriot who voluntarily and dutifully devotes himself to death for the sake of his country. Still, suppose the understanding is that the government may be permitted to sacrifice one man for the good of the multitude. In that case, I take that maxim to be one of the most hateful ever invented by tyranny, the most false that can be proposed, the most dangerous to be admitted, and the most directly opposed to the fundamental laws of society. Far from one dying for all, all have compromised their goods and lives to defend each other, so that individual weakness is protected by public strength and the whole State supports each member. After having suppressed one and sundry individuals, try to press the partisans of that maxim to explain better what they believe to be the body of the State. You will see that they reduce it to a small number of men who do not belong to the people but who are its officials, and who, taking a special oath to die for its welfare, then expect the people to die for theirs. (Discourse on Political Economy).

And yet, strange paradox! barbarous contradiction! The homage that for the last 20 years he has paid to liberty, sacrificing in its cause wealth and dignity, more often employed in flattering the pride and ambitions of men; who has visited every free country on Earth and lived in them for some time, consulting legislators and wise men to learn from their important science; who counts these great men among his friends and the despots among his enemies; who is notoriously known as an ardent follower of liberty in all Europe and America; who chased by Spanish despotism from one pole to the other, was called and came to France to defend that holy

[29] Miranda's note: An inhabitant of Caracas and Lima is no more Spanish, in whatever way he is considered, than an inhabitant of Connecticut or Boston is English.

freedom, and who has indeed defended it within his power: inconceivable singularity that this same man has been suffering for the last 18 months the most horrendous persecution in the home of France and in the name of the same nation he fought for, risking his life, and even so calumny has not been able to present in those 18 months one proof against him, whereas a significant number of the most honourable ones... exist in his favour.[30] If I were a prisoner of war, I would complain loudly about this persecution: so much more so, having been worthy of the Republic! History shows us, at the beginning of Rome, the most beautiful models of a free and republican people. With what magnanimity did they, after the great calamities of the Republic, express their gratitude to the foreigners, citizens and slaves, even the animals, who had paid them particular service during their misery? It shows equally to the shame of another rival nation of this people, which in a moment of anguish enlisted the able Greek General Xantipus, who served it well with his military prowess and rewarded him for this with manifestations of gratitude in the first moments of public joy, the people carrying him in triumph, but which a few days later, Xantipus having decided to sail back home to Greece in Carthaginian ships, he was drowned perfidiously at sea by a secret order of the same government. A policy that inspires such horror that the historian adds: "*Such wickedness is unbelievable even of Carthaginians*".

Then, citizens, what will you say after reading what has happened to me? I protest that not one but ten times would I have exchanged my destiny for that of the unlucky Greek instead of bearing the torments that I have suffered and continue to suffer to this moment. If Xantipus had the misfortune of being killed, so common in the army, he also had the joy of keeping his reputation and honour pure, a more precious object to a military man and any free man. Could I have expected that instead of the Roman magnanimity, I would have found the Punic faith in probably the most civilised nation on Earth?

Ah! Let us not call this the effect of a tyranny that has been destroyed. This may have been true until the 9 Thermidor, but after the Bastilles had been opened, and even public criminals have been granted the forms prescribed by the law for their defence [which is fair enough], why do you continue to refuse them to me? I complain about this to the nation's representatives and bring the issue to the attention of

[30] Note from Miranda: At the time of the process of the twenty-one deputies, the General Security Committee ordered the examination of all my papers, which are in the home of citizen Barrois l'aîné, among which is an exact diary of my life from adolescence, as well as my travels for 12 years, the only reading of which would suffice to shame the calumny and describe the most constant and most faithful friend of freedom. After the most meticulous examination of these papers, nothing but continual proof was found of my ardent love of liberty and my fondness for the arts. (They are their own expressions of the examining commissioners of the times of Amar and Robespierre) One could refer to the reading of these same pieces to the cowardly accuser André Amar, if a vile slanderer deserves to be dealt with. The illustrious and virtuous citizens who have been assassinated and defamed in their report of October 3, 1792 (old style) should regard this abominable monument of wickedness rather as a title of honour than of reproach. Let him present a single proof of the impostures that his impudence has launched against me and then he will be answered.

the world's people. I do not ask the Convention for favours. I demand the most rigorous justice for me and those who have dared, in a double attempt, to compromise the dignity of the French people, defiling its national representation.

F. Miranda

At La Force, 13 Nivose, in the third year of the French Republic.

6.2 Miranda's letter to the French Convention, Paris, prison La Force, 4 January 1795 (15 Nivôse)

Context:

Miranda remains in jail despite the fall of the Jacobins, who had condemned him. Two days after sending his memorandum to the Convention, he sent a complementary letter claiming his right to be freed. He was informed that the memorandum he sent to the President was not read to the Convention deputies but was only given to the committees, which did not make decisions, although they acknowledged the absence of culpability. Therefore, Miranda sends a shorter message which accuses the Thermidorian Convention of being as tyrannical as the Terror regime. At the same time, this present convention bases its legitimacy upon eradicating tyranny. This also explains the permanent hostility towards Miranda that the Thermidorian Convention and its prolongation under the Directory maintained, both sides of the coalition in power trying to capture rents and protect their own corruption.

Content:

Remarkable argumentation for its coherent juridical aspect and the eloquent style. He demonstrates that maintaining him in jail proves the despotic character of the Thermidorian Convention. This position reflects the lucid assessment Miranda makes about this undemocratic republic, that, indeed, the historical reality of this regime (and its extension in the Directory) proved to continue some tyranny by organising a "white terror" with the same method as the Jacobins used.

Sources:

Translated from French.

América Espera. Document 60. p. 175–176

Becerra. Vol. II. p. 437–439.

Colombeia. Vol. XVII. Document 3631. p. 61–63.

Archivo, in French, Vol. XV, f. 251. draft of this letter.

Text:

To the National Convention

15 Nivôse An III (4 January 1795)

Representative Citizens:

More than 18 months ago, I appeared before the Convention to denounce my arbitrary imprisonment. My complaint was referred to the Junta of General Security to seek justice, and the Junta has yet to question me. In accordance with the 18th Thermidor, which requires that each detainee be informed, as a general security measure, of the reasons for their detention, I requested to see mine, and the Junta replied that they had none.

All those who were detained as suspects by Robespierre's tyranny and are not among the cases excluded by the same law of 18 Thermidor have been put at liberty some time ago, and I find myself still in prison.

Various deputies, who have known me for some time because we shared the same misfortune in prison, demanded from the Junta a few days ago the application of this law in my case, and the secretary of the commission, Laumon, declared in his report that he had not found one document against me, and accordingly begged for my liberty to be granted. Still, for an indefinite policy, this matter has been postponed until the first meeting of the Three Juntas... Since then, the three Juntas have met several times without any change in my fortune.

What kind of policy is this? ... It can certainly not be that of freedom. The French Senate, which has made justice available, could it tolerate that through a policy worthy of the Couthons and the Robespierres, a man innocent before the law can be detained and chained by the mere will of another and that human rights and humanity are ignored. Is the law of nations violated in the name of the French people? No, citizens, I am persuaded that you will do justice by me and return a liberty I never believed to have lost.

Otherwise, I beg of you that which the laws grant every man and what justice does not even deny the wicked: a judgement as the sole legal means by which an honest man can keep his honour intact and be protected from infamous calumny or satisfy the public interest if he has had the misfortune to transgress the laws.

The existence of just one innocent citizen, laden with chains, in the knowledge of the constituted powers of any country, would be the most significant proof of despotism. If this man is authentically declared to be, as I have been, an excellent citizen and father of the soldiers, who for his services has been worthy of the fatherland and who is beyond suspicion,[31] this would be the utmost end of tyranny.

There is oppression against the social body when just one of its members finds himself oppressed. [Law of Nations,[32] art. 34.].

In La Force, 15 de Nivôse, Year III of the French Republic.

F. de Miranda

6.3 Miranda's Political Pamphlet [July 1795][33]

"Some Thoughts about the Present Condition of France and the Remedies for its Diseases"

[31] Miranda's note: see the Revolutionary Court: Trial to General Miranda, n° 36 y 37.

[32] Constitution of year I of the Republic (1793).

[33] The original title in French was: *Opinion du général Miranda sur la situation actuelle de la France, et sur les remèdes convenables à ses maux.*- 1795, París.

Context:

This critical text in political philosophy and constitutional law reflects the lessons learned from Miranda's experience serving revolutionary France. This exceptional political and human experience shaped his political and constitutional principles for the remainder of his life. He discovered the beginning of the manipulation of the popular power already under the Girondins' Convention,[34] which soon became a systematic abuse under the Jacobin Convention[35] (the Terror regime), having been jailed and condemned to the guillotine, making him share the "death corridor" with the primary victims of the Jacobin regime for 18 months; once freed, but being also critical to the new conservative regime, he was again suspected, arrested, escaped but proscribed and chased by the police, under a series of accusations of conspirations (alternatively for being considered as a monarchist, anti-Jacobins, spy of the British government, or potential dangerous rival to seize power), through a typical abuse of the executive power under the Thermidorian Convention and the Directory regime,[36] ending finally in the Napoleon dictatorship, which also accused and arrested him later when he came back legally to France in 1801.

In all these crucial events of the French Revolution, Miranda had the opportunity to verify concretely his fundamental hypothesis, which became his key political North: the successive constitutional imbalances impeding an effective separation of the three constitutional powers caused a tragic pendulum effect in the interpretation of the revolution principles from anarchy to tyranny.

- First, the moderate left Girondins' anarchy led to the extreme left tyranny of Robespierre's abuse of popular power, organised through the concentration of power in the legislative branch and an excessive decentralisation of the executive branch.
- Second, in reaction, sharp conservative opposition to the popular deliberative assembly, with the Thermidorian/Directory excessive strengthening of the executive branch,
- ending in pure dictatorship, reverting the revolutionary principles against democracy, captured by the "bourgeoisie" and the supremacy of private property.

Miranda disagreed with these four successive regimes that he considered antidemocratic for not respecting the genuine separation of powers. In particular, his perception of the disastrous effects of Jacobin ideology, which manipulates popular power with entirely deductive concepts based on philosophical postulates alien to reality. He perceived clearly the danger of erecting popular power above the other powers according to an abstract theory of the infallibility of united popular sovereignty. He detected that such a deductive method denies any separation of powers by ideological hypothesis, rendering it impossible to guarantee respect for human rights. He was able to verify personally the consequences of this ideology as both a direct

[34] See Chap. 4, Sect. 4.3 and Chap. 5, Sect. 5.1. note n°5, and document 5.2.2. in context, p.90.

[35] Ibid. plus note n°4 in Sect. 5.1.

[36] See Chap. 5. Sect. 5.2, note n° 24 p. 89.

witness and a direct victim of Jacobinism, sharing the fate of the moderate and Girondin revolutionaries. He forms a fundamental principle that direct democracy and popular power look attractive on paper but are counter-productive because they inevitably unleash a cynical anti-democratic manipulation of revolutionary idealism by a few activists in the name of an abstract people that serves to impose another type of absolutism.

For him, democracy, understood etymologically as a form of government by the people, was an unrealistic and dangerous ideology. The opposing interpretation, through the domination of executive power over the other two powers, was as hazardous as the domination of popular assemblies, ending in the same tyranny. He identified a mechanical, costly process of bloody action-reaction caused by the domination of one branch of power over the two others, leading to the destruction of democracy through the confiscation of popular power by a leader and his network of activists. His perception of the process of concatenation of successive imbalances deserves a detailed analysis:

First period: he observed his Girondins' friends who created some degrees of anarchy by an excess of deliberative bodies during the *Girondins' convention* in 1792–93 by overweighting the legislative influence upon the executive, with the result that any coherent policy of the government became difficult.

Second period: the resulting anarchy in a decentralised elective system provoked popular upheavals, allowing the Jacobins to take over (31 May/01 June 1793, coup by Robespierre) and imposing a further step in popular power by increasing the "democratic-popular" character of the Girondins' constitution project transformed into a new Jacobins' Constitution of the year I (1793). This constitution, voted on in June 1793 by the Jacobin Convention (1793–94), reinforced the imbalance created by the "assembleist" (Rousseau) ideology even further. This means a tyranny of the legislative "popular power" pretending to govern and rule justice by manipulating the mandates given to a few radical revolutionary activists in the name of direct democracy and popular power.

Third period: this tyranny provoked, in turn, a broad conservative reaction from both the left and the right sides of the Convention, but for opposite purposes (*Thermidorian Convention*). They all agreed to impede the return to Robespierre's tyranny by reinforcing executive power and limiting legislative power. They added a conservative senate, eliminated most of the deliberative local assemblies and restricted the voting rights and eligibility to a small elite and proprietaries ("censitarian" elections). The new constitution of the year III (1795) reacted to the Jacobin one (1793) by creating an opposite disequilibrium, concentrating much power in the executive without enough checks & balances. This regime, the Directory, established centralised control over the entire administration to prevent a return to past tyranny; however, in practice, it served the interests of the social elites and some corrupt ex-Jacobins. The local autonomy of the municipalities was lost, and all the main cities were under the direct control of the central executive to impede any return to a "communal power" similar to what happened in Paris from 1792 to 1794. Although the Directory could not dismiss the two legislative chambers, the constitution prohibited the primary assemblies in charge of the deputies' designation from deliberating on politics, and the Directory's commissioners strictly controlled the procedural aspects. The executive body concentrated almost all the nominations that were formerly elective and even assumed several roles of the judicial power (in cases of internal or external security), including control of the press and, through the Directory's commissioners, control of the courts and local administrations. This executive function was shared among five Directors, leading to a permanent struggle and shifting coalitions between the three main parties (Royalists, Girondins, and part of the Jacobins who joined the Thermidorians), which ultimately led to the elimination of Robespierre. Their main concern was maintaining control within their own class and protecting their past corrupt management. The resulting "particracy" game turned increasingly favourable to a conservative regime of "*republic without democracy*" in its quest to end the Revolution to the advantage of the newly enriched social elite, which profited from the revolution and the associated opportunities of corruption. The Directory years (1795–1799) were also precarious, deteriorating the governance and the economy, except for the dominant class, leading to several attempts from the left (neo-Jacobins) to restore the principles of the revolution. However, the legislative process hindered it due to the restrictions on eligibility conditions. At the same time, the conservative parties (royalists and moderate republicans) sustained the abusive concentration of powers to eliminate the left and confiscate the people's sovereignty. In this false left-right struggle, justified solely by remaining in or returning to power, several conspiracies and coups from both sides were attempted alternately, but this ultimately led to a more repressive policy. Each time, the Directory and the two legislative chambers changed their alliances from centre-right to centre-left, following a typical pendulum effect but without a stable solution. The Directory's purpose remained to "end the revolution" to benefit the new class of dominants. The fear of a return to the Jacobins' terror was abusively exploited, including by the neo-Jacobins, to justify a "white terror"[37] as well as election manipulations. This evolution confirms Miranda's diagnosis that the roots of

[37] The "Terreur Blanche" was the systematic repression against the Jacobins and those supposed to support an effective implementation of the Jacobins' constitution (of the year I, 1793), using abusive methods, not very different to Robespierre's tyranny. A first train of executions of Jacobin leaders and main actors (around one hundred executions of "Robespierrists") took place during the second semester of 1794. In early 1795, several royalist movements organised intense punitive expeditions against those pretending to return to the Jacobin principles; in March 1795, the Convention, who had reincorporated the expulsed Girondins, decided to arrest three ex-Jacobins (Barrere, Billaud-Varenne and Collot d'Herbois), and started to examine how to clean the Constitution for preventing a return to the "Jacobin Terror". The first measure was to enact a very repressive law in April against any popular movement or criticism of the Convention. In May 1793, a popular riot claiming the application of the 1793 constitution invaded the Convention in Paris. This event triggered severe repression, officially declaring the "White Terror", which arrested, deported and executed many political opponents of the Thermidorian Convention. This political maneuver eased the "Parliament coup" of the Convention, which had altered the Constitution (voted on in August 1795 as the Constitution of Year III) in an abusive manner. Later, the Thermidorian convention applied the "dry guillotine" or the territorial expulsion. Although this Terror had been less cruel and executed fewer victims, the abusive method and the lack of Human Rights were very similar to Robespierre's tyranny.

tyranny lie in the excess of power centralisation in one branch, either the popular legislative branch under the Jacobins or the bourgeois executive branch under the conservatives and some neo-Jacobins. Both methods inevitably lead to a vicious circle, increasing the need for even more centralisation, which ultimately leads to dictatorship, as it confiscates sovereignty and allows the new oligarchy to remain in power despite its unpopularity. Indeed, the Directory members, aware that its own Thermidorian constitution would not permit more "undemocratic" manipulations, decided to move to a direct dictatorship by organising a "self-coup", giving all the power to the Army of which Napoleon immediately seized this opportunity: the 18 Fructidor was a Jacobin self-coup (4 September 1797) by which the Directory became neo-Jacobin, and the 18 Brumaire coup (9 November) 1799 of Napoleon was organised by some directors of the Directory but eliminated the Directory itself.

Fourth period: Napoleon's coup allowed him to eliminate the two legislative chambers—which had a majority of moderate members opposed to the Directory—and to substitute the Directory with a consular commission with selected conspiration members, which designated Bonaparte as the first Consul (11 November). He named two commissions to propose a new constitution aimed at strengthening the new executive power. On 25 December, the constitution of the year VIII entered into force. This Consulate is the radicalisation of the centralisation of all powers in the executive branch. Inspired by the Thermidorian Convention, the Directory prepared this reaction and organised it as a conspiracy between unpopular Directors and Bonaparte. The purpose was to remain in power against the public opinion and the Chamber. It implemented an undemocratic return of the Jacobins under the pretext of preventing a return to monarchy. Napoleon further confiscated popular sovereignty with the Consular Constitution, ending the revolution by adapting it to the new dominant class of the bourgeoisie.

Miranda's political journey through these successive failures of governance marked him forever. He extracted "inductively" general principles explaining how freedom can be deviated into either chaos or tyranny when "deductive" beliefs are imposed on the real world without countervailing powers. For him, the root of the mistake is to impose "the truth" from a deductive "*yusnaturalism*", which, by definition, excludes any pluralistic debates. He translated this simple "common sense" into pragmatic formulas, making him an atypical revolutionary, for being the enemy of violence and idealistic ideologies. The paradox is that his realism was even considered utopian. His diagnosis of the French Revolution reaches a much higher analytical level than most historians.[38]

During his imprisonment, Miranda drafted several political texts for his defence while simultaneously drawing lessons from French mistakes. Freed by a press campaign he had organised with Delphine's help, Miranda attempted to contribute to France's political and economic stabilisation, participating in several political meetings and debates in Paris, where a new political balance was sought. In this

[38] In fact, it was only with the late awareness of the Soviet gulag that many French historians revised their understanding of the Revolution, and François Furet rediscovered Cochin's work (see note n° 17).

environment, as a new constitution was being elaborated to replace Robespierre's 1793 constitution, he published a French brochure in July 1795, proposing a political basis for the state of France.

Content:

Miranda's pamphlet was released a month before the debate at the Convention on the text of the new "*Thermidorian*" constitution, known as the "Constitution of the Year III" of the Republic. It establishes a diagnostic of the failure of the Jacobins, of the potential risks of the conquests and of caudillismo (the "*Alexandros and the Caesars*" as he knows personally the intentions of a military conspirator named Bonaparte), and of the alternative ways to a peaceful solution by establishing a "mixed" republican governance founded on the separation of powers but without taking away the means of action from the executive.

The exceptional lucidity on the excesses of the revolution, first by its left wing but also by feeding caudillo reactions, draws especially attention. In particular, he clearly warned against Bonapartism, which he saw as a real threat to European peace. This document is also the best synthesis of Miranda's political thought, faithfully defending a republican revolution capable of triggering an emancipation process through the rule of law, thereby warranting human rights. However, Miranda's text failed to effectively impact the third French constitution, which established an undemocratic bourgeois republic by creating an imbalance between powers precisely opposite to the previous one, inevitably leading to the erosion of democracy. In fact, the new constitution established by the Directory generated corruption, instability, and recurring coups, allowing a minority to maintain power. This behaviour paved the way towards the authoritarian and centralist reaction of Bonapartism.

Sources:

Translated from French.

Miranda, Francisco de (1750-1816). **Opinion of General Miranda on the current situation of France, and the Remedies for its Diseases".**- Paris: Impr. from rue de Vaugirard. 1794.

Archivo del General Miranda. Vol XIV, 1933. p. 387–400. Archivo original del General Miranda. Revolución Francesa. Vol. XVI. F. 47.

América Espera. op. cit. doc. n° 61, p. 177–186.

Antepara, José María (Comp.). (Guayaquil, 1770–1821): **South American emancipation: Documents, historical and explanatory, showing the designs that have been in progress and the exertions made by General Miranda for the South American emancipation during the last twenty-five years**.- London (England): Printed by R. Juigné. Sold by J. Richardson, Royal Exchange; B. Dulau and Co. Soho Square; L. N. Pannier, N°. 15, Leicester-Place - 1810.

Colombeia. Vol XVII. Revolución Francesa. 1795–1797. Document 3695. p. 215–236.

Becerra, Ricardo: **Ensayo histórico documentado de la vida de Don Francisco de Miranda. General de los ejércitos de la Primera República Francesa y Generalísimo de los de Venezuela**. - Caracas, Venezuela. Imprenta Colón. - 1896. 2 volumes. Include additional notes and an error list (p. 529–541). Vol. II. p. 444–455.

El Patriota de Venezuela. N° 2. "**Sobre la situación actual de la Francia; y sobre los remedios convenientes a sus males**. p. 326–342.

Rojas, Arístides: **Miranda dans la Révolution Française. Recueil de documents authentiques relatifs à l'histoire du général Francisco de Miranda, pendant son séjour en France de 1792 á 1798. Edition officielle, comparée avec l'édition primitive de 1810 publiée à Londres par ordre du Général Miranda, arrangée d'après un plan méthodique et chronologique, augmentée de documents omis dans l'Edition de 1810, enrichie d'un appendice dans lequel se trouvent des appréciations d'historiens français anciens et modernes, sur Miranda; et précédée d'une préface par Aristides Rojas,** *(Caracas, Venezuela).: 5-11-1826 – 3-1894), avec l' autorisation du gouvernement National.-* Caracas, Venezuela, Imprimerie et lithographie du Gouvernement National.- 1889 (Two different editions were published, one in French and another in Spanish, in memory of the International exhibition of Paris of 1889 and in honour of Miranda's role in the French Revolution. Also? a gold medal was issued with the bust of Miranda.

It also was published in Spanish in Caracas in the review "El Patriota", n°2, with the following comment:

> The little pamphlet that we present in translation is the opinion that the citizen General Miranda gave to France in the year 95, when this nation, torn to pieces by Robespierre's tyranny and submerged in anarchy by the factions that divided it, hesitated without finding Solid base of government on which to lean. Then this freedom leader, forgetting the resentments that should encourage him against a people that had paid so poorly for his services and that did not take into account having fought for the defence or his rights, took the pen to stamp these principles that are the foundations of the civil and political freedom of the peoples. We believe, therefore, that in making them known, we will do a service to all those good citizens who are engaged in the investigation of such an important matter.

Text:

"Some Thoughts about the Present Condition of France and the Remedies for its Diseases", July 1795, Paris[39]".

Paris, 2 July 1795.

Sed ea animi elatio, quae cernitur in periculis et laboribus, si justicia vacat, pugnatque non pro salute communi, sed pro suis commodis, in vitio est: non enim modo id virtutis non est, sed potius immanitatis, omnem humanitatem repellentis.

Cic. Offi. Lib. I. Cap. 19.[40]

[Translation: *The value shown in the dangers and the work is a vice, if justice does not accompany it, if the particular interest, and not the health of the Homeland, is the reason that makes it acts; so far from being a virtue, it is only ferocity that opposes all human feeling.]*

Every upright citizen's primary responsibility is to stand by their Fatherland in times of peril. Following the catastrophic upheavals instigated by tyranny and

---

[39] The original title is: *Opinion du général Miranda sur la situation actuelle de la France, et sur les remèdes convenables à ses maux.-* París: Impr. de la rue de Vaugirard. 1795. 23 p.; in-8.

[40] Cicerón, Marco Tulio: *Sobre los deberes*/Marco Tulio Cicerón; estudio preliminar, traducción y notas de José Guillén Cabañero. 2ª ed. Madrid: Tecnos, 2002. LVII, (Clásicos del pensamiento; 64).

disorder, which have pushed France to the brink of anarchy, the only beacon of hope for our nation and the many freedom-loving Frenchmen is the close alliance of virtuous and enlightened individuals. With the support of those who have suffered under terrorism, we can salvage our nation, overlook past grievances, and defend our imperilled freedom, even if it means setting aside personal animosities.[41]

Peace and Government: these are the goals that all voters aim to achieve.

Has such a unanimous agreement of wills expressed the needs of a whole country more decisively?

The unfortunate events of the revolution have nonetheless produced a good outcome: since public interest has become the most critical issue for each member of the social body, no other is known to them. People and properties have so often been the victims of private and public violence that even the coldest, most selfish person acknowledges the necessity of a protective authority and of an organisation that consists of several powers so that citizens need not fear the arbitrariness of their exercise.

Deep down, to ask for peace is to want a Government. Foreign powers will not trust our treaties when, as one faction is replaced by another, it can invalidate them. Therefore, only a wise division of powers can stabilise a government. All the constituted authorities will zealously watch each other because they are all interested in the permanence of the constitution from which they emanate, so they form a joint league against the enemy of any of them. Conversely, when all the powers are concentrated in one body, it will take upon itself the authority of the whole mass, and it will be enough for a faction to shoot against this sovereign mass to provoke, in fact, a revolution. The 31st of May[42] and the ninth of Thermidor[43] let the same National Convention subsist, yet both changed the face of the State because both forced power to change hands.

The dreadful tyranny of Robespierre and the former Committee for Public Safety was a product of this fatal confusion of powers. It is worth noting that the beginning of the iniquities and murders must be fixed at the time of the Convention when transferring all its strength to the Committee of Public Safety it banished the ghost of the executive power completely, a power which, although subject to the whims of the legislator, still posed a weak barrier. This committee took over the judicial power that the Assembly had already usurped in a grave situation. It was the Convention that, either through the influence of the Junta or alone, dictated the outcome of judgements, and even the shadow of civil and political freedom disappeared from this wretched soil.

Six years of revolution give us the excuse to seek in the history of different peoples the evils that confusion of powers brings about; we have committed the most horrible crimes, and we have suffered tragedies unheard of in the historical annals of the world, for no other reason that the Constitution granted itself an abundance of

---

[41] Paragraph indicated by Miranda in the original.

[42] Date starting the proscription of the Girondins by Robespierre.

[43] Date of the Robespierre fall, ending the Terror period.

powers more extraordinary even than those of a tyrant. Individuals who have oppressed their people have been stopped either by the customs, the laws or the beliefs of those they subjected; the Convention, on the contrary, trying to change everything, and upsetting all the principles, respected nothing, jumped over docks, slowed at no obstacle, and this tyrannical body ended by tearing to pieces anything that would not yield, and by destroying everything that went against its plans.

« *Les lois étaient sans force, et les droits confondus;*
ou plutôt en effet, L'Etat n'existait plus.»[44]

The happy revolution of 9 Thermidor dismantled chaos, but when light cut through the darkness, we were horrified to see the magnitude of the evil done and the inadequacy of the remedies. The relations between society were out of order, its ties were loose, there was no guarantee of personal security, and property had no solid base. The source of national wealth was exhausted, and its channels were obstructed, separated or broken. Anything the State took with one hand, it squandered with the other. Such are the effects of tyranny and the consequences of the confusion of powers.

It is convenient to sail in the opposite direction to return to the principles from which we have been so hideously torn away. Liberty should scrupulously divide them and prevent the monstrous confusion from happening again, and this is the first step in re-establishing order.

Two conditions are essential for the absolute independence of powers: first, that they emanate from a single source; second· that they continuously watch over each other. The People would not be sovereign if one of the constituted powers that represent them did not emanate from the people directly, and there would be no independence if one of them created the other. Give the members of the Legislative Power the capacity to name the members of the Executive, and it will exert over them an ill-fated influence that will destroy political freedom. If it names the judges, it will likewise influence the judgements, and the same will happen to civil liberty. Such is the case in England, where the Executive Power has an outstanding influence over the Legislative Power, and political liberty suffers considerably. The Judicial Power, although elected by the Executive, is protected from its pernicious influence because the Jury consists of the People, and the judges cannot be removed; for that reason, civil liberty has received no blows.

Only the executive power must have agents to carry out the functions assigned to it and must, therefore, appoint them. Since the other powers cannot delegate their functions, it is part of their essence not to be able to nominate employees. It would be absurd to think that the Legislative Power should appoint the ministers of the Treasury, as any matter concerning the finance of the State is a purely administrative function and, consequently, belongs to the Executive Power or to the agents it has appointed under its strict responsibility.

[44] "The laws were powerless, and the rights were denied or, rather indeed, the State did not exist anymore".

For more than a century, England has entrusted its Executive Power with the administration of the money collected from public contributions without the slightest inconvenience. Even though the Crown has often abused its Civil List to gain followers in Parliament, the State's funds have never been poorly managed. The Americans have equally entrusted this function to the Executive Power, and Hamilton,[45] designated as Secretary of the Treasury by the President of the United States, is well known for both his honesty and administrative skills. His talent and operations have re-established public credit to such an extent that paper money, which at the time of the celebration of peace was worth 10% of its value, has achieved under the current Constitution the value of 127%: a phenomenon that surprises all those who examine effects without taking their causes into account.

Powers must watch over and contain each other mutually, and none of them must assume the exclusivity of this commitment as they have all been nominated by the sovereign. If they have been trusted equally, why should we believe that one of them is infallible and incapable of corruption, whereas the others are subject to error and depravity? Nonetheless, it is an absurd mistake of those who suppose the legislative power is the natural observer of the executive branch and do not believe that the second has any right to inspect the first. Those who judge matters in this way obviously forget that the three powers are like sentinels in the vanguard, watching over the security of the State and that if one of them strays from its functions, the others must set off the alarm to warn the people, who will then see to its health and security. It is unlikely that three independent and zealous powers would ever coincide to betray the interests of the sovereign, and it is on this moral probability that the citizen's security regarding civil and political freedom has been founded.

A legislator must undoubtedly be immune to his opinions, and there would be no freedom in that nation in which a member of the Legislative Body could be tried for what he said or wrote in the exercise of his functions. But does this mean that the Executive Power cannot denounce before the people the attempts of the Legislative Body to trespass on its functions and become involved in the executive sphere, thus attacking political freedom? I do not believe so and think defending such a strange theory is challenging.

The strength of the Executive Power must be in direct proportion to the freedom of the people and the number of its citizens. All politicians agree that the larger the nation, the stronger the power that enforces the laws must be. However, not all agree that it should be made more vigorous the more significant the latitude the citizens enjoy in exercising their liberty. There is nonetheless a self-evident truth: that men's

[45] **Alexander Hamilton** (1757–1804). Colonel in the American Revolutionary Army. Aide-de-camp and Private Secretary of George Washington during the War of Independence. He contributed extensively to the American Constitution with his "Federalist Papers" [Hamilton & others, 1787]. As the first United States Secretary of the Treasury (1789–1795), he organised the Federal State Bank and guaranteed the Union's debt. Jefferson was hostile to his industrial and decentralisation policies. His antagonism with John Adams contributed to the failure of the Federalist Party. He becomes Miranda's friend in New York and cooperates with him on ideas for the South American liberation project. He dies in a duel provoked by Aaron Burr, sparked by political rivalries.

activity increases with their civil liberty and that it is, therefore, necessary for a more significant force of repression to contain them if they leave the path of reason. In free countries, citizens operate energetically and can do anything as long as they do not affect the rights of others; therefore, a sizable repressive force is needed to stop them from crossing this barrier.

Since France wishes to be the freest and most numerous of all existing republics, it is necessary to give it the most vigorous and firmest of governments; otherwise, it would be toppled immediately by the destructive action that the people would continuously exercise against it. From this truth, we can deduce that the Executive Power of the French Republic must not be numerous because, as Rousseau has said, '*The power of every government is inversely proportionate to the number of its members*.' In order to answer the questions of those who believe that extraordinary talents in the people in charge of such a vital function, let us observe that neither genius nor eminent talent should be considered essential qualities in the members in charge of the Executive Power, but prudence and justice, the President of the United States[46] (whom I know personally) has not gained the trust of his fellow citizens for his brilliant qualities, which he does not have, but for his consummate prudence and the rectitude of his intentions. This prudence and righteousness of judgement have dictated to him the selection of wise and skilful agents who have so effectively consolidated freedom and happiness in the country.[47]

One or two men at the head of the executive power[48] who ardently desire the nation's happiness and who choose six honest and talented ministers will have all they need to cooperate competently in the solid establishment of the liberty and joy of the French people.

It is also of the most significant importance that it should not be made up of only one chamber or part of the legislative or representative body, the one to have the initiative or right to propose laws, while the other is deprived of it, but in case this is the favoured system, the prerogative should instead go to the senate or council of elders, as a body that has grown old in the knowledge of business, well instructed and mature, by age, and not to the chamber or council of the 500 whose qualities are not these.[49]

---

[46] George Washington, who received Miranda in Philadelphia in 1783.

[47] Paragraph indicated by Miranda in the original.

[48] Underlined by Miranda in the original.

[49] Starting in April 1795, the Thermidorian Convention has been working on a new Constitutional text. This Constitution of the year III was enacted in the year IV (on September 25, 1795). Article V created the bicameral Legislative Power, which was instituted on September 23, 1795, and created the bicameral Legislative Power, which was initiated on September 23, 1795, made up of the Council of Elders and the Council of the Five Hundred. The Council of Elders, elected for a term of 3 years, comprised 250 deputies, of whom 1/3 were renewable each year, who were required to be at least 40 years old. It was incumbent on them to approve or reject the laws proposed by the Council of Five Hundred but not to amend them. The Council of Five Hundred comprised 500 deputies, who must have been at least 30 years old. They were elected for a term of 3 years and renewed every third year. He had the initiative of laws that had to be approved by the Council of

Only the senate proposed laws in Athens, and the people's assembly adopted or rejected them. In America, the Senate has the same rights as the House of Representatives, which, in imitation of the House of Commons in England, has the exclusive right to propose *money bills* or laws related to taxation. This excellent exception in a mixed government, such as the English, seems excessive in a democratic republic like the United States, where the people need not fear the impositions that an aristocratic body would wish to impose on them. And so, it seems to me more akin to the principles of democracy that these two chambers represent and to the general good that should result from the formulation of laws, that both should have the mutual right to propose and sanction them.[50]

PEACE

The confidence foreign powers can have in our government will be the surest way to enter into conferences that will give Europe peace and tranquility to the State. Still, it will not come before we declare loud and clear the *principles of moderation and justice*[51] that must guide the French nation after it has achieved liberty. Only justice consolidates states, as naturally, a league will form against those who usurp power, just as citizens of a country will form a league against anyone who wishes to infringe upon their rights. The glory of conquest is not worthy of a republic founded on respect for human rights and the great maxims of philosophy. The Alexanders, the Caesars and their like would be the dangerous citizens in it; the peaceful philosopher and the honest magistrate are the most necessary because they can always serve it.

The extension of France offers it enough means to defend its liberty and independence. Any accretion would only embarrass a government already too complicated in such a vast country that desires democracy and would only produce the effect of unprofitable jealousy on the part of her neighbours.

The natural glory of a country consists in its happiness and safety, not in the vain glory of its conquests. Let us see what Rousseau has to say on such an important matter:

Elders. When Miranda was writing his pamphlet, he was aware, through his friends' deputies, of the draft Constitution of Year III that was being prepared.

[50] Miranda's note in the original: One is surprised reading the article on the state of citizens in the draft of the constitutional act, that the service in the land or sea armies of the Republic is not enough to give a foreigner the right of citizenship. At the same time, every man who has lived 7 years on French soil becomes a citizen without requiring any service of him. However, if a brilliant and irrefutable proof of attachment to the cause of freedom can be given, this is spontaneously taking up arms for its defence; it is what the foreigner who fights for the Republic does. If a national who has served in the army is exempt from all the other qualities required to be a French citizen. What more excellent reason should this provision apply to one who voluntarily consecrates himself to a service that the native of the country is obliged to fulfil? England, the greediest of all the free countries in granting naturalisation, nevertheless gives it to all foreigners who serve for 3 years in the navy squads or for 2 years only in the troops of their colonies, and this even in times of peace. The law rejects this right to any other title unless a particular naturalisation bill has been obtained. (Digest. Angl. Vol. II, pages 239 and 240. Lond. 1791).

[51] Underlined by Miranda in the original.

> The greatness of nations, an extension of states! First and foremost, it is the origin of human suffering and, above all, of the innumerable calamities that undermine and destroy civilised people.
>
> In most small states, whether monarchies or republics, their citizens know and observe one another because the heads can see what mischief is done and what good can be achieved, and because their orders are carried out under their eyes. The large countries burdened by their own masses groan either in anarchy or under the yoke of lower-ranking oppressors, which, by the law of gradation, they will have. Only the Supreme Being could govern the world; superhuman faculties would be necessary to govern large nations.

Disapprove of the exaggerated pretensions that the Decemvirate presented as the vote of the nation; declare that France will circumscribe to its former borders, adding only a few war posts to keep its frontiers protected from insults: these must be the first diplomatic operations of the new government of the French Republic; and since the maxim is that no foreign power should interfere in its internal regime, likewise, she should not in principle, intrude in that of other people. Luxembourg, Mons, Tournay, Newport, Kasserlantern, Gezmezheim and other locations placed in the line of defence will make our borders easier to defend than if we extended them to the edge of the Rhine. The Alps, the Pyrenees and the Ocean must be the limits of France,[52] and always taking in the mountains, the line of demarcation to be the water courses, all the townships situated between our borders and the Rhine must be declared free, independent and friends of the French people. Those townships will form, so to speak, a double inaccessible barrier against the unforeseen attacks of our enemies, and their independence, guaranteed by France and the other belligerent powers, will assure their tranquillity. Thus, freedom under the protection of France (as in former times in the Netherlands) will produce a remarkable change in these simple and industrious localities.

A fair compensation will also be stipulated in favour of those sovereigns who have properties on this side of the Rhine and who shall be indemnified by the three electorates of Mainz, Trier and Cologne, which shall be given to them in exchange for their land on the right side of the Rhine. Once these electorates are eliminated, they will cease to be part of the College of the Empire. But as it is not fair that an individual should be dispossessed of the enjoyment of his rights insofar as is compatible with the general good, an income will be granted to the three electors so that they can live with decency and dignity for the rest of their lives.

Given that the free navigation of rivers is an inalienable right that nature grants those inhabitants of the countries they run through, that of the Lys, the Meuse, the Scheldt and the Rhine will be common to France and to those townships that have properties along the length of those rivers. They can sail freely up to the mouth of the Ocean.

[52] Miranda's note in the original: Those who would like to convince themselves mathematically of the strength, excellence and goodness, militarily speaking, of the borders of France as I have just indicated them, will be able to consult Lloyd, in his third volume, part five, London 1781.

Nonetheless, since the aperture of the Scheldt[53] should give back to Antwerp its former splendour and attract to that harbour the trade and riches of Amsterdam and other Batavian cities, and since France has no wish to harm the interests of her allies, it would be right to give over to the Batavians a part of the Earldom of Antwerp instead of the Dutch part of maritime Flanders, which by treaty is already attached to Belgium. This change would reconcile the interests and advantages of both peoples.

About our colonies, since their produce is of such interest to France, and since her manufacture and trade are based on them, we shall offer our lesser islands for the Spanish part of Santo Domingo and Puerto Rico, which will be given us in exchange for the strongholds that we occupy in Spanish territory.[54] By this one disposition, we would compensate our unhappy colonists for the many losses that the tyranny made them suffer. The cession of these two properties should not be onerous to Spain, given that it obtains no revenue from these two islands. On the contrary, maintaining the military posts is costly to the state because there is no trade or industry. This done, the land would be given to those of our brothers who, by an unfortunate error, or the terror of ferocious persecution, were forced to annex their country, and who, never having taken arms against their fatherland, expiate with long-suffering the mistake of an instant. With this conduct, we will avoid the unfortunate effects that Louis XIV provoked in France by revoking the Edict of Nantes,[55] forcing many industrious men to migrate to a foreign land whose work enriched their homeland, and the loss of which can still be felt.

A peace founded on that basis would somehow repair the evils that the French have caused humankind, destroy the disastrous effects caused by the Treaty of Westphalia,[56] and give the Protestant part of Germany the influence it should have because of its learning, philosophy, and adherence to the fundamental principles of liberty. Finally, the outcome of this war will be as valuable to humankind as the others have been unfortunate.

"Tunc genus humanum positis sibe consulat armis

[53] Key River that flows through the north of France and Belgium, where it is the strategic commercial haven of Antwerp. The Treaty of Münster (1648) granted the Netherlands the right to close the mouths of the Scheldt, which caused great harm to the city of Antwerp. Miranda's triumph in Antwerp allowed the Scheldt to open in November 1792.

[54] The peace treaty signed in Basel on July 22, 1795, between France and Spain, ceded to France the Spanish part of the island of Santo Domingo in exchange for territories that France had taken in the Basque Country.

[55] The Edict of Nantes, signed by Henry IV in 1598 to appease religious conflicts, established the status of Protestants in France. Louis XIV's revocation of this Edict in 1685 triggered a horrible war of religions, provoking a massive emigration of Protestants, who took their industry and wealth abroad, mainly to England, Holland and Prussia.

[56] This Treaty or Peace of Westphalia designates the negotiations and agreements that ended the Thirty Years' War in 1648. This war of religion was the bloodiest one in Europe, killing some eight million of persons. They laid the foundations for a Central European organisation that lasted until the French Revolution and the Empire. They weakened the Habsburgs, caused Germany's dismemberment, and affirmed France's preponderance.

Inque vicem gens omnis amet." VIRGILE.
[translation: "*Then the human race, laying down its arms, consoles itself*
And in turn, the whole nation will die"]

The current fate of Poland[57] should not be an object of indifference to France, as its political existence concerns it more than is commonly believed. Besides, Poland fought valiantly for the noble cause of liberty, and France encouraged her to lead a "diversion" in the North in her favour. The alliance of Russia, Austria, and England, as well as Prussia's aggressive behaviour towards unfortunate Poland, announces deep and dangerous intentions against France, and it is of the utmost importance to scrutinise them and prevent them in time.

How respectable would France be the day in which, abandoning all its conquests, she stipulated the good of humanity and prepared the way to irradiate *healthy liberty?* French people! Such an enviable fortune still awaits you! Fulfil your destinies! Posterity will one day place on balance the horrors of which you are to blame against the good deeds that must produce peace for men, and it will absolve you of your crimes in favour of these benefits.

The powers lured by this significant change will form a congress to dispose of and ratify these great interests, which, bringing together most of the continent, will be helpful, so to speak, to its future happiness. Then, you will enjoy a greater appreciation for your *wisdom*, *moderation,* and *justice* than that which your military prowess and the precarious luck of arms have brought you.[58]

After Europe admires your bravery, you will captivate it with your equanimity. You will prove to the universe that you only fought in defence of your freedom and that after you have saved it from peril, you generously put down your arms without demanding the great compensations you deserve from those who have so unfairly attacked you, not having one complaint to make against you.

FINANCE

One of the worst evils affecting the French nation is the enormous discredit into which its paper money has fallen. We can design any number of systems capable of bridging the distance between the nominal and actual values of the paper. Still, they would all be illusory unless a solid and stable government is established, and even when peace with Europe becomes a fact, the paper money will not acquire enough value without a sufficiently solid government. France finds itself in many of the same situations as the United States of America at the end of its revolution.

Congress's paper was then as unworthy of credit as ours, and it was not the peace and independence treaty but the final constitution that re-established its worth. The latter assured these people the highest degree of happiness and liberty that a nation had ever enjoyed. The same causes would infallibly produce the same effects in our midst. A wise constitution, based on the principles of philosophy and justice, and a government protected from the attacks of factions, would win back the trust of others and achieve the necessary credibility.

---

[57] Second partition of Poland, on September 23, 1793, between Prussia and Russia.

[58] Underlined by Miranda in the original.

It is not the wealth of a nation that inspires confidence but its justice and adherence to proper principles. A nation will display pomp to no avail unless it can prove that the possibility of paying creditors is accompanied by the strong will to fulfil its commitments with exactitude. Bad faith produces worse effects than insolvency because a poor state can get rich and become solvent, whereas it is unusual for an unjust government to keep its promises. A state's credit, like an individual's, is based on the payment of debts and having an opinion. The elements of this credit are, therefore, solvency and good faith. Still, neither will have a solid base until the state has become fixed and invariably consistent: this means until the government has been irrevocably constituted.

The less arbitrary a government is, the more complete the trust will be of those who trade with it because it cannot return to its promises. It is this that makes people prefer the paper money of North America to that of other countries, which established the credit of the English currency.

Without going into the complicated details of the plan that Hamilton presented to the American Government and was then perfected by Congress, I will briefly explain the basis of that excellent operation.

To begin with, Hamilton declared that the nation had a debt to pay and that justice demanded it should be obliged to pay it strictly.

Hamilton later presented the state of the whole consolidated debt, which he then stamped on the great book of the Treasury of the United States. He went on to propose to the creditors the exchange value of the paper in the most advantageous terms for them so that most of the debt would produce an interest of 6% per annum and the rest, a lower interest, 4.5% being the mean. By making it clear to them that the State's revenues by far exceeded the promised interest, he set their mind at ease about getting their money back. They were likewise allowed to exchange their capital against the credit stamped in the great book of the states, according to the value formerly fixed by their laws, or to keep them and demand payment according to previous agreements once the state, which at the time still lacked the funds, was able to do so. It was remarkable that when it was known that the nation had the means to make punctual payments and assure such a high interest rate to the creditors, none refused the change. In a moment, as if by a spell, the same debts, which had been reduced to 10% of their value, rose in a few weeks to 127%, showing that good faith and good administration in a state are a better guarantee of its credit than its wealth or greatness.[59]

In conclusion, peace, the establishment of a vigorous and free government, and public credit will open the sources of prosperity for our country, and France will bless the men who, after so many crimes and suffering, solve this complex problem: how to link freedom to calm and tranquillity.

May these short reflections call the attention of men well instructed in such vital matters so that thinking about these principles more profoundly and developing

[59] Note of Miranda: Those who wish to see in detail what I have just said, can consult the plan published in 1787 by Congress.

their ideas about the constitution that best suits France, they may restore the peace and tranquillity it needs to consolidate its freedom; and by doing so, create the future happiness of a nation so remarkable for its knowledge, taste and industry that it has always exerted influence on other peoples, and must therefore also influence the well-being of humankind.

"Tu Gale exemplo populos moderare memento"

*[*Translation*: 'Remember, Gaule that people are governed by example*

Francisco Miranda

In Paris, this Messidor, third year of the French Republic (2 July 1795).

References

Audoubert, N., [1988], *Un Bouffon sous la Terreur : les exploits du comédien Charles-Hyppolyte Labussière,*

Cochin, A., [1921], Les Sociétés de pensée et la démocratie moderne, Plon, Paris.

Custine, A. de, [1843], *La Russie en 1839*, ré-édition de Véra Milchina [2018], Classiques Garnier, Paris.

Furet, F., [1978], *Penser la Révolution Française*, Gallimard, Paris

Liénart, N., [1804], Charles-Hyppolyte Delpeuch La Bussière, ou Mémoires historiques de M. de La Bussière, ex-employé au Comité de salut public : servant de suite à l'Histoire de la Révolution française, avec des notes sur les événements extraordinaires arrivés sous le règne des Décemvirs, Paris, Marchant, an xii, 4 tomes - 2 volumes.

Maugras, G., de Croze-Lemercier, P., [1912], *Delphine de Sabran Marquise de Custine*, Plon, Paris.

Miranda, F. de, [1929-1950], *Archivo del General Miranda*, ed. Vicente Dávila/ Rubén González, Caracas/La Habana.

Parra-Pérez, C., [1925] Miranda et la Révolution Française, Librairie Pierre Roger, Paris.

Chapter 7
Paris Act, December 1797

Context:

This fundamental document can be seen as the first expression of an international law text, presenting Spanish America as a unified entity willing to negotiate freely with other sovereign countries. It was the first document to propose a coherent, autonomous instrument with a broad diplomatic scope and a geopolitical vision. The Act affirms both the pro-American identity and its right to self-determination, on which it establishes a platform of principles of international cooperation to form Treaties of geopolitical and economic alliances with the only two existing democratic countries. In addition, it marks the need for Miranda to appear with an official mandate and a minimal structure across a network of patriots from several cities in South America. This document creates the first coordination structure for the independence actions of the Spanish-American colonies ("the Board of Deputies of the Towns and Provinces of South America"). Its purpose is to grant an official mandate to its two commissioners (Miranda and Olavide).

The Paris Act was drafted in parallel with the second draft of the constitution to confer a more legitimate status on Miranda's presence and role in London and to submit it to the British government (Prime Minister Pitt, see Chap. 5, document 5.2.2.).

The circumstances of this Act (already explained in document 5.2.2 above) are linked to Miranda's decision in October 1797 to change his strategy and return to London. This change ended 5 years of intense struggle and continuous difficulties, thereby ending his illusions that France could be an ally in his emancipation plan for Spanish America. More precisely, the year 1797 concentrated a conjunction of factors very contrary to Miranda and his plan:

- the "monstrous alliance" of the Treaty of San Ildefonso between France and Spain against England
- his condemnation by the Directory to exile was decreed in July 1797

C. Ghymers, *Independence, Federalism and Regionalism in Latin America: An Analytical Anthology of Francisco de Miranda's Writings (1790-1811)*, United Nations University Series on Regionalism 34,
https://doi.org/10.1007/978-3-031-96938-6_7

- the Directory's decision to plan an invasion of Britain by entrusting it in October 1797 to the triumphant Napoleon, following his popular victories in Italy
- the endless political difficulties of Miranda in France since 1792 due to the instability of successive French regimes
- the self-coup organised by the Directory in September 1797
- the fact and impact of the republican conspiracy fomented in Caracas in August 1797, but the news of which reached Europe only in October,
- The capture of the Island of Trinidad (in front of Venezuela) by the British against Spain, offering an additional opportunity and a logistic argument for involving the British navy.
- The growing tensions between France and the United States were created by their non-neutrality with the British trade

All these factors made Miranda more aware of the urgency of making his plans explicit. Miranda realised that France was again evolving towards an expansionist dictatorship, something he had feared since 1792–93, due to the high probability that the Jacobins would attempt to seize the Spanish colonies. This would expose his homeland to the high risks of anarchy and tyranny, undermining his emancipation plan to establish a democratic federative republic based on education, human rights, and the rule of law. Two treaties between France and Spain had already been signed against England in 1795 (Treaty of Basel) and 1796 (Treaty of San Idelfonso). Miranda knew he could not convince the Directory regime to endorse or cooperate with his plan for American emancipation. Furthermore, the Directory had come into conflict with the USA over the non-neutrality of the United States in its trade with the United Kingdom and the looting by French corsairs of defenceless North American trading ships.[1] Miranda expected that in the event of a war, he would be in a better position to convince the interests of both the British and the United States to form the "Great Atlantic Alliance" he was promoting against the Jacobin expansionism that would attempt to seize the wealth of the Spanish empire. In fact, from the self-coup of the Directory manipulated by some Jacobins with Napoleon in

[1] This episode is known as the "**quasi-war**" (or the "**XYZ affair**") between France and the US. The French pirates seized American commercial ships, accusing them of trading with the English enemy, as a result of both the Jay Treaty (1794) between the United Kingdom and the United States and the US government's refusal to continue reimbursing the loan granted by Louis XVI to the French Republic. In 1796, some 316 ships were seized by French pirates, and France refused to receive the American Minister in Paris in December of that year. In 1798, the French Minister of Foreign Affairs, Talleyrand, blackmailed the US authorities by demanding a substantial personal bribe in exchange for not declaring war against the US, a tactic known as the "XYZ affair". In the hands of very strict observers of the ethical use of public money, the US government was very choked, and this episode marked a lasting perception of French politics. By the end of this pirate war, France had taken over 2000 American ships, causing significant damage to the US economy as well as to France's reputation.

September 1797,[2] and with the return of the corrupt Talleyrand[3] as minister of Foreign Affairs, the "quasi-war" with the United States was worsening, increasing the probability of interest of the new country in defending itself against a French invasion in South America.

After the publication of his moderate and peaceful pamphlet of July 1795 (see Chap. 6, document.6.3) that advocated for a republic with strict separation of powers, warranting human rights and the self-determination of neighbouring peoples, Miranda was persecuted by the royalists, the nationalists, and the warmongering Jacobins (especially Bonaparte). He was also a victim of slander from Thomas Paine and James Monroe (US Ambassador to Paris). He was even accused of conspiring with the Royalists (Vendemiaire riots) and arrested in November 1795, sentenced to exile for the first time (December 1795), but he reached to escape; he even argued on juridical arguments with the government through the press until he obtained a legal residence permit (April 25, 1796), he continued to discuss publicly and in the media against the Directory, the Jacobins and Napoleon, at the time Bonaparte's military victories and art pillages [Quatremère de Quincy 1989][4] in Italy had made this ambitious general very popular in Paris. It is possible that his love affair with Delphine de Custine would explain why he always reached to escape from the political police of Fouche[5] for 2 years, including, at the very last moment in January 1798, his flight to London at the last moment before being captured.

As a result of the self-coup of the (Jacobin) Directory on the 18th Fructidor (September 4, 1797), which concentrates even more powers and controls newspapers and political opinions, Miranda is banned for the second time by the Directory.

---

[2] The **18 Fructidore** coup (4 September 1797) was inspired by the left members of the Directory who were in conflict with the legislative power and about to lose their charges; they turned towards the Jacobins and asked Napoleon for his Army support for eliminating the right and the centre (see in Chap. 5, document 5.2.2., note n°29).

[3] **Charles-Maurice de Talleyrand-**Périgord (1754–1838), a cynical opportunist, used the Revolution as a way to obtain power and money; skilled diplomat, he had an essential role from the beginning of the Revolution, he proposed the nationalisation of the Church's assets in 1789, he was one of the authors of the 1791 constitution, then he fled and hid in England during the dangerous period of 1792–95, he skilfully managed with the Directory and the Jacobins to get back to the post of Minister of Foreign Affairs, which he held since 1797, with some discontinuities, despite the changes of regimes (First Consul, Empire, restoration, until Louis-Philip). He was not ashamed of being corrupt with perceived bribes from foreign countries for more than 60 million; one of his bribery attempts caused a "near-war" with the United States (and durable damage to the French reputation in the US) when he blackmailed the negotiators of the United States by asking for a bribe of several million for avoiding to declare war with France (the so-called «*XYZ case*» o "*quasi-war*").

[4] Miranda published heroic pamphlets against Napoleon's looting of works of art during his military conquests, being defended by the literary Quatremère de Quincy, with whom he had established friendships in the prison of Terror in 1794. See, Quatremère de Quincy (1794, 1989).

[5] Hypothesis of the author. There are no formal proofs, only deductions based on converging presumptions, since Delphine had many valuable contacts, especially when sharing the bed with Fouché, the police chief in charge of chasing Miranda. Another possibility would have been the corruption of the regime that Miranda and Delphine had used to escape. See more details in Chap. 5, note n° 49, in Chap. 6, note n° 17 & 21.

Still, he escapes again and hides in Paris to organise his return to London. First, he sent his Cuban disciple, Pedro Caro,[6] back to London with letters (dated October 15, 1797) for the British government through his friend and financier Turnbull.[7] Second, in order to gain credibility with the British authorities, he self-legitimises himself as the official representative of the Spanish colonies of America using documents he produced with two other patriots. He conceived and produced "official" documents, creating an itinerant coordinating college (which baptised the "Board of Deputies") and bringing together a few disciples or allies who had come to Europe at different times. With two representatives of them (Manuel de Salas and José del Pozo[8]) and on behalf of Pablo de Olavide[9] (absent), baptised "commissioners of South

[6]**Pedro José Caro** (?-1803), Cuban patriot, disciple of Miranda, in charge of negotiating with Pitt, with the President of the United States Adams and with the governor of Trinidad Thomas Picton, but who became a double agent, spying on account of the royalists in exchange for money from 1799. Miranda had total confidence in him and realised too late the treason. Picton, the governor of Trinidad, expelled him in 1799 as a suspect, and it was also Gual's opinion at the same time. It is proven that he traveled to Hamburg in 1799, where he sold information on Miranda's plans with the British government to the Spanish Ambassador, as well as details about Vargas' activities in London. He continued to betray Miranda on behalf of Spain, although hiding from the Spanish authorities in Madrid and Lisbon, until 1803, when he disappeared.

[7]**John Turnbull** (175? -1816) an English banker and businessman, very influential in British governments, was the financier of Miranda's plans and his lifelong friend. He met Miranda in Gibraltar in 1775 or 77 when Miranda was an official of the King of Spain, and they became close friends since these years; even Miranda appointed him his executor of his property and guardian of his children when he left London to set up his expedition landing to Coro. At his father's request, Turnbull's son tried to mount an expedition to free Miranda from the Spanish prison of La Carraca (Cádiz) in 1816, already paying 1000 pounds in the operation. He was, according to Miranda, the person who made possible his material stay in London, advanced him the necessary money so that he could carry out his plans and helped on several occasions to convince the British cabinet of the economic interest for England to support militarily and diplomatically to the Miranda option, the most positive for liberal democracy and free trade. In 1798, Miranda already received 2000 pounds of Advancement (according to a complaint by Duperon) and later about 60,000 pounds to organise a liberating army (according to Thomas Paine, letter to a gentleman at New York, 21 March 1806, p. 141, Miscellaneous Letters & Essays on various subjects, never published before in this country, edited by Carlile, Fleet Street, London, 1819.

[8]**Manuel de Salas** (1754–1841), a Chilean educator and pro-independence activist, travelled to Spain in 1777 and stayed for 7 years. During which he probably met Miranda, although there is no proof. However, he was likely present in Paris in 1797. **José del Pozo y Sucre** (1741–1819) was a childhood friend of Miranda from Caracas, and an officer in the Spanish army who met Miranda on expeditions to North Africa as well as in support of the North American Revolution in Cuba. He defended Miranda as a witness when he was wrongly accused of treason in 1783 in the Campbell affair. He was in London in 1790 on secondment, and he met Miranda there; his name appears in Miranda's "*Archivo*" as a colonel. Pozo worked with Pablo de Olivade. There was a debate about the presence (or even the existence) of these two persons and their nationalities; by mistake, their names appear as Jesuits in the archives of President Adams.

[9]**Pablo Antonio José de Olavide y Jáuregui** (1725–1803), called "the Frenchified". Count of Pilos. Born in Lima, educated in Spain, and protected by the Count of Aranda. Appointed Assistant of Seville and Intendant of the Andalusian Army (1767), he was tasked with developing a plan for colonising the desert lands of Sierra Morena, according to Thurriegel's initial idea, initially proposed for the virgin lands of South America, which involved bringing Swiss, Greeks, and mainly

America", he enacted the Act of Paris. His strategy formally diffused his geopolitical and economic principles, as opposed to the Jacobins and Napoleon, favouring England and the United States. On this basis, he grants himself an explicit mandate for diplomatic negotiations and military leadership, expecting to win more credibility in British opinion. His concern was to assure the government of his capacity to coordinate with other patriots and to justify the resumption of its cooperation with London. His strategy was also very opportune at the time, as an attempt at republican revolution in Caracas by Manuel Gual and José Maria España was known in Europe and a new war with Spain and a possible landing by Napoleon were emerging. This appears clearly from the letter he sent to London (via Caro) the day after the signing of the Paris Act, referring to the events in Caracas. Miranda contacted Manuel Gual and wrote to Thomas Picton, the governor of Trinidad, requesting his assistance in Gual's revolution. At the same time, Gual did the same in favour of Miranda with the British authorities.

Although conceived primarily to persuade William Pitt as a complement to his draft "constitution," this purely Miranda-style document exhibits an unprecedented coherence that reveals the Precursor's long-term geopolitical vision and foresight. The three other associated authors did not play any significant role. It could even be that Olavide - who had not yet responded to the invitation when the meeting took place - disagreed, as follows from his subsequent path of reconciliation with Madrid the year after.

In numerous books, the "*Junta de Diputados*" created by Miranda (Board of Deputies) is designated as the founding "Great American Union" of the lodge of the "Rational Knights", making the Paris Act the birth of a network of Masonic lodges in Latin America. Although it is proved that Miranda organised a vast conspiratorial network from London using specific techniques of the persecuted lodges and that it is also true that the Freemasons played an essential role in the revolutions in Latin America, it seems that merging these two facts is a later romantic interpretation - or recuperation - without any factual proof. It would be to confuse the political network of Miranda, an indisputable fact, with certain later Masonic lodges, also indisputable facts, which claimed, posteriorly to his death in 1816, to follow the republican thoughts of Miranda. Although it is true that certain lodges traced their origins to Miranda's ideology and that Miranda systematically relied on various Freemasons for their libertarian ideals, during Miranda's lifetime, there is no

German settlers to Andalusia. Accused of heresy and of professing the doctrines of the French philosophers (1778), he was sentenced by the Inquisition to 8 years in prison. He escaped and took refuge in France, living in complete secrecy for a few months in Geneva. Again, in France, he showed sympathy for the Revolution, and the Convention granted him the title of French Citizen. During the Terror, he is imprisoned, his assets confiscated, and he is released after the fall of Robespierre (9th Thermidor 1794). In 1798, he retracted his ideas and published his work, "The Gospel in Triumph or History of a Disillusioned Philosopher" (4 vols.) in Valencia. Carlos IV authorised him to return to Spain that same year, and the Holy Office cancelled the sentence that weighed on him. It appears that Miranda associated him with his plans in 1797, assuming he was still by his side, but there is no document proving a formal response to his appearance in the Act of Paris.

evidence that his exclusively political network was affiliated with Freemasonry or its rites. There is also no historical evidence to suggest that Miranda was a formal member of a Masonic lodge. However, there are clear indicators of interest in Miranda for the lodges, their ideas, and their members: he visited several lodges during his travels, and his thoughts demonstrated closeness and clear sympathies with the Masonry of his time. Furthermore, Miranda probably was reluctant to see his name appear in a lodge for security reasons. The only argument for supporting Miranda's lodge membership is deductive. Some supporters of this view (all of whom are Masons) argue that it would not have been possible for a Caracas man to establish so many high-level contacts without the support of Freemasonry in the US, as is the case in Europe. This argument consists of denying Miranda's own talents and considering that the "lover of freedom" would have agreed to enlist in a specific chapel, a somewhat incoherent deductive argument. This legend's responsibility relies mainly on Chilean-Argentinian romanticism (Bohórquez 1978), with historians who reconstructed a beautiful story from their own dreams, and later, the natural tendency to recuperate illustrious men to serve an ideological cause.

Content:

This fundamental document might appear as the first international law text for Spanish America, as it is the first attempt to propose a coherent legal instrument for the region with a broad diplomatic and geopolitical scope. The Act affirms both the Hispanic-American identity and its right to self-determination, establishing a platform of principles for representation and international cooperation to negotiate treaties of geopolitical and economic alliances with the two existing democratic countries at that time (the US and the UK). In addition, it creates an official structure for coordinating the independence actions of the Spanish-American colonies: the "Board of Deputies of the Peoples and Provinces of South America" or the "*Junta de Diputados*"). The document grants an official mandate to its two (self-proclaimed) commissioners (Miranda and Olavide). It also gives essential guidelines for free trade policy, territorial limits (with restitution of Florida and Louisiana to the US, while both allies (the US and the UK) could occupy Porto Rico, Trinidad and Margarita, and mutual assistance, both military and economic, including monetary cooperation between the central banks of the three countries.

The respective roles between the three present signatories and the absent are set. Miranda is designated as the "principal-agent". He is entrusted with Pablo de Olavide to negotiate with the UK and the US, as well as to borrow financial resources and appoint civil and military agents. Both give each other a mutual mandate in case one of them cannot act, and could then designate a deputy. This Paris Act must be read in conjunction with the second draft of the constitution submitted to Pitt (see Chap. 5, document 5.2.2).

Sources:

Written in French and Spanish,

Archivo, Vol XV p. 198–205

Colombeia. Vol XVII. Tercera Sección. Revolución Francesa. Document 3837. p. 575–584.

Colombeia. Vol XVIII. Cuarta Sección. Negociaciones. Document 3958. p. 54–63.

Becerra, Ricardo: op. cit. p. 54–61.

America espera, op. cit. doc. n° 68, pp. 194–199.

A synthetic version in English is available in

South American Emancipation, J.M. Antepara, ed. by R. Juigné, 17 Margaret Street, London, 1810, p. 18–19.

Text:

Paris Act

N° LXV[10]

Corresponding to N° 9 de 1797

Instruction

In Paris, 22 December 1797

We, the undersigned, Don José del Pozo y Sucre, Don Manuel José de Salas and Don Francisco de Miranda, having met in Paris on December 2nd 1797, having verified our credentials ("*poderes*"), have proceeded as follows:

Taking into account that Don Pablo de Olavide has not attended the meeting despite the invitation we issued him at his residence near Orleans

Taking into account that enough time has elapsed to allow for a reply,

Taking into account his precarious state of health, together with the revolutionary regime which currently exists in France, may have prevented him from having an active involvement in our deliberations;

Taking finally into account that the current circumstances are so pressing as not to allow the slightest delay, the below signatories delegates, have believed it necessary for the interest of our fatherland to continue with our task, and we have solemnly convened on the following articles:

1. The Hispanic-American Colonies, having unanimously decided to proclaim their independence and to settle their freedom on unshakeable foundations, now address Great Britain, albeit privately, urging her to support them in an enterprise that is as just as it is honourable. The reason being that if, in peace and without previous provocation, France and Spain acknowledged the independence of the Anglo-Americans, whose oppression was not comparable to that of the Hispanic Americans, England would not waver to help the Independence of the colonies of Southern America, being as it is at war with Spain and France, since the latter despite its open recognition of the sovereignty and freedom of the people, is not ashamed to consecrate in the article II and XIV of the Treaty of defensive and offensive alliance with Spain,[11] the most abject enslavement of 14 million people and their descendants; and this with a spirit of exclusion, all the more hateful compared to the avowal France makes of other people's non-negotiable right to give themselves the type of government they prefer.

[10] Error in the original is N° 45.

[11] A note in the original indicates that this Treaty was signed on 19 August 1796.

2. An alliance treaty similar to the one that His Most Christian Majesty[12] proposed to the United States of America must be taken as a norm to complete such an important transaction, with the difference nonetheless that the conditions stipulated for England would be more advantageous, fairer and honourable. On the one hand, England must agree to supply South America with sea and land forces to establish her Independence and protect her from strong political convulsions; on the other hand, America is committed to paying her ally a considerable sum, not just as compensation for the costs implied in its help, until the end of the war, but to pay off a good portion of its national debt. And to compensate, even to a point, the mutual benefit received, South America will pay England, immediately after independence has been established, the sum of …. Million pounds.
3. The naval forces to be requested from England must not exceed 20 warships; land forces will not exceed 8.000 infantry and 2.000 cavalry. In the defensive alliance to be signed, it will be stipulated that if England does not require infantry or maritime resources, America will compensate its naval contingent in monetary terms.
4. A defensive alliance between England, the United States and Southern America is indicated in such a way by nature, by the geographical situation of each of the three countries, by the produce, the industry, the needs, the habits and characters of these three nations, that the alliance must be long lasting, especially if care is taken to consolidate it by the similarities, in political form, of each government; that is, by the enjoyment of civil liberty wisely conceived and widely accessible. It can be said that it will be the last refuge of freedom, daringly attacked by the hateful maxims of the French Republic, the only way to create a counterweight capable of putting a stop to the destructive ambition of the French system.
5. A commercial treaty will be signed with Great Britain, conceived in the most advantageous terms for the British nation. Even though all notions of monopoly must be discarded, the treaty will naturally and reliably ensure that a vast majority of her manufactures are bought, as the population approaches 14 million inhabitants. It stocks foreign-manufactured products and consumes many European luxury items. English trade will also benefit by conveying all over the world, via its capital and factories, the precious fruits and abundant produce of Southern America. The basis of this treaty would be not to forbid the introduction of any commodity.
6. For a certain amount of years, in favourable but not exclusive conditions, Southern America will guarantee Great Britain the crossing or sailing of the Panama isthmus, which at some point will have to be opened, likewise the sailing of the lake of Nicaragua, which will also be opened to ease communication between the South Sea and the Atlantic Ocean, all measures that would greatly interest England.

[12] Designate the King of France.

7. In the current circumstances, there will be no commercial treaties with the allies of Southern America because the rights to import and export must be fixed following the common interests of the people that form the Hispanic American Colonies, especially of those regions known as the Viceroyalties of Mexico, Santa Fe, Lima and Río de la Plata, and of the Provinces of Caracas, Quito, Chile, etc., etc. We shall have to wait for the meeting of the deputies of these different countries in a legislative body to make, all in unison and in this respect, final arrangements. The current treaties will continue to operate on the same basis regarding those nations and the friendly powers.
8. The close association that the Bank of England can immediately establish with the Banks of Lima and Mexico for mutual support will be a significant advantage England will obtain from the independence of and the alliance with Southern America. This means that England's monetary credit will be based on solid foundations.
9. The United States of America can be invited to sign a treaty of friendship and alliance. If that were to happen, we would guarantee them the possession of the two Floridas and even Louisiana so that the Mississippi becomes the best border between the two nations that occupy the American Continent. In exchange, the United States would provide Southern America with an auxiliary force of 5,000 infantry and 2,000 cavalry while the war necessary to obtain its independence lasted.
10. In case Southern America, after the peace treaty, is attacked by any enemy, the United States, by the defensive alliance that is signed, will provide the number of troops stipulated in the former article. The contingent of Southern America will be presented as a sum of money.
11. About the islands that the Hispanic Americans own in the American archipelago, Southern America will only keep Cuba because the harbour of Havana - the key to the Gulf of Mexico - is indispensable to its security. The other islands, such as Puerto Rico, Trinidad, and Margarita, which hold no interest in Southern America, can be occupied by the allies, England and the United States, and will obtain remarkable benefits from them.
12. The crossing of the Isthmus of Panama and the lake of Nicaragua will also be open to the merchandise of American citizens; likewise, the export of produce from South America can be made in ships from that nation. The Americans should become for us what, for so long, the Dutch have been for the Northern powers, namely, the merchant navy.
13. The military operations in our American continent, and the arrangements made for these with the United States of America and England, in connection to the help that those allied powers may grant us to fight for our independence, will be trusted during the war to the consummate experience, expertise and patriotism of our compatriot and colleague don Francisco de Miranda, born in Caracas, in the province of Venezuela; the essential services that for the last 15 years he has rendered the cause of the independence of our country entitle him to unchallenged rights for that post. Accordingly, He will receive detailed instructions when he lands the first body of troops on the Hispanic American continent or

when the country's militia, totally or partially, is in arms. For the moment, we wish to express our desire to see the military operations begin on the Isthmus of Panama or firm land, not only because of the strategic importance of the locations, but also because those people are ready to fight for the independence of their country at the first signal. It would be convenient to have a fleet of eight or ten warships pass to the South Sea because we fear that Spain, which keeps naval forces in that sea, will put obstacles to our operations there.

14. Don José del Pozo y Sucre and Don Manuel José de Salas will depart without delay, following instructions, to Madrid to present themselves to the Junta, give an account of their mission in Paris and deliver a copy of this instrument. The Junta only awaits the arrival of these two delegates to be forever dissolved and to continue to different points of the American Continent. There, the presence of its members is necessary to provoke, as soon as the support from the allies materialises, a combined and general explosion of all the peoples of Southern America.
15. Don Francisco de Miranda and Don Pablo de Olavide are authorised to name civil and military agents to help them in their mission. Still, the appointments they make will, in this case, be provisional.
16. Don Francisco de Miranda and Don Pablo de Olavide are equally authorised to request loans in the names of those mentioned above, Hispanic American colonies, when they believe it necessary to fulfil the mission entrusted to them. They will pay the usual interest in similar cases and will be responsible for investing such sums, being accountable to the Government of Southern America when it so requires.
17. Don Francisco de Miranda and Don Pablo de Olavide have been commissioned to obtain in England without delay the following items:

    (a) A full artillery siege train consisting of at least sixty cannons in good condition and a hundred other light and position artillery pieces.
    (b) The full clothing of 20.000 infantrymen and 5000 cavalry with all the necessary riding gear.
    (c) Thirty thousand infantry sabres.
    (d) Ten thousand spears with their poles.
    (e) Conical tents to camp 30.000 men, and
    (f) Fifty field glasses

18. Don Francisco de Miranda will proceed alone if his precarious health or unforeseen circumstances prevent Don Pablo de Olavide from reaching Paris within the next twenty days, thereby continuing his mission to London. In that case, he will hold the same authority as if he were in the company of his colleague, benefiting from his help and advice. If forceful circumstances demand the support of a colleague, Don Francisco de Miranda can, if he judges it convenient for the good outcome of his commission, engage his compatriot Don Pedro Caro, currently employed by him in London, in a secret mission or any other person whose honesty and talents he can avow for. Conversely, if, due to the revolutionary French regime or the state of his health, Don Francisco de Miranda

cannot travel to London, Don Pablo de Olavide will have the right to continue this mission alone or in association with a colleague.

The under signatories, Don Francisco de Miranda, Don José del Pozo y Sucre and Don Manuel José de Salas, delegates of the "Junta" of Deputies of the peoples and provinces of Southern America, after a careful analysis of the articles above, we declare that those articles must be both a power and instructions to our commissioners Don Francisco de Miranda and Don Pablo de Olavide, envoys to London and if necessary, to Philadelphia. And we wish that these can supply any other instrument we omitted, given the difficult political circumstances that weigh upon this country. To facilitate negotiations, we have written two copies of this document, one in French and the other in Spanish, for the Junta in Madrid.

These are the only steps that at the moment we were able to take because our compatriot and leading agent, Don Francisco de Miranda, has had to live in absolute retirement to avoid being expelled, a punishment applied to all those citizens who distinguish themselves by their merits or talents, and which has been the only cause for the delay and other setbacks that we had to combat in the pursuit of our assignment.

Written in París on 22 December 1797, (L.S.) JOSÉ DEL POZO Y SUCRE
MANUEL JOSÉ DE SALAS, FRANCISCO DE MIRANDA
I confirm this text: F. de MIRANDA
DUPEROU, Secretary.[13]

References

Becerra, R., (1896), *Ensayo Histórico de la vida de Don Francisco de Miranda*, Caracas.

Burke, W. (1807), "*South American Independence: or the Emancipation of South America, the Glory and interest of England*", J. Ridgway, London.

Burke, W., (1808), *Additional Reasons, for our immediately emancipating Spanish America, deduced from the present crisis: and containing valuable information, respecting the late important events, both at Buenos Ayres, and in the Caraccas*, London. Reprinted by Creative Media Partners, LLC, 2015.

Bohórquez-Morán, C., (1998), *Francisco de Miranda, Précurseur des indépendances de l'Amérique latine*, L'Harmatan, Paris.

Mancini, J., (1912), *Bolivar et l'émancipation des colonies espagnoles, des origines à 1815*, Paris.

Miranda, F. de, (1929–1950), *Archivo del General Miranda*, ed. Vicente Dávila/ Rubén González, Caracas/La Habana.

Mitre, B., (1859), *Historia de Belgrano y de la Independencia Argentina*, Buenos Aires.

Quatremère de Quincy, (1989), *Lettres à Miranda*, Ed. Macula, Paris, 1989.

Vicuña-MacKenna, B., *Vida del Capitán General de Chile, Don Bernardo O'Higgins,* Obras Completas, Vol. V, Santiago de Chile, (1882/1936), p. 114.

[13] In the original the names of the Commissioners and their signatures, as well as some words and lines, are crossed out in the text.

Chapter 8
Extracts from Miranda's Leading Journalist Publications in London 1810

8.1 Antepara's Book on Miranda, "THE EMANCIPATION OF SOUTH AMERICA", London, 1810

Context:

At the beginning of 1810, a book under the name of the Ecuadorian revolutionary José Maria de Antepara[1] was published in London, dedicated to Miranda's constant efforts to emancipate South America and detailing his political ideas. In reality, this book, initially proposed by Antepara in 1809, was drafted mainly by Miranda. Tired of the repeated failures in his many years of efforts to convince the British government that his plan to liberate Spanish America was also in their own interests, Miranda changed his strategy by directly addressing British public opinion through a journalistic operation aimed at influencing the British government and Parliament to support his plan. However, his room for manoeuvre in London was narrow when the British authorities, under pressure from Spain, a forced ally facing Napoleon's threat, were inclined to expel Miranda if he continued his revolutionary activities in

[1] **José Maria de Antepara** (1770–1821), Ecuadorian independence patriot (Guayaquil), discovers Miranda's emancipatory argument in London in 1809 through the article published in the "Edinburg Review" followed by personal contacts; he becomes his friend and decides to change his plans to collaborate closely with Miranda in London and publish with him the magazine "El Colombiano" destined to organise information in Latin America from London, he also decided to defuse in English the arguments sustaining the combat of the Precursor to achieve the emancipation of Latin America. He accompanied Miranda in his negotiations in London with the Lopez Mendez, Bolivar and Bello's delegation. He travelled with Miranda when he returned to Venezuela at the end of the year 1810. In 1812, he escaped with the archives of the Precursor after Bolivar's betrayal in La Guira 1812. He will play a crucial role in Ecuador's identity, being a co-author of the constitutional regulation. He was killed in combat in Guayaquil in 1821, fighting for independence.

C. Ghymers, *Independence, Federalism and Regionalism in Latin America: An Analytical Anthology of Francisco de Miranda's Writings (1790-1811)*, United Nations University Series on Regionalism 34,
https://doi.org/10.1007/978-3-031-96938-6_8

London. Therefore, he was obliged to act behind the names of others. This was already the case in 1807, when William Burke interviewed him in detail and published under his direct influence "*South American Independence: or the Emancipation of South America, the Glory and interest of England*". Again in 1808, Burke published a complementary argument with Miranda's cooperation. In 1809, this was thanks to his friend, the economist James Mill,[2] co-writing an important article, published in the influential "Edinburgh Review" [Mill 1809], entitled "The *Emancipation of Hispano-America*." The next step was Antepara's book (1810), entirely dedicated to Miranda's ideas and his emancipatory project, written under the direct Miranda's instructions. Indeed, he was aware that he had exhausted his direct possibilities of influencing the British cabinets. Therefore, he undertakes a very modern propaganda strategy, with significant journalistic works for directly addressing British citizens and informing the public that the British government was not preserving longer-term economic and geopolitical British interests by not supporting his emancipation plan. At the same time, this strategy allows him to circumvent the authorities' control over his mail and personal attempts to foment rebellions in Latin America.

In parallel with the publication of this more than 300-pages book in English, Miranda launched in March 1810 his own newspaper in Spanish, "*El Colombiano*" [Grases 1966, Salcedo Bastardo 1982], a biweekly journal to be the vehicle for disseminating his emancipatory ideas throughout the Spanish Empire. Although he also edited it under the name of his friend Antepara to avoid problems with the British government and diplomatic protests from the Spanish Embassy, the government forced him to close it after five issues the same year [Miranda 1929].

Miranda's strategy worked. In June 1810, the press learned of and followed the events in Caracas on April 19; in July, the newspapers did justice to Miranda's tenacity and vision.

Content:

The excerpts below show the Precursor's extraordinary coherence and strategic vision. They also constitute an excellent synthesis of his chronological attempts and political, diplomatic, and constitutional thoughts. It is clearly a propaganda strategy, although the contents of these texts are based on a succession of proven facts and actions, and take up the ideas and geopolitical vision professed by the Precursor, as already presented in his constitutional projects, such as the Paris Act, and his opinion on the French Revolution.

After demonstrating the advantages that the UK could reap by helping Hispanic America achieve genuine emancipation and develop its full potential, the book illustrates the win-win scenario that would result for the world, including the projected benefits of the Panama Canal. The text revealed Miranda's chronological

[2]This article was published in the prestigious Edinburgh Review in January 1809 (Article 2 in n°XXVI). It was not signed by Smith but "attributed to him." Furthermore, textual parts will appear in the book, officially written by Antepara, which was also co-written with Miranda. **James Mill** (1773–1836), one of the founders of the school of classical economists, linked to Jeremy Bentham and Miranda, His son, the famous John Stuart Mill (1806–1873) was the founder of utilitarianism and one of the fathers of economic liberalism (and later contemporary neo-liberalism) but with an evolution towards social,

development and precise positions. His main principles are exposed in detail, from his conception that socio-economic development depends upon the good governance that was impossible under the Spanish colonial regime to the proposed constitutional formula based upon the local realities and institutions ("Cabildos") combined with some thinkers he referred to, passing through his fears that Napoleon could destroy his plan by confiscating the Spanish colonies.

Sources:

South American Emancipation, J.M. Antepara, ed. by R. Juigné, 17 Margaret Street, London, 1810.

Re-edited as **La Emancipación de la América del Sur**: documents, history and explanatory showing the designs which have been in progress and the exertions made by General Miranda for the attainment of that object during the last 25 years/ by J.M. Antepara; London, printed by R. Juigné, No 17, Margaret-Street, cavendish-Square, 1810, re-edition by David R. Chacón Rodríguez, Fundación Hermano Nectario María, Caracas 2005. Serie: (Francisco de Miranda; t. 2).

Also re-edited under the same title by Editorial Ayacucho, Caracas, 2009.

Text:

(extract)

SOUTH AMERICAN EMANCIPATION.
DOCUMENTS
HISTORICAL AND EXPLANATORY
SHEWING THE
DESIGNS WHICH HAVE BEEN IN PROGRESS
AND THE
EXERTIONS MADE
BY GENERAL MIRANDA,
FOR THE ATTAINMENT OF THAT OBJECT DURING THE
LAST TWENTY-FIVE YEARS
===============
By J. M. ANTEPARA
A NATIVE OF GUAYAQUIL
=============
LONDON:
PRINTED BY R. RUIGNÉ, NO. 17, MARGARET STREET,
CAVENDISH SQUARE;
AND MAY BE HAD OF ALL BOOKSELLERS
1810

....

3 [Importance of the Issue of the Emancipation of South America]

The brilliant prospects which seem to be opened up for our species in the New World, and the cloud which still thickens over the fortunes of the Old, presents at the present hour, a subject of contemplation to the thinking part of the British people; than which, excepting the great question of slavery or freedom, we know not if one more interesting can be imagined. We seize, with avidity, the present opportunity to communicate with them such information on this grand topic as we have been able to collect and doubt that our readers will partake with us in the deep interest with which it has inspired us.

After a tremendous struggle, to which the world has seen, perhaps, no parallel, the power of the despot of France now extends uncontrolled over almost every part of the continent of Europe. The hopes of the instability of that power, which so long continued to flatter the multitude who draw their conclusions not from reason but feeling, have given way to the fears that a series of tremendous successes has irresistibly engendered. We are now placed in the hazardous and most critical situation of neighbours to a power which combines against us all the resources of Europe and cuts off from us that important branch of our own, which we drew from her commercial intercourse. To the period, too, which may elapse before the affairs of Europe assume a condition more favourable to human nature or even to our security, foresight can assign no definite boundary. Even hope can hardly anticipate a very speedy termination. In this new and portentous condition of Europe, we are called upon to look more widely around us and to inquire whether, in the rest of the world, barriers can be found to resist the torrent whose pressure we must continue to dread, and resources to supply those, the channel of which is closed against us.

Taking this critical survey, we believe every eye will ultimately rest on South America. A Country, far surpassing the whole of Europe in extent, and still more, perhaps, in natural fertility, which has been hitherto unfortunately excluded from the beneficent intercourse of nations, is after a few prudent steps on our part, ready to open to us the immense resources of her territory, of a population at present significant, and likely to increase with most extraordinary celerity, and of a position unparalleled on the face of the globe for the astonishing combination of commercial advantages which it appears to unite. From the maturity for some beneficent change, which circumstances and events have for a series of years been working in those magnificent regions, and from the mighty effects they are capable of yielding for the consolations of afflicted humanity, it seems as if that Providence, which is continually bringing good out of evil, were about to open a career of happiness in the new world, at the very moment when, by the mysterious laws of its administration, it appears to have decreed a period of injustice and calamity in the old.

For the mighty benefits to be expected from a just and wise arrangement of the affairs of Spanish America, we are not left to the results of speculation, unambiguous as they are; we can appeal to experience and to fact. We have the grand experiment of North America before us, which the inhabitants of the south are so ambitious to imitate. The states of North America were our own colonies, and they had always been beneficently administered, yet has their independence been far more profitable to us than their subjection? What is the result concerning commerce alone?- The extraordinary fact is that for several past years, we have exported more British growth and manufacturing goods to the United States of America than to the whole of Europe. If such are the benefits resulting from the prosperity of the United States, how many times greater will those necessarily flow from the prosperity of South America?- How much more extensive is the country that the Spanish Americans possess? From enjoying a much greater diversity of climate compared to Europe, that country is much more prosperous and better provided with those commodities for which Europe presents the most eager demand. Of the soil of South America, a significant part is much more favourable to cultivation, much more fruitful, and cleared by nations who had made some progress in civilisation. Of all the countries in the world, South America possesses the most important advantages for internal navigation, being intersected in all directions by mighty rivers, which will bear, at little cost, the produce of her extensive provinces to the ocean. If the population of the United States, amounting perhaps to 6,000,000 souls, could afford so extraordinary a demand for British commodities, what way not the population of South America, extending already to no less than 16,000,000, be expected to afford? It is undoubtedly true that the moral and intellectual habits of the people of South America are not as favourable to improvement as those of North America. Their industry has been cramped; their minds have been held in ignorance by an evil government; hence, they are lazy and superstitious. But remove the cause, and the effects will cease to follow. So sweet are the fruits of labour, wherever the labourer enjoys them unimpaired, that the motives to it are irresistible, and his activity may be counted upon with the certainty of a law of nature. The deduction, therefore, is so minimal that, on this score, it will be requisite to make, that a very subordinate proportion of the superior advantages in soil and climate, which South America enjoys, will suffice to compensate the better habits with which the inhabitant of the United States commenced his career.

Concerning wants, the two countries bear a striking resemblance to one another. From the immense extent of uncultivated soil, which will require many ages to occupy, the whole bent of the population will be turned to agriculture, and it will be their interest, and their desire, to draw almost the whole of the manufactures goods, which their riches will enable them to consume, from other countries. The country to which the more significant part of this prodigious demand will come is unquestionably Great Britain. So far before all other countries, in respect to manufacturing advantages, does she stand that were the circumstances of Europe much more likely to encourage industry than unhappily they are, we could meet with no rival, and as we supply North America, so could we South, on terms which would infallibly draw to us the more significant part of her custom. With this magnificent source of industry and wealth, the channels Bonaparte can shut against us hardly deserve to be named since even the United States surpasses them all. With South America, then, under a free and beneficent government, --though we might weep for the calamities heaped upon our brethren of Europe by an insatiable despot, who, with the words liberty and good of humankind on his lips, would rivet this chains on the whole human race, and expend their blood and sweat for his own momentary pleasure or caprice, -- we might laugh the destroyer to scorn and enjoy prosperity which the utmost efforts of his power and rage could never disturb.

4. [Feasibility of Canal Navigation Across the Isthmus of Panama]

In enumerating, however, the advantages of a commercial nature, which would assuredly spring from the emancipation of South America, we have not yet noticed the greatest, perhaps of all the mightiest event, probably in favour of the peaceful intercourse of nations, which the physical circumstances of the globe present to the enterprise of man: -we mean, the formation of a navigable passage across the isthmus of Panama, -the junction of the Atlantic and Pacific Oceans. It is remarkable that this magnificent undertaking, pregnant with consequences so significant to humankind and about which so little is known in this country, is so far from being a romantic and chimerical project that it is not only practicable but easy. The river Chagre, which falls into the Atlantic at the town of the same name, about 18 leagues to the west of Porto Bello, is navigable as far as Cruzes, within five leagues of Panama. However, though the formation of a canal from this place to Panama, facilitated by the valley through which the present road passes, appears to present no formidable obstacles, there is still a better expedient. At the distance of about five leagues from the mouth of the Chagre, it receives the river Trinidad, which is navigable to Embarcadero; and from that place to Panama is a distance of about 30 miles, through a level country, with a fine river to supply water for the canal, and no difficulty whatever to counteract the noble undertaking. The ground has been surveyed, and not only the practicability but also the facility of the work has been entirely ascertained. In the next place, the critical requisite of safe harbours, at the two extremities of the canal, is here supplied to the extent of our utmost wishes. At the mouth of the Chagre is a fine bay, which received the British 74 gunships in 1740, when Captain Knowles bombarded the castle of St. Lorenzo, and at the other extremity is the famous harbour of Panama. Nor is it the only expedient for opening the important navigation between the Pacific and Atlantic Oceans. Further north lies Nicaragua's grand Lake, which, by itself, almost extends navigation from sea to sea.[3]

It falls into the Atlantic Ocean by a navigable river and reaches within three leagues of the Gulf of Papagayo in the Pacific. Mr. Jefferys tells us it was the instruction of the King of Spain to the governor of St. John's Castle not to permit any British subject to pass either up or down this lake, for if ever the English came to knowledge of its importance and value; they would soon make themselves masters of this part of the country.[4]

---

[3] For the accuracy of these statements, may be consulted a curious and instructive work, drawn up and published in 1762, by Thomas Jefferys, geographer to his Majesty; from the draughts and surveys found on board the Spanish prizes, from other accessible documents, and the statement of eye-witnesses. The title of the book, as it is now but little known, may be worthwhile to transcribe- "A description of the Spanish Islands and Settlements on the coast of the West Indies; compiled from authentic Memoirs: revised by Gentlemen who have resided many years in the Spanish Settlements; and illustrated with Thirty-two Maps and Plans, chiefly from original drawings taken from the Spaniards in the last war, and engraved by Thomas Jefferys, etc."

[4] See p. 43 of "A Description", etc., above cited. What Alcedo tells us is still more extraordinary, that it was even interdicted, *on pain of death*, to propose opening the navigation between the two seas. "During Felipe I time says he: "It was planned to cut it and connect the two seas through a canal, and for this purpose, two Flemish engineers were sent to explore it; but they found insurmountable difficulties, and the Council of the Indies represented the damage that would involve the monarchy, for which reason that Monarch ordered that no one should propose or try to do so in the future, on pain of death.". Alcedo, Diccionario Geografico- Historico de las Indias Occidentales, etc. ad verbum *Istmo*. A similar interdiction and penalty was ordained, respecting the navigation of the Atrato, where there is only an interval of a few miles between the navigable parts of the two rivers. It is navigable for many leagues, but navigation is prohibited under penalty of death, without

We are tempted to dwell for a moment upon the prospects that the accomplishments of this splendid but not challenging enterprise open to our nation. It is not merely the immense commerce of the western shores of America, extending almost from pole to pole, that is brought, as it were, to our door; it is not intrinsically important, though a comparatively moderate branch of our commerce, that of the South Sea whalers, that will alone undergo a complete revolution, by saving the tedious and dangerous voyage round Cape Horn;- the whole of those immense interest which we hold deposited in the regions of Asia, become augmented in value to a degree which, at present, it is not easy to conceive, by obtaining direct access to them across the Pacific Ocean. It is the same thing as if, by some great revolution of the globe, our Eastern possessions were brought nearer to us. The voyage across the Pacific, the winds both for the Eastern and Western passage being fair and constant, is so expeditious and steady that the arrival of the ships may be calculated[5] with almost the accuracy of a mail coach. Immense would be the traffic that would immediately begin covering that ocean by denoting the Pacific. All the riches of India and China would move towards America. The riches of Europe and America would move towards Asia. Vast depots would be formed at the great commercial towns, which would immediately arise at the two extremities of the central canal; the goods would be in the course of perpetual passage from one depot to the other and would be received by the ships as they arrived, which were prepared to convey them to their ultimate destination.

Is it too much to hope that China and Japan themselves, thus brought so much nearer the influence of European civilisation, much more constantly and powerfully subject to its operation, would not be able to resist the salutary impression but would soon receive significant changes in ideas, arts, manners and institutions? The hope rests, at least, on such strong foundations that it seems to rise even to certainty; and then, what glorious results might be expected for the whole of Asia, that vast proportion of the earth, which, even in its most favoured parts, has been in all ages condemned to semi barbarism, and the miseries of despotic power? One thing, at least, is sure: South America, which stands so much in need of industrious inhabitants, would receive myriads of laborious Chinese, who already swarm in all parts of the Eastern Archipelago in quest of employment and food. To her, this would be an acquisition of incredible importance. Thus, the connection between the two countries would still further accelerate the acquisition of enlightened views and civilised manners in China.

Such are a few of the results that one can expect from regulating the affairs of South America. Perhaps no nation has ever been offered the opportunity to effect such a profound change on behalf of humankind as Great Britain, through a

---

exception for any person, to avoid the damage that will follow to the provinces of the New Kingdom, due to the ease with which entrance is possible through it." Ibid, ad verbum *Atrato*.

[5] The reader may consult on the facility and importance of effecting navigation from sea to sea by this extraordinary lake, a curious memoir by M. Martin de la Bastide, ancient secretaire de M. le Comte de Broglio, published in the second volume of "*Historic Abrégé de la mer du Sud*, par M. de Laborde."

remarkable combination of circumstances, is now called upon by numerous motives to help South America achieve. The measure has, for a considerable number of years, been mingled in her councils, among the number of her resolves, and a short history, which, from peculiar circumstances, we are enabled to give with unusual accuracy, cannot be without interest, of what has been done in preparation towards an event which will hereafter occupy so great a place in the history of the world.

5. [General Miranda's Proposal to Mr. Pitt for the Emancipation of South America]

Though projects of hostility, some of them for plunder, some for permanent conquest, had been undertaken during the wars between this country and Spain against particular parts of the Transatlantic dominions, the first time, we believe, that a general scheme of emancipation was presented to the mind of the British minister, was at the beginning of 1790, when the measure was proposed to Mr. Pitt by General Miranda. He met with the minister with the most cordial reception, and, as the dispute respecting Nootka Sound was then subsisting, it was resolved that if Spain did not prevent hostilities by submission, to carry the plan into immediate execution. When an accommodation was effected, and peace was decreed at last, Mr. Pitt still assured the general that the scheme of emancipation in South America was a measure that would not be lost sight of but would infallibly engage the attention of every minister of this country.

6. [Brief Biographical Report on General Miranda]

The man by whom this important suggestion was made, and in whose breast the scheme of emancipation, not first conceived, seems at least to have been first matured, is a native of Caracas in South America, descended from one of the principal families in the country. At the early age of 17, he returned to Spain and, by the influence of his family, obtained a captain's commission in the Spanish army. Early smitten by the love of letters, he was eager to proceed to France to further his education, but permission was denied him, and he was forced to bring the masters, whom he could not find in Spain, from France at his own expense. It is an anecdote not unworthy of record that when the inquisition ordered his books to be taken from him and burnt, he applied to Count O'Reilly, inspector-general of the Spanish army, to see if the order could not be recalled. Still, the inspector told him that all he could do was to condole with him, for the same misfortune had happened to himself.

When France and Spain resolved to take a share in the war being carried on between Great Britain and her American colonies, it happened that Miranda was part of the Spanish army, which was destined to cooperate with the French. Acting thus and conversing with the members of a more enlightened nation than any he had yet seen, the ideas of the young American received that improvement, after which he aspired and in a scene where the cause of liberty was the object of all men's zeal and enthusiasm and in a country, the situation of which in so many respects resembled his own, a similar destiny for this last was naturally presented to his wishes. So deeply was the impression that he had dedicated almost all his life to this design and had been the prime mover in every scheme proposed for the emancipation of the Spanish colonies in America.

After the renunciation, or rather the postponement, of the design part of Mr. Pitt, the next project to change the condition of South America was started by the republican rules of France as part of their scheme for revolutionising the whole Spanish dominions. But Miranda foresaw the dangers with which that design was pregnant and, fortunately, had sufficient influence to persuade its renunciation. To prepare the reader sufficiently for the particulars of this curious affair, it may not be useless to run over hastily the steps by which the general had been brought to the situation in which he then stood.

At the end of the American war, he resigned his position in Spain's service and returned to Europe. He intended to study the institutions of the most enlightened nations and draw from them instruction for the benefit of his native country. For this purpose, he came first to Great Britain[6] and then proceeded to Prussia, Austria, Italy, Greece, and Turkey.

7. [Protection Provided by the Empress of Russia to General Miranda]

He then proceeded to Russia, where he met with Prince Potemkin at Cherson, whose notice he was attracted to, and through him, he was introduced to the Empress at Kyiv. A native of Spain, travelling in search of knowledge and improved by it, appeared to her in the light of a phenomenon. She invited him to remain in Russia, for in Spain, she said, he would be burnt – Spain was not a country for him. When Miranda opened to her, in reply, the views to which he had devoted himself on behalf of his country, she manifested the most substantial interest in the accomplishment of his scheme. She assured him that, in the event of his success, she would be the first to support the independence of South America. She transmitted a circular letter to her European ambassadors, affording him her imperial protection

[6] There is a curious proof of the notice that he and his cause were attracted to this country, even at this early period, in the "Political Herald and Review" for the year 1785, pp. 29, 30.

The flame which was kindled in North America, says the writer in that work, "as was foreseen, has made its way into the American dominions of Spain. That jealousy, which confined government appointments in Spanish America to native Spaniards and established other distinctions between these and their descendants on the other side of the Atlantic, has been a two-edged sword and cut two ways. If it has hitherto preserved the sovereignty of Spain in those parts, it has sown the seeds of a deep resentment among the people. Conferences are held, and combinations are formed in secret among a race of men whom we shall distinguish by the appellation of *Spanish Provincials*. The example of North America is the great subject of discourse and the grand object of imitation. In London, we are well assured, there is, at this moment, a Spanish American of great consequence who is possessed of the confidence of his fellow citizens and who aspires to the glory of being the deliverer of his country. He is a Man of sublime views and penetrating understanding, skilled in ancient and modern languages, conversant in books, and acquainted with the World. He has devoted many years to the study of general politics, including the origin, progress, and termination of different species of governments, the circumstances that combine and retain multitudes of humankind in political societies, and the causes by which those societies are dissolved and absorbed by others. Having visited every province in North America, this gentleman came to England, which he regards as the mother country of liberty and the school for political knowledge. As friends to freedom, we forbear to be more particular concerning this distinguished character. He is a conspicuous proof and example of the fact that it is our object to illustrate. We admire his talents, esteem his virtues, and heartily wish prosperity to the grandest pursuit that can occupy the powers of any mortal, that of bestowing the blessings of freedom on millions of his fellow men."

everywhere, and invited him to draw upon her treasury for his personal support. (See appendix, A.).

8. [Situation of General Miranda in the French Army]

It was after this tour through Europe, in which Miranda spent several years, that he returned, by the way of France, to England; and being by his friend, Governor Pownal, introduced to Mr. Pitt, proposed to him the plan of which the submission of Spain on the question at, issue prevented the execution. At the time when the prospect was thus, for an indefinite period, closed upon him in England, and the first promising movements of liberty in France were attracting the curious from every quarter of the world, Miranda returned to witness the great scenes which were there passing, and to obtain, if possible, from France in its new situation the same favour to South America, which in it had bestowed upon the United States. By his companions in arms, whom he had recently known in America, he was speedily drawn into some connection with the great leaders at that time in public affairs, and when the revolution was first called upon to draw the sword, he was invited and prevailed upon to take command in its armies. (See Appendix B.)

While he was serving with Dumourier in the Netherlands, the republican leaders first conceived the scheme for revolutionising Spain and her colonies. It was communicated to Dumourier by Brissot, in a letter which we have now before us, dated Paris, 28th November 1792, in the following terms:

> *Spain is ripening for liberty; its government is resuming its preparations, it is therefore necessary to make its preparations to succeed, or rather to naturalize liberty there. It is essential to make this revolution in both European Spain and American Spain. Everything must coincide. The fate of this last revolution depends on one man; you know him, you esteem him; it is Miranda. Recently, the ministers were looking for someone to replace Desparbés in St. Domingue; a ray of light struck me; I said, name Miranda. - Miranda first will soon have appeased the miserable quarrels of the colonies; he will soon have brought to reason these turbulent whites, and he will become the idol of the people of color. But then with what ease will he not be able to raise up, either the Spanish islands, or the American continent they possess? At the head of more than 12,000 regular troops who are now in St. Domingue and 10,000 to 15,000 brave mulattoes who will be provided by our colonies, with what ease will he not be able to invade the Spanish possessions? Having a fleet at his command, and when the Spanish have nothing to oppose him. The name of Miranda will earn him an army, and his talents, courage, and genius all guarantee us success....The ministers agree on this choice, but they fear you will refuse to give up Miranda, especially since you have chosen him to replace Labourdonnaye. I promised Monge this morning that I would write to you, and he gave me his word that he would name Miranda governor-general if you agreed to let him go. So hurry up and send your consent. I will add that our excellent friend Gensonné agrees; he will write to you about it tomorrow. Clavière and Pétion are delighted with this idea.*

9. [Project of France for the Emancipation of South America]

It will be readily acknowledged that there was here wherewithal to dazzle a man of ordinary ambition. Yet, the project damped and finally renounced employing Miranda, who began to fear that the revolution was proceeding too fast and too far. In the letter he wrote to Brissot, he presents himself with difficulties in answering his proposal's communication.

> *The plan,* he says, *that you form in your letter is really great and magnificent, but I am unsure if the execution would be certain or even probable. As for the Spanish-American continent and its islands, I am perfectly informed and in a position to form an accurate opinion. But for all that concerns the French islands and their current situation, I know almost nothing at all, and it would be, consequently, impossible for me to form a correct opinion on it. As outlined in your plan, this is the basis of the entire operation. Since it is from the French colonies that the active force must depart to mobilise the people of the opposite continent, we must be sure that this data is accurate and reliable. It also seems to me that my nomination and departure for Santo Domingo would be the alarm signal for the court of Madrid, and for that of St. James, and that the effects would soon be seen in Cadiz and Portsmouth, which would put new obstacles in the way of the enterprise, which, moreover, is too great, too beautiful, and too interesting, to spoil it or to cause it to fail by a lack of foresight at the beginning.*

After further correspondence and consultation, the pressure of affairs, combined with the discouragement offered by Miranda, led to the project being relinquished for the time being. (See Appendix C.)

10. [Extraordinary Advises of General Miranda to the People of France]

Some years after this occurrence, the matter was forgotten amid the violent struggles that agitated Europe. Many months had not elapsed when the reign of Robespierre began, and Miranda, with so many other virtuous men, was buried in the dungeons of the revolution. Though tried and clearly acquitted by the revolutionary tribunal, which declared that no shadow of suspicion was attached to him, he was still imprisoned. He escaped the guillotine only by one of those accidents by which so many others were delivered up to it. When he regained his liberty under the party that assumed power after Robespierre's death, he might still have become a leading figure in the revolution and was offered the command of an army. His answer, however, was that although he had fought for liberty, it was not his purpose to fight for conquest: if France would establish a free and moderate government, retire within her ancient limits, and sincerely offer peace to the whole world, he would willingly contend for her against all her enemies. This remarkable answer rests on as remarkable an authority, for Miranda had the fortitude to enlarge upon the same ideas in a pamphlet and to publish them at the very moment (1795) in Paris. (See Appendix D.)

11. [British Project for the Emancipation of South America]

About the same time, or a little after, Miranda received in Paris the visit of deputies and commissioners from Mexico and the other principal provinces of South America, who had come to Europe to concert with him the measures to be pursued for accomplishing their country's independence. It was decided accordingly that Miranda should, in their name, again repair to England and make such offers to the British government as hoped might induce it to lend them the assistance requisite for the great object of their wishes. The instrument, which was drawn up and put into the hand of their representative, as the document to the British government, of the proposals of the South Americans, is too remarkable an evidence of the views and plans of the leading members of the South American communities, not to deserve at the present moment the most serious attention.

The first article states that the Hispano American colonies having for the most part resolved to proclaim their independence, were induced to address themselves to the government of Great Britain, in the confidence she would not refuse them that assistance which Spain herself, amid peace, had not declined extending to the British colonies in America.

The second article stipulates that South America would pay Great Britain a sum of 30 million sterling for the required assistance.

The third article states the amount of the British force deemed requisite.

The fourth article is presented correctly in the words of the document itself.

A defensive alliance formed between England, the United States of America, and South America, is so recommended by the nature of things, by the geographical situation of each of the three countries, by the products, the industry, by the needs, the customs, and the character of these three nations, that this alliance may be of long duration; especially if care is taken to consolidate it by analogy in the political form of the three governments, that is to say, by the enjoyment of a civil liberty, wisely understood; one could even say with confidence, that it is the only hope that remains to liberty, audaciously outraged by the detestable maxims avowed by the French republic. It is the only means still to form a balance of power capable of containing the destructive and devastating ambition of the French system."

The fifth article relates to a treaty of commerce between Great Britain and South America.

The sixth article stipulates the opening of navigation between the Atlantic and Pacific Oceans by the Isthmus of Panama and the Lake of Nicaragua and the guarantee of its freedom to the British nation.

The seventh article respects the commercial arrangement between the different parts of South America itself, which is proposed to remain on its present footing until the assembly of deputies from the other provinces of the continent can arrange the terms of their union.

The eighth article points to some project to be devised, of a connection between the Bank of England and those of Lima and Mexico, for the purpose of mutual support and of giving England the advantage of that command of the precious metals which the country supplying them might have it in its power to yield.

The ninth and tenth articles relate to the alliance project between South America and the United States. The principal points are the ceding of Florida to the United States, with the Mississippi being proposed as the most advisable boundary between the two nations, and the stipulation of a small military force from the Anglo-Americans to aid in establishing independence.

The eleventh article, respecting the islands, states the plan of resigning all those which belong to the Spaniards, except only Cuba, the possession of which is rendered necessary by the situation of the Havannah commanding the passage from the Gulf of Mexico.

This document is dated Paris, December 22, 1797. The proposal transmitted to Mr. Pitt for the return of General Miranda to this country was acceded to with alacrity; the general had a conference with that minister in January. It accorded with the plans of Mr. Pitt at that time to enter with promptitude into the scheme proposed for the emancipation of South America. The outline of the proceedings was fully agreed upon, and so far had the preparations advanced, that General Miranda, in a letter to Mr. Hamilton, the much-lamented legislator of the United States, dated 6th April, 1798, thought himself authorised to write in the following terms:

> *This will be delivered to you, my dear and respectable friend, by my compatriot Don *******, charged with dispatches of the highest importance for the President of the United States; he will tell you confidentially what you wish to learn on this subject. It appears that the moment of our emancipation is approaching, and that the establishment of liberty on the whole continent of the new world is entrusted to us by Providence. The only danger that I foresee is the introduction of the French principles, which would poison liberty in its cradle, and would soon end up destroying yours.*

As arrangements advanced, on the 19th of October 1798, he wrote to the same gentleman in the following terms:

> *Your wishes are in some way fulfilled since it has been agreed here that, on the one hand, English troops will not be used for land operations since the auxiliary land forces must be solely American, while, on the other, the navy will be purely English. Everything is smoothed out, and we are only waiting for the fiat of your illustrious President to set off like lightning.*

In another letter, of the same date, to General Knox, he says,

> *What pleasure did I not receive, my very dear general, in learning of your nomination to the Continental Army of the United States of America? It appears that our wishes are finally being fulfilled, and that all possible circumstances are aligning in our favor at this moment. May Providence communicate to us enough wisdom to take advantage of it.* (See Appendix E.)

The proposal was that North America furnish 10,000 troops, and the British government agreed to provide the necessary funds and ships. However, the president, Adams, declined to give an immediate answer, and the measure was postponed.

At the dawn of 1801, a significant project was rekindled under Lord Sidmouth's administration. The government's far-reaching plans for South America, which were to be proposed to its people, were carefully considered and approved. Even the military operations were meticulously outlined and prepared for the expedition. However, the signing of the preliminaries of the peace of Amiens led to a postponement of the measure to a later date.

When war was again declared against France in 1803, the business of South America formed one of the principal designs of ministers, and measures were taken to carry it into effect, which was the moment when the peace still subsisting with Spain should be broken. This event did not occur till 1804, when Mr. Pitt was again at the head of administration. The measure was now prosecuted with zeal; Lord Melville and Sir Home Popham were employed in arranging with General Miranda the whole procedure details when the execution was again suspended by the affairs of Europe and by the hopes and exertions of the third coalition.

The prospect thus appearing shut upon them in Europe, the South American exiles from the Provinces of Caracas and Santa Fe, residing in the United States of America and on the island of Trinidad, pressed General Miranda and, at last, prevailed upon him to quit his residence in this country and make an effort in their behalf through the medium of America alone. Though the politics of Britain presented to him, at the moment, no prospect of active assistance, they appeared, at least, to promise the security that nobody of French or Spanish troops should cross the Atlantic to confirm the domination of the enemies of Britain. In these circumstances, he was induced to think that no great force- that nothing more, in short, than what might be requisite to impose respect upon the small number of troops in the Spanish garrisons and to afford some appearance of security to the people, was, in the known condition of the public mind, required to effect the revolution; and at the same time, the disputes subsisting between the United States of America and Spain, respecting Louisiana, afforded him hope in that quarter of all the assistance which the occasion demanded. With a complete understanding on the part of the government here and even, as it would seem, with the promise of support, he proceeded to America. Still, on his arrival, he found, to his mortification, that a compromise on the subject of Louisiana had already taken place and that the public aid of the government was not to be obtained. He was received, however, with cordiality and distinction by the president and secretary and from various quarters received encouragement to suppose that, by private exertions and resources, such means might be got together, as, with the help of good fortune, might be adequate to the enterprise. The government of the United States, from the obvious motive of exculpating themselves in the eyes of France, thought proper afterwards to disclaim all knowledge of the transaction and even to order the prosecution of two of the persons who appeared to have been principally involved in it, it came out upon the trial, to the conviction of the jury, when their upon acquitted the parties, that the government had been privy to all the proceedings of Miranda, and, by never so much as whispering their disapprobation, appeared of necessity, both to him and to his agents, to favour. However, they deemed it impolitic at the time to countenance his undertaking.

12. [General Miranda's Expedition to Caracas, in 1806]

The particulars of the expedition to Caracas are necessary for us to pass over entirely.[7] It failed, feeble as were the means employed in it, chiefly from the intelligence which had been treacherously conveyed to the Spaniards and by the misconduct of the American shipmasters, over whom the General had not sufficient control. But it had this in it of benefit, that the careful protection of person land property which Miranda maintained, removed every shadow of prejudice which the industry of the Spanish agents had been able to raise respecting the purity of his intentions, and had not the British commanders, who seconded his views; been induced to withdraw their support and to urge the dereliction of the enterprise, by the false intelligence which reached the West Indies of the conclusion of peace by Lord Lauderdale, - at any rate, had our government lent in minimal assistance;- not a

[7] The principal facts, together with the proclamations of General Miranda, documents of importance in forming a judgment of the whole bearings of this affair, may be found in a pamphlet, which we recommend as containing some correct information, not to be found anywhere else, entitled: "*Additional reasons for our immediately emancipating Spanish America*" by William Burke.

doubt can be entertained that the province of Caracas would have then declared its independence.[8] (See Appendix F.)

The part our country had in this expedition is still important to explain. The prospect of the vast advantages to Great Britain, from the independence of that part of South America, which was the object of Miranda's immediate views, induced the British Admiral on the station, Sir Alexander Cochrane, to enter into a formal stipulation for specific means of operation he was to afford to the undertaking, and certain advantages which were to be yielded to his country in return. The governors of Trinidad and Barbados allowed the General to recruit in these islands and even from the militia.[9] But after a bit of time, the Admiral wrote to him that by recent instruc-

---

[8] That this was the opinion of the best informed among the Spaniards themselves appears from the following extract of an intercepted letter from Don Dionisio Franco, director of the King's Revenues at Caracas, to the governor of Cumaná: "Un des hommes," says Depons (*Voyage à la Terre Ferme, t. 11. p. 293*) "un des hommes de l'Espagne qui connoit le mieux les interests de sa nation."

"Caracas, 16th of August, 1806."

"Miranda, despicable indeed, if left to his private resources alone, will, it appears to me, give us more to do than what we thought, if supported, as he appears to be, by the English, although the assistance they have until now given him be reduced to the not disapproving only of his enterprise."

"He effected his landing at Coro without any resistance because the garrison of that interesting point was reduced to 200 fusiliers of the militia alone; and although they might have armed more than 1000 men, they had no arms for the purpose; and in the same case, we find, are now all the inhabitants of these provinces."

"With this information, the Captain-General of the province has marched with all the armed force he could collect, but it will be a month before he can reach Coro, where he will probably already be entrenched and in a situation to make good his retreat. That, in my opinion, will be the least of the evils which may happen to us because if the English give him any assistance, let it be ever so little, and offer him support, his situation is the most advantageous of all those he could have chosen in all these coasts; as the peninsula of Paraguaná may afford them a situation to establish another Gibraltar, as long as they are masters of the sea; and it may happen that this spark of fire, that appears nothing, may finish *by devouring the whole Continent, &c.*"

(Signed) DIONISIO FRANCO

[9] The memorandum of Governor Hislop for the commanding officers of the corps of militia in Trinidad is so expressive of his honourable views on the occasion that it is worthy of being read.

It is desirable that a corps of light cavalry, infantry, and artillery should be formed to be put under the command of Count *de Rouvray*, as Colonel of the former, of Colonel *Kingston* of the infantry, and Captain *Harvey* of the artillery, who have volunteered their services with General Miranda; – the Governor will sanction, for this purpose, the offers of volunteers from each corps of militia, not however exceeding in number, twenty out of each hundred. Commanding officers of corps and other officers are expected not in any manner to discourage the voluntary offers of such of their men as may be desirous of going upon the proposed service from which the most important benefits may be expected to result to the British Empire, and in a peculiar degree to this colony; the prosperity cannot fail to be raised to the highest pitch by the success of the enterprise; which, under the skilful guidance of an experienced captain, such as General Miranda has proved himself to be, cannot be doubted; at the same time that the reflections of the possibility of their bitterest enemies getting possession beforehand of the Spanish neighbouring dominions, would not only be a most severe stab to the interests and welfare of Great Britain, but would place this island in a state of imminent danger, and at all events, blast the hopes of its future prosperity. These are considerations worthy of every reflecting mind. (Colonel Downie went in his place.)

tions received from England, he was directed to limit the assistance General Miranda was to receive from him to protection from the naval force of the enemy - to prevent succours being landed, - and to secure his re-embarkation, in the event of his being obliged to leave the shore, it is probable, that the negotiation at Paris, in which the ministers were then engaged, and their hopes of peace, were the sole motives of the reserve which they embraced on this occasion. That they had by no means determined against the grand plan of emancipation, as some of their enemies have been busy to insinuate, we are happy to be able to prove by the succeeding passage of the same letter.

I am further directed," says the Admiral,

> "*to send, by a fast sailing vessel, full details of the situation in which the continent of South America now stands so that his Majesty's ministers may finally decide as to the measures they may take. In consequence of the above,*" he adds, "*a schooner attends Captain Dundas of the Elephant to Coro, which schooner will receive on board your dispatches and immediately proceed to England.*" He concludes by saying, "*I think it proper to give you this early information, lest you should be led to expect a military force to arrive for your support - a circumstance I am ignorant of being in the contemplation of his Majesty's government; but, should any arrive, you may depend on its being forwarded to you without loss of time. In another letter, ten days later, he says, "I wish I could send you five or six regiments, and if the negotiations for peace blow off, I do not despair of a force arriving from England to place you in perfect security.*"

The extraordinary events which immediately followed the rupture of the negotiation at Paris and the removal from His Majesty's councils, which soon succeeded, of the ministers by whom that negotiation was conducted, afforded them no opportunity of recommencing any operation for the emancipation of South America. The facility with which they allowed themselves to be drawn into the support of the schemes of conquest, so injudiciously undertaken by Sir Home Popham, deranged all their views about that great object of policy. The history of the memorable expedition to Buenos Ayres is too well known to require any recapitulation. Its effects, concerning the great and salutary plan of liberation, have been twofold. It has undoubtedly shaken, and that violently, the confidence of the American people in the British government. They had been told by the highest authority that the views of that government were solely to aid them in procuring their independence, yet the first army they beheld came both for conquest and plunder.[10] However, it has had the fortunate

[10] A proclamation transmitted by Lord Melville, then secretary of state, and circulated on the coasts of Spanish America by the government of Trinidad in 1797, calling upon the inhabitants *to resist the oppressive authority of the Spanish government*, assures them "that measures have been taken to support them through the British naval force, and to supply them with arms and ammunition, merely to enable them to maintain their commercial independence, *without any desire, on the part of the King of England, to acquire any right of sovereignty over them, or to interfere with their civil, political, or religious rights*; unless they should any degree solicit his protection. Let us consider the effect this proposal was calculated to make upon the minds of the people of South America when contrasted with the conduct directed to be pursued in the instructions to the assailants of Buenos Ayres. In the instructions to General Whitelocke [Faulder 1808] (see the documents published in the Appendix to Whitelocke's trial, p. 8.) is the following passage: "*With the force above stated, you will proceed to execute the service entrusted to you, by the reduction of the province of*

effect of giving us, nationally, a much more just idea than we formerly possessed of the value of the South American population. It has aroused public curiosity more forcibly towards that quarter of the world and has afforded us some precious evidence of the desire that pervades South America to shake off the yoke of a forcing government and assume the guidance of its own affairs.

13. [Expedition Proposed by Sir Arthur Wellesley (Lord Wellington) in 1808 for the Emancipation of South America]

The politicians, who had succeeded to power when General Miranda returned to England, were prepared to embark on the scheme with real energy. After various delays, a force was at last assembled. It has been oftener than once publicly stated, we believe with perfect accuracy, that the expedition which was prepared at Cork previous summer and which was to be commanded by Sir Arthur Wellesley was intended to co-operate with Miranda in the long projected measure of emancipating South America; and had not the extraordinary revolution which broke out in Spain given to those forces a different destination, it is probable that, by this time, that critical measure would at length have been accomplished. (See Appendix, H.)

14. [Adequate Political Dissertation to Be Followed for South America]

We are now once more at peace with the Spanish nation, and, of course, all idea of using force to detach her colonies is out of the question. We are not only at peace but also in alliance with her. A generous sympathy with a people contending for their independence has had at least as much share in producing that alliance as our common hostility to their oppressor. Therefore, we are bound to abstain from every consideration of national honour. At the same time, this struggle lasts from any step that might be admitted as an injury or offence to our allies. Suppose the Spaniards, therefore, should succeed in repelling their invaders and should remain in peace and alliance with us. In that case, we must renounce, of course, all notions of emancipation of her colonies without her consent. Incalculably beneficial as such an event would be for us, and even for Spain herself, and impossible as it might be for any efforts of hers long to prevent its occurrence, still we conceive that the relations of peace and amity in which we should stand with that power would prevent us from interfering with promoting it, and tie up our hands from attempting to separate from her those dependencies upon which she still sets a value. However, she might derive no benefit from their possession and be guilty of their greatest oppression. If it were possible, therefore, for us to entertain those pleasing views on the probable issue of the present contest in Spain, to which some of our more confident compatriots seem still to adhere, we should only have to say that we should trust with some confidence, that the same spirit and intelligence which had been triumphant in Europe,

---

Buenos Ayres under the authority of his Majesty." On the next page, he is directed "not to introduce into the government any other change than that which must necessarily arise from the substitution of His *Majesty's authority for that of the King of Spain.*" In the instructions likewise to General Cranford respecting Chili, he is commanded to make no other changes "that that of placing the country under his Majesty's protection and government;" and told that "the form of the former government is to be preserved, subject only to the changes which *the substitution of his Majesty's authority for that of the King of Spain* may render inevitable." (See Appendix, G.).

would be just and generous in America; and that the amended government and enlightened councils of regenerated Spain, would relax the severity of its control over its remote dependencies, and yield, spontaneously, to its Transatlantic children, that emancipation for which they had hitherto relied, instead on the weakness, than the goodwill of their mother country.

However, these are speculations in which it appears to us that no sober man can now allow himself to indulge. We believe Spain's fate is decided, and that fine and misguided country has probably yielded, by this time, to the fate that has fallen upon the more significant part of continental Europe. Her European dominions have already yielded to the insatiable conqueror's unrelaxing grasp, and his ambition and greed have no doubt already scented their quarry in her American possessions. At this moment, we do not doubt that his restless intriguers are at work to poison the pure fountains of patriotism and concord in these distant regions, and forces are preparing to trample down those sparks of independence which the slightest stirring would now spread into an unquenchable blaze. A moment remains for us to resolve what may soon become impracticable.

The question, therefore, we humbly conceive, is not now whether Spain, a friendly, a neutral, or even a hostile power, shall retain her colonies, to their oppression and our significant disadvantage, but whether these colonies shall pass, with all their vast capabilities, into the possession of France; whether these immense and productive regions, the soil of so many hopes for the human race, shall be turned to the benevolent purpose for which they are fitted by nature, or whether they shall be seized by the arch enemy of the liberty and peace of mankind, and employed as an aliment of lawless power and universal oppression. About Great Britain, the question is not whether she shall secure to herself an immense advantage or neglect so to secure it but whether she shall take it to herself or give it to her unrelenting foe, her foe, already so powerful and so sure instantly to turn against her those potent means of which her negligence has allowed him to avail himself.

Bonaparte, by seizing the Spanish monarchy, has now brought the matter of deliberation to this narrow point -Whether the colonies shall remain, as before, attached to that monarchy- in other words, shall become his property- or whether those colonies shall be enabled, under the protection of Great Britain, to constitute themselves a free and independent nation.

We do not suppose it will be objected that we could, as another expedient, make a conquest of South America for ourselves, for we do not believe there is an individual in the country who thinks it would be advantageous to us as a conquest, or that the business of defence is not at present enough for us, without that of conquest, even if it could be supposed, which nobody we apprehend is now credulous enough to suppose; that it would be an easy conquest. We mention this idea, therefore, only to set it aside.

There is, however, another idea that deserves the most profound and respectful attention. If the King of Spain, or rather the late King of Spain, is stripped of his dominions in Europe, ought not his dominions in America to be preserved for him? This point is an unlucky circumstance, and to begin with, this ex-monarch is in the hands of Bonaparte. However, we are by no means convinced that this is a problematic and absolutely impossible task. We answer that, provided care is taken to secure liberty by diminishing sufficiently the power left in the hands of the King and placing a sufficient share in the hands of the people, we know of nothing so desirable as the establishment of a mixed monarchy for the government of South America. However, the nation has reason to believe it would prefer a constitution resembling that of its neighbours in the United States. If this preference should be very general and very decided, in this case, we hope there are no such bigoted partisans of royalty among us as to think that we should take up arms to force them to resign it and thus foment a civil war in South America (the inevitable effect of which would be, to throw the country into the arms of France), merely to prevent a great and remote nation from choosing their own form of government. If, however, the people could be brought to submit to it, few things would afford us more satisfaction than that a throne should be erected in South America, first for the aged ex-monarch of Spain and then for his son, for we can see no reason for respecting the feelings of the latter exclusively, and abetting all the revolutionary practices which have been used to dethrone the former.

At all events, however, it is our decided opinion that Great Britain is called upon, by the most imperious considerations of self-preservation, utterly to reject and oppose any proposition that Bonaparte may make –and we are by no means sure that one will not be made –for the erection of such a kingdom, either for Charles or for Ferdinand. If such an arrangement were to be adopted, who, we would ask, would be the persons who would accompany Charles and Ferdinand to South America and have the principal influence in their government?- Persons who leave behind their immense estates and dignities in Spain, and that Spain is in Bonaparte's hands. But is there anything more than a skilful intriguer would require to effect his purpose? Let him but affect the generosity of preserving to these men their estates and dignities in Spain, and is it not visible to every man what influence he has in his power to acquire immediately over them? Let him persuade them (and he is a great master in such arts) that he is not their enemy; that there ought to be no hostility, but rather a cordial union, between the empire of New Spain and the empire of Old; that there is no incompatibility between their holding their ancient and beloved patrimonies and dignities in Old Spain while they faithfully serve their master in the New; that it is for the interest of both countries they should be united, as it were, into one –and no way so effectual as an inter-community of properties and dignities; -let him, by these means, teach the great men who would follow the monarchs, to fix their hopes and affections upon their ancient condition and property in Spain, -and in these silken and golden cords he would hold them bound as fast as by chains of adamant. Then would the affairs of South America be governed entirely at the nod of Bonaparte, and it would be easy for him, under ready pretexts, to introduce into that country his troops till the time at last should arrive when he could declare it his own.

In endeavouring to form any opinion upon the nature of the change that should be attempted in these fine countries, the first thing to be taken into account is the disposition of the people. On this point, we have already presented fairly conclusive evidence, but it may be appropriate to bring together a few additional circumstances, which seem to us to place the matter in the most straightforward perspective.

Depons, whose work is in Caracas and the contiguous provinces, the reader will find a complete account at p. 378. Vol. VIII. of this Journal gives a history of an insurrection against the government, which he is highly anxious to represent as nothing serious. As a matter of course, this anxiety follows from the solid disposition to flatter the Spanish government, with which he evidently set out. Yet, he even lets many expressions escape him, which indicates the strong feeling he had of the spirit of disunion between the population of South America and the government of Spain.

Despite all these points of support, he says (p. 223, Vol. I), "*of Spanish sovereignty in the East Indies, it was, in 1797, on the point of experiencing a dangerous shock in the province of Venezuela.*" A little further on, p. 229, he says,

> *All the interrogations which the accused underwent, all the dispositions of the witnesses proved that the uprising had for its object to destroy the current government, and to replace it by a republican government; to no longer recognise the sovereignty of Spain, and to proclaim independence.*

At the bottom of the same page, he adds, "*If this dreadful project had not failed, it would have been the end of the Spanish possessions*".

The evidence of our officers having the same purpose regarding the business of Buenos Ayres is precise and unvarying. In a letter from Sir Samuel Achmuty to Mr. Windham, dated MonteVideo, March 6th, 1807, he says,

The seizure of the viceroy by the inhabitants of Buenos Ayres, an event undoubtedly significant in itself, first gave me insight into the views of many of the leading men and convinced me that, however inimical they were to us, they were still more so to their present government.[11]"

In the same dispatch, he says again, "*To the reports of this capture (of the viceroy) were added others still more important, &c.*

It was added that the royal court of Audienza was abolished, the King's authority set aside, and the Spanish colours no longer hoisted. These reports were circulated with avidity, and I soon found that they were acceptable to the principal part of the inhabitants. The person who before appeared hostile and inveterate now pressed me to advance a corps to Buenos Ayres and assured me that if I would acknowledge their independence and promise them the protection of the English government, the place should submit to me." Still further, in the same dispatch, Sir Samuel says,

> *The party now in power are mostly natives of Spain, in the principal offices of church and state, policy to inflame the minds of the lower order against the English, by every species of exaggeration and falsehood, and to lead them to such acts of atrocity as may preclude the possibility of any communication with us. The second party consists of natives of the country, along with some Spaniards who have settled there. The oppression of the mother country has made them most anxious to shake off the Spanish yoke. They aim to follow the steps of the North Americans and erect an independent state. If we were to promise them independence, they would instantly revolt against the government and join us with the great mass of the inhabitants. But though nothing less than independence will perfectly satisfy them, they would prefer our government, either to their present anarchy or to the Spanish yoke,*

[11] See trial of General Whitelocke [1808], Appendix, p. 51.

provided we would promise not to give up the country to Spain at peace. But until such a promise is made, we must expect to find them open or secret enemies.

Even in a copy of the instructions of the government to General Crawford, it is said,

The ruling consideration which long restrained his Majesty from invading any part of the enemy's territory in South America was the danger of erecting in that country, from the well-known impatience of the government felt by the inhabitants, a spirit of insurrection leading to the most sanguinary excesses.[12]

This is so absolute and strong and from so high a quarter that, taken in conjunction with the preceding testimonies, with the evidence furnished by the very pamphlet, of which in this article we have given an account. By those deputies who came to Europe to forward the object of emancipation, and of whose instructions to General Miranda, as the agent of South America, we have given a full detail; -it affords abundant proof of the disposition of the people to break off their dependence upon the government of Spain and to become a nation in their own right. Many other proofs, however, might still be added. In a note, for example, to the edition in 1801 of Politique de tous les Cabinets de l'Europe, pendant les Regnes de Louis XV, et de Louis XVI. t. Ii. P. 293, is the following sentence: "*During the last war, I passed through the region of Caracas, and I saw in this fertile province, the discontent carried to the highest degree.*[13]" In another note in the same volume (p. 302.), it is said, after mentioning the spirit of revolt manifested by the Indians, "*The Creoles themselves seem to have little attachment to the metropolis. I have heard several who, when speaking of the Spanish, referred to them as foreign foresters*."

The disposition of the people then, we may conclude with safety, is adverse to every idea of dependence but probably not yet attached to any particular free government plan. It is pretty generally known that they are enamoured of the happiness and prosperity which the Anglo-Americans appear to have procured for them, and the most precise conception they have formed of any line of conduct for themselves is probably that of following the steps of those envied neighbours.

Such, then, is the foundation on which we have to proceed; such are the materials we have to work with. The great question now is about the manner of the operation itself. In all questions of political change, there are two dangers of opposite

[12] See this copy of Instructions signed by Mr. Windham, *ibid.* p. 29. It is perhaps necessary to remark that it is the edition of Whitelockes' trial [1808], taken by Blanchard and Ramsay, which is here always quoted. On Whitelocke, see Chap. 11, section 11.3. note n°32.

[13] In the same note, the writer, who is Segur l'Ainé, tells us an anecdote, highly characteristic, and which might often be paralleled nearer home. He had remarked a particular instance of absurd and oppressive policy which, to use his own words, "*arretoît a la fois l'agriculture, la population, et la civilization. Ayant communiqué*," he adds, "*ces reflexions à un moine inquisiteur, fort consideré*", this monk answered me « La province *est bien comme elle est, et rend assec d'argent au roi; si, en laissant plus de liberté a ces gens-la, la prosperité et la population croissoient, bientôt la colonie secoueroit le joug de la métropole, comme les colonies Angloises.* ». Upset by his answer, I said to him: Father, I see an objection in the unfortunate case that fecondity would increase too much, making the population to grow dangerously".

descriptions to be considered. The first is the danger of doing too little; the second is the danger of doing too much. The first is by far the most common error, as timidity is a much more universal and powerful source of human misery than rashness. However, the evils produced by the second are more simultaneous and, for the moment, much more formidable.

As there are few evils in the mixed scene of human affairs without some corresponding good, the calamitous termination or change of the Spanish monarchy in Europe has removed many difficulties from the great measure of accomplishing the emancipation of South America. No contest is now to be maintained against the troops of Spain or the ministers of the Spanish government opposing the change. As those ministers can have no hopes of transferring the country's government to themselves individually, and as they will now look upon that country as their home, there is every reason to believe that they will cordially cooperate in effecting any beneficent arrangement in its general affairs.

How much happier is this situation than the one where the Dutch effected their independence when they revolted against the same Spanish monarchy? How much happier than that in which the Swiss revolted against the house of Austria; or that in which the North Americans rebelled against the monarchy of Great Britain; -than that even, in which the people of Great Britain revolted against the despotism of the Stuarts? Yet all these experiments turned out well and secured, at least for a long time, a more significant share of human happiness within the sphere of their operation than has ever been exhibited among any similar portions of the race. No difficulty appears to have been experienced in any of those instances of popular violence. How absurd is it, then, because one experiment, that of France, has failed to entertain a prejudice against all changes of government, however urgent the circumstance which call for them; when so many more have succeeded than failed; and above all, when the French attempt affords such instruction about the causes of its failure, that the same event can hardly ever happen again?

These successful experiments provide the most important instruction for the proper conduct of the change, which is being meditated for South America. Let us select Holland as an example. South Americans can hardly choose a wiser person; they possess this remarkable point of resemblance, and it was also a revolt against the Spanish government. What happened when the Dutch declared their independence? All those offices and powers emanating more immediately from the Spanish monarchy ceased to exist. These were the office of viceroy or governor, the great military commands, the office of intendant or master of the revenue, and some others. But besides these, there were other offices and powers which might more appropriately be considered as emanating from the country. These were the magistracies of towns and districts, the burgomasters, the officers of peace and justice, the barons and the landed gentry, with their natural influence. These remained when the others were struck off, and the country still continued as an organised whole. What, then, did the Hollanders do? They built upon this foundation. All the elementary organisations of the country stood united. It was only so far modified and altered as to accommodate it to the new institution, which was devised to supply the place of the powers rendered vacant by the expulsion of the Spanish authority.

Such is the sane and temperate conduct that the renovators of South America ought to prescribe to themselves. In this manner, the people, whose ignorance and irritability may be worked upon by men of evil intentions, require the most sage precautions in the crisis of any political change and are never called upon for their interference. They remain at their homes. Regarding the institutions primarily affected, the country appears to undergo no alteration. Their passions have no opportunity of being enflamed, and in every instance where matters have been conducted prudently on this plan, the quiet acquiescence of the people has followed as a thing, of course.

Political science has been largely obscured and has become prey to prejudices and false alarms by confusing distinct concepts. Thus, it is one thing to form a constitution; it is another thing, and a very different thing, to administer a constitution (or rather, the nation's business agreeably to the constitution) after it is established. Regarding the first, we adopt, to its full extent, the proverbial maxim, "*that as much as possible should be done for the people -but nothing by them.*" In this case, the people are not qualified to determine what is in their best interest. When forming a constitution, it is hardly ever the case that sufficient checks exist against popular violence. However, regarding the second particular, the conduct of national business according to the rules of the constitution, the case is widely different. Here, there is something that the people must do, or it is ridiculous to talk of doing anything for them. Whenever the interests of two sets of people are combined together in one concern if the entire management be left to one, it is perfectly clear that this managing set will draw, by degrees, all the advantages to their own side and throw all the disadvantages to the other; and if the joint-interest is so vast and unwieldy a concern as that of a nation, so far is this inequality sure to proceed; as to ruin the interest itself, and destroy all national prosperity; witness Sicily, Poland, and all other countries where a feudal aristocracy has swallowed up the power of the people. So far, therefore, is it from being true that in carrying on the business of a constitution, you can do no good with the cooperation and influence of the people that you can do no good without it? The constitution, too, can always be so contrived as to afford, in its exercise, after it is introduced, abundant checks against any irregular impulse of the people; so that the operation of the power which, in this second stage, is necessary to entrust to them, may be purely salutary.

Let us now see how these general principles apply to the particular and remarkable case before us. Upon the cessation of the Spanish authority in South America, which by the final subversion of the old monarchy, ceases of its own accord, what elements of organisation and government still remain in the country, upon which wisdom may opportunely seize for the prevention of disorder, and upon which it may build, with the least risk of confusion, a superstructure of government and freedom? The offices of the Spanish viceroys and governors, of the royal audiences, which were a sort of grand councils for a kind of mixed business, partly political, partly judicative; and the offices of the grand collectors and receivers of the revenue, with some others, fall to the ground. But there remains, as there remained in the case of Holland, the local magistracies of the country, and these of a constitution originally peculiarly good; and there remains the natural influence of the people of property and character in the country; altogether, -taken, as it must be, in conjunction with that extraordinary crisis which must unite, in a manner unparalleled, the views of all descriptions of the community in desiring a new and happy establishment of the national affairs, -affording a more secure basis whereon to proceed in new modelling a government, than was probably ever presented to legislative beneficence before.

The Cabildos,[14] for example, or what we would call the municipal corporations, afford an organisation so complete that the Kings of Spain themselves have, at times, entrusted to them the entire government of whole provinces. The Cabildos of Spain were established around the same time and for the same purposes as similar institutions, under the names of corporations in this country, communautés in France, and burgs in Holland, throughout Europe. In no country, however, was the constitution of those municipalities freer than in Spain, and in no country do they seem to have acquired such significant influence in the general government. The principal magistrates were of two sorts: the first Alcaldes, the second Regidors; the first, two in number always; the second varying in number according to the size of the municipality, but seldom exceeding 12, and rarely fewer than six; the regidors chosen by the people, and their office for life; the mayors ("*alcaldes*") selected by the regidors, and their office annual. "*It is probably*," says Depons,

> *The great respect that the Spanish nation had for its municipal establishments, which persuaded the conquerors of America that the government of their new possessions must necessarily have the Cabildos as a base; so they gave them to all the villages that they founded.*

This, then, is the acknowledged basis in America of the old government, which remains when the Spanish authority is overthrown and may become the basis of any new system that wisdom may choose to build upon. The Cabildos, too (and this may be considered an instance of how the feudal institutions of Europe produce new consequences when transplanted into new situations), spread their influence beyond the limits of the town to which they nominally belonged. In Europe, the power and influence of the baron extended throughout the entire country, and it would have been preferable for the city to maintain its own independence. In the new world, however, there were no barons; the influence of the Cabildo extended to the whole district. Therefore, the entire territory became divided among the Cabildos, and thus, the basis they formed for the erection of a new government is much more complete and satisfactory. The powers they had acquired, too, corresponded with their new situation.

"*It happened*," says Depons,

> *that, having no other tribunal as a counterweight, the Cabildos, in the provinces dependent on Caracas, gave their attributions more scope than they ever had in Spain. Everything, except the military, was their responsibility.*

It is abundantly evident from all this that there exists in South America such an elementary organisation, emanating from the country, as affords a security against

[14] Cabildos mean the equivalent of Municipal Councils.

confusion and a foundation on which to build -in all respects as good, to say the least, as existed in Holland at the time when she threw off her dependence upon Spain, and erected a comparatively happy government for herself.

The small extent, however, of Holland enabled her to proceed in a manner somewhat different from that which circumstances point out as the necessary course for South America. Her whole territory might be considered included within the jurisdiction of the seven principal municipalities, and it was easy for them to join together in a confederacy without tumult or confusion. On the other hand, it is evident that this is impracticable in a country of such vast extent as South America or even its great divisions. The representative system alone can ever afford a good government in circumstances like these. The problem, then, with South America is how the representative system can be grafted upon the Cabildos and upon that state of organisation which is rooted in the country.

The most important question here is whether the national representatives shall be elected by the Cabildos or by the electors of these members. Both plans are exemplified in the United Kingdom. In Scotland, it is the magistrates of the towns, corresponding to the members of the Cabildos, who vote for members of Parliament. In England, where the principles of freedom were always more powerfully asserted, the magistrates' electors, the townsmen themselves, generally choose the representatives.

Without entering into the details of this question, we shall state the grand principle which ought to guide all these kinds of deliberations. There is one danger in rendering the basis of a representation too broad. There is another danger in rendering it too narrow. In rendering it too wide, you incur the inconveniences of the ignorant and precipitate passions of the vulgar. In rendering it too narrow, you incur what is still worse, the mischief of bribery and corruption. If the Cabildos' electors formed a too-wide basis, there is reason to dread that the Cabildos themselves would form one too narrow. The difficulty, however, might probably be overcome by establishing provincial assemblies for the members, for which almost all the inhabitants might have a vote, while the great national legislature was elected by the members of the Cabildos alone.

Much, however, remains, and perhaps of the most delicate operations to the composition of a complete government. There is the appointment of that primary magistrate, who is called King, Consul, Inca, or by whatever name shall be most to the public taste, to whom those affairs are entrusted, which require an immediate decision and which a numerous assembly cannot perform. There is the provision of a fabric of responsibility -responsibility not in name only, but in fact- which hitherto has hardly been regarded as a part of legislation, but without which good legislation will never long prevail. There is the whole, too, of that most important department, the judicative, which still remains in so deplorable a state even in the best-governed countries. But we have already exhausted our limits. If it appears, as we trust it will, that our government is disposed to set about the great work in earnest, and if it seems, to men wiser than ourselves, that any good is likely to be derived from pursuing our speculations, we shall gladly resume the subject on a future occasion. In the meantime, we are anxious to warn those persons to whom the glorious task of regenerating South America may fall not to be duped by the common division, on which so many changes have been rung, of the powers of government into the legislative, the executive, and the judicative. It is a division not inconvenient for the ordinary purpose of discourse; but, at the bottom, so vague and inaccurate that some of the most deep-rooted errors and the most significant mistakes in politics have arisen from it. For complete information on this point, we refer our readers to Mr. Bentham, "Traités de Legislation," t. i. p. 319, par Dumont; and "A Fragment on Government," p. 96, published anonymously in 1776. For many other important objects connected with the same speculations, we would earnestly recommend another little book, published a few years ago at Edinburgh, entitled "Thoughts on Public Trusts," which we think entitled to far greater notoriety than it has ever attained, for it contains more of valuable thinking on constitutional legislation than most other books with which we are acquainted. Regarding the whole of the judicative branch, including tribunals and laws, invaluable instruction might be obtained from the works of Mr. Bentham, the man, unquestionably, of all who have ever lived, by far the best qualified to advise on this subject.

Concerning the particular mode in which it would be most prudent to employ the British influence at this crisis, it is not necessary, nor perhaps proper, that we should say much. One circumstance is peculiarly fortunate that the employment of troops has become, if not altogether, at least to a great degree, unnecessary. Another happy circumstance is that the influence of the country itself can be combined with that of Britain in making those fraternal advances to South America, which the exigencies of the time so urgently demand. There is a passage presenting some curious thoughts so applicable to the present occasion that we cannot forbear transcribing it, in a memorial of Governor Pownall, published so long ago as 1780, entitled, "*A Memorial, most humbly addressed to the Sovereigns of Europe, on the present State of Affairs between the Old and New World*;" the passage may be seen at p. 26, of a curious volume, entitled, "*Three Memorials, most humbly addressed to the Sovereigns of Europe, Great Britain, and North America, by T. Pownall,*" etc.

I would," says he,

> *by a detailed description of the nature of the country; of the application of the labour of the country to its capabilities; of the state of the community as it lies in nature, and as it is actuated; all compared with the constitution and administration of the government which is established there; with the spirit of the people, both Old Spaniards, Creoles, and Indians, show that South America is growing too much for Spain to manage; that it is in power to be independent, and will be so in act, whenever, and as soon as, any occasion shall call forth that power. Whenever such revolt takes place, it will not be in the manner or form of that of North America. Building on the foundation of its dominion as it lies in nature, North America has become a democratic or aristocratic republic. The falling off of South America will be conducted, in its natural progress, by the spirit of some injured enterprising genius taking the lead of a sense of alienation and a disposition of revolt to establish a great monarchy.*

It is indeed curious to contemplate what uniformity great men have everywhere and at all times, thought upon this subject. After some melancholy reflections upon the immediate consequences of discovering South America. Montaigne (Essais, liv. iii. Chap. 6.), exclaims,

> *That there had not fallen under Alexander, or under those ancient Greeks and Romans, so noble conquest, and so great a mutation and alteration of so many empires and peoples; under hands, which had gently polished and cleared what was wild, and had strengthened and promoted the good seeds that nature had produced there: mixing not only with the cultivation of the lands, and the ornament of the cities, the arts of this side, insofar as they had been necessary, but also mixing the Greek and Roman virtues, with the original ones of the country! What a reparation would it have been, and what an amendment to all this machine, if the first examples and behaviours of ours, which have presented themselves beyond, had called these peoples to the admiration and imitation of virtue and had erected between them and us, a fraternal society and intelligence! How happy he would have been to profit from such new souls, so hungry for learning and having such beautiful natural beginnings for the most part!-*

"*The Indies and Spain,*" says Montesquieu (Esprit des Lois, book xxi. Chap. 22), "*are two powers under the same master; but the Indies are the principal, Spain is only the accessory. In vain politics pretends to reduce the principal to the accessory; the Indies always attract Spain to themselves*".

Concerning the persons whom the unfortunate catastrophe of Spain may compel to seek refuge across the Atlantic but whose unwelcome interference would be attended with much inconvenience and perhaps disaster in the delicate moment of regulation and change, a very easy expedient presents itself. Let them be received into Cuba, where they may remain until the new constitution is established; afterwards, let them be admitted into the Continent upon the footing of citizens and brothers.

There is one other caution which we are still anxious to impress upon our compatriots. In looking to the advantages of friendship and commerce, which will flow spontaneously in such abundance from the freedom and prosperity of South America, let them not be too eager to stipulate for monopolies. Firstly, it will have an illiberal and rapacious appearance. Furthermore, it is not only unprofitable but also worse than unprofitable. Those merchants should still cry aloud for monopolies, which is not, perhaps, very remarkable; regarding this or that individual, what other men's loss may be their gain. But it is a matter of anger that anything in the shape of a ministry or of a legislature should need the demonstration to be repeated to them (for demonstration, it is complete as any in Euclid) of the elementary proposition that monopolies are disadvantageous. Since it is but too evident, however, that the repetition is necessary, it must, of course, be given. The effect, then, of any degree of monopoly in our favour, exacted from South America for the protection afforded them, would be to yield a more significant profit than usual to the merchants who would deal with them. However, one set of merchants is never content with having a small profit while their neighbours are making a large one. Any permanent enhancement of the rate of profit in any one branch of trade raises it proportionally in all others. Monopoly, therefore, afforded us in any quarter of the world, raises the price of all commodities at home, and that is precisely in proportion to the extent, or, in the vulgar idea, to the value of that monopoly. The consequence of this necessarily is to thrust us out of other markers. Therefore, creating a monopoly in our favour in one country is merely making a monopoly against us in all other countries – the monopoly of nature, which operates itself and requires no stipulations, coast guards, or revenue officers for its security.

In submitting these views and these details for our readers' consideration, we have been actuated chiefly by the desire to communicate to them those pleasing and comfortable impressions for which we would now look in vain in any other branch of political speculation. We have also been anxious, no doubt, to turn to the consideration of this most critical subject, the many powerful understandings to which it may not hitherto have presented itself and thus to secure to the undertaking the benefit of a more unrestricted and more extended discussion than it has yet had the fortune to receive. Something, too, may perhaps be gained by fascinating the nation at large in a project which has hitherto been almost exclusively the nursling of ministers and thus binding the government to more prompt and effectual exertions on behalf of a cause which may have become popular as well as influential. We have stated nothing that has not been long known to our enemies, both in Europe and in America, and nothing but good, it is evident, can result from its being generally known among ourselves.

8.2 Biweekly Newspaper "EL COLOMBIANO", London, May 1810

Context:

In London, the decision of the Portland cabinet in June 1808 to formally abandon Miranda's plan to counter Napoleon's expansionism in Latin America and instead fight him directly by supporting the Spanish resistance in Spain implied growing difficulties for Miranda's actions. Indeed, the government wanted the military expedition on the Peninsula to be perceived as a support to Spain against France, while intervention in South America would have appeared as hostile to the Spanish people and, therefore, would have increased the risks of some Spanish factions to join Napoleon's views. This context increased the constraints imposed on Miranda's exchanges with his South American allies, as formally expressed by Castlereagh and other Ministers to Miranda.

These pressures upon Miranda operations increased when Portland's Cabinet was changed, and the King chose Spencer Perceval as the new Prime Minister. Indeed, before Portland's resignation for illness on 4 October 1809, his cabinet was already in crisis due to the sharp opposition between the two strong Ministers Castlereagh (War & Colonies) and Canning (Foreign Affairs), the latter (also manoeuvring for becoming Prime Minister) being closer to Miranda's views than the first. Castlereagh's policy was also to fight Napoleon directly in Europe. His military expeditions in Portugal and Spain, and his disastrous expedition to Anvers, which ended in the Walcheren scandal in Holland, were strongly criticised by Canning, who secretly convinced Portland to dismiss Castlereagh. This internal dispute ended in the resignation of both parties after a pistol duel between them in

September 1809, allowing Spencer Perceval, the Chancellor of the Exchequer, to take over. This new Prime Minister, considered to be more intolerant and conservative, was not favourable to Miranda, whom he had already counteracted and confiscated some communications with Venezuelan patriots.

Therefore, Miranda was obliged to use either nickname (in the press as in its own newspaper) or friends' names to continue his crusade for emancipation. In parallel with Antepara's book in English, which exceeded 300 pages, Miranda launched, in March 1810, his own newspaper in Spanish, "*El Colombiano*", a biweekly journal, to be the vehicle for disseminating his emancipatory ideas. As for the book, he asked his equatorial friend Antepara to appear as director of this review, although most of the text comes from Miranda's hand. He reached the point of editing five "El Colombiano" issues from March to May 1810. Still, he was eventually obliged (even by his closest British allies) to stop because it was too notorious that he was behind this publication. These publications were issued before to get information on the revolution in Caracas on 19 April 2010. It was only on 22 June that the London press informed Miranda.

Content:

The selected text corresponds to the last issue, edited in May 1810, before it was prohibited. This extract is presented as coming from "an Englishman" and is the most emblematic of Miranda's political advice to his countrymen. It consists of essential and healthy advice for a successful revolution. The following main principles are underlined:

1. to make clear and absolute the self-determination of local people (people's sovereignty),
2. to temporarily deposit the government of America in the hands of the traditional Municipal Councils ("Cabildos")
3. to give legitimate representativeness to these Cabildos by choosing their members by popular election
4. to apply a strict separation between religion and politics
5. to warrant the security of persons and properties, making this principle the critical rule for making compatible revolution and individual freedom to make it possible to move successfully from an evil government to a better one.

Miranda would like America to become the counter-example of the French Revolution.

Sources:

El Colombiano de Francisco de Miranda y dos documentos americanistas, Instituto Nacional de Hipodromos, colección venezolanista, Caracas, 1966 (reproduction facsimil), p. 39–41

America Espera... document 161, P. 433–435

Text:

London, May 15, 1810. No. V. of "El Colombiano"

Thoughts of an Englishman on the state and present crisis of the businesses of South America.

"A people in the present situation of America, of which the chains that bound it to a distant country are broken by a foreign hand, finds itself in the best opportunity to form a beneficial government by itself, without finding itself in the need to support a struggle, has an unspeakable advantage, but although this advantage is very significant, there remains still some difficulties."

"The greatest danger the Americans are exposed to is the intrigues their current situation may cause. They are exposed to the intrigues of the agents and dependents of the old government, who will want to preserve their old authority. They could maintain it in case they could establish as sovereign of America, a representative or a branch of the old government; they could even increase it if they could form a government composed only of themselves. It is, therefore, left to the Americans to consider whether they should submit to the ambition and caprice of those men or if they have to force them to submit to justice and reason."

"If, like the inhabitants of the Colombian continent, they have the strength to force their opponents to submit and the necessary resolve to destroy all their hopes, they could achieve the happiness that would result from their autonomy; the sooner they take the appropriate measures, the fewer difficulties they will have to overcome, and the easier the enterprise of establishing a good government will be."

"The first step that the inhabitants of the Colombian continent had to take towards their independence was to take a measure that would ostensibly and decisively show their resolution to create a government that emanates only from themselves."

"The measure, which seems the most adequate and easy for this purpose, comes naturally from itself. Let the leading people of each district meet and declare *that as the old government has been dissolved by force of events, the government of the Americas is deposited temporarily in the natural authorities of the country, which are the municipal councils ("Cabildos")*. For these to win the authority and trust of the nation, it is necessary to place them under shelter and out of the influence of members and agents of the old and hated government. In order to preserve internal peace and to administer justice until the formation of a permanent government, the municipal councils must be composed of the principal inhabitants of the country, elected by the neighbourhood, to form, in this way, an interim national representation."

"This critical measure would produce two significant effects. Not only would it disconcert the intrigues of the French government of Spain and those of the agents of the former despotic government of America, but it would save the country from the danger of all the unjust and illegal acts that would result from an interval in which he found himself without a government, and of all the evils of a momentary anarchy, so challenging to avoid when passing from one government to another."

"The most dangerous influence that the enemies of happiness in America can employ is the sacred intervention of religion. Its mission is to direct souls and lead them to heaven. The mission of political institutions is to direct men's actions for the good of society in this world. To mix religion with political questions is to depart from its proper object and forge the chains of despotism; to enslave men under the pretext of religion is to profane it and betray the homeland."

"If the resolution of the peoples of America, as the news that we have in Europe seems to prove, is to be free, and if this resolution is firm enough to overcome all obstacles and destroy all intrigues, the first and grand object that must occupy their attention is the *safety of people and property*. Between the dissolution of the old government and the establishment of the new one, it is sometimes necessary to pass through this transition. This is a period of rehearsals, but everything will proceed smoothly, and there will be sufficient time to deliberate maturely if the security of the people and their properties is warranted. This sacred principle must be engraved in all hearts and followed with the most extraordinary rigour. When the blood begins to flow, when the property of individuals begins to be violated, when illegal prisons begin, freedom is lost, and the party of despotism begins to gain strength. Nothing is more important in the cause of liberty than protecting the safety of all individuals in society and their property. If this security is established and maintained, and it is demonstrated that whatever form or mutation is made in government, the protection of people and property is not at risk, then all obstacles to establishing freedom are almost overcome. All the men of goodwill then join this sacred undertaking since the greatest current obstacle to establishing independence is the fear many good men have of seeing their people and their properties compromised if the established order is changed. How much good could the Americans do for humankind if they could offer an example that destroys these ruinous fears and worries? How many misfortunes have the reformers of France produced, presenting so many hateful examples of violations of rights?"

"If when a people rise to destroy all that is opposed to the establishment of good government, it forms a firm resolve to respect people and property, it can be predicted that if it maintains this security, it will lead its project to success; but If you do not protect and maintain individual security, it can also be predicted that your revolution will not have a happy result; it will be able to change a lousy government for another; but it will indeed not form one that is good (...)."

References

Antepara, J. M. (1810), *South American Emancipation*, ed. by R. Juigné, 17 Margaret Street, London, (re-edited by Chacón, D., in 2005; Also by Editorial Ayacucho in 2009.

Burke, W. (1807), "*South American Independence: or the Emancipation of South America, the Glory and interest of England.*", J. Ridgway, London.

Burke, W., (1808), *Additional Reasons, for our immediately emancipating Spanish America, deduced from the present crisis: and containing valuable information, respecting the late important events, both at Buenos Ayres, and in the Caraccas*, London. Reprinted by Creative Media Partners, LLC, 2015.

Faulder, R. et al., (1808), *The trial at large of Lieut. Gen. Whitelocke, commander in chief of the expedition against Buenos Ayres. By court-in martial. held in Chelsea college, on Thursday, the 28th January, 1808, and succeeding days,* taken by Ramsey. Printed for.R. Faulder and Son, R. Lea, Wilkie and Robinson et al, Ed. Tipper, London https://dn790004.ca.archive.org/0/items/trialoflieutenan00whit/trialoflieutenan00whit.pdf

Grases, P., (1966) *El Colombiano de Francisco de Miranda y dos documentos americanistas*, Instituto Nacional de Hipódromos, colección venezolanista.

Miranda, F. de, (1929-1950), *Archivo del General Miranda*, ed. Vicente Dávila/ Rubén González, Caracas/La Habana.

Salcedo-Bastardo, (1982), *América Espera*, Editorial Ayacucho, n°100, Caracas.

Chapter 9
Miranda's Main Proclamations

Influenced by the impact of the "Letter to the Spanish Americans" written by Father Viscardo y Guzmán, whose edition and diffusion was organised by Miranda in 1799 (see Annex 1), he developed this communication method in his strategy for disseminating political ideas to the peoples and public opinions both in Latin America and in the international community.

The Miranda Proclamations were typical instruments he used from a perspective [Vattel] of "The Law of Nations" ["*droit des gens*"] to "*show the world that ... we are right and claiming justice*". He is characterised by the systematic use of this medium, which reveals the importance it gave to public opinions and citizen participation in realising its plans, as well as a precursor strategy of political propaganda. In this domain, Miranda, without being the inventor, manifests himself as a precursor in the modern use of Proclamations as an instrument of citizen participation. Above all, the content of his Proclamations reveals elegant syntheses of his political philosophy and his strong coherence about democracy.

9.1 First Proclamation, 1801: "Proclamation to the compatriots from London"

Context:

As explained in the commentary on the context of its 1801 constitution (see Chap. 2, document 2.3), Miranda's concern over the resignation of Pitt as Prime Minister and his replacement by Addington, who is favourable to a peace with Napoleon, stems from the fact that France and Spain have been allied since 1796. He had left London in September 1800, having noted again the procrastination and

C. Ghymers, *Independence, Federalism and Regionalism in Latin America: An Analytical Anthology of Francisco de Miranda's Writings (1790-1811)*, United Nations University Series on Regionalism 34,
https://doi.org/10.1007/978-3-031-96938-6_9

lack of support from the Pitt government, which had also denied him a visa to leave England. After 16 months of waiting for this visa, he travelled to Paris under the pretext of going to Caracas via Spain, where he was acquitted by the justice of old accusations. In reality, he intended to test the possibility of acting with Napoleon despite the risks of deviation from his plans by the Jacobins that he hoped to counter from the inside. The main explanation is that Miranda foresaw a Napoleonic expansion towards South America as inevitable [Antepara 1810]. According to his information from Venezuela, he did not want to be paralysed by British diplomacy when he expected the action to start on the ground. In addition, he likely wanted to demonstrate his determination to the Pitt government and, therefore, to make it explicit that the British government's procrastination was pushing him into the arms of the traditional enemy in order to achieve his plan of emancipation. He intended to make clear that the best thing for England would rather be to bet on him to prevent Napoleon from benefiting from his own plan. By going to France, he was trying to provoke a change in the strategy of the still-divided Pitt's cabinet.

However, his attempt with the First Consul, Napoleon, failed and turned very badly, resulting in his arrest by Fouché, condemnation, and banishment for the third time. Returning to London, he worried about being detained there as well, and therefore, he travelled back under a false identity on April 24, 1801. Thanks to his faithful friend Turnbull, he immediately secured an appointment with the new British government to try to convince them of the UK's interest in supporting his plans in America.

On April 29, he is presented to the Deputy Minister of Finance, Vansittart,[1] who becomes his best ally in the Addington cabinet and subsequent governments. Vansittart asks for his government program (the third project of the constitution, 1801) and some other documents within which this proclaims to his compatriots. Miranda [1929] wrote this first Proclamation, dated May 2, 1801, as a complement to his third draft of the federal constitution. In May and June 1801, the cabinet seriously considered Miranda's proposals. However, at the end of June, he learned that the English were instead preparing negotiations with France and Spain to reach a peace treaty. This Treaty, concluded in March 1802, was known as the "Peace of Amiens" and repeated precisely the same scenario that Miranda had already suffered under Pitt's government, without a war against Spain. England would not effectively support any of Miranda's plans and would not allow him to act from London.

Content:

It is worth emphasising the power and universalism of this text, a genuine anti-colonialist and anti-slavery pamphlet, which reveals Miranda's degree of advancement upon most of the opinions of his time. This text proclaims the common identity of all Hispanic Americans, whether they are Indian or white, denounces the perversity of the Spanish regime that builds its power upon an ignorant society

[1] **Nicholas Vansittart** (1766–1851), Pitt's political ally, member of the Parliament and financial expert, was quickly convinced by the opportunity of Miranda's plans, Vice Chancellor of the Exchequer in the Addington government and Chancellor of the Exchequer in Pitt's next cabinet in 1804.

intentionally divided by castes and ethnic segregation and sets the essential factors able to launch socio-economic development which are the combination of freedom, sovereignty, the rule of law, but under the condition to be organised into a single political entity through an open, integrated region. This combination will only result from the efforts of Americans once they enjoy "*equal rights, order and good laws*." Although ultra-synthetic, it reveals an economic development strategy based upon the combination of free enterprise and open trade, drawing on a legal framework that ensures stability and security. His doctrinal content follows the philosopher Emmanuel Kant's lines and announces economists' contemporary positions on "endogenous development". A similarity with the purpose of the European Union in terms of economic and social development might even be detected.

Sources:

Translated from Spanish

Colombeia. Vol XIX. Document 4572. p. 654–657

Archivo del General Miranda. Vol XVI, p. 104–107

América Espera, op. cit. document n° 96, p. 263

Text:

Compatriots

Three centuries have passed since the Spaniards conquered this continent by force. The horrors they committed in their conquest are well known by all and sundry, but the tyranny that they have exercised and continue to exercise only we know about and feel. Our rights as native Americans, as descendants of the conquerors, as Indians or as Spaniards have been violated in a thousand ways. To know this, it is not necessary to remember the violence carried out by the "visitadores" in 1781. Of the capitulations in Zipaquirá so solemnly sworn and so shamefully violated by the Spanish Government: of the ferocity with which our compatriots of Santa Fé and Caracas have been exiled and taken in chains to Spain in 1796 and 1797. These violent acts are so ordinary that there is not one of us who does not experience them daily. Forgotten about anything that might be of use to us, Spain only remembers us to exact tributes, to send a swarm of tyrants who insult us and dispossess us of our wealth to stifle our industry, forbid our trade, hinder our instruction and persecute every talented person in the country. For her, it is a crime to be born in America. In her eyes, every American is a suspect incapable of employment, born only to suffer.

Despite having a very fertile land, metals of all kinds, and all sorts of produce, we are poverty-stricken because the monster of tyranny stops us from enjoying those riches. The Spanish Government does not wish us to be rich or for us to communicate with the rest of the world, so we ignore the weight of their despotism. This cannot be exercised except on ignorant and miserable people. However, three centuries of oppression are a long enough lesson to teach us about our rights. These are personal security, freedom, and property, all essential to men living in society; but what freedom, what security can we have in our persons or our properties when the despot is the lord and master of lives and estates, and when their satellites deprive us of one or the other whenever it takes their whim to do so? When the slightest instruction, the most indifferent word, a vague complaint on the lips of one of us, is a capital crime that leads to torture, prison or death?

Compatriots: The world is too enlightened for us to suffer such outrages; we are too great to live under such an ignominious tutelage. Let us break the chains of this shameful thraldom and let the world know that we are not as degraded as Spain believes us to be. Let us follow the steps of our North American brothers by establishing a reasonable and free government like theirs; by doing so, we will obtain the same benefits they currently enjoy. They have been free for no more than 25 years, and yet what cities have they built during this period, what trade have they created, and what prosperity and contentment can you see in them? And we who are more numerous, who inhabit a more prosperous land, suffering what they never suffered, are we going to stick to our poverty, our ignorance and our slavery? The Appalachians will see their lower slopes cultivated by free hands, and the Andes that dominate the World will stay empty or inhabited by unhappy slaves; the Delaware and Potomac will be open to all the people of the world, whereas the Amazon and the Orinoco, and so many other majestic rivers that water our country will remain forgotten by men? Will the Arts and Sciences be foreigners to Southern America? No, my fellow countrymen, we shall be free, we shall be men, we shall be a nation. Between this and slavery, there is no middle ground; to deliberate about it is infamous. The only enemy who could oppose our emancipation is in chains in his peninsula, from where he cannot move nor avoid for a long time the punishment that an oppressed and insulted nation is preparing for him. The good Spaniards who groan about the estate of my fatherland see our liberty with relish. Our friends protect us powerfully and will stop the tyrant from making the slightest effort against us. We have our own arms and generals, who are accustomed to fighting for the cause of freedom. We have, above all, reason and justice on our side, which will provide the necessary vigour. So, fellow citizens, it all depends on ourselves. Let us unite for our liberty, for our independence. Let the odious distinctions between chaperones, creoles, mulattoes, etc. disappear among us. These can only be of use to the tyranny, whose objective is to divide the interests of the slaves so that they dominate one another. A free government looks at all its subjects equally; when the laws govern, the only distinctions are merit and virtue. Since we are all children of the same father, since we all share the same language, the same customs and above all, the same religion, since we have all been equally injured, so let us unite in the great work of our shared liberty. Let us establish over the ruins of an unjust and destructive government a wise and creative one: over tyranny, freedom, despotism, equality of rights, order and good laws.

Our suffering will stop with tyranny. Open to all nations, our ports will provide what we need in abundance and take away what we do not.

Our soil will support a wide variety of plants without restriction. There will be no more "estancos",[2] no more personal tributes, no more "alcabalas",[3] more guards,

[2]"**Estancos**" means here a monopoly granting (generally) to the State the exclusive right to sell and trade some products like tobacco at a higher price for the benefit of the fiscal colonial administration.

[3]"**Alcabala**" means an ancient indirect tax of Muslim origin that levied internal commercial transactions: the "alcabala" was a fundamental part of royal fiscal administration in Spanish America

nor any right to hinder commerce or the cultivation of the land. We shall harvest and trade for ourselves, not for greedy and unfair foreigners. What we now contribute to Spain to be further oppressed by her we shall employ in clearing our roads, making our rivers navigable, opening new canals for our traffic, and in establishments for the sciences and public care. To summarise, fellow citizens, we shall not be foreigners in our own country. We shall have a fatherland that appreciates and rewards us for our services. A Fatherland! Ah, this word will no longer be meaningless in our language. It will animate our hearts with the divine enthusiasm with which it animated many famous ancient and modern people. It will be joyful to live for the Fatherland and glorious to die for it. «*Dulce et decorum est pro patria mori* ».

9.2 Second Proclamation of 1801, "To the people of the Columbian continent (Alias Hispano-America)"

Context:

Identical to the first Proclamation and dated also from May 1801.

Content:

This text provides an insight into the potential of the Precursor's thought and his polemical ability. It is the most complete and brilliant legal argument of his time against colonialism and, in particular, against the "*abominable system with which Spain has governed these countries*." Miranda demonstrates, in terms of the law of nations (natural and voluntary), and with implacable logic, the lack of legitimacy of the Spanish crown over its American colonies, and therefore bases the right to claim and achieve the absolute independence of Spanish America. In addition to revealing himself as a foremost jurist, Miranda also appears to be a talented polemicist. He addresses the "entire Universe" and organises his demonstration in the form of a lawsuit in court to make clear not only the rights of native and Creole peoples to recover their legitimate sovereignty but also the imprescriptible crimes of the Spanish rulers for not having acted in the respect of the Christian principles they pretended to bring. At the same time, they impeded the legitimate development of indigenous peoples.

It is worth highlighting the pragmatism of this Proclamation, which is not limited to a simple legal dispute but also publishes a solemn Act that leads to a formal Proclamation of 4 articles of rights upon which rely the operational aspects of the basic principles of Miranda's strategy:

1. election of deputies (*representativeness*) to form a federal congress to organise an independent government (*operational unity for ensuring independence*),
2. abolition of the Inquisition, establishment of religious tolerance and separation of Church and State (*operational pluralism*),

---

and a symbol of colonial exploitation.

3. equality before the law for all Indians and free people of colour (no discrimination, *social integration by the rule of law*),
4. defensive military conscription according to a specific military regulation (rational organisation *of people's participation in the conquest of freedom*).

Drawing upon his military experience, Miranda drafted a military regulation annexed to this Proclamation, eradicating military privileges and publishing a detailed military code to organise an efficient state of war. He demonstrates that he is not naive and foresees the necessity of acting militarily.

Sources:

Translated from Spanish

Archivo, op. cit. Vol XVI, p. 108–120.;

Colombeia. Vol XIX. Document 4571. p. 641–654.

América espera, op. cit. p. 263–274.

Text:

Beloved and brave compatriots,

Many years ago, you asked us to establish your independence. Today, we are pleased to announce that the moment of your emancipation and liberty has come. We hope that our efforts will satisfy your noble desires.

These generous friends, finally convinced of the justice of our cause and yielding to your plea, are supporting and helping us establish a fair and independent government on a solid and well-balanced basis.

The time has come to throw out the Barbarians that oppress us and to smash the sceptre of an overseas government. Remember that you are the descendants of those illustrious Indians who, not wishing to survive the enslaving of their fatherland, preferred a glorious death to a dishonourable life. These illustrious fighters, foreseeing the misery of their posterity, chose instead to die under the walls of Mexico, Cuzco and Bogotá than to drag the chains of oppression. They were the victims of public liberty.

You will establish the independence of your fatherland over the ruins of an oppressive government. But given the importance of such an endeavour, one that will change the state of your situation, you must let the whole universe know the motives that feed your determination and prove indisputably that it is not hatred or ingratitude but the voice of justice and your sense of self-preservation that compel you to this memorable effort.

Instead of avoiding a broader discussion on this subject, show interest in provoking it. For what title does Her Catholic Majesty claim exclusively her right to own those domains?

Let us open the general history of the West Indies by Antonio de Herrera, and we will find in it that very famous statement made by H.C.M. in 1510 against the peoples of America.[4] There we find the following passage:

[4] Dec. 1. Lib.7. Cap. 14.

One of the past popes[5] that I mentioned, as lord of the world, that he was, donated these Islands and firm land of the ocean Sea to the Catholic Kings of Castile... So that, H.M. is King and Master of those islands and firm land by virtue of that donation, etc."

The same historian,[6] writing elsewhere about Spain's sovereignty over the West Indies and obviously concerned that it might be contested, declares that they were acquired in virtue of a concession made by the Pope in his capacity as Vicar of Jesus Christ.

So, H.C.M. has no other title to establish the right of ownership than a Papal Bull.[7] In truth, this title is so absurd and ridiculous that it would be a waste of time to refute it. Nations such as the French, English, and Dutch, much before you, and on more than one occasion, have shown the world how to respond to such peculiar donations. In this sense, those two Indian Chiefs from Darién, guided only by natural law, were right in saying that "to give, ask for and receive someone else's property, were as many acts of madness; and since they were the lords of the country, they had no affair with a foreign master[8]".

It may well be that the defendants of the Spanish Crown will argue the legitimacy of the right of Conquest. But before we examine if, in this particular circumstance, the right of conquest can be appealed to by H.C.M., it is necessary to point out that even if such were the case, this invocation would come too late because the Court in Madrid, when the Islands and the American continent were occupied, declared to have them only in virtue of the papal donation.

Besides, the brief stories of the expeditions of Cortés, Pizarro, Quesada and Soto irrefutably prove that if the right of conquest were to be accepted, it would belong to the descendants of those conquerors, who, with their own resources, attempted those risky and distant expeditions, without any investment from the Spanish Crown.

But suppose that the Court of Madrid wished to argue in favour of the right of conquest. Let us demonstrate that even in that hypothesis, this right would have no value whatsoever. According to the law of nations [Vattel 1758], a nation can occupy an empty, uninhabited land. Still, this same law of nations does not recognise the property and sovereignty of a nation except on those empty lands that it has really and de facto occupied, on which it has established a settlement, and from which it obtains something helpful. When sailors have found deserted land on which other nations had, on their way, erected a monument to claim it as theirs, they have taken

[5] Alejander VI, from the family Borja de Valencia, in Spain.

[6] Dec. 8 Lib.5. Cap. 16.

[7] De Luque quotes the Duke of Almodóvar, under the anagram of Eduardo, in the history of the overseas establishments of the European nations published in Madrid in 1790; he does not hesitate to declare in tom.5 cap.5 that *without the zeal of religion and the approval of the Pope,* the civilised and Christian nations would not be able to excuse the invasion of the Spaniards of the property of the West Indian inhabitants. One can see then that the Spanish publicists have no other basis to support their right of possession than the concession made by the Pope.

[8] Herrera Dec. lib 1. Cap. 2.

no more notice of this vain ceremony than of the disposition of the Popes to divide a significant portion of the world between the Crowns of Castille and Portugal.[9] However, it is undeniable that the Islands and the American continent were well inhabited, rather than deserted, and the Spaniards had no right to claim legitimate possession of them.

There is yet another consideration, taken from the necessary rights of people, that opposes even more strongly the admission of the right of conquest by H.C.M. Let us follow what on this topic the wisest and most famous of all modern publicists have to say[10]:

> *Unjust war gives the belligerent sovereign no rights whatsoever but turns him into a delinquent in the eyes of the enemy it attacks, oppresses, and kills, in the eyes of its own people as he is inviting them to be unfair, and in the eyes of humankind whose rest it disturbs and to which it gives a pernicious example. In this case, he who commits the injury must repair it or offer a just satisfaction if the evil is irreparable.*

Since the discovery of the New World, no one publicist has dared to sustain that the war of Spain against the people of America had been just. The nations of Peru, Chile, Mexico, and Bogotá, which were unknown to the Spaniards until then, could not in any way have offended them. Therefore, the aggressions of the Spaniards, initially unfair and atrociously executed, could not have granted them the slightest right. Since the evil produced by the Spanish Crown is itself irreparable, they have no other means, according to the disposition above, than to offer a fair satisfaction, that is, the immediate evacuation of their troops from the American Continent and the recognition of the independence of the people that until now have constituted the colonies called Hispanic American.

These are the fundamental principles, the eternal rules of justice, the dispositions of that sacred law that the necessary international law ("*Droit des gens*") imposes on the nations in virtue of people's natural rights. But because of a fatality that undermines the happiness of humankind, it is impossible to recur (alegar) to the natural and necessary law of nations, living the matter to the conscience of the sovereigns, we shall examine nonetheless what the voluntary law of nations, established for the health and advantages of society and sanctioned by the general consent of all civilised people, has dictated about the aspirations of the Catholic King.

In virtue of the voluntary law of nations, obligatory to all sovereigns, we find that only "*a war that has been formally declared can be seen to be in its effects fair on either side*".[11] Shall we now examine the circumstances that define a formal war and determine whether such a war existed on the part of Spain?

For a war to be formal (proper?), the aggressive power must first and foremost have a cause of complaint, given that it has repeatedly been denied a reasonable satisfaction and must have declared war. This last circumstance is de rigueur, as it

[9] Vattel: droit des gens. Lib.1. Cap. 18. Par. 207.

[10] Vattel: lib. 3 Cap. 11. Par. 183, 184 and 185.

[11] Vattel lib. 3. Cap. 12. P. 190.

has repeatedly been denied a level-headed satisfaction. Those are the requisite conditions of a formal war.[12]

Now we ask the whole Universe, and with these healthy and indispensable formalities in hand, we even ask the Court of Madrid whether it had complied with the requisites, and even if that had been the case, that the attacked power should have established its horrible domination over the ruins and rubble of our fatherland? Undoubtedly not: the last resource used to prevent the shedding of blood. Is it not necessary that in this declaration, Spain should have provided a proper cause of complaint, but how could this be when they were not known there even by name before the discovery of the New World? And not having offended them, not done any injury, how could they be obliged to offer any satisfaction?

The Kings of Castille and Aragon were well aware of these reasons. They knew they would not find legitimate causes or honest motives in the law of nations to justify their form of possession; therefore, they argued that the Spanish Pope's donation was instead.

It is evident that the Spaniards had no pretext to wage war and devastation on the American continent; it is also evident that they made no formal declaration of war. Their hostilities have been injustices, their victories assassinations, and their conquests theft and usurpation. The shedding of blood, the looting of cities, the destruction of provinces, these are their crimes against God and men!

Having lost the process of this critical question, the lawyers of the Spanish Court, as a last refuge, might say to us: "*How dare you challenge the government of H.C.M. when a prescription of 300 years gives him the most legitimate right over you and your properties?*

Compatriots answer the defenders of Despotism that there is no prescription in favour of tyrannical usurpation. Vattel shall again be our arbiter. "*The sovereign,* he says, *that believing himself to be the absolute master of a people's destiny, reduces it to slavery, fosters a state of war between him and the people.*" Have not the people of the Spanish colonies been groaning for the past three centuries under foreign oppression?

But even if the title of H.C.M. derived only from the papal gift is absurd and ridiculous, even though her Majesty's pretension over the vast empires that exist in Southern America is devoid of any right, we could ask whether the Kings of Spain, through a Government protective of the individuals and their properties, have attempted to obliterate the lack of a genuine title.

Do you remember the ferocity of Cortés, Pizarro, Quezada, Albuquerque, Toledo, Alderete and other similar monsters? That Don Rodrigo of Albuquerque, in virtue of his powers and of a Royal concession, confirmed later by H.C.M., disposed of the wretched Indians and their chiefs like vile heads of cattle, distributing them among

[12] Vattel lib. 3. P. 26. and cap. 4. P. 51, 54, 55 and 62.

his comrades as slaves?[13] That Vasco Nuñez de Balboa enjoyed throwing the chiefs and the Indians that had displeased him to be devoured by dogs?[14]

Do you remember that in commemoration of Jesus Christ and his Apostles, as they called them, they hung and burnt 13 Indians, whose only crime was to have been born Indians? (Las Casas 1552/1697).[15]

Do you remember that a successor of Montezuma, despite the most sacred promises made by Cortés, after inflicting upon him the most painful torments, was hanged from a tree next to two other Kings?.[16] So that for no further reason than a few vague words and innocent complaints, those Princes died, unfortunate vestiges of the ruling families of Mexico, a death sentence that, in justice, should have been applied to their executioners.

You probably remember that all the members of the Royal family of the Incas died a pitiful death and that Francisco de Toledo, Viceroy of the country, finished off the scene of these murders by condemning Tupac Amaru, the last Prince of the House of Manco Capac,[17] to death? And how brutal must Toledo's cruel ways have been when even Phillip II found him to have behaved like an assassin?[18]

We must not say that these cruel deeds were unknown to the Court of Madrid nor that the Royal dispensations (cédulas) were directed to foster the love and friendship of the American people. Let us consult all the personal procedures of the Kings of Spain, from the discovery of America to our days; let us consult the document quoted above; and we shall see that H.C.M. authorised the governors and other civil and military officers of the West Indies to take by force the wives and daughters of those Indians who would not subject to their will: to enslave those women and children: to sell them as such and harm them in all possible ways, killing them as disobedient and rebellious vassals.[19] That was the fatherly language of the Court of Madrid!

Ah! If the Kings of Spain and their people had professed the virtue, the Christian principles, and the humanitarian feelings of the illustrious Fray Bartolomé de las Casas, you would have loved their memory and wished to live as their subjects! If at least they had given you laws based on justice that suited both your character and interests, you might have forgotten previous usurpations and favoured a healthy government. Such was how the Romans, in similar circumstances, tried to make the

[13] Herrera. Dec. 1. lib. 10. Cap. 12.

[14] Id. Dec. 1. lib. 10. Cap. 1.

[15] Las Casas, B., Descubrimiento de las Indias Occidentales, Paris 1697, p. 12, translation, by Jean Baptiste Morvan de Bellegarde, of the author's: *Brevissima relacion de la destrucción de las Indias*, first printed Seville, 1552.

[16] Clavijero, lib. 10. Sect. 39.

[17] Hist. gener. del Perú de Garcilzao prt. 2. lib. 8. Cap. 18 and 19.

[18] Hist. gener. del Perú de Garcilzao prt. 2. lib. 8. Cap. 20.

[19] Herrera. Dec. 1. lib. 7. Cap. 14.

defeated nations forget their usurpations, offering in exchange for the liberty they had taken from them civilisation and good laws.[20]

But in your case, Compatriots, the Court of Madrid, rather than spread the rays of civilisation in your countries, has tried to extinguish or hide them, following the usual maxims of Despotism, whose tyranny can only rule over ignorant people. And do we not see nowadays that even the members of our noble class who are moved by a deserving ambition and wish to study the arts and sciences in foreign countries are forbidden to leave their fatherland without a special dispensation from the Crown, which is rarely granted? Are you not excluded from all the principal public offices to this day? Has not the most insatiable rapacity come to devour your money to enrich greedy foreigners at the expense of the natives? Do not all sorts of taxes, taken from your midst, have another aim than to strengthen the chains that bind your hands? And finally, are you not today, properly speaking, just servants disguised under titles that, for all their brilliance, are no less imaginary and indecorous?

Finally, when considering Spain's profound ignorance of these colonies, one cannot help but recall the Scythians mentioned by Herodotus, who removed the eyes of their slaves so that nothing distracted them from the task of churning their milk.

Who among you has not groaned under the oppressing reign of the Gàlvez, Areche, Piñérez, Avalos, and Brancifortes? Has H.S.M in the end, not shamelessly violated his faith and his most sacred promises, cancelling in 1783, without legitimate motives or even pretexts, the capitulation signed in Zipaquirà in 1781 between the Audiencia and the inhabitants of the Kingdom of Santafé, which had been ratified by the Court of Madrid in 1782?

Have we not also seen a general pardon in the province of Venezuela in 1797, an amnesty most infamously violated and without qualms by the Spanish Government? How can we, barely credulous Americans, believe the protestations of such a perfidious government?

If we add to this the fact that simply sailing the rivers, using many of the roads, communicating from one port to another of our coastline, or just proposing to open a navigation channel in the Isthmus of Panama are deemed capital crimes in the Spanish Code, then you will be able to understand the terrible system with which Spain has governed these countries.[21]

Fellow citizens, we must topple this infamous tyranny: the actual creditors must come into their usurped rights. It is essential that the reins of public authority, which a foreign power snatched from them, return to the hands of the inhabitants and natives of the country as it is clear (according to Locke) that the Government of such a Conqueror is the most illegitimate that exists and contrary to the Laws of Nature, and that it must be toppled immediately.[22] The most complete success will be the

[20] Nonetheless, it would have been very difficult to find in the world a more paternal institution and better laws than those that already existed in Peru at the time! See Garcilazo.

[21] Alcedo Diccion. Geograf. Histor. De la América. Madrid, 1790. palab. Atrato. Istmo.

[22] Del Gobierno Civil – art. conquista injusta. (Of Civil Government, art. unjust conquest).

reward of all your efforts, and if your brothers of Northern America, three million in all, have achieved their independence thanks to their bravery, virtue and perseverance, gaining the admiration even of their enemy, how can you not believe in your own success; when a population larger than ten million inhabitants are clamouring for it with justice, courage and decision?

In truth, with all the disasters that affect Southern America, how can it be an instructive example for humanity to see so many courageous Indian tribes which tenaciously protect themselves in their gorges and jungles, preferring a rootless and precarious life in the deserts and mountain tops of the American Alps than to subject themselves to the executioners of their families?

To conclude, do gather all under the banners of liberty. Justice fights for you, and if the soundest part of Europe approved the fearlessness with which the Dutch fought the ferocity of the Duke of Alba and the homicidal politics of his master, if it equally favoured the emancipation of the people of Portugal if it also applauded by principle the independence of Northern America, how can it reject its approval to the people of Southern America, victims of atrocities and assaults unknown to the other nations?

Moved by these considerations and feelings of honour and anger, you asked us to elicit aid to destroy that shameful and unbearable oppression. This aid is here. The land and sea forces that accompany me come to favour your plans: you will find in them generous friends who will only be fearsome to your enemies; that is, to the enemies of sound freedom and American independence. They renounce, and we respond for their "*loyal good faith*", all spirit of Conquest, dominion of monopoly of any kind, having no other wishes and intention than to contribute to your happiness, emancipation and political Independence.

But, citizens, as you build over the ruins of the oppressing regime the independence of your fatherland, remember that the fame of your deeds will reach the remotest regions, and you will record your names in the temple of memory. And since the endeavour is so great and glorious, you must dread soiling it with undue procedures. You must detest all kinds of crime and avoid the movements of anarchy at all costs. Remember that vengeance for offences done to you is dealt with at the law courts and that homicide is a homicide, no matter its origin. Do not imitate the tyranny of your oppressors as you confound them. Your idea is not to exchange one irregular government for another, to substitute an oppressive government with another, to destroy an ancient tyranny for a new one; in a word, to establish over the ruins of a foreign despotism, another despotism no less hateful, that of lack of control and anarchy. Finally, enlightened by those who have shone in antiquity, just as in modern times, you will never forget that just as a good cause produces beautiful effects, an impure principle necessarily leads to the most unfortunate results.

Wishing then to keep the countries safe from the terrible effects of anarchy and to maintain our joyful emancipation free from any action that goes against the Civil code, justice and public order in general, we announce the following articles:

Article 1

The Cabildos and Municipalities of Townships and Cities of the Colombian Continent will send their deputies to the main army headquarters without delay.

There, the deputies will choose the best place to meet and constitute the congress to form a provisional government that will lead the country to proper freedom and independence.

Article 2

The Roman Catholic Apostolic Religion will remain undisturbed as the national religion. Tolerance will be extended to all other cults; therefore, the Inquisition, which is useless in this context, will be abolished. The functions of the clergy, being of a sacred nature and needing daily study and occupation, will be incompatible with any other civil or military function.

Article 3

The personal tribute charged to Indians and coloured people for being hateful, unjust and oppressive will be abolished. The Indians and free people of colour will enjoy, from this moment, all the rights and privileges of other citizens.

Article 4

All citizens between 18 and 58 years of age are obligated to take up arms in the defence of their country; according to the circumstances and regulations, this will be published later.

"*Patriae infelici fidelis*" (Loyal to the unhappy homeland)

M_A.

9.3 Proclamation of General Francisco de Miranda to the Peoples of the American Continent, January 1806 (Destined for the Landings in Ocumare and Coro)

Context:

After lengthy negotiations with the Addington cabinet (Pitt's successor) involving even the Duke of Clarence (crown prince) in London to organise a military expedition from Trinidad, the English government, although interested, prevented Miranda from any concrete attempt against the Spanish colonies since England and Spain were not at war as a result of the Treaty "Peace of Amiens" signed in March 1802. In May 1804, William Pitt returned to power. Miranda asks him again to fulfil his previous promises and to allow him to travel so that he can undertake his own military expedition from Trinidad or the US alone. Using his recurring argument that it was vital for England to prevent Napoleon from acting first and seizing the Spanish colonies, Miranda submitted five new plans with different options for a liberation expedition in Latin America. Among the alternatives, one option was to let him act alone. Finally, in July, he obtained authorisation from Pitt to go to the US and Trinidad to undertake this risky option without British support. He left in September and arrived in the United States in November 1805, where he was received by President Jefferson and James Madison, Minister of Foreign Affairs. Madison was a friend of his. He had known him well during his participation in the War of Independence in 1783. However, for diplomatic reasons, the government was terrified and refused to provide him with any official aid. Instead, it would give only moral support and permission to let Miranda organise an exclusively private expedition, recruit troops, and buy weapons in the US.

In January, from New York, he wrote the Proclamation he would issue when he arrived in "Tierra Firme" after printing it on the trip with the printing press he installed on board his small navy of mercenaries and volunteers. In February 1806, he set sail with three ships for Northern Venezuela via Haiti, Barbados and Trinidad. After several difficulties and under the ad-hoc protection of the British fleet of his friend, Admiral Cochrane,[23] he undertakes his two landing attempts, first in Ocumare, where he confronts more powerful Spanish ships by the sea that were waiting for him as a result of denunciations (among others, probably due to Aaron Burr,[24] the Vice-President of the USA who had killed in 1804 in a duel Alexander Hamilton,[25] another friend of Miranda). Second, he seized the city of Coro, which was emptied of force by the Spanish military and religious authorities, which the betrayers had informed. For this reason, he could not execute his plan to recruit the patriots to form an army to grow up on its way to Caracas. The operation ends in a total failure. Miranda retreated to Trinidad, welcomed by Cochrane, where he constantly tried new efforts to receive support and recruit patriots until 1807 but was short of financial resources.

Content:

This is similar to the text of the second Proclamation of 1801, addressing Colombian Americans to recover "*their sovereign independence*", which only depends on their "will" and capacity to maintain "the Union". It establishes equal rights ("*we are all fellow citizens*") and a regime based on "*merit and virtue*". The Proclamation sets 10 articles to serve as the legal basis for the new order, in conformity with the constitution project: suspension of the functions exercised on behalf of Madrid, all powers handed over to the "Cabildos" (City Councils), which will send elected deputies to an Assembly in charge of forming a provisional government and a permanent one in reasonable time.

This Proclamation - written in New York on January 10, 1806 - was printed on board the ship "Leander" and dated March but crossed out by hand by Miranda at the time of landing (over-dated August 2 when arriving at Coro). It was intended to

[23] **Lord Thomas Cochrane** (1775–1860), a faithful ally of Miranda, one of the most famous British sailors; his fame comes from his talents in the maritime war against France and his political fight against corruption in elections and the Navy. Elected deputy, he bothered the oligarchy too much up to the point that the vested interests at stake managed to get rid of him in a financial scandal, causing him to be severely condemned, expelled and lose his titles of nobility. Cochrane then offered himself to Foreign causes dedicated to the independence of Latin America, taking a key role in the war against Spain as Admiral of Chile (1817–1822) in close cooperation with O'Higgins, liberator of Chile and disciple of Miranda, and later, in the independence of Brazil (1822–1827) and Greece (1827–28).

[24] Aaron Burr had a personal view and interest in undertaking a colonial operation in Mexico, to whom Miranda would mean a dangerous obstacle (see Chap. 5, document 5.3. Deductive Hypothesis…, and Chap. 10, document 10.4.1.

[25] **Alexander Hamilton**, one of the Funding Fathers of the US, see Chap. 2, section 2.2., note n° 9.

be disseminated and read in all churches and town halls of Venezuela, but was effectively posted only in Coro. The Catholic Church had condemned the "libertine" Miranda, prohibiting any contact with him as a fatal sin—the same as in the penal domain from the Spanish authorities.

The printed proclamation has a few manual corrections made by Molini, Miranda's secretary: in the first paragraph, where it said "*fellow citizens*" (paisanos), the secretary corrected it to "*friends*", and at the end of the section, he added: "*under the auspices and protection of the English Navy*". The end of the fourth paragraph is "tested" and ends as it is copied here. In the end, the word Coro is handwritten, as there is a blank space in the text for the location of the headquarters. It is dated by hand, 2 August, and the "march" is being printed. The numbered articles were in italics. The signature of Secretary Molini is an autograph, accompanied by a wax seal.

Sources:

Translated from Spanish

Archivo, op. cit. Vol VII, f. 174.

América Espera. Documento 135 p.356–359

Text:

Proclamation to the inhabitants of Columbian America,

Brave compatriots and friends:

Obeying your call and the repeated requests and cries from the Fatherland, to the service of which we have happily consecrated the best part of our life, we have landed in this Province of Caracas, the juncture and time seeming favourable to the fulfilment of our intentions; all the people in this Army are either friends or compatriots of yours; all of them have decided to give their lives if necessary to achieve your freedom and independence, under the auspices and protection of the British Navy.

With this help, we can undoubtedly say that once America recovers its sovereign independence, the day will finally come when her sons and daughters will be free to show their generous disposition to the rest of the world. The oppressive and senseless government, which obscured these beautiful qualities, slandering our modesty and character, is the same that maintained for three centuries its abominable system of administration. Yet, despite this, the government could never remove from our hearts the moral and civil virtues that a saintly religion and a code of conduct instilled in our habits, shaping us into an honest national character.

LET US MAKE USE of the same values so that once we have expelled the few hated government agents from Madrid, we can calmly establish the necessary civilian order to achieve such an honourable Enterprise. The recovery of our rights as citizens and our national glory as Colombian Americans will perhaps be the most minor benefit we shall receive from this just and necessary determination.

SO THAT the good and innocent Indians, just like the valiant "pardos" and free blacks, can firmly believe that we are all fellow citizens and that rewards will be given only on merit and Virtue. For that reason, they will infallibly obtain the military and civilian rewards they deserve by merit.

And if the people of Holland and Portugal were capable of shaking the yoke of despotic Spain; if the Swiss and our neighbours, the Americans, managed to establish their Freedom and Independence to the world's general applause, and for the benefit of their inhabitants, when each of those peoples amounted to no more than 2 or 3 million inhabitants, why cannot 16 million people likewise do it? Owners, as we are of the most fertile Continents, the most impregnable and the richest on Earth? The fact is that it all depends exclusively on our will, and just as wanting it will undoubtedly bring about our Independence, our Union will assure us permanence and ongoing happiness. Let Divine Providence so wish it for the relief of our unhappy compatriots, for the protection and benefit of humankind!

Those of you who, out of fear or lack of information, wish to know in depth the questions of justice and equality that require these procedures - together with the historical facts that prove the unbelievable ingratitude, unheard-of cruelties, and persecutions of the Spanish government, from the beginning of their discovery, let them read the letter written to his compatriots by D. Juan Viscardo of the Society of Jesus; and they will find in it the incontestable proofs and solid arguments in favour of our Cause, dictated by a Saintly Man at his deathbed, as he prepared himself to appear before the Creator of this Universe.

To act upon this plan with due effect, with assurance and efficiency, all the citizens, with no distinctions of class, property or colour (excepting priests where they are not specified), are to conform strictly to the following articles:

I. Every Military, Judicial, Civilian or Ecclesiastical Person who exerts authority derived from the Court of Madrid will ipso facto stop all functions, and he who continues exercising those functions after this publication, or he who obeys them, will be severely punished.

II. In the meantime, the Cabildos and City Councils in all the cities, towns, and localities will exercise responsibly, and according to the Laws of the Country, all government functions, Civil, Administrative, and Judicial, and the parish priests will not alter the exercise of their sacred functions.

III. All the Cabildos and City Councils will send one or two delegates to the Army Headquarters to attend the General Assembly, which will occur as soon as we arrive at the Capital. The purpose of this assembly is to create a provisional government that will eventually and in good time lead to a general and permanent government in agreement with the whole Nation.

IV. Every citizen between the ages of 16 and 55 will join this Army without delay, bringing with him the arms that he may procure, and if he does not have any, they will be given to him from the military warehouses of the Army; by his commitment, talent, age and education.

V. The citizen who basely follows the cause of the Agents of the Spanish Government or disports themselves with arms in the barracks, citadels, and forts possessing that government will be treated and punished like a traitor to the Fatherland. Those who are employed by Spain and, being fainthearted, believe it is honourable to serve against the Independence of their Fatherland will be expelled from the country forever.

VI. Conversely, those citizens currently holding military, civilian or any post who promptly gather under the Banner of the Fatherland will receive all sorts of honours and employment in proportion to the commitment and love they manifest for the Country at such a critical juncture: soldiers and sailors will be equally rewarded according to their capacity and zeal.

VII. The guardians of the Public Treasury will immediately make it available to the Cabildos and City Councils, which will name individuals capable of administering it. The goal is to supply the Colombian Army with whatever it needs for its maintenance and operations, not just money, but also provisions, clothing, fruits, carriages, mules, horses, and other necessary items.

VIII. To avoid insults or aggression from the people at war and in the advanced military posts, the Magistrates and Parish Priests from all cities, towns, and villages (under their responsibility) will fix the Flag or badge of the National Independence in the highest and most conspicuous part of the churches, and the citizens will wear on their hats the rosette that identifies them as such. Otherwise, they might not be respected and protected like brothers.

IX. The parish Priests and Magistrates will affix this proclamation on the doors of the Parish Churches and Council Houses so that its news swiftly reaches every inhabitant. Likewise, the letter above of C. Viscardo included in this proclamation will be read at least once daily in the Parish Churches and Council Houses.

X. Any impediment, delay, or negligence that hinders the observance of the nine articles above will be considered seriously detrimental to the nation. It will be immediately punished: Public health is the Supreme Law!

Date at the Headquarters in Coro, 2nd of August of 1806
FRAN. DE MIRANDA
There is a wax seal
(Signed) Thomas Molini.
(Rubric)
Secret:

9.4 Proclamation to People in Trinidad, July 1806

Context:

Before landing in Venezuela, Miranda's small fleet anchored in Haiti and Barbados to gather more forces and stock up. Miranda faced various difficulties with certain officers who organised riots. With the help of the British navy, discipline was restored, and Miranda issued this proclamation to motivate his troops about the purpose and challenge of the expedition.

Content:

Lyrical argument to convince the team of the meaning of the expedition. Miranda emphasises that, in addition to risking their lives for the emancipatory "sublime action," each individual will deserve fair compensation in terms of land and wages.

Sources:

Written in English

Archivo. op. cit. Vol. VI, p. 199–201

Miranda Documents, p. 71

América Espera. Document 133, p. 353–354

Text:

My friends and fellow citizens:

The glorious opportunity now presents itself of relieving from oppression and arbitrary government, a people who are worthy of a better fate, who ought to enjoy the blessings of the finest country in the universe, which bountiful providence has given them, but who are shackled by despotism too cruel for nature longer to endure; groaning under their present afflictions, they hail with extended arms, the noble cause of freedom and independence and call upon you to share with them in the godlike action of relieving your distressed fellow creatures.

Hasten to join the standard of one who is happy to call himself your countryman and is determined to rescue his country and shed the last drop of his blood in promoting its happiness, an object of which he has never lost sight for a moment in his life.

Land will be liberally distributed according to ranks at the expiration of 12 months, and privates will be entitled to provisions and clothing from the instant of their enrolment, with a quarter of a dollar a day of pay, not subject to any deduction.

And you, brave volunteers of the islands who here nobly come forward to partake with us our honours and share our prosperity, hasten to follow those officers under whose care you have already been trained and who are impatient to lead you on to victory and wealth.

The Gulf that Columbus first discovered and honoured with his presence will now witness the illustrious actions of our gallant efforts.

Trinidad, July, 1806

Vol. VII. Fol. 70 y 70 vto.

9.5 Proclamation to Be Issued by the Leaders of the Conspiracy Upon Landing in Brazil (Attributed to Miranda)

Context:

As explained in detail in Chap. 5, documents 5.3 (draft constitution for Brazil), a complete set of letters of denunciation in the Portuguese diplomatic archives by a Liverpool merchant about a liberating operation scheduled by Miranda for landing in Brazil in 1806 [Parra Perez 1943, Salcedo Bastardo 1982]. This military operation would have been launched just after a similar operation had succeeded on the coasts of Venezuela, and only if it had been successful there. Miranda would have prepared several texts, including a Proclamation in the context of his landing in Brazil. Although there is no formal historical proof of this Miranda's plan, texts and direct involvement of Miranda, there are several converging indices that argue in favour of the authenticity of this Proclamation and its author identity, even independently of the existence of a specific Miranda's plan scheduled for 1806, but as a potential eventuality.

These indices are:

- in the text of the Proclamation of the Independence of Brazil dated 1806 appears the reference to a prediction that Miranda was the only one to secretly warn the governments of England and the United States: the announcement that Napoleon would usurp the throne of the Braganza, which happened effectively much later, in December 1807, this means 16 months after this text was registered by the Portuguese authorities (in 1806). The French invasion resulted from the secret negotiation between Napoleon and Spain through the Treaty of Fontainebleau of July 1807. During his stay in France in 1795–97, Miranda had always opposed an invasion by France of Spain and Portugal. He was the first and only one to warn the British and United States governments about this risk of invasion. Still, his messages were addressed in a very reserved way and to the highest level of these states (see one of the warnings he had made in his personal correspondence to the President of the United States and also to the British government since 1798). It seems implausible that the whistleblower - a simple English merchant - could have learned of such a personal and not publicised prognosis of the Precursor. On the contrary, this information points to the thesis that Miranda contemplated very early the possibility of an uprising in Brazil in the case (inevitable according to his knowledge of Napoleon's character) of a French invasion of Portugal. Therefore, he would have secretly prepared the ground with documents ready to join these revolutions in case they occurred after his success in Spanish America.
- the content of this Proclamation develops not only Miranda's genuine philosophical conceptions but also in a style so close to that of the humanist that it seems impossible to have only been imitated or invented by swindlers, nor could fraudsters have drafted the subtly balanced philosophical positions in the Proclamation since that would imply an experimented knowledge and a perfect interpretation of original positions well advanced by this time. Miranda was alone in advocating for these ideas at that moment.
- The fact that this Proclamation does not correspond to excerpts from already existing Miranda texts for Spanish America (which would have been more logical in the case of being imitated by fraudsters), combined with the previous observations, leads us to think that this Proclamation was written by Miranda himself in prevision of an eventual extension of the movement that he was preparing for Venezuela and its extension to the whole Hispanic-America.

- The chronology of the denunciation letters fits perfectly with the Coro events on which the Brazilian expedition depended. This fact reinforces the hypothesis that this proclamation reveals genuine Miranda thinking - whether it is a scam from a very high-level traitor perfectly informed of the Precursor's ideas or a copy of an authentic proclamation written by Miranda himself and later destroyed to preserve his British support.

However, what remains impossible to clarify with existing materials is whether the Brazilian part of the conspiracy was effective or only expected and "extrapolated" by Miranda, who would have previously (maybe in London) drawn up a new constitution for Brazil as well as some proclamations in the case of the basic scenario of a Napoleonic invasion of Portugal could be associated with a contagion in Brazil of his Coro landing. In this hypothesis, the whistle-blower (or crook) would have had access to this hypothetical plan without a date or precise connections except for the connection with an operation in Venezuela; thus, upon learning of Coro's project, the crook would have extrapolated what he knew to present it as more concrete and already in course in parallel with the current plan for landing in Venezuela. This interpretation would imply that the crook was not a simple merchant but a top-ranking official from the British administration or even some US circles. It is a fact that the Spanish authorities had been informed, as evidenced by the trap set for Miranda's fleet at Ocumare and the compulsory evacuation of all citizens from Coro before his landing. There are also official messages from the Spanish spies in New York warning Madrid about Miranda's departure with soldiers. We detailed in Chap. 5 the hypothesis with some indices that Aaron Burr might be the brain of this denunciation.

Content:

Similar to the arguments and ideas developed for Coro (self-confidence in the legitimacy of independence, equal rights and no discrimination, universal suffrage, social status based only upon talent and virtue, religious tolerance and pluralism, respect for people and property, freedom and free competition, incentives to manufactures, agrarian reform, the importance of the rule of law and good governance, warning against violence,...) with some nuances in a nice romantic Mirandian style.

Sources:

Document received in English by Portuguese Ambassador in London, original letters accessible in Portuguese diplomatic archives, Torre de Tombo, Lisbon

América Espera, op. cit. p. 351–353, reprint of Spanish translation made by Parra-Perez, also published in Parra Pérez, C., ***Paginas de Historia y de Polémicas***, Lithografia del Comercio, Caracas, 1943

Text:

"Brave citizens of Brazil — Stand up! Hear the voice of Freedom and cast the ignoble chains by which you have been cruelly oppressed for so long."

Freedom, that supreme privilege of Man, is now within your reach. Determined to be free, and you will no longer be slaves. Look at our brothers in the United States, who can be placed among the first nations of the Earth, who just a few years ago were bound by chains as harsh as ours and in their fight for their birthright, they had to fight with a nation of gigantic strength both by land and by sea — but the cause for which they fought was more potent than several armies.

Who do we have to oppose in our glorious fight? A handful of poorly dressed and poorly fed slaves, miserable instruments of a weak and distant government, incapable of fighting with free, fearless and determined men. We have weapons, and we are men. The House of B no longer represents the Portuguese Government [Braganza]. The Tyrant of France has usurped that throne and intends to seize those rich and fertile provinces as part of his conquests, but will Brazilians have to submit their necks to the yoke of a tyrant? No. Let's all get up together and unite as brothers. We have brought weapons for your protection; run to the banners of Liberty, join hands and hearts in the glorious cause, and your names will be bequeathed to posterity as your country's most virtuous patriots and liberators.

In this region that Nature has enriched with a generous hand, manufactures will flourish without hindrance. We will no longer be forced to send our gold to Europe to acquire the necessary things that the children of Brazil can manufacture to a higher degree. Freedom will flourish without a license, Religion without fraud, Property will be respected, manufacturing will be encouraged, and Civil and political norms will be adopted for the benefit of the people in general and not to favour a few. Every intelligent and industrious man can be independent. We will not know of any other superiority that arises from talent and virtue, no distinction but that which patriotism and the public spirit make us creditors, and no other rivalry except in our struggle for the public good.

These motives will inspire us, and as long as we remain united in our hands and hearts in the cause of our country, we will be invincible.

May our struggles for the emancipation of this beloved Country not be stained with any unnecessary act of robbery or violence. Let us remember that we are fighting for Freedom and that every free man must be brave, generous and humanitarian; only cowards are slaves, cruel, rapacious and corrupt. May those who join our flag be received with open arms and participate in all the benefits of the alliance; that those whose age or particular circumstances prevent them from joining us but who nevertheless are well inclined to our cause be considered friends, and their persons and property are scrupulously respected; Those who appear to be enemies of the Freedom of their country will suffer the punishment established by their offended laws. There will be an equitable division of the lands among the brave who support this glorious enterprise, which they will enjoy under benign and just laws founded on principles and in strict justice and humanity. Every citizen will participate in the legislature. Laws will be made by those who must obey them, and no man will be above them or may transgress them with impunity; the poorest in the state will be under their protection as much as the richest.

Trade, industry, and the liberal arts will flourish in a land where Liberty has made its home, and this country will maintain such rank among the nations that boast it, of which it has been deprived for too long.

Brazilians: we are the heirs and owners of the land; therefore, do not allow the terror of being treated as rebels to influence your minds even for a moment. We will take precautionary measures by arresting those people who are the servile agents of the Government that oppresses us; they will have to answer in their persons for any outrage that they have committed against you. Let the glorious light of Reason illuminate your minds; let the love for your Country enliven your breasts; draw your sword, and swear that you will not enjoy rest or peace until your Country is free. It is better to live just 1 day and live it free than to languish in a long life of subjection and slavery.

Remember the long years in which you and your ancestors have led a miserable existence in slavery and submission, and allow that memory to stimulate you to perform acts of heroism that free you from the bitter chains that oppress you. Your parents, your wives, and your children cry out for you; Thousands not yet born will bless the efforts that ensured Brazil's freedom and prosperity. Let our slogan be Freedom or Death.

Your brothers, who have witnessed the blessed effects of Freedom in the countries where it presides, have come to you to preach the doctrine of Friendship, Fraternal Love, and Freedom. Hear their lively exhortations and convince yourself that nothing but accents of Truth flow from their lips and persuasion abides on their tongues.

Years of tranquillity, happiness and prosperity will follow the privations we must suffer in fulfilling this glorious undertaking; it is like sowing a rich and exuberant harvest."

[Whistle-blower's addendum: "*There was more, mainly about Miranda's supposed success in the Spanish provinces and exhorting Brazilians to follow their example, but I had no opportunity to copy it*".]

9.6 General Miranda's Proclamation to the Inhabitants of Valencia at the End of His Mission, Valencia, 22 October 1811

Context:

Miranda arrived in Venezuela in December 1810 at the instigation of Bolivar, who was sent to London by the Cabildo (Municipal council) mandate, which took power on April 19 1810. Once in London, faced with the requirement by the British government to give an appointment only if Miranda would be present, Bolívar was obliged to violate the instruction given to him by the Caracas oligarchy: "*above all not to involve Miranda*. Miranda's purpose was to lead the uprising against Madrid (at the hands of the French occupier) to channel it towards absolute independence from Spain but in union with the other cities and vice-royalties of the Empire. Being perceived as a radical revolutionary who could threaten the interests of the dominant Creoles, the new Caracas authorities received him with suspicion. However, they could not prevent him from participating in the nascent political life, and he was elected as a deputy to the constituent Congress that prepared the Constitution. He contributed decisively to the Declaration of Independence on July 5, 1811. A few days later, due to the uprising of the city of Valencia against the new republican government, Congress is forced, for lack of an alternative, to appoint Miranda, Chief of the Army, to subdue Valencia. Miranda wins after fierce fighting and restores order and discipline. Still, she is immediately criticised for his military decisions by local politicians, fearing that his military power would make Miranda a dangerous political competitor. They prefer to halt his efficient and successful anti-royalist campaign, thereby impeding his ability to submit to the remaining dissident regions. The purpose was to prevent him from gaining popularity and increasing his power. This reveals the significant ambiguity of the Caracas movement, which prefers to keep open the option of a return to the colonial order in the event of political and social reforms that would counteract their own feudal privileges. Miranda, respectful of the new constitutional order, obeyed this strategy, well aware that it threatened independence, but left Valencia pacified, issuing this Proclamation to clarify its position when accepting to return to Caracas.

Content:

This text's diplomatic and moral aspects dominate. It argues that he only fulfilled his limited mission in Valencia: to build a rule of law beneficial to all and respectful of freedom and Christian morality.

Sources:

Translated from Spanish

El Patriota de Venezuela.

In **Testimonios de la época Emancipadora**. Prólogo de Arturo Uslar Pietri. Caracas. 1961. p. 341–449. Biblioteca de la Academia Nacional de la Historia. Sesquicentenario de la Independencia. N° 37. Reprint of the texts n°s 2, 3, 6 y 7. p. 407–409.

Text:

Proclamation that General Miranda made to the people of Valencia on the occasion of his retreat from that city

Headquarters of Valencia, 22 October 1811

Dear compatriots and friends, this army came to bring you peace, tranquillity and order, and having fulfilled the duties for which it was sent, it leaves you now in quiet possession of your homes, your estates and your properties so that once back in the routine of your domestic occupations, you may find in them the same support and abundance that you enjoyed before, and that subjecting yourselves to the beneficial obedience to and command of the laws, we all live together in concord and with that unity of purpose necessary for the common safety.

The liberty and independence that divine Providence has given us today, after three centuries of disasters, injustices, and oppression, must be a new reason for us, united sons of Colombia, to eagerly undertake the creation of a constitution that secures our personal freedom and our properties and becomes a solid basis for permanent happiness.

One of the main advantages that free life and government bring to those with them is industry, as it eradicates the inseparable vices of idleness and improves their habits, making them good, wealthy and respectable. Agriculture is the first among the arts, and according to the Roman philosopher and orator, it is the one that benefits the free man: *nibil agricultura melius, nibil uberius, nibil dulcius, nibil bimini libero dignius.*[26] Let us live, then, content with our fortune, thanking the Creator of the Universe for having destined us to such an honourable profession, so valuable and similar to the system we have just adopted and also for having granted us probably the most beautiful climate and fertile soil of the earth.

The solid system of freedom rests on another fundamental basis, that of Morals, for as secular experience shows, those happy nations that had moral principles were, in fact, the simplest ones. Rome and Sparta among the ancient ones, Switzerland, Batavia [the Netherlands], England and America among the modern ones, and the moment the people corrupted them, liberty decayed and died forever. The loose and pernicious doctrines that some libertines publicise during the day against these immovable principles are obviously untrue and dire in their consequences.

Religion is the most efficient means of engraving from infancy those sublime principles in the heart of men, through which they learn to become Christians, valuable members of society and good citizens. For this reason, we must respect and revere the sacred precepts of religion, paying its ministers the due respect they deserve. I can assure you that all the parish priests I have met in the cities and places I have visited and are under my command are worthy men of the Church and excellent citizens. Many of them are imbued with severe judgment and true patriotism.

Finally, beloved fellow citizens and friends, allow one in the midst of you who for years has [sighed] longed for your happiness and who, in his travels and research, may have collected a little more experience than you in the affairs and businesses that affect you today, to give you this short and beneficial advice, coming as it comes from the warmth of his affection and his sincere patriotism, having so often offered his life to see you [unfinished].

Francisco de Miranda

By mandate of S.E. Carlos Soublette

References

Antepara, J. M., (1810), *South American Emancipation*, ed. by R. Juigné, 17 Margaret Street, London, Re-edited by Chacon, D. [2005] and also by Editorial Ayacucho [2009].

Las Casas, B. de, (1552/1697), *Descubrimiento de las Indias Occidentales*, Paris 1697, p. 12, translation, by Jean Baptiste Morvan de Bellegarde, of the author's: *Brevissima relacion de la destrucción de las Indias*, first printed Seville, 1552.

Miranda, F. de, (1929-1950) *Archivo del General Miranda,* 24 Vol. Caracas & La Habana.

Parra Pérez, C., (1943), *Paginas de Historia y de Polémicas*, Lithografia del Comercio, Caracas.

Salcedo Bastardo, J. L., (1982), *América Espera*, biblioteca Ayacuch n° 100, Caracas.

Vattel, E., [1758, 1916). *The Law of Nations* or the Principles of Natural Law Applied to the Conduct and the Affairs of Nations 26 and Sovereigns, Translation of the Edition of 1758 by Charles Fenwick with an Introduction by Albert de Lapradelle. Vol. III. Washington, DC: Carnegie Institution. p. xxx.

[26] *There is nothing better than agriculture, nothing more in general, there is nothing sweeter, nothing worthy of a free man.* Marco Tulio Cicero. De officiis (Duties), I, 150.

Chapter 10
Selection of Extracts from Miranda's Letters

10.1 Introduction

Miranda's letters, meticulously selected to serve as a necessary complement for analysing his thoughts and political strategy, provide a comprehensive view. Like a beacon of knowledge, this comprehensive view enlightens the reader about Miranda's geopolitical strategy and vision. These letters span two decades and bear witness to the extraordinary constancy of his efforts in a single direction. As a man of action, these letters demonstrate the continuity of his plan, offering precise details about the coherence of his ideas and their execution. Some were even written on the battlefields with a campaign writing desk. The selection process is rigorous, limited to parts that complement the texts presented in the previous chapters, ensuring the reader gains a more profound understanding without losing the context of the moment.

In addition to the content of geopolitical strategy that reveals, in real-time, thanks to the dates of the letters, the unusual degree of his capacity for analysis and vision, these letters testify to his permanent and selfless struggle not only to achieve independence of his homeland but also of his concern to insert it into an international alliance to strengthen democracy, the "ius gentium" and peace. The reader is actively encouraged to form their own opinion about both the coherence and the constant ethics of Miranda's attitude. Compared to W. Pitt's British behaviour, his integrity and ethical approach are evident in his letters. The ex-post analysis also allows for concluding the comparative capacity of both persons' geopolitical visions. Chapter 11 presents our thesis regarding Pitt's errors and cynical choices' direct responsibility in comparison to Miranda's fairness and concern for promoting mutually beneficial cooperation and international peace.

C. Ghymers, *Independence, Federalism and Regionalism in Latin America: An Analytical Anthology of Francisco de Miranda's Writings (1790-1811)*, United Nations University Series on Regionalism 34,
https://doi.org/10.1007/978-3-031-96938-6_10

In particular, these letters illustrate the "textbook case" of the "Prisoner Dilemma"[1] that Miranda tried to solve during more than two decades of tireless efforts. He demonstrated that active cooperation in emancipating Spanish America should have been a natural win-win game for Great Britain, especially in an alliance with the United States. Both democratic powers, constrained by their vested interests and static views, were unable to perceive their own dynamic interests and cooperate effectively with Miranda within a systemic worldview. Miranda's proposed cooperation was not just beneficial but also a potential game-changer in international relations, a vision that could have significantly reshaped the geopolitical landscape. A parallel with the challenging situation NATO is currently facing in 2024 could be drawn interestingly.

10.2 Period 1790–1797: London I & Paris

10.2.1 First Proposal of Miranda Presented to William Pitt as a Follow-Up of His Meeting[2] in Hollwood[3] on 14 February 1790

Context:

Upon returning from his four-year trip to Europe, Miranda chose London in June 1789 as the best place to implement his operational plan for the emancipation of Latin America, both for the existing democratic guarantees and for the socio-economic and cultural progress he observed in comparison to the rest of Europe. Under the protection of the Russian Ambassador in London,[4] he established numerous contacts, formed friendships, and gained access to government authorities. In September, he is invited to the table of William Pitt and his Minister of the Interior

[1] The **prisoner's dilemma** is a schematic model in modern game theory. It illustrates the paradox in decision analysis, where two decision-makers pursuing their own self-interests separately do not produce the best outcome for themselves. The relative incentives make it difficult to cooperate. If communication is not ensured, rational individual decisions do not lead either defendant to cooperate. Cooperative behaviour would yield a superior outcome, but it requires mutual trust (or formal commitments with transparent communication channels). In the face of uncertainty about the partner policy, both parties opt to protect themselves at the expense of their partner. As a result, both participants find themselves in a much worse outcome than if they had cooperated with each other in the decision-making process.

[2] This private conference lasted from 11:00 a.m. to 1:45 p.m.

[3] **Hollwood** was the country mansion of the prime minister of Great Britain, William Pitt the Younger, in Keston, near Hayes, in the London Borough of Bromley, on the road to Westerban. This house was destroyed after Pitt's death and a nice palace was built in 1823.

[4] As one of the favourites of Tsarina Catherine II of Russia, Miranda benefited from special protection against the Spanish spies in London who were trying to rapt him as a betrayer of the Crown

and Minister of India, William Grenville,[5] at a banquet organised for the London Mayor. A war between Spain and England seemed inevitable at this time due to the sovereignty conflict with Spain in the Pacific Northwest (Nootka Sound). In February 1790, British opinion became aware of the Spanish aggression against English ships in this region and demanded retaliation, thereby opening an opportunity for Miranda's plan. On February 14, 1790, on the recommendation of one of his friends in London, Thomas Pownall,[6] he visited William Pitt, Prime Minister, for the first time at his country home in Hollwood, Kent. As a result of a 3-h meeting, Miranda writes a substantiated memoir, which he sends to Pitt along with an annexe.

Content:

It is a synthetic text that already contains most of the principles he will develop later and throughout his life. He sets out in unambiguous terms the legitimacy of emancipation with British support for ensuring the socio-economic development of the whole region. The coherence of the arguments and the advancement - in the world of 1790 - of his conception of a possible catching-up of these colonies through popular education and good governance should be emphasised. In particular, the absence of discrimination between Creoles and Indians and the implicit affirmation of a genuine American identity are already clearly perceived. It also expresses a modern geopolitical vision of the necessary alliance of economic progress and democracy between England and Spanish America. Miranda will always follow this clear line, which integrates the best ideas of Enlightenment philosophy, subsequently adapting them to reality in a visionary projection of the contemporary world.

Sources:

Written in English, French and Italian. The original version is in his Archivo. Vol. I. Fol. 128. Negociaciones.

- **Archivo del General...** op. cit., Vol. XV, p. 111–117
- **Colombeia**. Vol IX. Document 1232. p. 38–42
- **América Espera**. Translated in Spanish, Document 39. p. 104–106.

Text:

Proposal of 5 March 1790

Follow-up to the Conference at Hollwood on the 14th February 1790

South America requests, that England would assist her to shake off the infamous oppression in which Spain keeps her, refusing to the natives of all ranks the civil, military & ecclesiastical posts of any Consideration & given it to the sole old-Spaniards of a low class in general, that come there with the only View of enriching themselves, ill-use, and oppress the unhappy Inhabitants with an inexpressible Rapacity- forbidding also to the American Nobility to pass to Spain, nor to any other foreign Country, without an especial License from the King, that very seldom is granted; by which means they have become in fact prisoner without cause, or any

[5] **William Grenville** (1759–1834), Tory politician, later became a Whig, conservative, very reticent towards Miranda's democratic ideas, and opposed to military operations overseas; see Chap. 11.

[6] **Thomas Pownall (1722–1805)**, a member of the British Parliament, former governor of Massachusetts and of other American states, Miranda's ally. See Chap. 5, section 5.2.1., note n°6.

apparent motive!- and what is worst yet, to oppress their Minds by the infamous tribunal of the inquisition, that forbids them the reading or having any valuable books or publication that may me capable of illustrating the human understanding; whom by those means they pretend to degrade, to make superstitious & despicable, merely by a gross Ignorance.[7]

The People of different Provinces in South America, coming to despair with the excessive taxes, injustice, & all sorts of abuses, revolted at various periods, but without obtaining the redress they wanted because, in the end, they submitted themselves to fair promises, which instead increased their misery. (a) Caracas revolted in the year 1750.- Quito in 1764.- Mexico was converting his independence from England in 1773.- Peru was in an open revolution in March 1781- and in June of the same year (1781), the Kingdom of Santa Fe de Bogotá expelled the Viceroy with all the European troops, the natives remaining the Masters of the Country.- they came to a Capitulation afterwards, by which the King promised everything they demanded & as soon as he recovered his authority again, and had forces sufficient broke the stipulation, forfeited his promise, & treated them with cruelty going so far as to imprison other persons of the first Rank & Distinction all over the Continent by arbitrary orders, or Letters de Cachet, without the slightest motive or apparent reason.

In this situation, South America thinks herself with a full right to repulse a Domination both oppressive & tyrannical- & to form for herself a government free, wise & equitable in the form that may be more adaptable to the Country, Climate, genius & manner of its inhabitants &. And more so, when doing that, not the least usurpation or Injustice is offered to the Kings of Spain… All the World knows how little they contributed to the expense of the discovery of the New World & nothing surety to the Conquest… for which, however, they made themselves very essentially paid! If they don't pretend to plead as a fundamental right (being the heirs & Successors of D. Fernando the Catholic), the curious Donation of the Spanish Pope Alexander the VIth, which subject is instead of a ludicrous than of a serious Disquisition.

South America might by herself execute the mentioned expulsion, being superior in Population & more so in wealth to Spain, but considering the extension of that Continent & the great distances from one Capital to another- Considering that there are no roads to communicate by land, being necessary to go by sea from one province to another- and what is more yet, that there is not in all the Spanish Dominions on that hemisphere a single Newspaper as a medium of Communication between one province & another;- is very obvious the impossibility of acting unanimously & of course the necessity of having a maritime force that may preserve the communication open, & resist those that Spain might send to obstruct the Design.

No power can do this with more excellent facility than England, and under the principles of justice, perfect reciprocity regarding Spain & for her own

[7] Miranda's Notes: The **Scythians**, says Herodotus, gouge the eyes of their slaves so that they patiently churn the milk, which is their ordinary nutriment (Lib. 4°). But Spain, still refining its cruelty, takes away, so to speak, the eyes of understanding from the Americans to hold them more subject.

welfare.- South America has a very extensive trade to offer with preference to England; has treasure for to pay with punctuality the services that she may receive….& even for to pay an essential part of the national debt of England- for which reason conceiving this critical subject of mutual interest to both parties, South America hopes, that being united by a solemn compact with England, establishing a free and similar government, and combining a plan of commerce reciprocally advantageous, these two nations might form the most respectable & preponderant political union in the world.

Considering the analogy that exists in the character of these two nations, & the effects that naturally must flow from Liberty and a good government, giving an instruction to the general mass of men that will progressively expel the religious prejudices that imbue the minds of that People….otherwise honest, hospitable & generous[8]- we must expect to see soon growing up a respectable, and illustrious Nation, worthy of being the intimate allies of the most enlightened and celebrated Power upon earth.

The adjoined Statement will show the population, wealth, and actual products of South America, her consumption from Europe also, and a comparative plan of Old Spain at present, by which it may be conceived the disparity that results in favour of the former and the impossibility in which Spain is of making any efficacious opposition if the Stated combination should take place.

The practicability of all the military operations (for which purpose only 12 or 15,000 men inf. and 15 sail of the line are required) is subject to be explained afterwards, if needed- as well as the possibility of making without much difficulty a canal of navigation across the Isthmus of Panama, that will facilitate the commerce of China & the South Sea, with innumerable advantages for England & America &.

D. Francisco de Miranda.

T. I, f. 128 Negociaciones

10.2.2 *Letter from Miranda to William Pitt, London, 28 January 1791*

Context:

This letter is a note delivered to William Pitt, who wanted to know Mr. Don Francisco de Miranda's opinions shortly after the Agreement of Nootka Sound with Spain in October 1790, which allowed the UK and Spain to avoid a war. This diplomatic agreement meant Miranda's hope of getting British military support for his emancipation plan collapsed.

[8] Said writing confirmed me more in the assent to the truth that a long time ago, by dealing in part by word and much more in writing, with some Indian gentlemen, I had understood, that is, that culture in all kinds of letters among those who are not professors by destiny, flourishes more in America than in Spain, etc. (Feijoo (1764). "Erudite Letters." Volume V. Chap. 10).

In 1808, as a similar change by the government occurred, Miranda [1929, 1978] ironically sent a copy of this note to Lord Castlereagh,[9] indicating that, again, he was declining the proposal of accompanying Sir Arthur Wellesley when his scheduled expedition to Venezuela was suddenly redirected from Cork towards Spain.[10]

Content:

Miranda's offer of services to the British government. Still, it excluded fighting directly against Spain (something that A. Wellesley-Wellington would propose to Miranda in 1808, which he would categorically reject). He also proposes to Pitt that the services of the former American Jesuits, exiled by Spain, be utilised as a valuable source of American human capital for a future independent administration that would need to ensure the socio-economic development of Hispanic America. Pitt took this advice into account when asking the British consul in Tuscany to locate Father Viscardo y Guzman,[11] alias Paolo Rossi, author of the "*Letter to the American Spaniards*" (see Annex 1), which Miranda published later in 1799 and 1801.

Sources:

Archivo, op. cit. Vol. XV, p. 128–129 ..,

Colombeia. Vol IX. Document 1245. p. 66–67

América Espera, op. cit. Document 41 p. 109, as well as in **Ensayo Historico...** Becerra, Vol. II, p. 346–347

Text:

N° XVI

Corresponds to N° 1 of 1791

To Mr. William Pitt,

London, 28 January 1791

My only views now & always were to promote the happiness and liberty of my own Country (South America), which was excessively oppressed- and in so doing,

---

[9] **Lord Castlereagh** (1769–1822), Minister for War and Colonies from 1807 to 1809. See Chap. 5, document 5.2,4., note n° 68.

[10] **Arthur Wellesley** (1769–1852), Duke of Wellington, general-in-chief, conqueror of Napoleon in Portugal (1809), Spain (1812–13), France (1814) and Waterloo, Belgium (1815), was also a British politician (and younger brother of the British Foreign Minister from 1809 to 1812), Miranda was his advisor until 1809 to help defeat Napoleon. See Chap. 5, document 5.2.4. Note n° 65.

[11] **Juan Pablo Viscardo y Guzmán** (1748–1798), a half-blood Peruvian Jesuit, was jailed and expulsed as 3.000 other members of the Jesuit company from Hispanic America by the Spanish King Charles III in 1767 for being critical of the colonial regime. All were condemned to live in exile. In 1781, from Italy, where he was in exile, he attempted to secure British assistance in freeing Peru from Spanish tyranny after learning about the indigenous rebellion led by the Inca Tupac Amaru. Miranda was aware of him in 1786, when he visited the exiled Jesuits in Italy and gave him the nickname Paolo Rossi, advising Pitt to invite him to London as an adviser. Thus it was, and he lived in London from 1790 until he died in 1798. He drafted the famous "*Letter to the Hispanic American*," which influenced Miranda, who translated and published the letter in French first in 1799 and Spanish in 1801. This letter (see Annex 2), which firmly claimed the emancipation of the Spanish colonies, played a significant role in developing the sense of American identity among Hispanic Americans as a basis for independence. See Annex 2 at the end of this book.

to offer also significant commercial advantages to England, as stated in the Proposal[12] presented on the 5th of March 1790, and so forth.

Upon these principles, I should be pleased to offer and continue my services to England- that in pursuing the advantages already obtained by the last Convention, some judicious arrangements may be made to forward & bring to maturity, in a future period, the same generous and benevolent Plan above mentioned, for the happiness and prosperity of South America; for the grandeur and opulence of this Nation!- Very few individuals of the Ex-Jesuits natives of Chili & Mexico, now exiled and ill-used in Italy, might be of very excellent service; both to direct the new settlements, and commercial intercourse to be formed between the English, and natives upon the granted Costs of South America; and for establishing some communications with the great Spanish towns on the continent, through their own relations, & friends.

I should mention that my personal situation requires competent annual support to be granted to me—as I have been deprived for a long time of receiving any income from my own estates in Caracas. Any sums of money that may be granted to me, on any account whatsoever, either for services done or expected from me after, shall be repaid by me when I may come to the possession of my property in South America.

And it is expected that the intention being purely Patriotic, with the wishes only of producing services to my Country and promoting the interest and advantages of Great Britain, as perfectly compatible in this point of view, that services must not be requested from me against Spain, with any other motive! Being a point of delicacy with me, although authorised by the rights of Nations, and the example of many great and Virtuous men in modern and ancient times.

London the 28th January 1791.

Francisco de Miranda.

N: T. I, f. 135–237.

10.2.3 Letter from Miranda to William Pitt, London, 17 March 1792

Context:

As a result of the Peace Treaty between England and Spain signed in October 1790, which prevented British military support for Miranda's plan, he decided to try to interest revolutionary France, claiming freedom and thereby opening himself up to his ideas of emancipation. In addition, France had remained neutral in the Nootka Sound conflict despite the Bourbon alliance between France and Spain.[13] Before

[12] Miranda's first written proposal to William Pitt, see above, document 10.2.1.

[13] The Bourbon kings of France and Spain had several successive "***Pactes de famille***" from 1733, formally ending with the first French Republic in 1792. Under the constitution of 1791, which entered into force in September 1791, Louis XVI continued to occupy the throne as constitutional

travelling to Paris and serving the Revolution and the traditional enemy of England, Miranda wants to recover the documents delivered to Pitt in 1790. After sending repeated letters and taking actions through intermediaries to recover them in 1791, Miranda loses patience and sends this letter, arguing in harsh terms with Pitt.

Content:

Logical argumentation against Pitt's attitude, with a sense of honour, from someone who pursues "*an object above any personal interest.*"

Sources:

Translated from French

Archivo, op. cit. Vol. XV p. 142–144

Colombeia. Vol. IX. 1988. Document 1258. p. 90-92, reprint en **América Espera.** Document 44, p. 114–116

Text:

To the right, Honourable Mr. Pitt

From Francisco de Miranda

London, 17 March 1792

Having patiently waited six months for a reply to my letter dated 18 September 1791, or at least for the return of the papers that I had the honour to entrust you with, I have no more doubts about the course of action I must take. No matter how strange your behaviour seems to me, I understand it.

It is beyond my means to provide conclusive proof of what happened between you and me, and even if I could do so, the confidential nature of the objective of our interviews would render it impossible.

But, do you believe it is a fair and honourable thing to do to keep someone else's property and to default on commitments you made in the name of your nation? Because it was to the English nation through your ministry that the communication of a plan believed to be worthy of her was made and not to the honourable William Pitt, and that you should think you have the right to do what you consider appropriate with my projects, once I have left the country?

No, Sir, all the ideas contained in those plans, I hope you shall not forget this, were communicated to you with the express intention of fostering the Liberty and Prosperity of the Hispanic American peoples and for the advantage and honour of England, as these two objectives are perfectly compatible. But, if you have in mind to make a different use of them, be persuaded from now on that my compatriots will find the means to stop your sinister intentions, even if you wish to execute them promptly because I am well aware that there are agents who inform you of what is going on in Southern America. In that case, I would be obliged to show the world which of the two of us, in the course of these negotiations, has conducted himself according to the principles of justice, equality and honour and has lifted his eyes only to benefit his fellow citizens, for the Felicity and prosperity of the Fatherland!

---

monarch until its suspension on August 10, 1792, and the Monarchy was officially abolished on September 21, 1792, with the proclamation of the Republic by the Convention. Spain joined 1793 the first coalition against France but was defeated and signed the Peace of Basel in 1795. Nevertheless, in 1796, Spain became France's ally again to fight England through the Second Treaty of San Ildefonso. See Chap. 5, notes n° 25 and 31.

Your secretary, Mr. Smith, gave me only four of the ten documents I had the honour of entrusting you with the other day, claiming it was impossible to find the rest. Sir, that papers handed personally to the English Prime Minister, considered by him of the utmost importance, should go… missing! Allow me not to reflect on the singularity of these circumstances. After that, Mr Smith told me that he had been instructed to give me 800 pounds on the condition that I should sign a receipt acknowledging that I had received them from Mr Pitt; refusing the signature of my agent here, I have signed to avoid any difficulty on my part concerning these mean pecuniary agreements and to see this embarrassing affair over and done with.- And Mr. Smith must have informed you that I decided not to include in this receipt, or the one for the previous 500 pounds, the condition that I should have these sums at your disposition as soon as possible.

Money has never been the object of my worries, as you may well know by the refusal I have given to offers of employment and honours that the most generous and distinguished monarch on earth has had the kindness to make me, occupied as I am by an objective which goes beyond my personal Interest.

Sir, with all due regard and respect, I am your most obedient and humble servant.

F. de M.

P.S.: Also, I leave the convenience of finding the papers I gave you for your judicious deliberation, sir. They are being returned to me in full, or at least with the Declaration that they have not been copied… and with the hope that you will prevent a later requisition from me by giving them sealed to my friend Mr Turnbull. I shall make a short journey, hoping to find them in my hands on my return.

10.2.4 Letter from Miranda to Joseph Servan,[14] French Minister of War, About His Conditions for Serving France, Paris, 24 August 1792

Context:

Miranda arrived in Paris from London on March 23, 1792, and began discussions with the Girondins, who were[15] in charge of the government. He realised France was contemplating exporting its revolution to Spain (and the rest of Europe) rather than liberating Spanish America. He tried to convince the French authorities that it was not advisable to attack Spain, but he needed to prepare thoroughly and coordinate with them to undertake a larger project in South America in a sequential manner. Upon returning to London in August 1792, Miranda was blocked by the new

[14] **Joseph Servan** (1741–1808), career officer, Girondin revolutionary, appointed Minister of War in May 1792 in the Girondin government. He resigned in October 1792 as minister to command the army of the Pyrenees; he was arrested by Robespierre during the Terror and released after the tyrant's fall. He re-joined the army until his retirement in 1807.

[15] **Girondin**: moderate left-wing political movement, pro-revolution and majority in the French Parliament from 1791 to 1793. See Chap. 5, note n° 5.

Jacobin[16] plot to end the monarchy, with the taking of the royal palace and the massacre of August 10. His Girondin friends insistently asked him to enlist as a general in the Army to repel the invasion of the Austrians and the Prussians (First Coalition) to save the revolution, France, and the royal family, and so to get later the help of France in America. After four days of reflection, Miranda accepted the offer under the underwritten conditions.

Content:

Miranda's commitment to defend freedom by enlisting himself in the service of the attacked Revolution, not as a mercenary but as a defender of the freedom of France, was conceived as a step to bring freedom to his homeland in Latin America, both objectives being dependent on the success of the French Revolution.

Translated from French

Sources:

Translated from French

América Espera. Document 45, p. 117.

Colombeia. Vol. I. Document, p. 36–37.

Text:

Paris, 24 August 1792

To José Servan, Minister of War

Persuaded as I am that the French nation is defending its sovereignty with justice and kindness and of the glory attained by those who will have the honour of joining her in defence of freedom, the only source of human happiness, I agree to serve her faithfully and to be intimately united to her under the following circumstances:

1. I must enter the French Army under the degree and salary of a Brigadier General.[17]
2. A nation must always attend with justice and equity to those who serve her faithfully. At the war's end, I will be given an office (in the military or elsewhere), allowing me to lead an honest life in France (25,000 L.t.).[18]
3. Since the freedom of people, in general, is an objective that interests the French nation, and especially that of the people who inhabit Southern America (or the Hispanic American Colonies), who in their trade with France consume many of her goods, and who would also like to shake off the yoke of oppression to join her; it is necessary that France efficiently protect their cause since it is the cause of freedom, and that I should be allowed (at the right moment) to occupy myself mainly with their happiness, establishing the liberty and independence of their countries. I have voluntarily taken charge of this, and the United States and England have promised their support at the first favourable opportunity.

[16] **Jacobin**: radicalised revolutionary movement, see Chap. 5, note n°4.

[17] This means General in Europe (but not in the US Army).

[18] France never paid Miranda's wages. The accumulated arrears officially acknowledged by the "Comité de Salut Public" amounted to 35.000 Libras in assignats y 21.700 Libras in metallic money, see *Archivo*, [1929–1950], Vol. XIV, Introduction, p. VIII.

N.B. I have enlisted in the service of Free France under these express conditions and in that spirit, which has been guaranteed (on behalf of the representative government) by the ministers (of war) Servan, Le Brun, and Clavière and also by the patriotic mayor of Paris, Pétion. They have all promised to witness this before the whole world if necessary.

F.[19] Miranda

10.2.5 Letter from Miranda to Russian Ambassador Woronzoff in London, Count Woronzoff, 30 August 1792

Context:

Before the massacre in Paris on August 10, Miranda planned to travel to Saint Petersburg to greet and thank his protector, Tsarina Catherine the Great. He benefited from the efficient diplomatic protection of Russia against the manoeuvres of Spain to arrest him or expel him from London, in addition to the financial generosity of the Tsarina, who paid him a significant rent, in addition to having cancelled his substantial debt with his English bankers when he was admitted in the restricted circle of her courtesans at the Court in Saint Petersburg in 1787. His move to Paris in the service of the French Revolution and his military role against the crowns of Austria and Prussia was poorly perceived by Catherine, who, deeply upset, cut off his income, his rank as a Russian colonel in her imperial military staff, and the corresponding diplomatic protection and passport.

Content:

Miranda attempts to justify his decision to join the French revolutionary army by putting himself at the service of his "favourite divinity," freedom. He also shows his preoccupation with preserving his letter and documents by recommending that they be delivered to Mr. Turnbull in case this Ambassador leaves London.

Sources:

Translated from French

Russian Academy of History. Letters from Francisco de Miranda in the Leningrad Archive. Armario VII. Carpeta. 68.

América Espera. In Spanish, Document 46. p. 118.

Text:

To Woronzoff

Paris, 30th of August, 1792

My dear count,

At the very moment when I expected to have the pleasure of seeing you and talking to you about the current affairs of Europe, etc., here I find myself a general of the French army, of the army of freedom, and on the brink of leaving to take command of a division at the frontier.

[19] The particle "de" before the name Miranda is crossed out in the original document.

You cannot be surprised that I should have joined the Defenders of Liberty, as you well know that it is my favourite divinity and that I have devoted myself to its service long before France thought of occupying herself with it... But what has most forcefully induced me to accept has been the hope of being useful 1 day to my poor country, which I cannot abandon.

Only motives as powerful as these have stopped me from thanking Her Majesty the Tsarina personally for all the goodness she has bestowed on me, and you know, count, how sincere my acknowledgement is... I hope you will transmit this to her as soon as an opportunity appears!

Next winter, I hope to obtain leave to spend some days in London, attending to my affairs. I, therefore, beg you to let the honourable Mr. Charles Fox know that my feelings remain unaltered and that I am still fully committed to our stipulation..., as it is under this condition that I have entered the service.

My sincere greeting to my friend General Clark (who may find it scandalous that an old Castilian has become a sans culotte) and Lord and Lady Benning, and many greetings to Mr. Kochebei, Likazovich, the chaplain, etc..... A kiss to both of your charming children, and I wish you, with them, much happiness. Wish me good luck... and goodbye.

Yours,

Miranda,

Field Marshall

PD, Keep this letter. I will send it to someone who departs today and whom I know. If you have to leave England, even temporarily, you can give my papers to Mr. Turnbull.

10.2.6 Miranda's Draft Proclamation Sent to French Deputy Gensonné,[20] October/December de 1792

Context:

Miranda fulfils his commitment agreed with France against the invaders of the First Coalition (Austria and Prussia), managing to stop the Prussians in Ardennes, near the Northern border with Belgium, on September 12 (victories of Morthomme and Briquenay), giving a first victory to the Revolutionary army, and saving the French Army from a defeat in Valmy that provoked the Prussian retreat, transformed into an important psychological victory that saved the Republic.[21]

[20] **Armand Gensonné** (1758–1793), moderate Girondin, partisan of the rights of the blacks, president of the Convention, unjustly guillotined by order of Robespierre without proof as many of the other deputies, under the false accusation of complicity with Dumouriez.

[21] After having already stopped the Prussian cavalry on 12 September, Miranda also played a role in this crucial victory of Valmy on 20 September 1792 by falling by chance (being disoriented) with his cavalry on the rear of the Prussian troops, creating panic. Nevertheless, the Valmy victory seems difficult to understand, as does the fact that Dumouriez let the enemies withdraw safely.

Promoted to Lieutenant-General for his role in the Ardennes to expel the Prussian invaders, Miranda is called to Paris by the Girondins, who contemplate a plan to extend the revolution, starting by sending an expedition to the Caribbean to re-establish the authority of the Republic over the French part of Santo Domingo. In executing his contract with France, Miranda proposes his own emancipation plan, which he had previously submitted to Pitt, involving a move from England to France and the United States. Shortly after, Deputy Brissot proposed in November that Miranda, who was busy liberating Belgium from the Austrians with Dumouriez, be appointed head of this expedition. However, it was not at all the emancipation plan Miranda wanted; instead, it was a colonial operation favouring France. Furthermore, Miranda also feared the growing power of the Jacobin movement, whose governance principles would spoil his plan for the democratic emancipation of his land. Therefore, he declined the offer diplomatically.

Content:

Excellent synthesis of the chronological stages of Miranda's plan, from the Tupac Amaru revolt in 1781 to the Brissot plan of 1792. He expresses, among other points of interest, his sceptical position in the face of the (cultural) excessive tendency of the French Revolution ("*... typical of the national character*") but offers opportunities to act in favour of the freedom of Latin America. Above all, this text reveals his conviction and prediction that revolutionary France would inevitably tend to "*extend its principles to the continent*", especially against the Iberian Peninsula, thus exposing his fatherland to significant changes in regime. Miranda explains his position: he disagrees with the French territorial aggressiveness against Spain, but he does support the idea of helping to emancipate the Spanish colonies on the condition of being able to orient the governance system without French interference.

Sources:

Translated from French

América Espera. Document 49. p. 119–121.

Colombeia. Vol. X. Doc. 1674. p 269–272.

Textos sobre la Independencia. p. 45–48.

Text:

Draft for Gensoné

Paris 10 October 1792

Fellow citizen:

Although I was summoned by you in 1781 to come to the aid of our fatherland, troubled as it was then by the humiliations and extreme oppression that Minister D. José de Gálvez had imposed on its unhappy inhabitants through his agents and

---

Various explanations were formulated, among which was the hypothesis of bribery given by Danton to the Prussians, allegedly paid for with the Bourbon crown jewels. Other historians observe that this victory was not immediately perceived as a significant event, but was instead transformed into a myth and symbol many years later. However, Valmy had an effect on the Prussian side. W. von Goethe, who participated in this battle, wrote "*from this place and from this day dates a new epoch in the history of the world*". See Elise Meyer (2020).

"visitadores", whose unrestrained behaviour had provoked a general insurrection in the kingdom of Santa Fé de Bogotá,[22] in Peru and even in the province of Caracas, I could not in those circumstance run to the help of my country, partly because I was tied to a superior rank in the army of H.C.M, at war then with England, and partly because I realised that in all those movements of insurrection there was no general plan: a fact that became evident after I received the Capitulations of Zipaquirá (8th June 1781), which bore witness on one side to the simplicity and inexperience of the Americans and on the other side, to the cunning and perfidy of Spanish agents; and so I thought it was best to suffer for some time, and to wait patiently for the independence of the Anglo-American colonies, which would become in the near future the infallible preliminaries of ours.

With this in mind (and to avoid the intolerable persecutions of Minister Gálvez), I resigned from my post in the Spanish army after the Peace was published and went on to make a comparative analysis of the United States of America.[23] It was there that in 1784, in the city of New York, the current project of the emancipation and liberty of the whole Hispanic American continent was formed, with the cooperation of England, all the more interested since Spain had already given the example by forcing her to acknowledge the independence of her colonies in the same continent.

With this objective, I travelled to England in 1785. Still, the nation's extreme embarrassment and difficulties following the loss of its colonies, as well as the high costs of the recent war, gave me little opportunity to address affairs of such magnitude. So, I decided to bide my time by carefully examining the various governments and political systems of Europe. For five years, the arts, sciences, religions, industries and effects of the different types of republics and mixed governments occupied my attention until 1789,[24] when I returned to England, not without having endured risks in my personal security, as the Madrid agents (apparently considerate and friendly) never stopped plotting treacheries. In St. Petersburg,[25] they took off their mask and, expecting to impose their will on the sovereign, asked for me to be delivered to Spain without any articulate motive, except that the Spanish Empire was under threat, to which Catherine II magnanimously answered that she knew of no crime committed by me and that if the Spanish Empire was at risk with my presence, I could not be better placed than in Russia, where my presence would always be agreeable; they attempted something similar in Stockholm, and even in Paris by clandestine means, without any success.

Finally, in February of 1790, this grand project was presented to the Prime Minister[26] of H.B.M and accepted in the exact terms of the day (in case the two nations went to war), that is, for the absolute emancipation of the Hispanic American Colonies, in similar terms to those of France and Spain when they acknowledged

[22] *Colombeia*, Vol. VI, doc. N° 955 y tomo IX, doc. N° 1259.

[23] *Colombeia*, Vol. III, doc. N° 529 "Viaje por los Estados Unidos".

[24] *Colombeia*, "El Viajero Ilustrado".

[25] *Colombeia*, Vol. V, "Diario de Rusia".

[26] *Colombeia*, Vol. IX, "Negociaciones con Pitt".

that of Northern America; on the following 6th of May, the hostile declaration of England on the happenings of Nootka Sound, came for the purpose, and it was convened the same day that this project would be immediately carried out if the war (as seemed likely) was declared between the two nations. They invited some of our ex-Jesuit compatriots, whom I had seen and prepared in Italy for this matter, to come to London, and success seemed near at hand when, not long after, the agreement between Spain and England ended the dispute and, for the time being, put a stop to our desires.

The French Revolution was swiftly progressing towards a system of freedom, although with a certain exaggeration typical of the national character. I had news from one of our fellow citizens who was in Paris at the time that the new government was already extending its principles to Spanish America, to protect its independence. With this purpose, I travelled to Paris in March 1792 and found that, indeed, the ideas of the Government were directed to a continental war and that the plan was to stir Spain via Catalunia and Vizcaya and, similarly, the colonies of Spanish America; I contested with success the first part of the project and managed to postpone the second until a better opportunity, leaving its leadership to me, since the aim was emancipation and independence.

Soon after, as I was preparing to leave Paris on my way back to England, the fatal day of the 10th of August of 1792 arrived, and with it, the fall of the French throne. The same ministers who had promised to cooperate with our independence then came to me insisting that all would be lost, the Royal family itself, if the enemy armies which were approaching from Champagne reached Paris; that the happiness of my country and the salvation of France depended on the Prussian and Austrian armies leaving French territory, as then all agitation would stop and everything would return to order: and that as an interested party, I should take the rank of general in the French army and together with Dumouriez join the endeavour upon which everything depended. These are the motives and reasons for my entering the service of the French nation on the 24th of August of 1792.[27]

The enemies were driven out after joining General-in-Chief Dumouriez in Gran-Pré and acting closely and in agreement in this campaign. I was promoted to the rank of Lieutenant General and subsequently to Commander of the Northern Army. At this stage, I was ordered to lead an army against Spain, which I refused to do for the abovementioned reasons. On December 19, 1792, I received the news that the Minister had appointed me Commander-in-Chief to Saint Domingue, and that an army of 25,000 men and a squadron were there waiting for me to operate in the Spanish American Revolution and independence.

[This document is not complete as of the original.]

T. I, f. 8. Revolución Francesa.

[27] *Colombeia*, Vol. IX, doc. N° 1439.

10.2.7 Extract of a letter from Miranda to French Deputy Pétion,[28] Valenciennes, 26 October 1792

Context:

Jérôme Pétion (1756–1794) was an influential Girondist deputy, at this time President of the Convention (holding legislative and constitutional power from 1792 to 1793), a friend of Miranda, and an opponent of Robespierre. Miranda writes a long letter to him from the battlefield, facing the enemy, stating that he is about to fight the day after his division invades Belgium, at the order of Dumouriez,[29] to expel the Austrians from Belgium and the Netherlands.

After the insurrection of the Paris Commune of August 10, 1792, prepared by the Jacobins, the Legislative Assembly decided to call elections for electing, by universal suffrage, a "national convention" that would decide on the new institutions after ending the Monarchy. These elections are organised very quickly at the beginning of September, but this "universal suffrage" excludes women and domestics. In addition, participation is minimal (10%), the elections taking place in a period of popular overflow and massacres, skewing the result in favour of the partisan minority of ideological, radical regime change (the royalists being de facto excluded by the events of July, August and September, and the threat launched by the foreign crowns at war with the republic). However, the Convention remains deeply divided between a majority of moderate revolutionaries (Girondins led by Brissot, Vergniaud, Pétion and Roland) and a nucleus of very active and organised extremists in the Jacobin club (led by Robespierre, Danton, Marat and Saint-Just) supported by influent political clubs[30] shaping and manipulating public opinion. In this conflicted situation, moderate revolutionaries were either excluded or chose to exclude themselves. The first decision of the Convention, which concentrates legislative and executive powers, is to eradicate the monarchy and proclaim the republic.

In such a context, Miranda, at the beginning of a military campaign, perceives the risk of a concentration of power and popular violence that could weaken the French Revolution and undermine his plans for freedom. He is struck by the fact that those leaders do not perceive the risks of division and that, in particular, by excluding women, they condemn themselves to an unbalanced and more violent society. Significantly, he writes this advice for rebalancing policy decisions through the fair role of women from a battlefield just before the start of a bloody invasion of

[28] **Jérôme Pétion** (1756–1794) was a revolutionary lawyer, ex-Jacobin, Girondin, see Chap. 6, note 7.

[29] Dumouriez launched the attack against the Austrian in Belgium on the 27th of October, 1792, the day after Miranda's letter to Pétion.

[30] The clubs were named the "**Sociétés de pensée**," gathering a new oligarchy of political activists who pushed for a radical Revolution; see Chap. 6, document 6.1, note n° 14.

Belgium. At that time, among the men, only Condorcet[31] proposed giving women voting rights.

Content:

Miranda shared his fear with the President of the Convention about four related crucial issues: the risks of division in the Army due to the lack of a clear single mandate, the still present danger of the Jacobins, the intention to send an expedition against Spain that he considers premature, and the lack of political rights for women which unbalances the search for fundamental changes in French society. It is remarkable that Miranda already perceived the weaknesses of the Girondins' governance in October 1792: the risk of anarchy in the army stemming from the executive's weakness in the face of a too-powerful legislative branch, where the Jacobins act against public interests.

Furthermore, this letter deserves to draw attention to the critical role he attaches to female emancipation for the revolution's success and fundamental societal changes. It is psychologically interesting that he is writing from the battlefield on the eve of an essential combat in which he will face the risk of death. This implicit, contrasting link between Jacobins, war and women's rights emphasises that Miranda put the finger - well in advance - upon the connection between gender inequality, war, and Jacobins' radical ideology and cultural machismo, which constituted a real handicap for reaching an inclusive and peaceful society. His preoccupation is not new, as he also refers to a file of accumulated documents from his trips and previous exchanges dealing with the gender issue.

This letter is also an example of his skilful epistolary technique to convince his reader: first, the way he wants to capture the attention of his influential politician (asking him to take time to read the letter or reporting past events, giving him importance); second, the serene tone and scope of his concerns by combining strong positions for imposing his will with expressions of modesty and respect.

Sources:

Translated from French

América espera. Document 50. p. 122–124.

Archivo del General Miranda. Vol. XV. p. 453–456.

Colombeia. Vol. X. Document 1675. p. 272–276.

Text:

To Pétion

At Valenciennes, 26 October 1792

The first year of the Republic

(Do not read this until you have 20 minutes free, as it would be helpful if you would read it entirely and carefully)

---

[31] **Nicolas de Caritat, Marquis de Condorcet** (1743–1794), a scientific and political person, initially Jacobin, moved close to the Girondins, promoting democracy and equal rights for people of all races. He was condemned by Robespierre but committed suicide. He was the first French revolutionary who proposed gender equality (with voting rights for women). Of course, several heroic women had pleaded before for their political rights. Still, the French revolutionaries restricted their rights, and Napoleon ensured no return even more with the "Code Civil" of 1804.

My dear and worthy friend,

You may be surprised not to have had further news from me since I last wrote to you through our common friend, General in Chief M. Dumouriez. – As it turns out, I have been rather ill until now, when I feel well enough to take command of the second division that the General in Chief has entrusted to put under my charge.

Anyway, our vanguard has successfully entered enemy territory. The rest of the army will enter the day after tomorrow ... Our plans to drive out the enemy and invade the Austrian Netherlands are often and judiciously combined, it seems to me, for our worthy General Dumouriez, who, as I have already had the honour to tell you, makes all the arrangements himself ... but is it that the other bodies, which must cooperate, will fulfil their duty and act with drive? Here is what I fear!

To prove to you that my fear is not entirely unfounded, here is a copy of the impertinent letter that one of those who must essentially cooperate has just written to Mr. Dumouriez, who, however, has not wanted to notify the Minister of War, believing that with his restraint he will lead these officers to their duty, sacrificing their foolish vanity to the public interest. It is with the most significant difficulty that I have been able to obtain this copy, begging you not to show it to anyone, and that I am sending you only to convince you of the absolute necessity to get a single military authority able to remedy all these disputes and entanglements that could very well end up ruining public affairs ... Anyway, do what you consider best. I have already discussed this subject with you on other occasions.

Let's move on to something else. General Dumouriez told me that you were planning to send a force against Spain and that, for this reason, they wanted me to return to Paris, etc. It is a delicate matter on which I dare to request a voice before anyone else and before you make the slightest decision. First, I must inform you of the progress England has made in this matter since I acted as an agent of South America in favour of its independence and freedom over the last 3 years. Second, what were the North American positions concerning the same subject? Third, the effective means I had prepared in Italy, with some American Jesuits who had become enlightened men and implacable enemies of Spain. Fourth, 12 years of fatigue, travel, and meditation on the same subject gave me a kind of right that I confidently claim.

This same reason is, moreover, the leading cause (as I had the honour to tell you in another opportunity) why I preferred to settle in France and be a French citizen, to any other advantage that I could obtain in North America, Russia or England. On this point, I can provide essential services to the Republic and simultaneously bring happiness to my country, which is the ultimate goal of human happiness. Thus, you must not doubt my complete self-denial for one thing and another ... I know only two duties in my present situation, the first towards France, as a legitimate member of the nation and a faithful servant of the Republic, to whom I have sworn an inviolable oath; the second, towards my poor oppressed country, which extends its hand to me from a distance and shows me the chains with which it, unfortunately, groans under the most cruel and infamous despotism. This idea tears at my heart every time I think about it ... but I don't lose hope. I encourage virtuous men and benefactors of humanity; posterity will bless you eternally!

The following singularity seems to me as a good omen at this time: the year 1785, when I travelled through Prussia, etc., Spain and France, who viewed my "principles" and my ideas with evil eyes, informed by Mr. La Fayette that I had to pass through Paris, on my way back to England, they had prepared my accommodation for me at La Bastille, with the complicity of Mr. de Aranda, Montmorin, Floridablanca and Louis XVI ... They ultimately failed ... as the first is in Spandau, the other on the precipice, another one beheaded in the Chátelet, the fourth in the Castle or Bastille of Segovia and the last in the Temple, while this Miranda is, sword in hand, in the Armies of Liberty. This is a reflection that I would have already made for Mr. La Fayette if his situation had allowed him to receive it. For the rest, my friend, I beg you not to formulate for me purposes other than those with which the Republic can best use my limited knowledge. My duty devotion is complete and very sincere.

As regards legislation – I'm pleased to see that Demagogue Robespierre fell into oblivion where he should have always been for the sake of public affairs – to which he did much damage – but I see with anger that you are suffering others even more infamous such as Marat, Cha, etc...., who are slandering with impunity virtuous men, the Nation and the National Convention! Remember that with the same mistake, the last legislative assembly lost its credibility in the eyes of the nation and the entire European continent, ultimately losing any authority. The Legislative Committee seems very well integrated, and maybe those nine members know more about this critical matter than all other men put together!...

On my part, I recommend you one thing, wise legislator, the women ... Why is it that in a democratic government, half of the individuals, that is, the women, are not directly or indirectly represented, whereas they are subject to the same severity of the laws that men make at their own will? Why are they not consulted about the laws that most concern them, such as those related to marriage, divorce, girls' education, etc.? I confess that all these things seem to me to be unbelievably pressing and worthy of being taken into account by our wise legislators... If I had my papers at hand, I would find a few comments that I made on this issue in conversations with some American and European legislators, who have never given me a satisfactory answer, most of whom are happy to acknowledge such an injustice, etc.

Miranda

To Citizen Pétion, member of the National Convention

(letter written in Miranda's own hand)

10.2.8 Letter from Miranda to Alexander Hamilton,[32] París, 4 November 1792

Context:

Alexander Hamilton, who had served as aide-de-camp and secretary to Washington and played a key military role in the war for US independence, met Miranda, who was in the United States in 1783 to analyse the US strategy of independence and its system of governance. They became close friends. It was there in New York in 1784 with him that Miranda formulated his plan for the emancipation of South America. In 1792, Miranda informs his influential friend that revolutionary France is contributing to the advancement of his emancipation plan. Miranda sent his plan to Pétion in October, proposing absolute independence based on a French alliance with the US. Throughout his independence struggle, Miranda constantly tried to involve the US in his strategy. Hamilton was sensitive to Miranda's arguments, which later attracted upon him criticisms from Adams (second President), Jefferson (third President) and his vice-President, Aaron Burr.

In his letter, Miranda refers to the nomination of a new French Ambassador (Edmond-Charles Genet), a translator in the French Ministry of Foreign Affairs, when France contributed to the US War of Independence. However, this Ambassador arrived much later due to the trial against the King in Paris, since the French government would have sent the King to the United States with the new Ambassador in case of being condemned to exile.

Content:

This is an example of the reactivation of Miranda's North American connections, given the resumption of its plan for South America, which is supposed to receive support from the USA. Significantly, Miranda informs his friend of the favourable prospects he finds in France to obtain political-military support from the government. The letter's tone indicates that Miranda remained optimistic about the possibility of getting military support from the French government until the end of 1792.

Sources:

América Espera. Translated in Spanish, Document 51, p. 124.

Archivo del General Miranda. Vol. XV. p. 145–146.

Colombeia. translated in Spanish, Vol. X. 1989. Document 1678, p. 278.

Text:

N° XXVIII

Corresponds to N° 2 of 1792

D. Francisco de Miranda to Mr. A. Hamilton, secretary of the Treasury.

Paris November the 4th, 1792.

The 1st year of the Republic.

My dear friend,

[32] **Alexander Hamilton** (1757–1804), constitutionalist, one of the most important founding fathers of the USA and its constitution, first Minister of Finance of the USA (1789–1795), the principal author of "*The Federalist Papers*", see Chap. 2, section 2.2., note n° 9.

The affairs & success of France take a happy turn in our favour…I mean in favour of our dear Country America, from the North to the South- the official communications from the newly appointed Minister of France & the Information our friend Col. Smith[33] shall give to you will show how things are grown ripe & into maturity for the execution of those grand & beneficial projects we had in contemplation, when in our conversation at New York the love of our Country exalted our minds with those ideas, for the sake of unfortunate Columbia.

I am sincerely yours,
Francisco de Miranda
T. I, f. 141 Negociaciones

10.2.9 Letter from Miranda to Deputy Brissot,[34] Liège, 19 December 1792

Context:

The deputy Brissot, an influential moderate revolutionary, head of the Girondists at the Convention, and an advocate against the slave trade, had proposed that Miranda lead an expedition to reconquer Haiti and then continue against the Spanish colonies. Being in Liège, Miranda, having achieved the expulsion of the Austrian army, which began on 27 October, is informed by Dumouriez on December 18, 1792, of this proposal. Miranda, who had already received an offer in this regard and who had travelled to Paris in October 1792 to guide France towards his own plan (which was very different as opposed to any colonial aspect), is opposed to the French strategy, which he considers inappropriate as neo-colonial, and uncertain according to his criteria, in particular, because he already perceived the risk to expose Spanish America to a violent and doctrinal revolution in case the rising Jacobins doctrine would control such an expedition. His emancipation plan is intrinsically associated with institutional governance, which is incompatible with the Jacobins' views and even those of his Girondins' friends. Subsequent events

[33] **Colonel William Stephen Smith** (1755–1816), an official of the US Army during the War of Independence, met Miranda in London when he was secretary of Ambassador John Adams, with whom he made part of the trip to European courts. In 1805–06, Smith, as Surveyor of the port of New York, helped Miranda to organise his expedition to free Venezuela. Smith's son was among the volunteers and was captured by the Spanish army in Ocumare and condemned, but he managed to escape.

[34] **Jacques Pierre Brissot** (1754–1793), a lawyer, prepared the French Revolution through his publications, travelled to London, the USA and the Netherlands in 1788–89, founder of the "Society of Friends of blacks", participated in the revolution and was elected to the Assembly of 1791 and the Convention in 1792, becomes chief of the Girondins, a leading activist of the declaration of war on Austria and of equality between whites and blacks. He was a Miranda supporter and a leading opponent of Robespierre; he was arrested with the Girondins in Robespierre's coup and sentenced to the guillotine in October 1793.

demonstrated that Miranda was absolutely right to be cautious in the case of Saint Domingue/Haiti, particularly given French support.

Content:

Firm but skilful rejection of the risky Girondins' offer that does not guarantee the emancipation that Miranda seeks. He does not close the door to the idea entirely but asks to rethink the French plan based on his own plan, mentioning that this plan is available in the hands of his friend Pétion. However, he gives two objections: he does not know sufficiently the situation of the French islands upon which the whole strategy would be based and the risks that his involvement would produce reactions and contra-strategy by both the Spanish and the British governments, damaging his emancipation plan, that subtly he refers to by mentioning it.

Sources:

Written in French

Archivo del General Miranda. Vol. XIII, pp. 168–170.

Colombeia. Translated in Spanish, Vol. X. Document 1686. p. 287–289.

América Espera. Translated in Spanish Document 53. p. 125–126.

Text:

N° XXXII

Corresponds to N° 6 of 1792

Liège, 19 December 1792

The first year of the French Republic

General Miranda to Citizen Brissot, National Convention, and the General Defence Committee member.

I have just read the letter you sent to General Dumouriez about me, dear citizen.[35] Thank you for the flattering expressions you used about my modest knowledge and the friendly influence you induced the Executive Power to trust the government of Sto Domingo to me, etc. I only learnt this piece of news yesterday because, despite the summons that General Dumouriez sent me on November seventh to meet him in Liège, where he had interesting things to communicate to me, it was impossible for me at that time to abandon the army that was under my care. After all, we were engaged in an essential but complex operation towards Ruremonde.

The plan you have outlined in your letter is of the utmost importance and magnificent; nonetheless, I wonder whether it can be carried out securely or whether it is even possible. I am well aware and informed about the Hispanic American continent and the adjacent islands and quite capable of expressing an exact opinion about them, but I am ignorant, on the other hand, of all that concerns the French islands and their current situation; it is, therefore difficult for me to foresee adequate criteria on this topic.

Given that this plan is based on these French islands, it is essential to gather more information to ensure that this strategy is the right one. As the attack force must originate from the French colonies to mobilise the people of the oppressed continent, it is necessary to obtain more information to confirm that this approach is the

[35] Miranda note: Document N° 1680.

correct one. It seems to me as well that such a nomination and my departure to St. Domingo would send an alarm signal to the Court of Madrid and that of St. James; the effects would be immediately felt in Cadiz and Portsmouth, and this would place new obstacles to that endeavour, which is far too brave, beautiful and captivating to spoil it or lead it to fail because of some unforeseen circumstance from the beginning!...

Nonetheless, since you are better informed than I am about the internal movements of the Cabinets in Europe and of the situation of the French Colonies, as well as their internal affairs, you will be able to appreciate the issue more precisely than I do. All that I have the honour to tell you on this matter must be interpreted as something other than observations to be considered in the conceptual frame of the general plan.

I would not wish anyone to believe my purpose is to avoid or reject an office that the Executive Council considers I should undertake. When I embraced the cause of freedom in France, I fully committed myself to either winning or dying for it and in my position, obeying was my first duty.

Thankful and respectful, I remain yours,

Miranda

PS. The papers that contain the plans I presented to the British Government in 1790[36] regarding Southern America's independence have been in Paris for a while and are in the power of my intimate friend Pétion. It might be convenient to examine them before establishing the grand plan that you suggest in your letter; if taking advantage of a leave (during the stationing of our troops next month), we could induce the Executive power to grant me the permit to go to Paris, we could then set up a definite plan.

T. I, f. 142 vto. Negociaciones

T. III, f. 136 R.F. Traducido del francés.

10.2.10 Letter from Miranda to A. Hamilton,[37] Paris, 1 April 1797

Context:

After the Thermidorian coup of July 1794 against Robespierre and the Jacobins, the Convention eliminated the most radical deputies, which led to the establishment of a republic in the hands of an executive whose powers were concentrated by the new Constitution of Year III (1795), marking the transition to the Directory. Miranda, who continues to be persecuted politically for his criticisms against this non-democratic republic, considers the new regime as a continuation of the tyranny

[36] See Chap. 5, document 5.2.1.

[37] **Alexander Hamilton** (1757–1804) was one of the Founding Fathers of the US; see document Chap. 2, section 2.2, note n° 9 and Chap. 6, document 6.3. note n° 45.

because it is a reaction to the Jacobins' excess of power concentration in the hands of the legislative (Convention and other local deliberative assemblies) by falling into the opposite error of an excess of power concentration in the hands of the executive. Disappointed by the evolution in France, he tries to reconnect with his US friend Alexander Hamilton (he knew him very well during his participation in the US revolution in 1783–84) for a double reason: first, his permanent geopolitical preoccupation to involve as much as possible the US in his strategy for emancipation; second, to warn Hamilton about the manoeuvres undertaken by Thomas Paine[38] against him and Knox.[39]

Indeed, the occasion to send this letter to Hamilton was triggered by a strange message he received from the US Ambassador in Paris, James Monroe,[40] in a letter dated 17 March 1797, (Syrett, H. 1974),[41] affirming that Thomas Paine was telling that Hamilton and Knox would have given a written mandate to Miranda to undertake negotiations with the British government for organising the independence of South America. Ambassador Monroe asked Miranda to deliver to him the alleged documents that Paine had seen in Miranda's house in Paris. While it is true that Miranda has been looking for an alliance with the US since his 1783–84 trip, he never received a mandate or documents from Hamilton or Knox. In a factual answer to Monroe, sent by letter on 2 April,[42] Miranda flatly denied these facts, reminding that it could only have been simple conversations in New York in 1784, when Hamilton and Knox were not in charge of US policy, since Paine had seen Miranda in France only once in 1793. These letters were sent as an attachment to the letter to Hamilton. Miranda suspected Paine, whom he strongly opposed ideologically when

[38] **Thomas Paine** (1737–1809), a famous English political philosopher, and critic of the British monarchical regime, travelled to America in 1774 to act in favour of American independence, wrote influential pro-independence pamphlets, published in 1776 "The Common Sense" that had considerable impact for the dissemination and argumentation of republican and independence ideas, he returned to England in 1787, militated in favour of the French Revolution, condemned in England for his republican ideas, was exiled and settled in France in 1792, which offered him nationality and elects him deputy of the republic, during the Terror he is arrested by Robespierre and released with the fall of the Terror regime in October.

[39] **Henry Knox** (1750–1806) was a pivotal military figure in the US Revolution and a key player in the government, as well as an influential constitutionalist. He served as Secretary of War for the United States from March 8, 1785, to December 31, 1794. In January 1784, he met Miranda in New York. He was pro-federation and shared political opinions with Miranda on the need for a solid but controlled executive branch, as well as supporting Indigenous rights to land as the prime occupants and by fundamental natural law. He was also responsible for managing the nation's relations with the Native Americans, but failed to convince Congress, the colonists, as well as the Indians. He left the government in 1795.

[40] **James Monroe** (1758–1831), anti-federalist and future President of the USA from 1817 to 1825, was Minister Plenipotentiary in France from 1794 to 1797 (officially, he went to Holland in January 1797 but returned to Paris in March and April 1797 before embarking for the USA from Bordeaux). Miranda had greeted him personally when he was released from jail in 1795.

[41] Letter dated March 17, 1797, from Monroe to Miranda. In ed. Syrett, H. (1974), *The Papers of Alexander Hamilton*, vol. 21, April 1797–July 1798, Columbia University Press, 1974, pp. 4–5.

[42] Miranda's letter to Monroe 2 April 1797, ibid., vol. 21, April 1797–July 1798 pp. 5–6.

Paine was unquestioningly supporting the Jacobins in Paris, of undertaking manoeuvres to counter his support for a strategic alliance with the United States and England towards a complete but non-violent revolution in Latin America. Miranda especially feared that Paine would return to the USA and counteract his plan and Hamilton's role. Paine's trip was postponed due to the state of war between France and England up to the Peace of Amiens in 1802. At this time, Paine was betting on Napoleon to impose a popular power that could extend the Revolution to England. Miranda's fears were verified, but much later, as evidenced by the letter Paine (1819) sent to New York in 1806[43] to harm Miranda.

The second reason for contacting Hamilton – in line with Miranda's permanent geopolitical strategy to involve the US – was taking on even more relevance in April 1797 with the worsening of the conflict between France and the USA over the payment of the debt contracted by the USA with the King of France during the war of independence, combined to the French purpose to harm the US trade with Britain. This conflict degenerated into a "quasi-war" - given that it remained maritime - and formally broke out in July 1797 with the termination of the Treaties with France due to the seizing by pirate attacks of the US merchant ships by France (the US had no maritime armed force) in retaliation for the non-payment of the debt contracted by the US to the French crown.

Regarding Miranda's relations with Hamilton, he had already sent him a first letter on April 7, 1791 (Syrett, H. 1965),[44] that is, during his stay in London after his tour throughout Europe (1785–1789). In this letter, he congratulated Hamilton on his good governance and policies as Chancellor of the Exchequer. Other letters followed: arriving in London at the beginning of 1798 (letter from Miranda of February 7, 1798 (Syrett, H. 1974),[45] in which he proposed to use Rufus King,[46] the US Ambassador linked to Hamilton and with whom Miranda had already won trust in London.

In 1797, Hamilton, who had left his post as Chancellor of the Exchequer in 1795, was engaged in politics before being named Major General of the Army (the highest

[43] Letter from Thomas Paine 1806, in Paine, T. (1819), *Miscellaneous Letters & Essays, on Various Subjects*, Ed. Carlile, R, p. 140 and 141.

[44] Letter from Miranda to Hamilton, Chancellor of the Exchequer of the United States, dated April 7, 1791, Syrett, H. (1965), *The Papers of Alexander Hamilton*, op. cit., Vol. 8, February 1791–July 1791, p. 245–246.

[45] Not reproduced in this book, it is found in French in Syrett, H. (1974), *The Papers of Alexander Hamilton*, Vol. 21, April 1797–July 1798, op. cit. p. 348–350.

[46] **Rufus King** (1755–1827), also considered one of the "founding fathers" of the United States and its constitution, a close friend of Hamilton and political activist in the federalist ranks, was appointed Ambassador in London by G. Washington where he will perform brilliantly from 1796 to 1803. He will adopt positions favourable to Latin American emancipation; he received the documents from the Peruvian Father Viscardo, who distrusted Miranda, but the Ambassador entrusted Miranda and gave these documents to him (see annex 1, Letter to the Americans), supporting the Precursor in his plans from London in front of the US administration (that never wanted to help Miranda). See Theodoro Hampe Martinez (1999) and Merle Simmons (1986, 1989).

position in the army) under the Adams Presidency, when the United States went into quasi-war with France.

Content:

This is an additional diagnostic of the Jacobins' betrayers of freedom who deviated from the French Revolution, with references to a new book.

Complaints about the slanderous accusations of the Jacobins against Miranda influenced his relations with Thomas Paine and James Monroe, two of his opponents, in an effort to garner the United States' support for his plan. Miranda is rightly trying to dissociate himself from the reputation-damaging Jacobins, who constitute a totalitarian threat —a view fully shared by Hamilton. However, he clarifies that the common ideology of freedom he shares with Hamilton is persecuted in France, where only a small minority tries to resist.

As explained above, the precise reason for this letter was to warn Hamilton of possible manoeuvres against his friendship with Knox and him by the Jacobin Paine upon his probable arrival in the United States. This letter was sent with copies of the letters from Monroe (and his assistant Prevost) requesting the delivery of documents with an alleged remittance from Hamilton to Miranda for negotiation with Pitt.

Sources:

Translated from French.

Archivo del General Miranda. Vol. XIII. p. 174–175.

Colombeia. Vol. XVIII. Document 4001. p. 143–145;

América Espera. Document 64. p. 187–188.

The Papers of Alexander Hamilton, vol. 21, April 1797–July 1798, ed. Harold C. Syrett. New York: Columbia University Press, 1974, pp. 4–5-6

Text:

To Hamilton

Paris, 1 of April 1797

My dear and respectable friend:

After 4 years, I take up my pen to let you know that I am still among the survivors who remain in France after the tyranny... I have sent you a book recently published by Desodoards[47] on the French Revolution. It contains all the main facts and mentions the causes - in my opinion - with knowledge, impartiality and moderation. All those who are familiar with the revolution in-depth have endorsed my view, which I formed by reading the book in the first place. Read it immediately and pass it on to the new President,[48] if he has not read it already. Mister Pain and M-e, who have returned to their country, may not share this assessment, but I think they know the Jacobin system better than the French Revolution.

[47] **Antoine Etienne Nicolas Fantin des Odoards** (1738–1820), French historian. The book sent by Miranda was Fantin-Desodoards, A. (1797), *Histoire philosophique de la révolution de France*, Perlet (Imprimeur). 4 Vol., Paris.

[48] **John Adams** (1736–1826) Second President of the EE-UU 1797–1801.

Well, my friend, it is undoubtedly, President Washington who made a severe mistake in sending as ambassadors Messrs. Morris[49] and Monroe, both extremists in opposite senses… The first is indeed infinitely more cultivated and less extravagant than the other. Paine has become a real Marat… Let us hope that he does not harm the New World as much as the other did to France.

Goodbye! my dear friend. Keep up the courageous struggle to maintain the Cause of liberty that so many rascals and ignoramuses have been dishonouring for the last 5 years, arguing that they love it and are defending it. Here, I am still linked (and therefore persecuted for it) to the small group that knows it well and sincerely defends it. Let's hope! Providence will be good to us for the happiness of this country and, at least, for the peace of mind of the rest. Please give me news of our friends Knox and W. Duer.[50] Greet them in my name and let them see the section of this letter that you deem most apposite, as well as the Book. Please present my respects to General Washington, as well as to all my friends in New York, etc.

Yours sincerely,

Also, I have received a letter from Mr. Monroe through his secretary, Prevost, at this very moment. The content of this letter makes me suspect some cabala or intrigue from Mr. Messrs Paine and Monroe [crossed out] (with whom I have never had dealings). In haste, I send you a Copy of this short correspondence so that you can answer the calumnies that are the weapons of the Jacobite sect.

Vol. XVIII, f. 174 R.F.

10.3 Period 1798–1805: London II

10.3.1 Letter from Miranda to John Turnbull,[51] 12 January 1798

Context:

[49] **Governor Morris** (1752–1816) was an American statesman. He represented Pennsylvania at the Constitutional Convention of 1787. He was also the author of part of the United States Constitution and one of its "signers." He is widely recognized as the author of the document's explanatory memorandum: "*We, the People of the United States, in order to form a more perfect union* ..." and has been called the "*Penman of the Constitution*". As Senator, Minister Plenipotentiary to France from 1792 to 1794, and Chairman of the Erie Canal Commission from 1810 to 1813. He met Miranda in Philadelphia in 1783.

[50] **William Duer** (1743–1799) [1], British-born American lawyer, member of the Continental Congress (1778–1779), active on financial and war aspects, became a speculator.

[51] **John Turnbull**, powerful businessman and well-connected banker in London, Miranda's faithful ally and moneylender. See details in Chap. 2, note 27.

The Directory banned Miranda[52] after the self-coup of September 2, 1797, which led to increased political repression in France, particularly under the political police of Fouché, who acted to arrest Miranda for both personal and political reasons. Miranda had been banned from France again on September 4,[53] after various political difficulties the Precursor had faced since his publication in July 1795[54] and his reluctance to cooperate with the Thermidorians, who confiscated the revolution. Miranda was especially frightened by the "*monstrous alliance*" between the Republic and the Spanish absolutist regime, as well as the irresistible rise to power of the warmongering, expansionist Napoleon, who was already contemplating invading England to end parliamentary democracy. These circumstances pushed Miranda to decide in October to return to England, now at war with Spain and directly threatened by Napoleon, who was appointed in October by the Directory to head the "Army of England" (landing plans in England, for more comments, see Chap. 5, document 5.2.2. in context).

After preparing his return to London through his personal envoy (Pedro Caro[55]) with letters to the British government, to his friends, and with the Paris Act (see Chap. 7), Miranda once again mocked the political police of his personal enemy Fouché, escaped from Paris [Parra-Perez 1950] on January 3[56] and embarked on January 7, 1798 with disguise and under a false name to Dover. Contrary to his previous stay in London from 1789 to 1792, Miranda no longer had diplomatic

[52] The **Directory** is the formula of republic that succeeds to the Convention. After the coup against Robespierre ending the "Terror" (July 1794) the Convention tried in reaction against the excesses of a popular power through manipulation of a too dominant legislative power, to anchor a bourgeois republic based on freedom and property and making the popular power almost to disappear. To this end a new constitution was drawn up and approved in 1795, which established a strong executive power dominating the two other branches but in a collegial form without any mechanism in case of internal conflict. The executive was composed of 5 non-re-eligible directors who has to change by one each year, the legislative branch had two chambers elected in restrictive census form (very few voters with respect to the two previous constitutions) and also renewed by fraction. This formula was a political failure, alternating centre-right and centre-left coalitions with several royalist plots justifying Jacobins coups in reaction, but for maintaining in power the same group of corrupted persons.

[53] He had already been proscribed in 1795, accused of taking part in the royalist conspiracy and the events of the 13th Vendemiaire, when in fact he was defending the opposing band of republicans. He had managed to escape and outwit the police for several months, before finally being acquitted and declared innocent again after months of negotiations and proceedings.

[54] See Chap. 6, document 6.3.

[55] **Pedro José Caro**, Cuban patriot who betrayed Miranda, see Chap. 5, document 5.2.2., note n° 26 and Chap. 7, note 6.

[56] A plausible explanation of Miranda's ability to escape on time to the French police would be the information he got from Delphine de Custine, his lover since 1795, who was also in love affair with Fouché. See Chap. 5, document 5.2.3., notes n° 49 1 50, and Chap. 6, document 6.1, notes n° 17, 20, 21. Among other indices available in this sense is in a letter from Delphine that refers to an intimate scene the day Miranda had to leave Paris: "*… remember the woman who combed your hair on the day of your escape from Paris, to whom you gave a box with a heart...*" letter from Delphine to Miranda, of May 1798 quoted by Parra Pérez, C. (1950) in *Miranda et Madame de Custine*", Paris.

protection from Russia, while still being followed and persecuted by Spain, in addition to Fouché's police.

Content:

He briefly explains his situation to his friend and protector in London and requests a passport through this merchant's influential contacts.

Sources:

Translated from French,
América Espera. Document 70. p. 201–202
Archivo del General Miranda. Vol. XV. p. 206–208.
Colombeia. Vol. XVIII. 2004. Document 3962. p. 70–72,

Text:

To John Turnbull- Esquire
Dover, 12 January 1798

Here I am, my dear friend, recently arrived from Calais. I had been forced to abandon France like a common criminal the last 18 Fructidor.[57] By very fortunate circumstances, I could escape from the Directory's claws!

Given the uncertainty in which I find myself in an asylum (my great protector, Catherine II,[58] who has passed away), I decided to come here under the name of Mirandow, American, having used an old Russian passport for this purpose. Nonetheless, when my real name was found out after the careful inspection of my luggage, I had no choice but to identify myself to the Customs Inspector, who behaved very decently and who reported the fact immediately to the Government, to which he also sent a very brief letter that I conveyed through our friend Smith.

In the same letter, I requested an interview with the Minister to update my knowledge as to what England had done during my absence or what it was prepared to do

---

[57] **Coup of the 18 Fructidor** (4 September 1797), the date of the Jacobin coup against the results of their electoral defeat. The moderates and the royalists won a majority. This coup was designed to prevent the Jacobin members of the Directory from losing their office by using Napoleon's army in a "preventive action" intended to prevent a royalist coup. Still, in reality it was to increase the repressive powers of the executive and give the Directory the means to impose the illegitimate orientation of the Jacobins.

[58] **Catherine II of Russia**, also known as Catherine the Great. Her real name was Sophie Friederike Auguste von Anhalt-Zerbst. She was born in Szczecin (Stettin), Pomerania, now Poland, in 1729 and died in Saint Petersburg in 1796. She seized the throne from her incompetent husband in 1762 and managed it until she passed away after 34 years as an illustrated despot with many results, allowed Russia to impose itself as an international power, expanded the Russian territory over its neighbours and ensured the beginning of economic development. She was a sovereign protector of progress and the arts, cultured and open to the ideas of the Enlightenment philosophers. She modernised Russia with a policy of education but without daring to reform the feudal order in the countryside that remained underdeveloped. Miranda, who visited her and belonged to her court in 1787, was especially well received by the Tsarina, with whom he had a very close relationship. She approved and supported his plans for the emancipation of Latin America, protected him from the manoeuvres of Spain and the Inquisition, made him an official of her Army, paid his enormous debts and gratified him with a life annual rent as a member of her staff, offered him to stay at his service and despite Miranda's refusal, she gave him a Russian diplomatic passport so that he could continue his project of emancipation of Latin America with less risk. However, she withdrew her support in 1792 when Miranda joined the French Revolution.

for the Spanish American colonies, to which he, in 1790, had promised (as stipulated in Hollwood), that in the case that Spain went to war with England, the latter would support them in their quest for liberty and independence, just as France had done with the North American colonies in 1778.

This idea was so publicised throughout the country that I was informed that an insurrection was about to start in Santa Fe, Caracas, Mexico, and even Chile! I confess that although I wish for the liberty and independence of the New World, I fear equally and maybe even more, anarchy and the revolutionary system! God forbid that those beautiful countries turn, like St Domingo, into a bloody and murderous scenario under the pretext of liberty; let them instead remain for another century under the idiotic and barbarous Spanish oppression!

I know that besides the two Spanish Americans currently in London, other respectable people have arrived since I was last here. I have also met some other South Americans in Paris. They all coincide with the main principles of absolute liberty and independence, such as the United States of America obtaining and paying England well for the services it could offer us without meeting any demand for a trade monopoly.

We greatly wish for the cooperation of the North Americans. They are our neighbours and brothers in freedom and even our own compatriots…

I will show him some instructions I carry with me that confirm what was done in Hollwood in 1790.

I hope that England and the United States of America will adopt a judicious and liberal plan—similar to the one that France had made in 1792 and that we were about to implement when Robespierre's infernal character came to undo everything—jointly today for the good of humankind and the triumph of true liberty.

For this reason, I have requested safe conduct. I hope you will intervene before the government so I can have them by the day after tomorrow. I make the same request for an official to accompany me, who is not accused of anything and for whom I respond.

Goodbye
Bond Street No. 40
M-a.
T. II, f. 21 Negociaciones

10.3.2 Extract of Miranda's Note Reporting His Conversation with W. Pitt in Hollwood on 16 January 1798

Context:

See the previous document as well as Chap. 5, document 5.2.2 (second draft constitution for Spanish America).

Content:

A precise report of the exchange with Pitt in which Miranda's strategy to seduce the Prime Minister appears clearly, first with the representativeness that Miranda had attributed to himself by enacting the "Act of Paris" (see Chap. 7), and second with a British-style monarchical constitution to fit in with the English anti-French and anti-Republican political context, and so regaining credibility in London after he supports the French Revolution. On the other hand, Pitt's compelling interest in Miranda is also verified due to his government's geopolitical threats at this delicate moment. Miranda confirms, through direct testimony, the growing risk that Napoleon poses to the UK and its political regime.

Sources:

América Espera. Document 72. p. 203–207.

Archivo del General Miranda. Vol. XV. p. 264–269.

Colombeia. Vol. XVIII. 2004. Document 3968. p. 79–85.

Text:

Finally, after waiting more than three months in Paris for the response of Don Pedro Caro and Mr. Turnbull of London, without receiving any news or knowing positively what to attribute it to, I resolved to leave myself for England, both to fulfil with my duty in a commission of such magnitude as by the persuasion in which I was that hospitality in this country would not be denied me. Undoubtedly, the risks and difficulties of executing my mission were significant. Still, I had obtained a passport that my friend Legrand, with muriatic oxygen acid, had falsified by changing the sign and signature, and also a wig and green glasses to disguise myself.

I left Paris on January 3, 1798, in the Calais stagecoach, where I arrived on the 7th. I was fortunate to meet a kind Jacobin innkeeper for whom I had brought a recommendation, his name was Detant, at the "Grand Cerf". He managed the control process for my Passport at the Municipality and the shipment of my chest with great skill and expertise, considerably reducing my risks. And indeed, I embarked on the 11th at 6 p.m. on a Danish ship. The same Detant and my faithful housekeeper, Françoise, accompanied me to the boat.

We then set sail and entered Dover at the tide of the next day, January 12, before the day. The customs collector, Mr Newport, visited us, and we went to the inn until noon, when we returned to make our declaration and inspect the luggage.

A double bottom was discovered in my chest, and inside were several papers and some printed matter on which my name was featured on the front. The guard was a little surprised and said to me, 'Are you perhaps General Miranda? 'I replied, 'It could be! And I told him to come with all the papers to the room of the Chief, Mr. Newport, to whom I explained positively who I was. ... He welcomed me with great pleasure; we put all my papers in a package, without anyone having read a single word, and he begged me to seal them with my seal for my safety. I wrote immediately from there to my friend Joseph Smith, announcing my arrival and the purpose of my trip, charging him to ask Mr. Pitt for a passport, and Mr. Newport was in charge of sending my letter, separating us afterwards with pleasure and much civility. When I got to the inn, I found that all the companions had already given me up for lost and were glad to see me arrive free and healthy. We ate pleasantly, and I still wrote like Smith to Mr. Turnbull in London.

On Sunday (14) at 9 a.m., Mr. Newport came to my inn with the Passports that I had requested and begged me not to take them with me but to take them with the indispensable persons. He would open the customs office (even on holidays) so that my luggage could be delivered later, and the people who were supposed to accompany me were executed on time. I wrote to my friends in Paris, and at around noon, I set off with my friend Combray. The fact was that Mr. Pitt, to whom Mr. Newport's letter was presented, knowing my handwriting in the overwritten letter from Smith (who was in Bath at the time), opened it and had the Passports dispatched immediately.

I did not arrive in London until Monday the 15th, because I slept on the road because of the thieves who walked on it and had robbed others 2 days before. I got off at Dantan's Inn, Panton Square, around 4 a.m., and after lunch, I went to see Mr. Turnbull (42 Broad Street), who was waiting impatiently for me. We talked a little about my business, and he communicated to me the two letters (Nos. 47 and 48) from Mr. Pitt's Secretary, Carthew, from whom I learned that the Minister had been waiting for me that day in Downing Street and that he was expecting me tomorrow without fail at his country house in Hollwood, for a conference, what did I wish for!

On the 16th, at 11 in the morning, I departed in a post carriage to Hollwood, where I arrived around 1:00 in the afternoon. The porter announced my arrival immediately to Mr. Pitt, who came to me without delay and immediately received me, with expressions of joy and friendship, complimenting me on my safe arrival and reminding me that 8 years ago, we had met for the first time in that same place to talk about the same essential subject; that now circumstances were very different because England was in open war with Spain…! I replied that these circumstances were precisely the reason to repeat, or rather, resume the negotiations of 1790 on the same subject; everything is fine, he told me, but in the name of who and by whom is this authorisation given, and whether we could not write a document that (hopefully) would be like a power of attorney, in order to proceed in an orderly fashion with the matter. I replied that we had foreseen both objections and that to remedy them as far as we could, we had agreed that my instructions were powers in themselves, that these were given by the commissioners, deputies and representatives of the Spanish Colonies, and that all this was contained in a sheet that I had already prepared, having the note and the attached document LXV and L. He read both with great attention, and when he reached the part of the alliance with the United States of America, he exclaimed, with sincere joy, we are happy to act together with America in this venture…! Do you know if any particular propositions have been made to America yet?- I don't think so because they would not ask me to make them if they had. I promise you not to take any particular step until I have your decision or answer: very well, he said to me with a nod, and he went on reading; he was surprised to find out that the population was over 14,000,000, and he asked what the Roman swords and the sarisas laudemonas were? A short sword used by the Roman infantry in imitation of the former Spanish sword, I replied, and the sarisa is a 13 ft long pike; in the article where we request from England 20 ships of the line, he answered aghast, if it meant 20 boats in the West Indies? I replied that not only there but also in the South Sea and other places…. very well, he said to me, because in that case, the negotiation would stop here as we can't provide such forces! But as for the whole, there will be enough!

And coming to another point, he added (although England does not intend to get mixed up on any account with the Government of the country), which is the form or type of government you are considering establishing in the country? I replied that it would be very similar to Great Britain's because it would consist of a House of Commons, another one of Lords, and an Inca as the hereditary sovereign! Very well, he said, because if you tried to introduce in the country a French style system, I could assure you (he replied with vivacity) we would instead the Spanish Americans continued for another century to be the obedient subjects under the oppressive government of the king of Spain than to see them immersed in the calamities of the abominable French system!... Very well, I said, it is precisely to avoid such contamination, and to guard ourselves against the Gallic influence, that we have thought of emancipating ourselves immediately; and to make alliances with the USA and with England in order to combat unanimously (if it were necessary) the monstrous and horrific principles of the alleged French liberty!… And so that you know that these are the same opinions that my own compatriots believe in, I have the draft of the project for a Constitution that we think best accommodates the spirit and views of us Americans and that the commissioners of that region have sanctioned. He read everything with great care, and when he got to the article on the hereditary Inca, he assented, lowering his head, and in the end, he said, all this is fine. There is no embarrassment on the whole, but as it is such a momentous issue and for the time being, I can't tell you more- in a short while, you will have a formal and decisive answer! I observed that the sincerity and simplicity with which I had acted allowed me to expect the business to be handled quickly and with me as well. Indeed, he replied, and this is the best way to conclude business soon and to mutual satisfaction. He went on to ask me when I had arrived in London. I answered that only yesterday after five! This question, it seemed to me, could have been made to find out whether I had written, here, after my arrival, the project of Constitution &… But my quick reply apparently left him satisfied. I insisted that he keep the constitution draft in a safe place, as I had no copy. I only let him have it because of the urgency of his request… Point taken!...

Then, leaving this aside, he asked about my thoughts on French affairs and if I was convinced they might land in England. Here we entered the broad road of the French Revolution, and in passing, I informed him about the motives that took me to Paris in 1792 and the accident that produced my entering the service of France; in short, so that nothing should be attempted against the Hispanic American Colonies (as would have happened had I not gone to Paris at the time) and so that liberty could be introduced by soft means and sanity, if that were the case.. etc. I also made him see the reasons that kept me in France after I recovered my liberty, as a result of the death of Robespierre and the return of the rest of the party of La Gironde to the Legislative Body after 9 Thermidor, that the object was peace, and to re-establish order in France no matter how. They had thought of me for the first object: peace. And that the proposal for the terms of this peace were in a small document that I had published then in Paris "*Opinion du General Miranda sur la situation actuelle de la*

France, et de convenables remèdes à ces maux...[59]" He replied that, in fact, he had read the piece and that he remembered very well how moderate and sensible were the terms in which it was conceived!... Then, I added that the intention was to engage Empress Catherine II in being the mediator and pacifier of the universe and that the matter seemed more plausible to me under her will since she was the intimate ally of England at the time! It is very accurate, he replied, and there is no doubt that it would have been the most appropriate person for this task of the sovereigns of Europe! I also talked about the wish that some Deputies of my acquaintance, expelled on 18 Fructidor, had tconsidered coming to England to escape persecution if they were assured they would not be repelled... He asked me their names. I mentioned *Quatremère, de Quincy* and *Boissy d'Anglas*; even though he showed no disgust when hearing their names, he did not reply but changed the subject. Speaking of Bonaparte, he said, among other things, that he believed he did not want to accept responsibility for the military operation against England. I said I was unaware of the contrary but that he could be persuaded that Bonaparte would send him whatever was agreeable to Barras and all the Jacobins or murderers of France. To prove this, I would tell him an anecdote on the subject... Just before leaving Paris, I said he had called for a meeting of merchants to take out a loan of 25 million pounds (liv. tor.) for the fastest expedition against England! Bonaparte was present in the assembly and spoke about the advantages that the conquest of England would bring, especially for French trade. It was fair and necessary that they make the first down payments for the landing on the island's coast, because once this was over, the rest would soon follow. To this, he replied, smiling, to be sure! This is for you to see, I said, whether it is probable that Bonaparte will refuse that commission. He also asked me: and how is it that you have escaped under so much risk from France at this moment? And I replied with a passport adapted to my person by chemical means, and with the help of some disguise... Finally, with friendship and mutual satisfaction, we separated around 3:30 in the afternoon...I remained quite surprised by the warm welcome and the total oblivion of the strong reply given to these affairs at the beginning of 1792, when I went to Paris, and finally, at 6 in the evening, I returned to London.

T. I, f. 151 Negotiations

10.3.3 Extract of Miranda's Letter to W. Pitt, London, 20 March 1798

Context:

Miranda, already disappointed by the British delay in executing the purpose of the January meeting with W. Pitt, who does not answer his interview demands, fears that Napoleon would logically invade the Iberian Peninsula. According to his

[59] See Chap. 6, document 6.3.

analysis, this would open the door to anarchy in the colonies if he were not prepared to implement it, considering both his constitutional and institutional dispositions, as well as his military plan. Pitt was attempting to break the alliance between Spain and France, and therefore was excessively cautious not to irritate Spain. Pitt's position was heavily influenced by that of his cousin, Lord Grenville, the aristocratic Foreign Secretary (Minister of Foreign Affairs), who was the leader of the party that focused on fighting Napoleon on the continent, in strong opposition to the faction of the Secretary of War (Minister of War), Henry Dundas, who had on economist view with consideration of longer-term, and therefore, was favouring war at sea and in the colonies.[60] Dundas was a supporter of Miranda, who also had economic and geopolitical views and a strategy for the longer-term interests of Britain. On the contrary, Grenville, who had a static vision focused only on the Continent, was reluctant to trust Miranda, whom he perceived as a Jacobin republican.

However, Miranda was unaware of the British treason that had already been decided against him. Naively, he was confident in the word of the prime minister of a nation he believed was once again endowed with democratising intentions and a superior geopolitical vision, along with some civilising ethics. Still, he ignored that the British cabinet had already taken a position. This secret position is revealed in a coded letter from Rufus King,[61] the US Ambassador in London, to his Minister of Foreign Affairs, Timothy Pickering, dated February 26, 1798 (Syret, H. 1974).[62] King explained that England would prioritise not breaking an alliance with Spain to not lose Spanish support in the face of the worrying French threat. Therefore, the British government won't support Miranda as long as Spain can resist France. However, if they saw France invading and taking over Spain and its colonies, they would apply Miranda's plan, adapted to their own interests; that is, they would openly support the revolution throughout South America and seek direct support

[60]The **"Blue Water"** policy is based on maritime supremacy to achieve international and commercial supremacy. For detailed explanations, see Chap. 5 section 5.2.4., note n° 66 and Chap. 11, section 11.8.

[61]**Rufus King** (1755–1827). American lawyer, politician and Ambassador of the United States in London. He was in close contact with Miranda and the author of the "Letter to the Americans", Viscardo, the Peruvian Jesuit in exile, whom Miranda had already recommended to William Pitt in 1790. Miranda recommended inviting the Jesuit to London and employing him as an advisor from 1791 to 1798 (the year he died). Father Viscardo handed over his papers and the famous letter to the US diplomat for dissemination when he died. The Consul entrusted it to Miranda shortly after, and Miranda published it in French and Spanish (see Annex 1). Rufus King, a friend of Hamilton in the Federalist ranks, was this party's candidate after Hamilton's death for both Vice President (1804, 1808) and President of the United States (1816). It facilitated Miranda's trip to the United States in search of support for his failed expedition in 1806.

[62]Confidential letter from Rufus King, dated February 26, addressed to Minister Pickering, sources: copy [decripted], RG 59, Despatches from United States Ministers to Great Britain, 1791–1906, Vol. 7, January 9–December 22, 1798, National Archives, quoted in an editor's note in the publication of Miranda's letter sent to Hamilton on February 7, Syrett, H. ed. (1974), *The Papers of Alexander Hamilton*, op. cit. Vol. 21, April 1797–July 1798, p. 348–350. It also appears in a letter from John Adams to James Lloyd on March 14, 1815.

from the US in their own strategy. In this case, they had already decided to exclude Miranda, who would be previously arrested under any pretext.

Content:

This letter reveals three significant features of Miranda's thinking and positions:

- the constant, rational and transparent Miranda's vision about the necessity of support from a tactical alliance with both the UK and the US governments,
- but it contrasts with Pitt's cynical strategy and Miranda's naïve idealisation of the British and US political leaders. He still believed these policymakers would be interested in escaping the prisoner's dilemma and choosing the win-win game of common interests over selfish national goals.
- Miranda shows remarkable clairvoyance in perceiving 10 years in advance the Napoleonic invasion of Spain and the disastrous impact that this would automatically cause in the colonies in case they were not ready to channel the revolutions through new institutions able to establish the rule of the new law. He has already expressed, and will continue to do so as a permanent obsession until the end of his life, his main fear, which is the probability of French Jacobin influence during the vacuum that could occur between the fall of Spanish authority and the implementation of a new system.

Sources:

Translated from French

América Espera. Documento 74. p. 210–219.

Archivo del General Miranda. Vol. XV. p. 212–214 y 216–225.

Colombeia. Vol. XVIII. 2004. Document 3973. p. 92–94.

Text:

N° LIII

Correspond to

N° 7 de 1798

Attached: Political overview of Spanish America by Francisco Xavier Clavijero.

From Francisco de Miranda to Mr. Pitt

London, March 20, 1798

The undersigned, principal agent of the Hispanic American Colonies, has learnt through specific reports and public opinion that Spain is currently in a critical situation, given the imminent entry of French troops into her territory. This aggression threatens the government with an anarchic convulsion, and this will be transmitted to the New World, as the Spanish Colonies, finding themselves then alienated from their link to the Metropolis, will be obliged to seek a new form of Government. In that case, it seems inevitable that in the intermediary period between the fall of the old and the functioning of the new system, the anarchic and subversive principles of the French system should furtively introduce themselves there unless efficient and quick measures are taken to avoid it; it is with this in mind, that the members of the committee and compatriots have sent the undersigned before the ministries of H.B.M and of the United States of America, to prevent a catastrophe so costly to the New World as fatal to the Old one, by applying the right and firm measures.

He regrets the time (probably indispensable) the government takes to grant him an interview or a response to the frank proposals he had the honour of submitting on January 16 to the very honourable William Pitt. He conceives that a simple aid from England of six or eight ships, with four or five thousand troops that the United States could easily supply, would be sufficient and that it is all that is needed at the present moment, admitting the probability of a not too distant break between them and France.

For this same reason, the undersigned has believed that he could not better comply with the intentions of his commissioning constituents than by sending one of his Compatriots, who is currently with him, to Santa Fe de Bogotá to inform the other constituents of the current situation verbally and to put them in a position to react accordingly or to send him other directives. The same person will go to Philadelphia (with letters from the Minister Plenipotentiary, Mr. King) to make proposals and offers to the American government that articles 9, 10, 11 and 12 of his Instruction prescribe.[63]

The undersigned hopes that his preparatory measures will deserve the approval of the most honourable Minister and will be executed within eight to 10 days, the date on which the ship that must transport Don Pedro Caro to Philadelphia will leave; any correction or any change that Mr. Pitt purposely would judge helpful would be made without inconvenience before this date.

The undersigned begs the most honourable Minister to accept the assurances of his high consideration and the perfect esteem with which he has the honour of being his very humble and very obedient servant,

M.

P.S.: The attached list of Spanish America's population, products, etc., has been provided to you by some country commissioners who prepared it using the most exact and recent data.

T. I, f. 153 Negociaciones

T. II, f. 41 Negociaciones

10.3.4 Miranda's Letter to John Adams,[64] President of the United States of America, 24 March 1798

Context:

As mentioned in his letters to Hamilton, Miranda does not limit his strategy to England, whose primary concern is to re-establish good relations with Spain,

[63] Act of Paris, December 22, 1797. See Chap. 4.

[64] **John Adams** (1735–1826), second President of the United States (March 4, 1797 to March 4, 1801). In 1789, he was Vice-President of the United States after being the first Ambassador of his country in London (1785–1788). In his memory, he reveals that he considered Miranda as a dangerous idealist who dreamed of an impossible democracy given the cultural underdevelopment of Latin Americans (see following note).

thereby dividing its alliance with France and paralysing the direct British support Miranda needs. Furthermore, he has always believed in an alliance with both Anglo-Saxon democratic countries. He does not limit his demands and contacts to his direct friends, either, and he also addresses President Adams, who is opposed to his Federalist friends but is a crucial decision-maker for obtaining any support.

Following his first-hour resolutions, with the Paris Act, and with his conversations with Pitt, Miranda wants to involve and lean on the United States, not only because it is the leading country and neighbour but also because it is American and anti-colonial. In addition, Miranda observes the growing tensions between France and the US, which began in connection with the Treaty of London (1795) between the US and England, which France regards as a breach of the US's neutrality concerning the French war against England. This perception was sharpened in September with the self-coup within the French Directory, which gave a Jacobin orientation to the French executive and reinforced hostile positions towards the US. In addition, the conflict over the non-payment of the US debt to France presents an opportunity to blackmail the US government by seizing US merchant boats and their assets. Talleyrand, the French Minister of Foreign Affairs, requests personal bribes to prevent France from declaring war and to facilitate negotiations with the US. The talks in Paris failed, and the so-called "XYZ Affair" broke out, provoking damage to the reputation of the French regime and a lasting anti-French reaction in the US (which had previously been pro-French due to French support for their independence war).

Against this backdrop, Miranda sent his representative, Pedro Caro, to Philadelphia and wrote to John Adams, who was sceptical of the Republican regime. Miranda will have no result, being considered by Adams as an unrealistic adventurer.

When he did not receive a reply to his letter to Minister Pitt sent on March 20, 1798, in which he annexed Data on Spanish America and the Act of Paris, Miranda became very worried by his analysis that the French troops would be tempted to invade the Spanish territory and provoke an anarchic convulsion in the new world. Miranda's priority was to ensure the timely implementation of a new form of government. Therefore, he asked the British Government for aid of 6 to 8 ships, upon which 4 or 5 thousand troops of the United States could cooperate to achieve independence and sovereignty, as stated in the reserved instruction dated Paris on December 22, 1797 (Paris Act).

President Adams never took a positive view of Miranda, whom he regarded as a dangerous idealist who sought to involve the United States in a costly and unappealing adventure. Furthermore, Adams was informed of Miranda's connections and convergent views with Hamilton, Rufus King, and Knox, all of whom were political opponents of his government. This also explains the radicalisation of Adams against Miranda's views. These reactions are documented in Adams' memoirs and in subsequent letter exchanges, in which he makes numerous and insightful comments on

Miranda, his ideas, and his contacts in the US. Adams' motivations for opposing any US aid to Miranda were multiple, according to several of his letters (1815)[65]:

1. Miranda's lack of credible official representation (he questioned the Paris Act and the signatures of the two Jesuits who appear in the Act); although it was confirmed that Paris Act was a self-made-justification that could not have been more official than under a private pact between conspirators, given the Spanish regime, it is strange that President Adams did not take into consideration that it would not have been possible to act otherwise with an absolutist regime that did not allow official opposition or debates and that sent spies against Miranda. This evidence should have been a sufficient argument;
2. the cost to the US budget for supporting Miranda's plan;
3. the neutrality of the USA with any conflict between Europeans, and especially the fact that Miranda wanted to prevent France from seizing the Spanish colonies, risking a war with France, and as a result, reinforcing the British positions in Europe and its industry and weapons;
4. Adams' weariness with the revolutionary process and the threat of a Creole Jacobinism that could be even worse than in France;
5. Adam's judgement on Miranda (1815): he saw him as a dangerous utopian, believing that democracy could be effective in South America, revealing a very negative perception of his Southern neighbours.[66]

Content:

A remarkable synthesis of Miranda's strategy, written in a diplomatically flattering manner:

- Transparent attempt to get the US support in cooperation with the UK, betting upon some degree of competition between them
- making the former feel that the latter expects the former to make decisions,
- ideal combination of the advantage of getting British naval supremacy with the importance of seeing only American troops (non-colonial character) on the grounds,
- He made an identical warning against the French political proselytising of the Jacobins' republic that he had made simultaneously to William Pitt regarding Napoleon's ineluctable expansionism in South America, which would be a disaster for the Americas.

[65] See in particular the exchange of letters between John Adams and James Lloyd, especially the letter dated 6 March 1815, in: *Founders Online*, National Archives, *The Adams Papers* op. cit.

[66] John Adams' letter to James Lloyd of March 26, 1815, is very explicit: "*The People of South America, are the most ignorant the most bigoted the most Superstitious of all the Roman Catholics in Christendom.... Could Such a Plan as Miranda's of a free Government and a Confederation of Free Governments be introduced and established among Such a People over that vast Continent or any part of it? It appeared to me more extravagant than the Schemes of Condorcet and Brissot to establish a Democracy in France; Schemes which had always appeared to me as absurd as Similar plans would be to establish Democracies among the Beasts Birds or Fishes»*. Source: *Founders Online*, National Archives *The Adams Papers.*

- Stress that the possibility of ruling out the Jacobin threat in the Americas depends on his decision
- A brief presentation of his constitutional form of "mixed government" for Latin America, in coherence with Pitt's purposes, but also justified for seducing the (paradoxical) reluctance of the conservative President of the United States about the Republican regime.

Sources:

Translated from French.

América Espera. Doc. 75, p. 219–221.

Becerra. Vol. 1. p. 21–23.

Colombeia. Vol. XVIII. Negotiations. 1797–1799. 2004. Document 4005. p. 149–152.

Text:

N° LIV.

Corresponds to N° 8 de 1798.

To His Excellency John Adams, President of the United States of America.

London, March 24, 1798

Mr. President:

On behalf of the Spanish American Colonies, I am honoured to send the attached proposals to Your Excellency. These have also been presented to the Ministers of HBM, who have received them very favourably, expressing great satisfaction at acting in a similar case to that of the United States of America. It seems to me that the delay that I am experiencing - truly distressing at such a time pressing - comes precisely from the expectation in which the English government appears to be seeing North America determined to break definitively with France because of the desire it has to make common cause and cooperate for the absolute independence of the entire Continent of the New World.

As the spirit of justice, generosity, and adhesion of my Compatriots to the United States is best expressed in the document that serves as my powers and Instructions, I wanted to attach a complete copy to you, convinced that this demonstration of friendship and frankness will serve more effectively to speed up the decision ... always counting on the indispensable reserve in everything that does not directly concern the United States. If any of the articles contained in this Instruction (or anything else that is related to it) needs explanation, Don Pedro José Caro, one of my Compatriots, also Commissioner of the Hispanic-American Colonies and in charge of delivering to your Excellency this letter, will be able to fully and completely answer to you and satisfy everything.

After receiving Your Excellency's orders, his mission is to move without delay to the Hispanic-American Continent to inform our Constituents and Compatriots of the current state of the negotiations that they have entrusted to us and of the political situation in Europe.

I beg your Excellency to please provide everything he might need for this critical purpose so he can immediately go to the Province of Santa Fe de Bogotá.

I do not hide from Your Excellency, Mr. President, my concern about the forthcoming entry of the French troops into Spain: fear that a convulsive movement in the Metropolis will produce anarchic shocks in the Colonies and that the abominable system of France will find its way among us if we do not take swift and efficient measures to avoid this. "Dii avertant!" Anyway, I hope that with the bit of help we need to begin, which is reduced to six or eight ships and four or five thousand troops, we will easily find both in England and America ... My wish would be for the Navy to be English and ground troops to be American. May Providence wish the United States to do what the King of France did for them in 1798 for its Compatriots of the South in 1778!

I always congratulate myself on seeing at the head of the American Executive Power, the distinguished man who, through his courage, made his country independent and, with his excellent sense, later gave it a stable government, thus saving Liberty. We will certainly take advantage of the wise lessons of your Excellency, and from now on, I am pleased to manifest to your Excellency that the projected form of government is mixed ... with a hereditary head of the Executive Power, under the name of Inca and, what I like the most, chosen within the same family. A Senate composed of noble families, but not hereditary, and a House of Commons elected from among the other citizens with sufficient property. Such is the outline of the form of government that seems to gather the majority of votes on the Hispanic-American continent, and that will prevent the inevitable fatal consequences of the French-Republican system that Montesquieu calls extreme Freedom.

Addressing these propositions directly to Your Excellency, I believe I should use all the required reserve in a matter as extraordinary as necessary.

I also have the honour of annexing to these a statement of the population, products, exports, and consumption of Spanish America, which, having been made under the most accurate and recent reports, seems to me to deserve the attention of your Excellency.

With sentiments of the highest consideration and most perfect esteem, I have the honour, Mr. President, of being the humblest and obedient servant of Your Excellency.

F. de M.

T. I, f. 154 Negotiations

10.3.5 Miranda's Letter to Hamilton 6 April 1798

Context:

A third letter from Miranda (see comments in document VII.12) requesting support from his friend, Hamilton, a renowned constitutionalist and influential US politician. However, Miranda received neither a response from Hamilton (of the opposition Federalist Party) nor from President Adams (who was opposed to Hamilton, although within the same party). The best option for implementing Miranda's emancipation plan was to get broad political support from the US in a coalition with England. So, he sought the personal participation of other friends who were former soldiers in the US independence campaign, in case he would have to act without government support, which was ultimately the case in 1806 (see documents 10.37 & 10.38). Miranda's disciple, Pedro José Caro, who Miranda sent as a personal messenger, did not fulfil his mission. He went via Trinidad to Bogotá and betrayed Miranda.

Miranda tries to take advantage of the political tensions between France and the United States that have worsened since March 1797 as a result of the suspension of payments of the American debt to France (contracted during the war of independence with the French crown) and the French aggressive response which seizes the US merchant ships (800 ships taken between 1797 and 1800) causing significant economic damages to the US. The probability of war between the US and France is reinforced by the political change in the Directory on September 4, 1797, with the Jacobins taking over in a self-coup, initiating a policy against the United States. Hamilton and his Federalist Party favour declaring war against France to reinforce the alliance with England and to contain the expansion of the Jacobins. This option would support Miranda's geopolitical thesis, which tirelessly denounces the risk that France poses to both England and the United States, as well as his plans for Latin America. With the breaking of the treaties with France, Hamilton was appointed in July 1798 as the head of the US Army by Adams (at the insistence of G. Washington). However, Adams managed to avoid war through new negotiations.

Content:

Miranda shows optimism again, expecting his friend to join a movement that fits his political convictions: freedom that should be protected from French Jacobinism, thanks to a constitution that balances a "mixed government," which means a way to protect the government from an abusive popular power. Hamilton and Miranda share these constitutional principles. He also asks Hamilton to contact his other friends, General H. Lee and General Knox.

Sources:

Translated from French

América espera, document n°76, p. 221–222

Archivo..; Vol. XV p. 234–236

The Papers of Alexander Hamilton, Vol. 21, April 1797–July 1798, ed. Harold C. Syrett. New York: Columbia University Press, 1974, pp. 399–402.

Text:

From Francisco de Miranda to Alexander Hamilton Esqr. In New York.

London, April 6, 1798

This present letter will be delivered to you, my esteemed and respectable friend, through my compatriot, Mr. Pedro Joseph de Caro, in charge of the mission of the highest importance to the President of the United States. He will inform you confidentially about what you want to know. It seems that the moment of our emancipation is approaching, and the establishment of freedom in the entire continent of the New World is entrusted to us by Providence. The only danger I intuit lies in introducing French principles, which would poison the incipient Liberty, soon ending its own. However, if we take wise measures in time, everything can contribute significantly to success. May he teach you my instructions on the matter so you can add what I have forgotten?

It has been previously agreed that a mixed form of government should be implemented, which, in my opinion, seems to suit the country perfectly. I will have the opportunity to raise it for your consideration in due course. Although I warn you that we would like to have you with us for such a transcendent purpose, this is the desire of my compatriots, as informed to me in this regard. So I hope he won't reject us when the time comes ... His predecessor, the Greek Solon, certainly wouldn't have done it!

Of this, I am sure! And possibly find it myself.

There is another person in your country that I know by reputation who, in my opinion, could very well help us in a significant military way: General H. Lee of Virginia. Having received at the beginning of the revolution in France (through my friend Colonel W. Smith) a letter from him by which he stated his intention of entering the service of the Republic, I boast that he will not shy away from us either when it comes to the true Freedom that we all love, as well as the happiness of his compatriots in Peru and Mexico.

Please do me the favour of warning him so that he will be ready to accompany us and advise him of the always indispensable discretion. Will our friend Knox want to join us? This would please me greatly, although I fear it may not be so.

Good luck, dear friend; give me your news by writing to me at the address of Mr. King, your Minister plenipotentiary here. Present my respectful regards to Mrs. Hamilton. I remain in your memory, forever and invariably,

Your sincere friend.

F. de M.

10.3.6 Miranda's Instructions to Pedro José Caro. London, 6 April 1798

Context:

Miranda sends his assistant, Pedro Caro, on a mission to Philadelphia after having fulfilled the same mission in London and before continuing to Santa Fé de Bogotá in preparation for implementing his England-USA-Colombia tripolar alliance strategy. Ultimately, Caro will not travel to Philadelphia and will go directly to Santa Fe. Later, Caro betrays Miranda.

Content:

This is an interesting example of how Miranda organised his influence and recommendations of prudence to his envoy, although without excluding anyone, except for the Jacobins, who have shown themselves to be the gravediggers of freedom in France and constitute the most dangerous threat to America. Miranda draws a contrast between the French and American revolutions.

It is also important to note his concern for receiving confirmation of his representativeness and mandate from various parts of Spanish America. He also appears aware of the disadvantage that his compatriots still face as being "still indolent."

However, it is disheartening to know that Miranda did not realise Caro's betrayal, and that all the well-conceived organisation of this crucial mission failed; this wise advice only served to betray him.

Sources:

Translated from Spanish

América Espera. Document 77. p. 222–224.

Colombeia. Tomo XVIII. 2004. Document. 4031. p. 192–195.

Textos sobre la independencia. p. 59–63.

Text:

N° LIX

Corresponds to N° 13 de 1798

Instructions for the agreement and the best orientation of P.J. Caro's mission.

Upon your arrival in New York, you will deliver the letter you are carrying to Mr. Hamilton, the only one to whom you can speak with confidence on the matter. And then, without wasting time, you will leave for Philadelphia. Here you will deliver the letters you have from Mr. Turnbull to the Dealers, Messrs. Thomas Willing & Company, who should assist you with whatever you need; and without loss of time, also deliver Mr. King's letter to the Minister of Foreign Affairs, who will immediately request a hearing to give to the President, in his own hand, the dispatches for which he is in charge; or if some reason prevents it at the time, he will send these dispatches through the Minister to the President, requesting that they be presented to him privately, as soon as possible.

In the conference with the President, you will endeavour mainly to insist on a prompt reply (or at least to know his opinion) on the familiar matter, both to instruct our Compatriots in America and to write to me here immediately; let's be clear that all letters addressed to me will be duplicated; One copy will come here under the cover of Mr. Turnbull & Forbes, and the other will remain in Philadelphia in possession of the businessmen for whom you have the recommendation of Mr. Turnbull or the Minister of Foreign Affairs, Mr. Pickering, as you deem more convenient so that in case I have left for America, I will always find your letters in Philadelphia.

Above all, it is necessary to leave (once the document has been placed in the hands of the President) for Santa Fe, whose mission is the most important of all ... I cannot sufficiently recommend to you discretion, seriousness, prudence, activity, caution, resolution, audacity and courage, that in time and with judgement is necessary to use in the handling of a matter as delicate, serious and important as this one. Your talent and patriotism will help you discern what is convenient rather than any other explanation. Still, it is necessary that after you engage with the chiefs and prominent people of the country, you make them feel the need to prevent by all possible means the introduction of the Jacobin principles or system in our Continent because by this means, Liberty instead of the cradle will then find the grave, as the entire history of the French Revolution proves and as it is experienced, unfortunately at present, by the unhappy republics of Switzerland, Venice, Genoa, Lucca, etc. than all of Europe more or less. By informing them of the current state of Europe and the favourable disposition of England and the United States of America regarding our independence, make them understand they have to try to form a single position and wait with resolution and firmness (since up to now they have had the laudable patience to wait for this most favourable situation) the moment of our appearance in the points and places agreed to proclaim our Independence and Sovereignty. Then, we'll demonstrate that under a wise, just and well-balanced form of government, we become the happiest and most respectable nation on earth in a very short time.

Immediately, it would be helpful to send me some people of respect and capacity, both to Philadelphia and the island of Trinidad, so that they can help me both in the military and the political, with which they will also try to send new powers more legalised than the antecedents or, at least, a broad confirmation of these, taking as a general rule never to use current man, since having nothing to lose everything they venture will end by ruining the very building that they had wanted to raise. The French Revolution is the best proof of this assertion! On the contrary, if you select men of consideration and integrity, all they will undertake will prosper due to their own interest to consolidate a government of Laws that is the protector of property and personal freedom, the basis of all civil happiness, and in which the general utility of all is precisely gathered. The proof is the revolution of America, which is the most evident testimony and the most substantial contrast that could be opposed to the French atrocity, without trying to exclude the virtues and talents in any individual, they are found. *To command science is necessary, to obey a natural direction, and sometimes ignorance alone is enough*, says Saavedra. Nor will foreigners be employed except those perfectly known by ourselves or recommended by the English or American government who, interested in the company's success, will not recommend someone unworthy of it. For the same reason, the people recommended by our main agents in London or America should be reliable.

All shipments coming from the American Continent will be in triplicate, one to London, another to Philadelphia and another to the island of Trinidad, under the cover of our agents in these parts. Mr. Turnbull will also give letters to Trinidad (Francis Isnardi Esquire).

Finally, to that part of our compatriots (which is not tiny) whom indolence still dominates, despite their good wishes for the public cause in which we are committed, it will be necessary to repeat the maxim of the Romans: *audaces fortuna juvat, timidosque repellit,*[67] and to all the sensible that other quote from Saavedra ... "*Few businesses overcome the impetus; some the strength; many the suffering and almost all the reason and interest. Reason is the one that best arranges business; Few loses who knows how to use it*".

Enjoy your mission, and after a happy trip, achieve all the success in your tasks that your affectionate friend and attentive servant wishes you sincerely and warmly.

In London, April 6, 1798

[67] "*Fortune helps the bold and repels the timids.*"

See note[68]
Francisco de Miranda
T. I, f. 159 vto. Negotiations

10.3.7 Miranda's Letter to William Pitt. London, 21 May 1798

Context:

Miranda is convinced of the urgency of acting in South America and implementing the tripolar democratic alliance among England, the United States, and Colombia, and becomes impatient and disappointed. His constant concern is that France and its "abominable Jacobin system" could overtake him and create chaos that would degenerate into tyranny or anarchy in his homeland.

Content:

In a new, well-argued attempt to make England aware of its own interests, he provides an account of his efforts with excellent transparency and demonstrates his unwavering determination. This includes the veiled threat of being forced to act even without the help requested, but then with violence and to the detriment of the UK. He also explicitly formulated his wishes for a joint strategy between Great Britain and the United States.

Sources:

Translated from French
Archivo del General Miranda. Vol. XV. p. 269–271.
América Espera. Document 78, p. 225.
Colombeia. Vol. XVIII. 2004. Document 3977, p. 99–101.

Text:

N° LXVII
Corresponds to N° 21 de 1798
To the Honourable William Pitt
London, the 21st of May, 1798
Great Pulteney St. N. 1

The undersigned reminds the most honourable William Pitt of the answer he kindly promised to give regarding the proposals made to him in Hollwood on January 16th[69] in the name of the Spanish American Colonies of Southern America.

All the information received by the undersigned since then corroborates the hypothesis of the impending emancipation of those Colonies. Since the object of his mission is to prevent the dire consequences that the revolutionary French principles cause almost everywhere else by applying pre-emptive measures, he believes that the moment for the colonies to act has arrived. Otherwise, they would

[68] Miranda's note at the margin: 9 de octubre de 1798. See *Colombeia*. Vol. XVIII. Document 4068. p. 253–254.

[69] See document 10.3.2. Miranda's report on his meeting with W. Pitt.

fundamentally compromise their destiny as well as that of posterity. If they remain as passive spectators between France and the United States of America, they would later become (as they are to Spain) the vile slaves of the great republic, if not the infamous instruments of French tyranny.

To this end, and in order not to neglect a matter of this importance, the undersigned has already sent his compatriot Don P. Caro to South America to inform his constituents of the current state of affairs and of the negotiations in Europe as well as to make the preparations on the American Continent that have been agreed in advance, having also sent to the President of the United States the proposals and possibilities on behalf of the Spanish-American Colonies that his Instructions prescribe, as he had the honour to notify in time to the very honourable Minister in his note of last March 20.[70]

In this situation, the undersigned does not fear the disapproval of being untimely in requesting an immediate interview with the most honourable Minister to submit some essential observations that seem to need a prompt decision and to act unanimously with the United States of America in this critical business.

My compatriots are fully aware of the valuable assistance that England and the United States of America could provide them at this moment, supporting them in establishing their independence and forming a responsible government based on a solid and permanent foundation, protected from revolutionary convulsions. If, by misfortune and against their expectations, the proposals, procedures and other noble openings that the Colonies have made to England and the United States are not honoured by their previous commitment (I must repeat), they will be forced to obtain it by violent means, following the example of their Northern compatriots, rather than accepting the shameful and unhappy destiny of Switzerland, Holland and the governments of Italy, and of other governments at the present moment.

…

F. de M.
T. I, f. 163 to. Negotiations
T. II, f. 95 Negotiations
Translation from French

10.3.8 Military Plan Elaborated in London in August 1798: Memorandum

Context:

Despite the British authorities' lack of response and total silence, Miranda continued to press the government to launch a joint military expedition between the UK and the USA.

[70] See document 10.3.3. Letter to W. Pitt.

Content:

A synthesis of the joint operation that Miranda proposed to England and the United States in close coordination with his own network of agents, ready to give the necessary domestic support to the external intervention. This text demonstrates the author's sense of tactics, excellent preparation, and consideration of mutual interests that should prevail among the UK, the US, and the patriots. His global vision is impressive and undeniably demonstrates his quality as a great geopolitical and military strategist who manages even the minor logistical aspects of a continental military campaign. It ends with a clairvoyant summons from Turgot.

Sources:

Translated from French

Archivo del General Miranda. T. XV. p. 287–296.

América Espera. Document 80. p. 227–233.

Archivo del General Miranda. T. XV. p. 287–296.

Colombeia. Tomo XVIII. Document 3979. p. 102–113.

Text:

Memorandum

Military plan conceived in London in August 1798

The emancipation of Spanish America, requested more than 18 years ago by most of the country, is a political endeavour that could never be carried out as successfully as in the present circumstances. In a time when almost all French and Spanish ports are blocked and when North America, declaring itself openly against France, and therefore against Spain, her ally, is determined in agreement with Great Britain to cause as much damage as possible to the two hostile powers, what could be a more accessible and more powerful means to obtain this desired end than to separate from Spain a vast territorial extension, the population of which exceeds 15,000,000 souls, and whose produce and wealth are a mass of resources, which would otherwise benefit France, in whose interest Spain has unthinkingly thrown herself?...

On the assumption that the British government and the United States of America are determined to cooperate in agreement in the execution of this significant undertaking, we will indicate the procedure that should be followed in military operations to carry it out successfully. The prospect of success, adopting the means that we propose to develop below, is found:

1. On the intimate and secure knowledge that we act according to the wishes and dispositions of the inhabitants of the country;

2. On the nature and strength of the means of defence with which the main points towards which it would be convenient to go first are currently available;

3. On the opinions and favourable dispositions of the most significant number of the leaders who rule there and over whom we are interested in obtaining the most exact information in advance.

The tendency of Spanish Americans towards emancipation, which would make them completely independent of the metropolis, is evident in the efforts they made to this end at different times, particularly in 1781. These efforts could not be stifled except by addressing the main complaints that motivated their insurrection. Their current dispositions to return to the same object in a more determined way than ever necessarily derive from the deep resentment that the violation of the Capitulation signed by the members of the Audiencia and the Archbishop of Santa Fé, the June 9, 1781,[71] and ratified by HMC the 21 of January of 1782, as well as the kidnapping of several respectable personages taken prisoner to Spain by the simple suspicion of having been won by the general feelings. Some of these unfortunate victims (as well as other equally innocent individuals from Peru, etc.) have perished or are now lying in dungeons.

In short, the character that the manifestation of the discontent of the Hispanic-Americans had already begun to dominate, having been such that the government had believed over time that it could not prevent a general split except by granting reparation to the complaints that were the apparent motives, all announces that when these vast provinces decide to be independent, they will be against all opposition. On the other hand, the imprudence committed by not fulfilling the commitments contracted with them no longer allows for believing that the people would again accept any proposal for conciliation that Spanish authorities could formulate.

Let us now examine the means of defence that the Spanish government could use to oppose the companies that had as their objective the establishment of independence in South America.

There are no European troops throughout the country. Two particular types of warfare make up all security.

The first comprises what are called regulated troops, of which almost all the soldiers are taken solely from among the inhabitants. Most of its officers have been sent from Spain. However, it is worth noting that these same officials are often closely tied to the country's interests through their marriage ties. These ties have made them owners, taking away any idea of ever returning to the metropolis, from which a large number had only left with the hope of making a fortune. There is thus reason to believe that very few of them are opposed to establishing the new projected order of things.

The second type of troops consists of regulated militias, whose officers and soldiers (except a part of the general staff) are all equally from the country and, therefore, even more likely to share the desire for change with the rest of the inhabitants.

You will find two reports attached, one on the regulated troop corps (No. 1) and the other on the regulated militias (No. 2) currently distributed in the different places of the Viceroyalty of Santa Fé, a province with many strategic places on which we will then propose to focus our attacks, which must infallibly decide the fate of the rest of South America.

Another type of Militia is designated as urban militia. It comprises a selection of city, town, and village inhabitants most apt to bear arms. They are armed but not subject to any military discipline. The Viceroyalty of Santa Fé alone could supply 30,000 men of this type.

[71] *Colombeia*. Vol. VI, document 955 and Vol. IX, document 1259.

Regarding the chiefs who lead in the various districts where it would be advisable to act first, a third list (n° 3) is attached here, in which the names and grades of those distributed in each place are registered. Those who are reliable to our cause have been marked with an asterisk.

We still have to expose the procedure that should be followed to execute the Project in question.

Everything having been agreed in advance between the British government and the United States of America, to seek to distract the enemy's attention by taking ostensible provisions that seem to have Veracruz or Cuba as their object and to give more appearance of reality to an alleged expedition against Cuba, to reveal the uncertainty about the choice of the particular point by which we would propose to attack this island, which would leave the alternative between Havana and Santiago de Cuba.

The Isthmus of Panama is the district where we think it would be most advantageous to settle initially. The possession of this tongue of land that brings together the two continents of America would allow communication with the Atlantic Ocean and the Pacific Sea at the same time; from this excellent position, one could, with equal ease, take on the flank all the establishments of the northern coast of South America and those of the western coast of the same peninsula. On the other hand, the most populated establishments in this vast expanse of the country are precisely the closest to the Isthmus, a well-pronounced movement in this part would, in a short time, give successive impulse to all the rest.

One could not be the owner of the Isthmus without first seizing C — e, a seaport located at the mouth of the river of the same name, which crosses over two-thirds of the width of the Isthmus in its course. C — e being the first agreed point of attack, the British government and the United States of America should take as their meeting place the island of Trinidad or that of Granada; the latter is provided with a safe and comfortable harbour, and the climate is the healthiest of all the Antilles.

The North Americans will be in charge of transportation, with a convoy of transports, approximately 5000 infantrymen, and 2000 cavalry, all armed and equipped. The only thing that should not be transported are horses, which can quickly be supplied on the South American continent.

There, an English squadron of 8 or 10 ships of the line with a proportionate number of frigates will join us, having under their escort a convoy for the transport of a 20-piece siege artillery train, 25 position pieces and another 30 battalion pieces, plus six shells of the most robust calibre to be used as mortars, with cast irons of all the preceding calibres as well as a sufficient quantity of gunpowder. A proportionate number of artillery companies accompanied all this. With this, weapons and luggage would be needed for the equipment of an Army Corps comprising 20,000 foot soldiers and 5000 cavalrymen, along with camping equipment in proportion; several own tools would be required to remove the ground, sufficient to put to work around 6000 sappers. Roman spades and swords, the model of which will be supplied, to arm 20,000 men. England would not need to deprive herself of any regular corps of troops now.

With such a formation in Granada or Trinidad, it would be impossible for the inhabitants not to suspect some thoughtful enterprise against some of the settlements in South America. Those of Trinidad, in particular, being Spanish and having the possibility of communicating every day with the continent's inhabitants, from which they are not separated except by a very narrow channel, their suspicions would soon be disseminated there.[72]

Then, the new measures to deceive at least about the actual point of this coast where a landing would be thought would be to circulate that we are going against Caracas. The moment's circumstances would concur in accrediting that rumour propagated with care and without affectation. The province in which this city is the capital is generally the most dissatisfied with the Spanish government. The chiefs, thus authorised to consider this point as the first to be considered, would not neglect to drive back the more significant part of their forces there, which could not take place without at the same time reducing the means of defence of the points actually threatened.

C — e is a bicoca whose garrison is weak, and the Commander is inclined to favour the company in question. While the squadron would have the castle and forts at the port's entrance at bay, the cove, where the filibusters landed in 1670, would offer a comfortable place for the troops to land. These would go immediately to the city, which is not fortified. The castle that dominates it could not put up a long-lasting resistance, assuming it wanted to defend itself, which it probably would not, as the Commander is a man to be trusted.

Owners of C-e, a proclamation should begin to circulate in the country to explain the purpose of the operation to the inhabitants and encourage them to join the American troops as soon as possible.

We have every reason to believe that the Commissioners currently distributed in these vast regions to prepare the consciences there will have brought things to the point that the first appearance of a force will prompt the people to rise en masse and join it. The city of Tolú on Morosquillo Cove, very close to Zispata Bay,[73] will also be indicated as the central meeting point.

First of all, C — e will have to be deposited all the munitions and supplies of war. It will also be the starting point for all subsequent operations. Until we have seized other maritime posts further east, it will be the primary outlet for communicating with England and the United States of America. It will therefore be advisable first to place the post protected from any attack, both on the seaside and in the countryside. Regardless of a garrison in the castle, it would be good to establish a kind of entrenched Roman camp to the city's right, spacious enough to contain a Corps of 4 to 6000 men. This Corps should be composed mainly of the country's militias to which some detachments of North American veterans will have adequately joined

[72] Miranda's Note: There is a document from the Parliament that converts the port of Trinidad into a free port, or to put it neutral, where the inhabitants of the continent can trade as freely as the nations in peace with Great Britain.

[73] Miranda's note: Militias of the country to which some detachments will come together.

to train and accustom them to service. Command should be entrusted to the most experienced and capable officers.

Head with all the possible diligence towards Panama. Communication is straightforward, and the distance is not more than 10 to 12 leagues.[74] The fortifications of this place are inadequate and poorly preserved. It would not be able to put up a prolonged resistance. Although the two principal officers who command there are not men with whom it is convenient to count, the rumour of the surrender of C. and the manifestation, not equivocal, of the inhabitants' feelings. The few people in this place, together with the impossibility of receiving aid from anywhere, will soon determine whether they will surrender.

As these developments continue, the fermentation will spread in the province where the first two attack points are located. This province is Santa Fe, which is very rich and the most populated on the entire continent. The individuals attached to the Spanish government –which could not be but the Viceroy, the members of the Audiencia and some officials- seeing themselves to the point of being abandoned by the armed force, as they were in 1781, will surely follow the same path that they followed in the mentioned time, that is, they will take Cartagena as their place of refuge. In effect, Cartagena is a solid maritime place from which they could count on help from the metropolis and from which they could also obtain an advantageous capitulation if all hope of help is forbidden.

Present yourself in front of this fortress. But since a company against Cartagena would not know how to be followed by success until we had taken over the navigation of the Magdalena River, which has its mouth to the east of the place in the Bay of Santa Marta, it would be advisable before any demonstration of attack, to establish in Tolú as we have said above, and where probably all the country's militias will have already surrendered to meet with the army, all the more so that we can believe that the magistrates of this city are in the best possible dispositions, as well as in Santa Marta itself.[75]

Santa Marta is an entirely open maritime city on the land side, whose defence, which we can quickly correct on the seaside, would increasingly secure the country against any foreign company. Supported on the right by the Santa Marta Post and the left by the Tolú Post, we would immediately settle on the island where Cartagena is located. This operation can be carried out much more efficiently by sea because there is no opposing current from Chagre to Tolú and Santa Marta.

As we must wait for resistance in the Cartagena attack, we should not present ourselves before the walls without having a siege artillery train at hand. If nothing has been achieved using persuasion, it will be convenient to form your attack in the most abrupt way possible, establishing its first parallel, which should be the last

---

[74] Miranda's note: There are two routes: one maritime to Cruces, the other land from the landing stage to Panama on a uniform terrain and a good road.

[75] Miranda's note: In Tolú, as mentioned above, where all the country's militias had already arrived to join the army, because everything suggests that the city's magistrates have the best possible dispositions.

one, as close as possible to the body of the stronghold without neglecting, however, to take all the usual precautions to protect men.

The English squadron, patrolling or anchoring within sight of the port, would powerfully help with its presence to support land operations and hasten the surrender of this place, depriving the garrison of any hope of being assisted by sea.

Once Cartagena's fate is decided, its neighbouring provinces, such as Caracas, Cumaná, Paria, etc., will not take long to pronounce themselves.

However, although we are sure of the inhabitants' dispositions, we will not have to neglect anything proper to strengthen them in their determinations. To this end, immediately after the surrender of Cartagena, it was convenient to send three ships of the line to Buenos Aires, accompanied by some frigates, to prevent the Spanish government from making this significant departure, from which they could reach Chile and even Peru by land.

It will also be necessary to obtain, as soon as possible, from the British government the dispatch of a squadron of four ships of the line and some frigates to patrol in the Pacific Ocean from Lima to Acapulco.

Undoubtedly, the spirit of independence will spread quickly from one end of South America to the other. The province of Caracas to the north and that of Chile to the south, which are more or less the two extremes of the Continent, generally pass for being the two regions whose inhabitants aspire with more ardour to emancipation.

As for Mexico and other northern provinces of South America, hitherto subject to Spain, it can be assured that the peoples that inhabit them are at least as mature for independence as those we have just designated. It will even be observed that the manifestation of their wishes in this regard has an older date, since in 1773, they made a request to the British government tending to obtain from it help to achieve this profitable goal, and if we have not proposed to start with Mexico the execution of the projected company, the main reason is that an operation of this type started first in that part, although accompanied by the tremendous success, would have the inconvenience of notifying the Spanish government to prepare for the South American side that, due to its situation and the nature of the localities it presents would provide more accessible means to deflect the blows that would be prepared for it or at least to delay the effects.

Therefore, it was convenient to leave Mexico for last. Establishing independence in that rich region will crown the vital work we propose to execute here. Its proximity to the United States of America and the ease with which the leading establishments can be taken along with Acapulco will ensure success infallibly.

I will finish with the sensible and philanthropic reflections of a well-known publicist directed to the European powers on the emancipation of the Spanish American Colonies that he foresaw in 1776. "*It would be a useful thing maybe, he said, to be prepared in advance to confront events that are to be expected*". *Sensible and happy is the nation that is also the first to subordinate its politics to the new circumstances and agrees to consider its colonies as allied provinces. Sensible and happy is the nation that is also the first to convince itself that all policy about trade consists of putting all its land to use in the manner most advantageous to its owners, all its arms in the most beneficial manner to each working individual, that is, in the manner in which everyone, guided by their own interests employs them as they believe is right; that everything else is but illusion and vanity.*

When the total separation of America has obliged everybody to acknowledge this truth and has eliminated the commercial jealousies of the European nations, there will be less cause for war among men, and it would be difficult not to wish an event that would procure this good for humanity, Mr. Turgot.

T. II, f. 112 Negotiations

10.3.9 Miranda's Advice to the Young O'Higgins: Advice from an Old South American to a Young Compatriot on His Return from England to His Country. Breviary for the Young Bernardo O'Higgins, London, March 1799

Context:

Bernardo O'Higgins (1778–1842), the Liberator of Chile and the First Supreme Director of the Republic of Chile, was Miranda's disciple and essential assistant in London before returning to his homeland in 1800. At that time, Bernardo only used his maternal surname, Riquelme, being the natural (and secret) son of the Vice-King of Peru, Ambrosio O'Higgins (1720–1801). Ambrosio had a love affair with a young Creole of only 17 years old when he was Governor of Concepcion, in charge of the Empire's southern borders. In the colonial regime, the King's top officers were prohibited from marrying Creoles, so Ambrosio did not recognise the son but took charge secretly of his education.

Miranda found him in London, where his father had secretly sent him to study, and he converted him to his cause, making O'Higgins his most faithful follower in the pursuit of Chile's benefit and the cause of American integration. The spies of the King of Spain discovered the young disciple actively supporting the conspirator. This information led to the King's decision to castigate his father, Ambrosio, by dismissing him from his office as Vice-King of Peru. However, the Vice-King died shortly before the messenger's arrival with the dismissal order. On the day of his death, Ambrosio called his notary and recognised his son, making him his heir. The fact that Miranda bet on the secret son of the enemy's power to make him one of the main Liberators does not seem to be a pure coincidence: the Hellenist Miranda saw an opportunity for a symbolic myth worthy of the Greek tragedies, and he was also not wrong. O'Higgins became his most faithful disciple, and he managed to stabilise Chile on constitutional principles directly inspired by Miranda (Ghymers, C., 2002).[76] The precursor understood that the same enlightened Ambrosio O'Higgins,

[76] On this position, see Ghymers, C. (2002), "Influencia del Maestro sobre el Discípulo: el papel de Miranda y O'Higgins en la singularidad del caso chileno y de su gobernabilidad", in *Revista del Instituto O'Higginiano de Chile*, n. 19, Santiago.

open to reforms and frustrated by the Spanish regime, by sending his unique son to be educated in the strategic centre of the enemy of the Spanish Empire, secretly acknowledged that the future lay in the British parliamentary democracy rather than in the absolutist colonial regime. It was as if a personal projection of the necessary reforms that the father had failed to carry out during his tenure as Vice-King was being made.

Content:

This affectionate yet insistent advice to a disciple reveals the importance the person of his young disciple held for him and the high hopes he placed in his destiny. The peculiar effort to perpetuate his influence on a disciple without fortune or name, only 20 years old, is striking. This reinforces our hypothesis of Miranda's plan to make the son of the enemy power a democratic Liberator, thus carrying out a symbolic Cornelian coup. It also highlights interesting aspects of Miranda's core values, including his pragmatic personality and open-mindedness, as well as the atmosphere of struggle and suspicion surrounding Miranda's cause within the Empire.

Sources:

Translated from Spanish

The original of this precious document has disappeared. Miranda ordered that his addressee destroy it at the end of his navigation back to Chile, given the importance of keeping his relationship with the natural son of the Vice-King secret. However, witnesses of the time said that O'Higgins disobeyed and kept it hidden for several years, always carrying it with him, sewn into the inner lining of his hat. A copy would have been found in the documents inherited from O'Higgins and discovered by the Chilean historian Vicuña Mackenna, who published it. Nevertheless, the original remains not found.

This text is taken from: Vicuña Mackenna, Benjamin: ***Obras completas de Vicuña Mackenna*** published by the Universidad de Chile. Volumen Quinto. Vida de O'Higgins. La Corona del Héroe. Santiago de chile: Talleres de la Dirección General de Prisiones. 1936. Capítulo III. p. 61–64.

América Espera. Document 85. p. 242–244.

Becerra. T. II. p. 472–474.

Chacón Rodríguez, David.: **Miranda y los consejos a O'Higgins**.- Caracas: Fundación Hermano Nectario María para la investigación histórico-geográfica de Venezuela.

Text:

My young friend:

My ardent interest in your happiness prompts me to offer you advice as you enter the vast world that has drawn me in its waves for many years. You are familiar with my life's history, and you can judge for yourself whether it's worth listening to or not.

By manifesting an unlimited trust in you, I have given you proof of the highest esteem in which I hold your honour and discretion. By making these reflections, it should be clear how much I value your good sense, as nothing is more insane and even more dangerous than advising a foolish person.

As you leave, do not forget for one instant that outside this country in the whole world, there is no other nation where you can talk about politics to anyone other than the proven heart of a friend, unless that nation is the United States.

Choose then a friend, but choose him with the most excellent care, for if you make a mistake, you are lost. I have often given you the names of several South American men whom you could trust if you were to cross paths with them, which is improbable, as you live in different regions.

Not having but very imperfect ideas about your country, I cannot give you my opinion on the education, knowledge and character of your fellow compatriots, but judging by the most significant distance from the Old World, I would believe them to be the most ignorant and the most preoccupied. You are the only Chilean I have met in my long connection with South America. Therefore, you know little more about the country than what its recently published history presents, which tends to portray it in a favourable light.

Based on the facts referred to in that history, I would expect much from your peasants, especially those of the South, where, if I am not mistaken, you will try to establish your residence. Their fights with their neighbours must make them capable of using arms, whereas the difficulty of being a free people must bring to their spirits the ideas of liberty and independence.

Going back to the point of future confidence, beware of any man older than 40 unless you are sure he is fond of reading, particularly those books forbidden by the Inquisition. In the others, the worries are too ingrained for there to be hope of change or a safe remedy.

Youth is the age of ardent and generous feelings. Among people of your age, you will easily find those who are ready to listen and are easy to convince. But on the other hand, youth is also the time for indiscretion and rash actions: you must beware of this defect in the young as much as shyness and worries in the old.

It is also an error to believe that every man, because he has a crown on his head or sits on a priest's chair, is an intolerant fanatic or a decided enemy of the rights of men. I know from experience that the most enlightened and liberal men of South America exist in that class. The difficulty lies in finding them. They know what the inquisition means, that their slightest words and facts are weighed in its scales, and that it more easily forgives the sins of irregular behaviour than those of liberal ideas.

The pride and fanaticism of the Spaniards are invincible; they will despise you for having been born in America, and they will hate you for having had an English education. Stay far away from them.

The Americans, inpatient and communicative, will avidly demand stories of your journeys and adventures. From the nature of their questions, you can make a rule to discover the character of the people who address you. Showing some indulgence to their profound ignorance, you must value their character, the degree of attention paid to you, and the greater or lesser intelligence they show in understanding you and accordingly grant them your trust. Never allow disgust or despair to take hold of your state of mind. You cannot serve your country if you give way to those feelings.

Conversely, strengthen your spirits with the conviction that once in your country, not a day will go by without there being events that will fill you with discouraging ideas about the dignity and judgment of men, the loss of spirits increasing with the apparent difficulty of putting a stop to those evils.

I have always tried to pass these principles on to you in our conversations, and I would like to remind you of them every day, every hour, and every moment.

You love your fatherland! Nurture that feeling constantly, fortify it by every possible means, because only through its duration and energy will you be able to do good.

The obstacles to serving your country are so numerous, formidable, and invincible that only the most ardent love for it will sustain your endeavours for its felicity.

You are familiar with my ideas about your country's probable destiny; even if you choose to ignore them, this is not the right place to discuss them.

Read this paper during your sea journey and destroy it immediately. Do not forget the inquisition, its spies, its robes and its tortures.

Francisco Miranda

10.3.10 Miranda's Letter to William Pitt, 19 March 1799

Context:

Since arriving in London in January 1798, Miranda has unsuccessfully made intensive diplomatic efforts with both the British and US governments to organise a joint operation in South America. However, neither of the two governments is convinced, and even England is not favourable to the operation that Miranda is promoting with the United States, because the British government fears that it would reinforce American interests to the detriment of those of England. This situation, typical of a "prisoner's dilemma", combined with the distrust of the British aristocrats towards the liberal Miranda, who was suspected of republicanism, blocked his plan in London. Disappointed, Miranda made what he considered his last attempt to cooperate with Pitt at this moment before abandoning the idea of involving the British government and deciding to forego England in favour of seeking exclusive backing from the US. In fact, to impede this option, Pitt denied him the passport he needed to travel until September 1800.

Despite this deception, Miranda will try - tirelessly but with ups and downs - again in February, March (when he announces to Gual that he is preparing with the most incredible secret ... an expedition to these places[77]" and also in June (he will

[77] "Very reserved" letter from Miranda to Manuel Gual dated March 4, 1800, *Archivo*...op. cit. Vol. XVI p.

even announce to Caro that he is about to leave for Trinidad at the end of June[78]) and December 1799, as well as in January and February 1800, again in April / May 1801, in June / August of the same year (he will also announce to Gual his arrival through Jamaica in November 1800 with 12,000 soldiers to attack Maracaibo and continue to Santa Fé de Bogota[79]), and in all the following years with a pathetic succession of sad disappointments and new hopes depending on the changing geopolitical events and also for avoiding to be used by imperialist interests. Finally, in 1805, he realized that the only remaining option was to launch a military expedition on his own, without external governments, but with the hope that British interests would react positively when the movement became a reality.

Content:

The most eloquent and diplomatic synthesis of Miranda's successive steps and efforts to achieve the emancipation of his homeland, with interesting arguments to convince, once more, the British government that it is overall in their own strategic interest to implement his emancipation plan before Napoleon invaded the Peninsula (his obsessional prediction since 1798) to seize the Spanish and Portuguese colonies for dominating the world. He also mentions his agent (a "young Peruvian", Bernardo O'Higgins, given that Chile depended on the viceroyalty of Peru), whom he sent. He is about to leave for America to implement his plan on the Pacific coast.

Sources:

Translated from French
Archivo del General Miranda. Vol. XV. p. 344–352.
América Espera. Document 86. p. 244–249.
Colombeia. Document 3984. p. 117–127.

Text:

Great Pulteney Street
19 March 1799

The undersigned has the honour of reminding the very honourable William Pitt of the vital matter of the Spanish-American Colonies that he submitted for his decision on January 16, 1798,[80] and of which the very honourable Minister (after examining the proposals and an in-depth exchange of views on this matter) was kind enough to undertake to promise to give a frank and prompt reply.[81]

From that time, the undersigned has never ceased to give this negotiation the impetus he mentions in his instructions, as per the agreement of January 16th, and has done his best to keep Mr. Pitt well informed about any fact or procedure undertaken. Since then, he has requested several appointments to communicate to the Minister the fundamental news he has received from the Spanish American

[78] Letter from Miranda to Caro dated June 3, 1799, *Archivo…* op. cit. Vol. XV p. 412–423.

[79] Letter from Gual to Abad, reproduced by Meza Dorta G. in *Miranda and Bolivar….* op. cit. p. 34–35.

[80] *Colombeia*. Vol. XVIII. Document 3970. London, January 16, 1798. p. 87–89.

[81] Miranda's Note in Original: The undersigned, having gone to Mr. Pitt's house in Hollwood, negotiations for the Independence of the Spanish-American Colonies began with this Minister in February 1790.

Commissioners in Madrid, Lisbon, Paris, and other locations. However, I am sorry to say that he has not received a single answer. Nonetheless, the feelings expressed by the ministers of H.B.M. in both Houses of Parliament concerning Switzerland, saying that: "*being this nation the only one, besides England, that has dared to oppose the destructive principles of France, they deserved their admiration and support. And that the same case could happen about other countries in close connection to England*" gave the undersigned some hope, as the principle goal of the Colonies was to oppose these same principles, forming a stable government on radically opposite foundations to the French system; and that the help demanded could not be at the cost of England, since it only was six warships and some artillery troops, the cost of which would have been amply paid for.

All these transactions have been transmitted regularly to the Spanish American continent by the commissioners of the same country. At the same time, they extolled the provinces to wait patiently for the appropriate moment for this declaration rather than expose themselves to the fatal effects of the partial movements of Santa Fe de Bogotá in 1781, of Chile and Caracas, etc. We recommended them especially to observe the strictest vigilance so that under no excuse no agent of the French revolutionary system entered the Spanish American country, as there were reasons to believe that the foreign help needed to start the enterprise could be found quickly and swiftly from England and the United States of America if - as we thought - these could break links with France, which would also mean war with Spain, given the existing alliance treaties between the two powers.

Even though the undersigned has not received a direct response from the American Government on this matter, he had reason to believe, from information that was mainly directed to him, that the project would also be well received in the United States and that the Declaration of war against France would be the signal to proclaim the Independence of the Spanish-American Colonies. He believed that he had to send this critical information to the colonies through a respectable person who was considered in the country and aware of the political movements of Europe.

Pedro Caro, one of the American Commissioners, left for the Continent on the 20th of November, 1798. The undersigned has learned of his happy arrival through a letter dated January 11,[82] written by himself. It is thought that at this time, he will have seen the primary agents of a part of the Colonies who, having sent the information to the other Provinces, will have put them in a position to know the status of the negotiations at the time of Mr. Caro's departure, to act together and in agreement in any event.[83]

Such was the state of affairs when Mr. Turnbull showed to the undersigned a letter written by the Under-Secretary of State, Mr. Hammond, in response to another that the former had written to him (without the undersigned having the slightest knowledge of this) dated February 18 last, requesting Mr. Hammond's opinion on

[82] *Colombeia*. Vol. XVIII. Documents 4086, p. 277. and 4089, p. 281–283.

[83] Miranda's note in the original: Don Pedro Caro, one of the American Commissioners, left for the Continent of South America (via Trinidad) in November 1798.

the probability of any return whatsoever to continue to provide the undersigned with the assistance necessary to meet the expenses inherent in this negotiation, having already extended its delay for more than 1 year. Mr. Hammond peremptorily indicates to Mr. Turnbull that, having submitted his letter to Milord Grenville, he was charged with telling him that he could not give him the slightest hope of such support.

This letter certainly does not provide a direct response to the undersigned. Still, it is the only one that he has been able to obtain for more than a year, which implies the total rejection of all support or cooperation on the part of this country for the Independence of the Spanish-American Colonies, which would be a manifest contradiction of everything that has happened between the Prime Minister and the undersigned; that the critical situation in which these Colonies find themselves at present requires that they really know what to expect, to make a quick and decisive determination about their interests, not having a moment to lose, the undersigned would believe that he was essentially failing in his duty if He should not make this genuine and sincere action, to prevent the unpleasant consequences that a misunderstanding on his part, or an unfounded hope on the part of his compatriots, can bring about on the Colonies.

The very honourable William Pitt knows very well that for a long time the undersigned has not had as his goal but to serve his country, being commissioned in 1782 to petition England for the Independence of the Spanish-American Colonies, that the conduct of Spain made it legitimate and reciprocal in all respects, declaring war on England for the independence of its own, which today form the United States of America[84]; that it was in February 1790 when he had the honour of making his proposals to Mr. Pitt and that after a deep exchange of opinions it was stipulated that he [Miranda] would submit the entire project in writing, with the political and commercial data of the country that they should accompany him, under the solemn promise that this project would be undertaken without fail by England, in the event of war with Spain and solely for its absolute independence as had been obtained by the United States of America, which was promptly executed and delivered to Mr. Pitt by the undersigned[85] on March 5, 1790.

[84] Miranda's note in the original: His country has commissioned the undersigned since 1782 to request support from England for its absolute independence.

[85] Miranda's note in the original: Proposals were made to Mr. Pitt at his country house at Hollwood in February 1790, and the result was a formal stipulation by which England is bound (in the event of any war with Spain) to help the "Colonised" to obtain their absolute independence. They promised in return to England an advantageous trade agreement, without monopoly or exclusion of other nations. For this purpose, the undersigned was required to deliver to the Minister the reports, plans, and military and commercial data that had been agreed upon, which took place on March 5, 1790.

From that time, the undersigned continued the same communications with the very honourable Minister until the Nootka Sound Agreement[86] with Spain, which put an indefinite term to the previous stipulations by England.[87]

However, being informed shortly after, the French Government was busy offering support to the Spanish colonies to incite them to Independence under its protection; the undersigned went to Paris in 1792. There, he found that the Project was indeed about to be launched. He reached out to convince the government to postpone this plan by promising to run the expedition himself at a more favourable time, the only reason that led to his entry into the service of France. In November 1792, the French government appointed him Commander General of the Islands in America to execute this project. But he did everything possible again to defer it to another time, believing the moment unfavourable and fearing that the anarchic principles that were already fermenting were not a sinister omen for the operation, which probably then saved the Colonies from the fatal influence of this system and safeguarded so the New World perhaps from a total disaster.[88]

The monstrous Alliance that had ensued between Spain and France since then, in 1797, together with the declaration of war between the former and England, immediately suggested the idea of resuming the negotiations of 1790 regarding the Spanish American colonies. He wrote to the Minister in this respect through M. Turnbull, having left France shortly after that in January 1798.[89]

Upon his arrival in Dover, he was honoured to receive a kind invitation from Mr. Pitt to come to see him in London as soon as he arrived.[90] On January 16, 1798, he had the satisfaction of being received for a very long interview at Hollwood, in which the Minister's first word was to repeat the initial promise made in 1790: "Now we are at war with Spain, which puts us in a situation of acting *better than*

[86] Miranda's note in the original: Nootka Bay on Vancouver Island is located in the Pacific Ocean, on the northwestern coast of North America, and was recognised by Cook in 1778. The English tried to colonise it, causing a conflict between Spain and England that was resolved peacefully in 1790. This agreement between the two countries broke Miranda's plans.

[87] Miranda's note in the original: The Nootka Sound Convention with Spain, having put an indefinite term to the previous stipulation and the undersigned having also learned that the French Government was also dealing with this (the freedom of the peoples), went to Paris in March 1792 and managed to postpone this project.

[88] Miranda's note in the original: As a result of the previous agreement, he entered the service of France and was appointed, in November 1792, Governor General of Santo Domingo for the execution of this project; but the Robespierre system having occurred, it caused the undertaking to be deferred to more favourable times.

[89] Miranda's note in the original: The treaty of alliance that took place after the peace between Spain and France and that condemned (by articles 2 and 15) the Spanish-American Colonies to perpetual slavery, suggested to him the idea of resuming negotiations of Hollwood in 1790 and left France permanently to return to England in 1798.

[90] Miranda's note in the original: Upon his arrival in Dover, he writes to Mr. Turnbull, who sent his letter to Mr. Pitt, and he immediately receives ministerial permission and safe conduct to come to London with his companions, etc.

before ". The undersigned presented his new instructions[91] drawn up in Paris by Commissioners who had come from the Spanish Colonies and which summarised the same propositions made earlier in 1790 at Hollwood, also confirmed, in his absence, by other American agents who had come to London for the same subject - while the undersigned was in France - such as the Marquis of Casa Montalvo,[92] of Havana, Mr. J. Palacio y Ortiz,[93] of Santa Fe, Mr. Pedro Caro[94] of Mexico, and others.[95]

In the same interview, the entire plan and project were discussed again, as well as the projected form of government, which the Minister found very promising. And everything was concluded with the assurance on the part of him that he *saw no obstacle for the moment, but that in a matter of such great importance, it was then impossible for him to say more about it; that in a very short time, he would give an answer and that the frankness that the undersigned had shown in his management was always the safest as well as the fastest means of reaching the goal happily,* etc.

Having patiently waited for a response for 2 months, the undersigned believed it indispensable to make the same proposals to the Government of the United States of America, according to what was prescribed in his Instructions and with so much more confidence that the Minister, in the preceding interview, had openly declared to him that *it would be with the most excellent satisfaction that England would act with the United States of America in a similar undertaking*, it being well understood that the undersigned would not communicate to the Americans until after having received the Minister's reply, or in any case to prevent it in advance, which the undersigned did on March 20, 1798.[96]

It appears that the reports previously communicated by the undersigned to the American continent have arrived to calm the spirits, as the different movements have already manifested themselves in the provinces of Caracas and Mexico. They have calmed down since then, and everything announces at present the best dispositions for a spontaneous and general movement as soon as the promised aid reaches the determined points.

What will be the impact of making known after the long wait and committed support from England that this country says today that not the lightest assistance

---

[91] Act of Paris of December 22, 1797.
In: *Colombeia*. Vol. XVIII. Document 3958. p. 54–63.

[92] Miranda regularly visited the Count of Casa Montalvo in Havana. He was precisely on his estate, "Ojo de Agua. He was precisely on his estate called "Ojo de Agua" when he was accused of having shown General Campbell, in 1781, the fortification of the Prince's Castle. (Colombia, Volume II).

[93] **Ortiz** was the secret nickname for Antonio Nariño, see note n° 46 in Chap. 5, document 5.2.3.

[94] Pedro Caro was from Cuba.

[95] Miranda's note in the original: He is invited by Mr. Pitt immediately after his arrival to come and see him, and having presented his Instructions to resume and proceed with the Hollwood negotiations of 1790, the same guarantees previously offered with promise are repeated of a prompt reply.

[96] Miranda's note in the original: Not having received a response by March 20, he notified the Minister that he had made the same proposals to the American Government following his instructions.

could be warranted, while the American agents in London had been receiving English commitments for 14 months?

It is difficult to foresee the effect that desperation could trigger in such a case. Still, it is clear that educated people who were proud to see a system of order and morality implemented throughout the entire American continent to counter the disorganising principles spread by France will lose any hope and will be diminished in American public opinion. It is also clear that the future interests and security of the United States of America will be deeply compromised, and that the trade and strategic advantages provided to Great Britain by this vast continent will become actual losses. On the other side, considering what the perverse instinct of the French Directory could undertake for meeting its purposes of general invasion and for extending its perfidious vengeance to the United States of America as well as to Great Britain thanks to the immense revolutionary power it, unfortunately, enjoys at this moment, one will be naturally frightened for the sake of humankind[97]! He warns the Minister about the imminent danger for these colonies, making him personally responsible for the unfortunate consequences of any delay.

The most recent news from France indicates that the deployment of French troops to Portugal and the revolutionary operations in Spain have been suspended, pending the implementation of measures to secure support from the Spanish and Portuguese colonies. For this purpose, several Spanish residents in Paris had entirely submitted to the Directory and were about to be sent to Spanish America to condition the People's minds. With flattering promises and perfidious insinuations, they expected to attract them to the French interest when the invasion occurred.

This information may be accurate or not, but it seems evident that in the unfortunate case of the New World, France would undertake this plan, while England would be rejected unexpectedly and humiliatingly. It would be highly probable that France would attempt to seduce these simple people (furthermore, those who had been excessively badly treated for three centuries) first by making false promises about freedom and happiness to dominate them and those of the United States in the same way it had already done with the most excellent part of the Old World.

The undersigned does not want to reflect on this issue and the magnitude of its consequences. The very Honourable Ministry has more than anybody else the ability to do it. Nevertheless, it is fair to discard any doubt about such a significant issue, with each one taking their own responsibility. The undersigned will be obliged to communicate without any delay the answer to this memory that Mr. Pitt wishes to give – whatever in a written way, verbally or tacitly – to the American commissaries who will diffuse it to the different provinces of Spanish America. A copy of it will also be given to the President of the United States of America to inform him of the current state of the negotiations, as he was initially informed of their starting point, and to prevent being accused of omission or misinformation in his opinions.

[97] Miranda's note in the original: He pointed out to the Minister the imminent danger in which these colonies find themselves, making him fall all the responsibility for the dire consequences that may result from the delay.

A young Peruvian currently resident in London would be glad to carry over the decision England would make about this critical issue, in case this resolution would be favourable or meaningful for his compatriots.

In any case, the undersigned takes this opportunity to bear witness to the most honourable Minister the pure sentiments of his deep appreciation for the favourable reception and the honourable protection that he has seen fit to grant him upon his arrival in England, the memory of which will always remain engraved on his heart.

The undersigned has the honour of being, with the most profound respect and highest consideration, the very honourable Minister, the very humble and very obedient servant.

T. I, f. 181. Negociaciones

10.3.11 Miranda's Letter to Manuel Gual[98]: London, 31 December 1799

Context:

In July 1797, a republican conspiracy led by Manuel Gual and José María España failed in Caracas. Manuel Gual was a liberal Republican in contact with Miranda, who was indirectly linked to this conspiracy, as demonstrated by G. Meza Dorta (2012).[99] Indeed, Miranda was in close contact not only with Gual but also with his accomplices in Caracas in the attempt of 1797, Cortés, Sorondo and Zinsa. Miranda's interventions to the British Minister of Foreign Affairs, H. Dundas, in 1797 warranted British support from Trinidad Island to Gual. After the failure of the Caracas uprising in July 1799, Manuel Gual, who escaped to the island of Trinidad, occupied by the English since 1797, made contact with Miranda through a letter (accompanied by documents), which would not reach Miranda until December. Immediately, Miranda answered him, given that Trinidad was one of the possible places he considered for setting up a liberating expedition, especially if it had finally received British military support. In later letters (not reproduced here), Miranda will specify his plan via Trinidad to the extent that he would receive this pending support.

Content:

This letter shows that Miranda wants to keep in contact with the author of the conspiracy in Caracas. The insistence to preserve the Homeland from French Jacobinism, to imitate the US Revolution and to impede the domination of any third power on Hispanic America are clearly expressed. The intangible persistence of the values and the fidelity to the principles defended by Miranda from the beginning are observed despite the recurring disappointments he faces.

[98] **Manuel Gual** (1759–1800), Venezuelan pro-Independence activist, co-author of the first attempt of a republican revolution in Caracas in 1797, Miranda's remote collaborator, was assassinated envenomed by agents from the Spanish regime on Trinidad island on 25 de October 1800.

[99] Meza Dorta, Giovanni, *Miranda y Bolivar: dos visiones*, bid & co. Editor, Caracas, 2012, p.30–36.

It is also observed that Miranda still did not understand at the end of 1799 that his envoy José Caro was a traitor, which is why the English governor of Trinidad (T. Picton) threw him off the island, and not because Picton would be against Miranda, as he wrongly believed at the time.

Sources:

Translated from Spanish

Archivo del General Miranda. T. XV. p. 404.

América Espera. Document 89. p. 253.

Colombeia. Tomo XIX. Fourth section. Negotiation, 1799-1801. Document 4327. 2006. p. 222–224

Text:

to Gual

London, December 31st, 1799

…

…..About the Governor of Trinidad, I must warn you that I have believed him a friendly man and favourable to our independence, but recently, I have revised my judgement; therefore, it would be convenient for you to conduct yourself with caution and reserve with him. If he ever wanted to upset you or mistreat you (as he did with our commissioner Don P. Caro), try to go to the United States of America and present yourself there in my name to General Hamilton, who is the second Commander General of the American Army, and will certainly give you an honourable reception. You can also open up entirely to him because he is perhaps the most faithful friend that our Freedom and independence have in the whole world. However, nothing should be precipitated at this critical moment, and please wait until you receive my later news.

The English government's promise to help us promptly gives us such hope that it would be foolhardy not to wait a little, but it has also been such a long time, entertaining us with its beautiful promises, that I have almost lost my confidence. I expect more from the United States of America (because they are very interested in our Independence) and above all from ourselves than from any other! This results from the incalculable damage the Gallican Anarchy has done to Liberty worldwide!

For the first time, I will send you a magnificent map of South America, which we have engraved here for our use. It was worked by Cruz in Madrid in 1775 and immediately collected by the government so that the world would ignore the beauty of nature in that hemisphere. A geographical-historical Dictionary of our America was also published in Madrid by one of our compatriots (Don Antonio de Alcedo) in five volumes in quarto, a handy and rare work for the same reason. I will send you a second copy if I can find one.

As for me, my friend, I'm always invariable at the service of the Fatherland. For this, I have already made numerous sacrifices that would make leaving the company seem absurd now. Any position that is pointed out to me will be very acceptable and honourable for me, provided that everyone marches toward the same and only goal of our Freedom and independence, without the domination of any foreign Power trying to fix or mix its authority in the Country, because in that case we will be the greed and very soon the spoil of all the others that having any maritime force will also want to have part in the Division. Dii avertant! In short, my friend, the true glory of all Americans consists in the achievement of society and vice versa ... Two great examples we have before our eyes are the American Revolution and the French. Let's quietly imitate the first; let us carefully avoid the fatal effects of the second!

M-a

T. II, f. 218 vto. Negotiations.

10.3.12 Miranda's Letter to Napoleon Bonaparte, First Consul of France, 29 January 1800

Context:

Napoleon, strengthened by his military victories in Italy and the Egyptian campaign, intervened in internal politics with the aim of seizing power. Already before his campaigns, in 1795, he had demonstrated his ability to engage with the Army against the royalists (Vendémiaire riots). From Italy, he had managed, in conspiracy with the Directory, a first self-coup for preventing his Jacobins' friends, members of the Directory, from losing power after the unfavourable elections of 1797 (self-coup of 18 Fructidor year five). In November 1799, he organised again a coup with the direct complicity of the Directory (1795–1799) on the 18 Brumaire of the year VIII (November 9). This third military intervention enabled him to close the Directory regime and its constitution, thereby creating the Consulate (1799–1804). The purpose was to respond to popular demand for ending the revolution, but to emerge as the providential leader, and for his own benefit. His purpose was to become rich, as he had already entrusted Miranda and others when the future emperor was a poor conspirator in Paris. He planned to stabilise France in order to generate the means to conquer Europe and end the British parliamentary regime, as well as its economic superiority and military and geopolitical dominance. To this end, his objective was to establish a dictatorial regime, legalised using a new constitution (called the Constitution of the Year VIII), tailor-made for him by his accomplice, the Jacobin Sieyés. He wants to centralise all the powers in his hands fast and perpetuate it for at least 10 years. This new constitution was elaborated by a commission under his control in a few weeks and implemented as of December 26, 1799. His new power as First Consul began on January 1, 1800. Napoleon immediately used his power to destroy the political factions and the divisions, seeking primarily to control the threat of the Jacobins (he strengthened the political police of Fouché, ordered the closure of 60 newspapers and sent into exile many opponents) and temporarily restored peace with foreign powers while authorising the previously exiled to return.

Miranda, who knows the character and the risks of Caesarism, perceives him from the first moment as a genuine threat to Europe, as well as to his homeland and its democratic emancipation. He has been convinced and warned for several years that the dictator will inevitably be tempted, in his expansionist and proselytising zeal, to seize the Spanish colonies for economic and geopolitical reasons, despite the Treaty of Alliance between France and Spain of 1796.[100] However, given that England refuses to support Miranda's plan and does not let him leave England so as not to push Spain into the hands of France - the most dangerous enemy of the UK - he envisions that Napoleon could represent a possible option, first to increase his pressures upon Pitt to demonstrate him the reality of the risks for Britain if his government continues to refuse the win-win game of his plan, and, second, as the ultimate way to escape from the status quo imposed upon him by the short-termism views of London. At this moment, he feels paralysed when fearing that the Jacobins' risk to his emancipation plan would be higher if he stayed silent in London, as the government's procrastination would incite Napoleon to act by surprise in the colonies. This is why he considers now that if he had been part of Napoleon's strategy, he would have had more chances to counteract the virus of the French system from inside than being trapped in London. Therefore, he tries to interest the First Consul in his plans, which would open an opportunity for him to act directly on the ground with a military opportunist who is a risk-taker and possesses all the powers. Miranda sent two letters to the First Consul, one in January through the intermediary of his disciple Vargas,[101] who could travel from London to Paris, and one in July 1800.

Content:

Diplomatic manoeuvre by Miranda to try to re-establish his relations with France through the First Consul Napoleon Bonaparte, who concentrates all the powers. He assesses that he could at least give him a chance to regain his rights (among others, his salaries as general of the revolution that had not been paid as a result of the Robespierre coup and the accusations he was a victim under the Directory) and his credibility (he had been unjustly banned under the allegation of involvement in the bomb attack in Saint Nicaise street against Napoleon). His purpose was also to show his differences with the UK government, not to be assimilated into British power. The arguments are well-balanced and clearly express his major preoccupation with freedom, which Napoleon's power directly threatens.

Sources:

Translated from French
Archivo del General Miranda...op. cit. Vol. XVI p. 58–60
América Espera, op. cit. p. 254–255

[100] The **Treaty of San Ildefonso II** (1796), negotiated by the Directory, is a military alliance between Spain and France against their common enemy, England, which followed the restoration of peace between revolutionary France and the Spanish absolutist regime after 2 years of war (1793–95). It was like a return to the old Bourbon's "family Pact". France needed Spanish support against the first coalition promoted by England, while Spain was the target of the British military fleet in the American colonies. Napoleon complemented the Treaty in 1800 (San Ildefonso III) with secret clauses to attack England using Spain's American resources.

[101] **Pedro Firmin de Vargas** (1762–1811?), Colombian independentist and economist linked to Antonio Nariño. He went to London to meet Miranda and worked with him for a while. He then travelled to Trinidad, where he conflicted with Governor Picton. He returned to London in 1803. Miranda broke the relationship when Vargas tried to convince William Pitt to adopt an alternative plan for Mexico rather than the one Miranda had prepared for Venezuela.

Text:

Near London, the 10th Pluviose,
8th year of the French Republic,
(29 January 1800)
Citizen Consul,

Allow one of the oldest Republic and French Citizen soldiers to claim his rights before you, openly violated on 19 Fructidor, year 5.

That attack was all the more treacherous for me since my name does not appear, and they do not even mention me in the records that served as evidence for the Conspiracy, true or not, that the Triumvirs used as a cause for such a strange measure.

The fact that the alleged leaders of the plot are entirely unknown or personal enemies makes the accusation even more absurd.

Invited by the French Government to defend the noble cause of Liberty in extremely critical circumstances (in August 1792), I enlisted under honourable conditions and was formally hired, certified by the Minister of War himself.

The strict investigation that they demanded regarding my conduct, as a consequence of the disastrous events originated by the defection of Dumouriez, made it clear to the entire Nation that I had faithfully fulfilled this commitment and that France owed to whom had the honour of defending it gloriously at the head of its armies.

The tyranny and arbitrary system that more or less weighed on France from the time of the famous "Comité de Salut Public" to the last Directory followed, of course, the reverse path and instead of granting me what was justice, they continued to accumulate one persecution after another, until placing my name on all the ban lists, starting with the Girondins to those of Danton and Pichegru, in addition to depriving me of my luggage and horses, denying me the payment of the salaries that were owed in their almost totality since the beginning of the war.

My library, which could have been saved by chance, was inevitably also ransomed, obliging me to resort to compulsory borrowing.

Today, when the august empire of Justice and moderation is finally proclaimed loudly, under happy auguries, I hope to obtain through your supreme authority what many others, under similar conditions, have already justly received and that my formal caveat with France is finally fulfilled.

The love of Freedom for which I made so many sacrifices, I made in other parts induced me to refuse to live in my native country, perhaps the most oppressed of all those on Earth, and it determined my intimate connection with France.

For the same reason, before the French Revolution, I sought refuge in England, and this ancient connection was the cause of granting me asylum, as the French rulers violently excluded me from their country on Fructidor of the 5th year. However, for about a year, I have been anxiously requesting permission to leave this country with the intention of moving to the United States of America, which I have not been able to achieve!!! ... This means, Citizen Consul, that this letter is not addressed to you from a neutral country.

Hopefully! May the gifts of freedom be extended to all of our fellow men who yearn for it, and may France enjoy, after so many sacrifices, a lasting and glorious peace based on the priceless good that constitutes a judicious and perfect Freedom; these are and always will be my sincere wishes.

Health and respect.

M — a.

Allsops buildings

10.3.13 Miranda's Letter to William Pitt, London, 11 February 1800

Context:

Miranda despairs about the lack of reaction from the British government despite a more favourable international context for the UK government (France stabilises) while the threat of a Napoleon operation to seize the wealth of the American colonies is rising.

Content:

Miranda subtly argues to Pitt that the significance of his plan is so clear and straightforward that the Prime Minister could not fail to make a decision very quickly. Therefore, Miranda claims to be received, acknowledging that other patriots, besides himself, could be received as an alternative, clarifying that the goal supersedes his person.

The letter includes an Annex, which is a brief memorandum outlining the logic that compels the UK to act, positioning France and the UK as competitors for securing an arrangement with the US to capture the trade income from South America. Due to France's actions, he demonstrates that the UK has no other rational choice but to support the revolution in South America to prevent France from gaining power.

Sources:

Original in English, but translated from the Spanish version in Salcedo-Bastardo **Archivo**... op.cit. Vol. XVI p. 51_53

América Espera...op.cit. Document 91, p. 255–256.

Text:

11 February 1800

Sir:

I realise that I have bothered you a lot regarding the affairs of South America. However, I hope I will not be charged with being importunate; the question's significance will justify me against such a charge.

The subject is now so reduced conceptually and so clear and perceptible in execution that the papers I have to offer you will not take more than half an hour of your time to make you fully aware of the matter on which you must decide.

Therefore, allow me to reiterate my request for the hearing that you were kind enough to promise me, and I kindly request that you designate a day for me.

If there were other people, and I am not unaware that there are, who understand and can better explain this matter and who are more confident in communicating it than I am, after 9 years of conversations on this subject, I would not feel the slightest regret or disgust[102] for the precautions I have taken, having been able to withdraw from it safely to my honour from the beginning of this business and also now.

I cannot conclude without adding that I trust you will be pleased to have seen me, my Lord.

Any appointment that you would do me the honour of granting me, you will find me in Knightsbridge.

Brief summary P.M. (to Mr. Pitt, February 11, 1800).

Without providing a general explanation, much less a detailed one, of the civil or military plan regarding this matter, this summary only presents the current critical situation, based on my information. To express the current circumstances with which you are connected in the present and the consequences that make it absolutely necessary to take a decision.

The present object of consideration is no less critical than if Great Britain and France had the alliance of the Hispanic peoples of South America to dominate their sources of income and possess their commerce.

If Great Britain or France could, through these means, include the United States in their alliance due to a shared interest.

The people of South America, both individually and in their civil communities, are and have been for some years ready to obtain independence:

Insurrections:

Caracas 1750–1797 Gual

Quito 1764

Mexico 1773

Peru 1781

And the revolt of Santa Fe, 1781–1796

Therefore, that power in Europe that has the fortune to give permanent naval assistance and protection to this operation will own the sources of income and commerce and maintain dominance in any great Atlantic maritime system that emerges or is formed in the future.

(a) What the French are doing.
(b) What the United States is willing to do.
(c) That Britain is reduced to the dilemma of acting while the matter is currently advanced. Whether it will act by its own power or decision, or if it will submit to what an imperative need forces it to decide. Lack of resolution.. . their effects. Negligence. its consequences.

[102] Miranda's note: Willing to give them the place; but I must in justice to myself beg that this be told to me, as I am.

10.3.14 Miranda's Letter to William Pitt, Gravesend, 21 April 1801

Context:

Miranda was expelled from France by Fouché at Napoleon's instruction. He was accused of being a foreign agent conspiring against Spain, an ally of France since 1796 (see Treaty of San Ildefonso II, Chap. 10, document 10.3.12, note n° 103). He left France on March 22 to Anvers first, then to Holland to sail to England, where he arrived on April 21, 1801. He was not even informed that Pitt's government had fallen on March 14 (after 17 years in power). He wrote to his friend Turnbull to request assistance and keep the secret about his return to England. He was worried about possible official reactions, using a false name, and asked him to give a letter to Pitt to explain his return. On April 23, Charles William Flint of the British Foreign Office requested that Undersecretary Hammond consider allowing Francisco Miranda, who was in France, to return to London. Turnbull persuades the new Prime Minister, Henry Addington, to authorise and introduce him to his new cabinet. Miranda was, in fact, welcomed quite well until the negotiations with Napoleon led to the Peace of Amiens in 1802, which meant once again the end of British support for Miranda.

Content:

Miranda requests authorization "without delay" to travel via London to his homeland or the USA under the alias Martin, in order to take measures against the Napoleonic invasion plan of Spanish America and prevent it from leading to a governance disaster similar to what happened in Santo Domingo.

Sources:

Translated from the French

Archivo...

América espera ...op. cit. Document 99, p. 284–285.

Text:

(extracts)

Gravesend, 21 April 1801

To the Right Honourable William Pitt,

Sir,

The imminent dangers that threaten the Spanish-American continent today, as well as the already operational expeditions in the ports of the French Republic, which are preparing to invade it, motivate my arrival in this country and are the reason that obliges me to request authorisation to stay (incognito) for a short time in England, to embark on board a neutral ship bound for the Coast of my homeland ("Terrafirme") or bound for the United States of America...

Unfortunately, if the current French government were to interfere in the matter, it would cause the country to be in absolute disarray, and if correct, prompt, and firm measures were not taken in advance, it would throw the country into disasters similar to those of Santo Domingo.

10.3.15 Miranda's Letter to Senator Lanjuinais,[103] Hamburg, 8 June 1801

Context:

Miranda turns to his friend and faithful supporter in France, Jean-Denis Lanjuinais, who has helped him enter France and, especially, leave despite the persecutions of Fouché and Napoleon. He wants to thank him and explain that he has left France again but, suspecting censorship and to prevent creating problems for his friend by sending him a letter from an enemy country, he does not indicate that he is back in England, but rather, for misleading the Fouché's spies, he suggests in his letter that he is in Sweden, a neutral country. He puts Hamburg as the city of dispatch of this letter.

Content:

Clear adherence to his concepts of freedom and justice as opposed to the Jacobins' doctrine. He wants to appear ready to fight against the Jacobins again to defend freedom and eradicate the guillotine and proscriptions.

Sources:

Translated from French

Archivo... op. cit. Vol. XVI p. 243–244

America espera, op. cit. Document n°102, p. 292–293

Text:

(extracts)

Hamburg, 8 June 1801

A Lanjuinais,

... you can be very sure that my love for Freedom and my unfailing dedication to Justice, far from diminishing, have only intensified since then ...

When I speak of Freedom, I am not referring to the one that Robespierre, Sieyes, and Fouché wanted to establish but rather to the one that Montesquieu and Locke clearly defined. When I speak of Justice, I am not referring to what Danton and Merlin have been teaching us in France but to what Malesherbes, you, and L'Hospital have generously sacrificed.

If the fight between Liberty and his opponents continues for a longer time, they might see me actively participate and appear for the second time on the side of the Saar brandishing arms (although this does not seem likely to me). But then, undoubtedly, you could conclude that healthy Liberty had a Party that worshipped it, defending it without Bastille, Guillotine, looting, and proscriptions....

---

[103] **Jean Denis Lanjuinais** (1753–1827), lawyer, Girondin senator elected to the Convention in 1792, republican but one of the fiercest opponents of Jacobins. Robespierre arrested him but escaped and was hidden in Bretagne, reincorporated to the Convention in March 1795. He was a moderate politician who opposed tyranny, although he supported the Directory and the Constitution of year V (1795).

10.3.16 Memorandum to See How the Fruitless Negotiations Established with England Can Be Repaired: London, 29 April 1803

Context:

Miranda arrived again in London from Paris in April 1801, where he undertook encouraging negotiations with the new Addington government and Minister Vansittart, who supported him and requested his government plan. In two days, Miranda writes for Vansittart his third draft of the federal constitution, as well as a Proclamation and a military regulation. After several secret meetings with Vansittart and Evan Nepean,[104] the Minister of the Navy, they devised a plan of military operations in May 1801, which consisted of concentrating military forces in Curacao and landing in Coro to liberate Venezuela and then, proceeding towards the other viceroyalties. He sends a letter to Gual so that he can be ready with the patriots from the Antilles.

However, in June, everything came to a standstill again; Miranda insisted on sailing, even without British support, with the idea that he could provoke the initial uprising, allowing the British government to justify intervening in support of an endogenous emancipatory movement already underway. At the end of June, he was informed that the government had decided to relaunch the peace negotiations with France, which implied refraining from action against Spain, which had been allied with France against England since 1796. At Miranda's insistence, the talks on his plan resumed in secret in July. Still, the government imposes that the head of the expedition is a British military man and not Miranda. He categorically refuses to allow a foreign military man to be given authority over Latin America. This would undermine the movement's credibility, as its purpose was to implement an emancipatory democratic regime, not establish a new British colony. In fact, the British lobby favouring intervention in South America was already considering its own project for taking over the Rio de la Plata for commercial reasons before any other argument. This lobby was already composed of Dundas[105] (Lord Melville) and Home Popham.[106] It was not necessarily opposed to Miranda, assuming that the importance of his objectives would allow for a compromise.

---

[104] **Evan Nepean** (1752–1822), was a military officer in the Royal Navy who entered politics as Vice Minister of the Interior until 1791, became Vice Minister of War (until 1794), and was appointed Minister of the Navy until 1804.

[105] **Henri Dundas** (1742–1811) Ministry of War until March 1801, and First Lord of Admiralty from 1804 to 1805.

[106] **Home Popham** (1762–1820), a senior officer in the British Royal Navy, Commodore since 1803, Member of Parliament since 1804, linked to Lord Melville (Dundas) and William Pitt, made Contra-Admiral in 1814 after their battles against Napoleon with Wellington in Spain. In 1803, in contact with London merchants, he designed the first plan for the government. In 1804, he received a mandate from the Pitt government to study and prepare for the military operation proposed by Miranda. However, instead of supporting Miranda, he betrayed him (see detail in Chap. 11, section 11.2) and used Miranda's information to conceive an alternative colonial operation, convincing the

In September 1801, the new government, led by Addington, did not want to expose its negotiations to any risk of association with Miranda. A pre-agreement between the British government and France had already been reached in London on October 1. The negotiations started in December, and the "Treaty of Amiens" was formally concluded on March 1802 between Great Britain (also representing the Ottoman Empire) on one side and France, Spain and Holland on the other.

Consequently, Miranda resigned to continue negotiating, betting on the expansionist Caesarean ambitions of the First Consul and expecting war to break out between France and the US (the quasi-war of the Directory's time continued), which should push Spain to accompany France. In this case, England would be forced to resume the expedition plan to Spanish America. His hopes rested on his anticipation of the inevitable Napoleonic expansionism towards the Iberian Peninsula, which would be verified, but only too late, in 1807.

In 1803, he resumed his preparatory contacts with Vansittart, who introduced him to Home Popham, Pitt's adviser to the Navy, candidate for deputy and linked to British business interests in Latin America, who said he was interested in supporting Miranda's ideas in Parliament, and even presented a first military plan [Robertson, W. S.][107] to the government. With Fullarton and Davison,[108] government military contractors, and others, Miranda pinpoints his military plan for immediate implementation. In fact, as he had foreseen, the precarious peace between France and England collapsed on 17 May. It is no surprise to Miranda, as evidenced by the fact that his plan was formulated before, on April 29, 1803, foreseeing the inevitability of a new war with France due to French expansionism and protectionism. He also attached to his plan an "appeal to the English Ministers", dated May 17, 1803, the very same day the war between England and France erupted again. However, this letter was written in April when England and Spain were not yet at war. In October 1803, Spain proclaimed neutrality with Great Britain. However, there was a secret

---

government that the easiest and safest way was to betray Miranda, who would have been an obstacle to the colonial interests of England. This is why he secretly organised a military landing in the South, using Miranda's information and networks. Furthermore, he used the fact that Miranda was preparing his own landing in Coro, which should divert Spanish attention to the North of the Empire, allowing England to benefit from a surprise effect in Buenos Aires. Popham's operation was a total disaster, and he was court-martialled for taking a military initiative without political backing from the government. However, this condemnation and other accusations did not affect much his career. He made significant scientific contributions to the navy, the best known being the design and implementation of the system of numerical naval signals with flags (1803).

[107] See the details of the negotiations and successive plans in William Spence Robertson (1929), *The Life of Miranda*, Chap. 11. University of North Carolina Press, 1929.

[108] **Alexander Davison** (1750–1829), a prosperous English businessman, Nelson's friend and supplier of the Navy, was acquired by Miranda's geopolitical vision, which gave him a glimpse into a juicy business in America. A friend of Popham, he offered himself in 1803 to finance and organised part of Miranda's expedition, arming 3 or 4 ships in exchange for future commercial advantages and on condition of the protection of a military vessel of the British Navy. He also financed Miranda's expenditures for preparing his planes for £ 10.000 during 1801 and 1802. (Robertson, W. S., 1929).

clause in the Treaty[109] between France and Spain by which Spain committed to indirectly defending France against England through the resources of its American colonies, committing to allocate most of its income from Spanish America to the French Army. When informed of this secret clause, the British Navy launched an attack on October 5, 1804, on the Spanish convoy[110] carrying gold and silver from Montevideo, which was destined for France, thereby provoking a new war between Spain and England in December 1804. This context means that the central argument for the British government to block Miranda's plan should no longer be valid.

Content:

Once again, Miranda reaffirmed the urgency of military action, given the "*danger of falling under the abominable yoke of France*". This report highlights the astute understanding of the geopolitical aspects that the British government could and should benefit from by following its plan. It also establishes the principle and priority of capturing Caracas to organise a consultation of the inhabitants by convening a General Assembly and confirming the will for independence that would be sent with negotiators to Spain to try to arrive at a peaceful settlement. This arrangement should guarantee absolute independence and free trade. It even contemplates two hypotheses: if there is a war between England and France, it is necessary to prevent France and its Spanish ally from having the resources of the American colony, and if there is peace, England will benefit from free trade with these new markets. In both cases, England was a beneficiary under the necessary conditions to prevent the French revolutionary leaders from seizing these lands and resources. In addition, the US should be welcomed, as it would increase economic and political benefits, as it is convenient for them to align with England in the geopolitical interests of democracies, a constant view in Mirandian thought.

Sources:

Translated from the French

America espera, op. cit. Documents n° 109 y 110, p. 301–303

---

[109] **Treaty of San Idelfonso III**: A secret treaty signed between Spain and France on October 1, 1800, that specified the existing treaty in favour of Napoleon's expansionist ambitions. He promised the creation of a State in Italy that would depend directly on Spain in exchange for having the Spanish Navy at his disposal to support his war against England and to recover Louisiana, which had been occupied by Spain since 1763. Furthermore, Spain declared war on Portugal, a traditional ally of the United Kingdom, thus initiating the so-called "Orange War." The Treaty was clarified by subsequent agreements that ensured France of military and financial assistance, thanks to the American colonies, to contribute to the war against England and the recovery of Louisiana, which had been held by Spain since 1763. Furthermore, Spain agreed to declare war on Portugal, a traditional ally of the United Kingdom, thus beginning the so-called "*Orange War*."

[110] **Battle of Cape Santa Maria** (Portugal), in which four Spanish frigates were taken by four British frigates. The frigate *Mercedes* was sunk with a valuable gold and silver treasury, which was discovered in 2007 by a US company, worth several hundred million dollars. After a 5-year court battle, a U.S. federal judge awarded the treasure to Spain and ordered Odyssey Marine to relinquish it to Spanish authorities, despite a claim by Peruvian authorities arguing that the metal comes from Peru. In the sinking of the Mercedes, the Alvear family had perished, except the Father and the son, Carlos de Alvear, future Supreme Director of Argentina in 1815. See also note n° 115 in document 10.3.21.

Archivo del… Vol..XVI, op. cit. p. 290–93 y 296–97

Text:

London, 29-4-1803

The purpose of this Report is to show that it is possible to repair, using a prompt and decisive effort, how much has been lost since 1790 during the fruitless negotiations with England with a view to the Independence of the Spanish-American Colonies.

The matter becomes all the more urgent since these Colonies are in danger of falling under France's abominable yoke if they are not promptly helped. The fate experienced by those in Florida and New Orleans is merely the prelude to an evil plan that Napoleon is pursuing with determination. This is its favourite purpose after the French troops evacuated Egypt.

February 6, 1803.

The most recent and reliable communications that have reached us from the Caracas coast report that discontent is total in that province; that to suppress in a certain way the spirit of revolt, they limited themselves to sacrificing a prominent figure in the country, a junior officer from the regular troops and three more from the militia, belonging to the coloured class of people. Agents of the Spanish Government hesitated to go further, contenting themselves with apparent submission for the moment. For the rest, all the people were indiscriminately disarmed, both in the cities and in the countryside, and all communication with the outside world was interrupted through the application of horrendous and even unknown penalties during the most critical times of the War. These facts contribute more than anything else to the fermentation that must exist in the country! The undersigned is convinced that the same state of mind should prevail in the neighboring province of Santa Fe, as on similar occasions, both provinces have always acted in concert, corroborating these circumstances based on all the news that has reached us.

The communications that have also reached us through Trinidad and Hispanic Americans currently living on the island lead us to believe that their compatriots only require additional support in arms and a few men under the command of an experienced military leader to achieve their goals at this time. This would give an impulse capable of mobilising the country's inhabitants, who anxiously await this signal.

So, to finally fulfil this purpose and general aspiration, we respectfully submit the following request for consideration.

"A sufficient loan for the acquisition of some ships armed as pirates, which are currently for sale both in Liverpool and on the River Thames, as well as an armament for 6 or 8 thousand infantry and cavalrymen; and also for the recruit of some 1,200 to 1,500 men who must enlist to smuggle off the coast of Spanish America under the patronage of a respectable Trinidad trading house that will hire them for this specific purpose."

Counting on such force, we are convinced that it will be feasible to take the city of Caracas and the port of La Guaira by surprise. This city is totally open and devoid of any defence, and La Guaira does not present any obstacle if it is attacked from the flank or from behind. Once owners of these two points, we are, in fact, the owners of the entire province.

It will then proceed to the convocation of a General Assembly. If the majority of the inhabitants are actually determined to support their independence, a report will be drawn up with the documents of the case, and a ship will be dispatched to take them to Spain, along with the most respectful proposals for the mother country, urging it by all the means to reach a friendly and reasonable arrangement, provided that the absolute independence of the government of the Colonies and, therefore, its free trade with the rest of the world, is the fundamental basis of said stipulation.

Meanwhile, aid will continue to be provided to all the forces we find in Caracas, extending the same operation to the province of Santa Fe. Agents duly authorised by the provisional government of the province will be sent to both England and the United States of America to achieve amicable mediation in an equitable arrangement with Spain, or, if this is rejected, to obtain the adequate aid necessary to help us successfully sustain our honourable independence.

If the current negotiations between Great Britain and France culminate in some peaceful settlement, England can only benefit from the success of our Independence. If their conclusion is war, then there is a common cause, and both Spain and France would be deprived of these immense resources. In any case, France (or some French revolutionary leaders) will be prevented from taking over those beautiful lands. In turn, the United States of America will have to be bound by our cause by agreeing to antagonise France, a country whose only goal is probably to deceive them. In this way, they might become linked with England through a common interest.

Regarding the cost of armaments, they would surely pay hundreds of times in case of success, or if, due to unpredictable misfortunes, everything went to the ground, ships and arms would return to British ports.

The friends of our independence in the United States of America also offer help to sustain us quickly, which is highly encouraging for our later operations and to instil respect in our enemies if, unfortunately, we had them».

Annexe: Appeal to English Ministers Dated 19/03/1803

The current state of war between England, France, and their allies gives the undersigned the most reasonable hope of receiving the help and support that the Ministers of H.M. British had promised their compatriots in South America, with the intention of quickly achieving their independence and establishing a sound and reliable government. The only preliminaries of peace signed by England and France in 1801 would then have made possible the suspension of the expedition in progress, ready to be launched for that purpose, and the sole resumption of the war has been able to give us the same advantage again. At least, this is what the government's respectable agents repeatedly assured us.

In this case, and using the notices emanating from the American agents in the Provinces of Caracas and Santa Fe that are currently on the island of Trinidad and dated March 19 and 30, I submit to the consideration of the Ministers of HM British the following request:

Some weapons and ammunition of war.

Some troops of people of colour, of whom those currently on the island of Trinidad.

Some ships were destined to transport them to the shore, and, if possible, one or two warships would escort them.

This force, however insignificant it may seem, would be enough to give the necessary impulse to the Continent if one takes into account that the general mass of the inhabitants eagerly awaits it to join the movement and that the majority of the Spaniards living in Trinidad offer to join us for this purpose, as evidenced more clearly in what is extracted from the letters from Commissioner Vargas that we will give below…

…. This elementary exposition will suffice to convince the Ministers of H.M. British about the need I find myself to obey the voice of the country that cries out for me to help it in critical circumstances. Therefore, I hope you will be kind enough to grant, without delay and with certainty, the transfer of my person to the island of Trinidad, with the aid that you rightly deem convenient to agree upon us.

10.3.17 Miranda's Secret Letter to William Pitt and His New Cabinet, London, May 16, 1804

Context:

The Addington government replaced Pitt in 1801 due to a conflict with the King over the protection of Irish Catholics following Ireland's union with the United Kingdom. But Addington's government fell in April 1804, and Pitt was called back to power on 10 May. However, he headed a much weaker coalition than before.

Immediately, Miranda - who had once again been deceived by Addington, despite his friendship with Minister Vansittart, with whom he had prepared in detail the military plan from Trinidad since 1802 - once more - his strategy with Pitt. Miranda returned to his original plan, which the government had already approved, although it had been cancelled on April 7, 1804. However, at this moment, England is still officially at peace with Spain, which explains Pitt's prudence, who again does not want to confront Spain for fear of pushing it into the hands of France.

Content:

Miranda emphasises two reasons for a swift British intervention: his impassioned argument against the irrepressible Napoleonic expansionism in Spain and England, and his confidence in the advanced preparations of the patriots with their plan of revolt, which he believes is about to erupt. He implies that the government must choose whether to support the movement in its self-interest, but the movement is presented as already underway.

Sources:

Originally written in English but here translated from the Spanish version from América Espera (Salcedo-Bastardo)

Archivo…. Vol. XVII. p. 21–22

América Espera document 113, p. 306–307

Text:

To Pitt and members of the British Cabinet

(Secret)

The undersigned takes the liberty of addressing promptly the new Ministers of H.M. for two reasons, which he hopes are sufficient to justify his attitude. The first concerns the need to prevent the enemies of this country from taking advantage of the time allowed, from seizing the ports of Caracas and Santa Fe de Bogotá, in order to oppose the independence movement that both provinces are currently about to undertake. The second is that the preparations organised for this purpose, both here and in New York, Boston and Trinidad, are already ready, as well as the people gathered for this purpose, who are anxiously awaiting the signal or the arrival of the subscriber in the established points; Therefore, it should be avoided that these patriots do not fall into confusion and disorder, as no decision has reached them until now.

Negotiations on this matter with the last Ministers of H.M. are continuing. They had already reached the point of final execution when they were abruptly suspended on the 7th of the previous month. However, the Under-secretary of State appointed by the very honourable Mr. Addington to handle this case informed the undersigned, on the occasion of an interview they just held, the importance and even the need to see the new Ministers of His Majesty as soon as possible to obtain your opinion about such a tremendous and transcendental matter for the interests of the Country. For this reason, the undersigned hopes that the hearing he requests for this purpose will be granted as soon as possible, or at least the appointment of a person from the Government who, instead of Mr. Vansittart, is in charge of tackling this delicate and vital case on the right track as time is running in this critical moment.

The military plans, the connections with the agents of the American country, and the state of progress of these operations will be submitted for consideration by the person designated for this purpose. He trusts that, based on this examination, the continuation of the project will surely be approved by the new Ministers since all the expenses and the preparations have already been made; on the other hand, only the Government will be responsible for deciding in the first place or not, to participate or not, as it deems appropriate.

Fr. de M___a

London, May 16, 1804. Grafton Street (27)

10.3.18 Miranda's Memorandum Dated June 12 1804

Context:

Miranda is growing increasingly worried about the procrastination of Pitt's cabinet in the face of the threat posed by the tacit Spanish-French coalition, as several converging pieces of information from America lead him to expect a possible upheaval by the patriots.

Content:

This memorandum highlights again the rising risks of the anarchic situation in Spanish America and the need for him to be sent there immediately to prevent an unmanageable problem. Miranda is mainly preoccupied with possible violent uprisings, which could take the form of ethnic cleansing in case of a lack of leadership and a structured legal order for all the vice-royalties that he might provide there. He underlines his potential role, like in a promotional pamphlet, which multiplies the references to the requests addressed to him for triggering the insurrection.

Sources:

Translated from French

Textos sobre la Independencia, Biblioteca de la Academia Nacional de la Historia, n°13, Caracas, 1959

America espera.... Document 114, p. 307–309

Text:

(Selective extracts)

The current situation in the Spanish-American Colonies is highly critical and precarious for the time being. The Provinces of Caracas and Santa Fe Bogotá are only pending the agreed password to reject the government and to implement their own one which favours their independence; Such a measure is becoming more and more urgent as mulattoes and free people of colour make up a substantial part of the current urban population, which are already armed and grouped into militia corps, pressing for such a blow. and threatening to appropriate all power themselves.... The power of the Spanish Governors is almost non-existent today in these provinces, as stated in letters 1 and 2, which assert, through relatively recent communications, that Mexico is experiencing a similar situation.

All the natural officers of those provinces, as well as the other people who, as a result of the different commotions that occurred in these countries in the last 10 years, are scattered throughout the various islands of the American archipelago as, in the United States of America, that is, on the island of Trinidad or in New York; from these places, they are waiting for the latest information or the arrival of the subscriber to start up and act in concert. Among them stand out engineers, officers of the Spanish royal navy, as well as powerful landowners of the American country.

They have even managed, through their envoys, to attract and group for the same cause missionaries, monks and ecclesiastics who have significant influence among the Indian tribes of the Orinoco, Río Meta and Apure, Spanish Guiana, & c. v. No. 3.

The newly appointed Ministers of H.M. have been encouraging the undersigned with great hopes on several opportunities, having even promised aid that is about to be sent (v. n°7). Those various occurrences were regularly broadcast to the American Agents in Trinity and New York, so that everything was up to date at the time. If the undersigned did not arrive as soon as possible, the movement would leave without its leadership and without that general consensus, which is essential to ensure successful and firm outcomes.

... If the Government manifests its desire to collaborate with a little more efficiency, those indicated in Note No. 6 will be entirely sufficient, especially if they were under the orders of Sir Home Popham, an officer who contributed under the responsibility of the last ministry to achieve the naval arrangement since we are convinced that in addition to his military and political knowledge, he is credited with great enthusiasm and self-denial for the success of the operation, to such an extent that it would be tough to find similar qualities in another person....

In any case, the subscriber only asks that his departure be made as soon as possible. Any delay in the current circumstance is considered very damaging and must be avoided with all available means and a plan before his departure, covering a general operation at the level of the entire H. American Continent, the Pacific Ocean, and., subsequently, take possible action in all eventual events concertedly and based on the same plan.

Addendum dated August 3 1804:

(Extract)

...The patriots in America... realising that the English Government has not decided and that the delay is already unbearable...are so distrustful that they suspect the said government as insidious and insincere (v. 11–12) and beg the undersigned to leave England and join them. According to recently arrived information, the same is desired by those also gathered in New York and Philadelphia in the United States.

To all this, we add the impact that the arrival of Lecourbe-Macdonald and other French officials will not fail to produce among the impatient exiles who, due to the advent of the new imperial regime, are currently leaving French territory. On the way to the United States, the need to act promptly will become palpable if these Jacobin Chiefs are not soon to be seen spreading their hateful doctrines throughout Mexico and this beautiful continent.

10.3.19 Miranda's Letter to William Pitt, London, September 29 1804

Context:

Miranda is informed that Spain's neutrality with England is not respected, and he foresees that the conditions for a new war are met. This will oblige Pitt's government to support his military and political plan in South America. Therefore, he renewed his requests to Pitt, fearing that he might arrive too late if the Patriots made unprepared or chaotic attempts and/or Napoleon could act at any time.

Content:

To Miranda's standard arguments - advocating for the urgency of British intervention in support of his plans for South America - this letter introduces an additional subtle psychological manoeuvre that warns Pitt that the patriots are about to organise an uprising with "coloured people" from Santo Domingo. He uses the fact that Pitt was very afraid about the recent Haitian/San Domingo ethnic revolution that could affect the whole Caribbean (so the British islands, too) to make clear that if he could act on time, his plan based upon constitutional order would prevent any calamity.

Source:

Archivo.... Vol. XVII p. 97–98.

América espera, document n° 116, p 310–311

Text:

To Mr. Pitt,

Grafton Street, September 29, 1804

Mister:

It seems to me that the time has come when I must resort to your sacred promise to help and provide benevolent support to my native country (in the event of war with Spain) to obtain its emancipation and independence. My friend, Mr. Evan Nepean, recently provided you with several documents related to the same matter. After careful examination and consideration of this whole matter, he informed me that you wanted me to wait until you knew the outcome of specific pending negotiations in Madrid, etc. This has already happened, as I understand it. Consequently, I come to beg you with all deference for your permission to travel to Trinidad, where my compatriots and friends have gathered on the island (with the acquiescence of the last Ministry), awaiting me for the same purpose.

My departure from England is all the more necessary since what was a conjecture when I made my last request to you 2 months ago has now become a fact. From reports brought from Trinidad by Mr. Fitzwilliam, a respectable merchant who recently arrived in London, it seems that the commissioners of the province of Caracas have already passed through that island, sent to Santo Domingo, the last Spanish colony, requesting support of the coloured peoples of said colony to obtain independence and form an alliance with them. I do not need to demonstrate to you the fatal consequences that this unexpected measure (in case it would be carried out before our arrival) will cause in the colonies of South America and, from then on, in the entire group of the West Indies.

I trust, Lord, that your patriotism and prudence will prevent this evil and save the New World, as well as the Old, from the calamities and ruin that threaten both of you at the present critical times.

The preparations required for this purpose are well advanced thanks to the zeal and activities of Mr. Davison, a person recommended by Mr. Evan Nepean, whose instructions he followed in completing them. Lord Melville has the list of what is required for your approval and yours. According to the plan submitted to you by Mr. Evan, the forces needed for this operation must be mainly in Trinidad, as I had the honour to tell you and Lord Melville in my letter of 27 of the current.

With sentiments of higher respect and consideration, I am yours, sir, a very obsequious servant,

10.3.20 *Miranda's Memorandum for Pitt's Government, October 14 1804*

Context:

At a ministerial conference in Wimbledon dedicated to addressing policy options in the war against Spain, held in October 1804, Pitt and Lord Melville (Minister Henry Dundas) decided to charge Miranda with preparing the option of cutting Spain off from its budgetary resources derived from America. The flows were mainly used to finance Napoleon's war ambitions against England. Miranda wrote a lengthy explanatory memorandum that provided all the valuable information.

Content:

Below is a brief synthesis of Miranda's arguments, which justify that the best way to eliminate Napoleon's threat was to eliminate Spanish domination of Spanish America before any French action could do so.

Source:

Archivo.... Vol. XVII p. 85–96.

América espera, document n° 117, p. 311–319

Text:

(short extract)

Before going any further with the details of the operations, I will ask a few simple questions:

- Is Spain independent from France? It is not!
- Is she virtually under the dominion and control of that New Empire? Yes, she is!
- Will she allow France to have peace relations with Great Britain for a moment longer than Bonaparte's criteria and projects dictate? No!
- Does France get any income from South America through Spain? Yes, and a lot!
- Would it not put France in material trouble if that source of wealth is cut off? Yes!
- Would it not materially benefit Great Britain to establish that source on its own scale and open new channels for exporting its European and Asian manufacturers? Yes!
- What sustains the Spanish army with which the French are now intimidating us in a certain way? The treasures and wood of South America! And the training offered by foreign trade to its sailors.

Therefore, I will ask whether the independence of South America will perhaps render the Spanish navy ineffective, thus opposing us with a less cohesive force in any future war. If this argument is accepted, then I can affirm that the third naval power in Europe would be destroyed and that this power would consider France the cause of the damage, seizing any opportunity for revenge that could arise in the extraordinary fluctuations of European politics.

10.3.21 Miranda's Letter to Evan Nepean, London, February 5 1805

Context:

As stipulated by the secret clauses of the Third Treaty of San Idelfonso[111] of October 1800, Spain had promised to help France in the event of war with England. Spain committed to deliver 72 million francs annually to Paris to prepare for the war against Britain. In September 1804, the English Ambassador in Madrid and the English spies informed the Pitt government about the preparations for a joint operation of the French and Spanish fleets against England. Pitt – who has been again Prime Minister since May 1804 - immediately commissioned Admirals Cochrane and Cornwallis to intervene. The British Navy attacked by surprise on October 5, 1804, a Spanish convoy of four frigates loaded with 3 million metal pesos off the Portuguese coast of the Algarve (known as the Battle of Cape Santa Maria[112]). The confiscation of the treasure by the British fleet led to the declaration of war between the two countries in December 1804.

Therefore, once more, Miranda believed that his plan could finally meet the ideal conditions for its implementation, as was already the case in 1790, 1798, and 1802. Indeed, this was again the case since Pitt ordered Popham on October 12 to prepare the plan discussed with Miranda. This preparation took place on October 14, 1804, in a ministerial meeting, and on the 16th, Pitt had a meeting with Miranda, Dundas and Popham. However, the government continued to hesitate and block the effective launch of the plan.

Facing such paralysis and a status quo attitude, Miranda was determined to create an opportunity for British intervention by provoking the beginning of insurrection, betting on the selfish character of Pitt's policy. This would put him in a position such that, observing the events, he could not resist taking advantage in the interest of British trade and increasing his geopolitical power.

Content:

Miranda begs to be allowed to leave for the Antilles as soon as possible to launch his own military plan. He asks the minister to grant him material aid in arms and ships, arguing that it is in England's direct interest to do so. He also insists, once again, on the mutual interests of cooperation and urgency, given that if it is delayed again, the Patriots might not be able to offer any advantage to England.

Source:

Translated from French

---

[111] See document 10.3.16., note 112.

[112] See also note n° 113 in document 10.3.16. Four British frigates attacked the four Spanish ships carried back from South America a total of 4,286,508 Spanish dollars in silver and gold coin, as well as 150,000 gold ingots, 75 sacks of wool, 1666 bars of tin, 571 pigs of copper, seal skins and oil, although 1.2 million in silver, half the copper and a quarter of the tin went down with the main ship, the "Mercedes". Still, the remaining ships and cargo were assessed at a value of £900,000 (equivalent to £69,103,000 in 2023). The sunk part was recovered in 2007 by a treasury hunter, but after a long trial, the gold and silver were attributed to Spain.

Archivo.... Vol. XVII p. 144–146
América espera, document n° 119, p. 320–321

Text:

To Sir Evan Nepean
Grafton Street, 5 February 1805
My dear Sir Evan:

After patiently waiting for the open conflict with Spain, as the condition set by the ministers of H.M for taking a final resolution on the affairs of South America, I have no alternative - seeing that this important matter, it seems, has been postponed once again, ad infinitum, despite the incontestable evidence I gave the government about the imminent dangers to which the country is exposed - that I beg you to request on my behalf the Right Honourable William Pitt and Mr. Melville, a passage to the Windward Islands, aboard of any warship, and to be allowed by order of the governors of His Majesty on these islands, to act unhindered against the common enemy. I believe it is infinitely wiser to act on our own while there is still hope for a solution, rather than to seek all the help England could offer us too late, once confusion and disorder are introduced between us.

If it is compatible with the intentions of the ministers of H.M. that the English negotiations would offer voluntarily to provide us with aid in arms and ships - so that we can obtain an independence equal to that which Spain and France gave to the Anglo-American colonies of the North, in exchange for some commercial advantages in case of success - could be done without obstacle from the government, it would be our only wish at this time to ensure a safe triumph beneficial for both sides. These trade benefits would be unequivocal proof of our sincere friendship and would foster a growing mutual interest, guaranteeing that it would become permanent in the future.

However, I beg you, Sir Evan, that this proposition, whatever capital and importance it may be to the commerce of England and the interests of South America, be not an obstacle to my immediate departure because any delay is, at this time, the worst of the evils since it is highly possible that within some time, the peaceful colonised of America will not have any property or commercial interests to offer to England.

With the utmost respect and sincere appreciation, I am Sir Evan, your most humble and obedient servant.

10.3.22 Miranda's Letter to William Pitt, London, June 13 1805

Context:

Months have passed without a clear position from the British government, and Miranda, still unable to leave London, is growing increasingly impatient. The delay is frustrating and significantly impacts the mission to Trinidad.

Content:

Miranda's heartfelt plea to defend his cause and his integrity in the face of baseless accusations is a testament to the injustice he is fighting against.

Sources:

Translated from French

Archivo…. Vol. XVII p. 215–219

América espera, document n° 120, p. 321–323

Text:

(extract)

To Pitt

Grafton Street, 13 June 1805

Sir,

The request that I had the honour of raising for your consideration through Sir Evan Nepean, to authorise my immediate departure for Trinidad, responds to the desire to meet my compatriots who are currently on that island, waiting with great anxiety for my arrival, to undertake the critical enterprise of their emancipation. They are fully prepared to start it on their own account since the promised aid from England tends to take too long, and the present moment is the most promising that can be desired.

The same person who gave me your answer on this matter gave me to understand that, in reality, it was not a lack of goodwill on your part that caused such a delay but the insane approaches taken by some of my compatriots that led the Government to express certain doubts as to the decision to be taken in this matter.. . I do not doubt that ... wickedness and even calumny have come to disturb the march and prevent a happy conclusion…which would have been in the interest of a large portion of humanity who thus becomes its victim….Allow me to remove any doubt in this regard to destroying these treacherous innuendos since, having not given up for a single moment the political and moral principles that gave rise to our first political connection in 1790; I would not have the slightest difficulty in bringing down even the shadow of suspicion or the inconsistency of any accusation.

When one has dedicated 25 years of his life uninterruptedly to a single and unchanged goal, which is the study of the correct principles that lead men to happiness, to apply them for the benefit of the Nation, it seems to me that one should not doubt their own principles….I have the honour to propose you designate two or three persons of your trust…and ask them to assess my behaviour and the rightness of all the information I presented to HM government….

Miranda's Note, dated July 5, 1805

The response to this Letter has been a verbal message by Sir Evan Nepean (and also sent to me by Vansittart) in which Mr Pitt assures me that he does not have the slightest concern or suspicion about such rumours - for his opinion about my integrity and honesty is invariable, notwithstanding what could have happened years past in times of more turbulence that he wished to be buried in perpetual oblivion - and he begged me to be well persuaded of the best appreciation and perfect confidence that I deserved him &, &, &, - my friend Vansittart agreed with me, however, that there had been some foundation, and that my justification was well laid out in any case, for what it was worth. And there is no doubt that the impression must have been strong since the apparent fierce ones have suddenly been transmuted into gifts and satisfactions.

10.3.23 Miranda's Letter to Evan Nepean, London, July 9 1805

Context:

Unchanged: Despite the state of war against Spain, which was supposed to justify British intervention in South America, and the growing risks to Napoleon's strategy towards the Americas, nothing progresses.

Content:

This is a five-point summary of the agreements that have been prepared. Within these points, the reference to a plan with "Liverpool merchants" is noted, which must be taken into account regarding the supposed operation to Brazil that will be denounced by a Liverpool merchant to the Portuguese authorities (see Chap. 5, document 5.3).

Sources:

Translated from French

Archivo…. Vol. XVII, p. 243–245

America espera, document n°121, p.324–325 _

Text:

To Nepean

Grafton Street, 9 July 1805

Sir,

After waiting a long time and patiently for the decision of His Majesty's Ministers, in relation to the many times promised aid by the Government of this country to the Spanish-American Colonies with a view to their emancipation; after communicating and agreeing with said Ministers the plans and measures necessary to implement this valuable undertaking; after seeing the Squadrons set sail and witnessing the departure of the troops of our enemies towards America, with the purpose (in my humble opinion) of overthrowing and frustrating these very plans that had cost us so much preparation and to which they were linked in a way the more significant political and commercial interests of England for the future; After finally waiting these last days with the most profound anxiety, the measures to be taken around the problem that was to decide the fate of the island of Trinidad (together with all the people who, according to my communication and under the recommendation of the Ministers of His Majesty, was congregated in the referred island) and, consequently, that of the provinces of Caracas, Santa Fe, Quito, & c .... that divine Providence, apparently, as well as the glorious efforts deployed by the British Navy seem to have saved for this time! After all this, allow me, Lord, through your intermediary, to beg the Ministers of His Majesty to reach a very prompt decision since it is impossible for me to extend my stay in this country beyond the time necessary for the granting of my passports and the necessary arrangements for my transfer to the islands on a warship, as you can realise yourself in the light of all the events that have happened so far and especially as a result of the war against Spain.

But, in any case, to make it clear, the purpose of this exhausting and lengthy negotiation has never deviated from the goal set from the beginning…that is, to make the interests of America as a whole mutual with those of England, since this is entirely compatible with the happiness of both countries. It is a more necessary measure today, as it can help restore the political balance that was completely destroyed in Europe by France. Perhaps this could be the only way to achieve this rebalancing safely, benefiting England and its Allies. The following arrangements are proposed, which, without the need for a significant deployment of forces, can facilitate the means sufficient or, at least, indispensable to achieve such an important goal; taking advantage, moreover, of the promising opportunity of the moment, which, in such undertakings, is often preferable to force itself.

I. The plan already combined with My Lord Melville and Sir Home Popham, consisting of a ship of the line, two frigates and two transports, with 3000 men of colonial troops and an armament for 20,000 men to be recruited from the people of the country, immediately after disembarking us.
II. The Plan formed with Sir Evan Nepean included two war frigates, two corvettes, two colonial cutters, and an armament for 10,000 men, as well as a transport carrying 1500 troops recruited in the country after our landing.
III. The plan was agreed upon with Mr. Davison, who offered to equip two 350-ton ships, embark a complete armament for 5000 men, and recruit about 1000 volunteers and people of colour on the island of Trinidad. Upon landing on the coasts, they would be reinforced by 5000 inhabitants of the country.
IV. The plan proposed by Liverpool merchants consisted of supplying two good ships armed as privateers with an armament for 10,000 men. These ships would be taken to Trinidad and disembarked on the opposite continental coast at the indicated site.
V. Simple letters of recommendation for the Governors of Trinidad and Curaçao (if this island is taken) to allow those who wish to embark voluntarily on neutral or armed ships in privateering among the inhabitants to do so without inconvenience and carrying with them weapons and ammunition of war &. &;

I have perfect appreciation and the sincerest devotion, &. &. &.

Miranda

To the R. H. Sir Evan Nepean.

10.3.24 Miranda's Letter to Pitt, London, July 18 1805

Context:

Miranda continues to be blocked by W. Pitt, who asks him for more patience under the pretext of essential negotiations. Miranda confirms his firm resolution to act without waiting for England and to leave for New York and Washington. Two days ago, he wrote a personal memorandum (see document 10.3.23 above) given to Minister Nepean to communicate his arguments to Pitt.

Content:

Miranda again insists on convincing Pitt with the same two main arguments: the urgency to act before their "common enemy" on the American continent and the mutual benefit for Britain and his fatherland.

Sources:

Translated from French

Archivo…. Vol. XVII p. 245–246.

Text:

(short extract)

….General Miranda...begs him [Prime Minister] to read the attached copy...that has been deserving his attention for so many years... It is a matter of carrying out the same idea before the common enemy can render it impractical, and we intend to use the means that would provide the country itself ... if we are fortunate enough to still arrive in time to prevent the entry of "*modern Gauls*" into the American continent.…

… May the divine Providence - by seconding my views - make England, as well as my native land, ever independent, friendly and happy.

10.3.25 Miranda's Personal Notes About His Negotiations with William Pitt in London, 16 July–5 August 1805

Context:

In 1801, Miranda had convinced the Addington cabinet (after the fall of Pitt) to participate in the military expedition (with the Royal Navy and British troops) of his precise liberation operation, starting with a landing in Coro, Venezuela, from where the whole Spanish American colonies would be freed in a domino effect. However, in parallel with seriously considering Miranda's plan, the British government launched an alternative strategy by attempting to negotiate a peace Treaty with France and Spain. This latter plan yielded temporary results, leading to the "*Peace of Amiens*" (September 1801), contrary to Miranda's expectations and advice. From then on, Miranda decided to act independently and wanted to travel to Trinidad Island, which was under the rule of the UK, where he had friends and support. However, the government wanted to keep Miranda under its control in London, as per Plan B, maintaining the expectation that a future military operation would occur once the diplomatic conditions were favourable, specifically only if Spain broke the peace. Nevertheless, Miranda continued to try to organise his own expedition. This was a way to put pressure upon Pitt while attempting to create a competitive alternative through the involvement of the United States by asking for help through his North American contacts, which the British government continued to oppose.

In May 1804, Addington's cabinet fell, and Pitt returned as Prime Minister, creating hopes to return to Miranda's initial plan. Indeed, the relations with France and

Spain shifted towards a new war, which would clear the way for Miranda's invasion with British troops, all the more so that Napoleon had an obvious interest in seizing the Spanish colonies and their critical financial resources necessary for invading Britain. Indeed, the war against Spain started in October (officially in December). Still, Pitt renewed his diplomatic procrastination and postponed his answer to Miranda again, who became very upset, feeling not only betrayed by the British for four whole years but also by the government's choice of the wrong option for Britain and the future of democracy.

Miranda is obsessed with his vision of possible initiatives of the French Jacobins through Napoleon's geopolitical expansionism against the Iberian powers and their prosperous colonies. If Napoleon were faster than he and his Anglo-Saxon allies, Miranda's plan for organising democratic emancipation would be destroyed, and the political balance across the Atlantic could turn against democracy.

Content:

Despite being fully aware that Pitt and the government had betrayed him, he remains convinced that the British authorities could not be so irrational; thus, he can turn his feelings into brilliant argumentation, which rationalises his doubts and clarifies diplomatically the kind of obstacles he has been facing for years. He drafted this argument note to give to his friend, Minister Evan Nepean, who has direct access to Pitt, to discuss it with him and bring Pitt's attention to his suboptimal choices. This report makes clear the coherence of Miranda's argumentation and his pathetic attempt to unblock the situation by forcing Pitt to choose between giving him a clear explanation for the delays so that he could accept holding out for longer or letting him leave London and undertake his own strategy, which would be beneficial to the UK. Indeed, Miranda finally won. Three days later, through his other friend, Minister Vansittart, he received the positive answer that Pitt finally accepted, authorising him to implement his plan, but without any British official support.

In his notes, Miranda shows that he is well aware that Pitt used him as an instrument of diplomatic blackmail by showing that he controlled his actions in a cynical deal with Spain and Portugal, which is deeply unethical concerning his commitments with Miranda: either these two colonial powers remain neutral with the UK and Pitt would impede Miranda to disturb their Empires, or he would authorise Miranda to organise the revolution in South America as a sanction.

Sources:

Translated from Spanish

Archivo.... Vol. XVII p. 246–249.

América Espera document n°122, p. 326–327...

Texts:

Note from his diary

10.3.26 *Miranda's Report on the Message Sent via Nepean on 16 July 1805*

The answer that Sir E. Nepean has transmitted to me to this note, after having conferred at length with Mr. Pitt on the matter, is that he advised me to wait for a while because the political affairs of Europe were not yet in the appropriate degree of maturity to start our expedition; if my lack of patience, made me run over everything, I didn't leave them any alternative ...therefore they consider that they should not be blamed etc. ... To this, I answered, that I could not be accused of precipitation after so many years of patience - nor lack of confidence when within the space of 1 year alone, I had experienced four breakdowns of promises given by the same ministers of H.M.? Furthermore, the most notable aspect was that the reasons for the occurrence were not even explained to me, instead being covered up with mysterious pretexts of negotiations, etc. But so that not even this pretext could ever be argued against me, I offered a way that would level everything and safeguard my right: that the secret motive be communicated to my friend Mr. Vansittart together with the persons that Mr. Pitt would appoint for his part, and if after this conference, my friend assured me that I should accept to follow Mr. Pitt's advice, because it would be compatible with the interest and honour of my Fatherland, I would be ready to submit and wait as long as Mr. Pitt would judge it necessary; and if, on the contrary, the decision would be against the opinion of Mr. Pitt, and in favour of my resolution, then it should be agreed that the reason was on my side, that the passports and means necessary for my departure be given to me — that we should remain good friends, and consequently await the result of my operations, to provide me with any times the aid that was promised to me, and that in a way was owed to me after so many personal sacrifices as I had made for it.

It was agreed that my proposal was fair and very just. I should communicate it immediately to Mr. Pitt and promptly implement it.

10.3.27 *Miranda's Comments on the Received Feedback from Pitt on 19 July 1805*

Indeed, on the 19th of the current month, I received the attached note from Mr. Vansittart with the decision in my favour. I was with Sir Evan the next day. He told me that Mr. Pitt did agree, acknowledging to submit himself to the decision - that he wanted to be fulfilled on time what the government, through Mr. Vansittart, had initially promised me, and that he only felt my departure - because he was the greatest friend of my plans and projects that I could imagine (here Nepean told me, to my satisfaction, a curious anecdote – "Well, when Mr. Pitt heard my resolution to leave he said – '*if the money were of consideration for him, we would stop him at all costs, but his thoughts are so far above that that it would be useless to think about it*'... and thus he left the other colleagues who were present absorbed". This is what Nepean told me so that I would have a reasonable opinion and a good name to leave behind me in the government of this country. Finally, we agreed that I would prepare whatever was necessary for my departure, etc.

10.3.28 Miranda's Comments on Pitt's Attitude on 5 August 1805

I have been with Nepean for my office - and we have seen Mr. Cooke, who is prompt and friendly – however, Nepean informed me that Mr. Pitt wanted me to receive £ 1600 from the Treasury for my expenses and that this was not in compensation of my pension of £ 700, since whenever I returned to England, I would have my current pension in the same terms as at present and that this should convince me of the fair intention of the ministers and of the favourable judgment that I deserved from the government etc. ... Again he began to repeat to me how much he regrets to see me to leave without being able to give me the least possible assistance... To this, I replied that the war was beginning with more vigour, and thus, it seemed strange to me that what was more practicable 5 months ago was impossible now. He replied that this was precisely the case, however. This confirms to me the idea that Mr. Pitt has been negotiating with me and using me for a long time ... and that today he has offered Portugal that as long as Spain keeps him in his neutrality and independence, England assures Spain not to disturb her colonies or to allow her Islands [n.a. Trinidad] to give the slightest help to the continent etc. ... nor that Russia believes that England wants to arrogate to herself the commerce of all the America - when so much is declaimed in the day against the ambition of France: what my friend Vansittart believes equally as I do, is the reason for this apparent incongruity and apathy. Add to this that Nepean agrees that the interests of my country may require a speedy move, although this is not in any way advantageous to England in its present position; indeed, to initiate a revolution in South America at this time would disrupt the English strategy in Europe. However, we have agreed that I give notice to the English Squads that are found in those places and that I send agents with powers here, that we maintain secret correspondence and that I should be persuaded that the government intimately wishes me tremendous success in this company, and will not stop supporting us with all its power and efforts, once the operations begin. This is also the opinion of my friend Vansittart; he assures me that I should be deeply persuaded that the ministers have more hope at this point in the Enterprise that I am going to execute in South America than in the entire continental coalition of Europe. Etc.…

10.4 Period 1805–1811

10.4.1 Miranda's Notes About His Negotiations with Minister Madison[113] and the US Government, December 11 1805

Context:

After another series of up-and-downs of enthusiasm and deep disappointments about Pitt's attitude using him in a geopolitical deal with Spain and impeding him from launching his own military expedition, Miranda finally managed to set sail from Gravesend on September 2, 1805, for the USA on the ship "Polly". His decision to abandon his plan with England was not new. Still, it had been skilfully countered by the hopes that the successive cabinets since 1801 (Pitt, Addington, Pitt) have distilled for him in terms of diplomatic and military relations in the triangle of England-France-Spain. Starting in 1805, the growing tensions between Spain, France, and the United States allowed the Precursor to foresee a new case of conflict that would help him obtain direct US military support for his project, reinforcing his determination to act without England at least initially.

Miranda landed in New York on November 9, where he made contacts before entering into negotiations with the US government. On his way to Washington, he met in Philadelphia with Aaron Burr (the former vice-president who had killed Hamilton, Miranda's friend, in a duel 1 year before). This US politician had a secret plan to remove Mexico from Spain (and for personal interests), but Burr, who saw Miranda as a potential obstacle because he was able to denounce his imperialist operation in Mexico, did not want to cooperate. This was reciprocal. Miranda regarded him as an untrustworthy person who had already betrayed him in the past. It is highly possible that Burr informed the Spanish authorities about Miranda's expedition.[114]

Miranda arrived in Washington on December 6. The next day, he was received at the White House by President Jefferson, and on December 11 by Minister Madison, and then again with Jefferson for dinner on December 13. Miranda's minimum goal was to gain at least tacit approval from the United States, so that he could arm his military expedition by recruiting soldiers in the United States and potentially secure some US military support. Quickly, he understood that, despite receiving a positive welcome to his plan, he would only achieve the minimum, as the US, being very strict with diplomacy and not at war with Spain, would be obliged to repress any

[113] **James Madison** (1751–1836) was one of the "Founding Fathers" of the United States and the primary author with Hamilton of the "Federalist Papers" and the federal constitution. Named Minister of Foreign Affairs by President Jefferson in 1797, he was elected the fourth President of the United States from 1809 to 1817. He was in close contact with Miranda in 1783–84 and they remained friends.

[114] Even worse, he could be the operation's mastermind behind the denunciation of the operation to Spain, followed by the blackmail exerted on the Portuguese authorities regarding the landing of Miranda in Coro and then in Brazil (see Chap. 5, section 5.3. on the Brazilian constitution, Deductive Hypothesis). However, this remains to be investigated (no formal proof yet).

formal act against Spain, as well as any illegal operation. However, a space for action was left open if it was limited to exclusively private and legal activities, given that individuals were free in the territory of the USA. Miranda accepted this minimum, which made it feasible to arm his expedition, which he always saw as a way to trigger momentum, and that British and US interests should push their governments to join.

Content:

Miranda reports his conversation with Minister James Madison, who confirms that the US government could turn a blind eye to its liberation operation, including the fact that financing comes from private US citizens, under the condition that it respects the law. Official support was not feasible, as the young federal republic was not at war with Spain and was cautious about establishing international credibility.

Sources:

Translated from Spanish

Archivo…. Vol. XVII p. 283–293.

América Espera document n°124, p. 333…

Text:

(extract)

December 11, 1805

At 7 p.m., I came to the Secretariat, and then Mr. Madison and I locked ourselves in. He received me with great pleasure and friendship, and he assured me that he had an order from the President to receive my communication with the necessary secrecy and reserve; I proceeded to frankly express to him the efforts that I had made for more than 20 years both in England and France to seek a solid and absolute Emancipation of the Hispanic-American Continent, in the same terms as his Country had obtained from England - and to achieve it at this time, it only needed the tacit consent of the Government, at least it turns a blind eye because we had friends in New York and Boston who offered to advance funds and how much was necessary for the matter provided that the government gave its consent and approval. I felt that he was glad about this proposal, corroborating my suspicions in the bad faith of England that if we took possession of any part of the continent, it would want to treat us like East India - and telling me that the individuals of this Country could very well help in the process, since the Government applies the Law of Nations, and did not respond to the facts or undertakings of individuals!. He asked me carefully which provinces were ready to start the revolution. Having told him the name of the Three, he seemed to agree; from this, I infer that they have their own sights set on Mexico or are dealing with the Mexicans on the matter. In short, I drew his attention to the importance of the matter for all reasons and the need not to delay the answer; he agreed to it and told me to come back after morning at the same time, and the answer would be ready. – Once at home, I found the invitation to visit the President &….

10.4.2 *Miranda's Letter to the Minister of Foreign Affairs, James Madison, New York, January 22 1806*

Context:

After his interviews in Washington in December 1805, which won him only the tacit approval of the US government, Miranda gave the green light, explaining that "*the authorities would close their eyes on the support received from private agents provided that the laws of the United States were not openly violated.*" He provided instructions on how to complete the preparations and related purchases. He received funding of about US $ 45,000 from American businessmen and activated the Turnbull and Vansittart credit for £ 2000, complaining that the English were less enterprising. Thus, he could arm three ships and recruit about 200 men in New York, who set sail on February 2, 1806, for Haïti. There, he received aid and supplies, adding two ships to his navy. He then began new negotiations with English ships. In Barbados, he added one more frigate and negotiated with Admiral Cochrane[115] for British naval support in exchange for a future Treaty. In Trinidad, he was authorised by Governor Hislop to recruit about 100 additional soldiers.

However, when the new cabinet formed by Lord Grenville (after Pitt's death) learned of Cochrane's support, contrary orders were sent on July 15. Cochrane informed him on July 30, but secretly assured Miranda that he would protect him in case of a disproportionate maritime attack.

Meanwhile, Spanish spies discovered Miranda's ongoing expedition in the US. The military authorities in Venezuela were informed, and Spain officially lodged a complaint. Madison was forced to prosecute Miranda's associates, but North American justice acquitted them.

Content:

Thank you letter for sealing the agreement to keep the tacit support received secret. The book he presented to President Jefferson was The History of Chile by the Jesuit Molina.

Sources:

Translated from French
Archivo.... Vol. 17. p. 347–348
América Espera document n°128, p. 340–341

---

[115] **Lord Thomas Cochrane** (1775–1860), 10th Earl of Dundonald, was a British naval officer, peer, mercenary, and politician. He was famous for his maritime success against the French Revolutionary and Napoleonic Wars. Nicknamed the "Sea Wolf" by Napoleon. In 1806, he gave crucial support to Miranda's expedition to Coro. He was dismissed from the Royal Navy in 1814 after a controversial financial affair on the London Stock Exchange. Expelled from the Parliament and rejected by the British aristocracy, he offered his services to organise and lead the revolutionary navies of Chile and Brazil during their respective wars of independence during the 1820s. In 1818, he became a Chilean citizen, being appointed Vice-Admiral of the Chilean Navy. In 1820, with O'Higgins, he organised the Liberating Expedition of Peru in application of Miranda's plan. In 1832, he was rehabilitated by the Crown with the rank of Rear-Admiralty of the Navy.

Text:

To Madison

New York, 22 January 1806

Sir:

Allow me to say two words to you as I am about to leave the United States: Thank you for the kind attention you gave me during my stay in Washington. The essential things that I had the honour to communicate to you then will remain, I do not doubt, in the most profound secret until the final result of this delicate matter. I acted under this assumption, fully agreeing with the government's intentions, which I hope I have understood and carried out with accuracy and discretion.

The attached letter contains a book I promised the President of the United States, and I beg you to send it.

Please extend my respectful greetings to Mrs. Madison, and be assured that I am, with appreciation and high regard, your most humble and obedient servant.

Fran. de M.

To the Honourable

James Madison, Esquire, etc.

10.4.3 The British Invasions of Plata River in 1806–1807: Miranda's Letter to Commodore Home Popham, Trinidad, 7 April 1807

Chapter 11 presents a detailed analysis of the context in which this letter was written, along with an analysis of the evolution in British policy with Latin America and the relations of the successive cabinets with Miranda.

Context:

Miranda, who had left England in September 1805, sailed from New York on 2 February 1806 to Haiti as the first step in his private military expedition to Venezuela. He wanted to act independently, as he understood that the British government had been manipulating him as early as 1798. He attempted to overcome the diplomatic procrastination of the successive Pitt and Addington administrations by creating a beneficial opportunity for British interests, both military and commercial, illustrating what the British geopolitical interests could lose in the event of no intervention. His calculation was based upon the hope Pitt would follow in case of success. His plan was the same as what he had proposed to Pitt as early as 1790, which was reformulated in early 1798 and finally officially approved by Pitt in 1804. The plan was to land on the northern coast of Venezuela and, from there, be joined by local citizens to trigger a domino effect towards the general emancipation of Spanish America (and possibly also of Brazil), with the British joining in once the movement had become credible and successful. Indeed, Miranda discounted that Pitt could not resist the pressures of both the British business circles to make up for the growing Napoleon's protectionism and also form part of his cabinet, especially the Minister of War and Colony, Henry Dundas (Lord Melville), his friend Nicholas

Vansittart (secretary to the Treasury) and commodore Popham. They headed a group of politicians opposed to fighting Napoleon on the continent to transform this war into a maritime-imperial conflict where Britain had clear superiority and could succeed in cutting off the financial resources from Spanish colonies and also impede the French from taking military and commercial advantages of British hesitations and to be tempted to seize the Spanish colonies. This Dundas group supported Miranda's attempts to convince Pitt (and the following Prime Ministers after Pitt's death in January 1806) and the successive Ministers of Foreign Affairs (Harrowby, Mulgrave, Fox, Howick). It resulted in internal friction in the British government, which is a key feature explaining the British external policy (see development in Chap. 11), and even, according to some historians (Ferell, J. S., 2006), *"Dundas' efforts to prevent Britain from getting militarily involved [on the Continent] provide a prime example of the foreign policy that Britain would follow for almost two centuries"*.[116]

In his personal expedition, which Miranda had difficulties financing with only private sponsors, he reached, thanks to his connections, only timid maritime support from Admiral Cochrane (Caribbean fleet) and Governor Hislop (Trinidad) and also implicit authorisation from the US government to hire private mercenaries in New York with private local sponsors.

The reality was callous to Miranda:

- First, the minimum support that was committed by the British authorities and the US participants was even less than expected, with the Navy refusing any intervention on the continent (see document 10.4.5. dated 10 January 1808), while *"the bad faith of the Agents of the United States Government, who betrayed the secret to our Enemies, but also to the infamous and treacherous conduct of the American Officers, entrusted with the command of the Ships composing the Expedition"*.
- Second, Miranda was betrayed by Popham, one of his close collaborators in the preparation of these expeditions, who abused his own confidential plans and information for organising a secret parallel expedition with pirate intentions in June 1806 in the River Plate, at the very moment that Miranda was sailing to Venezuela.
- Third, and the worst, the British government, led by Lord Grenville after Pitt's death in January 1806, tried to benefit from the opportunity given by the unauthorised Popham's act of piracy on Buenos Aires by launching immediately direct colonial operations on the Southern cone. Minister of War W. Windham and the Duke of York, Commandant-in-Chief of the Army, decided to send military reinforcements, not only to the River Plate to consolidate the Popham's conquest of new territories but to undertake a complementary operation to control the critical port of Valparaiso on the Chilean coast of the Pacific, pretending to annex so the whole Southern cone as a colony under the British crown. The

[116] Ferrell, J. S. (2006), *The Pivotal Roles of Henry Dundas and William Pitt in the British Cabinet Fiasco of 1800*, University of Tennessee Honor Thesis Project, Spring 4.

treason against Miranda was double: (i) refusing him significant military support to his own expedition on the Northern coast at the exact moment they decided on a substantial military invasion on both ocean sides of the Southern cone, but (ii) with ambition opposed to Miranda's emancipation goal, by annexing the Southern cone in a colonial conquest with the explicit order to impede any domestic and political changes.

Therefore, Miranda's strategy was turned against him, betraying his emancipatory purpose of independence and democracy. This caused severe damage to his reputation since he was accused in Latin America of being a mere spy serving British colonial interests. At the same time, Miranda also lost credibility in London, and the rejection by the Argentinian Creoles of British invasions showed that Miranda's thesis that the local populations were about to reject the Spanish authority was wrong. Despite these damages, after more analysis, Arthur Wellesley and Minister Castlereagh [1807/1851] acknowledged - but too late - in 1807 Miranda's thesis: "*The liberation of South America must be accomplished through the wishes and exertions of the inhabitants...*".[117]

However, such a shocking degree of shameless strategy, organised by British interests, has some explanations. Therefore, further contextual analysis with complementary information is necessary. Assessing the exact dimension of daring to betray such a fair ally like Miranda is difficult. An attempt in this direction is made in Chap. 11, which shows that the British positions relied mainly on gross mistakes resulting from Pitt's procrastination, amid deep divisions within the British government. This mismanagement contributed to Napoleon's victories on the European continent as well as to establishing the bad reputation of the "perfidious Albion".

Content:

Despite his disappointment at having been betrayed by someone who thought he was a friend and who used abusively his confidence for his own profit, Miranda demonstrates with British phlegm a cynical and firm position by reminding Popham that he had warned him of the error of preferring to conquer rather than supporting his plan of effective emancipation. Miranda expresses his satisfaction at learning from Popham that the Creoles have confirmed they want independence and reject any "new owner." He transforms his letter into a cynical call to cooperate again with Popham and Davison for common interests once they are acquitted in London for their errors in Buenos Aires.

Sources:

Translated from French
Archivo.... Vol. XIX p. 9–10
América Espera document 140, p. 362

Text:

To Sir Home Popham
Trinidad, 7 April 1807

[117] Vane, C.W. Marquis of Londonderry (1851), *Correspondence, Despatches, and other Papers of Viscount Castlereagh*, London, VII, p. 385.

My dear Sir Home:

Some time ago, I had the pleasure of receiving your letter dated July 20, 1806, from Río de la Plata. I am delighted to hear from you that the attitude of the country's inhabitants upon your arrival was as favourable as I predicted to you at Wimbledon in the presence of the respectable Lord Melville. However, I never believed that anything solid could be established in this country, much less expect to stay for a long time among the inhabitants without declaring their absolute independence.

Indeed, how do you want 18,000,000 inhabitants established on the largest and most impregnable continent on Earth, located some four or six thousand miles from Europe and possessing treasures and immense resources, to be conquered and subjugated today by a handful of people who come to send them as if they were owners? No, my dear friend, the thing is not natural, feasible, or possible, and as a guarantee of this assertion, we have today the very result of your enterprise.

However, I hope that as soon as you get rid of the charges against you today, you will be in a position to join us and cooperate in these sensible and liberal plans that we had maturely combined in England, with a view to the happiness, freedom, and independence of my native country, as well as to the prosperity, glory, and security of yours.

Please pay my respects to Lady Popham and our friend Davison, whom I wish to see soon honourably acquitted, as you were once acquitted of a similar indictment.

To Sir Home Popham

10.4.4 Miranda's Letter to Viscount Castlereagh: Trinidad, 10 June 1807

Context:

Miranda's naval invasion of the North of Venezuela (Coro) on 31 July 1806 was a total failure, as the Spanish authorities had removed the entire population, impeding him from recruiting patriots to take Caracas. He had no choice but to abandon his position in Coro on August 12. Furthermore, Grenville's cabinet decided at this moment to abandon Pitt's plan. He arrived in Aruba first, from where the English begged him to leave and rejected any new support. He then went to Granada on October 21, where Cochrane welcomed him very well, assuring him that his friends in London could reverse the wrong position of the Grenville government. Miranda sent letters to Grenville (Prime Minister, but ignoring that his cabinet had fallen on March 31, 1807) and Dundas (Lord Melville, Minister of the Navy, who had been impeached in 1806). In November, he settled in Trinidad, hosted by Governor Hislop, where he still waited for a renewal of British cooperation. He sent his trusted officer, de Rouvray, to London with instructions to negotiate with the government and letters to solicit support from his allies, Nepean, St Vincent, and Vansittart.

However, the Popham disaster in August 1806 prevented rapid changes, with the Grenville government demanding that Latin Americans first rebel as a prerequisite for any intervention. However, due to Napoleon's continental blockade, the industrial lobbies exerted pressure when they realised that they urgently needed new markets outside the French reach, whose dominance on the continent was clear. At the same time, it was not the case outside Europe thanks to the British Navy's supremacy. At the end of 1806, debates had taken place in Parliament to define a more transparent policy towards South America.

British government opinion slowly reverses its favourable attitude towards Miranda's theses in the face of mounting Napoleonic perils.

De Rouvray met with the Grenville cabinet, which welcomed Miranda's messages and clarified that they needed Miranda to return to London. The Prime Minister criticised the lack of a clear line in the Parliament. In February 1807, Sir Arthur Wellesley (the future Wellington, winner of the Battle of Waterloo against Napoleon) delivered a report proposing an attack on Venezuela to overthrow the Empire and counter the Napoleonic threat, directly inspired by Miranda's ideas. When the government seemed to support this option in March 1807, King George III dismissed Grenville's cabinet following a political conflict over Catholic rights in Ireland. The new Prime Minister, the Duke of Portland,[118] appointed Lord Hawkesbury to the interior, George Canning to Foreign Affairs, and Lord Castlereagh to war and colonies. As a result of the debates provoked by the Miranda attempt in Coro and the Popham disaster in La Plata, the new Minister Castlereagh issued a report for the government in May 1807 explaining that it was necessary to intervene in South America, either to achieve liberal emancipation of South America or more directly for dominating the region, while William Burke[119] met Miranda and published a pamphlet "*South American Independence: or the Emancipation of South America, the Glory and interest of England*" advocating support for the Miranda plan in the interest of Britain.

These elements once again moved Miranda to tirelessly relaunch his efforts from Trinidad, hoping that his presence near the coast of Venezuela would facilitate a change in British policy. As usual, the UK's options oscillated between a defensive strategy for facing the growing Napoleonic threat (an invasion fleet was being

[118]The **third Duke of Portland**, William Cavendish-Bentinck (1738–1809), was twice Primer Minister.

[119]**William Burke**, an Irishman, ex-official from the British army and writer promoting Miranda's ideas. He met him for writing in 1807 his book "*South American Independence: or the Emancipation of South America, the Glory and interest of England*" advocating that this emancipation was in the British interests. In 1808, he published a second book (with Miranda's cooperation) "*Additional reasons for our immediately emancipating Spanish America*". He went to Venezuela to support the April 1810 movement, publishing many articles in the "Gazeta de Caracas". He escaped from La Guaira on the boat "Saphire" (that Miranda missed due to Bolivar treason), and died in Jamaica at the end of 1812. Miranda's friend, not to be confounded with Edmond Burke. James Mill mentioned William Burke in his article in the Edinburgh Review and n°26, published in January 1809, "Emancipation of Spanish America".

prepared on the French coast off England) and a preventive offensive in South America to prevent the transfer of Spanish funds to Paris.

Miranda sent several letters to his political and military contacts and completed his strategy with a letter to the new Minister of War, Castlereagh.

Content:

This is a sound synthesis of Miranda's argumentation. It relies on Castlereagh's speech to Parliament, but insists that conquering and dominating his people would be counterproductive for both British interests and the reduction of the French threat. However, a British intervention is essential, mainly due to the internal difficulties present in the US, which currently do not constitute an alternative.

Sources:

Archivo…. Vol. XIX p. 55–58

América Espera document n°141, p. 362–364

Text:

A Lord Vincent Castlereagh

Trinidad, 10 de junio de 1807

My Lord,

The last letters I received from England informed me of the change in Administration, and the recent Papers informed me of Your Lordship's Appointment to the Colonial and War Department. At the same time, as my agent in London told me, I was expecting the decision on some critical Business I had before His Majesty's Cabinet and which resolution was favourably promised. I now take the liberty to address this letter to your Lordship on the same subject.

This Business was established under the administrations of the late Mr. Pitt and the Addington (now Lord Sidmouth). The Right Honourable Nicholas Vansittart, My Lord Melville, and Sir Evan Nepean have been the Chief Persons with whom this confidential Business has been communicated and transacted. To them, I refer to your Lordship for more information on the subject.

Count de Rouvray, an Officer of Rank, who served with me in the late Expedition on the coast of Caracas, and Mr. Turnbull, Chairman of the Manufacturing Towns of Great Britain, have been appointed our agents near His Majesty's Ministers. Through them, we have received various communications relative to this Business. I hope they have, by this time, waited on your Lordship and made all the necessary applications to obtain a speedy dispatch of this important affair. And if I am to judge by the favourable and just sentiments Your Lordship expressed in Parliament towards the beneficial effects this Expedition will produce to the interests of Great Britain and the favourable opinion and views that I know Lord Melville possesses on the same subject, I ought to premise a speedy and favourable result.

The present situation and disposition of the People in the whole Province of Caracas (as I am lately informed) is very favourable to this undertaking, yet, notwithstanding the terror that the government tries to inspire, by few executions and the tremendous pursuits of the Inquisition, made a tough political tool on this occasion. The general orders given to the commanders of the principal towns of this province, except La Guaira and Puerto Cabello, are to evacuate them in case of my landing with a substantial force and the inhabitants retire to the country. Still, they have told me they will not do so when the opportunity arises. 200 French Troops are now at Caracas with the view of employing them in defence of La Guaira or Puerto Cabello, and I am afraid that some more may be sent from Martinique, where two French Frigates, I am told, have lately arrived from France; as the Governor of Caracas appears to be much alarmed with the late capture of Curaçao, conceiving it to be a preliminary step towards the invasion of the Province of Caracas.

The late transactions at Buenos Aires have produced no good or favourable impression on the part of the People of South America towards the British Nation. I already thought that the project of conquest was unpopular in the Country, impracticable to any considerable extent, productive of much mischief and confusion in the internal parts of South America, and the most odious that could be presented to the Priests and religious Peoples of the Country. At the same time, the Independence would meet with the approbation of every class of society, except the Agents of the Spanish government and some wretched or despicable contraband Traders on the Coast and in the Islands of Trinidad and Jamaica.

I actually perceive an incalculable mischief in the delay of this proposed operation, for if we do not subtract and protect the continent of South America from the influence and domineering ambition of France, the whole will very soon and ultimately be absorbed in the same fatal and universal dominion. Some of their Troops are already in the Country. Although their exertions towards converting the People's Minds in favour of France have not produced much proselytising in the Province of Caracas until now, it is doing incalculable mischief already. It will ultimately succeed in achieving the nefarious views and intentions. I pray you, My Lord, on these considerations to take some prompt and definitive measure that may put a stop to this incalculable evil or release the American People from the dangerous exertion in which they are embarked by opposing the French and Spanish governments' views, which ultimately must be fatal to themselves, if not effectively supported by the Government of Great Britain.

My own exertions on this Island are almost at an end if I do not receive the promised support from Great Britain soon. I have been keeping here at my own Expense the ship "Leander" as well as the Officers and Men that went with us and were tried in the late Expedition, as they may be of excellent service in going again on the same ground possessing besides the language and knowledge of the Country and having relations and friends in it.

Another danger that appears to me to be rising against South America is the present state of anarchy and confusion that the Western country of the United States is bringing to the banks of the Ohio and Mississippi. By the latest accounts I have seen of North America, nothing appears to me more probable than a dissolution of the confederacy at the approaching election for the next President. In this supposition, we cannot expect anything from that quarter; instead, we can expect mischief instead of assistance and benefit. Your Lordship, however, is a better judge than I on this object and may place this Hypothesis in the scale of benefits or evils that have to be met in the future progress of this undertaking.

I have the honour to, with high consideration and respect, My Lord, Your most Obedient and most humble servant.

(Signed) Fr. de Miranda

P.S.,- To add to our present distress, the last Packet has been taken Windward of Barbados and carried to Martinique.

To the Most Honourable Lord Castlereagh

10.4.5 Miranda's Letter to Viscount Castlereagh, London, 10 January 1808

Context:

Miranda's messenger in London (de Rouvray) and his allies (Turnbull and Vansittart) inform him that Castlereagh is convinced about Miranda's views of the need to act to "*prevent South America to fall into the Grasp of the French, which can be only done by procuring for them Independence, and to be affected, but by the means of General Miranda*[120]", with whom he has consideration. However, he forbids him "*to appear in any way as an agent of the British government*[121]".

As a result of this information, Miranda decides to return to London to resume the diplomatic initiative with the new administration. He left Trinidad via Tortora on October 24, 1807, and arrived in Portsmouth on December 21. Arriving at his house on Grafton Street on January 1, 1808, he went to Lord Castlereagh's house on Sunday, January 3, where he delivered information and requested an appointment. On January 4, he is received by the Minister of Foreign Affairs, George Canning, and on January 5, by Castlereagh. In parallel, he resumed contact with his suppliers, such as Davison, for the logistics aspect. He appears pretty convinced that this time, the government made a favourable decision, given that Napoleon invaded Portugal in November 1807 and, in fact, had already ruled Spain. In this context, the press[122] believes that the French threat is at its maximum and that British interests advocate in favour of the approach of Miranda, which is again endorsed publicly by W. Burke [1807].

In this favourable context, Miranda wrote this letter that had to be sent to the Provinces of South America by the Minister of War and the Colonies, Lord Castlereagh. But the Minister refused, arguing that he was not the Prime Minister, the only one who could send such a letter to Foreigners.

This formal argument attempts to conceal the continuation of the British government's cynical use of Miranda's plan in their European diplomatic policy. Miranda is involuntary, a British instrument against Spain, designed to demonstrate that they control him as long as the Spanish administration does not disrupt the geopolitical

[120] Turnbull's letter to Minister Vansittart, dated 25th of September 1807, *Archivo,* Vol. XX, page 376.

[121] Ibid.

[122] London Times article of January 9, 1808, and a new publication by W. Burke (1808) entitled "*Additional Reasons for our Immediately Emancipating Spanish America.*"

balance in Europe, especially by not joining France against England. In such a case, they could adopt Miranda's plan and destroy their colonial empire.

Content:

The lengthy yet excellent and rigorous synthesis of his actions and strategy, based on the ups and downs of the international scene between England, Spain, France, and the USA, explains Miranda's approach to overcoming the successive obstacles to implementing his plan. The argument is brilliant, skilfully using the failure of Popham's expedition in Buenos Aires to put in evidence, on the one hand, the mutual interests of England and his plan, and, on the other, the heavy responsibility of the British Military authorities who failed to support him when necessary. He also explains the failure of his landing in Coro by the betrayal of some of his agents in New York who informed Spain in advance, together with the "*treacherous conduct of the American Officers*" on the ships of his expedition.

It contains in a few lines the essentials of his government formula, the integrating advantages of having a homogeneous region, and the military plan it advocates.

He adds a note at the end about Castlereagh's objection to Miranda's demand that the minister send his letter to his contacts in South America (as Pitt had already done in the past).

One week later, Miranda also sent Castlereagh the Military Memo he had announced, which contained extensive data and strategic information on Venezuela, Santa Fé (Colombia), and the Pacific area.

Sources:

Archivo.... Vol. XXI. p. 18–27

América Espera document n°142, p. 365–371

Text:

(extracts)

To Castlereagh

London, 10 January 1808

My Lord,

I first proposed the emancipation of South America to the English Ministers as far back as 1790, promising to grant them Independence under the same conditions that France and Spain stipulated with the English colonies in North America. The Convention with Spain about the Nootka Sound ended the measures at that Time for carrying this Plan into execution (see Note A).

France undertook it soon after, in 1793, to give them absolute independence on the same terms. Still, the exaggerated doctrines propagated at that period by the anarchical party in France put a stop to it through my own persuasion and effort and by my demanding further explanation about the actual state of Santo Domingo, which I apprehended would have contaminated the Continent, and instead of bringing Liberty, would have introduced anarchy and confusion. The retreat of the French armies from the Netherlands that followed soon after put an absolute stop to this Plan (see Note B)

As soon as Spain abandoned the Coalition and renewed her connections with France, I turned my views again towards England and, soon after, quit France. — When I arrived in London in 1798, the British Government, under the same Ministry as Mr Pitt, renewed the Negotiations to put the same Plan into execution, assisted by the cooperation of the United States of America, which was invited to furnish a Land force of 10,000 Men — while Great Britain would have found the money and ships necessary for carrying into execution this grand Operation. President Adams, however, disappointed us on this occasion, and the subject was postponed until now (see Note C).

At the beginning of 1801, during Mr Addington's administration, the same negotiations were renewed. The Government plan was to be recommended to the people of South America, and the Military operations were combined and agreed upon. The Expedition was at the point of sailing when the Preliminaries of the Peace of Amiens stopped it, and the execution, of course, was again suspended until an opportunity occurred to realise this grand Plan at some future Period (see Note D).

Following the declaration of war against France in 1803, the same plans were resumed, and the administration prepared to carry them into execution when a declaration of war with Spain was made. This event only occurred in 1804 under Mr Pitt's third Administration, when preparations were immediately resumed, and an extensive and detailed Plan was arranged with Mr Pitt and Lord Melville, Sir Home Popham being consulted on the Naval Part of the intended expedition (see Note E).

These measures, however, were suspended by the manoeuvres of Spain and by Russian intrigue when the reiterated instances of the South American exiles from the Provinces of Caracas and Santa Fe, residing in the United States of America and on the Island of Trinidad, forced me to quit England and to attend to their call; with the view of obtaining some assistance from the United States of America (which were at that time expected to be soon involved in a War with Spain on account of the differences respecting Louisiana) having previous to my departure obtained permission and assurances from Great Britain, of being supported in case of success, in the attainment of our independence agreeably to our primitive stipulations.

This attempt failed due to the bad faith of the United States Government agents, who betrayed the secret to our Enemies, and the infamous and treacherous conduct of the American Officers entrusted with the command of the Ships composing the Expedition (see Note E).

The subsequent attempt upon the Coast of Caracas, in the districts of Coro, in August 1806, supported by some Ships belonging to the squadron of the Winward Islands, under the command of Sir Alexander Cochrane, with whom a formal stipulation in favour of Great Britain was agreed and signed; would have been successful, if the Commanders of the Navy had not peremptorily refused to carry on any operations whatsoever upon that Coast, and force us to retire; under the false apprehension that the Preliminaries of Peace with France must have been signed by Lord Lauderdale at Paris by that Period (see Note F). By the evidence of those who were on the spot at that time and by the intercepted Correspondence from the Principal Agents of the Spanish Government in the Province, it appears that the point on the Coast was judiciously chosen: their own evidence says: [extracts]"*....Miranda despicable indeed if only left to his private resources, appears to me likely to give us more to do, than what we thought...the situation is the most advantageous of any that he could have possibly chosen on all the Coasts...where they may form a* *second Gibraltar...So that this spark of dire, which appeared nothing, may ultimately devour the Continent, if the English assist him*"...(see the original letter from Don Dionisio Franco[123]) ...

...

And that the difficulties of the Captain General & Intendant [of Venezuela] due to lack of money were so great that it forced them to adopt the odious and violent measure of seizing some of the sacred Property of the Churches with all the Deposited Money Belonging to the Poor, Death & etc.; so that if Great Britain had given us decided support of any kind, not only those Provinces, but the rest of the Continent of South America, would have been now totally emancipated from the dominion of Spain (see mainly the letters of Don Dionisio Franco, Administrator of the Province, and Lieutenant Murray of the Royal Navy).

From these documents and the information I have collected on the Island of Trinidad during these last 12 months, it appears that the disposition of the People of the Provinces of Caracas and Santa Fe in favour of Independence is the same. Still, their anxiety increased significantly, with rumours being transmitted from both Spain and France that the Island of Puerto Rico and the Province of Caracas had been ceded to France by secret stipulations with Spain. And as long as I was at Coro, I found there a letter from the Secretary of Government in Caracas mentioning, "*that France would conquer Portugal and give it to Spain in exchange for that Province.*" (see Note H)

These apprehensions significantly increased when 180 French troops were stationed at the capital of Caracas, while Old Spain appeared to be in the hands of France. In this alarming situation for South America, I came to England to reclaim from His Majesty's Ministers that assistance, so long and so repeatedly promised, of supporting the independence of Spanish America. As it was natural for the inhabitants of Caracas to suppose that orders from Spain would soon arrive, calculated to promote French interest and the submission of the whole Province to their New Masters, they could only have avoided their fate by speedily adopting measures for a productive and successful opposition. In my opinion, this step would be the highest degree of absurdity were the inhabitants of those Provinces to venture unsupported and unprepared to contend with France and Spain united without efficient maritime and Land support. In this case, I would imagine it more prudent for them to make the best terms and arrangements with France rather than become victims of French rapine and conquest. I now conceive of favouring independence, as dangers and difficulties must always unite men. I do not perceive, by what I know of the Province, that any difference of opinion existed on emancipation if Independence was fairly and openly offered to them. The delicate point of their Religion must be carefully attended to. The late Events in Buenos Aires are certainly unfavourable, as they encourage the Agents of the Spanish Government to oppose resistance and the Strangers in the Country to aspire to those high and elevated situations that **Liniers** and his followers have obtained in another quarter. On this account, I think the force

[123] Chapter 8, document 8.1., note n° 10.

to be employed now to secure this operation ought to be greater than any that has yet been received.

The population of the *Colombian* continent is considered by the best authorities to be between 15 and 20 million, and it is disseminated over four Grand territorial divisions. first Mexico and Guatemala, as far as the Isthmus of Panama, containing seven million. 2d Santa Fe, Caracas and Quito, four million. third Peru and Chile, four million. fourth Buenos Aires and Tucumán, three million. The total Mass of this Population is chiefly composed of Native Indians, Free People of Colour, slaves and Whites. The Indians and Slaves are supposed to represent the two-thirds: the People of Colours and the Whites, the remaining third. This statement, which appears to me to be the most accurate, is evident that each of these departments, or divisions, based on its territory, population, and resources, is susceptible to having a separate, independent government.

I do not perceive from the information that I have been able to collect in these 20 years that the people of that Country have shown any preference for a particular form of government; all their wishes have tended to obtain their Emancipation and to preserve, by that change, the solid and essential principles of Civil Liberty, which have rendered the Swiss and Dutch People happy and flourishing for the last three centuries (see Notes I).

I do not believe this to be a point that is difficult to settle by simple persuasive means, as the people are mild and incorruptible yet. Still, if *compulsion were* employed in any manner, the result would be opposition and intestine divisions. Considering their great advantage in having a uniform and general Code of good Laws — a single Language — Religion — Form of Administration, the difficulty of a change without convulsions is greatly diminished, and little is to be apprehended. Depons, in his judicious and exact observations on Terra Firme, remarks that the *Cabildos* or Municipal organisations of the Civil Government of South America, are the most popular and best-calculated institutions to administer and govern the country (see Depons, volume II, article Cabildos, Paris, 1806).

The Department of Caracas, Santa Fe, and Quito may be called, by the similarity of its Position and Physical structure, the Switzerland of South America: completely separated from Mexico by the Isthmus of Panama; from Peru by the Cordillera de los Andes; and from Brazil by the immense Rivers, Amazonas and Orinoco, there can be no apprehension of its interfering with the arrangements that may now take place in Brazil.

If we meet with success in this Province, and regulations are immediately introduced, wise in their tendency and acceptable to the People, we may expect to see, in a very short time, the same example followed in Mexico through the Isthmus of Panama and Guatemala; in Peru, through Quito; and ultimately at Buenos Aires, through Peru and Chile.

The Land and Naval Force that I conceive sufficient to put in execution this Plan, beginning by the Province of Caracas, is 10,000 Men of all Arms and a competent Naval Force to co-operate with it — leaving the Military details of this operation for another Memoir; which I shall be immediately in readiness to submit to Your Lordship.

The greatest danger, I now apprehend, is the arrival of some French Chief in the Province, with a Military Force and a set of intriguers well calculated to delude the simple South Americans, as they probably have done by this time, at Buenos Aires. To prevent such risks and dangers, *celerity* in executing this Plan is what I should conceive as the most essential and material point, as that country is in the utmost danger now. — first Suppression (I have already executed Your Lordship's Commands by transmitting to our confidential Agents at Trinidad, through the care of Governor Hislop, the following message: "*I have seen His Majesty's Principal Ministers of State who requested me to assure our affectionate countrymen that the Business is actually in hand; and that the next Packet without fail would transmit to them positive information, (if not the definitive Official resolution) of the critical affair, that brought me to this Capital.*

....

....Let me be permitted to say a few words about the current state of the Trade between South America and the Metropolis, carried under the American Flag, through the exclusive interest of the Intendants and the Governor of those Provinces. It appears by a voluminous correspondence lately intercepted in a Packet from Europe, and actually in my Possession, that all the productions of South America are now cheaper in Spain than they ever were in times of Peace and that merchants of South America, as well as the European Spanish Traders, complain very highly about it. — Also, the Species and Money transactions between Mexico, Havana, Cartagena, etc., are chiefly carried by North American merchants, whose immense profits have turned them from Friends into Enemies of our Independence. They can only, I presume, be brought back to our friendship and interests when they shall see themselves deprived of that immense Trade, which they now almost exclusively enjoy. (see Note L).

In times when guilt and usurpation are upon the Throne, and Virtue seems oppressed almost everywhere on the Continent, let me be allowed to say a few words in answer to some illiberal insinuations and infamous calumnies which I find have been thrown out to the public. — My personal views and interests will be highly gratified, and my labours are ideally rewarded if I can see the People of these Provinces enjoying a sufficient Portion of rational, civil liberty under a solid, permanent form of Government that will maintain it and promise them Happiness. The situation of a private Citizen, then, will be, to me, not only a congenital & eligible one but a good example, I hope, to others by showing that the true character of a Patriot consists in being submissive to the Laws of his country, and a valid Member of that Society to which he belongs.

I have gone rapidly over the narrative of this important affair, presuming that the annexed Documents (mainly the Plan presented to Mr. Pitt and Lord Melville in 1804) will supply the deficiencies, and I have to apologise to Your Lordship for the unavoidable delay, my Papers not having come to hand before Thursday last.—The Documents I have now by me are numerous and interesting, but the apprehension of being diffuse and tedious has made me select a few only, leaving the others for the inspection of any confidential person that Your Lordship may think proper to appoint for inspection and examination. For the sake of brevity and dispatch, I have also transmitted some original documents whose preservation is absolutely vital to me; I request that Your Lordship have the goodness to return them after His Majesty's Ministers have perused them.

I have the honour to be with the highest consideration and respect,

My lord, your most obedient and most humble servant,

To the Right Honourable Lord Viscount Castlereagh & & &.

NOTE.— This message was objected to by Lord Castlereagh when the papers were put into circulation in the Cabinet because, not being a Prime Minister, he could not take it upon himself (as Mr. Pitt did before) to transmit it to the Provinces of Southern America; where in fact it had already been sent; though he agreed that the communication was correct and desirable but ought to be taken upon myself & omitted in this Memoir: with which explanation and suppression, this Document was returned and accepted.

10.4.6 Miranda's Letter to George Canning, London, 26 May 1808

Context:

The Grenville cabinet, which succeeded Pitt's government after he died in early 1806, fell in March 1807 on the Catholic emancipation question, and the Duke of Portland formed the new cabinet (1807–1809) with Pitt's followers, among whom were Castlereagh (War) and Canning (Foreign Affairs). Castlereagh and Canning were in personal conflict over various strategic issues. The former, along with the views of the previous Grenville cabinet, considered that Napoleon had to be stopped on the continent, not overseas, as proposed by the latter, who supported Miranda's plan. Castlereagh was more cautious and reluctant to promote independence and democracy in Latin America, whereas Canning aligned with Miranda in preventing Napoleon from seizing the Spanish colonies and was also an anti-Jacobin. General Arthur Wellesley (before becoming Duke of Wellington), closer to Canning, offered Miranda to be his advisor in his anti-Napoleon crusade, charging him with the military preparation of an expedition to South America along with his plan for the emancipation of Spanish America.

Content:

Miranda, who has been waiting for 4 months for an appointment with the Minister of Foreign Affairs to warn him about the consequences of Napoleon's Spanish occupation, wants to draw his attention to the imminent risks for the UK and Latin America. Once again, Miranda's forecasts proved to be accurate a few days after this letter, with the Spanish Revolution of May and the formation of the Juntas by the municipal Cabildos.

Sources:

Archivo... Vol. XXI, p. 178.

America Espera... document 145, p. 377–378.

Text:

London, 26 May 1808.
27 — Grafton Street
May 26, 1808.
To George Canning.
(Private)

General Miranda presents his greetings to the Right Honourable George Canning and reiterates his request of January 11 for an interview on a matter that he had the honour to communicate to you previously and that, due to the last tremendous events in Spain, has now become not only decisive in Europe but also of the most alarming consequences for the future fate of the Hispanic Colonies in South America.

It considers that the present moment is so essential for executing any measures relating to its emancipation and independence that any further delay could be materially detrimental, both to the interests of Great Britain and to the preservation of South America. Convinced of this, he would consider himself highly guilty if he now omits every effort within his power to ensure the success of such a desirable and fundamental purpose.

10.4.7 Miranda's Letter to the Marquis del Toro,[124] Absent, to the Illustrious Cabildo and City Council of the City of Caracas, London, 20 July 1808

Context:

As anticipated and feared by Miranda for more than 10 years, Napoleon implemented in November 1807 his plan for the invasion of the Iberian Peninsula, starting with Portugal, a traditional ally of England, and then usurping the Spanish throne with the two objectives of imposing his continental blockade and also to divert the American resources for financing the French wars. Napoleon's plan was executed by step, first in October 1807, using his military agreement with Spain to decide to occupy Portugal in November and implement by force his continental blockade against the UK, but without even consulting his Spanish ally, and acting de facto as the supreme authority of the Peninsula, considering that by bringing modernisation to Spain he would benefit from popular support against the corrupt absolutist government. However, Napoleon was utterly wrong; the people reacted against the foreign occupier and the vulgar usurpation of the royal power (on April 30, 1808) that he organised in Bayonne when he betrayed the royal family. The rebellion of the

[124] **Francisco José Rodríguez del Toro e Ibarra**, (1761–1851), Mayor of Caracas and Attorney General of Venezuela, Marquis del Toro. Do not confuse him with his nephew, Francisco José Rodríguez del Toro e Ibarra (1761–1851), who was an independentist, the first general of the Republican army, and a signer of the Independence Act of 1811.

Spanish people, which began in March 1808 in Aranjuez against Carlos IV and his government, culminated in the revolution of May 2, 1808, in Madrid, triggering the atrocious war against the French occupation troops and the formation of the "Junta" of the rebel cities.

Miranda knows that these events signify a fatal decapitation of the institutional structure of the Empire that implies two historical opportunities for Spanish America: an opportunity for the widespread extension of the rebellion to the vice-royalties in America and an opportunity for the British government to justify a military intervention to prevent French expansionism and cut off the monetary flows the French army could organise from South America.

Unfortunately for Miranda, the British government seizes this opportunity to fight Napoleon's troops without opposing Spain by supporting the Spanish people's resistance to the French occupation. This decision means that Wellesley's military expedition in preparation for South America, according to Miranda's plan, was stopped at the last moment in June 1808 and redirected towards a direct intervention on the Iberian Peninsula, focusing all the attention and absorbing all the resources on this war for many years before eradicating Napoleon's regime.

Miranda is distraught by this change, and he measures the high risks of anarchy and civil war that the situation could unleash in the absence of adequate coordination with institutional preparation. His main concern is to ensure that a shared constitutional and democratic structure is built upon the municipalities, utilizing the traditional city councils—the "Cabildos"- from the old colonial rights of the Habsburg era. Therefore, aware of the British incapacity to join his project, he turned again towards an alternative: to address directly the prominent Creole leaders in the capitals of the vice-royalties to warn them about the risks they would expose themselves to if they did not take the initiative to pursue independence and apply his proposal for a constitutional plan. He sent reciprocal copies to all capitals. He begins on July 20 with his city of Caracas, writing to the Marqués del Toro, who was the military man who fought him when he landed in Coro in 1806, followed by letters to the Buenos Aires Cabildo on July 24 (and requesting that it be transmitted to Peru, to Chile and Quito), and on September 10, 1808, to the Cabildos of Havana and Mexico.

Content:

Miranda warns the local authorities of Caracas to beware of the opposed Spanish and French factions, the latter being the most dangerous. He recommends that the most representative of the Creole oligarchy take the initiative to call the "Cabildo" (Municipal Council) to form a representative local government—the "Junta"—but take distance from the rebel Juntas formed in Spain, whose interests are opposed to those of America.

Sources:

Translated from Spanish

Textos sobre la Independencia...op. cit. p. 100–101.

América Espera document n°146, p. 378–379

Text:

To the Marquis del Toro

London, 20 July 1808

Mr Marquis:

Allow me, My Lord, that you deliver this message to the Cabildo and the City Hall of that Illustrious City of our Country in these most critical and dangerous circumstances that have ever occurred for America since the establishment of our ancestors in it.

Spain is now without a sovereign and in the hands of various factions, which either ally with the French or others with England, and are trying to establish the party that best suits their particular views through a civil war. Naturally, they try to attract us each to their party so that we are also involved in general dissension, exposing us to the risk of being subjugated by France (which is the most probable result, although less desirable). As a result, the Colombian Continent could be subjected to the same calamities that the lack of prudence, or leftover misconduct, has brought down on the unfortunate, oppressive and corrupt Spain.

In this assumption, I plead with Your Lordship very indeed that by forming a representative municipal body that would take charge of the Government of that Province and by sending as soon possible authorised people to this capital capable of handling such essential matters, we will see with this government what it should be done for the security and future fate of the New World; in no way should Your Lordship look for the advice of interested parties, in hostile resolutions, or offensive alliances that can bring such dire deals for our country, as the Spanish authorities have brought on mine; without having even consulted or offered us the slightest advantage in their vain and foolish projects with the other powers of Europe. The truth is that the views or interests of the recently formed "Juntas" of Oviedo, Seville, Madrid, etc., have minimal compatibility with the interests and authorities of our Provinces in America.

I would also beg Your Lordship (if you deem it convenient) to send a copy of this message to the other neighbouring provinces (Santa Fe and Quito) so that, making adequate use, we march unanimously for the same purpose. In my opinion, disunity would put our salvation and independence at risk.

For Your Lordship, from his most affectionate countryman and humble servant.

Francisco de Miranda.

10.4.8 Miranda's Letter to the Illustrious Municipal Council of Buenos Aires, London, 24 July 1808

Context:

Like the previous letter sent to Caracas, Miranda, aware of his inability to obtain military support from Europe or the United States, attempted to address the local authorities of the main cities directly. He faced an additional handicap: Popham's military invasion of Buenos Aires 2 years ago had unduly associated Miranda with this neocolonial attempt. This British betrayal of Miranda's emancipatory ideal, a grave injustice, seriously damaged his reputation and credibility.

Content:

The same advice was diplomatically introduced with reference to the official British positions at the highest levels, demonstrating that Miranda had succeeded in convincing the British to support his emancipation project. This support and influence could have a significant impact on the project's success.

Sources:

Translated from Spanish.

Textos sobre la Independencia...op. cit. p. 102–105.

América Espera document n°147, p. 379–381.

Text:

To the Magistrates of Buenos Aires.

Sirs:

Not doubting that your Lordships are aware of the commitments and efforts with which I have tried to promote the Freedoms and Independence of the Spanish-American Continent, and having the honour of being one of its most minor and most faithful citizens, I address the attached notice so that, making the use that seems to your Lordships convenient, let's get, if it is still possible, to avoid the severe and imminent risks that currently threaten our dear and beloved Country.

D. Manuel Padilla reported to me with all the details, the extraordinary events in Buenos Aires and Montevideo, the results of which were the evacuation of the English troops and the withdrawal of the Squad with which they attacked both cities last year, 1807; in these events, I have had the double satisfaction of seeing, that my previous admonitions to this government, regarding the impractical project of conquering or subjugating our America, were not only well-founded but also that after your heroic success for repelling such an odious attempt, your Lordships offered at the same time peace and friendship to the enemy, under the honourable condition of solid and free independence. These facts are so glorious and memorable in the annals of the New World that they constitute immortal monuments for the people and magistrates of the City of Buenos Aires.

To proceed with the pulse and maturity that require a matter of such magnitude, it seems to me you should keep in mind and meditate on the following documents:

I. The declaration of His British Majesty addressed to the Province of Caracas on April 8, 1797 (following the agreement made by me on behalf of the Spanish-American Colonies on February 14, 1790, with the very honourable Minister William Pitt).
II. The instructions to the Mayor General Whitelocke, by the Secretary of State Windham, March 5, 1807.
III. Secret instruction of the same Secretary Windham to General Craufurd, October 30, 1806.
IV. The speech of His British Majesty to the Houses of Parliament, July 4, 1808.
V. The orders of the private Council of His British Majesty, relative to the Spanish Nation, July 4, 1808.

With these official pieces, which essentially portray our America, your Lordships will be able to form a fair judgement on the views of the British Government towards the mutual interests of this nation, particularly with our opulent establishments on the American Continent.

2° May Divine Providence give to your Lordships the indispensable union and success required for matters of such magnitude and interest to ourselves and to the human race in general.

Concordia res parvae crescunti discordia maximae dilabuntur.

[with harmony, small things grow; with discord, the greatest perish].

(Salust. De Bel. Jug.)

To your Lordships with the utmost affection and high regard.

Your most obedient servant and compatriot.

Q.S.M.B.A.

Francisco de Miranda.

P.S. addressed to Dr. D. Saturnino Peña,

Absent, to be followed by his wife in Rio de Janeiro or Montevideo.

I think sending this office to the Kingdoms of Peru, Quito, and Chile would be very timely.

10.4.9 Miranda's Letter to the Vice-King and Cabildo of Mexico and the Capitan General and Cabildo of La Habana, London, 10 September 1808

Context:

It is similar to the two previous letters, as the British government's intentions became clear regarding the political and logistical impossibility of favouring the independence of the Spanish colonies.

Content:

Miranda attempts to mitigate the damage to his strategy caused by the successive betrayals that occurred in Buenos Aires and during his own Venezuelan landing.

He explains that, anyway, British and Spanish-American interests are converging, but he cannot communicate the complex and secret reasons that underlie the British positions in a letter. He asks for their trust while waiting to provide them with all the explanations in person.

He also annexes a note explaining that he refused to participate in Wellesley's military expedition to Portugal.

Sources:

Translated form Spanish

Archivo.... Vol. XXI p. 353–354

América Espera document n°148, p. 381–382

Text:

London, 10 September 1808

Grafton Street No. 27 - Fitzroy Sqr.
(Reserved)
Sirs.

The attached Notice (1.2A.) Already communicated to some Provinces of our America, on the occasion of the Revolution that occurred in the Spanish Government and the Monarchy, may be helpful to you under the present circumstances — and for this reason, I am sending it now to that Capital. The latest news from Spain and Portugal sufficiently indicates the outcome of my well-founded conjectures: I mean that Europe can no longer govern the Colombian Continent, whose political, moral, and civil systems are entirely different and perhaps incompatible with our serenity and well-being in America.

The political plans of England towards those countries, which are about to be carried out, have changed their orientation due to the unforeseen events that have recently occurred in Spain. Still, I think the views are the same: France has also changed its mind at various times, as can be seen from Document B, and thus, it is not necessary to be muddied with these political aberrations when the interests between us and Great Britain are *solid, reciprocal and highly advantageous* to both parties; despite the bizarre policy with which the government conducted itself here both towards Buenos Aires, as well as in my Patriotic Expedition to the Province of Caracas! These hidden causes and secret springs ask for information and knowledge that neither you can acquire at that distance, nor do I prudently communicate from here in writing: In which course, I invite you earnestly to pay attention and credit to a citizen and compatriot, whose fate is entirely tied to yours having consecrated all his life, and even sacrificed very considerable personal interests, for the good and happiness of his expensive country.

As soon as it would be possible and opportune to meet you, you will have me in your company, always remaining with genuine affection and pleasing will.

To you from your most attentive Countryman and humble servant.
Q.S.M.B.
Francisco de Miranda.
Mr. Captain General - and Illustrious Cabildo of the City of la Habana.
Your Excellency, Sr. Viceroy, and Illustrious Cabildo of the city of Mexico.
P.S.

Note 10.C contains the reasons why I did not consider it convenient to accompany this country's last expedition to Portugal and Spain

10.4.10 Miranda's Letter to the Cabildos of Buenos Aires and Caracas, London, 6 October 1808

Context:

The Spanish people's opposition to the French usurpation turned into a cruel war and political disorganisation.

Content:

Miranda warns again of the inevitable anarchy that always results from a lack of clear institutional organisation, as recent history shows, as well as in Greco-Roman Antiquity. He joins his letter with 12 annexed documents, among which is his fourth version of the federal constitution for Spanish America (see Chap. 5, document 5.2.4)

Sources:

Translated from Spanish

Textos sobre la Independencia... p. 106–111

América Espera document n°149, p. 382–385

Text:

(extracts)

To the Cabildo of Buenos Aires, Marqués del Toro and Cabildo of Caracas

London, October 6, 1808

Grafton Street No. 27.

Fitzroy Square.

Sirs:

…I am very worried, if your detail is correct, that the diversity of opinions between the European Governors and the American people will produce a fatal conflict for the former and not very advantageous for the latter if the People (and not its competent and virtuous men) were to take over the Government. Consider the events in France with the revolutionary government and the recent developments in many parts of distressed Spain. The truth is that the strength of a state resides essentially in the People collectively and that without it, one cannot form vigorous resistance anywhere; furthermore, if obedience and subordination to the Supreme Government and its Magistrates is lacking *in our case*, instead of preserving and defending the State, it will infallibly destroy it by anarchy: as we have just palpably seen in France as well as in history, in Italy, Greece, etc.

The Directors of the present Revolution of Spain, for lack of a Representative organisation in the beginning, are now forced, it seems, to form an imperfect one (since the Nation did not elect the Provincial Boards), and so late that they will hardly have time to agree on a general Défense and Organization Plan before the enemy has invaded most of the Kingdom, while the people of more weight and authority in the country, disgusted with the excesses of anarchy, are reluctant to the point of not wanting to take part in the common cause. These errors surprise me all the less, since we have seen people of much greater experience and wisdom in France make the same mistakes, often due to a lack of practical knowledge in matters of this nature. The attached outline, No. 12 of the Representative Organization for the Governance of our America, was formed here some years ago and has received the approval of the best specialists in this field, who have examined it subsequently, both in England and in the United States of America. Therefore, I recommend it for your consideration at this opportune moment….

… Documents 3, 4, 5, 6, 7, 8 and 9, although in personal matters, also contain facts and circumstances related to the negotiations and efforts that we have practised both in this country, as well as in France and the United States of America, to obtain the freedom and independence of those countries; it is the primary object in the day and that attracts the attention of almost the entire human race, for which reason I pray you to scrutinise them, for they are toils and results of many years of study, accompanied by a practice acquired in the great Revolutions that have upset almost all the governments and ancient institutions of Europe. I will always consider myself happy if I can contribute in any way to the relief and prosperity of my country, together with my beloved and virtuous compatriots….

….

with high regard and great affection

I remain your most attentive servant and faithful compatriot.

ingenti Patriae perculsus Amore.

[startled by the immense love of our country]

Francisco de Miranda

N. B.

The attached documents are copied in the language in which they were written due to a lack of time to translate them, for which I beg your pardon, and I will translate them, if necessary.

N. B. (to Buenos Aires)

The primary Documents cited in this letter were sent to you some time ago by the hand of Don Manuel Padilla, who requested them for this purpose. Still, this subject's strange and reprehensible behaviour later makes me doubt his veracity and honesty. It is a pity that such individuals now appear here with the name of Americans, to the shame and disgrace of their homeland.

Doctor D. Saturnino Peña, who seems to me to be a subject of merit and integrity, very different from Padilla's character, is the channel through which they addressed you the antecedent documents, which I do not doubt he remitted to you punctually and with honour.

To the Marqués del Toro and Ill° Cabildo of the City of Caracas.

10.4.11 Miranda's Letter to Lord Castlereagh, London, 24 March 1809

Context:

The Portland's cabinet (March 1807–October 1809) continues the ambiguities concerning South America in Pitt's line. As the Ministry of War and the Colonies, Lord Castlereagh hesitates between direct continental and indirect actions overseas, like his predecessors. Temporarily convinced by Miranda about the danger of Napoleon's capture of Spanish colonies, he asked Miranda and A. Wellesley to prepare for military intervention in South America. However, at the last moment, the government decided to assist the legitimate Spanish rebellion against Napoleon. This new alliance with Spain impedes any aggression against their colonies. In June 1808, he announced this sudden policy change to Miranda, who was very upset and refused his invitation to accompany and cooperate with this British Iberian war, which started in August 1808 in Portugal against the French Army.

During the remainder of 1808 and 1809, Miranda failed to convince Wellesley and others of the win-win game that the independence of South America could launch. Still, he knew that without a war against Spain, the British administration could not adopt his plan. Therefore, he developed an active presence in the press and intellectual circles to disseminate his views on the win-win game that Britain is missing as an alternative way to pressure the government. He exchanged various letters with the patriots (despite Castlereagh's prohibition) and his British supporters (Hislop, Cochrane). He met various British writers who were interested in his project, including Jeremy Bentham, James Mill, William Burke, and William Thomson.

At the beginning of 1809, the Alliance with the Spanish rebellion was sealed by a Treaty with the Central Junta, giving Miranda once more hope that the Spanish American Juntas created against the usurped authorities in Madrid could be part of a cooperation with Britain. However, Spencer Perceval, Chancellor of the Exchequer in the Portland administration, strongly reprimanded Miranda for transferring his revolutionary pamphlets through the Treasury services in Trinidad towards Venezuela. Under Spanish pressure, the British authorities intercepted several of his messages, and intense pressure was placed upon him to prohibit him from continuing to communicate with South American patriots.

In 1809, the British expedition sent by Castlereagh against Napoleon's naval base at Antwerp turned into a total disaster due to strategic mistakes, worsening the long-standing divisions in the Cabinet between Ministers Castlereagh and Canning. This division prolonged the traditional opposition between a continental view versus a maritime one, which handicapped the British strategy and allowed Napoleon's fast and spectacular victories, strengthening his domestic as well as external power. In March 1809, Canning manoeuvred secretly to require the dismissal of Castlereagh, leading to a duel in which Canning—who had never learned to shoot a pistol - was wounded. Both Ministers were forced to resign from office, precipitating the fall of the Portland cabinet in October 1809.

Content:

Miranda believes that the historical window of opportunity presented by the Peninsular War in Spain may be lost. He again attempts to use the government's official responses to highlight its own contradiction and the risks to British geopolitical and commercial interests that new delays are exacerbating. Knowing the logistical constraints imposed by the Iberian War, he nevertheless attempted a more diplomatic strategy without a military expedition. So, he reminds his proposal made in January 1809 to Prince Ernest Augustus[125] (Duque of Cumberland) to be sent together with two British commissioners to convince the local authorities of Mexico and La Havana to make an alliance with the UK to get their independence.

[125] **Ernest-August de Hanover**, (1771–1851), duke of Cumberland, fifth son of George III, became King of Hanover in 1823 when his brother King William IV died.

Sources:

Original in English but here translated again from a Spanish translation

Archivo... Vol XXII, p. 246–250

América Espera document n°151, p. 387–390

Text:

(extracts)

My Lord,

London, March 24–1809

My Lord

Allow me to request Your Excellency's attention to the message that Sir Arthur Wellesley transmitted to me last June. In it, he meant "*that other matters (that is, the suspended operations and negotiations relating to the South American Colonies) would be decided after knowing the result of Spain ...* " which I had the honour of exposing to him in a letter dated August 19, 1808.

Now, when I think that this predetermined epoch is entirely over and that the dangers of those Colonies have increased considerably, I would consider myself deficient in zeal towards my native country - and in the sense of duty towards those whose political interests have been entrusted to me for not a few years. - if I were not to exercise my ability and resources at this critical time in favour of their just and honourable cause. In fact, I have always shown so little inclination to meddle in the affairs of Old Spain (for the reasons set out in my note, which was transmitted to Your Excellency through Sir Arthur Wellesley on the occasion of the proposal to accompany you in the recent expedition to Spain and Portugal, v. Copy of letter A.), as I have been passionate and zealous in promoting the freedoms and independence of the Colombian Continent - and even more in preventing its submission by the new alleged King of the Indies, Don José Bonaparte, as the central provinces of Old Spain call it and proclaim it!

Quo die omen avertent

Be convinced, Excellency, that the old Spanish Government, formed by the evil genius of Felipe II of Spain, never had in view the welfare of these Colonies and has ended up destroying its own supporters and agents on the principles of politics and alleged tenderness towards his children in South America. After keeping them for three centuries in a state of imbecility and degradation unparalleled in the annals of humanity, he now wants, it seems, to hand them all over to the benevolent race of Bonaparte and his humanitarian legions of administrators!

I have every reason to believe, from the information I have recently received from various parts of South America, that the majority and the best-informed classes of the inhabitants of those Colonies detest the idea of becoming subjects of the French or any other foreign nation, and they very much desire emancipation and a better form of Government, organised by themselves: the Viceroys and Governors, the Audiences and the Intendants are entirely of different opinion, because their families and property being based in Old Spain, the meridian of Madrid always influences and directs their conduct. - One month, they proclaim for Fernando VII, the next for Don José Bonaparte, another for the Supreme Board, and finally, they will recognise King José if the people of South America do not interfere and prevent it. This course of things is so natural and evident in human affairs that it does not require many arguments to prove it. Some events, however, have occurred recently and since the revolution in Old Spain, which is worth citing as corroborative evidence....

....Under these impressions, I visited Sir A. Wellesley last January 26 - and after having shown him all the important letters that I had received from various Provinces of South America and all that I had written to that Continent as a result of recent events in Spain and up to that time, I offered my services to Great Britain with the purpose of proceeding without delay to Mexico or Havana in the company of one or two English Commissioners who could explain to the constituted authorities of the country the favourable provisions of Great Britain. Britain made them, and after hearing and discussing in the presence of the English representatives the interests of both parties, reached a decision following their instructions and on which we can make a general and firm plan based on which we act in future operations for taking from now on the measures for the independence of that Continent. – His reply was "*that His Majesty's Ministers could not for the moment enter to continue discussing the matter, while the Spanish attempt was pending, but as soon as that question was finished, he supposed that the matter would be resumed and the promised answer would be transmitted to me.*» We agreed, however, that my communication would be transmitted without delay to Your Excellency and that I would send you a copy of two letters that I had received and read to you from South America for the same purpose, adding that you would always be happy to see me, etc.

Weighing all these circumstances and seeing the squadrons of France and El Ferrol ready to sail, with one of them already sailing in the direction of South America, my anxiety increases; indeed, it is an alarming degree! Several of the Spanish elements that a few months ago took from our hands an armament ready to be dispatched by sea and enough to have achieved for this time the independence and happiness of South America, under cover and through false promises that they would rescue Spain and the Colonies wholly under the oppressive yoke of France, are now recognised traitors and deserters in favour of Bonaparte's cause. They try by all means to acquire the entire Spanish monarchy for him. Could it be that the own sons of South America, corrupted by those men, such as Solano, Caso, Calvo and O'Farrel, have taken the side of the French oppressors and tried to hand over their native country to the abominable invaders and oppressors of humanity? Even Asanza, whose administration in Mexico announces a benevolent, disinterested and enlightened disposition; Saavedra, who is remembered with affection in the Provinces of Caracas, Havana, etc.; and Jovellanos, whose patriotic writings and persecutions place him among the benefactors of humanity ... the former has evidently betrayed the cause of freedom in Spain and the latter two have shown such inertia that against the grain we are led to accuse them of lack of zeal and energy in the glorious cause they deserved to have embraced. I hope, however, that my fears are unfounded and that these two distinguished characters will continue on their path in life and deserve the best that their native country has to offer. These sad examples and painful reflections convince me more and more, Excellency, that the well-being and happiness of South America can never come from Spain but from its own incorrupt children!

It amazes me that a plan of this importance and so essentially related to the interests of this country was on the verge of being executed by a series of governments from the year 1790, beginning with Mr. Pitt, fervently adopted by Lord Sidmouth and Saint Vincent; retaken by Mr. Pitt and Lord Melville and finally accepted by his Excellency and his colleagues. By a fatality that is inexplicable to me, he has been defeated with equal frequency!

Therefore, I earnestly beg you to grant me an audience so we may resolve this fundamental, decisive, and interesting matter as soon as it is compatible with Your Excellency's occupations. I much dread the consequences of delay because what seems practicable now could be insurmountable at any other time.

I have the honour to subscribe, with high respect and consideration, to Your Excellency, the most obedient and humble servant,

(Miranda's draft)

To the Most Honourable

Lord Viscount CASTLEREAGH

etc., etc., etc.

10.4.12 Miranda's Report on His Conference with the Duke of Gloucester, London, 24 April 1809

Context:

At this date, the British government continues to postpone its decision regarding Miranda's plan, but Miranda continues his tireless lobbying.

Miranda maintains good relations with the Royal Family through several members, from the King's sons, the Duke of Clarence, Prince William (1765–1837), who will become King William IV in 1830, and the Duke of Cumberland, Prince Ernest Augustus (1771–1851), as well as others like the Duke of Gloucester and Edinburgh (1776–1837), who was the grandnephew of King George III (1738–1820). The Duke influenced the British Army and reorganised it, especially to prepare the Island's defence against Napoleon, a member of the House of Lords. He also introduced Miranda to ministers and politicians, particularly to promote the abolition of slavery.

Content:

Miranda reports a long meeting at the Duke's request. The Duke wanted to secretly discuss his plans for America with him, which he considered necessary to "*execute for the good of humanity*" and that he would continue to influence the Parliament in favour of.

Sources:

Translated from Spanish

Archivo... Vol. XXII, p. 299–303

America espera... document 153, p. 392–395

Text:

After a long conference (about 2 h) in which, with mutual apparent satisfaction, we explained ourselves about the important matter that was mainly dealt with, relative to the Independence of the Colombian Continent..... Above all, the Duke was delighted with everything that happened in our conference this morning. He said to me: "*Well, friend, here you see that we have prepared everything for the execution of our plan on South America if these men enter, as is possible, in the ministry promptly and even if they did not enter the government, their influence would always cooperate advantageously to our views and ideas in Parliament. This was what I wanted, and for this reason, I advised you to come here today. I hope the results will be favourable in the future and let's go for a walk together*".....

We indeed went towards Bond Street and Piccadilly, and here I said goodbye, leaving him with other friends of his that we met along the way, and that by accident, having heard my name mentioned, they spoke with praise of the article on South America in the latest issue of the Edinburgh Review....

10.4.13 Circular Letter from Miranda to His Agents in South America, London, 24 March 1810

Context:

The British government holds firmly on its official line of neutrality with Spain, where the British Army under Wellesley's command is directly challenging Napoleon, who had brought with him his "*Grande Armée*" from Germany to Spain in only a few days in November 1809. This war became the very first priority of British policy. During 1809, the internal rivalry between Ministers Castlereagh and Canning had worsened to the point that the cabinet virtually ceased functioning. In September, the two men fought in a duel, forcing both to resign. The Prime Minister was already ill and resigned on 4 October, being replaced by Spencer Perceval. This Prime Minister, famous for his intolerance against Catholics, was not inclined to help Miranda, considered an embarrassing ally whom he wanted to control more strictly. Miranda was already prohibited from maintaining correspondence with Spanish Americans by Castlereagh, decides to circumvent these orders to pursue his promotion of emancipation by using other Latin American residents in London, like Antepara, who signs Miranda's book "*South American Emancipation*" (published in January 1810) addressing the British public opinion, and also appears (in March 1810) as the editor of the biweekly review "*El Colombiano*", the newspaper created by Miranda for diffusing his ideas in Spanish America (see Chap. 9, document 9.2). He also uses nicknames in the press and asks the readers to send their comments to a neutral address in London. It is precisely the case of this circular that he sends to South American contacts with the first issues of "*El Colombiano*", his newspaper edited in London in Spanish.

Content:

This circular delivers as an attachment (not reproduced here; see Chap. 8, document 8.2) the first issues of Miranda's new journal explaining the justification for independence and offering advice on preventing the risks of anarchy through people's sovereignty and democratic elections. In the circular, Miranda offers to be the point of reference for organising a network for emancipation.

Sources:

Translated from Spanish

Archivo del General Miranda. Vol. XVIII. p. 367–368.

América Espera. Document 162. p. 435–436.

Text:

Circular

London 24 March 1810

N° 27 Grafton Street, Fitzroy Square

Dear Sir.

The purpose of the printed attachment is to communicate to our Americas those Official Documents and news that seem most beneficial for their interests and security so that, by taking the most prompt and necessary measures in the current crisis, they could be with instruction and sanity in condition to avoid the imminent risks to which they are exposed.

For the same reason, I wrote more than a year ago to the Cabildos and Town Halls of the different Capitals of those Vice-Kingdoms so that, anticipating on time the dire consequences of the manoeuvres and intrigues of the various governments in Spain, they would be able to look for their safety and Emancipation. These are essential points that do not admit the slightest doubt today.

My home in this city (as in any other part) is, and will always be, the fixed point for the Independence and freedoms of the Colombian Continent.

God keeps you,

(Draft of Miranda unsigned)

If, for greater security, you would like to put the answer under the cover of a merchant in this City, it is the following— Messrs. Boehm & Tayler. London.

10.4.14 Miranda's Letter to N. Rodríguez Peña,[126] London 15 August 1810

Context:

[126] **Nicolas José Rodríguez Peña** (1775–1853), Argentinean patriot who played an essential role in preparing the independence of the Spanish colonies, closely related to Miranda, anti-Jacobin too and pro-English, his home was one of the centre of conspirators during the revolution against the Spanish domination, with H. Vieytes, J. J. Castelli, M. Belgrano and others, he was member of the militia resisting to the British invasions. However, his brother, also in contact with Miranda,

Miranda is preparing for his trip to Caracas after the Venezuelan delegation, sent by the new authorities of Caracas, led by Simón Bolívar, visited London in July 1810. Miranda introduced the delegation to the British authorities. Bolivar, who returned to Caracas in August, invited him to return to help establish an authentic emancipation. Miranda contacted the other cities and sent messages to spur the creation of local Juntas based upon elected representatives in municipal councils ("*Cabildos abiertos*").

In Buenos Aires, he was in contact with the brothers Rodriguez Peña, who shared his vision of claiming complete independence and establishing a constitutional order that would impede Jacobin deviations. Nicolas Rodriguez Peña's house was the centre of the patriots preparing the emancipation revolution. In mid-May 1810, the official information of the Spanish submission to the French arrived in Buenos Aires. Nicolas' house was the place where the start of the May Revolution and the Declaration of Independence was decided.

When Miranda sent this letter, Rodriguez Peña was engaged in a military campaign inside Argentina to extend the revolution to the whole colony.

Content:

Miranda manifests his support for the River Plate revolution and provides advice for ensuring genuine independence. He also expresses his preoccupation with the rule of law: *"Freedom is nothing other than justice wisely administered."*

Sources:

Translated from Spanish

Archivo del General Miranda. Vol. XXIII. p. 524–525.

América Espera. Document 172. p. 446–447.

Text:

To Rodríguez Peña

London 15 August 1810

Dear friend and Sir.

I have received with great pleasure the news from you that D. R. Larrea communicated to me, whom I have treated with appreciation because he seems to me to be an honoured subject and of estimable attitude - I have also seen and treated Mr. Mathias de Yrigoyen, Deputy for the city of Buenos Aires sent to deal with this Government: and from what I get from his reports it seems to me that the matters of the Río de la Plata promise no less success than those of Caracas, and it is remarkable that these two cities, so distant from each other, and with a difference of only 30 days, without the slightest communication, went through all the same steps, and have taken his own political steps in executing his glorious revolution! Be careful, my friend, to sustain what has been done because all retreats now would bring fatal consequences for them and the Independence of those Countries. The only thing

---

was also cooperating with Beresdorf by allowing him to escape, abused by the British spy James Burke. He promoted and financed the May Revolution of 1810, fought in the liberation army in key battles, and was named governor of Alto Peru (Bolivia) after the victory of Suipacha in 1810. He then acted in the ups and downs of creating the independent republic, being a member of the masonic Logia, which became the "*Logia de Lautaro*". He was closely associated with San Martin's expedition to free Chile and Peru.

that I disapprove of in these events is that you have left the members of the Audience in the Count and the other people who had a part in the infamous and scandalous events of Goyeneche and his henchmen with the citizens and patriots of La Paz. Freedom is nothing other than justice wisely administered, and where heinous crimes are committed with impunity, true freedom cannot take a seat.

According to what Mr. Larrea has informed me, I am convinced that you have already left to meet with your worthy brother in Buenos Aires. Therefore, you work with zeal and activity in laying the foundations of an excellent civil and representative Government, allowing these institutions to mature progressively. Thus, you will have done to your country the most significant benefit that men can do to their fellows: redeem them from slavery and leave them free and independent! May Providence grant you complete success in such a noble undertaking and, to them, the enjoyment of such high happiness!

I have received flattering news from my compatriots and relatives in Caracas, who have called me urgently. We have already obtained what they wanted from this government: We will probably leave in a few days, together with the Deputies of said Province, towards that continent, but this will still depend on what happens in the interim. Anyway, I will notify you of my departure, as I always stay everywhere.

Your faithful friend and sure servant.

(Draft of Miranda unsigned)

To the

DOR. DN. SATUR: PEÑA. Rio de Janeiro.

10.4.15 Miranda's Letter to the Supreme Board ("Junta") of the New Kingdom of Granada, Caracas, 22 January 1811

Context:

As Miranda recommended and expected, the Viceroyalties in Spanish America created Juntas elected by the Municipal Councils. The first was made in Venezuela and Buenos Aires, and was imitated by Santa Fe (Bogotá) and other cities in 1810. However, as Miranda feared, the juridical vacuum opened internal conflicts about governance's independence and federative aspects.

Miranda arrived in Venezuela in December 1810 and was actively involved in the debates on the form of government and the degree of independence to be decided in Caracas. Faced with intense internal disputes between local autonomists and central federalists, and the risk of fragmentation of the Spanish Empire, he was always preoccupied with the centrifugal forces that exposed the independence to the difficulty of defending a divided territory in the event of reconquest by Spain. Therefore, he advocated for the urgency of organising the cooperation of the provinces through a federation, both to prevent civil wars and to organise common defence and ensure constitutional stability. For this purpose, Miranda sent from Caracas to Santa Fe

(Bogota) his reliable Chilean disciple, Father Cortés Madariaga,[127] who played a vital role in the April 1810 event of the Caracas Cabildo proclaiming independence. In Miranda's line, Cortés considered the union of the different provinces as essential for ensuring stable and genuine emancipation. He concluded and signed on 28 May 1811 the "*Treaty of Alliance and Federation*" between Cundinamarca (Colombia) and Venezuela.

Content:

Miranda congratulated the Junta of Cundinamarca (Santa Fe de Colombia) for resisting manipulations from the bishop of Cuenca and announced the dispatch of a special representative with a mandate to negotiate a political agreement for the unity of the two independent entities for mutual security.

Sources:

Translated from Spanish

América Espera. Documento n° 173. p. 447–448.

Las primeras misiones diplomáticas, López Mendoza, Cristóbal. Vol. II. p. 106–107.

Text:

To the Supreme Board ("Junta") of the New Kingdom of Granada

Caracas, January 22, 1811.

Lords and Fathers of the Nation.

Allow me, my Lordships, as a citizen of the Province of Venezuela who deeply admires, respects, and recognises the illustrious works that the Supreme Junta of Santa Fe de Bogotá has carried out in favour of our freedoms and rights, to respectfully come to thank you for such high and beneficial favours.

We have just received, with inexplicable joy and applause, the response that this August Senate has given to the Bishop of Cuenca in defence of the sacred rights and sovereignty of the Colombian people and how the solid foundations and reasons that justify our holy cause, we also hope, gather in one voice all its inhabitants, so that they easily repel the tricks of our enemies, who like Cortabarría and the Prelate of Cuenca, do not omit the indecent means to deceive or hallucinate the simple and honest inhabitants of these distant Provinces.

The Father Dr. José Cortés Madariaga, who recently left this city for that capital and is in charge of a very important commission, will tell your Lordships (what I could highly suggest you listen to) about a political treaty between the kingdom of Santa Fe de Bogotá and the Province of Venezuela so that by forming together a single social body we now enjoy greater security and respect and in the future to get

[127] **José Cortés de Madariaga** (1766–1826), priest and political activist in the Venezuelan independence movement. A native of Chile, Cortés de Madariaga arrived in Venezuela by accident in 1802 and obtained a canonry in the Cathedral of Caracas. He played an active role in the events of 19 April 1810 in Caracas and was a member of the Junta Suprema of Caracas, close to Miranda's views. At the republic's fall in 1812, he was sent to the military prison at Ceuta, in Africa, from which he escaped 2 years later. When Venezuela regained its independence in 1817, he returned and promoted the founding of a representative federal government. This plan was disclaimed and condemned by Simón Bolívar. Cortés de Madariaga later travelled to Jamaica, where he again worked for independence.

glory and permanent happiness. This subject is a man of high merit and distinguished patriotism, for which reason I will not say more now about this important project.

You are left with sentiments of the highest consideration and respect. By your Lordship,

Your most obedient and attentive servant,

(Signed) Francisco de Miranda

To the Supreme Board of the New Kingdom of Granada. Santa Fe de Bogotá.

References

Burke, W., (1807), *South American Independence: or the Emancipation of South America, the Glory and Interest of England*. J. Ridgway, London.

Burke, W., (1808), *Additional Reasons, for our immediately emancipating Spanish America, deduced from the present crisis: and containing valuable information, respecting the late important events, both at Buenos Ayres, and in the Caraccas*, London. Reprinted by Creative Media Partners, LLC, 2015.

Fantin-Desodoards, A., (1797), *Histoire philosophique de la révolution de France*, Perlet (Imprim, 4 Vol., Paris.

Ferrell, J, [2006], *The Pivotal Roles of Henry Dundas and William Pitt in the British Cabinet Fiasco of 1800*. University of Tennessee Honors Thesis Projects.

Ghymers, C., [2002], "Influencia del Maestro sobre el Discípulo: el papel de Miranda y O'Higgins en la singularidad del caso chileno y de su gobernabilidad", *Revista del Instituto O'Higgiano de Chile*, n° 19, Santiago.

Hampe Martínez, T., (1999), "Viscardo y Guzman en Londres o los albores de la independencia hispanoamericana (1791—1798)", en *Juan Pablo Viscardo y Guzman (1748) 1798) El hombre y su tiempo*, Fondo editorial del Congreso del Perú, Lima.

Meyer, E., (2020), "Valmy, la victoire à contretemps", *Annales historiques de la Révolution Française*, 2020/4, n° 402, Armand Colin, Paris.

Meza Dorta, G., (2012), *Miranda y Bolívar: dos visiones*, bid & co. Editor, Caracas.

Miranda, F. de, (1929-1950), *Archivo del General Miranda*, ed. Vicente Dávila/ Rubén González, Caracas/La Habana.

Miranda, (1978 – still in publication), *Colombeía*, edición de la Presidencia de la República, Caracas.

Paine, T. (1819), *Miscellaneous Letters & Essays, on Various Subjects*, Ed. Carlile, London.

Parra-Pérez, C., (1950), Miranda et Madame de Custine, ed. Bernard Grasset, Paris.

Robertson, W. S., (1929), *The Life of Miranda*, University of North Carolina Press.

Salcedo-Bastardo, (1982), América Espera, Editorial Ayacucho, n°100, Caracas.

Simmons, M., (1986), "Viscardo y Guzman's two sojourns in London: new documentation", *Archivum Historicum Societatis Iesu*, Vol. 55, Roma.

Simmons, M., (1989), "More about Viscardo y Guzman's sojourns in London", *Archivum Historicum Societatis Iesu*, Vol. 58, Roma.

Syrett, H. ed. (1965/1974), *The Papers of Alexander Hamilton*, Columbia University Press, New York

Vane, C. W., Marquis of Londonderry, (1851), *Correspondence, despatches, and other papers of Viscount Castlereagh: second series: military and miscellaneous*, W. Shoberl, London.

Chapter 11
Assessment of the British Policy with Latin America and Towards Miranda

11.1 Historical Context of British Policies in Hispanic America

The emerging British colonial empire had been accumulating many conflicts with the already powerful Spanish empire since the sixteenth century. During the first decade of the seventeenth century, England began to establish a growing presence in Florida. Additionally, it attempted to access the Pacific coast, first through the slave trade and pirate expeditions (Hawkins, Drake, Raleigh), which involved seizing Spanish convoys carrying precious metals, and second, with a few attempts to establish settlements (Guyana, Suriname, Darien), but without achieving significant success. However, their sailors slowly acquired the skills and technology to match and challenge the Spanish navy. Britain had long aspired to gain access to the vast markets of South America. Nevertheless, Spain maintained its dominance in South America. The eighteenth century saw the extension of intra-European rivalries to the Caribbean and South America, marked by several treaties, and the progressive emergence of Great Britain as a geopolitical and military power. Despite public opinion's reluctance to strengthen the state and its army, which was perceived as a risk of despotism, this shift occurred. On the contrary, the maritime force, although more costly than infantry, was positively perceived, favouring the adoption of a "blue-water"[1] policy (complementarity between naval power and trade expansion), as already proposed by Walter Raleigh's maxim [around 1600]: "*Whosoever commands the sea, commands*

[1]The so-called "***Blue Water***" strategy, initially coined by the Portuguese in 1508, was adopted by Great Britain in the seventeenth century. It means developing the ability to exercise long-distance sea control for commercial and military control purposes. From the eighteenth century, it became the geopolitical doctrine on which the British empire was built. See Chap. 5, section 5.2.4, note n° 66.

C. Ghymers, *Independence, Federalism and Regionalism in Latin America: An Analytical Anthology of Francisco de Miranda's Writings (1790-1811)*,
United Nations University Series on Regionalism 34,
https://doi.org/10.1007/978-3-031-96938-6_11

the trade, whosoever commands the trade of the world, commands the riches of the world, and consequently the world itself'.[2] The British strategy began to strike a fluctuating balance between foreign intervention through allied nations and British naval power protecting trade. In the second half of the eighteenth century, priority was given to strategic establishments and the growth of international and colonial markets [Baugh 1994]. Military expenditures increased significantly more than in Spain or France (Brewer, J. 1994; Minard, P. 2018), rising from 9% of GDP in 1710 to 14% in 1780,[3] and were primarily dedicated to naval power.

This rising potential power overseas favoured plans of intervention in Spanish America, even before Miranda's first proposal of 1790, both for cutting a source of strength for Spain and responding to private lobbying for increased manufacturing exports. Following the devastating British intervention in Santo Domingo/Haiti from 1793 to 1797, these plans were generally postponed due to government procrastination stemming from the fear of triggering further uncontrollable political upheavals. However, with the radicalisation of the French Revolution and Spain joining France against Britain,[4] the government sent troops to the Caribbean. It envisaged an expedition to South America, along with Miranda's ideas. The initiative came from the Secretary of War, Henry Dundas,[5] the leading advocate of overseas operations, together with Nicholas Vansittart,[6] who elaborated in 1796 a plan for an ambitious "*expedition from Cape to the Plata*" for moving later to Chile and Peru. This plan was officially approved in January 1797. The proposal aimed to sever the Spanish colony from Madrid, thereby enhancing British commercial interests and potentially gaining a strategic advantage by cutting Spain's financial resources. However, the deterioration of the situation in Europe frightened Pitt, who cancelled this plan. In parallel, the expedition in the Caribbean captured the island of Trinidad in February 1797, but failed to seize Puerto Rico and Saint-Domingue. Dundas sought to utilize Trinidad as a platform for subverting Spanish rule and

---

[2] Raleigh, W. (1600), *A discourse of the invention of ships, anchors, compass*.

[3] Until the Glorious Revolution, England was the less militarised power, with an army of around 30.000 soldiers, against 70.000 for Spain and 120.000 for France. From 1680 to 1780, military expenditures were multiplied by 15, reaching ¾ of the public budget against only ¼ in France. Furthermore, the British GDP per capita was already higher than elsewhere, as were fiscal resources. See Brewer, J. (1994), *The Sinews of Power. War, Money and the English State, 1688–1783*. See also Minard, P. (2018) "L'État militaro-fiscal anglais au 18th siècle", in *Revue d'histoire moderne & contemporaine,* 2018/4 (n° 65–4) 2, p. 162 à 177.

[4] The **Second Treaty of San Idelfonso**, signed on 19 August 1796 between the Spanish Empire and the First French Republic, set that. France and Spain became allies and combined their forces against Great Britain.

[5] **Henry Dundas** (1742–1811) was a Scottish jurist and politician, close to Miranda. He was Home Secretary from 1791 to 1794, in charge of the Ministry of the Indies from 1793 to 1801, Minister of War from 1794 to 1801 and First Lord of Admiralty from 1804 to 1805. He was elevated to the title of Viscount of Melville in 1802. His policy was to develop the "Blue Water" strategy, i.e. betting first on global sea control and not so much on the European continent.

[6] **Nicholas Vansittart** (1776–1851), Pitt's political ally, quickly attached to Miranda's plans, becoming Miranda's personal friend, Deputy Minister of Finance (1801–1804) in Addington's Government (who succeeded Pitt in 1801), Chief Secretary for Ireland (1805), Deputy Minister of Finance (1806–1807) and future Finance Minister (1812–1823).

fostering independent movements. In 1798, Miranda returned to London, attempting to reactivate his plan. Still, William Pitt's reservations increased with the Napoleon campaign in Egypt and the potential danger to the British interests and trade with the East India Company. In 1800, a Scottish Major General, Thomas Maitland,[7] a friend of Nicholas Vansittart, revised Vansittart's plan and issued: "*Plan to capture Buenos Aires and Chile, and after to emancipate Perú y Quito*", (Terragno, R. 1998).[8] This version followed Miranda's views, which were implemented between 1817 and 1820 (after his death) by Bernardo O'Higgins, his disciple, with the assistance of San Martin. Vansittart planned to send two expeditions, one to Venezuela and the other to Buenos Aires, to cross the Andes and converge on the Pacific coast, to seize Lima. The British Government approved it under the name of the Maitland plan, but like the previous Miranda plans, it was again cancelled. Until he died in 1806, *Pitt's procrastination* became a constant attitude based on two linked fears when having to decide on a military intervention promoting a change of political regime: the dread of socio-ethnic upheavals impeding benefit from stable trade with Britain and implying spending excessive forces oversea on the ground, and the uncertainty about the ability of the American inhabitants to organise and accept a substitution of the Spanish authority for the British one.

It was not until 1806 that two successive British military expeditions attempted to invade the River Plate, aiming to capture the cities of Buenos Aires and Montevideo as part of a broader plan to control the entire South Cone of America. These colonial attempts were decided to betray a Miranda who was precisely in the same period organising in full knowledge of British authorities - but without their help – a non-colonial emancipating landing in the North of Venezuela. These colonial British attempts were rapidly defeated and humiliated by a fast reconquest by the Argentinian patriots. Analysing the circumstances and antecedents of these failed colonial projects provides essential information on British mismanagement and the military strategic context in which Miranda attempted unsuccessfully to launch his emancipation project.

This Chapter attempts to understand the ambiguous relations the "*perfide Albion*" had with Miranda. Still, it also provides an opportunity to demonstrate that his precursor degree can be assessed without being influenced by today's values and ideas. The reason is that this case compares two historical facts from the same era: Miranda's analyses and forecasts with those of the British administration, and what actually happened during the French Revolution and the Napoleonic Wars. As

[7]**Thomas Maitland** (1760–1824), a British Army officer, was in charge of trying again to conquer St Domingo in 1797 but failed. He then bargained a secret Treaty with Toussaint l'Ouverture, the head of Haitian forces. Several times elected to Parliament, he became a "Privy Councillor" of the King in 1803. Governor of Ceylon from 1805 to 1812.

[8]According to Rodolfo H. Terragno (1998), in his *Maitland & San Martín*, Universidad Nacional de Quilmes, 1998, the Maitland plan is considered the plan that Libertador San Martín applied for crossing the Cordillera and freeing Chile and Peru. However, the initial ideas come from Miranda. San Martin only accepted Miranda's views and implemented this plan after failing with his several expeditions to Lima through Bolivia (Alto-Peru).

explained by John Lynch (1969), "*No British government would promote a revolution for independence if it was likely to unleash a social revolution*".[9] Thus, it is easy to compare "objectively" (i.e. without interference with present ideas) this dogmatic choice with the alternative proposed by Miranda for drawing attention to their difference in relevance for both the British and South American interests. These differences allow us to assess objectively who, at that time, had the best capacity to perceive and anticipate existing geopolitical challenges, risks and limitations. Above all, the reader can evaluate for himself who made the best forecasts, Miranda or the British government, when considering the facts of what happened afterwards.[10]

The arguments developed in this chapter demonstrate how the British government systematically overlooked the best options for its own interests, thereby facilitating the prolongation of the highly damaging Napoleonic successes. Miranda's strategy would have probably yielded a better outcome not only for UK citizens but also for the general interest of the world as a whole.

Contrary to several current views, this analysis pretends to show that the failure of Miranda to get the needed British military support was not so much due to the imperialist strategy and the priority given to British interests but rather to British strategic mistakes which impeded maximising these selfish interests, mainly being beneficial to the Napoleon's power and expansionism. Furthermore, our argument goes well beyond, daring to issue the "uchrony" hypothesis[11] that the prolongation for years of the bloody and costly European wars is a consequence of the conservative fears upon which the procrastination of British governments was based. It is even plausible that such a geopolitical paralysis by the Hegemon might bear part of the responsibility for the exacerbated future development of nationalist reactions inside the whole of Europe. For the same reason, this probable responsibility might be extended to the anarchical civil wars in Spanish America and their durable results on their political systems and under-development.

---

[9] Lynch, J. (1969), "British Policy and Spanish America, 1783–1808", *Journal of Latin American Studies,* Vol. 1, No. 1 (May 1969).

[10] Although controversial, our method allows us to propose an explanation beyond the mere succession of observed facts, breaking the stochastic uncertainties. See the arguments explained in Chap. 3, section 3.6.

[11] Uchrony means alternate history or the reconstruction of history not as it was but as it might have been under alternative events.

11.2 The Popham's[12] Pirate Expedition to Buenos Aires in June 1806

Popham indeed organised his expedition without official authorisation, as demonstrated by the government's embarrassment, the first order sent by Castlereagh,[13] the dismissal of Popham and his trial on court martial in London. However, he was eventually not effectively sanctioned, despite being responsible for a pirate expedition organised by a group of officials who were behind the financial, commercial, and colonial arguments for hiding personal profit goals.

Nicholas Vansittart introduced Commodore Popham to Miranda in 1803. Minister Dundas and Commodore Popham shared Miranda's idea of organising a military landing in the Spanish colonies to prevent the Spanish Empire's financial resources from being used to support Napoleon's plan to challenge British power and, primarily, to compete with the British Navy. Popham was also a candidate for deputy in the British Parliament, where he wanted to support Miranda's actions.

Miranda's plan had already been presented to Pitt in 1790, but a diplomatic deal between Pitt and Spain prevented war, without which the British government was unwilling to attack Spanish colonies. The defeat in 1795 of the first coalition against France led Spain to reverse the alliance, joining France in its war against Great Britain (Treaty of San Idelfonso, 1796) when Miranda was in France (1792–1797). This allows Henry Dundas, Minister of War and Colony in the Pitt's cabinet, to formulate an invasion plan to Mexico and South America, but by using Miranda's argument of independence from Spain for taking control of these regions and their trade potential. However, the purpose was very different. Miranda wanted political independence to introduce radical political changes by laws that Britain feared due to the recent Caribbean upheavals. Dundas's purpose was a geopolitical conquest for both security and commercial reasons: "*...destroying the colonial resources of our enemies and adding proportionately to our own commercial resources, which*

[12] **Sir Home Riggs Popham** (1762–1820) was a Royal Navy commander who fought against the French during the Revolutionary and Napoleonic Wars. He created a signal code for boats adopted by the Royal Navy in 1803, which was helpful to the Trafalgar victory in 1805. He was a Member of Parliament from 1804 to 1812. Between 1787 and 1793, he was engaged in commercial ventures in the Eastern Sea, including contraband. From 1794, he was active in the war against France in Flanders, Denmark, and the Red Sea. In 1804, Pitt commissioned him to work on Miranda's plan to contribute to the emancipation of Spanish colonies. In January 1806, he recovered the Cape of Good Hope from the Dutch, where he conceived his pirate expedition to La Plata, betraying Miranda (see this Chapter) and attempting a colonial conquest, ending in a total disaster. He was dismissed by the Navy and sent to the Spanish war against Napoleon, where he won various battles, being promoted to Rear Admiral in 1814.

[13] **Robert Steward, viscount of Castlereagh** (Dublin, 1769–1822), Irish Tory, Minister for Ireland (1798–1801), Minister for India (Board of Control), Minister of War and Colonies (1805–1806) and (1807–1809), Minister for Foreign Affairs (1812–1822). He opposed Miranda's plans and Dundas' maritime strategy despite his disastrous continental operations from 1805. He also betrayed Miranda by managing with Pitt the spy James Burke (see below note n° 36) to South America before the British invasion in competition with Miranda's operation in Coro.

are and must ever be, the sole basis of our maritime strength....", (Ingram, E. 1970)[14] His idea was not merely a "colonial conquest" (Dundas 1796–1797)[15] but also to get British military and commercial control of the region with the political purpose of giving guidance for preventing the spread of the Jacobin principles and even to control or, if necessary, oppose Miranda's political revolution. A key element for assessing Miranda's vision of the future – and in opposition to Dundas - was about evaluating the maturity of Creoles for managing themselves: history shows that he was wrongly too optimistic, but the British administration fell into the opposite with a traditional feeling of superiority. The Dundas' imperial plan had already been discussed secretly with Nicholas Vansittart, Robert Brooke,[16] and Popham. However, with the rising threat from France, a sceptical Pitt stopped this plan by focusing his meagre military resources upon the European theatre.

Dundas made no secret of his opposition to Pitt and the Foreign Secretary (Pitt's cousin) Lord William Grenville's[17] choice to intervene only on the continent. Dundas promoted, instead, as Miranda, a strategy of economic and financial power based upon the British maritime advantage for defending and extending British rule, which was also the source of long-term political power for Britain. He consistently argued against military intervention on the continent, maintaining that British prosperity in both war and peace depended on sea control, rather than continental control. He was also a constant opponent of peace with Napoleon, believing it was premature (Mackesy, P. 1984). "*By success in the West Indies alone, you can be enabled to dictate the terms of peace.*"[18]

On 12 October 1804, when the war against Spain was restarting, Prime Minister Pitt invited Popham and Miranda to a dinner at the villa of Henry Dundas, Miranda's supporter and head of the Admiralty. Dundas was also convinced that to mitigate the effects of Napoleon's protectionism on Great Britain's commercial interests, it was necessary to open the harbors of South America, especially on the River Plate.

---

[14] Edward Ingram ed. (1970), *Two Views of British India*, p. 206.

[15] In 1796 and 1797, Henry Dundas explained to the House of Commons that British operations in the West Indies aimed not at conquest and financial reward but at Britain's security. Henry Dundas' speeches of February 18, 1796 and May 18, 1797, Parliamentary History, vol. 32, col. 752; and vol. 33, col. 584, quoted by Golding C. (2017), op. cit. p. 35.

[16] **Robert Brooke** (1744–1811) was a lieutenant-colonel in the Army of Bengal and governor of the island of St Helena from 1788 to 1800.

[17] **William Wyndham Grenville** (1759–1834), cousin and Interior Minister of William Pitt in 1790, before becoming Pitt's Foreign Affairs Minister from 1791 to 1801 and returning as Prime Minister after Pitt died in 1806. Grenville was very influential in Parliament, pro-aristocratic, and suspicious of Miranda, who was Republican and had fought along Washington's side in the US against the UK. Contrary to Miranda, Grenville was in favour of military intervention in Europe and an opponent to his colleague, Minister Henry Dundas, who was always a supporter of Miranda's plan of a maritime war in America in order to get a lever upon France and to establish English supremacy at a lower cost. (Not to be confounded with William Windham, Minister of War in Pitt's government from 1794 to 1801).

[18] Mackesy, P. (1984). *War Without Victory: The Downfall of Pitt 1799–1802*. Oxford: Clarendon, p. 12.

Among the topics discussed were Spain's hidden agenda, which was building a fleet in Ferrol despite its neutrality commitment and an ultimatum from the British government. They saw this as additional proof of the nation's future intention to ally with France against the UK. Such a French-Spanish military alliance was perceived as a severe threat to the security and the future of the Kingdom. In this context, Pitt asked Popham to write a memorandum on the matter; therefore, the next day, 13 October, Popham met with Miranda, with whom he drafted the memorandum and presented it to Minister Pitton the 14th. It was only signed by Popham and delivered to the home of Navy Minister Dundas on the same day. On 16 October, Pitt invited Dundas, Popham and Miranda to a luncheon to discuss the strategy. Miranda suggested that the River Plate should be protected for some time with a garrison in Montevideo, the main port, and another one in Maldonado to protect the entrance to the River. The reason was that the Vice-royalty of the Río de la Plata was crucial to the economy and budget of the Spanish Crown, as gold and silver were transferred from Potosí to Buenos Aires and later to Montevideo, from where they were ultimately shipped to Spain. This route was preferred because it did not risk sinking when crossing the Magellan Strait.

A British naval presence in the River Plate would allow the future independent nation to be organised under British protection, preventing Spain from attempting to regain the territory and dissuading Portugal from trying to control that riverbank, according to the information Miranda had received. The memorandum established that 20 million pounds (more than £2 billion today) was the annual income from exports, and that two-thirds were earmarked for the military effort offered to France. This secret conspiracy between Spain and France, in violation of Spain's neutrality in the event of a war between France and England, was uncovered by English espionage in 1804 as secret clauses of the Treaty of San Ildefonso, signed in 1800 between the two nations.

Popham used the information extracted from Miranda and Pitt along other data from William Pio White, a US trader based in Buenos Aires, with whom he was involved in unclear trade business and traffic. White had informed him of the ease of stealing the treasury of the Company of the Philippines, which had been accumulated in the vault of Buenos Aires, without significant military defence. In July 1805, Popham received orders to escort the David Baird[19]-led expedition against the Dutch colony of the Cape of Good Hope. As the Cape had fallen with Holland under Napoleon's control, the official purpose of Popham's mission was to impede French troopships from controlling this key haven on the road to India. Before attacking

[19] **David Bear** (1757–1829), a British officer, distinguished in the campaigns in India, became a rival of Arthur Wellesley but failed. He fought in Egypt and the Middle East against Napoleon, named Lieutenant-general, he commanded the expedition against the Cape of Good Hope with complete success, capturing Cape Town and forcing the Dutch general Janssens to surrender. He was then soon associated with the Popham piracy project on Buenos Aires and was recalled in 1807. However, he was quickly re-employed as a divisional general in the Copenhagen expedition of 1807. He was made Colonel and sent to the Spanish war against the French army. In 1809, he was ennobled, becoming Baron and upgraded to General in 1814.

Cape Town, their expedition traveled through the eastern coast of America in November 1805. In January 1806, the expedition conquered Cape Town, with Baird becoming the Governor and General Beresford[20] nominated in charge of the Army at this place. In the meantime, the Spanish-French fleet was destroyed at the Trafalgar battle in October 1805. It seems that Popham had received new orders from the admiralty to patrol the east coast of South America, from Rio de Janeiro to the Río de la Plata, in order to detect any attempt to counter-attack the Cape. But Popham convinced Bair to give him part of the garrison (1.600 soldiers) under the command of General Beresford. These soldiers had indeed become idle after the victory of Trafalgar. Popham planned to use them in exchange for a significant share of the booty from his pirate plan, which aimed at personal enrichment by seizing the colonial treasure stored in Buenos Aires under the guise of an anti-Napoleonic operation. In addition, Popham also hoped to garner public opinion support by sending some of the money to London and leveraging the press to highlight future advantages for British exports and business.

On 14 April 1806, Popham sailed towards Argentina, landing and Beresford's troops taking over Buenos Aires at the end of June 1806. Popham seized an important stock of gold and silver indeed (for US $2 million or US $ 50 million in purchasing power in 2023), sending five tons of silver to London (about US $3 million in 2023) and keeping the rest for him and his accomplices, Baird and Beresford, as well as smaller parts for the other officers and the soldiers.

This pirate operation[21] was organised without any official order from the Navy or the government. Additionally, it was based on confidential information that Miranda had released in their memorandum to Pitt. However, Popham neglected the critical recommendation made constantly by Miranda, that no sustainable result could be obtained without the adhesion of local citizens, warning the British that a colonial operation would fail anyway. So it was. Furthermore, Popham took this initiative knowing perfectly that Miranda was undertaking his own landing on the northern coast around the same period. He probably considered that the simultaneity of both operations would increase his own chances because Miranda would attract Spanish attention to the North, all the more since Miranda's expedition had been denounced from the beginning by betrayers to the Spanish army.[22] Popham was also perfectly

[20] **William Carr Beresford** (1768–1854) British military and politician. He was a general in the British Army and a Marshal in the Portuguese Army. He was appointed general to participate in Popham's operation in Buenos Aires, which he managed to take for a few weeks, proclaiming himself governor of the British colony of Buenos Aires (from the end of June to the beginning of August 1806). The Argentine patriots reconquered Buenos Aires, and he was captured. However, released by chance during his transfer, he regained his rank in the war against Napoleon, cooperating with Wellington in Spain and Portugal.

[21] Grenville used even the term "buccaneer" operations.

[22] Miranda sailed from New York on February 1806, and the Spanish authorities were fully informed a few days later by the Consul of Spain in New York that the Leander - Miranda's boat - left for Santo Domingo. This information enabled the Spanish governor of Venezuela to take measures to defeat Miranda by ordering the evacuation of the populace from Coro and the Bishop to warn the people against the dangerous "*libertine Jacobin moral*", prohibiting any cooperation with

aware that the purpose of Miranda's expedition was not to extend British colonies but to establish genuine independence, although with a free trade and military alliance with the UK. He was a formal part of the commitment between Miranda and the British authorities to operate continuously in close coordination, as the official position of the governments was that any possible British intervention could only occur after the success of Miranda's invasion or in the event of local rebellions against the Spanish regime. In coherence with Miranda's views, Grenville's cabinet (Pitt's successor) had confirmed this critical commitment that any British intervention would be decided only after a local revolution against Spain had previously occurred. Therefore, it was a clear case of conscious and *direct betrayal*. Popham was even so shameless that in July 1806, after capturing Buenos Aires, he wrote to Miranda to invite him to join his conquest in the River Plate!

The Popham invasion operation of the Rio de la Plata failed miserably in July/August 1806, as the Argentinian Creoles sought independence, not a new coloniser, as Miranda had formally and repeatedly warned Popham and the government, demonstrating the superior predictive capacity of the former compared to British stakeholders.

11.3 The Second British Invasion of the River Plate in 1807

The British press was informed in September 1806 about Popham's colonial conquest of Buenos Aires at the end of June 1806 (the travel used to take some 70 days between Buenos Aires and England). Miranda's operation in Coro failed in mid-August 1806; however, the information did not arrive in London until the end of October. The Popham's success provoked enormous popular enthusiasm and an immediate favourable response from the business sector, to which Popham had also written from Buenos Aires. These positive reactions, along with the diplomatic impact favourable to the British bargaining position in its negotiations with France, explain why Grenville endorsed this illegal initiative afterwards despite his traditional opposition to overseas operations.

In fact, when arriving from the Cape in their intermediary stop at St Helena island in late April 1806, Popham learned of the death of his political patron, William Pitt, and felt the necessity to justify his expedition by writing to Dundas[23] and William Marsden,[24] Secretary of the Admiralty, that there was an urgent need to

him. See also our possible assumption of Aaron Burr's betrayal, Chap. 5, section 5.3, in Deductive Hypothesis.

[23] Although Dundas was not anymore First Lord of Admiralty in the Pitt's cabinet, having been impeached by an accusation of corruption in 1805, of which he was acquitted in June 1806. Popham shared Dundas's views on the conquest of South America but interpreted it as a personally lucrative colonial conquest.

[24] **William Marsden** (1754–1836) was a famous Irish orientalist, numismatist, and linguist who served as Second Secretary to the Admiralty (1795–1804), then First Secretary to the Admiralty

ensure the grain imports from Buenos Aires haven upon which the South African basis of The Cape was dependent, on top of the economic benefits for the British industry by granting it access to "*a great proportion of the wealth of Chili and Peru.*".[25] These letters had reached London on 24 June Golding, C. (2017), causing embarrassment in the Cabinet. Only 1 month later, Minister of War Windham[26] instructed Beresford not to take territories, prevent involvement in local revolution, and send the unnecessary forces back to the Cape. At the same time, the admiralty charged Rear Admiral Charles Stirling[27] to relieve Popham of command and implement Windham's orders with Beresford.[28] In parallel, however, Windham secretly charged Brigadier General Samuel Auchmuty[29] on the same day to sail with 2000 men to reinforce Beresford.

Nevertheless, Grenville's cabinet again blocked the preferred continental strategy after Napoleon's military successes (Austerlitz, December 1805). Peace discussions with France had already started when the "official" news of Popham's capture of the River Plate was known in September 1806. This immediately strengthened the British negotiators' grip on France.

At this moment, Lord Grenville, impressed by the unexpected impacts of these operations, radically changed his mind, acknowledging finally that this time, Miranda and Dundas' strategies were appropriate to the situation: South America provides leverage over Spain and France for buying peace at lower costs. First, knowing that River Plate had become a British dominion, Lord Grenville had in mind using it to bargain for the cession of this new conquest in exchange for concessions, such as the restoration of Naples and free trade. Buenos Aires was seen as a

(1804–1807), succeeding to Evan Nepean.

[25] Popham to Dundas, April 30, 1806; and Popham to Marsden, April 30, 1806, in Royal Navy in the River Plate, 28–9, and 26–8. Cited by Golding, C. (2017), *At water's edge: Britain, Napoleon, and the world 1793–1815*, p. 194.

[26] **William Windham** (1750–1810), British Whig statesman and Parliament member, close to Fox and E. Burke, anti-Jacobin and opposed to peace with Napoleon, was Minister of war in Pitt's government already in 1794 and resigned with Pitt in 1801, being again appointed as Minister of war in the Grenville cabinet after Pitt's death, from 1806 to 1807. Not to be confounded with Lord Grenville (William Wyndham Grenville).

[27] **Charles Stirling** (1760–1833) Navy Officer, participated in naval operations against France, sent to Jamaica, promoted to rear admiral, was charged with the reconquest of Montevideo and Buenos Aires in 1807, ordered to take up the office of naval Commander-in-Chief at the Cape of Good Hope Station, appointed in 1810 as Commander-in-Chief of the Jamaica Station, named Vice-Admiral in the second war against the US in 1812, recalled to London under accusation of corruption in 1813, was first condemned in Court Martial, but in appeal recovered part of his titles.

[28] Windham's instructions to Brigadier-General Beresford, July 24, 1806, WO 6/3, pp. 3–7, BNA.

Admiralty to Popham, July 28, 1806; and Admiralty to Rear-Admiral Charles Stirling, July 28, 1806, in ADM 2/1364, pp. 15–16, and 16–20, BNA, cited by Golding, C. (2017), *At water's edge...* op. cit. p. 196.

[29] **Samuel Auchmuty** (1758–1822) was adjutant-general to Sir David Baird in Egypt. He was made brigadier-general for participating in the second invasion of the River Plate, promoted to major-general, sent to India and then promoted in 1810 to the rank of lieutenant general. In 1822, he became Commander-in-Chief, Ireland.

lever for winning other French concessions. However, in London, public opinion and commercial lobbies were pressuring the government not only to retain what appeared to be an easy conquest but also to extend this policy to the entire Spanish colony, to the point that the government revised its instructions in September 1806. Although confirming the dismissal of Popham for judging him in court martial for unauthorised actions, at the same time, Minister of War and Colony William Windham decided to changed partially the previous instructions to Stirling and Achmuty, reinforcing their troops and ordering them to manage their parallel expeditions for consolidating the Beresford's conquest, placing the whole territory under the authority of H.M. of the UK, although maintaining the previous conservative order to prevent any social revolution.

At the beginning of October 1806, Grenville, previously the champion of the preference for continental war, suddenly became the impromptu champion of colonial conquests, to the point that he even considered the possibility of taking control of Mexico and the West coast of South America. This option continued to be considered by Grenville up to February 1807, with the presentation of a plan (Golding, C. 2017) that even contemplated the capture of Manila[30]! Therefore, at the beginning of October, Grenville launched a second top-secret expedition commanded by his secretary, Brigadier-General Robert Craufurd,[31] which carried 4200 soldiers with written colonial instructions to conquer the Pacific coast and Chile simultaneously. For logistical reasons, this more ambitious expedition was delayed to the end of October 1806 and finally sailed only on 12 November 1806, a few days before being informed by rumours that Buenos Aires had been lost. The Argentinian forces and inhabitants had forced the British troops to surrender, and all were captured, except by pure coincidence, Popham and his fleet.

On 3 February 1807, Montevideo was captured by more than 10.000 British forces. King George III appointed General Whitelocke[32] in February 1807 to take command of the two main fleets already in the River Plate, and Minister Windham nominated him to assume the new colony's civil governor functions. The colonial

[30] Lord Grenville to Buckingham, October 3, 1806; and "*Spanish America Memorandum*," likely written in February 1807, in *Royal Navy in the River Plate*, 128–29, and 157–60. Cited by Golding, C. (2017), *At water's edge*...op. cit. p. 200.

[31] **Robert Craufurd** (1764–1812), British Officer, sent to the Prussian court to study military tactics, engaged later in the South Indian wars (1790–1792) under Lord Cornwallis, sat in parliament for East Retford from 1800 to 1805, became friend of W. Windham who took him in his staff at the Ministry of war and colony in 1806, ordered to invade River Plate with the prospect to become Brigadier-General, he fought in Montevideo and Buenos Aires, but failed, accusing his General Whitelocke of cowardice and treason for surrendering in Buenos Aires. Sent on the Iberian wars against Napoleon in 1808, with David Bair, he won the confidence of Arthur Wellesley. He was promoted to Major-General in June 1811. He died during the conquest of Ciudad Rodrigo, a key victory for Wellesley against the French Army, which opened the way to Salamanca and Badajoz.

[32] **John Whitelocke** (1757–1833), British Army officer, served in Jamaica and San Domingo, then South-East England. He was appointed Lieutenant-General and Inspector-General of Recruiting in 1804 and promoted to General in charge of the South American expeditions. He surrendered to the Argentinean forces and was brought before a court-martial in London in 1808. Condemned, he was expelled from the Army. See his trial [1808].

character of this mission was thus formally set. Again, written secret instructions were explicitly given by the Secretary of State, William Windham, "*not to introduce in the government any other change than that which must naturally come from the substitution of the authority of the King of Spain by that of H.M.*[33] (Faulder, R. et al. 1808). Whitelocke brought additional troops, and on July 1, under his mandate, 13,000 soldiers attacked Buenos Aires. The strong resistance of the Argentinians, combined with General Whitelocke's incompetence, contributed to the rapid and complete failure of the expedition. This General had to accept a humiliating armistice on 7 July 1807. As Miranda had warned the British authorities, a military invasion in South America without an emancipation plan acceptable to the local people was not sustainable. Again, let's observe who was right.

11.4 British Expeditions to the River Plate Were an Explicit Colonial Betrayal of Their Commitment to Miranda

At the exact moment of the expeditions to the River Plate, the government was perfectly informed about Miranda's attempt to land on the Northern coast of Venezuela. Still, any support had been refused, and this error was not even considered rectified. This confirms that both Popham and Grenville committed a premeditated betrayal against Miranda's emancipation projects. Furthermore, these operations demonstrate an impressive combination of what could be characterised as strategic blunders in both political and military aspects. These strategic blunders, such as the Buenos Aires invasion being a mere colonial extension without any political vision and the contradiction with the own commitments of Grenville's cabinet, invite a critical analysis. The audience is invited to ponder over what would have been the British position in case Miranda's landing in Coro, probably followed by an upheaval in Brazil, had been successful?

The revealing fact is that, once informed of the loss of Buenos Aires and Montevideo, the British authorities confirmed the expeditions with orders to reconquer the River Plate cities, thus acknowledging the purely colonial purpose of the expeditions. An order was given to divert the second fleet, initially destined for the Pacific coast, to join the first, focusing their attacks on the River Plate on the Atlantic coast with more than 11,000 soldiers.[34] In contradiction to the basic principle announced by Grenville, that only in the case of popular support would a military intervention take place, the British strategy clearly revealed its genuine colonial purpose. Indeed, denying any support to Miranda at precisely the moment indicates the *cabinet's hidden opposition to the emancipation of South America.* Of course,

[33] Faulder, R., et al. (1808), *The trial at large of Lieut. Gen. Whitelocke...* Ed. Tipper, London, in Appendix containing Official Documents, 5 March 1807, Secret Instructions, p. 2.

[34] Wellington recognised in 1808 that a minimum of 10,000 soldiers would have been necessary for Miranda to be successful.

the British government opposed the Spanish regime. Still, it did not adhere to Miranda's project, either due to colonialist reasons or fear of regime change for the South American people, which was considered politically immature. However, this fear of regime change should not have been the sole reason for their actions. The audience should feel the shortsightedness of the British government's fear of regime change. The written instructions given to Whitelock [Faulder 1808, Beverina 1939] stipulated explicitly the importance *"to prevent...any revolution"*.[35] They only wanted submission to their geopolitical domination, i.e. an imperialist order. This meant a frontal treason and the instrumentation of Miranda. However, it also represents a short-sighted view of an administration unable to perceive the more significant benefits that an independent Hispanic America would have brought to industrial activity and, in turn, to the UK and global prosperity.

The British government's manipulation of Miranda is a grave injustice. The chronology of the first invasion in 1806 reveals that Popham's expedition was a voluntary betrayal of Miranda's partnership. The chronology of the second invasion project further demonstrates that the British government's involvement in Popham's illegal initiative was a deliberate attempt to profit from it. First, by immediately sending reinforcements to the River Plate to transform Popham piracy into a colonial conquest of new territories. Second, by extending the operation far beyond, pretending to seize the whole Southern Cone with a complementary project to control the key port of Valparaiso on the Chilean coast on the Pacific side. Third, by projecting control over Santiago to facilitate a merger with Beresford in Buenos Aires afterwards, and owning such a large colony in South America. In addition, the persistence of trying to consolidate a colonial invasion despite being informed that the Argentinian people were unanimously united in rejecting British domination is definitive proof of the nature of these failed colonial attempts and of the intention to use and manipulate Miranda as a mere instrument. Additional evidence of the unfair attitude towards Miranda is that the British government had already sent in 1804 a professional spy from the British army, James Burke (Pyne, P. 1998),[36] to Buenos

---

[35] See note n° 33 above, also in Beverina, Juan, [1939], *Las Invasiones Inglesas al Rio de la Plata*, Vol. II, p. 123, Circulo Militar, vol. 249–250, Buenos Aires.

[36] **James Florence Burke** (1771–1826), is not to be confounded with Edmund Burke or William Burke. He was an Irish military serving in the French army in Haiti in 1792 in the Dillon Regiment. In 1793, his regiment was captured by John Wittlelocke, who proposed that he defect and join the British army. Although almost unknown, he was one of the most talented spies in history due to his ability to win the confidence of key stakeholders. From 1794 to 1804, he was employed in undercover operations in Europe, particularly in Germany, reporting directly to the Duke of York, Commander-in-Chief (the son of the King). He efficiently managed his spy activities, especially in Buenos Aires and Rio, from 1804 to 1806, under direct instructions from the British government, without informing Miranda, who had told him that he was preparing his own military expedition. His introductions extended to the top level of the Viceroyalty and the prominent families of Buenos Aires, as well as a small group within the pro-independence party. He travelled to Montevideo, Chile, Peru and Bolivia, arriving in Rio, where he stayed until June 1806. Returning to Europe, he was sent to Prussia, where he became confident in cavalry general Blücher, one of the war party leaders in Prussia in 1805, as they fought against Napoleon. Later, in France, in the court of Napoleon's wife, Josephine, in Portugal and Spain, where he won the confidence of the King and

Aires to secretly inform about a possible British intervention in the event of war with Spain. Burke established contacts with the Viceroy's court while presenting himself as Miranda's agent to the independentist circles. To these Argentinean patriots, he disseminated the idea that a British army landing was intended to free them from the Spanish colonial regime, as part of Miranda's plan. Such a strategy produced results for the small group of independentist activists. In particular, Saturnino Rodriguez Peña,[37] one of Miranda's prominent supporters and independent leaders, acted in favour of Beresford, even organising his escape after his capture, convincing him that this was useful for Miranda's plan. Later, Rodriguez Peña admitted having been betrayed.

These perfidious operations culminated in an astonishing, spectacular loss-loss game for the British and South American interests. They significantly damaged the cause of Miranda among the Creole patriots, being accused of acting as a mere British agent who was going to implement another colonial domination, as well as the British officials who doubted that the Latin Americans would have been able to follow Miranda in an operation against Britain. The British reputation suffered seriously both on the geopolitical side by demonstrating not only its dominant imperialist option but also its cynical abuse of its allies and the lack of respect for their word. The reputation damage was also severe on the military side, as the Royal forces were quickly defeated by inferior forces that lacked critical logistics.

11.5 Contextual Interpretation of British Geopolitical Strategy

Any attempt to analyse Miranda's thinking and his constant strategy requires an understanding of the complex relations he maintained with the British powers, despite a cycle of successive ups and downs, with converging views alternating with intense confrontations, from the first Pitt administration in 1790 to the following

his wife before Napoleon's usurpation, Back to England, he was in contact with Arthur Wellesley, preparing his expedition to South America up to June 1808 when Britain became allied to Spain for forestalling France. Burke was sent to South America again to diffuse the new British-Spanish Alliance's information against Napoleon and spy on the French activities there. He even became Carlota's lover (the Portuguese Prince Regent's wife and daughter of Charles IV), exercising political influence on her and reporting to Castlereagh. Arriving in Buenos Aires, where his ex-mistress, Ana Périchon, had become Viceroy Linier's mistress, was vehemently opposed to Carlota's plan to pretend to be the Regent of the Spanish colony. Burke was denounced as a British spy and sent back to Rio, where he also faced difficulties and was eventually obliged to return to London in 1809. He was again sent to the European continent, where he was in close contact with essential governments from 1810 to 1812. Then, it wasn't easy to follow his activities. He retired in 1826, but his talent continued, as evidenced by the fact that he remained on the payroll for many years after his death. See Pyne, P. (1998) and Roberts, C. (1938).

[37] **Saturnino Rodríguez Peña** (1765–1819), Argentinean patriot, Miranda's ally. See Chap. 10, document 10.4.14, note n° 129.

cabinets until 1810. This unstable cycle in the relations between Miranda and the successive British authorities was not due to the versatility of the respective characters. Their conflicts correspond to the respective constraints that both sides faced in the context of the fundamental geopolitical conflict between Britain and France. External and domestic conflicts were closely intertwined, with variations in both the external and domestic coalitions. Therefore, analysing Miranda's strategy inevitably requires referring to the domestic forces and struggles in each country and their impacts on the respective management of their external constraints.

Miranda presents this additional particularity to be probably the only stakeholder of his time having played an active role in the most profound conflicts and features of both enemies simultaneously: his political actions were fully inserted into the British identity debate "continental versus imperial-maritime" or "Blue Water" policies (Baugh, D. 1988; Black, J. 2005)[38] as well into the related French ideological debates "Girondin versus Jacobin". In both cases, he correctly anticipated the risks and subsequent development by choosing a strategy to counter the French Jacobin threat to democracy, which involved moving to London and opting for the imperial-maritime potential of the UK as a less damaging and more realistic way to halt the Jacobin threat for Britain, Europe, and the Americas. His idealism was rooted in a firm belief in the ultimate triumph of human cooperation in a win-win game for all. Therefore, it is worth investigating the contexts and determinant factors of the complex British strategy, which evolved from an indirect "containment" purpose in response to the Jacobin and Napoleonic threats to a direct "overthrow" goal aimed at mitigating their menace.

The respective contexts in France and the United Kingdom differed significantly, subject to opposite political and institutional constraints. In turn, these limitations were changing according to the respective socio-economic evolution resulting from geopolitical events and changing coalitions, but also as a function of the fundamental differences between two competing political regimes that determined very different management of the respective strategies:

- On the British side, a very stable constitutional monarchy with parliamentary elections imposing public debates and countervailing powers in a conservative but quasi-modern democracy, and with an already imperial-maritime culture based upon a naval power combined with the emerging manufacturing and financial superiority, but exposed to a high reliance upon safe and stable external markets. Associated with an insular and pragmatic culture, these features meant that the *price of war was much higher than in France*, resulting in it being a key parameter from a political and economic point of view.

[38] The debate between continental and maritime strategies is an old one, typical of Great Britain, dating back to the second half of the seventeenth century. On the development of imperial-maritime—"Blue Water"—strategic thought, see Daniel A. Baugh (1988) "Great Britain's 'Blue-Water' Policy, 1689–1815," *The International History Review* 10:1 (February): 33–58. On Britain's relationship to the Continent, see Jeremy Black (2005), *The Continental Commitment: Britain, Hanover, and Interventionism, 1714–1793*, Routledge.

- On the French side, an emerging centralist republic, based upon the *culture of central absolutism* turned towards ideological radical options for imposing changes in a rural economy, with a violent messianic ambition to export the revolution as a necessary narrative for consolidating domestically the centralist power, which was seen as a vehicle for its modernisation; this ambition was made possible thanks to a demographic surplus that made it possible by mobilising and exploiting a "Grande Armée", several times (five to seven times!) bigger in terms of the number of infantrymen (Brun, J. F. 2009; Burnham, R. n.d.) compared to the United Kingdom.[39] These features indicate that the war's political and economic costs were significantly lower than elsewhere, making it an attractive political tool for both domestic and external objectives.

The conflict between these two antagonistic ambitions and political cultures was inevitable (something very similar to the 2022 Russian invasion of Ukraine and conflict with present European democracies). It evolved progressively into a hegemonic struggle that spread beyond Europe to a quasi-world war with a structural disequilibrium: the *political and economic cost of war was much lower in the French regime*, which was undemocratic and needed external conquests and wars to fuel popular support to its dictatorial powers, while in Britain the war had a much higher political and economic cost, with a reduced army and geopolitical and budgetary decisions subjected to the slow parliamentary process and the collegiality of the government, exposed to internal political rivalries under divided public opinions (again something very close to what occurred in the European Union in 2024). In addition, the British insular culture limited its expansionism to controlling a stable environment, without attempting to impose it overseas. On the contrary, the messianic vocation of the French culture tends to export ideologies.

[39] Napoleon's army, thanks to the conscription in a non-democratic regime, was composed of around 250.000 soldiers in the initial period of the Consulate (1799) and reached 500.000 men when Napoleon was scheduling the invasion of Britain from Boulogne in 1804. During the Empire, the Grande Armée was increased to close to one million in 1809, of which 20% were foreigners, reaching a maximum between 1.200.000 and 1.400.000 in 1812. See Jean-François Brun (2009) "Les unités étrangères dans les armées napoléoniennes: un élément de la stratégie globale du Grand Empire", in *Revue historique des armées,* 229. The British army had no conscription. It had only 40.000 soldiers in 1793 and had to be increased to 133.000 in 1804 when Napoleon concentrated more than 100.000 troops in Boulogne to invade Britain. The problem for Britain was that it had to maintain a significant share overseas to protect its colonial empire, making available a smaller margin of troops. Furthermore, this margin was less mobile than the French one because they had to cross the Channel before being offensive. For example, when Wellesley was fighting in the Iberian Peninsula, he could only transfer a total of 60.000 soldiers. At its peak, the British army reached a maximum of 250.000 in 1813, of which 20% were foreigners. See Robert Burnham, "The British Army in the Napoleonic Wars: Manpower Stretched to the Limits?" in Napoleon Series, https://www.napoleon-series.org/military-info/organization/c_casualties.html.

11.6 Miranda and the Hegemon's Hesitations: War Versus Negotiations and Continental Versus Overseas Expeditions

After his unsuccessful attempts in 1790–1792 to bet on the British imperial-maritime culture and business interests, Miranda shifted to the French side, betting on the expansionist vocation to ensure continental supremacy of the revolutionary ideal he saw as a mere step before exporting it to South America. He discovered and confronted the inner viral danger of Jacobin ideology, which persisted after Robespierre's elimination, as he realised its connection to deeply rooted aspirational imperialism as a cultural feature that he saw as potentially perverse and fatal to his entire emancipation project. On the contrary, he perceived British commercial imperialism as manageable because it was more liberal and economically more rational. Although opposed to British imperialism, he saw that the British regime was not systemically opposed to his project and could even be economically rational. His inner idealism led him to perceive a possibility of compatibility with Spanish American emancipation, as long as conditions for a win-win dialogue could be found.

Therefore, in 1797, comparing the risks between the Jacobin ideological imperialism and the more liberal commercial imperialist bias of the British policies, he decided to come back to the British side, not only to enjoy in London a safer place for pursuing his own emancipatory plan but as the only place where he could find the global overseas culture and the means his project did require. Indeed, he wanted to integrate his South American plan into a global geopolitical alliance between Britain, the US and his future Colombia, aimed at countering the French Jacobin system, both at the military, commercial and monetary levels, demonstrating that he already possessed a very systemic analysis.[40]

This visionary global strategy, anticipated in 1797, foresaw the outcome of the Anglo-French conflict as a total war, in which the necessary precondition for lasting peace was a regime change in France, rather than a negotiated peace. In this struggle, Miranda confirmed that for staying on the democratic side and the economic progress, the British side was the least damaging. Posterior events show he was totally right, again as a forerunner.

Although Pitt shared most of Miranda's perspective on Britain's strategic interests and the usefulness of the imperial-maritime roots of British power in fighting against France, he was always reluctant to follow Miranda's plan, being trapped in several constraints that he often used to procrastinate, being rarely able to make a clear choice between a continental strategy or an imperial-maritime,[41] (Fortescue,

---

[40] See Chap. 7, Act of Paris.

[41] According to some British historians, this reluctance came from the British early disasters on the island of St Domingo in the Caribbean: "*The secret of England's impotence for the first 6 years of the war may be said to lie in the two fatal words, St. Domingo.*" J. W. Fortescue (1915), *A History of the British Army* (London: Macmillan and co., vol. 4. The losses of soldiers during the expedition to Haiti reached more than 50.000 only for the years 1793 to 1796. This represented a severe

J. W. 1915; Geggus, D. 1983). His choice emerged only during his second cabinet (1804–1806), when he opted for overseas operations late. This strategy was confirmed after his death as a progressive evolution explained by the shift of the centre of gravity of the Anglo-French conflict away from Europe to maritime colonies and external trade under the pressures of the events. Until the end of the period of residence of Miranda in London (1810), the British cabinets were trapped in a succession of crossed hesitations: a diplomatic one between war and peace concerning France as well as with Spain, combined with a military tactical succession of hesitations between choosing to counteract directly on the Continent the rising French rival or to launch overseas operations by exploiting the British comparative advantage of the Royal Navy for extending the colonial empire as an indirect way to impede Napoleon to get more financial means by capturing these means and placing so Britain in positions able to dictate peace conditions to France.

This combination of British hesitations must be explained all the more that they created a detrimental asymmetry compared to the sharp French strategy and the faster decisions permitted by a dictatorship. The British hesitations could be analysed as successive attempts to optimise British interests under logistical and economic constraints, much like a system of equations to be solved with changing relative prices between "peace versus war" and "Continental versus overseas" expeditions. Nevertheless, in a parliamentary regime, unlike the French dictatorial regime, the changing composition of British cabinets and the personal preferences of influential ministers led to damaging internal divisions. Combined with the slower decision-making process in a parliamentary regime and the heavy bargaining power, these factors explain some incoherent and suboptimal decisions. The net result of these differences contributed significantly to explaining Napoleon's rapid victories on the continent. *To what extent did British mistakes contribute to consolidating Napoleon's image of military genius*?

The successive attempts at strategic optimisations by British authorities were very complex. They fluctuated based on a series of objective parameters, mainly the relative prices between war and diplomatic arrangements, but with many interdependencies according to international events affecting the relative prices between continental war and overseas expeditions:

- On one side, the cost of peace with the Jacobin republic and its Napoleonic deviation was on a rising trend, meaning that war was progressively preferred to peace because the latter option would have meant giving oxygen to the French regime, which was (rightly) perceived as inherently in conflict with the British regime for dominating and eradicating it ("*The Kingdom of Great Britain and the French Republic cannot exist together.*" Napoleon, 1800). The main factor behind this opposition to peace was the growing perception among the elite of a direct threat to their own fate, should Napoleon succeed in spreading his radical ideas and methods, and thus suffer the same fate as the French aristocracy. However,

reduction in the capacity of the British army, obliging to accelerate unpopular recruitments. See also Geggus, D. (1983), "The Cost of Pitt's Caribbean Campaigns, 1793–1798." 699–706.

peace was accepted by the elite only temporarily, and only when social and economic constraints also threatened the British regime (clearly the case in 1801, leading to the error of the Amiens Peace).

- On the other side, the cost of war against France was a positive function of the degree of alliance between Spain and France. This aspect lowered the price of peace with Spain. Peace negotiations with Spain were thus a diplomatic way of preventing or breaking a Spanish-French alliance and significantly reducing the cost of war against France.
- The net result of these two functions explains Pitt's attitude that overseas war against Spanish colonies would only be desirable if Spain were previously in open war with Britain.
- This perceived relative cost of overseas war against Spanish colonies was a decreasing function of two factors: (i) sharply down as far as Spain joined France or in case of rising probability that Napoleon could take control of the Spanish colony's resources; (ii) also down as far as Creoles would reject the Spanish crown and would opt for British presence and free trade, making logistically feasible a cheaper extension of the British empire by mobilising less military forces and no need for a domination policy.
- This second factor on resources was weighted mainly and explained that additional overseas heavy operations were logistically incompatible with simultaneous continental operations: the British population was only one-third of the French one, which, in addition, had a vast potential to recruit on its continental conquests. Around 1800, according to Golding, C. (2017) the UK forces could reach only 80,000 soldiers, of which more than 10.000 were blocked for the Ireland situation and about 20,000 for colonial protection (India), leaving only 50,000 for the UK defence, of which a maximum margin of about 25,000 could be withdrawn and transported for overseas additional operations.[42] This contrasts with the "Grande Armée", which quickly reached one million soldiers, the mobility of which was higher than that of the British, which was constrained by the bottleneck of the naval transport capacity across the Channel. This army was well-prepared to engage in a local war, dependent on its sea power. Indeed, the government had made significant military investments since 1790 to secure its dominance of the seas. The maritime forces increased from 40.000 to 120.000 in 1800, but these forces were not operational in a continental war and absorbed budgetary resources, impairing the infantry.
- But the British authorities and politicians generally had in mind that for reaping better net benefits for the British trade and diplomatic reputation with a minimum of military resources, overseas operations could not be involved in local revolutions against existing social and ethnic orders, except in case that these

[42] The British Army grew from a mere 40,000 men in 1789 to 250,000 by 1814. The Royal Navy swelled from 16,000 seamen in 1789 to 140,000 in 1812. See Linda Colley (1994), "The Reach of the State, the Appeal of the Nation: Mass Arming and Political Culture in the Napoleonic Wars," in Lawrence Stone, Ed., [1994], *An Imperial State at War: Britain from 1689–1815*, Routledge, New York, p. 165–84. Quoted by Golding C. (2017), op. cit. p. 247.

people would accept freely to join the British empire and its free trade; for some, this meant to undertake overseas expeditions only once such a local revolution would have occurred and demonstrated an ability to an effective stable self-governance. This idea was fueled by memories of the disastrous experiences with their expeditions to the Caribbean in the 1790s, which were marred by ethnic upheavals provoked by the ideas of the French Revolution.

Rational optimisations based upon these objective parameters would show easily that Miranda's thesis was not only objectively compatible with the British interests but also could have been *the first best option on both sides*. Only the last constraint (on local political regimes) allowed conflictual interpretations. However, considering them officially as convergent for being implicitly complementary in the *formula Miranda had agreed (naively?) upon with the government*: he would get responsibility for implementing his internal governance project, while the British partner would ensure military protection in exchange for the resulting free trade. Miranda pretended that a robust constitutional order based upon the local municipal councils could peacefully channel the weight of the colonial past. Of course, in his view, the British support and presence would have to remain commercial and dedicated to external protection for the benefit of both sides. Dundas (as well as Miranda) believed that expanding British trade and commerce was the primary purpose of the empire rather than conquest (Golding, C. 2017).[43] The British government, however, was less optimistic about Miranda's ability to maintain control over populations in the event of such a regime change. Still, it used this argument to justify a de facto colonial ambition in South America as a means to control social revolution, as evidenced by Windham's instructions for the second invasion of Buenos Aires. However, these instructions also demonstrated that the government sought to benefit from Miranda's argument, claiming that the desire for independence would be a valuable vehicle for ensuring easier British penetration and control with fewer troops than would otherwise be required. Nevertheless, the government never explicitly committed to respect independence, but only in a few moments to help end the Spanish domination.

11.7 A Loss-Loss Game: Miranda's Fiasco and British Mismanagement

The British authorities found themselves in a challenging position. They attempted to leverage the independence movements for their imperial expansion while maintaining a stance of non-interference in overseas political revolutions to minimise the military forces they sent abroad. These two options were fundamentally at odds, creating a logical contradiction that the strategy could not escape. This complex

[43] Golding, C. (2017), op. cit. p. 67, see also Fry, M., [1992], *Dundas Despotism*, p. 62–3, 198.

situation was a critical factor in the failure of the British authorities' expeditions to Buenos Aires and the subsequent failures of Miranda's efforts.

Our analysis suggests that a win-win game for both parties could have been achieved if purely coherent behaviour had prevailed over domestic disputes. However, history shows the contrary with a series of disastrous failures that are difficult to explain, except by the absence of competent optimisation by the authorities, leading to a dramatic dynamic loss-loss game for all the parties, Miranda, the British, the South Americans, and the European due to the prolongation of the Napoleonic wars. The task of historians is to try to explain these wrong decisions and consider feasible alternatives.

Responsibility for this historical mistake is clearly not on Miranda's side; instead, it lies with British tactical errors resulting from a lack of vision in a context of *dissensions within British cabinets*. Miranda was in a weak position in London, being obliged to adapt his strategy successively to all the maritime hegemon's logistical constraints and political arbitrages, whatever the degree of adequacy with his own options. These options, however, were nevertheless in line with most British interests. He permanently warned his British allies in their own interests against:

1. the inner danger of the Jacobin French system,
2. the potential spread of violent socio-ethnic revolutions,
3. the unsustainability of a military operation without sustaining the local independentist forces,
4. the inevitability of Napoleon's invasion of the Iberian Peninsula and, therefore, the rising risk of the Jacobins' attempt to control South American resources.

Miranda had developed the thesis of the feasibility of an emancipation path of South America – in conformity to British maritime advantage and identity, in Dundas and Vansittart's lines - that would maximise the British interests:

- allowing Britain to get at much lower costs a peaceful extension of free trade and prosperity for both sides,
- compatible with a minimum of military presence overseas, just for protecting, and not dominating the newly independent state
- and therefore, without the necessity to withdraw essential forces from the European theatre,
- while eradicating any risk of an attempt by Napoleon to seize the American colonial resources.
- Finally, accepting the British reserve about the risks of local revolution with ethnic upheavals, he submitted himself to the government condition by organising himself the first landing in Venezuela in 1806 in the hope that fulfilling this requirement would imply that British commercial interests and imperialism would push the government to join or support his own expedition.

This ideal triple dividend repetitively advocated by Miranda was, however, weakened by two doubts from his opponents:

- first, his adamant definition of complete emancipation (that is, independence plus political changes) that most British politicians did not actually share, having in mind, either hypocritically, an opportunity for extending the crown colonial empire or hiding this ambition behind the need to prevent socio-ethnical upheavals with firm control and numerous occupation troops;
- second, some conservative politicians and opinions in London had a biased perception of the idealistic republican options of his emancipation plan. Either they perceived him as a dangerous utopian who would be unable to control the socio-ethnic explosion he could trigger among immature populations, or they continued to see him as a hidden Jacobin, based upon his controversial[44] past military role in favour of the US and French Revolutions, like Lord Grenville. In particular, they feared the risk of Miranda's abolition of slavery. The difficulties faced by the British in the Caribbean when the French abolition of slavery by the Convention in 1794 threatened the British plantations also explain the rising racial fears in the British circles, as well as their opposition to Miranda's political plan. This plan was supported by Dundas, who had initiated debates in the Army and Parliament regarding the abolition of slavery. He favoured the recruitment of slaves and offered limited rights to them[45] in order to compete with the French ideology, which pretended to provide equal treatment to the slaves.

11.8 Analysis of the Successive British Mistakes Along with the Changing Balances Inside the Governments

Analysing in more detail the complex evolution of the balance of powers between the different options of the successive cabinets allows us to understand better how the British authorities spoiled the option that would have been the best solution for Great Britain, which was the formula promoted by Miranda. A slow, progressive evolution is observed in favour of overseas expeditions, which, when finally decided upon and operationally prepared, were ultimately cancelled in June 1808 as a result of the King's decision to support the Spanish patriots opposed to Napoleon's usurpation of the Spanish throne. Despite multiple warnings issued by Miranda over the years, the British authorities were caught off guard and decided to revert to a continental strategy, swapping the Wellesley / Miranda expedition at the last minute for a landing on the Iberian Peninsula. Thus began a long continental war, marked by numerous military setbacks, which ended only with Waterloo after 7 years of costly

[44] General Dumouriez (1794), who was in exile, used to publish against Miranda's role, as well as others.

[45] Dundas's positions as regards slavery were, as the whole British colonial policy, very cynical and purely "economic". Although he understood the inevitable trend towards abolition, he considered it as "temporarily" inopportune for tactical and economic reasons as an opportunist politician. His exact role in the abolition law is still an object of debate.

damage in terms of military, financial, and political consequences. Four steps can be observed:

1. During the extended *first Pitt's Cabinet (1783–1801)*, two opposed visions were permanently competing between the two dominant ministers shaping the British external policies. On one side, Minister Lord Grenville (Foreign Affairs 1791–1801) focused on the fighting on the continent through coalitions with continental allies against French enemies as the key to obtaining victory over France; on the other, Minister H. Dundas (Secretary of State for War 1794–1801 but also responsible for East India policy) who favoured war overseas and in the colonies, first in Western (America) and Eastern India,[46] but also in Malta, Egypt, and the Cape to protect the access to India. Dundas complained repeatedly about the subordination of the West Indian expedition to events on the Continent. The result was a recurrent indecision in the cabinet arbitrages between Dundas and Grenville. Pitt did not rationally optimise cabinet decisions in managing the strategy according to the events. As explained by J. Ehrman (1983) "*Almost every action taken by the Cabinet was decided upon by a 2 to 1 vote [Pitt was always on the winning side] with Dundas and Grenville splitting the decisions amongst themselves*". This constant internal dissension was very damaging, making both strategies inefficient and effectively putting Britain's security at risk.[47]
   (a) During the *first part of this period (1793–1796),* which started with the war against France and the formation of the first coalition (Austria, Prussia, Spain and Britain), Pitt applied a "*containment strategy*" to the Jacobin risks: he mixed both kinds of expeditions: marginal interventions on the continent with overseas ones in the Caribbean. Pitt still considered the French Revolution unsustainable for fiscal and social reasons, and believed that financing the first coalition would be sufficient to contain the republican threat, convinced of the British financial advantage over revolutionary France.[48] The three of Grenville's continental operations failed successively (the Netherlands in 1793, Toulon in 1793, and the West of France in 1795), as did those of the First Coalition, which ended with the Peace of Basel in 1795. On the contrary, the Dundas' maritime expeditions, economically minded, were relatively more successful with the capture of France's West Indian possessions in the Caribbean (1794 Martinique, Guadeloupe, St Lucia, and St Domingue, with financial loss for France) although followed by some setbacks (loss of Guadeloupe and St Domingue) with a very high

[46] In addition to Minister of War and Colony, Dundas remained the minister primarily responsible for overseeing the management of the East Indies through the Presidency of the "Board of Control" from 1793 to 1801.

[47] On the thesis that Pitt lacked a clear strategy see John Ehrman, *The Younger Pitt, Volume Two: The Reluctant Transition,* London, Constable, 1983, p. 348.

[48] In 1794 and 1795, the British government provided a total amounting to £8,095,315 in subsidies to the Continental allies of the first coalition.

human cost due mainly to the yellow fever, and the spread of French revolutionary ideology which threatened also the slave regime in English Caribbean. Dundas was also successful in his campaigns towards East India: the capture of the Dutch colonies (the Cape and the equivalent port of Trincomalee in Ceylon) because France had previously annexed Holland. From August 1795, Pitt started to understand that the French revolutionary regime was resilient and considered embracing the Dundas' "Blue Water[49]" option as a matter of necessity rather than a choice.

(b) *From 1796*, an evolution towards an "*overthrow strategy*" in the fight against the French Jacobin threat. Britain being alone against France, a progressive evolution favourable to Dundas' maritime strategy was imposed by the facts: (i) impressive supremacy of France, (ii) new aggressive military alliance of Spain with France (Second Treaty of Idelfonso) which allowed to outnumber the British fleet in the Mediterranean, threatening the India road, (iii) French attempt to land in Ireland. Pitt was worried but again did not opt clearly for one strategy against the other: on one side, Dundas's arguments scored points progressively despite Grenville's opposition, and an operation against Spanish America was again considered in 1796–1797 as an imperial-maritime war against Revolutionary France; but on the other side, the high cost in human lives of his campaigns in the Caribbean (Duffy, M. 1987, cited by Golding, C. 2017)[50] brought strong criticisms in the Parliament and the public opinion, together with the fears that the French attempt to land in Ireland would give new arguments to Grenville and George Spencer,[51] the First Lord of Admiralty, for maintaining the Navy operational in the Channel.

Dundas' position was clear-cut and based upon the British historical aversion to being drawn into continental complications, [which also characterises the events of the next two centuries, including Brexit], but also on the longer-term strategic view that the war against France would be won (Dundas, H. 1795) on an economic basis.[52] In 1796, he declared, "A *com-*

[49] The "***Blue Water***" strategy, initially coined by the Portuguese in 1508, was imported into Britain in 1650 (see Chap. 5, note n° 66. It means to get the ability to exercise sea control at a long range for the purpose of trade and military control. "*Whosoever commands the sea commands the trade; whosoever commands the trade of the world commands the riches of the world and consequently commands the world*", Walter Raleigh (1600).

[50] The British army suffered 42,250 deaths in the West Indies and 62,250 total casualties—70 per cent of all British officers and men dispatched to the Caribbean, according to Duffy, M. (1987), *Soldiers, Sugar, and Seapower*, p. 333–34, quoted by Golding, C. (2017), op. cit. p. 83. This very high cost in human lives was mainly due to yellow fever and the slave revolts resulting from the emancipation decided by the French convention in 1794. Public opinion criticisms tempered the other successes of his colonial option.

[51] **The Earl of Spencer** (1758–1834) was a British Whig politician who served under William Pitt the Younger as Lord Privy Seal in 1794 and as First Lord of the Admiralty from 1794 to 1801. He was later Home Secretary from 1806 to 1807 under Lord Grenville's cabinet.

[52] Unsigned memorandum, attributed to Dundas, [1795], Melville Papers, fol. 1, WCL, quoted by Golding, C. (2017), op. cit. p. 59.

plete success in the West Indies is essential … No success in other quarters will palliate a neglect there … By success in the West Indies alone you can be enabled to dictate the terms of peace".[53] He prepared Miranda's reconciliation with Pitt, which will give him additional support. Unfortunately, this change and support occurred only in January 1798, when Miranda acknowledged that France was definitively not reliable to support his emancipation ideal. In early 1797, the British victory of Cape St Vincent (Portugal) re-established British command of the Mediterranean. It allowed the blockade of Spanish trade to decrease the arrival of silver and gold from America significantly. The Dundas' strategy also affected the French trade with Western India. Indeed, the Caribbean "*trade contributed significantly to the economies of both Britain and France. In 1790, it constituted 15.5% of total British trade. For France, the sugar produced by the colony of St. Domingue and its other West Indian islands accounted for nearly a third of all the nation's foreign trade*".[54] In 1797, the island of Trinidad, located off the Venezuelan coast, was captured by the Royal Navy. In 1798, Nelson won the Battle of the Nile (Aboukir Bay, Egypt), destroying the French fleet.

Dundas, like Miranda, relied upon a triple argument:

(i) First, the solution to the war against the Jacobin France was economically dependent[55] and had to be organised from seizing the French and Spanish colonial resources, weakening their armies while strengthening the British one and financing also the budgetary subsidies to the necessary continental allies for containing the French expansion;

(ii) second, this policy provides new markets for British exports and the safety of essential imports for the Navy, as well as the manufacturing sector and cheaper food;

(iii) third, the British military capacity was insufficient to risk being entrapped in a complex continental war from which he could not withdraw sufficient troops and vessels to sustain more strategic overseas operations.

The Dundas military approach was fundamentally economically minded, considering that the worst threat to Britain in the war with France was not so much a direct French invasion but rather the damage to Britain's imperial trade and commerce. The British could compel a French army to evacuate the home islands, even once they landed. Still, French naval actions against British colonies and trade could be more

[53] Mackesy, *War Without Victory*, p. 12. In this year, 1796, Dundas engaged almost half of the British battalions only in the Caribbean theatre (see Golding (2017), op. cit. p. 82, Dundas to Duke of York, October 5, 1795, WO 6/131, p. 80).

[54] Christopher T. Golding (2017), *At water's edge op. cit.*

[55] Dundas had been closely related to Adam Smith.

devastating and potentially permanent for the British power (Golding, C. 2017). In March 1800, Dundas wrote a full report on his proposals.[56]

The ex-post observation of the facts suggests that Dundas and Miranda proposed the most effective strategy for Britain during the 1790s. However, Dundas was not sufficiently supported by Pitt and Grenville, all the more so that Miranda's plan was considered too revolutionary for Grenville and the conservative politicians. Realising that the French Revolution was an enduring reality and a direct threat to the British ruling class, a consensus appeared on the need to oppose the geographical spread of the Jacobin virus. Nevertheless, there was no consensus on the means, leading to incoherent strategies. In particular, there was no agreement on Miranda's arguments that the pro-active organisation of independence could be better and safer for Britain than hoping naively for the inhabitants to welcome spontaneously the British domination or to let them overthrow alone the Spanish crown, something they saw as exposing to more risks of ethnic cleaning than Miranda's care for the rule of law.

In 1798, Pitt finally opted for the direct continental strategy against Dundas and Miranda, who had arrived in London, having escaped from French police in early 1798. Pitt had favourably welcomed him, but after listening to him, he postponed any decision until the second half of the year, keeping Miranda in reserve in case of a return to the Dundas' strategy. Indeed, in April, Dundas supported Grenville's expeditions to Ostend and Walcheren (Holland), but these expeditions turned into total disasters, provoking Dundas' opposition to any new initiative from Grenville. He even presented his resignation to Pitt, who refused it. In May 1798, Napoleon sailed from Toulon and took control of Malta on the road to invade Egypt, to attack later British India or damage British trade with Asia. However, these facts favourable to the Dundas option were offset by the outbreak of a new rebellion in Ireland. Frightened by the Irish risks, Pitt changed his mind again and ruled out any maritime operation in South America as inopportune. Furthermore, he was hesitating between sending troops to the Eastern Mediterranean to stop Napoleon in Egypt and defending the road to India, as required urgently by Dundas, or seizing the opportunity for continental landing, as Grenville insisted again. Finally, the destruction of the French fleet at Aboukir in August 1798 and Napoleon's return to Paris to overthrow the Directory reopened the idea of a direct intervention on the continent in a new, coordinated coalition. He charged Grenville to form and finance this second coalition against France (associating Austria,

[56] Dundas, H (1800), *Memorandum for the Consideration of His Majesty's Ministers* March 31, 1800, Box 5, Henry Dundas Melville Papers, 1771–1831, Rubenstein Library, Duke University. Quoted by Golding, C. (2017), op. cit. p. 208.

Russia, Ottoman Empire, Portugal, Naples, various German monarchies and Sweden).

Logically, Dundas was distraught and disagreed with Pitt and Grenville. In 1799, he worried that if there were a rebellion in South America, the United States might seize the opportunity to extend its influence there, potentially to the detriment of British trade. He was angry for not having been supported sufficiently by Grenville, and, unfortunately, Pitt was unable to impose a clear option and stop the dispute. Dundas unfairly undermined Grenville's strategy when, effectively, a rapid continental operation appeared to present a historical opportunity to stop Napoleon in Italy by strengthening the Austrian ally at this very moment. Although in terms of strategic vision, Dundas (like Miranda) had been right most of the time, the circumstances in early 1800 provided a real possibility for a successful Grenville's continental expedition within the commitments of the second coalition. However, Dundas sabotaged it to demonstrate that any continental operation was doomed to fail, thereby ensuring that his overseas option would remain valid. Even though Pitt and Grenville ordered Dundas to implement the second coalition commitment by sending a support expedition to the Austrian forces in Italy, Dundas worked actively against this order, which he saw as condemning any successful operation in Western India. His insubordination undermined this order up to the point of demonstrating that a continental victory was indeed impossible. In his memorandum (Dundas, H. 1800),[57] he advocated undertaking an expedition on both sides of South America soon. Specifically, he expected to launch his own initiative to absorb the few available troops, directly competing with Grenville's plan. Therefore, he concealed the actual size of the available army and resources, significantly weakening the British invasion force intended to land in Italy by reducing its size and sending part of it to Malta, which was part of his priorities for protecting the road to India. The internal dissension explains that Pitt's cabinet lost the fragile window of opportunity by sending too few troops too late. Pitt himself supports the responsibility, not only for having been unable to make a clear decision within his cabinet but also for delaying the decision to send additional troops until mid-June. This explains the Austrian defeat at Marengo, which occurred precisely in mid-June, when Pitt finally, but too late, ordered the sending of additional forces. According to military criteria, Napoleon's success at Marengo was largely due to the absence of the necessary and timely British support. If the British troops had been deployed as planned, it is clear that Napoleon's army, already outnumbered by Austria, would

[57] Dundas, H. (1800), "*Memorandum for the Consideration of His Majesty's Ministers*," op. cit. p. 208.

have lost, thereby preventing the collapse of the Second Coalition. That would have changed the course of the war and its costs.

Additionally, as a result of his divergence with Grenville, Dundas was also responsible for the withdrawal of Russian participation in the coalition, stemming from disagreements over policies regarding Malta and the Baltic Sea. Dundas' manoeuvres and Pitt's indecision made the Austrian-French new alliance inevitable, prolonging Napoleon's wars for at least one decade.

In July 1800, Pitt's cabinet eventually acknowledged that Dundas was right; continental attempts were useless. However, he decided to operate first in the Mediterranean against El Ferrol and Cadiz, as well as against the French troops blocked in Egypt. The Cadiz operation failed in October 1800.

On 10 October 1800, Miranda, seeing Pitt's implicit objections to his plan despite the British tactical failures on the continent, left London for Paris with the ambiguous intention to try to attract French interest in his plan and so to put Pitt under such competitive pressure. In the meantime, the Irish question drew considerable attention and led to the fall of Pitt's cabinet in March 1801, as the King refused the Catholic emancipation proposed by Pitt. At the same moment (March 1801), the last initiative taken by Pitt and Dundas against the French army in Egypt (Canopy battle) was a success, but it benefited the next cabinet entirely.

2. *Thus, in March 1801, at the end of Pitt's first cabinet, the remaining options* were either imperial-maritime strategy or peace negotiations. Although the imperial success partially compensated for the continental repetitive failures, Britain felt at a considerable strategic disadvantage (Ferell J. S. 2006): "*French control of western and southern Europe posed a considerably greater threat to British interests than British command of the sea did to French... it was clear that the French had a better chance of successfully invading Britain, than the British did of invading France*".[58] Therefore, and also under the social and business pressures resulting from the economic consequences of the war against France (obstacles to trade, grain crisis, food riots, insurrection threat, Ireland revolutionaries, financial crisis), the *following cabinet, Henry Addington* (1801–1804), to which neither Dundas nor Grenville were no longer part, had no other choice than to revert logically Pitt's preference for war[59] as well as Dundas "Blue Water" imperial view. Addington was obliged to look immediately for a peace Treaty with France. The negotiations were fast, and an agreement was reached in the fall of 1801, with the formal final Treaty in 1802 ("Paix d'Amiens").

In such a context, Miranda's plan was clearly excluded:

[58] Ferrell, J. S. (2006), *The Pivotal Roles of Henry Dundas and William Pitt in the British Cabinet Fiasco of 1800*. University of Tennessee Honors Thesis Projects.

[59] In 1801, Pitt himself, who proposed Addington as his successor, acknowledged that peace was inevitable at this moment.

- before the peace, because Pitt considered that the British army was not sufficient for sending an expedition to South America while acting inside the second coalition and having to stand by to prevent Napoleon's invasion;
- after the Peace, because the UK had tied its hands diplomatically and had handed over the French Caribbean colonies with the Peace Treaty.

- Nevertheless, this period of official peace allowed Britain to clearly see that the Napoleonic regime was using peace to continue its expansionist ambition, which confirmed it to be a real threat to British imperial interests and its ruling class. Thus, it moved from a containment strategy to an overthrow one in a Francophobic unanimity.

3. *When Pitt returned to power in 1804*, the war with France had already started again in May 1803. It was about to be extended to Spain too, providing the necessary conditions for Miranda's plan again, but also with Dundas back in the cabinet (in charge of the Royal Navy until 1805) as an opportunity for an imperial extension. Viscount Castlereagh was the Minister of War and the Colonies. The cabinet reinitiated the war against Spain and opted to prepare expeditions in South America at this time, asking Commodore Popham and Miranda to prepare the secret report proposing the expedition (Golding, C. 2017).[60] In parallel, betraying Miranda, Pitt and Castlereagh sent the talented spy, James F. Burke, an officer working for the Duke of York, commander-in-chief of the British Army, to prepare an invasion of Buenos Aires.

   However, the main cabinet's concern rapidly shifted towards preventing a French invasion of Britain, as intelligence indicated that Napoleon was preparing invasion troops in Boulogne. In December 1804, a combined operation with Russian soldiers ended in a disastrous defeat in Holland. Pitt shifted back to a defensive strategy, combining it with his traditional subsidies to allies, to promote a third coalition against Napoleon on the continent. Once again, Miranda was convinced that Pitt's changes in priorities were an abusive use of his person and ideas. Therefore, he decided to break this intolerable situation by acting independently - without any British support - and was eventually granted (reluctantly, after being denied several times) a passport to leave London for New York. From there, he planned to organise his own military expedition to liberate Hispanic America, with the idea that British commercial appetites would compel the government to join in once his landing had achieved its ends. He sailed on 2 September 1805 and arrived in New York on 9 November.

   Nelson's victory at Trafalgar (October) over the combined Spanish-French fleets repelled the danger of a quick French invasion. Still, Napoleon's spectacular successes in Ulm (October) and Austerlitz (December) effectively destroyed the Third Coalition and ensured a strengthened French hegemony in Europe.

[60] "Secret Paper on South America," Popham to Secretary Yorke, November 26, 1803, *Castlereagh Corr.*, 7: 288–93. Quoted by Golding, C. (2017), op. cit. p. 207.

4. *Grenville's cabinet (1806–1807)* succeeded Pitt (dead in January) in February 1806 for only 13 months. It was a disastrous period marked by incoherent policies, high ministerial turnover in the cabinet, and several humiliating military failures, especially in South America, where this cabinet undertook unprepared expeditions in opposition to Miranda's plan and ultimately betrayed him. This lack of a coherent agenda favoured the consolidation of Napoleon's expansionist ambitions. In the Spring of 1806, a British blockade of French trade was implemented, to which Napoleon retaliated with his own continental blockade (Berlin Decree). The British economy suffered seriously from this commercial war. The new Minister of Foreign Affairs, Charles Fox, engaged in peace talks with Napoleon when Grenville's government was informed about an unauthorised mission's capture of Buenos Aires, which advocated that the expedition implement previous plans prepared with Pitt's cabinet. Paradoxically, Grenville, traditionally opposed to these overseas operations, finally understood (what Dundas and Miranda had been arguing for a decade) that this was an unexpected lever strengthening his bargaining power in the peace discussions. Therefore, he endorsed this initiative almost immediately by sending additional forces. Nevertheless, he confirmed the colonial purpose with explicit instructions to prevent any attempt at local revolution except for the change of imperial dependence. A few weeks later, he extended the purpose to an ambitious colonial expedition to conquer the whole Southern Cone of America. Between November 1806 and February 1807, Major-General Arthur Wellesley [1807] exchanged with Lord Grenville [1807] several letters (Golding, C. 2017) considering positively these military projects.[61]

   The reason for such a radical change was not a conceived strategy but a sum of incoherent reactions to external and internal constraints in a combination of three facts:

   (i) the impossibility to compete with Napoleon on the continent, but also to agree upon a beneficial peace with France
   (ii) the need to find new markets and raw material providers, especially for facing the "Berlin decree" (November 1806), establishing the continental blockade and
   (iii) The general mood favouring the "Blue Water" dream of imperial conquests over risky continental battles confirms popular support for these expeditions.

   Nevertheless, this change revealed the explicit opposition to the Miranda emancipation expedition on the northern coast of Spanish America. Such discrimination between the two expeditions indicates Grenville's pro-colonial policy, contrary to the initial Dundas' plan. This attitude regarding Miranda was not only treasonous but also naive incoherence in British policy, despite Miranda's warnings: how could Grenville imagine reaping the

[61] See in particular, "*Memorandum on the Subject of a British Expedition to New Spain*" January 25, 1807; Major-General Sir Arthur Wellesley to Lord Grenville, February 17, 1807; and Reports by Wellesley to Lord Grenville [numerous], in *Dropmore Papers*, 9: 22–25, 41–45, and 479–93. Quoted by Golding, F. (2017), op. cit. p. 213.

benefits of the claim for independence from Spain by sending troops to extend the empire's domination while impeding any other change? The disastrous military and political outcomes were the inevitable consequence of such a lack of geopolitical vision. Once again, Miranda appears to be forecasting the future correctly.

5. *Lord Portland's cabinet (1807–1809)* drew some lessons from this failure and confirmed, first, an option of overseas strategy and second, an orientation closer to Miranda's views, despite scandalously betraying him. His Ministry of War and Colony, Viscount Castlereagh [1807], one of Pitt's disciples, wrote in early May 1807 a memorandum to the cabinet explaining that British strategy should assume the role of enabler and protector of South American independence[62] and not that of the conqueror, acknowledging so that Dundas (1800)[63] and Miranda were correct, writing (cited by Lynch, J. 1969) "*the liberation of South America must be accomplished through the wishes and exertions of the inhabitants, but the change can only be operated under the protection and the support of an auxiliary British force*",[64] and his memorandum preparing the expedition in June 1808 "*the attack has to start by Venezuela, where Miranda will address to the people*".

   Further proof of this acknowledgement was that, through Miranda's contacts in 1807, Castlereagh suggested that Miranda return to London from Trinidad, where he was in refuge after his disastrous failure in Coro (August 1806). He left Trinidad in October and arrived in Portsmouth on 21 December 1807. He immediately assisted W. Burke with his publication on South American emancipation in January 1808. In February, he was asked by the government to prepare a new military plan for Spanish America, working alongside Arthur Wellesley, who was designated to lead this new liberation expedition. However, since the end of 1807, French troops had been invading Portugal, and in March 1808, Madrid was also taken, followed by Napoleon's usurpation of the Spanish crown. In May, the Spanish popular uprising against French occupation began. Miranda had forecasted such events for over a decade and should have dictated a swift British reaction with an expedition to prevent the South American colonies from falling under the Jacobins' control. Castlereagh and Wellesley were favourable to Miranda's position until Spanish delegates representing the rebellion against Napoleon's usurpation came to London in June 1808, asking for assistance. On

[62] Castlereagh papers, "*Memorandum for the Cabinet, Relative to South America*" May 1, 1807, in Castlereagh Corr., 7: 314–24. Quoted by Golding, F. (2017), op. cit. p. 214.

[63] Dundas had already expressed the same position in his memorandum to the King, arguing in favour of a South American operation but excluding any plan of conquest or colonisation, but for opening trade and organising entrepots. See "*Memorandum for the Consideration of His Majesty's ministers*" March 31, 1800, Box 5, Henry Dundas Melville Papers, 1771–1831, Rubenstein Library, Duke University. Quoted by Golding, F. (2017), op. cit. p. 208.

[64] Castlereagh papers, edited by Charles W. Vane, Vol. VIII p. 385, London, 1848–53, cited by Lynch, J. (1969) "British Policy and Spanish America, 1783–1808." *Journal of Latin American Studies* 1:1 (May 1969): 1–30.

15 June, Canning, Minister of Foreign Affairs, announced to Parliament Britain's commitment to support the Spanish rebellion as representing the legitimate power. On 4 July, King George III ordered the stoppage of the war against Spain, which had become a strategic ally against Napoleon, and to initiate the Iberian Peninsula wars. On 12 July, Wellesley sailed from York, shifting at the last moment the South American expedition prepared with Miranda towards the Iberian Peninsula. Miranda was distraught and felt once again betrayed by the British partner. This bloody war[65] extended from mid-1808 until the beginning of 1814, ravaging durably Spain and Portugal. Although this war played an indirect role in the costly final victory against Napoleon in 1815, it is legitimate to ask whether a different plan, such as cutting financial resources to Spain and France from their colonies, would not have shortened the Napoleonic Wars.

In conclusion, Portland's cabinet, although trying to correct some mistakes of the preceding cabinet, fell into the same misjudgment as the previous administrations by sending unprepared naval operations with an underestimation of the limitations in transport capabilities for these maritime expeditions. Castlereagh's decisions to seize Antwerp Haven ended in a total disaster in Walcheren, and the Iberian War suffered costly reverses in 1808 and 1809, provoking political and popular reactions in London.

6. *Spencer Perceval's cabinet (1809–1812)*

This Prime Minister, famous for his intolerance against the Catholics, was not inclined to help Miranda, considered an embarrassing ally whom they wanted to control more strictly. Miranda had already written to Perceval when he was Minister of Finance under Portland's cabinet, soliciting his support for his views. The official alliance with Spain implied that Miranda was under stricter control, as the Spanish Ambassador in London addressed official requests to the government for Miranda's activities and messages sent to the patriots in Spanish colonies. Being prohibited from maintaining correspondence with Spanish Americans, he was fully aware of the need for a more diplomatic approach, seeking British political support rather than military intervention. He then decided to circumvent the British controls and orders by pursuing his own promotion of emancipation by using other Latin American residents in London. This was the case of Antepara, who signed Miranda's book "South American Emancipation" addressing British public opinion, as well as appearing as the editor of the biweekly review "El Colombiano", the newspaper created by Miranda for diffusing his ideas in Spanish America (see Chap. 8, document 8.2).

He also uses nicknames in the press and asks readers to send comments to a neutral address in London. This circular is precisely the one he sends to South

[65] Napoleonic wars cost around 300.000 dead and missing British soldiers. The total number of soldiers killed among the belligerents remains controversial; however, it could be estimated between 2.500.000 soldiers and five million, in addition to at least two million more civilian victims. This tragic liability left serious marks in Europe and impacted the development of nationalism in Europe with consequences on the world.

American contacts with the first issues of "*El Colombiano*," his newspaper edited in London in Spanish.

The last months of Miranda's residence in London indicate a change in strategy, dedicating his efforts to convincing both in London and Latin America the intellectual circles of the need for an orderly change in political regimes based on municipal autonomy and the need for implementing a new "rule of law."

This overview of the successive periods of British strategy sheds a worrying light on precise errors in the authorities' duty to rationally optimise their policies for the sake of British interests. Although one can understand the arguments of both sides, it is difficult to argue that the government chose the best option for its own interests. Therefore, we consider that the negative outcome concerning both Miranda's plan and British strategy against Napoleon was not so much imposed by facts but rather by gross mistakes in British policy and military options that had made progressively more impossible to correct, prolonging so the war for many years, with a huge but evitable human and economic costs.

Examples of critical mistakes, among others, could be observed in missed opportunities for overseas and continental operations. In 1799, after the doble naval success of Cape St Vincent (1797) and Gibraltar (1798) and the formation of the second coalition, which was well coordinated (contrary to the first one), the Dundas's plan presented already in 1796–1797, and reformulated with Miranda when he was back to London in 1798, seemed eventually made consensus, except Pitt's approval, who blocked the priority for maritime expedition again. Grenville's optimism about his continental projects convinced Pitt to postpone an opportune operation in Spanish America again, which would not require absorbing the troops reserved for supporting the second coalition allies. This first mistake amplified the second one, in turn, due to Dundas' fight with Grenville, which led to the worst mistake committed by Dundas and Pitt when they failed to send sufficient forces in time for the landing in Italy to assist the Austrians before the Battle of Marengo in June 1800. The results of this fundamental division within Pitt's cabinet, unable to impose a clear strategy, explain the failure of both options: Napoleon's expansionism in Europe was strengthened by his Marengo victory, and the Spanish American resources continued to finance the French-Spanish war cooperation and rebuild a French fleet against Britain.

Another example of a damaging mistake is the two British colonial expeditions to Buenos Aires in 1806–1807, showing that the rejection of the fourth condition was a deliberate choice by British politicians. It led to catastrophic military and geopolitical consequences for Britain, with damaging repercussions for Miranda's reputation in South America and the United Kingdom. Errors, succeeding errors, made it more difficult each year to fulfil the conditions for the Miranda joint operation, which would have been the best for the world.

11.9 Conclusions: Confirmation of Miranda's Forwardness Views in Geopolitics

The complex relationships between Miranda and the British hegemon enable a new interpretation of the British strategy towards Spanish America. This specific analysis, when placed in its geopolitical context, reveals interesting elements that contribute to understanding the Precursor's behaviour during this fascinating period of the revolutions that shaped our Western world.

The ability of the Precursor to conceive an advanced geopolitical strategy is confirmed and can be assessed in comparison to those of British and French authorities. More specifically, this analysis defines the set of objective conditions that would have had to be met simultaneously for the British authorities to have fully implemented the Miranda plan. These simultaneous conditions to maximise British interests facing Napoleon's ambition, while fitting perfectly with Miranda's objectives, were:

(i) a state of open war between Spain and Britain,
(ii) a priority given to the option of military overseas expedition versus continental operations within coalitions with allies, or compared to undertaking peace negotiations
(iii) a creole explicit will to reject Spanish authority and access to freer trade with Britain
(iv) a British offer of protection and support which would not appear as a colonial conquest purpose but for preventing chaos and promoting security and trade

The first three conditions were objectively met with a sufficient degree in several opportunities. Still, the fourth one tended to remain ambiguous or unmet when the other three were, and it became satisfied when the other three were weakening. The respect for independence was promoted only by a part of the cabinet, whose dissensions explain that it took too many years to be acknowledged. The negative experiences of the double disaster in the River Plate demonstrated that this fourth condition was not effectively fulfilled before 1808. However, when this condition was eventually met, the probability of being easily welcomed in South America after the Popham/Beresford colonial precedent was lower than ever. Furthermore, when the condition for appearing as a British positive support was finally considered met simultaneously with the three others under Portland's cabinet (1808), Napoleon's usurpation of the Spanish crown caught the English strategy off guard, despite Miranda's repeated warnings. As a consequence of the popular rebellion in Spain against the French usurpation, the British government (Canning) changed the strategy again, invalidating the two first conditions: the Spanish rebels turned to ally Britain against Napoleon, impeding the attack the Spanish colonies and implying a preference for a continental military campaign on the Iberic peninsula again.

Although at first glance, the failure to implement a joint Miranda-British expedition and its potential global win-win game appears explicable and, therefore, rational, this would limit the analysis to a succession of facts and actions-reactions.

However, understanding history requires more than an ex-post mechanical analysis of what happened. We consider it essential to assess historical facts by confronting them with potential alternatives and explaining why these alternative options were not adopted, primarily when the best results did not occur. This serves to measure the genuine degree of rational optimisation, not for re-writing history but for assessing the quality of the adopted decisions, and for the purpose of this work, to be able to compare the British strategy against that of Miranda and deduce who had the most adequate and earliness vision considering what actually happened afterwards.

This method provides an explanatory complement based upon a deeper ex-ante analysis, thanks to a forward-looking view. It shows that the failure of Britain to cooperate with Miranda's plan is not so rational because it resulted not so much from the impossibility of meeting the four objective conditions but rather from the inabilities and tactical mistakes of the British authorities who impeded "subjectively" these four "objective" conditions to be fulfilled at the right moment. This leads us to the conclusion that the British authorities made successive wrong choices, ultimately to their detriment. Therefore, the apparent optimisation was made on wrong à-priori in the context of exogenous events, resulting in a catastrophic strategy made up of a succession of historical mistakes that France was able to exploit brilliantly.

All these years of close relations between Miranda and six successive British administrations from 1798 to 1810 lead to clear conclusions: the divergences of views between Miranda and the British governments do not reflect so much differences in legitim opposed interests, but rather differences between proper and wrong geopolitical analysis, between *rational long-term optimisation and conservative short-term status-quo*, between economically based arguments and individual political interests, between general interests and particular vested interests.

Of course, the decision-making process in a parliamentary regime is a handicap when facing a military regime. Nevertheless, our analysis clearly shows that the British authorities accumulated an impressive collection of strategic mistakes that prolonged the war for many years. A notable gap appears between the short-termism of British politicians and Miranda's transparent and indefectible "*avant-garde*" ideal, which bet on the rational superiority of mutual benefits and their economic results. Of course, Miranda's pathetic conviction that the positive-sum game Britain could reap from his emancipation plan would overcome the "perfidious Albion" behaviour remains a paradoxical excess of naivety on the part of a man of action. The cruel reality is that British policymakers were unable to understand the economic and diplomatic benefits that would have been brought about by the proposed implementation of people's auto-determination, *combined* with free trade and peaceful international cooperation through law and fairness. Miranda consistently overestimated the British government's ability to comprehend its long-term interests in promoting the emancipation of South America. We consider this defect also as the expression – and the proof - of the degree of precocity of his analysis. In fact, rather than the choice of British authorities, as explained by Golding (2017), the governments were driven by the events as "*the Napoleonic wars* [that] *spawned an imperial transformation of the British state*".[66]

This conclusion could even lead to some *uchronic exercises* by raising three worrying interrogations resulting from the failure of a combined Miranda-British military intervention in South America, which would have allowed to prevent both civil war in Latin America and new Napoleonic wars by cutting Spanish resources from America and financing with them the British coalitions:

(i) Would a timely expedition, allowing Miranda's plan to establish a peaceful federal republic in Spanish America, have prevented the bloody and chaotic wars of independence, which led to caudillismo and further underdevelopment in Latin America?
(ii) Would the British repeated procrastinations in their strategies against the French global expansionism be responsible for prolonging several years of Napoleon's military successes?
(iii) Could this extension of French dictatorship have sown the seeds of the belligerent and revengeful nationalism that led to the world and ideological wars of the twentieth century and a lasting deepening of the intra-European divisions?

Although alternate history (uchronia) is neither proof nor history, it helps to provide a broader scope for understanding historical analysis, the challenges Miranda faces, and to assess his degree of foresight. The complex relations of Miranda with the British government bring an additional piece of thinking for assessing how much Miranda's geopolitical vision correctly perceived on time the risks of Jacobin "totalitarianism", and especially the global threat of Napoleon, with his inevitable will to capture Spain and Portugal, to try to finance with their colonies his own imperial domination strategy. This Precursor's ability to forecast explains his rational risk-taker behaviour, which was missing in the British cabinets. It was indeed a calculated risk to propose to "*Perfide Albion*" in early times, supporting Latin American independence in a strategy conceived in economic and logistical terms as a global win-win game with the imperialist hegemon: offering freedom under British protection and free trade. This offer would have allowed the British authorities to reap net benefits without withdrawing many troops from Britain or Europe while efficiently hitting the Spanish Treasury and its financial transfers to the French army. Simultaneously, Spanish America would have benefitted from an association with the British empire, like the US, but in a triple financial and technological synergy. Finally, British presence would permit the prevention of anarchical turmoil and bloody ethnic revolutions. Unfortunately, the British short-term selfishness led to betraying its fair and transparent ally. Therefore, the two key questions to arrive at are:

(i) Could it be that the British incapacity to adopt the full Miranda/Dundas proposal (to reach an objective first-best strategy) would have played an objective

[66] Golding (2017) op.cit. p. 8. Once again, a worrying parallel with the 2025 new US imperialist strategy against Ukraine and Europe that Trump's presidency triggered might be observed, short-term personal and mercantilist interests outweigh outrageously longer-run rational interests.

responsibility in resulting in massive human and economic costs for Latin America and the world?

(ii) Could Miranda's constitutional strategy have allowed for democratic emancipation, avoiding the bloody turmoil of the wars of independence in Spanish America and the consequent caudillismo?

References

Baugh, D., (1988), "Great Britain's 'Blue-Water' Policy, 1689-1815." *The International History Review*, 10:1 (February°: 33-58.

Baugh, D., (1994), "Maritime Strength and Atlantic Commerce: The Uses of 'A Grand Marine Empire.'" In *An Imperial State at War: Britain from 1689–1815*, edited by Lawrence Stone, 185-223. Routledge, New York.

Beverina, J., (1939), *Las Invasiones Inglesas al Rio de la Plata*, Vol. II, p.123, Circulo Militar, vol. 249-250, Buenos Aires.

Black, J., (2005), *The Continental Commitment: Britain, Hanover, and Interventionism, 1714-1793,* Routledge, New York.

Brewer, J., (1994), *The Sinews of Power. War, Money and the English State, 1688-1783*, London, Unwin Hyman, re-edited Routledge,

Brun, J. F., (2009), "Les unités étrangères dans les armées napoléoniennes: un élément de la stratégie globale du Grand Empire", in *Revue historique des armées*, 229.

Burnham, R., (n.d.), "The British Army in the Napoleonic Wars: Manpower Stretched to the Limits?" in Napoleon Series, https://www.napoleon-series.org/military-info/organization/c_casualties.html

Castlereagh, R., (1807), "Memorandum for the Cabinet, Relative to South America" May 1, in Correspondence, Castlereagh Papers, 7: 314–24.

Colley, L., (1994), "The Reach of the State, the Appeal of the Nation: Mass Arming and Political Culture in the Napoleonic Wars," in Lawrence Stone, ed., *An Imperial State at War: Britain from 1689-1815*, Routledge, New York, p. 165-84

Duffy, M., (1989), "Pitt, Grenville, and the Control of British Foreign Policy in the 1790s." In Knights Errant and True Englishmen: British Foreign Policy, 1660-1800, edited by Jeremy Black, 151-77. John Donald Publishers, Edinburgh.

Duffy, M., (1987), *Soldiers, Sugar, and Seapower: The British Expeditions to the West Indies and the War against Revolutionary France*. Oxford: Clarendon Press.

Dumouriez, C. F. (1794), Mémoires du Général Dumouriez, Vol II, Elmsly, London

Dundas, H., [1795] Unsigned memorandum, attributed to Dundas, in Melville Papers, fol. 1, WCL, quoted by Golding, C. [2017], op. cit. p. 59.

Dundas, H., [1796–1797] Speeches of February 18, 1796 and May 18, 1797, Parliamentary History, vol. 32, col. 752; and vol. 33, col. 584, quoted by Golding C. [2017], op. cit. p. 35.

Dundas Melville, H., (1800) "Memorandum for the Consideration of His Majesty's Ministers" March 31, Box 5, Melville Papers, 1771-1831, Rubenstein Library, Duke University.

Ehrman, J., [1983] *The Younger Pitt*, Volume Two: The Reluctant Transition, London, Constable, p. 348.

Faulder, R., et al., (1808), *The trial at large of Lieut. Gen. Whitelocke, commander in chief of the expedition against Buenos Ayres. By court-in martial. held in Chelsea college, on Thursday, the 28th January, 1808, and succeeding days .. …* Ed. Tipper, London. https://dn790004.ca.archive.org/0/items/trialoflieutenan00whit/trialoflieutenan00whit.pdf

Ferrell, J, (2006), *The Pivotal Roles of Henry Dundas and William Pitt in the British Cabinet Fiasco of 1800*. University of Tennessee Honors Thesis Projects.

Fortescue, J., (1915), *A History of the British Army,* Macmillan and co., London.

Geggus, D., (1983), "The Cost of Pitt's Caribbean Campaigns, 1793-1798." *The Historical Journal* 26:3 (September): 699-706.

Golding, C. (2017), *At water's edge: Britain, Napoleon, and the world 1793-1815*, Doctoral Thesis, Temple University, Philadelphia.

Grenville, Wyndham W., Baron, (1894), *The Manuscripts of J. B. Fortescue*, Esq., Preserved at Dropmore … 10 vol. London: Printed for H. M. Stationary Office by Eyre and Spottiswood.

Ingram, E., (1970), ed. *Two Views of British,* The Private Correspondence of Mr Dundas and Lord Wellesley: 1798-1801. Adams & Dart, Bath.

Lynch, J., (1969), "British Policy and Spanish America, 1783-1808", *Journal of Latin American Studies*, Vol. 1, No. 1 (May), https://www.jstor.org/stable/156483

Mackesy, P., (1984), *War Without Victory: The Downfall of Pitt 1799-1802*. Oxford: Clarendon, 1984.

Minard, P., (2018), "L'État militaro-fiscal anglais au 18th siècle", in *Revue d'histoire moderne & contemporaine* R 2018/4 (n° 65-4).

Miranda, F. de, (1929-1950), *Archivo del General Miranda*, ed. Vicente Dávila/ Rubén González, Caracas/La Habana.

Pyne, P., (1998), "A soldier under two flags. Lieutenant-Colonel James Florence Burke: officer, adventurer and spy", in: Études irlandaises, n°23-1, p. 121-138.

Raleigh, W., (1600), *A discourse of the invention of ships, anchors, compass, manuscript*, Yale University, Beinecke Rare Book & Manuscript Library, Beinecke MS 566.

Roberts, C., (1938), *Las Invasiones Inglesas del Rio de la Plata (1806-1807) y la Influencia Inglesa en la Independencia y Organización de las Provincias del Rio de la Plata,* ed. Jacobo Peuser, Buenos Aires.

Terragno, R., (1998), *Maitland & San Martín*, Universidad Nacional de Quilmes.

Wellesley, A., (1807), "Memorandum on the Subject of a British Expedition to New Spain" January 25, Sir Arthur Wellesley to Lord Grenville, February 17, 1807; and Reports by Wellesley to Lord Grenville [numerous], in Dropmore Papers, 9: 22-25, 41-45, and 479-93.

Chapter 12
Deputy Miranda's Interventions in Venezuela Constituent, 1811

12.1 Extracts of the Parliamentary Interventions of Deputy Miranda in the Supreme Constituent Congress of Venezuela, Caracas, July 1811

Context:

Miranda sailed back to Venezuela in October 1810 and arrived in La Guaira (the port near Caracas) in December 1810, a few days after Simón Bolívar, who came to welcome him with the brother of the President of the Supreme Junta de Caracas. However, some official circles are critical of, or even opposed to, Miranda's return due to ideological conflicts, not only over his independentist views but also his federal, republican, and social plans. He immediately engaged his efforts to transform the Caracas revolt against Bonaparte's usurpation of the Spanish throne into a complete emancipation through a democratic republican constitution. Indeed, the Caracas movement against Bonaparte's invasion of Spain was merely an opportunistic means to seize the posts and the salaries of the civil servants in the metropolis without altering the absolutist regime.

In March 1811, Miranda was elected as a deputy to the First Constitutional Congress and served on the committee responsible for drafting a written constitution [Academia de la Historia 2011]. He played a decisive role in drafting the Declaration of Independence and was a significant contributor to the development of a republican constitution [La Constitución Federal de Venezuela y Documentos Afines 1811]. However, he could not achieve all his objectives, particularly the sufficient degree of central federal power (namely for the army) that he considered crucial for the sustainability of the sovereignty [Parra Perez 1959].

C. Ghymers, *Independence, Federalism and Regionalism in Latin America: An Analytical Anthology of Francisco de Miranda's Writings (1790-1811)*, United Nations University Series on Regionalism 34,
https://doi.org/10.1007/978-3-031-96938-6_12

Content:

Eloquent replies made by Miranda in the constitutional congress to several objections on critical aspects of the design of the constitution of Venezuela: the strategic need to declare absolute independence from Spain, the need for starting with this point before reaching unanimous support by all the provinces, the democratic nature of a regime depending more of separation of powers than from an elective parliament with reference to historical examples of "elective tyranny". He also corrected some misinformation diffused during the debates about the United States precedent.

Sources:

América Espera. Documento 174. p. 448–454.

Libro de Actas del Supremo Congreso. Vol. 1. p. 105, 109, 111, 119, –120, 123, 132, 136, 138, 139, 140, 155–156, 167, 171, 185, 186, 189, 190, 211, 212, 217.

Text:

SESSION OF JULY 1

....

Mr. Miranda vigorously supported the need for robust security measures and duly demonstrated the absolute necessity of unity of action within the Executive Power. Believing the general health of Venezuela to be the supreme law, he thought that the vast majority of its provinces could coercively compel those who would resist to cooperate for the happiness of the others, citing the example of the United States, in which the nine united provinces forced the two who wanted to separate. He concluded by presenting a written motion to ask the Executive for the data contained therein.

SESSION OF JULY 2

....

Mr. Miranda supported the reasons alleged by Mr. Sata as a complete demonstration of the inconveniences that would follow from removing Congress outside of Caracas and concluded by opposing it.

....

M. Miranda: I leave Mr. Sata the work of challenging and dispelling the fallacies that the pre-opinion has brought up, but I cannot allow it to be said in this assembly that 40 men can't abuse authority. It is very inappropriate to us that he openly clashes with such notorious and recent historical events. Even children who have read history know that 1200 men chosen in France, as we have been, assumed all powers, became evil, and flooded their homeland with blood, mourning and desolation. No one doubts that there were 30 tyrants in Athens and that the big English parliament, that rampart of despotism, gave Cromwell the authority to tyrannise the nation. This ignorance of history cannot be very advantageous to a legislator, and if public opinion were better heard and that of that Patriotic Society so unjustly denigrated, it would be seen that similar errors were not incurred there. The opinion that has spread, claiming the Congress of North America had all the powers and that the Executive commissioned George Washington, is false. I want the dates and facts to be quoted to me. I was present when the chief of arms handed over his authority to Congress at the war's end. He had no authority other than military: during the war, he was authorised to raise troops and collect food and other supplies from the provinces. Upon peace, he resigned his command, presented his accounts, and proceeded to distribute the expenses among all the States. Our arguments must be based on facts: we have divided the powers because we have believed it necessary; we must be very cautious in sustaining this division; with it, Caesar would not have abused the freedom of Rome, and Athens would have been in danger earlier if she had been less severe; It is, therefore, necessary to bear in mind the past examples and those of our neighbours. Collegiate bodies can be tyrants when there is no exact division of powers.

SESSION OF 3 JULY

……………………………………………………………………………………

Mr. Miranda, whose speech could not be taken literally due to an unforeseen accident, argued for independence with solid reasons, delivering an energetic and lengthy speech. One of the main ones in which he supported his opinion was the ambiguity that our conduct induced in the calculations of England and other powers capable of helping us. All of them, he said, want to know positively what the actual state of our relations with another power is to which we have been united so far, so as not to expose themselves to arm ourselves against themselves if the order of events unites us again, by will or by force, with Spain. In our present situation, the nation helping us cannot surely count on our reciprocity if it were to need our assistance, perhaps against Spain, whose rights over us have not yet been cut. We must be independent and accept the risks and enjoy the advantages attached to such independence so that secure pacts can be formed with us that do not risk serving to directly increase the forces against the nation, which helps us. Otherwise, it would be to pretend that they should strengthen the arm that, sooner or later, could be used against them with the same weapons they had given to us. This, I believe, is a potent reason in favour of our Independence.

…………………………………… ……………………………………

Mr. Miranda: This discussion, the most knowledgeable and essential perhaps that Spanish America has witnessed since the sad days of its slavery, shows us that almost all members of Congress agree on the usefulness and advantages that result from the prompt declaration of our absolute independence and that only for two opinions appear difficulties that I do not think are of the most significant importance. Mr. Maya has said that the confederation had to precede independence necessarily, that there are no powers in Congress to declare them, and that the province of Mérida, whom he represents, expressly told him in its instructions that such a declaration was not appropriate for now, so he was in a certain way prevented to accept it; Mr. Yanes has wholly dissolved the first difficulty and I will omit to speak anything about it; as for the second, it is more relevant from sophistry than accuracy.

SESSION OF JULY 5

…………………………………… …………………………………… .

Mr. Miranda supported the Executive's opinion with excellent reasons, asserting that the news about the political state of Europe, the withdrawal of Massena, and the situation in the Peninsula made it necessary to make a clear decision and give a clear sign that it saves us forever or sacrifices us all for the happiness of the Homeland.

…………………………………… …………………………………… .

Mr. Miranda got up and, in a long and energetic speech, responded to Mr. Roscio's objection about our small population to declare ourselves independent. He stated that when the United States of North America perfected their great and immortal enterprise, they did not have the three million inhabitants of which he had previously spoken since the number of slaves only amounted to 400,000; that their territory, in addition to this, was twice as extensive as ours, manifested in its main cities, where, however, there were no more lights and illustration, than in Caracas, that the excesses of Europe were not applicable to America since it divided into small States, the usurpation could not have an effect, nor the conquest that the Republics mentioned by Mr. Cabrera of Luca and San Marino barely counted 500,000 inhabitants, that that of Ragusa, whose virtues he had admired when he was in it, since without land and with no other resources than sterile rocks, made industry shine, manifesting the precious effects of freedom, had no more than sixty to eighty thousand inhabitants, that Genoa, which had such a distinguished role in history, did not have more than a million inhabitants; Sweden was circumscribed to two million, and Denmark was less than Sweden. The population of the Electorate of Hannover was not more than ours. That the circles of the German Empire, taken individually, were not more considerable either. That the seventeen United Provinces of the Netherlands had three million populated souls, although those that promoted independence and achieved it were five or seven provinces, which having no more than one million inhabitants, they repelled all the power of the tyrant Philip II and the Duke of Alba and that since we were bordering with the new Kingdom of Granada, which had given us peace and unity, our fears should cease by declaring immediately the Independence.

SESSION OF 11 JULY

....

Then Mr. Miranda got up and, satisfying the objection proposed by the previous gentleman, observed that in France, only the nobles emigrated, and not the rest of the people, since most of them reflected that their prerogatives had ceased and that their Ideas of greatness and preponderance were absolutely vain and imaginary; they saw no other choice than to provide themselves with an asylum where those ghosts that they so idolised would not have disappeared, the crass ignorance that reigned among this class of citizens and the sad prospect that they had infinitely contributed to this resolution. They were offered the option not to exercise this right in the future, which was a privilege they had enjoyed during the time of kings. As for us, the speaker continued, I am firmly convinced that we will have no other emigrations than those of some European Spaniards, who do not suffer from our freedom and will always oppose our just regeneration. And what evils can come from such men leaving the country without ever being remembered? On the contrary, this would be the happy moment of our perfect calm. Embark, then, congratulations, go to Puerto Rico and join that King in commission with that certain Cortabarría, who will surely do us less harm there than they can cause ourselves. The various conspiracies uncovered in this city and Cumaná, the scandalous act of Captain Feliciano Montenegro, and numerous other examples, which I omit, have been the payment and remuneration for our suitable treatments and the considerations we have maintained for them. I repeat, then, that some individuals who are so demoralised and whose union with us is in all respects unaffordable leave as soon as possible.

However, I distinguish between the good Spaniards and the bad, and I do not think that I intend to confuse the criminal with the innocent. On the other hand, it is positive that all those who have come to America with ideas of command and authority have been tyrants, ungrateful and unknown, which serves as a lesson to us, so we always receive them with the severest circumspection. It seems to me, then, that I have satisfied the objection proposed by Mr. Maya.

12.2 Miranda's Objections to the Federal Constitution of 1811: (Federal Constitution for the States of Venezuela in General Congress, Federal Palace of Caracas, December 21, 1811)

Context:

Miranda failed to convince Congress about the exact meaning of a federal republic. The other deputies opposed central power, understanding federalism as a decentralised regime, while Miranda insisted that Venezuela also needed some limited central powers for the executive federal government. These federal powers, of course, had to be strictly controlled by the autonomy of the other powers. In particular, he experienced the weakness of the governance regime when the government asked him to submit to the rebellions organised against the republic while denying him the necessary power. He, therefore, wanted a possibility of central power in case of war, enabling a federal army to be efficient under a mandate accountable to the authority of parliament and the judicial power. Again, the fall of the first republic will demonstrate only a few months later, in 1812, that he was right. Still, the local oligarchies remained reluctant, preferring to maintain some military and political room for manoeuvre, which indicated a lack of genuine consensus on the proposed emancipation path.

Content:

Miranda wants to warn that this constitution is inadequate for ensuring independence and social inclusion, clarifying that he disagrees with the fundamental points of the balance of powers and with its failure to unite Venezuelan society, thereby exposing its independence and security. Miranda foresees that in the event of a Spanish invasion, this constitution would not provide adequate cohesion for defending independence, as the events would soon prove.

Sources:

América Espera. Documento 175. p. 455.

La Constitución Federal de Venezuela y Documentos Afines. p. 223.

Venezuela. Constitución, 1811.: Constitución Federal, para los Estados de Venezuela, hecha por los Representantes de Margarita, Mérida, de Cumaná, de Barinas, de Barcelona, de Trujillo y de Caracas, reunidos en Congreso General. - Caracas: En la Imp. de Juan Baillío, impresor Sure. Congreso de los Estados Unidos de Venezuela, Ano segundo de la Independencia, 1812.

Venezuela.: La Constitución Federal de Venezuela de 1811 / Estudio preliminar por C. Parra Pérez.- Caracas: Academia Nacional de la Historia, 1959. 231<4> p.: il.; p.: facsims; 23 cm. Biblioteca de la Academia Nacional de la Historia. Sesquicentenario de la Independencia; 6. Contenido: Observaciones preliminares --Acta de la independencia --Constitución Federal para los Estados de Venezuela.

Text:

Protest by Francisco de Miranda

Considering that in the present Constitution, the Powers are not in the right balance, nor the structure or general organisation sufficiently simple and straightforward so that it can be permanent; on the other hand, it is not adjusted with the population, character and customs of these countries, that instead of meeting us in a general mass or social body, it divides and separates us, to the detriment of the common security and our Independence; I put these objections in compliance with my duty:

Francisco de Miranda.

References

Academia de la Historia, (2011), *Libro de actas del Supremo Congreso de Venezuela 1811-1812*, Colección Bicentenario de la Independencia, Vol. I, Caracas. http://en.rettalibros.com/shop/catalogs/show_material_details/47068.

La Constitución Federal de Venezuela y Documentos Afines. (1811). https://www.cervantesvirtual.com/obra-visor/constitucion-federal-de-los-estados-de-venezuela-21-de-diciembre-1811/html/86de8dbc-4b14-4131-a616-9a65e65e856a_2.html.

Parra Perez, C., [1959] La Constitución Federal de Venezuela de 1811 y documentos afines, Academia de la Historia, Caracas.

Annex 1 Father Viscardo y Guzmán's Letter addressed to Spanish Americans

Published in French by Miranda in London (1799) and in Spanish (1801)

Context:

Miranda ensured in 1799 the dissemination of a fundamental document for the emancipation of Spanish America. This letter had been entrusted to him by the US Ambassador in London, Rufus King,[1] in 1798. This Ambassador had received it in February 1798 from its dying author, Father Juan Pablo Viscardo y Gúzman (1748–1798), a Peruvian Jesuit. The text was probably written in 1791, as the author says the fourth century is about to begin. It must have been completed before October 12, 1792, to commemorate the tricentennial of the discovery of the New World, also known as the "Encounter of Two Worlds."

Viscardo was one of the Jesuits exiled to Italy in 1767, when the Spanish colonial regime ordered the arrest and expulsion to Europe of more than 3000 religious of this order who questioned the absolutist colonial regime for their philosophical positions that legitimised the resistance to the oppression, even against the King if it did not ensure the right to development and happiness of its peoples. The Jesuits also advocated for the respect of the identity of America and its inhabitants, who were considered inferior beings by European writers such as Buffon, de Pauw, and Robertson.[2] This expulsion of thousands of Creoles, members of the

[1] Chapter 5, Sect. 5.2.2, note n° 40 & Chap. 10, Sect. 10.3.3, note n° 62.

[2] These authors diffused the Eurocentric anthropological view that Americans were degenerated races by their laziness and apathy, as well as their natural fauna and environment. Several Jesuits in exile put their scientific knowledge at the service of American anthropology, defending the value of American nature and Indigenous identity, creating an insurgent consciousness.

C. Ghymers, *Independence, Federalism and Regionalism in Latin America: An Analytical Anthology of Francisco de Miranda's Writings (1790-1811)*, United Nations University Series on Regionalism 34,
https://doi.org/10.1007/978-3-031-96938-6

"developmental" elite closely tied to the people, had dramatic consequences for the population, affecting directly their education and standard of living, to the point that it is considered to be one of the determinants of the awareness of the need for independence by the Creoles. Miranda (1808), condemned the unfair colonial regime, stating that "*the Jesuits have done more good for South America than any other group of people or religious order ... the real reason for their expulsion.*"[3]

Miranda and Viscardo knew each other, at least indirectly, and the latter played a significant role in the ideology of the former, while, reciprocally, Miranda made Viscardo's residence and cooperation with the administration in London possible. Furthermore, Miranda allowed Viscardo's Americanist thinking to be known by organising its publication and active diffusion. However, there is no proof that Miranda managed to meet personally with Viscardo in Italy in 1786 when he was seeking contacts with the American Jesuits in exile. Miranda knew that Viscardo and many Jesuits actively supported emancipation from Spain. There are indeed indices that Miranda looked for him. His pseudonym "Paolo Rossi" appears in Miranda's papers. During his trip to Italy in 1786, he curiously diverted his journey to Livorno, where Viscardo resided. When he was informed of the 1781 uprising in Peru led by Túpac Amaru, Viscardo contacted the British consul to request English support for the rebellion. The residences in London of both pioneers coincided twice, respectively, in 1791–1792 and the 4 weeks preceding Viscardo's death in 1798. According to Ambassador Rufus King's diary, Viscardo, dying, learned of Miranda's return to London but bequeathed his manuscripts to Ambassador King, telling him that "*he did not trust Miranda.*"[4] However, King, who realised that the dying man was suffering instead from paranoia and wanting to be helpful to the independence ideology of Viscardo, decided a few days later to deliver these documents to Miranda, who met all the criteria to take advantage of them for the benefit of America and for continuing Viscardo's mission. It was Miranda who published and made famous the "Letter to the Spanish Americans", first in French in 1799, with a false place of publication in the United States to avoid problems with the English government, which demanded neutrality with Spain.[5] A second edition, translated into Spanish by Miranda, was published in 1801. Miranda disseminated this document widely, among other occasions, during his landing in Coro in 1806.

[3] *Archivo*... "Carta al Dr. William Thomson del 16 de julio 1808", op. cit. Vol. XXI, pp. 313–314. Montesquieu (1757) wrote the same assessment in his *Esprit des Lois*, liv. iv, ch. 6 honouring the Jesuits as the chief benefactors of Spanish America (quoted by James Mill (1909) in the *Edinburgh review* n° 26), reproduced in Annex 1, note n° 43.

[4] According to Teodoro Hampe Martínez (1999), who studied King's archives deposited in the library of the "New York Historical Society" (Manuscript Department, Rufus King papers, vol. 73, February 10, 1798). Extract reproduced in "Viscardo in London or the Dawn of Spanish-American Independence", in Brading, Gutierrez, Marzal and others, (1999), *Viscardo and Guzmán: the man and his time*, Vol. I, Fondo Editorial del Congreso del Perú, 1999, pp. 167–187.

[5] Pitt was trying to improve its relations with Spain in order to get Spain to end its alliance with France, which was of great concern to the British government. See Chap. 5, Sects. 5.2.2 and 5.2.3 in contexts.

In 1808, Miranda convinced William Burke [1807, 1808][6] to include this letter as an annex to the book they were writing together, "*Additional Reasons for our immediately emancipating Spanish America...*". In 1809, an extract was published in the article "*Emancipation of South America*" (Edinburgh Review[7]) written by Miranda with James Mill, and in 1810, Miranda also included the letter in his book, written with Antepara [1810].[8]

Miranda was probably involved in the origin of Viscardo's second trip to London, as a consequence of having given to William Pitt in 1790 a list of the American Jesuits living in Italy after their expulsion of 1767, with the proposal to use them as advisers and agents or administrators to manage the future new states post-colonial period efficiently. Effectively, on May 11, 1790, Francis Osborne, Secretary of State for Foreign Affairs of the British government, sent a secret letter to the English ambassador to the Tuscan court, entrusting him to find a "gentleman named Paolo Rossi [Viscardo's pseudonym]".[9] Between June and November 1790, several British officials sought and persuaded Viscardo to settle in London to work for the Pitt government.

According to the study of other Viscardo texts, the ideas in this pamphlet emerged well before 1798 and would have been formulated between 1781 and 1790. Miranda acknowledged that the date of its writing was unknown, but he estimated it to be 1791. He published it in London but indicated Philadelphia, USA, as the place of publication to avoid problems with the English government, which could receive diplomatic complaints from Spain and complicate Miranda's stay in London. This dissemination had a very significant impact on the degree of awareness in favour of independence in both Latin America and Europe.

It is a fundamental piece of American libertarian thought. Taking advantage of the imminence of celebrating the third centenary of the discovery, he makes a fiery defence of the principle of people's self-determination. He summarises the three centuries of colonialism with four words: "*ingratitude, injustice, servitude and desolation*". It is the first political document to propose total independence and justify it with convincing arguments. His influence on the men of his time was decisive in reinforcing Miranda's ideology and articulating his argument, thereby broadening his support in public opinion in Europe and the United States.

Like Miranda, Viscardo oriented his life towards realising his vision of a Spanish America independent of the Spanish colonial regime, "*which actively harmed the prosperity and well-being of the settlers ...*". However, the separatist thinking of the

[6] **William Burke**, another author who published Miranda's ideas and information to convince British opinion it was in British interests to support the emancipation of South America. See Chap. 10, Sects. 10.4.4 and 10.4.5, notes n° 122 and 125.

[7] Edinburgh Review, n° XXVI, January 1809, Article 2 https://books.google.be/books?id=XRkVAAAAQAAJ&pg=PA277&redir_esc=y#v=onepage&q&f=false

[8] Chapter 8, Sect. 8.1.

[9] Merle Simmons (1989), "More about Viscardo y Guzmán's sojourns in Londres", en *Viscardo y Guzmán: el hombre y su tiempo*, Vol. 1, op. cit. p.45.

Arequipa Jesuit precedes that of Miranda. According to Luis Miguel Glave Testino (1999),[10] his educational context in a region that cultivated an Indigenous heritage rooted in the Inca past and several Indigenous rebellions prepared him for an early sensitivity to independence. Furthermore, he was educated by the Jesuits, as was Túpac Amaru, who defended the indigenous people. Their expulsion from America triggered a reaction for independence. Indeed, upon learning of the uprising in Peru by Túpac Amaru in 1780–1781, Viscardo immediately took steps (Vergara Arias, G.1999) so that England would decide to support[11] and participate in the emancipation of Peru, while Miranda, also attentive to these events, received requests from Caracas to support the rebellion. Still, it was not before 1783 that Miranda took the straightforward option of independence.

As regards his political doctrine, Viscardo was a man of the Enlightenment, a disciple of Montesquieu, Raynal, and Adam Smith, "*considered part of the liberal movement of the eighteenth century*"[12] (Ruiz Zevallos, A.1999) and had many other points in common with Miranda: he admired the English regime and free trade that led to tolerance and peace, he considered the "*market ... eroding of servile relations*",[13] contributing to emancipation, he condemned the absolute monarchy and the political use of religion to subdue the people, he was an internationalist humanist, he feared the French, especially from 1789, considering that their revolutionary ideas could attract and deviate the Creoles towards an illusion, preventing the realisation of a better pro-English plan. Contrary to Miranda, he was not a Republican; instead, he was convinced that the settlers of South America were culturally more inclined towards the monarchy, which is why he proposed that the future sovereign of Hispanic America be elected from "*the English Royal House*."[14] Rather, he represented the Creole provincial nobility. However, like Miranda, he had a dynamic vision of inter-ethnic relations in colonial society.[15] On the other hand, and it is the most significant difference with Miranda, Viscardo did not formulate any proposal or indication of how free Spanish America should be ideally governed, and he trusted that independence and free trade would be the automatic remedy to all the ills of the colonies, which indicates a degree of simplicity and naivety in comparison to the structured governance system and the subtlety of

---

[10] Glave Testino, L. M., (1999), Un niño en el Cuzco, la formación de la menoría peruana de Viscardo, in *Viscardo y Guzmán: el hombre y su tiempo,* op. cit. Vol. I, p. 279–305.

[11] Letter of September 30, 1781, addressed to John Udny, English consul in Italy, quoted by Gustavo Vergara Arias (1999), "Viscardo and Guzmán: Reflections and Fears about their independence project and its execution", in *Vizcardo and Guzmán: the man and his time*, op. cit. Vol. I, p. 191.

[12] Augusto Ruiz Zevallos, (1999), "Un Precursor de la República Criolla? El Liberalismo Democrático en Juan Pablo Viscardo y Guzmán", in *Viscardo y Guzmán: el hombre y su tiempo*, Vol. I, p. 340.

[13] *Ibid.* p. 349.

[14] As Viscardo wrote in his letter of 28 March 1793, quoted by Gustavo Vergara Arias, (1999), op. cit. p. 201.

[15] *Ibid.* p. 348.

Miranda's sociological vision. His main contribution, expressed in the "*Letter to Spanish Americans*", which possibly helped to reinforce Miranda's[16] already similar arguments and positions, was to develop, from the critique of current absolutism, an argument in favour of a new pact for social integration based on two complementary axes: citizen freedom understood as the ability to protect the natural rights of each individual as a person and as a producer, and the creation of Creole American identity, a quasi-continental reality, which allows to base the right to separatism regarding of the Metropolis and the formation of a new nation: "*The New World is our homeland, its history is ours ...*".[17] These two axes were already in the doctrine of Miranda, who will be able to transform them into a proper political system by complementing them with operational constitutional provisions.

Sources:

Merle Simmons, *Los escritos de Juan Pablo Vizcardo y Guzmán, precursor de la independencia hispanoamericana*, Universidad Cátolica Andrés Bello, Caracas;

Brading, Gutierrez, Marzal y otros, *Vizcardo y Guzmán: el hombre y su tiempo*, Tomo I, Lima, Fondo Editorial del Congreso del Perú, 1999;

Archivo op. cit. Tomo….;

Antepara, José María (Comp.): South American emancipation: documents, historical and explanatory… op. cit.*Extract of the original manuscript of Viscardo's pamphlet:*

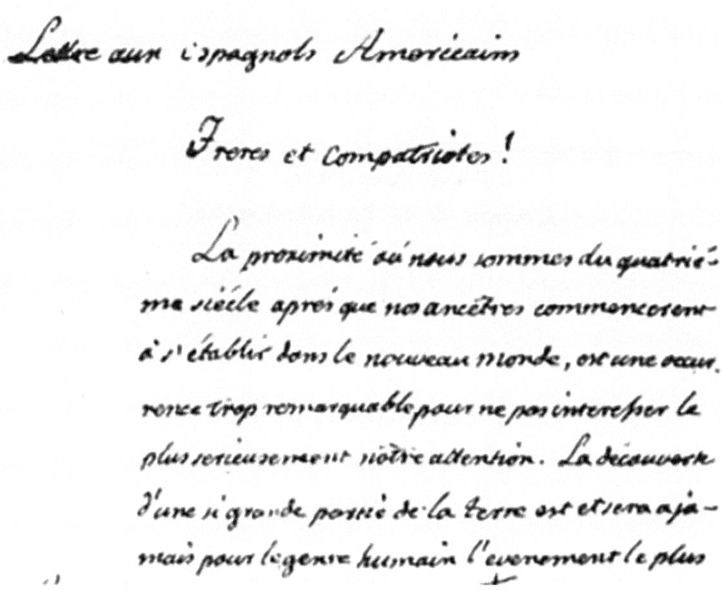

Lettre aux Espagnols Americains

Freres et Compatriotes!

La proximité où nous sommes du quatrième siècle après que nos ancêtres commencerent à s'établir dans le nouveau monde, est une occurrence trop remarquable pour ne pas interesser le plus serieusement nôtre attention. La découverte d'une si grande partie de la terre est et sera à jamais pour le genre humain l'evenement le plus

[16] Miranda's political doctrine was already explicitly shaped in 1790, while the Viscardo pamphlet was written in 1791 and delivered to Miranda only in 1798.

[17] "Carta a los Españoles Americanos", quoted by J. F. Gálvez Montero (1999), "Viscardo, un espíritu de libertad e independencia: entre las reformas y la ruptura del Pacto Regio", in *Viscardo y Guzmán: el Hombre y su Tiempo*, Vol. I op. cit. p.369.

LETTRE

AUX

ESPAGNOLS-AMÉRICAINS.

PAR

UN DE LEURS COMPATRIOTES.

Vincet Amor Patriæ.

« L'Amour de la Patrie l'emportera."

A PHILADELPHIE.

MDCCXCIX.

CARTA DERIJIDA

À LOS

Españoles Americanos.

POR

UNO DE SUS COMPATRIOTAS.

Vincet amor Patriæ.

"El Amor dela Patria Vencera."

IMPRESO EN LONDRES POR P. BOYLE,
VINE STREET, PICCADILLY.
1801.

Text:

Letter[18] addressed to Spanish Americans[19]

Brothers and Compatriots:

The fourth century of our ancestors' establishment in the New World[20] is about to begin. Although it is a highly remarkable occurrence, it fails to capture our serious attention.

The discovery of such a large portion of the earth is and will always be the most remarkable event in the human race's annals. Still, for us, the inhabitants of that continent, and our descendants, it is the object of the greatest significance.

The New World is our Homeland, and its history is ours, and that is why our interest and duty oblige us to examine our present situation and its causes so that we can resolve, after careful study, which party we should take for the conservation of our rights and those of our successors.

[Although our history of three centuries, in its causes and effects, so worthy and exciting for us, is uniform and notorious, it can be condensed into four words—*ingratitude, injustice, slavery, and desolation*; it is necessary to study it more carefully[21]].

When our ancestors withdrew at an immense distance from their native country, renouncing not only food but also the civil protection that belonged to them and which could not reach them at such great distances, they exposed themselves, at their own expense, to procure a new subsistence, with the enormous fatigue, and with the most significant dangers.

The grand event that crowned the efforts of the conquerors of America gave them, apparently, a right, which, although it was not the fairest, was at least better than that of the ancient Goths of Spain, to appropriate the fruit of their courage, and their jobs; but the natural inclination to their native country led them to pay him the most generous homage of his immense acquisitions; not being able to doubt that a gratuitous service, so important, ceased to deserve a proportionate recognition, according to the custom, of that century, of rewarding those who had contributed to extending the dominions of the nation.

---

[18] Designates a writing that reflects and testifies to a legal act. For the medievalist, the letter constitutes a privileged (and often unique) source of economic and social history, at least in Western culture.

[19] The letter was originally written in Spanish, but Viscardo himself translated it into French. Miranda, editor of the two versions, includes the list of exiled Jesuits and an extensive quote from Fray Bartolomé de Las Casas.

https://www.congreso.gob.pe/Docs/FondoEditorial/bicentenario/vizcardo_guzman_v1/index.html

[20] This writing was probably made in 1791, since the author says the fourth century is about to begin, etc. He must have finished it before October 12, 1792, the celebration of the tricentennial of the discovery of the New World, also called the Encounter of Two Worlds.

It was included by Miranda in the French edition entitled *Lettre aux espagnols Américains*. (Philadelphia, 1799), and omitted in the first Castilian edition (London, 1801).

[21] Paragraph included in Antepara.

Although these legitimate hopes have been frustrated, their descendants and those of the other Spaniards, who have successively passed to America, although we do not know any other country than this one, on which our subsistence is founded and that of our posterity, have nevertheless cordially respected, preserved and loved, we have nonetheless cordially respected, preserved, and loved the attachment of our ancestors to their first homeland; it is to him that we have sacrificed infinite riches of every kind, lavished our sweat, and gladly shed our blood for him. Guided by blind enthusiasm, we have not considered how much effort in favour of a country which is foreign to us, to whom we owe nothing, on whom we do not depend, and from whom we can expect nothing, is a cruel betrayal against the one in which we were born, and that supplies us with the necessary food for us and our children; that our veneration of the affectionate sentiments of our fathers for their first country is the most decisive proof of the preference we owe to ours. Everything that we have lavished on Spain has thus been usurped on us and our children, our simplicity being so much that we have let ourselves be chained with irons that if we do not break in time, we have no other recourse than to endure this ignominious slavery patiently.

If, as sad as it is, our present condition were irremediable as lonely, it would be an act of compassion to hide it from your eyes, but having in our possession its surest remedy, let us uncover this horrible picture to consider it in the light of truth. This teaches us that any law that opposes the universal welfare of those for whom it is made is an act of tyranny and that to demand its observance is to force slavery, that a law that was directed to destroy the base of the prosperity of a town directly, would be a monstrosity superior to all expression; It is also evident that a people, who are deprived of personal liberty and the disposition of their property, when all other nations, in equal circumstances, put their most significant interest in extending them, those same people would find themselves in a state of greater slavery than an enemy can impose in the frenzy of victory.

Once these indisputable principles have been accepted, let us examine how they apply to our reciprocal situation with Spain.

An immense empire, treasures that exceed all imagination, glory and power superior to all that antiquity knew—those are our titles to the recognition of Spain and her government, our titles to obtain her protection and justice.

However, our reward has been such that it treats us with the greatest injustice, as if we were guilty of the most heinous crimes. Today, Spain banishes us from the entire ancient world and distances us from the societies to which closer ties bind us. Adding to this usurpation is the deprivation of our personal freedom and the confiscation of our property.

Since men began to associate for mutual benefit, we were the only ones forced by the government to buy what we needed at the highest possible prices and sell our products at the lowest prices. To make this violence the most successful, we have been locked up in besieged cities. We have been isolated, so we cannot obtain the goods necessary to us at moderate prices and in equitable exchanges from other countries.

[Government taxes, employee bonuses, and the greed of merchants authorised to exercise the most desperate and unbridled monopoly deprive us of everything, yet the government prohibits us from turning to industry to supply our most urgent needs without having a choice. This mercantile tyranny forces us to chain our industry.[22]]

The effects of this detestable trading plan could not be observed without anger, the details of which would be incredible if those who have given us impartial and trustworthy people did not provide us with decisive evidence to judge the rest. Without the eyewitness of Don Antonio Ulloa,[23] it would be challenging to persuade Europe that the price of articles, essentially necessary everywhere, such as iron and steel, would be in Quito, in peacetime, regularly higher than 100 pesos, or 540 pounds Tournois[24] per quintal of iron, and 150 pesos or 810 pounds per quintal of stee;[25] the price of the first being not in Europe but from 5 to 6 pesos (25–30 pounds) and that of the second in proportion; that in a port as famous as Cartagena de India[26] and also in peacetime, there has been such a significant shortage of wine that they were obliged not to celebrate Mass, but in a single church, and that generally this shortage, and Its excessive price, prevent the use of this drink, more necessary there than in other parts, due to the unhealthy climate.

For the honour of humanity and our country, it is better to pass in silence the horrors and violence of another exclusive trade (known in Peru by the name of *Repartimientos*[27]), which the Corregidores[28] and Alcaldes Mayores[29] arrogate to desolation and the particular ruin of the unfortunate natives and *mestizos*.[30] Besides, what wonder is it then if with so much gold and silver that we have almost satiated the entire universe, we hardly have enough to cover our nakedness?

[For what use are so many fertile soils if, in addition to the lack of tools necessary to till them, it is useless for us to do so beyond our own benefit? So many

[22] Paragraph included in Antepara.

[23] **Ulloa Torre-Guiral, Antonio de (1716–1795)**, a famous Spanish scientist and sailor, participated in various scientific expeditions in South America; he published several important reports on Spanish America and scientific observations. In particular, his book "*Noticias Secretas de América, about the naval, military and political state of Peru and the province of Quito*" (1748), whose edition was prohibited by the Spanish government but issued later in London in 1826. He was critical of the Spanish administration and tried to promote scientific research, participating in various projects and the creation of several institutions, among others, the Museum of Natural Sciences of Madrid.

[24] Silver coin minted in Tours, central France, and of usual circulation there, was equivalent to one peseta.

[25] Ulloa, Jorge Juan & Antonio, *Viaje a la América Meridonial*, Vol. I Book 5. Chapter VII (Historical Relation of the Trip to South America), Madrid. 1748. 5 Vols.

[26] Ibid. Tomo I, Libro I, Capitulo VIII.

[27] Land distribution to the Spanish settlers.

[28] Judicial authority that governed the Indian towns entrusted to the Crown.

[29] Lawyers, Superior judges who hear on appeal, the sentences given by the Ordinary Mayors, or minor justices.

[30] Spanish descendent with Indian.

goods, as nature lavishes on us, are entirely lost because of the tyranny that prevents us from taking advantage of them and distributing them to other people].[31]

It seems that, without giving up all feelings of shame, nothing could be added to such great outrages. The ingenious policy that, under the pretext of our interests, had deprived us of liberty and property should at least suggest that it was necessary to leave us some shadow of honour and some means of reestablishing ourselves to develop new resources. This is why humans grant rest and food to the animals that serve them. The economic administration of our interests would have consoled us for the other losses and would not have brought advantages to Spain. The interests of our country, being none other than ours, its good or bad administration falls necessarily on us, and it is evident that it is to us alone that the right to exercise it belongs, and that alone we can fulfil these functions, with reciprocal benefits for the country and ourselves.

How dissatisfied did the Spaniards show us when some flamingos, vassals like them, and also compatriots of Carlos V,[32] occupied some public jobs in Spain? How much did they not murmur? With how many requests and uprisings did they demand that those foreigners be fired, without their small number, nor the presence of the monarch, being able to calm the general unease? The fear that the money from Spain would go to another country, although belonging to the same monarchy, was why the Spaniards insisted on their demands with more ardour.

What a difference between that momentary situation of the Spanish and ours for three centuries! Deprived of all the advantages of the government, we have not suffered from their part but the most horrible disorders and the greatest vices! With no hope of ever obtaining immediate protection or prompt justice at a distance of two to three thousand leagues, without resources to claim it, we have been given over to the pride, injustice and greed of ministers, so greedy for what less like the favourites of Carlos V. Implacable towards people they do not know, and who look like foreigners, trying only to satisfy their greed, with the perfect assurance that their wicked behaviour will go unpunished, or ignored by the sovereign. The sacrifice of our most precious interests for those of Spain has been the particular merit with which they all seek to honour themselves, to excuse the injustices with which they end us. But the misery into which Spain itself has fallen proves that those men have

[31] This paragraph appears in Antepara's book.

[32] **Carlos V** (1500–1557) First Spanish monarch of the House of Austria, he was born in Ghent on 24 February 1500. He was the son of Philip the Handsome and Joanna of Castile and the maternal grandson of the Catholic Monarchs. Due to his mother's incapacity, he inherited the throne of Spain upon the death of his grandfather, King Ferdinand, in 1516. In March of the same year, Charles of Ghent was proclaimed King of Castile and Aragon in the church of Saint Gudula in Brussels. Charles was educated in Ghent by **Guillaume de Croy**, Lord of Chièvres (1458–1521), and Adrian of Utrecht, who would later become Pope under the name of Adrian VI. In 1519, upon the death of his paternal grandfather, Emperor Maximilian of Austria, he inherited the states of the House of Habsburg. He was crowned Holy Roman Emperor in Aachen, at the tomb of Charlemagne, on 20 October 1520, thus becoming the most powerful ruler in Europe. Suffering from gout and diabetes, he died on 21 September 1558 of malarial fever contracted from mosquito bites in Yuste. His remains rest in the Monastery of El Escorial.

never known the true interests of the nation or that they have only tried to cover, on this pretext, its shameful procedures, and the event has shown, *once more than ever, that injustice never bears solid fruit.*

So that nothing would be lacking in our ruin and our ignominious slavery, deprivation, greed, and ambition have always supplied Spain with a swarm of adventurers who pass to America, resolved to retaliate there, with our substance, of what they have paid to obtain their jobs. The way to compensate for the absence of their homeland, its penalties, and its dangers is by doing us all possible evils. Renewing every day those scenes of horror that made entire towns disappear, whose only crime was their weakness, these turn the splendour of the greatest conquest into an ignominious stain for the Spanish name.

Thus it is that after having satisfied the theft, palliated with the trade name, the exactions of the government, in payment of its *distinguished benefits*, and the rich salaries of the innumerable multitude of foreigners, who under different denominations, in Spain and America, they are lavishly satisfied with our goods; what we are left with is the continuous object of the stalking of so many proud tyrants, whose greed knows no other term than that which they want to impose on him their insolence and the certainty of impunity. Thus, they consider, while in the Court, in the armies, in the tribunals of the monarchy, riches and honours are poured out to foreigners of all nations, we alone are declared unworthy of them and incapable of occupying, even in our own country, jobs that strictly speaking belong exclusively to us. Thus, the glory that cost our parents so much pain is for us an inheritance of ignominy and with our immense treasures, we have bought only misery and slavery.

[If we travel across our unfortunate country from one end to the other, we will find wherever we want the same desolation, greed as excessive as it is insatiable, wherever we want the same horrific traffic of injustice and inhumanity, on the part of the leeches employed by the government, for our oppression. Let us consult our annals of three centuries, and there we will see the ingratitude and injustice of the Court of Spain, its infidelity to fulfil its contracts, first with the great (Christopher) Columbus,[33] and then with the other conquerors who gave him the New World empire, under solemnly stipulated conditions. We will see the posterity of those generous men beaten down with contempt and stained with hatred that has slandered, persecuted and ruined them. As some superficial peculiarities could make doubt of this persecuting spirit, which at all times has been pointed out against the

[33] **Christopher Columbus** (1451–1506) was born in Genoa, Italy. His origins are an absolute enigma. Some historians maintain that he came from the Kingdom of Aragon, the Kingdom of Galicia or the Kingdom of Portugal, from Felanix, among others. He died in Valladolid, Spain, on May 20, 1506. Sailor who, in the service of the crown of Castile, found a western route to the Indies but thus made Europe aware of the existence of the American continent, arriving there on October 12, 1492.

Spanish Americans, read only what the true Inca Garcilaso de la Vega[34] writes in the second volume of his Commentaries [1609, 1965],[35] Book VIII, chapter 17].[36]

When the viceroy Don Francisco de Toledo,[37] that fierce hypocrite, determined to make perish the only direct heir of the empire of Peru, to ensure Spain the possession of that unfortunate country, in the process that was established against the young and innocent Inca Tupac Amaru among the false crimes with which this prince was charged, Garcilaso says:

> ...[against] *those who were born in the country of Indian mothers and Spanish fathers, conquerors of that empire; It was alleged that they had secretly agreed with Tupac Amaru and the other Incas to excite a rebellion in the kingdom, to favour the discontent of those who were born of the royal blood of the Incas, or whose mothers were daughters, nieces or first cousins of the family of the Incas and the Spanish parents, and of the first conquerors, who had acquired such a reputation; that these were so little cared for that neither the natural rights of mothers, nor the great services and merits of fathers, gave them the slightest advantage, but instead that everything was distributed among the relatives and friends of the governors, leaving those exposed to die of hunger, if they did not want to live on alms, or become highwaymen, and end up in a gallows. These accusations were made against the children of the Spaniards, born to Indian women. They were arrested, and all those who were 20 years old or more, capable of bearing arms and who were then living in Cuzco were imprisoned. Some of them were subjected to torture to force them to confess to something for which there was no evidence. Amid these fury and tyrannical procedures, an Indian woman whose son was condemned to torment came to the prison and, raising her voice, said: My son, since you have been condemned to torture, endure it courageously as a man of honour; do not accuse anyone falsely, and God will give you strength to suffer it; He will reward you for the dangers and pains that your father and his companions have suffered to make this country Christian, and to bring its inhabitants into the bosom of the church ... This magnanimous exhortation, uttered with all the vehemence that That mother was capable, she made the most excellent impression on the viceroy's spirit, and she separated him from his plan to kill those wretches; However, they were not acquitted, but were sentenced to a slower death, banishing them to various parts of the New World. Some were even sent to Spain as well.*

Such were the first fruits that the posterity of the discoverers of the New World received from Spanish gratitude when the memory of the merits of their parents was still fresh. The Viceroy, that bloody monster, then seemed to be the author of all

[34] **Inca Garcilaso de la Vega** (1539–1616), the natural son of a Spanish conquistador and a royal Inca mother, produced the first literature by an author born in the Americas to enter the Western canon for his chronicles of Inca history, culture, and society. See in English (1965) *Royal Commentaries of the Incas*, (1609) trans. Harold V. Livermore.

[35] The second volume corresponds to the second part of Los Comentarios Reales (Lisbon) by Inca Gracilaso de La Vega (1609), published under the title *Historia General del Perú* (Cordoba). The description of the persecution of the mestizos is taken from Book VIII, Chapter XVIII of his work.

[36] Paragraph included in Antepara.

[37] **Francisco de Toledo** (1515–1582), Count of Oropesa, descendant of King Alfonso XI of Castile, fifth of the Viceroys of Peru (from 1569 to 1581), established the foundations of the colonial system in Peru. He destroyed the Inca culture and religion, imposing settlements, taxes, and forced labour on the Indians. He introduced the Inquisition and forced Christianization. He executed Túpac Amaru, the last Inca. The Spanish authority jailed him for accusations of financial mismanagement.

injustices, but let us be disappointed about the feelings of the Court if we believe that it did not participate in those excesses; It has delighted in our days to renew them throughout America, tearing a much larger number of its children from it, without even attempting to disguise its inhumanity: they have been deported even in Italy.

After throwing them into a country that is not their domain and rejecting them as vassals, the Court of Spain, through a contradiction and an unprecedented refinement of cruelties, with a fury that can only inspire in tyrants the fear of sacrificed innocence, the Court has reserved the right to persecute and oppress them continually. Death has already freed most of these exiles from the miseries that have accompanied them to the grave. The others lead unfortunate lives and are proof of the cruelty of character that the Spanish nation has been accused of so many times, although this stain should only fall on the despotism of its government.[38]

This government has had three entire centuries during which, without interruption or any variation, the same conduct concerning us is the complete proof of a thoughtful plan which sacrifices us entirely to the interests and convenience of Spain but, above all, to the passions of its Ministry. However, this is less evident that, despite the multiple efforts of a false and evil policy, our establishments have acquired such consistency that Montesquieu, that sublime genius, has said: "*The Indies and Spain are two powers under the same owner, but the Indies are the essential and Spain is nothing but the accessory. In vain does politics try to reduce the main thing to the accessory; the Indies always attract Spain to them*".[39]

This means, in other words, that the reasons for tyrannising us are increasing every day. Like a malevolent guardian who has become accustomed to living in splendour and luxury at the expense of his ward, the Court of Spain sees the moment

[38] In the year 1785 there were still in Italy the following (313) ex-Jesuits, natives of Spanish America. This list is taken from the General Register of Rome when Don Francisco de Miranda was travelling in that country. As in the Spanish edition of this work, which appeared in 1801, some of the names of the Jesuits appear incorrectly. We have corrected and modernised their spelling by comparing it with those that appear in the list of the compilation made by Fr. Rafael de Zelis of the Society of Jesus in his Catalogue of the subjects of the **Society of Jesus** that formed the Province of Mexico on the day of the arrest, June 25, 1767; formed in Rome, which appears on p. 231 and 293 of the work of Cuevas, Mariano, S. J. (Editor)].: Documentary treasures of Mexico: 18th century: Priego, Zelis, Clavijero, Francisco Javier (1731–1787)/[foreword by Fr. Mariano Cuevas, S. J. (1879-1949)].—Mexico: Edit. Galatea, Higinio Arias Urray, 1945.—405 p., 5 h. of plates, 1 h. of folded plan, 1 h.; 24 cm.—(Collection of unpublished or very rare documents, by Fr. Mariano Cuevas). Foreword taken from p. 9, Contains Letter from a religious... to a sister of his... of the Convent of Santa Catarina de La Puebla de los Angeles/written [by Fr. Antonio López de Priego]. Travels in exile of Father Rafael de Zelis of the Society of Jesus. Description of the city of La Puebla de los Angeles or Angelopolis/[by Father Francisco Javier Clavijero]. See: Annex 1. In the original manuscript of General Miranda's Archive it appears in volume 1, fol. 121. It was reproduced in Colombeia, Volume IV, Document 721 (List of American Jesuits currently residing in Italy, expelled from their homeland. Rome, February 23, 1786. This list was given to him by the ex-Jesuit Tomás Belón), p. 299–303.

[39] From Montesquieu's book *De l'esprit des lois, Paris 1748,* Lib. XXI. Cap. 22.

that nature, reason and justice have prescribed to emancipate us from such tyrannical tutelage.

The vacuum and confusion that the fall of this lavish administration of our assets will produce are not the only reasons that the Court of Spain encourages perpetuating our minority and aggravating our heavy chains. The despotism it exercises with our treasures on the ruins of Spanish freedom could receive a mortal blow with our independence, and ambition must prevent it with the best efforts.

The claim of the Court of Spain to blind obedience to its arbitrary laws is founded mainly on the ignorance that it seeks to encourage and entertain, especially about the inalienable rights of man and the indispensable duties of every government. This has succeeded in persuading ordinary people that it is a crime to reason about the matters that matter most to each individual and, therefore, that it is a continuous obligation to extinguish the precious torch that the creator gave us to light and guide us. But despite the progress of such a disastrous doctrine, the entire history of Spain constantly testifies against its truth and legitimacy.

After the memorable era of arbitrary power and the injustice of the last Gothic kings, who brought ruin to their empire and the Spanish nation, our ancestors, when they re-established the kingdom and its government, did not think of rebelling against it. Absolute power to which our kings have always aspired.

With this design, they concentrated the supremacy of justice and the legislative powers of peace, war, subsidies, and currencies in the Courts. The courts represented the nation in its different classes and should be the custodians and guardians of the people's rights.

To this solid barrier, the Aragonese added the famous magistrate, known as the Justice, to oversee the protection of the people against all violence and oppression, as well as to repress the abusive power of the kings. In the preamble of one of those laws, the Aragonese say, according to Jerónimo de Blancas[40] in his commentaries, p. 751, that *the sterility of their country and the poverty of its inhabitants are such that if freedom did not distinguish them from other nations, the people would abandon their homeland and go to settle in a more fertile region*. And so that the king would never forget the source from which his sovereignty comes, *Justice*, in the solemn ceremony of the coronation, addressed the following words to him: *We, who are worth as much as you, make you our king and lord, provided that you keep our rights and liberties; and if not,* not, as the famous Antonio Pérez, Secretary of King Philip II, relates. It was, therefore, a fundamental article of the Constitution of Aragon that if the king violated the rights and privileges of the people, the people could legitimately not recognise him as their sovereign and, in his place, appoint another, even if he were of the *pagan religion*, according to Jerónimo de Blancas himself.

---

[40] **Jerónimo de Blancas** (1530–1590) was a Latinist and an influential legal historian active in the Crown of Aragon whose Commentaries on the affairs of Aragon, published in Latin in 1588, aroused the distrust of the Council of Aragon and of Philip II. Blancas, apart from elaborating a history of the kings of Sobrarbe, ranging from García Jimeno to Fortún II, condenses the supposed Fueros of Sobrarbe into six laws, which he presents in Latin and the style of the XII Tables.

It is to this noble spirit of freedom that our ancestors owed the energy that made them finish such great enterprises and that, amid so many onerous wars, made the nation flourish and filled it with prosperity, as is observed today in England and Holland. But after the king passed the limits that the Constitution of Castile and Aragon had prescribed for him, the decline of Spain was as rapid as the power acquired, or better to say, usurped by the sovereigns had been extraordinary, and this proves enough that absolute power, to which arbitrary power always joins, is the ruin of states.

[Then he explains the solid principles of liberty that are initially included in the Spanish Constitution and affirmed by the spirit of the people; he declares with great discernment, in the brief passage that follows, the miserable and misleading cause of the loss of these principles at its origin:

The union of the crowns of Castile and Aragon as well as the great States, which at the same time touched by the inheritance of the Kings of Spain and the treasures of the Indies, gave the Crown a strong unforeseen preponderance that became so powerful that in a very short time, he transformed all the obstacles that the prudence of our grandparents had opposed to ensure the freedom of their descendants. The royal authority, similar to the sea when it leaves its margins, flooded the entire monarchy, and the will of the King and his Ministers became the universal law.

Once despotic power was so solidly established, the very shadow of the old Cortes no longer existed; there was no other safeguard for the natural, civil and religious rights of the Spanish than the arbitrariness of the Ministers or the old formalities of justice called "*Vias legales*" (legal channels). The latter has sometimes opposed the oppression of innocence without thereby preventing the proverb that says: *there go the laws, where the kings want*].[41]

A successful invention finally provided the most fruitful means of eliminating these troublesome obstacles. The supreme economic power and the *reserved motives in the genuine soul* (expressions that will amaze later), finally discovering the vanity of all the illusions of humanity about the eternal principles of justice, about the rights and duties of nature and society, have deployed their irresistible effectiveness on more than 5000 Spanish citizens[42] in a single stroke. Observe that these citizens were united in one body, that to their rights of society,[43] as members of the nation, they united the honour of public esteem, deserved by services as valuable as necessary.[44]

---

[41] Paragraph included in Antepara's book.

[42] This refers to the arrest and exile of all the Jesuits from Spanish America, decided by Carlos III in 1767, with confiscation of all their properties. Viscardo was one of the more than 3000 Jesuits who were expulsed to Italy, prohibited from working, and condemned to poverty and starvation.

[43] The Jesuit order, named the "Company of Jesus", created in 1540.

[44] Paraguay (says Montesquieu (1748)) *can furnish us with another example. It has been attempted to commit a crime against the company which considers the pleasure of commanding as the only good in life, but it will always be sublime to govern men by making them happier. It is glorious that it was the first to show in those countries the idea of religion united with humanity. By repairing the devastations of the Spaniards, one of the most significant wounds the human race has yet*

Omitting the reflections that arise from all the circumstances of such a strange execution and leaving aside the unfortunate victims of that barbaric attack, let us consider it only about the entire Spanish nation.

From this painting of desolation and slavery, the author goes on to demonstrate the basis of the freedom of a country. Considering his education, the country from which he was born, and the society of which he was a member, the timeliness and fairness of his sights are worthy of approval:

[The conservation of natural rights and, above all, the freedom and security of people and farms is unquestionably the cornerstone of all human society in any way combined. It is, therefore, an inescapable and indispensable duty of every society or government that represents it to respect and effectively protect each individual's rights].[45]

Applying these principles to the current issue, it is clear that 5000 Spanish citizens, who until then public opinion had no reason to suspect any crime, have been stripped by the government of all their rights without any accusation, without any form of justice, and in the most arbitrary manner. The government has solemnly violated public safety, and until it has made the entire nation aware of the motives that made it act so despotically, there is no particular individual who, instead of the protection due to it, does not deserve to be submitted to such oppression, all the more so since his individual weakness exposes him more quickly than in the case of an essential organisation for which the entire nation was interested in many aspects. Such a serious and well-founded fear naturally excludes any idea of security. The government, guilty of having destroyed it throughout the nation, has made instruments of oppression and ruined the means entrusted to it to protect and preserve individuals.

[If the government believes itself obliged to revive public security and the nation's confidence in its administration's correctness, it must manifest the justice of its cruel procedure concerning the 5000 individuals who were just spoken in the most precise legal form. Meanwhile, he must confess his crime against the nation, violating an indispensable duty and exercising an implacable tyranny].[46]

[But if the government believes itself superior to these duties towards the Nation, what difference is there then between that society and a herd of vile animals that a simple whim of the owner can loot, sell and sacrifice?].[47]

The cowardly and timid silence of the Spaniards about this horrible attack justifies the discernment of the Ministry that dared to embark on a complex and unjust undertaking. And if it happens in the political diseases of a State, as in human

received has begun to heal. This company's exquisite feeling for everything it calls honour and its zeal for a religion that humiliates those who listen to it much more than those who preach it have made it undertake great things and achieve them. It has brought scattered peoples out of the forests, it has given them a secure subsistence, it has clothed them, and if, with this, it had done nothing but increase industry among men, it would have done a great deal. Esp. des Loix, IV, chap. 6.

[45] Paragraph included in Antepara's book.

[46] Paragraph included in Antepara's book.

[47] Ibid.

diseases, which never seem more dangerous than when the patient is insensitive to the excess of evil that consumes him, indeed, the Spanish nation, in its current situation, has reasons to take comfort in your sorrows.

The progress of the great revolution that we have just outlined and that has been perpetuated to us in the Constitution and government of Spain is following national history. Let us examine the influence we must expect or fear from this revolution.

When the known causes of any evil worsen without relaxation, expecting the opposite good from them would be folly. We have already seen the ingratitude, injustice and tyranny with which the Spanish government exhausts us since the founding of our colonies. This is when it was far from the absolute and arbitrary power to which it later came. Now that he knows no other rules than his will and that he is used to considering our property as a good that belongs to him, all his attention consists in increasing it to our detriment, always colouring with the helpful name of the *mother country*, the infamous sacrifice of our rights and our most precious interests. This logic belongs to highway robbers, which justifies the usurpation of others' property with the utility that results from it for the usurper.

The expulsion and ruin of the Jesuits had, to all appearances, no other motive than the fame of their wealth. But being these exhausted, the government, without compassion for the disastrous situation to which it had reduced us, still wanted to aggravate it with new taxes, particularly in South America, where, in 1780, they cost Peru so much blood.[48] We would still groan under this new oppression if the first flashes of anger, so long suppressed, had not forced our tyrants to desist from their extortions. *Generous Americans of the New Kingdom of Granada! If Spanish America owes us the noble example of the intrepidity that should be opposed to tyranny and the splendour that accompanies its glory, will it be in the splendour of humanity that it will be engraved with immortal characters, that your weapons protected the poor Indians, our compatriots, and that your deputies stipulated for their interests with the same success as for yours! May your magnanimous conduct serve as a valuable lesson to all humanity!*

The Ministry is very far from giving up its plans to gobble up the miserable remainder of our assets, but bewildered by the unexpected resistance he encountered in Zipaquirá, he has changed his method to reach the same end. Adopting, when least expected, a system contrary to that which his distrustful policy had invariably observed, he has resolved to arm the American Spaniards and instruct them in military discipline. Undoubtedly, he hopes to obtain from the American-regulated troops the same aid he finds in Spain with bayonets to make himself obeyed. But, thank heaven, the depravity of the principles of humanity and morals has not reached its height among us. We will never be the barbarous instruments of tyranny, and before staining ourselves with the slightest drop of blood from our

[48] Viscardo refers to the **Túpac Amaru Revolution** in Peru and the following waves of rebellions, which began in March 1781 and were resolved by the capitulations of Zipaquirá. The Jesuits educated Tupac Amaru before their expulsion, and Viscardo was in contact with him, and he undertook contact with the British government from Italy to help this Inca revolution. See *Juan Pablo Viscardo y Guzman (1748–1798) El hombre y su tiempo*, (1999) (varios autores) op. cit.

innocent brothers, we will spill all of ours for the defence of our rights and our common interests.

A powerful navy, ready to bring us all the horrors of destruction, is the other means that our past resistance has suggested to tyranny. This support is necessary for the government to conserve the Indies. The decree of July 8, 1787, orders that: *the revenues of the Indies (except for tobacco) be prepared to provide sufficient funds to pay half or a third of the enormous expenses required by the royal navy.*

Our settlements on the New World continent, still in their infancy and when Spanish power was in its most significant decline, have always been sheltered from enemy invasion. Our forces are now much more considerable, and it is clear that the increase in troops and the navy is an expense as enormous as it is useless for our defence. Thus, this formal declaration, announced with so much frankness, does not seem to indicate otherwise but that the *paternal vigilance* of the government for our prosperity (whose sweetness it has made us like until now) intends to give us new proofs of their zeal and love.[49] Listening only to the ideas of justice, which should be opposed to any government, one could believe that the funds that we must supply *to pay for the enormous expenses of the Royal Navy* are destined to protect our trade and multiply our wealth so that our ports, in the same way as those of Spain, will be open to all nations and that we will be able to visit the most distant regions, to sell and buy there first-hand. Then our treasures will no longer come out like torrents, never to return, but circulating among us, they will increase incessantly with industry.

The more we could surrender to these beautiful hopes, the more they conform to the *system of union and equality*, the establishment of which between us and the Spaniards of Europe, the government wishes in its royal decree what a vast field will then be opened to obtain in the Court, in the armies, and the courts of the monarchy, the honours and riches that have been so constantly withheld from us! The European Spaniards, having hitherto had exclusive possession of all these advantages, it is quite right that the government, to establish this perfect equality, begin to put them on the same foot in which we have been so long. We alone should frequent the ports of Spain and be the owners of its trade, wealth, and destiny. It cannot be doubted that the Spanish, witnesses of our moderation, will calmly stop submitting to this new order. The system of equality and our example wonderfully justify it.

What would Spain and her government say if we serenely insisted on implementing this beautiful system? And why do they insult us so cruelly by speaking of union and equality? Yes, equality and union, like that of the animals in the fable, Spain has reserved the role of the lion. Then, is it not until after three centuries that the possession of the New World, our Homeland, is owed to us and that we hear about the hope of being equal to the Spaniards of Europe? And how and by what title would we be stripped of that equality? Ah! Unfortunately, it is our blind and cowardly

[49] Note in original: whenever the Spanish government announces a benefit to us, one cannot help but remember what the executioner said to Felipe II's son when he put the noose around his neck: Peace, peace, Señor Don Carlos, everything is for your good.

submission to all the government's outrages. It is the one that has given rise to such a despicable and insulting idea.

Dear brothers and compatriots, if no one among us does not know and feel their grievances more vividly than I could explain, the ardour that is manifested in our souls, the great examples of your ancestors, and your ardent courage, they prescribe you the only resolution that befits the honour that you have inherited, that you esteem and that you do above your vanity. The government of Spain has already indicated this resolution to you, always considering us as a different people from the European Spaniards, and this difference imposes on you ignominious slavery. We consent for our part to be a distinct people; let us renounce the ridiculous system of union and equality with our masters and tyrants; let us renounce a government whose vast remoteness cannot procure, even in part, the advantages that every man must expect from the society of which he is a member; to this government that, far from fulfilling its indispensable obligation to protect the liberty and security of our people and property, has made the most significant effort to destroy them and that, instead of trying to make ourselves happy, accumulates all kinds of calamities upon us. Since the rights and obligations of the government and its subjects are reciprocal, Spain has breached all of its duties to us: it has severed the weak ties that could have united and strengthened us.

[When he finally asks his compatriots to become masters of themselves from a joint perspective of the nature of things and their own particular circumstances, for example, the famous revolt in the province of Holland, that everyone admires, against the tyranny and oppression of Spain; that of Portugal against that same country; the recent independence of the North American colonies—an event which had, unsurprisingly, the most profound impression upon them. And, in a tone of sublime piety and genuine love for humanity, which is worthy of admiration, embracing each of the nations, including the Spaniards themselves, in their generous vision of the blessings that would flow from prosperity and freedom of a part of the world, concludes the following:

> *Nature has separated us from Spain by immense seas; the son who was at such a distance from his father would undoubtedly be a fool if, in order to proceed in the least, with regard to his interests, he always awaited the resolution of his parents. Natural law at that distance emancipates the child. Why are numerous people who do not depend on other people in any way, of whom they have no need whatsoever, subject to them like the vilest slaves?*

The distance between places, which by itself proclaims our natural independence, is even less than that of our interests. We essentially need a government in our midst so that the distribution of its benefits is the object of social union. To depend on a government located two or three thousand leagues away is the same as renouncing the usefulness of our rights, and this is the interest of the Court of Spain, which only aspires to give us laws, to dominate our commerce, our industry, our goods, our people and to sacrifice everything to its ambition, pride and greed.

Anyway, whatever the point of view for assessing our dependence on Spain, it will be evident that all our duties oblige us to finish it as soon as possible.

We must do by gratitude to our ancestors, who did not shed their blood and sweat so that the theatre of their glory or their works became that of our miserable slavery. We owe it to ourselves for the indispensable obligation to preserve our natural rights received from our creator.

Precious gifts that we have no right to alienate and that they cannot unjustly take from us under any pretext whatsoever. Can man involuntarily deprive himself of the use of his reason? Can your judgment be forcibly taken away? Personal freedom does not belong to him, even less the essential use of reason. You cannot eliminate it; no one can take it away from you. It is the free enjoyment of the priceless inheritance of our parents, and we must transmit it intact to posterity].[50]

It would be a blasphemy to imagine that the supreme benefactor of men allowed the discovery of the New World so that a small number of *rogues and malicious imbeciles* would always be charged to desolate it and of having the atrocious pleasure of dispossessing millions of men, who have not given them the slightest cause for complaint, of the essential rights received from his divine hand; to imagine that his eternal wisdom wanted to deprive the rest of the human race of the immense advantages that such a great event should bring them in the natural order and condemn him to wish that the New World had remained unknown forever. This blasphemy is nevertheless put into practice by the law that Spain arrogates to America, and human malice has perverted the natural order of the Lord's mercies, not to mention the justice due to our particular interests for the defence of the fatherland. With all our strength, we are obliged to fulfil the hopes that, until now, the human race has been deprived. Let us once again discover America for all our brothers, the inhabitants of this globe, from where ingratitude, injustice and the wildest greed have exiled us. The reward will be no less for us than for them.

The various regions of Europe, which the crown of Spain has been forced to renounce, such as the kingdom of Portugal, placed in the very enclosure of Spain, and the famous Republic of the United Provinces, which shook off its yoke of Iron, they teach us that a continent infinitely larger than Spain, more prosperous, more powerful, more populated, should not depend on that kingdom when it is so remote and even less when it is reduced to the harshest slavery.

[The courage with which the English colonies of America have fought for their freedom, which they now enjoy gloriously, covers our indolence with shame. We have let him take the floor as they have crowned the New World, the first, in independent sovereignty. Added was the effort of the Courts of Spain and France to support the cause of American English. That courage accuses our insensitivity. May it be now that the encouragement of our honour has been caused by outrages that have lasted three centuries.

There is no longer an excuse for our apathy, and if we suffer longer the humiliations that destroy us, it will be rightly said that our cowardice deserves them. Our descendants will curse us and heap bitter imprecations upon us. When they bite in vain on the brake of slavery they have inherited, they will remember the moment

[50] Paragraphs included in Antepara's book.

when, to be free, it was only necessary to love it. This moment has arrived. Let us take advantage of it with all the sentiments of precious gratitude, and no matter how little effort we make, wise freedom, a precious gift from heaven, accompanied by all its virtues and followed by prosperity, will begin its reign in the New World, and tyranny will immediately remain exterminated].[51]

Encouraged by such a great and just motive, we can confidently turn to the eternal principle of order and justice, implore him in our humble prayers for divine assistance, and, hoping to be heard, console ourselves in advance of our misfortunes.

This glorious triumph will be complete and will cost humanity little. The weakness of the only enemy, interested in opposing it, does not allow him to use open force without accelerating his total ruin. His primary support is in the wealth we supply him, that these be refused to him and that they serve our defence, and then his rage will be powerless. On the other hand, Our cause is so just, so favourable to the human race that it is not possible to find among the different nations any that is in charge of the infamy of fighting us or that, renouncing its personal interests, that is to contradict the general desire in favour of our freedom. The wise and virtuous Spaniard, who groans in silence for the oppression of his country, will applaud our company in his heart. National glory will be reborn in an immense empire, converted into a safe haven for all Spaniards, who, in addition to the fraternal hospitality they have always found there, will still be able to breathe freely under the laws of reason and justice.

Please, God, this day be the happiest that has ever dawned; I am not saying for America, but for the whole world. Please, God, that it arrives without delay! When to the horrors of oppression and cruelty, the kingdom of reason, of justice, of humanity succeeds; when the fear, anguish and groans of 18 million men give rise to mutual trust, the frankest satisfaction and the purest enjoyment of the benefits of the Creator, whose sacred name is no longer used to disguise the theft, fraud, and ferocity [Las Casas 1697].[52] When the hateful obstacles that the most foolish selfishness

[51] Paragraphs included in Antepara's book.

[52] What just motive could the Spanish government have to declare war on the Indians—says the virtuous Las Casas—who had never done any wrong or disturbed it in any way? They had never seen them, nor known them, nor had they landed on their lands to wreak havoc there; in them, they had never professed Christianity, like the Moors in the new kingdom of Granada. Nor can the Indians be accused of being declared enemies of our faith, nor of doing works to destroy it with open persecutions or with hidden persuasions, forcing Christians to renounce their faith to force them to become idolaters. Divine and human laws have never allowed nations to wage war under the pretext of establishing faith among them unless one does not want to maintain that the gospel law, full of charity, sweetness, and humility, should be introduced in the world by force like the law of Muhammad… There are no places in the world where men and animals multiply as much as in the Indies because the air breathed there is temperate and favourable to generation. But the Spaniards have found the secret of completely depopulating the regions filled with an infinite multitude of men and women, whom they have unjustly killed to seize the gold and silver they possessed; the others have made them perish by making them work excessively or by forcing them to carry hefty heavy loads for a space of 100–200 leagues, so much so that in order to have wealth, they sacrificed the lives of the Indians. We say nothing untrue and still do not say half of the things

opposes to the well-being of the whole human race are overthrown, sacrificing its true interests to the barbarian pleasure of preventing the good of others, What a pleasant and sensitive spectacle the fertile shores of America will present covered with men of all nations, exchanging the productions of their countries with ours! How many, fleeing from oppression or poverty, will come to enrich us with their industry, with their knowledge and to repair our so weakened population! In this way, America will reunite the earth's extremities, and the common interest of a single Great Family of Brothers will unite its inhabitants.[53]

Annex to the Letter of Viscardo: Miranda [1929] compiled a list of names of exiled Jesuits who could be helpful to the cause of independence

Provincia de México

Abaurrea, Miguel; Achica, Agustín; Adonaegui, José; Aguirre, Juan; Alegre, Javier; Alegría, Francisco; Alegría, José; Almela, Miguel; Almón, Juan; Anaya, José; Aramburu, Ignacio; Arenas, Manuel; Armesto, Juan; Arnés, Victoriano; Arriaga, Blas; Arriaga, José; Arrieta, Juan; Arriola, Lorenzo; Arroyo, Simón; Arsdekin, José; Ascarza, Domingo; Ascencio, Ramón; Barco, Miguel; Barreiro, Diego; Barroso, Antonio; Begert Santiago; Belmont, Juan; Berens, Juan; Bermeo, Juan; Bernárdez, Francisco; Blanco, Ignacio; Blanco, Juan; Bolado, Pedro; Borda, José; Borrote, Agustín; Boz [Baz?] Miguel; Brito, Manuel; Brito, Rodrigo; Cabo, Andrés; Cabo, Lorenzo; Calderón, Fernando; Calderón, Francisco; Calderón, Mariano; Callejo, José; Callejó, Matías; Calvillo, Antonio; Cañas, Bartolomé; Cantón, Pedro; Caro, José; Caro, Pedro; Casanova, Antonio; Castañiza José; Castaño, Santiago; Castilla, José; Castillo, Javier; Castillo, José Manuel; Castro Agustín; Castro, Antonio; Castro, Joaquín; Castro, Miguel; Cedano, José; Cedano, Juan; Cia, Joaquín; Ciorraga, Manuel; Clavijero, Ignacio; Clavijero, Javier; Col[¿ll?]azo, Manuel; Colón, Manuel; Contreras, Javier; Coronel, Santiago; Cosío, Domingo; Cosío José Gregorio; Cuervo, Pedro; Cuevas, Eduardo; Díaz, Cosme; Díaz, Vicente; Díez, Domingo; Díez, Juan; Doménech, Francisco; Domínguez, José; Doporto, José Ignacio; Doporto, Juan; Echeverría, Garbiel; Egusquiza, Juan; Encinas, José; Escalante, Francisco; Escobar, Marcos; Espadas, José; Esparza, Domingo; Esparza, Juan; Esparza, Tomás; Fábrega, José-Lino; Fabri, Manuel; Fernández, Eligio; Flores, Blas; Flores, Juan Nepomo [¿Nepomuceno?]; Flores, Manuel; Fondevilla, Estanislao; Franco, Javier; Franyuti, Antonio; Franyuti, Esteban; Franyuti, Felipe; Frejomil, Atanasio; Frejomil, José; Frenero, Antonio; Fuente, Andrés Prudencio; Gadea, Miguel; Gallardo, Pedro; Gavuza, Pedro; García, Diego Sebastián; Garnica, Lorenzo; Gil, Maximiliano; Gómez, Ignacio; González (Cantabna), Manuel; González, Andrés; González, Claudio; González, Cruz José; González, Isidro; González, José Domingo; González, Juan Ignacio; González, Miguel Gerónimo; González, Narciso; González, Tomás; González, Javier; Gradillas, Ignacio; Guebel, José; Guerrero, José Maximiliano; Gutiérrez, Miguel;

we have seen. D. Bartolomé de las Casas: Chiapas, Mexico– Seville 1414 – Madrid, July 17, 1566: *La Découverte des Indes occidentales par les Espagnols*, Paris: A. Pralar, 1697.

[53] Printed in Londres by P. Boyle, vine street, Piccadilly.

Herrera, Manuel; Hijtl, Antonio; Hostel, Lamberto; Ibáñez, José; Inaama, Francisco; Illanes, Francisco; Irízar, Martín; Iturriaga, José Maximiliano; Iturriaga, Pedro; Jiménez, Antonio; Jimeno, Custodio; Labat, Juan Bautista; Laguinazábal, Joaquín; Landívar, Rafael; Lartundo, Juan; Latas, Felipe; Lava Legaspi, José; Lezaun, Antonio José; Llantada, Juan; Llorente, Juan; Lomana, Nicolás; López, Manuel; López, Salvador; Lozano, Antonio; Lozano, Miguel; Lucena, Andrés; Lugo, Antonio; Lugo, Juan; Maestri, Matías; Maldonado, José; Malo, Enrique; Malo, Juan; Malo, Pablo; Malo, Pedro; Maneiro, Juan; Márquez, Mariano; Márquez, Pedro; Martín Arrivas, Manuel; Martínez, Javier; Martínez, Juan; Martínez, Tomás; Martínez, Víctor; Matheu, Santiago; Mendoza, Manuel; Miguel, Andrés; Miralla, Gaspar; Miranda, Francisco; Miranda, Manuel; Miranda, Tomás; Montalbán, Manuel; Mota, Juan Ignacio; Muñoz, Agustín; Muñoz, Antonio; Muñoz Cote, Manuel; Muñoz, Juan; Muñoz, Manuel; Nava, Juan Antonio; Navarrete, Pedro; Noriega, Antonio; Noroña, Nicolás; Núñez, José; Oceguera, Nicolás; Ocio, Magdaleno; Olague, Martín; Oliveros, Pedro; Ortiz, Ignacio; Padilla, José; Palacios, Hilario; Palacios, Rafael; Patiño, Benito; Peñalver, José; Pereira, José; Pérez Acal, Pedro; Pérez, Ignacio; Pérez Morales, Pedro; Pérez, Tomás; Piedra, José; Pimentel, Luis; Pineda, Francisco Sales; Poggio, Ramón; Portillo, Atanasio; Poveda, Antonio; Pozo, Bernabé; Pozo, José; Prendis, Antonio; Priego, Antonio; Quintana, Mariano; Quintanilla, José; Quintanilla Juan; Ramírez, Policarpo; Ravanillo, Juan; Real, Agustín; Remirer, Antonio; Rendón, Javier; Restán, José; Reynoso, Sancho; Rincón, José; Rivera, Rafael; Rivero, Javier; Rodea, José; Rodríguez, Domingo; Rodríguez, Gil; Rodríguez, Manuel; Rodríguez, Javier; Rojo, Andrés; Romeo, Benito; Roset, Juan; Ruiz, Juan de Dios; Sacrameña, Juan; Salazar, Julián; Sánchez, José; Sandoval, Vicente; Santa Cruz, Gabriel; Santoyo, Luis; Sarmiento, Bernardo; Sebastián Félix; Serrano, Juan; Serrano, Juan Manuel; Sierra, José Luis; Silva José Vicente; Sola, Miguel; Solar, José Basilio; Soldevilla, José; Souza, Matías; Tarros, Ramón; Tejedor, José; Terán, Manuel; Toledo, José; Tovar, Vicente; Turpin, José; Ugarte, Domingo; Ugarte, Hilario; Urbina, Benito; Uría, Joaquín; Uriza, Francisco; Uriza, Miguel; Urízar, Miguel; Vaquera, Pedro; Valdés, Bernardo; Vallarto, José; Vargas, Gregorio; Vasoazábal, Andrés; Vega, José Honorato; Velasco, Benito; Velasco, Maximiliano; Ventura, Lucas; Vidal, Francisco; Vidaurri, Jorge; Villalta, Manuel; Villaurrutia, Francisco; Villavies [¿c?] a, Juan; Vivar, Francisco; Vivas, Luis; Zamorano, José; Zapata, Juan; Zarzosa, Bernardo; Zayas, Joaquín; Zelis, Rafael.

Varios ex jesuitas del Perú: Ríos, Maximiliano; Ríos, José; León, Manuel; León, Miguel; Gutiérrez, José; Zubizarreta, Tomás; Arguedas, Juan; Santos, Martín; Santos, Mateo; Bohórquez, Casimiro; Cardona, Casimiro; Bustamante, José.

Del Paraguay o Buenos Ayres: Rivadavia, José; Rospigliosi, Ramón.

De Quito: Lorenzo, Tomás; Aguirre, José; Eguer, Antonio; Hacha

De Chile: Palazuelos, Antonio; Molina, Ignacio; Boza, Mateo; Aguirre, José; Suma total-333. D2.

Annex 2 Miranda as Prematurely Professional Revolutionary

John Dunn,
King's College,
Cambridge

Intervention to the "Panel on Miranda" organised by Professor James Dunkerley, in the "Institute for the Study of the Americas" of the University of London, May 2006.

Long before the aspiration degenerated into a mildly bovine slogan, General Miranda gave a striking example of what it is to interpret and think about politics in a way which was unmistakably global and act within it on a basis which was conspicuously and for a time quite effectively local. Seen through the murky prism of the history of Western political ideas, accordingly, he comes out a figure with a distinct air of magical realism. The point of the slogan, after all, is to invoke a counter-intuitive felicity in execution which is always open to suspicion but which at least aims, with prima facie coherence, to address two very differently specified levels and domains of jeopardy at once and by doing so to avoid a categorical denial in the first instance of fundamental features of the political predicament which already, by the date of Miranda's birth, with whatever variations in intensity, faced all reasonably ambitious political agents beyond the narcissistically self-sufficient imaginations of Europe's greatest powers. That felicity, wherever it plausibly has obtained in retrospect, is explicitly contingent and always, hence in the outcome, potentially overwhelmingly forlorn. It is, at most, an ambition, never a proven capability. To act in politics is necessarily to risk failure (Dunn 2000). To act with globally specified ambition and due local awareness is to run simultaneous risks in two conspicuously and avowedly incommensurable dimensions.

C. Ghymers, *Independence, Federalism and Regionalism in Latin America: An Analytical Anthology of Francisco de Miranda's Writings (1790-1811)*,
United Nations University Series on Regionalism 34,
https://doi.org/10.1007/978-3-031-96938-6

It is hard to recover from the text of Miranda's writings a firm judgment of how realistic his picture of the continent, which he dreamed of changing, really was. The line between fantasy and cognitive grip (always a hazy one in politicians of any drastic importance—think of Churchill or de Gaulle, Lenin or Khomeini) is especially hard to pick out from texts alone, and South America, of all the continents has always shied away from drawing it too sharply. Even the grandest of Miranda's immediate successors, Simon Bolivar, still an emblematic figure for the travails of the continent nearly two centuries later and ideological prize in very active contention amongst aspirants to lead it forward (or backwards) today, left minimal reliable indication of just where he took it to run. Despite the far ampler and more protracted contextual evidence on his agency and its consequences and the rich hoard of personal commentary on his own responses to that tumultuous experience, even his gifted and patient biographer, after a lifetime of scholarly labour, finds it hard to go beyond the turmoil of hurt, frustration, disappointment and confusion in which his gigantic struggle ended (Lynch 2006). The General in his Labyrinth. As Bolivar himself put it as early as 1824 in a letter to a friend: "*The Spaniards will soon be finished; but when will it end for us* ?" (Penalver 1824). As he entered his final year in 1830, he reached a bitter conclusion: "*I am ashamed to admit it, but independence is the only benefit we have gained, at the cost of everything else.*" (Constituent Congress, Bolivar 1830).

In Bolivar's own case, the key experience was plainly revolutionary politics itself—the process and outcome of vast, violent and overwhelmingly confused struggle on a continental scale, and the key relevant comparisons must be with the experience of revolution on the part of other great revolutionary leaders within unmistakably world-historical struggles. By these standards, Miranda had very little such experience in the continent he loved and hoped to rescue, and the little he did have ended unprepossessingly and in failures which others at the time, however unjustly, could readily view as his own personal fault (Lynch 2006). (Within revolutionary politics assessments are characteristically and exaggeratedly moralistic and very weakly tempered by concern for personal justice.) With Miranda, in contrast with Bolivar, what is principally clear is the purposefulness (and in some measure the skill) with which he set about the diplomatic task of broking between the global and the severely local, and finessed the necessarily somewhat precarious relationship between a goal which was continental in scale and perhaps in point, and the discomfortingly confining contexts in which he found himself attempting to pursue it.

Within the confines of personally powerless exile, these contexts varied dramatically, between the private house of Britain's remarkable young Prime Minister William Pitt, correspondence with America's formidable Secretary of the Treasury Alexander Hamilton, Catherine the Great's Ambassador to Britain, and the Girondin leaders Pétion and Brissot in the thick of France's Revolution late in 1792, to finding himself more narrowly immured in Jacobin and Thermidorian jails, and then in renewed correspondence with Pitt and at least one further visit to the latter's house in the closing years of the century. Between these sharply contrasted settings, he had contrived to believe himself offered the governorship of Santo Domingo, seen prominent service in France's revolutionary armies, and found himself disastrously discredited by the open treason of his immediate military superior General Dumouriez, despite stalwart refusal to desert the republican cause for a restored monarch (Racine 2003).

Navigating these very different contexts required a markedly different touch as he moved from one to another, and at least the tactful intimation of very different assumptions (assumptions which they might actually share) as he addressed his shifting audiences. It is less than surprising that the Constitution which he sketched out to Pitt for the Hispanic American colonies in the event of independence, once it had vindicated the territorial scope on the mainland to which he hoped to apply it, should have moved on promptly to underline the commitment that the latter's form of government must be mixed and similar to Great Britain's own, with a hereditary monarch (the Ynca) holding executive power, and an Upper Chamber, nominated by the monarch on the basis of prior service and serving in this new role for life unless dismissed for misconduct by the classically inspired Censors, alongside a Lower Chamber manned by popular election.

It is equally unsurprising that in denouncing his own unjust imprisonment in France without clear charges and with no sustainable evidence of wrongdoing brought against him, he should have summoned up the authority of Jean-Jacques Rousseau (not a natural reference point for Pitt) to denounce the Jacobin abuse of the doctrine of *raison d'état* and its imperturbable continuation by their Thermidorian replacements. Context alone explains that contrast very amply, but it does not perhaps wholly exonerate Miranda of a degree of inconsistency. Rousseau is summoned up again quite effectively through the pages of the 1755 *Discourse on Political Economy* in Miranda's *Manifesto to the French People* to denounce the clear individual injustice of Jacobin principles in action. But he is summoned up as the gravest and deepest authority on democracy and very much on democracy's terms. Not only is monarchy nowhere in sight, and aristocracy no longer of practical relevance, but there are no surviving traces of any commitment to mixed government, and the bitter attack on the Thermidorian regime comes out not as a rejection of its structure of authority, or of the arbitrary relation between that authority and the society from which it supposedly derived, but from its espousal of a flagrantly unjust principle of action with a French provenance which, far from being a Jacobin innovation, went back at least as far as Cardinal Richelieu (Church 1972).

The indeterminacy of Miranda's historical status—Precursor clairvoyant or largely inadvertent, and precursor to just what? Dedicated revolutionary *avant* as well as *après la lettre*, and hence potentially professional only in the light of his own or our hindsight—is less a fact about the opacity of external circumstance than a reflection of the political history of language. When the Duc de La Rochefoucauld-Liancourt answered his royal master's anxious query, "Is it a revolt ?" as the disorderly Parisian deputation debouched on Versailles, with the celebrated apophthegm, "No, Sire, it is a Revolution.", it is far from clear how prescient he was showing himself about the vicissitudes to come. What he unmistakably was presaging was a dramatic transformation in political vocabulary. Before 1789, no one could be a professional revolutionary because no one spoke or thought of revolution in a way that could intelligibly view it as a vocation. The ancien regime in continental Europe, in Britain itself, just as in North and South America, elicited an ample array of enemies to political incumbents. Some of these enemies developed elaborated intellectual critiques of the regimes they opposed, whether in order to pin down their infamy or for the more invigorating prospect of reforming them and bringing them to rights. Over half a century of sustained scholarly endeavour has had very little success in clarifying which forms of imaginative commitment and cognitive conviction could and did shape these oppositional attitudes into something like a vocation (Mornet 1954). The most widely touted recent candidates have been Republicanism (Skinner and van Gelderen 2002) or Radical Enlightenment (Israel 2001). Miranda is an implausible vessel for either even inter-continentally, being at best fair weather (or diplomatic) republican and scarcely mistakable for a rapt devotee of Spinoza. In political orientation, he perhaps came closer in judgment to the substantial body of opinion in France, Britain and elsewhere, which saw the incipient crisis of the ancien regime as geopolitical and economic in origin and powered above all by a deepening global vortex of commercial, naval, military and colonial competition between states of increasingly precarious legitimacy, sinking ever deeper in debt (Hont 2005).

Revolution, in its post-1789 acceptation, embodies an ambitious political judgment. It asserts (or repudiates in accordance with political taste and conviction) a canonical sequence in which the pre-guaranteed disintegration of a political and social order beneath the weight of its own evident accumulation of failures or before the angry assault of its inveterate internal enemies somehow elides into the reconstruction of a supposedly superior order already latent in its derelict predecessor. The collapse or overthrow of incumbent regimes had ample European precedents in 1789, above and beyond the plentiful instances of dynastic usurpation. What was novel in the wake of 1789 was the vision of comprehensive replacement issuing ineluctably from the womb of the old. It was this vision which Burke correctly discerned would lend new virulence to civil war and domestic political competition and conjure up counter-revolutionaries with every augmentation of its own strength (Burke 1989). There was always a large element of delusion to this judgment, but what is very evident is that this delusion had drastic and very conspicuous consequences (Dunn 2008). The vocation of the professional revolutionary was not to jeopardise incumbency for its own sake (still less for his or her own sake), but to reinforce or accelerate the prospects for this imagined transformation. The scale of the revolution's consequences was, in large part, a measure of the destination's magnetism and the fluctuating plausibility of reaching it.

Miranda may have been a stalwart Republican in preference, but he was no Jacobin Ultra. There is little sign (less perhaps than with Bolivar) of his feeling the allure of a distinctively revolutionary consummation and definite signs of misgiving at the prospective costs of incontinent efforts to enact one. Where he does appear to have discerned something politically momentous and devoted his life to realising its political potential was in his judgment of regime vulnerability in ancien regime

Iberian America, itself a reflex of the acute vulnerability of Spain's own domestic ancien regime. He had an excellent opportunity to see this for himself early on in adult life as an officer in the Spanish army posted to Cuba, in direct conflict with the British at Pensacola, and perhaps as a fund-raiser for the voyage of Admiral de Grasse's French fleet into the Chesapeake Bay en route to reinforce Cornwallis's momentous surrender at Yorktown (Elliott 1990), although the extent of Miranda's contribution is sharply disputed (Racine 2003, p. 23-24). From this instructively geopolitical exposure, and from the debacle of the Comunero rising in New Granada shortly after (Phelan 1978), he drew the twin conclusions—firstly that the political naivete and inexperience of his own compatriots, alongside the obduracy and perfidy of Spain's imperial governors, made it essential to wait for the victory of Britain's North American colonists before mounting their challenge, but also, secondly, that once the latter had duly and inevitably triumphed, his own compatriots were just as certain to follow inexorably in their footsteps (Elliott 1990).

This was a cool and, as it turned out, by then, a prophetic verdict on the geopolitical vulnerability of two very different imperial structures and the eventual collective efficacy of their American subjects in the face of that vulnerability. The one thing he seems to have been clear of virtually from the outset was that Spain's time in the Americas had gone. What was far from clear was what would succeed it. It is reasonably obvious that Miranda himself drastically underestimated the disruptions unleashed by evicting it and had little zest for the scale of conflict consequent on the more ambitious transformative projects which featured within it. He remained prudently discreet on the political (and also the social, economic and cultural) character of the regimes which he expected to supplant it. Even nearly two centuries later, a degree of discretion is still very much in order in specifying the character of its successor regimes in many instances and quite obtrusive in the analytical unease and ideological irresolution of their most sophisticated current assessors. The Atlantic transfer of European political categories and modes of political interpretation remains a hazardous voyage, and on landing and taking root, the categories themselves continue to befuddle as readily as they illuminate. Nor do they gain noticeably in reliability by routeing in via North America (Centeno and Lopez-Alves 2001).

How far, then, is it reasonable to Francisco de Miranda as a precursor not merely to Venezuela's republic (Bolivarian or otherwise), but also to the professionalisation of revolution? By the standards of Luncharsky's lapidary verdict on Lenin—"an opportunist of genius"—Miranda showed little prowess in the role. Neither Coro nor La Guaira compared favourably with the victory of October 1917 (Racine 2003), even without their dispiriting sequel. But occupying a role does not require success within it. Nor is the nebulousness of Miranda's conceptions of forms of government an evident disqualification for a revolutionary. From early on in his adult life, Miranda showed himself acutely sensitive to the limitless array of political opportunities opened up to would-be political agents by the context of global geopolitical struggle and the slender thread of rationality which those opportunities imparted to lives devoted to seizing them. Where, like any true revolutionary, new and old, he showed less sensitivity was to the endless array of dangers which accompanied them.

Annex 3 Miranda's military role in the independence of Venezuela

Miguel Castillo Didier
University of Chile

Purpose of this annexe

It is crucial to revisit Miranda's role in the military aspects of Venezuela's independence, as historical misinterpretations have clouded his actual contributions. Many historians have unfairly attributed the fall of the First Republic to him, labelling his return to the homeland as an adverse event. The narrative that Miranda '*suffered a series of defeats*' and that his return '*would have tragic consequences for both him and the country' misrepresents the facts.*

Correcting the misinterpretation of Miranda's series of defeats is crucial to accurately reflecting his military actions. He played a heroic leadership role when in charge, achieving significant results in the First Republic's defence, despite the government's obstacles to his plan and actions. He participated in two main armed confrontations and emerged victorious in both. He gave the patriots their first triumph, beating the royalist insurrection in Valencia in August 1811. He was immediately stripped of command and only reinstated when everything was lost at the end of April 1812. Even at the end of May, he had not yet received the necessary authorizations. All the government errors were fatal, mainly because they did not want Miranda to march to Coro and Maracaibo after his victory in Valencia. After that victory, in August 1811, Miranda's other armed action in the fight against the invader took place in June 1812, with which he managed to stop Monteverde's advance towards the capital. The invader could not take the city of La Victoria, which was the key

C. Ghymers, *Independence, Federalism and Regionalism in Latin America: An Analytical Anthology of Francisco de Miranda's Writings (1790-1811)*, United Nations University Series on Regionalism 34,
https://doi.org/10.1007/978-3-031-96938-6

to Caracas. There was no other armed action in which Miranda intervened. The invasion of Monteverde began in Coro, as Miranda had warned, but he was impeded from being successful. Nevertheless, the realist army advanced rapidly in the independent territory, thanks to several 'patriots' defections. Miranda was only called back too late when the Spaniards had managed to take Valencia, the second city in the country. However, Monteverde lacked the necessary gunpowder and weapons. Monteverde managed to take control only with Bolívar's defeat in early July 1812, when he abandoned the fortress of Puerto Cabello, where the Republic's reserves of weapons and food were stored. He seized "*400 quintals of gunpowder, lead in abundance, and three thousand rifles*" (Miranda's words, according to Pedro Gual's testimony*). Consequently, with the government's unanimous support, Miranda undertook negotiations for a truce and obtained an approved, satisfactory treaty that should have allowed the patriots to save themselves and continue the fight from Cartagena and Santa Fé de Bogotá.

*Testimony and declaration of D. Pedro Gual, in Salcedo-Bastardo, *América Espera*, op. cit., document n° 187.

Upon returning to his homeland in 1810, the Precursor worked actively in favour of the declaration of total independence. He played a crucial role in founding the Patriotic Society, which he helped establish and presided over. Simon Bolivar and other patriots were also active in it. In July 1811, the First Congress of Venezuela was convened, and Miranda served as a deputy, making a decisive contribution to the proclamation of independence. However, Miranda failed to convince the people of the need for a strong central government. A federal regime was adopted with insufficient central power. Miranda [1929] voted against it and made clear his reservations that this was inconvenient at a time when the union and cohesive action of the provinces were required.[1] The warning would, unfortunately, prove prophetic.

The royalist insurrection in Valencia marked a significant shift in Miranda's military role. Initially, the command was given to the Marquis del Toro, who was unsuccessful. Miranda was then called upon, and despite the challenges of divisions, resentments, envy, and pettiness, he managed to take the city, securing the first significant military victory for the patriotic cause. Despite the subsequent criticism of his measures to punish the rebels, this victory underscored Miranda's leadership and the challenges he overcame.

Miranda's strategic vision as a victorious general was evident when he proposed an immediate attack on the royalists in Coro and Maracaibo. Initially, the Government agreed, but Congress's opposition, driven by fear of Miranda's growing prestige,

[1]Chapter 9, Sect. 9.2. Miranda justified his position on the Constitution, saying that it "*is not adjusted to the population, customs and habits of these countries and that instead of uniting us in a common mass or social body, it could divide and separate us to the detriment of common security and our independence.*"

proved fatal. Miranda's warnings about the consequences of this refusal were tragically accurate. Esteemed historian Caracciolo Parra-Pérez commented on this (1925, 1992), emphasising the weight of Miranda's warnings and the missed opportunity for the revolution. This fact should evoke a profound sense of loss about the chance that slipped away.

> *Such an attitude had mortally wounded the Revolution: the moment of victory had passed, and the opportunity that the far-sighted Miranda wanted to seize would not present itself again. The absurd attitude of the revolutionary authorities is enough to explain the failure of the 1812 campaign and its disastrous consequences.*[2]
>
> *The best opportunity to destroy the main centres of royalist resistance in the country was thus lost due to the malice of a few irresponsible individuals. The majority of the deputies seriously neglected the interests of the Republic and pursued as their primary goal the removal of military command from Miranda, fearing that he would also usurp civil power after achieving some decisive victory and unifying the provinces under the independent flag. Selfishness and narrow-mindedness then deprived the Revolution of its natural leader and caused irreparable harm.*[3]

Bolívar would later speak of "*the senseless weakness of the Government concerning the city of Coro*," the Spanish headquarters in Venezuela.

From this misstep, which today seems incredible, everything went badly for the First Republic. The military situation worsened. There was no regular army but undisciplined militias. Desertions began. The terrible earthquake of March 26, 1812, mainly buried the patriotic cities and was used by a significant part of the clergy to present it as divine punishment for the country's rebellion against the King. The establishment of paper money encountered fierce opposition and increased distrust. The provinces did not fulfil their obligations to the central government. The panorama of anarchy was growing day by day.

> "*The Republic was, then, completely undermined from within,*" says Mijares (1964), "*when a frigate captain, Don Domingo de Monteverde, who had arrived in Puerto Rico with some troops to reinforce the royalists in Coro, obtained permission to advance into the interior of the country. An Indian named Juan de los Reyes Vargas Vargas left the advanced forces of the patriots and defected to the enemy near Barquisimeto, and shortly after, two Spaniards in the service of the Republic—José Martí in Guanare and Bernardo Goroyza in San Juan de los Morros—followed his example. These betrayals and the inexperience of the republican leaders, whose troops were frequently dispersed without fighting, created an atmosphere of vague distrust that the few officers who were beginning to become veterans tried in vain to counteract with prodigies of courage and vigilance.*"

---

[2] Parra-Pérez, C., (1925/1989) *Miranda y la Revolución francesa*, II, 395.

[3] Parra-Pérez, C., (1992), *Historia de la Primera República de Venezuela*, II, p. 75. We reproduce here note 17, which cites the opinions of other authors: "Palacio Fajardo, loc. cit., p. 117. Zea, in his History of Colombia, is also categorical in this regard: *from the moment that force was resorted to, it was necessary to use it to the extreme: the government denied Miranda permission to continue the operations* (Cited by Mancini, p. 362). See also Azpurúa's testimony: The general "*wanted to continue the western campaign to secure Coro and Maracaibo, a support point from which the enemy could undertake [sic] to the centre of the Republic, which occurred... Congress disapproved that thought, and consequently, the general returned to Caracas*" (Doc. IV, 68)."

This author (1964) considers the earthquake *"the greatest catastrophe, which seemed to open the grave of the Republic."*[4] And of the bitter divisions among the patriots, Bolívar will say: *"Our division, and not the Spanish weapons, returned us to slavery."*[5]

But Miranda was not wanted. On the contrary, he was isolated, watched, and excluded.

> "*It is astonishing*," says Augusto Mijares (1964), referring to letters from Juan Germán Roscio to Andrés Bello [1984],[6] "*to observe through his imprudent outbursts how such a thorough and cruel siege could be established around a man who had been fighting for American emancipation for nearly thirty years; how they sought to—and succeeded in—making each of his steps suspicious; they excluded him from any action; and even his evident necessary political actions became reasons for suspicion and new pretexts to immobilise him*[7]."

More than a month after the earthquake and the fall of the critical city of Barquisimeto, Miranda was reluctantly appointed generalissimo on April 23. It was too late. Miranda accepted lucidly, exclaiming: *"I am appointed to preside over the funeral of the Republic."* However, it was not until May 16 that Miranda managed to bring together the Federal Government and the Province of Caracas to take measures against the growing anarchy. Martial Law was declared, and the Constitution was suspended to allow the generalissimo to appoint military leaders. However, in mid-June, the Government of the Province of Caracas still refused to accept this law. While Miranda was held back in Caracas by the oppressive political negotiations and insisted on the need to reorganise the army,[8] Valencia had fallen into the hands of the royalists following the betrayal of a leader, Juan Montalvo, who deserted in the middle of the battle. All the important cities, except Caracas, were already in Spanish hands. However, opposition and intrigues against Miranda continued. On June 12, Luis Delpech wrote to him: *"All, my general, except for a small number, seem to be conspiring to destroy the country that you want to save"* (cit. by Mijares, A. 1964).[9]

Adding to the gloomy panorama was the black slaves' uprising in favour of the King and against the patriotic Creoles, which soon threatened even Caracas.

---

[4] Mijares, A., (1964), *op. cit.*, 205.

[5] Bolívar, S., [1811-1830, 2007], *Proclamas y discursos del Libertador 1811-1830*, 17: "Memoria dirigida a los ciudadanos de la Nueva Granada por un Caraqueño", 15.XII. 1812.

[6] See in this regard the long letter from Juan Germán Roscio to Andrés Bello, dated April 9, 1811. In Bello, A. [1984] Obras completas de Andrés Bello. Tomo XXV, Epistolario - 2ª ed. - Caracas : Fundación La Casa de Bello , 1984., pp. 27-40. A good part of the extensive text is dedicated to trying to discredit and tarnish the figure of Miranda.

[7] Mijares, A., (1964), op. cit., 211.

[8] Parra-Pérez (1992) says in his History of the First Republic of Venezuela, Vol. II, pp. 236–237: "*Miranda undertook the organisation of his army with the same spirit with which San Martín, as a professional soldier, carried out that of the troops that in 1814 entrusted him with the government of Buenos Aires, in Tucumán. After the defeat of Belgrano, San Martín made an entrenched camp and dedicated himself to instructing officers and soldiers. The same, with the good success that is known, was carried out by the Argentine general in* ***Cuyo****. Only San Martín's troops did not desert and the royalists were far away.*"

[9] Cit. por Mijares, A., (1964), *op. cit.*, p. 213.

Confusion and discouragement became general. But Miranda believed that there was still a fight to be had. On May 29, he proclaimed to his compatriots:

> *"Inhabitants of the province of Caracas: The time has come to offer the country the sacrifice of your rest and fulfil the sacred vow you have made so many times. The enemy has penetrated the heart of the province; it has sacked the towns, devastated the fields and committed horrible excesses. Some of your compatriots' seduction, fanaticism and imbecility have procured them advantageous positions, and many rest peacefully on the edge of the precipice. But others fight gloriously on this field of honour, which is the current theatre of war: they raise the Fatherland in their arms and show it to their enemies majestic and terrible [...]*[10]".

At the end of June, Miranda was still fighting. Concentrated in the town of La Victoria, he repulsed the royalists. From the 20th to the 29th, he received attacks from Monteverde. On the last day, the royalist leader reinforced his men with veteran troops recently brought from Puerto Rico. The offensive seems unbeatable.

"However, the patriots repulsed him,[11]*causing him heavy losses, and this triumph came to be regarded as a definitive victory."* Above all, it was beginning to be appreciated that the courage and enthusiasm of the Republicans could essentially make up for what they lacked in knowledge: "*Without any concert or formation,*" observed Colonel Austria,

> *"The infantrymen arrived at the fire, their rifles armed; the artillery moved its pieces and trains with urgent speed; the officers and chiefs, full of courage and without paying attention to their corresponding position, with a noble dispute over danger, inflamed the troops. At the head of some lancers, the Generalissimo threw himself into the thick of the fray: all advanced with heroic courage and exhaustion until they forced the royalists to seek their salvation in a disorderly and shameful flight."*

Father Martel, also an eyewitness, noted that *"the soldiers admired the serenity and smiling countenance that Miranda displayed."*[12]

This last heroic action seemed to indicate that the words of the Generalissimo were finally being heard. The enemy had been stopped. Now, it was necessary to do what he had proposed to the Government in August 1811, when he defeated the royalists and took the city of Valencia. He calls his compatriots:

> *"Let us march, my comrades, to Coro, Maracaibo and Guayana. Let us destroy these dens of bandits that infest the country of the first-born sons of Colombian freedom; then we will rest; then we will embrace each other; father, son and husband will renew the sweet bonds of nature and love, interrupted by the urgent needs of the Fatherland; she calls you, citizens,*

---

[10] F. de Miranda, (1959), *Textos sobre la Independencia,* p. 159. La proclama citada más abajo en la p. 161–162.

[11] It is possible, then, to see that Miranda fought until the end of June and did not surrender in that month. The idea of capitulation, which was not exactly a surrender, arose after, on the night of July 5, it became known that Puerto Cabello and its arsenal had fallen into the hands of the Spanish. On July 12, the idea was approved unanimously by the members of the Government and was put into practice on July 25. The Precursor had not "surrendered" in June, holding back the invader, who for the first time in his march from Coro encountered resistance. Miranda and his forces saw the possibility of defeating and expelling Monteverde. Then came the Bolivar's fall of Puerto Cabello.

[12] Mijares, A, (1964), *op. cit.* pp., 216–217.

> *and her voice, more imperious than the conscriptions and forced enlistments dictated by law, resounds in your hearts; listen to her and obey her; take up arms, abandon your private interests for a while; run to the refuge of armed freedom and do not return to your homes until you have firmly established it."*

Therefore, Miranda's two military actions in Venezuela were not defeated: the first was the victory in Valencia in August 1811. After containing the invaders throughout June 1812, his attitude shows the opposite of a loser and a heroic leadership that was little recognised.

And then came the final blow, the coup de grace for the First Republic. Palacio Fajardo writes about it:

> *"Miranda's wise conduct was beginning to restore order in Caracas and discipline in the army when the Spanish prisoners in the citadel of Puerto Cabello took possession of it*[13]*."*

This "castle," the fortress of Puerto Cabello, was the arsenal of the Republic: gunpowder, arms, ammunition, and food fell into royalist hands on June 30, when the Spanish prisoners concentrated there, with the help of traitors, took control of the fortress and began to fire on the city, surprising Simon Bolivar, who commanded the square, with an appointment made by Miranda. The Bolivar's failure to distribute the royalist prisoners in different places at that time was fatal. According to some sources, Bolivar would not have been at his post, as he was participating in a dinner in the city. The future Liberator fought from the town below the fortress until July 6, when he only had 40 men left. It was the final blow for the Republic, and Bolívar and Miranda acknowledged this fact.[14]

Precisely on the night of July 5, when the first anniversary of the proclamation of independence was being commemorated at the General Headquarters in the city of La Victoria, the news of the capture of the castle of Puerto Cabello arrived. Miranda's words, transmitted by witnesses, are eloquent. "*Venezuela has been wounded in the heart.*"

Days later, the generalissimo will read the letters of Colonel Bolívar, which express his despair in the face of the disaster. On July 12, the now ex-commander of Puerto Cabello wrote:

> *"My general, my spirit is so sad that I do not feel like commanding a single soldier; my presumption made me believe that my desire to succeed and my ardent zeal for the country would make up for the talents I lack to command. So I beg you to either assign me to obey the lowest officer or give me a few days to calm down and recover the serenity I lost when I lost Puerto Cabello [...]. I did my duty, my general, and if I had been left with a soldier, I would have fought the enemy; if they abandoned me, it was not my fault. Nothing was left for me to do to contain them and commit them to saving the country, but it has been lost in my hands*[15]*."*

---

[13] Cit. by Mijares, A., (1964), ibid, p. 217. Underlined is ours.

[14] The Bolivar's written confessions, acknowledging his fault in the military disaster, converge with Miranda's feeling that independence was dead.

[15] *Archivo*, XXIV, p. 415–417.

Two days later, on July 14, the colonel presented his report with a letter no less pathetic, in which he stated: *"I wish I had not saved my life and had left it under the rubble of a city that should have been the last refuge of freedom and glory of Venezuela!"*.[16]

Rodriguez de Alonso (1974) concluded, *"It was no longer in Miranda's hands, or in anyone else's, to save the existence of the First Republic."*[17] The majority of the population, including the black slaves who, in the first days of July, were already threatening Caracas itself, joined the royalists.[18] The idea of reaching a capitulation that would allow saving human lives and resources to continue the fight later was shared by all the representatives of the Government, who, on July 12, decided to enter into talks with Monteverde. Pedro Gual's testimony regarding the Generalissimo's thoughts is clear. On July 19, he told him:

> *"I have just entered into an honourable capitulation with the enemy, in agreement with the Government. Since you left the General Headquarters, I have received only the most unpleasant news from all sides [...]. Let us then turn our gaze to New Granada, where I have Nariño [...]. With the resources we receive from here, including officers, ammunition, and so on, and those we will likely obtain there, we will return to Caracas [...].*[19]

This was precisely what Bolívar would do later. In 1813, with his Admirable Campaign, he liberated the Province for a short time, establishing a Second Republic (which would disappear in December 1814, just as the First Republic had, after the successive victories of Boves and his brave plainsmen).

The capitulation would establish respect for persons and property, the liberation of prisoners, and the departure from the country of those who wished it. The armistice was signed in San Mateo on July 19, 1813. July 25. Miranda, who had participated as a victor in three capitulations during his military career (the one in Pensacola, the one in the Bahamas, and the one in Antwerp), thought that they would be respected in this case as well. But it was not so.

On the night of July 30–31, a group of patriots, dominated by ambition, passion, or confusion, and rumours, arrested their Generalissimo. Among the conspirators was Colonel Simón Bolívar, who, according to his version, intended to have Miranda shot, accusing him of losing Venezuela through treason. But on the morning of the 31st, the city was handed over to the royalists, with whom Miranda remained in the hands of the Spanish, who, violating the capitulations, kept him in prison until his

[16] Ibíd, p. 430.

[17] Rodríguez de Alonso, J., (1974), *op. cit.*, p. 109.

[18] Parra-Pérez (1992), states: *"From April or May 1812, it would have been necessary to send to prison or shoot, for royalism, three-quarters of the inhabitants of Caracas, among them, a large number of employees of the Republic [...]. Bolívar's campaigns in 1813 and 1814 are perhaps the most daring and admirable of his glorious military history. Nevertheless, the genius of the man and the concentration of powers and resources in his hands were as impotent as they had been, against Monteverde, the first government and its Dictator. Bolívar did not manage to save his Second Republic from the onslaught of the plains masses led by Boves. Many texts demonstrate that general opinion was, in Venezuela, until 1820, hostile to Independence."*

[19] Cit. por Rodríguez, J., (1974), *op. cit.*, 111.

death. The compatriots of the Precursor had facilitated to the Spanish what they had been seeking for decades. Bolivar was awarded a Spanish passport for Miranda's capture, although he pretended later that he dared to refuse it.[20] The facts are that he actually took and used it for escape.

Nothing is more unjust than the accusation of treason and incompetence that the future Liberator made against Miranda. And nothing is more contradictory to the self-incrimination of the latter, made 20 and 18 days before, when he believed the country had been lost in his hands. In reality, Venezuela was not lost only by the fall of Puerto Cabello, nor much less by the capitulation of San Mateo. It was finally lost by the fall of the port. It is unnecessary to go to some historians who repeated the accusation of treason without further examination to prove that there was no treason. It is precisely Bolívar himself who agrees with Miranda in his Cartagena Manifesto of December 15, 1812. It is true that in his Exposition addressed to the Congress of New Granada on November 27, he had insisted on accusing Miranda of cowardice, affirming that *"he returned us to the yoke of our former tyrants."* But in the December Manifesto, the future Liberator, in total contradiction to his November Exposition, analyses with great lucidity the causes of the fall of the First Republic, agreeing—except in one—on all points with the criteria that Miranda had expressed in Congress and the Barracks.

These causes pointed out by Bolívar, which confirm Miranda's diagnosis, are: 1) the adoption of the federal system, which was "*what weakened the Government of Venezuela the most*"; 2) the failure to form a disciplined army, but rather "*the establishment of innumerable bodies of undisciplined militias*", which "*made the Government odious*"; 3) the impunity in which the crimes of State committed shamelessly by the discontented were left; 4) the subdivision of the Province of Caracas, which "*awakened and fomented a bitter rivalry in the cities* [...] *against the capital*", 5) the dissipation of public revenues in frivolous and harmful objects; 6) the establishment of paper money (a consequence of the above), which "*seemed to most people to be a manifest violation of the right of property*," so they preferred that the commander of the Spanish troops "*come to free them from a currency that they viewed with more horror than servitude*"; 7) the earthquake of March 26, which "*certainly upset both the physical and the moral, and can be properly called the*

[20] The victorious Spanish leader, Domingo de Monteverde, gave Bolívar a passport to leave the country, saying that this was a reward for the capture of Miranda and that he had informed the King in these terms. But in the interview in which the Spanish leader affirmed this—according to his Spanish protector—Bolívar would have reacted by refusing to accept this passport, putting the granting of the passport in danger, risking his own safety. The quick and intelligent intervention of the peninsular friend who protected him, Don Francisco Iturbe, saved the situation. Felipe Larrazábal, (1918), musician and, historian, biographer of the Liberator, heard from Iturbe himself (Bolívar's friend) the narration of the scene in which Monteverde said to his secretary: "*A passport is granted to the gentleman (looking at Bolívar) in reward for the service he has done to the King with the imprisonment of Miranda.*" Faced with the young man's reaction, Iturbe said he tried to humour the situation by saying: "*Come on, don't pay attention to this scoundrel; give him the passport and let him go.*" *Vida de Bolívar*, v. I., p. 132. However, this single version defending Bolivar's honour comes from his friend and is not verifiable.

immediate cause of the ruin of Venezuela" (a significant part of the patriotic forces were buried); 8) the ecclesiastical influence that had "*after the earthquake a very considerable part in the uprising of the subordinate places and cities and in the introduction of the enemies of the country*"; 9) the divisions, "*the internal factions that in reality were the mortal poison that made the country descend to the grave.*"[21]

> *"Bolívar's criticism of the system and the vices that the Republic rapidly acquired is [...] amply justified, and, by a coincidence that could be called ironic and until now never pointed out (1939), appears as the best defence of the opinions and purposes expressed by Miranda in Congress and at headquarters."*[22]

However, Bolívar's analysis requires two fundamental criticisms:

First, the fall of Puerto Cabello disappears, as he forgets his initial judgments about that tragic episode. Still, if this event can be considered the coup de grâce for the Republic, it is clear that all the other causes he lists had already been at work. Therefore, Bolívar was realistic in acknowledging his mistakes on July 12 and 14, 1812. He was not at his post, in the fortress, but below, in the city, for questionable reasons, when the Spanish prisoners took it, and he was absolutely unfair in blaming Miranda. As Parra-Pérez and other historians point out, the genuine causes of the fall of the First Republic are the nine listed by the future Liberator, to which must be added the fall of Puerto Cabello—the padlock controlling access to Caracas—but only as a final "*coup de grace*". But it could have been avoided if Bolívar had dispersed the hundreds of prisoners and had been in his command post, in the fortress and not down in the city. None of these causes is attributable to the "Generalísimo".

Second, Bolívar indicates an additional but fundamental cause in his "*Manifesto of Cartagena*" of December 1812, which blames Miranda, although without naming him, for the fall of the first republic. It is a criticism subtly associating the government's errors with some of Miranda's ethical aspects, even though Miranda shared these criticisms. However, the result is not relevant to Miranda's military conduct:

> *"The most consistent error that Venezuela committed... was, without contradiction, the fatal adoption of the tolerant system... certain good visionaries who, imagining aerial republics, have sought to achieve political perfection, presupposing the perfectibility of the human race. Thus, we had philosophers for leaders, philanthropy for legislation, dialectics for tactics, and sophists for soldiers."*[23]

Such additional criticism reveals the young man's deep-seated need to dispel any doubt through a divergence in political strategy. Complementing his attempt to disguise his betrayal with an ideological reason allowed him to clear his conscience and justify his ambition for power. Arguing an ideological divergence as a cause for the disaster was—consciously or not—a self-justification of his act of betraying his leader by stating that, in any case, he alone represented the correct strategy for the future. Thus, he could open his path to a future Liberator without worrying any

[21] Bolívar, S., (2007), *Proclamas* y *discursos...*, 11–2.

[22] Parra-Pérez, C., (1992), *op.* cit., II, 407.

[23] Bolívar, S., (1812), *Manifiesto de Cartagena*, 15 December 1232.pdf (biblioteca.org.ar)

more about the usurpation he had carried out. There was indeed a divergence of political options between the Jacobin Bolívar and the humanist Miranda, although it has no relation to the military disaster. One cannot blame the military leader Miranda for errors in his defence campaigns, which were never tolerant or sophisticated. On the contrary, he demonstrated himself to be a lucid visionary and a pragmatic leader, without any airy rambling; however, subsequent events proved that he was entirely right. Bolívar himself recognised his own failure at the time of his death.

Miranda fought tirelessly against all the other evils pointed out by Bolívar despite difficulties, indiscipline, divisions, intrigues, and slander from his compatriots.

Bolívar was decisively unfair to Miranda. If, in the first days of July, he said that the country "was lost" in his hands, how can he, 20 days later, accuse Miranda of having lost it? And how can he, in November of the same year, in Bogotá, accuse Miranda of cowardice and incompetence, insisting that Miranda had lost Venezuela, and the following month list nine causes of the disaster, none of which is attributable to the Precursor? The desire to exonerate himself from the responsibility he had confessed to Miranda led Bolívar to commit such a great injustice and insist on it. Perhaps this same desire is at the root of the fact that he omitted the fall of Puerto Cabello when listing the causes of the fall of the First Republic in New Granada. The capture of this city and its fortress, along with its depot of arms and gunpowder, by the royalists was a significant contributing factor to the disaster in Venezuela, for which Bolívar alone bears responsibility, although this was not the only cause of the disaster. But the future Liberator silences it in his analysis. The loss of the Republic's arsenal, its gunpowder, its cannons, all its weapons and reserves was undoubtedly fatal in circumstances where, despite the small territory not reconquered by the enemy, Miranda and his forces had stopped Monteverde's advance and had successfully repelled the royalist attack throughout June. Bolívar omits all this in his Cartagena Manifesto of December 1812.

Not a few historians have affirmed that Bolívar handed over the Precursor; many others, however, take up the Liberator's explanation that his attitude in arresting his mentor had been an act of emotional patriotism.[24] A heavy doubt looms over and aggravates the reality of this tragedy: it is an incontestable fact that the tireless apostle and fighter for Spanish American independence was handed over by patriots to the enemy.[25] After decades of fruitless pursuit, the Spanish finally had him in their

[24] On this controversy, see Ghymers' analysis in Chap. 4, Sect. 4.8.

[25] The victorious Spanish leader, Domingo de Monteverde, gave Bolívar a passport to leave the country, saying that this was a reward for the capture of Miranda and that he informed the King in these terms. But in the interview in which the Spanish leader affirmed this—according to his Spanish protector—Bolívar would have reacted by refusing to accept this passport, putting the granting of the passport in danger, risking his own safety. The quick and intelligent intervention of the peninsular friend who protected him, Don Francisco Iturbe, saved the situation. Felipe Larrazábal, (1918), musician and, historian, biographer of the Liberator, heard from Iturbe himself (Bolívar's friend) the narration of the scene in which Monteverde said to his secretary: "*A passport is granted to the gentleman (looking at Bolívar) in reward for the service he has done to the King with the imprisonment of Miranda.*" Faced with the young man's reaction, Iturbe said he tried to humour the situation by saying: "*Come on, don't pay attention to this scoundrel; give him the passport and let him go.*" *Vida de Bolívar*, v. I., p. 132. However, this single version defending Bolivar's honour comes from his friend and is not verifiable.

power: not because of any action from the Spanish enemies, but thanks to the actions of a group of "patriots," among whom Bolívar played a significant role. Thus, Miranda's figure was made to disappear under the weight of slander and buried in Spanish dungeons. At the same time, Bolívar, free and provided with the passport granted by the "reconquistador" Domingo de Monteverde, could begin his upward career, leading him to be identified as the Liberator.

References

Adelman, J., (2006), *Sovereignty and Revolution in the Iberian Atlantic,* Princeton University Press and "An Age of Imperial Revolutions", *American Historical* Review, 113 (2008), p. 319–40 (focused more specifically on the disintegration of Spain's empire).

Antepara, J. M. (1810), *South American emancipation: documents, historical and explanatory…* op. cit.

Bailyn, B., (1967), The Ideological Origins of the American Revolution, Harvard University Press

Bello, A., (1984), Obras Completas, Epistolario Vol. XXV, Fundaci6n La Casa de Bello, Caracas.

Bolivar (1830), Message to the Constituent Congress, Bogota, 20 *January* 1830, cited by Lynch, *Simon Bolivar*, p. 294

Bolivar in particular, after a measure of sympathy in the wake of the debacle at Coro in 1806, took this view pretty harshly after Miranda's surrender to Monteverde and flight to La Guaira in 1812 (Lynch, *Simon Bolivar*, p. 53-64).

Bolívar, S., (1812), *Manifiesto de Cartagena*, 15 December, 1232.pdf (biblioteca.org.ar)

Bolívar, S., (2007), *Proclamas* y *discursos,* Fundaci6n Ayacucho, Caracas. https://archive.org/details/discursos-y-proclamas/page/VIII/mode/2up

Brading & others, (1999), *Vizcardo y Guzmán: el hombre y su tiempo*, 3 Vol. Fondo Editorial del Congreso del Perú, Lima.

Burke, W., (1807), *South American Independence: or the Emancipation of South America, the Glory and Interest of England.* J. Ridgway, London.

Burke, W., (1808), *Additional Reasons, for our immediately emancipating Spanish America, deduced from the present crisis: and containing valuable information, respecting the late important events, both at Buenos Ayres, and in the Caraccas*, London. Reprinted by Creative Media Partners, LLC, 2015.

Burke, E., (1989) *Writings and Speeches*, VIII, *The French Revolution 1790-1794*, ed Mitchell, L., (1989) Clarendon Press, Oxford, effectively endorsed by Mayer, A., (2000), *The Furies* Princeton University Press.

Centeno, M. & Lopez-Alves, F., (eds), (2001), *The Other Mirror: Grand Theory through the Lens of Latin America,* Princeton University Press & Forment, C., (2003), *Democracy in Latin America 1760-1900*, Vol 1, University of Chicago Press.

Church, F., (1972), *Richelieu and Reason of State* Princeton: Princeton University Press.

Dunn, J., (2000), *The Cunning of Unreason* Harper Collins, London.

Dunn, J., (2008), Revolucao?, *Lua Nova* (Sao Paulo), 75, p. 199-214 (in Portuguese)

C. Ghymers, *Independence, Federalism and Regionalism in Latin America: An Analytical Anthology of Francisco de Miranda's Writings (1790-1811)*,
United Nations University Series on Regionalism 34,
https://doi.org/10.1007/978-3-031-96938-6

Elliott, (1990), *Empires*, 367.

Elliott, J., (2006), *Empires of the Atlantic World: Britain and Spain in America 1492-1830,* Yale University Press (the Transatlantic dimension is set out magisterially).

Furet, F., (1981), *Interpreting the French Revolution* Cambridge University Press.

Glave Testino, L. M., (1999), Un niño en el Cuzco, la formación de la menoría peruana de Viscardo, in Branding & others, *Vizcardo y Guzmán: el hombre y su tiempo*.

Hont, I., (2005), J*ealousy of Trade*, Harvard University Press (background is best presented synoptically).

Inca Garcilaso de la Vega, (1609), The Royal Commentaries of the Inca, edited by Alain Gheerbrant, http://www.archive.org/details/incasroyalcommenOOvega

Israel, J., (2001), *Radical Enlightenment*, Clarendon Press, Oxford (gives the most powerful and sustained presentation), and also *Enlightenment Contested*, (2006), Clarendon Press, Oxford.

Koselleck, R., (1988), *Critique and Crisis: the Pathogenesis of Modern Society,* London, Berg.

Langley, L., (1998), *The Americas in the Age of Revolution 1750-1850,* Yale University Press.

Larrazabal, F., (1918), *Vida del libertador Simón Bólivar*, Edición modernizada, con prólogo y notas de R. Blanco-Fombona, Ed. Ayacucho, Caracas.

Las Casas, de, B., (1697), *La Découverte des Indes occidentales par les Espagnols*, written by A. Pralar, Paris.

Lynch, J., (2006), *Simon Bolivar: A Life* New Haven: Yale University Press.

Mijares, A. (1964), *El Libertador*, Fundación E. Mendoza/ Shell, Caracas.

Miranda, F. de, (1929–1950), *Archivo del General Miranda*, ed. Vicente Dávila/ Rubén González, Caracas/La Habana.

Miranda, F. de, (1959) Textos sobre la Independencia, Academia Nacional de la Historia, Caracas

Montesquieu, C., (1748), *De l'Esprit des Lois*, Partie IV, chapitre 6

Mornet, D., (1954), *Les Origines intellectuelles de la revolution francaise* 5th ed Presses Universitaires de France, Paris.

Michael Sonenscher, M., (2007), *Before the Deluge,* Princeton University Press.

Pagden, A., *Spanish Imperialism and the Political Imagination* Yale University Press, Spanish, p. 131–32

Parra-Pérez, C., (1925), *Miranda et la Révolution Française*, Librairie Pierre Roger, Paris.

Parra-Pérez, C., (1992), *Historia de la primera república de Venezuela*, Editorial Ayacucho, Caracas.

Penalver (1824), Letter to Fernando Penalver, 10 November 1824, cited by Lynch, *Simon Bolivar*, p. 270.

Phelan, J., (1978), *The People and the King: the Cumunero Revolution in Colombia 1781* University of Wisconsin Press, Madison, (who emphasises the historical depth and local density of the sources and character of the closest prior counterpart to the challenge which Miranda envisaged to Spain's imperial authority. He definitely did not have in mind the drastic threat to Creole wealth and privilege presaged by Tupac Amaru or Hidalgo.

Racine, (2003), *Miranda*, chapters 5 & 7 op. cit.

Racine, K., (2003), *Francisco de Miranda: A Transatlantic Life in the Age of Revolution* Wilmington: Scholarly Resources.

Rodriguez de Alonso, J., (1974), *Le siècle des lumières conté par Francisco de Miranda*, Ed. France Empire, Paris.

Ruiz Zevallos, A., (1999), "Un Precursor de la República Criolla? El Liberalismo Democrático en Juan Pablo Vizcardo y Guzmán", in *Viscardo y Guzmán: el hombre y su tiempo*, Vol. I.

Simmons, M., (1983), *Los escritos de Juan Pablo Vizcardo y Guzmán, precursor de la independencia hispanoamericana*, Universidad Cátolica Andrés Bello, Caracas.

Skinner, Q., & van Gelderen, M., ed. (2002), Republicanism: a shared European heritage 2 Vol., Cambridge University Press (gives a recent conspectus of the available resources across Europe over several centuries). The trail was blazed most influentially by Pocock, J., (1975), *The Machiavellian Moment* Princeton University Press, and the case has been developed most systematically, in face of sustained criticism, in relation to the fledgling United States, notably in Bailyn, B., (1967), *The Ideological Origins of the American Revolution,* Harvard University Press and Wood, G., (1969) *The Creation of the American Republic,* University of North Carolina Press, Chapel Hill.

Skocpol, T., (1979), *States and Social Revolutions,* Cambridge University Press (For the structural significance of geopolitics and international political economy in social revolution, and the special significance of war in state breaking).

Sonenscher, M., (1997), "The Nation's Debt and the Birth of the Modern Republic", *History of Political Thought* , 18, p. 64-103 & 267-325 and *Before the Deluge* (For France more specifically).

Vergara Arias, G., (1999), "Viscardo and Guzmán: Reflections and Fears about their independence project and its execution", in *Viscardo and Guzmán: the man and his time*, Vol. I.

Name Index

C. Ghymers, *Independence, Federalism and Regionalism in Latin America: An Analytical Anthology of Francisco de Miranda's Writings (1790-1811)*, United Nations University Series on Regionalism 34,
https://doi.org/10.1007/978-3-031-96938-6

Q

R

Geographical Places Index

C. Ghymers, *Independence, Federalism and Regionalism in Latin America: An Analytical Anthology of Francisco de Miranda's Writings (1790-1811)*, United Nations University Series on Regionalism 34, https://doi.org/10.1007/978-3-031-96938-6

MIX
Papier aus verantwortungsvollen Quellen
Paper from responsible sources
FSC® C105338

If you have any concerns about our products,
you can contact us on
ProductSafety@springernature.com

In case Publisher is established outside the EU,
the EU authorized representative is:
Springer Nature Customer Service Center GmbH
Europaplatz 3, 69115 Heidelberg, Germany

Printed by Libri Plureos GmbH
in Hamburg, Germany